HOW TO PREPARE FOR THE TOEFL* TEST

Test of English as a Foreign Language

Eighth Edition

PAMELA J. SHARPE, Ph.D.

Associate Professor of
English as a Second Language
and Bilingual Education
Northern Arizona University in Yuma

BARRON'S

*TOEFL is a registered trademark of Educational Testing Service. Barron's Educational Series, Inc. bears sole responsibility for this book's contents, and is not connected with Educational Testing Service.

To my former students
at home and abroad

All inquiries should be addressed to:
Barron's Educational Series, Inc.
250 Wireless Boulevard
Hauppauge, New York 11788

Library of Congress Catalog Card No. 95-25617
International Standard Book No. 0-8120-9407-7 (book only)
International Standard Book No. 0-8120-8470-5 (book with disks)
International Standard Book No. 0-8120-8420-9 (book with cassettes)

Library of Congress Cataloging-in-Publication Data
Sharpe, Pamela J.
    Barron's How to prepare for the TOEFL : test of
English as a foreign language / by Pamela J. Sharpe.—
8th ed.
    p.   cm.
    ISBN 0-8120-9407-7
    1. English language—Textbooks for foreign
speakers. 2. Test of English as a Foreign Language—
Study guides. 3. English language—Examinations—
Study guides. I. Barron's Educational Series, Inc.
II. Title.
PE1128.S5   1996
428'.0076—dc20
                                                    95-25617
                                                    CIP

PRINTED IN THE UNITED STATES OF AMERICA
98

CONTENTS

To the Teacher   v
Acknowledgments   vii
Timetable for the TOEFL   viii

INTRODUCTION

Study Plan for the TOEFL   3
Suggestions for Success   6
Questions and Answers Concerning the TOEFL   6

REVIEW OF LISTENING COMPREHENSION

Getting a Good Start   21
Overview   21
Types of Problems in the Listening Comprehension Section   22

REVIEW OF STRUCTURE AND WRITTEN EXPRESSION

Overview   35
Strategies and Symbols for Review   35
Types of Problems in the Structure and Written Expression
   Section   37

REVIEW OF READING COMPREHENSION

Overview   263
Types of Problems in the Reading Comprehension
   Section   263

TOEFL MODEL TESTS

Model Test 1—Short Form   277
Model Test 2—Short Form   297
Model Test 3—Short Form   317
Model Test 4—Short Form   337
Model Test 5—Short Form   357
Model Test 6—Short Form   377
Model Test 7—Short Form   397
Model Test 8—Long Form   417

ANSWER KEYS FOR THE TOEFL REVIEW EXERCISES AND MODEL TESTS

Answer Key—Exercises for Structure and Written Expression   443
Answer Key—Exercises for Reading Comprehension   458
Answer Key—Model Tests   462

EXPLANATORY ANSWERS FOR THE TOEFL MODEL TESTS

Model Test 1—Short Form   469
Model Test 2—Short Form   478
Model Test 3—Short Form   487
Model Test 4—Short Form   496
Model Test 5—Short Form   504
Model Test 6—Short Form   513
Model Test 7—Short Form   522
Model Test 8—Long Form   530

THE TEST OF WRITTEN ENGLISH (TWE)

Questions and Answers Concerning the TWE   545
Review of Written English   547
Example Test   548
TWE Model Tests   550

APPENDIX: *Transcript for the Listening Comprehension Sections of Model Tests 1 through 8*   557

To the Teacher

Rationale for a TOEFL Preparation Course

Although *Barron's How to Prepare for the TOEFL* was originally written as a self-study guide for students who were preparing to take the TOEFL, in the years since its first publication, I have received letters from ESL teachers around the world who are using the book successfully for classroom study. In fact, in recent years, many special courses have been developed within the existing ESL curriculum to accommodate TOEFL preparation.

I believe that these TOEFL preparation courses respond to three trends within the profession. First, there appears to be a greater recognition on the part of many ESL teachers that student goals must be acknowledged and addressed. For the engineer, the businessperson, the doctor, or the preuniversity student, a satisfactory score on the TOEFL is one of the most immediate goals; for many, without the required score, they cannot continue their professional studies or obtain certification to practice their professions. They may have other language goals as well, such as learning to communicate more effectively or improving their writing, but these goals do not usually exert the same kinds of pressure that the required TOEFL score does.

Second, teachers have recognized and recorded the damaging results of test anxiety. We have all observed students who were so frightened of failure that they have performed on the TOEFL at a level far below that which their performance in class would have indicated. The standardized score just didn't correspond with the score in the gradebook. In addition, teachers have become aware that for some students, the TOEFL represents their first experience in taking a standardized test with a test book and a separate answer sheet. The concepts of working within time limits, marking an answer grid, and guessing to improve a score are often new and confusing to students, and they forfeit valuable points because they must concentrate on unfamiliar procedures instead of on language questions.

Third, teachers have observed the corresponding changes in student proficiency that have accompanied the evolutionary changes in ESL syllabus design. Since this book was first written, we have moved away from a grammatical syllabus to a notional functional syllabus, and at this writing, there seems to be growing interest in a content-based syllabus. Viewed in terms of what has actually happened in classrooms, most of us have emphasized the teaching of functions and meaning and deemphasized the teaching of forms. As we did so, we noticed with pride the improvement in student fluency, and with dismay, the corresponding loss of accuracy. Some of our best, most fluent students received disappointing scores on the test that was so important to them.

Through these observations and experiences, teachers have concluded that (1) students need to work toward their own goals, (2) students need some time to focus on accuracy as well as on fluency, and (3) students need an opportunity to practice taking a standardized test in order to alleviate anxiety and develop test strategies. In short, more and more teachers have begun to support the inclusion of a TOEFL preparation course in the ESL curriculum.

Organization of a TOEFL Preparation Course

Organizing a TOEFL preparation course requires that teachers make decisions about the way that the course should be structured and the kinds of supplementary materials and activities that should be used.

Structuring

Some teachers have suggested that each review section in this book be used for a separate class; they are team teaching a TOEFL course. Other teachers direct their students to the language laboratory for independent study in listening comprehension three times a week, checking on progress throughout the term; assign reading and vocabulary study for homework; and spend class time on structure and written expression. Still other teachers develop individual study plans for each student based on previous TOEFL part scores. Students with high listening comprehension and low reading scores concentrate their efforts in reading labs, while students with low listening comprehension and high reading scores spend time in listening labs.

Materials and Activities

Listening comprehension. Studies in distributive practice have convinced teachers of listening comprehension that a little practice every day for a few months is more valuable than a lot of practice concentrated in a shorter time. In addition, many teachers like to use two kinds of listening practice—intensive and extensive. Intensive practice consists of listening to problems like those in the review of listening comprehension in this book.

By so doing, the student progresses from short conversations through longer conversations to mini-talks, gaining experience in listening to simulations of Parts A, B, and C of the TOEFL examination. Extensive practice consists of watching a daytime drama on television, listening to a local radio program, or auditing a class. Creative teachers everywhere have developed strategies for checking student progress such as requiring a summary of the plot or a prediction of what will happen the following day on the drama; a one-sentence explanation of the radio program, as well as the name of the speaker, sponsor of the program, and two details; a copy of student notes from the audited class.

Structure and written expression. Of course, the focus in a review of structure and written expression for the TOEFL will be on form. It is form that is tested on the TOEFL. It is assumed that students have studied grammar prior to reviewing for the TOEFL, and that they are relatively fluent. The purpose of a TOEFL review then, is to improve accuracy. Because accuracy is directly related to TOEFL scores and because the scores are tied to student goals, this type of review motivates students to pay attention to detail that would not usually be of much interest to them.

Among ESL teachers, the debate rages on about whether students should ever see errors in grammar. But many teachers have recognized the fact that students *do* see errors all the time, not only in the distractors that are used on standardized tests like the TOEFL and teacher-made tests like the multiple choice midterms in their grammar classes, but also in their own writing. They argue that students must be able to recognize errors, learn to read for them, and correct them.

The student preparing for the TOEFL will be required not only to recognize correct answers but also to eliminate incorrect answers, or distractors, as possibilities. The review of structure and written expression in this book supports recognition by alerting students to avoid certain common distractors. Many excellent teachers take this one step further by using student compositions to create personal TOEFL tests. By underlining four words or phrases in selected sentences, one phrase of which contains an incorrect structure, teachers encourage students to reread their writing. It has proven to be a helpful transitional technique for students who need to learn how to edit their own compositions.

Reading comprehension. One of the problems in a TOEFL preparation course is that of directing vocabulary study. Generally, teachers feel that encouraging students to collect words and develop their own word lists is the best solution to the problem of helping students who will be faced with the dilemma of responding to words from a possible vocabulary pool of thousands of words that may appear in context in the reading comprehension section. In this way, they will increase their vocabularies in an ordered and productive way, thereby benefiting even if none of their new words appears on the test that they take. Activities that support learning vocabulary in context are also helpful.

In order to improve reading, students need extensive practice in reading a variety of material, including newspapers and magazines as well as short excerpts from textbooks. In addition, students need to check their comprehension and time themselves carefully. Many teachers are using preparation books for the General Education Degree (GED) in special reading labs for students preparing for the TOEFL. Books such as *Barron's How to Prepare for the GED* contain passages at about the same level as those on the TOEFL, and include comprehension questions after each passage. Teachers report that passages on natural science, social science, and general interest only should be assigned because literature passages often require that the student read and interpret poetry and plays and these literary readings do not appear on the TOEFL. Again, it is well to advise students of the advantages of distributed practice. They should be made aware that it is better to read two passages every day for five days than to read ten passages in one lab period.

Networking with ESL Teachers

One of the many rewards of writing is the opportunity that it creates to exchange ideas with so many talented colleagues. At conferences, I have met ESL teachers who use or have used one of the previous editions of this book; through my publisher, I have received letters from students and teachers from fifty-two nations. This preface and many of the revisions in this new edition were included because of comments and suggestions from those conversations and letters.

Thank you for your ideas. I hope that by sharing we can help each other and thereby help our students more. Please continue corresponding.

Pamela Sharpe
10253 Del Rico Street
Yuma, Arizona 85367

Acknowledgments

It is with affection and appreciation that I acknowledge my indebtedness to the late Dr. Jayne C. Harder, Director of the English Language Institute of the University of Florida, who initiated me into the science of linguistics and the art of teaching English as a foreign language.

I am also very grateful to my parents, Robert and Lilly Sharpe, for their enthusiastic encouragement during the preparation of the manuscript and for their assistance in typing and proofreading this and each of the previous editions; to my late husband, Tom Clapp, for the love, support, and confidence that I gained from our relationship; to Ms. Carole Berglie of Barron's Educational Series, Inc., for her insights and guidance in seeing the first edition of the manuscript through to publication, and to all of the editors at Barron's for their contributions to later editions, especially Ms. Liza Burby whose creativity contributed to making this the best edition yet.

With the permission of Mr. Frank Berlin, Sexton Educational Programs, New York, explanations for the listening comprehension problems have been adapted from previous work by the author.

With the permission of Educational Testing Service, the test instructions contained in this publication for the various sections of TOEFL have been reprinted from the *TOEFL Bulletin of Information*. The granting of this permission does not imply endorsement by ETS or the TOEFL program of the contents of this publication as a whole or of the practice questions that it contains. Since the types of questions in TOEFL and the instructions pertaining to them are subject to change, candidates who register to take TOEFL should read carefully the edition of the *TOEFL Bulletin of Information* that will be sent to them free of charge with their admission tickets.

Timetable for the TOEFL

TIMETABLE FOR THE TOEFL: SHORT FORM*
Total Time: 120 minutes

Section 1 (40 Minutes)	Listening Comprehension	50 Questions
Section 2 (25 Minutes)	Structure and Written Expression	40 Questions
Section 3 (55 Minutes)	Reading Comprehension	50 Questions

TIMETABLE FOR THE TOEFL: LONG FORM*
Total Time: 150 minutes

Section 1 (50 Minutes)	Listening Comprehension	80 Questions
Section 2 (35 Minutes)	Structure and Written Expression	60 Questions
Section 3 (65 Minutes)	Reading Comprehension	70 Questions

*Note: Actual times will vary in accordance with the time the supervisor completes the preliminary work and begins the actual test. Format and numbers of questions may also vary from one test to another.

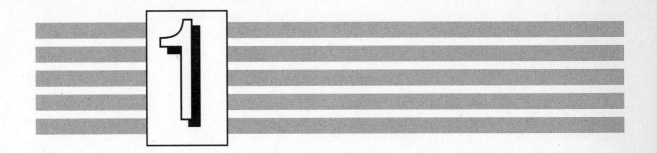

INTRODUCTION

Study Plan for the TOEFL

Many students do not prepare for the TOEFL. They do not even read the *Bulletin of Information* that they receive from Educational Testing Service along with their application forms. You have an advantage. Using this book, you have a study plan.

Barron's TOEFL Series

There are three books in the Barron's TOEFL series to help you prepare for the Test of English as a Foreign Language. Each book has a different purpose.

Barron's Practice Exercises for the TOEFL. A book for learners at an intermediate level who need preview and practice for the TOEFL. It includes a general preview of the TOEFL examination, a preview of the most frequently tested problems, and more than a thousand exercises. A separate cassette tape accompanies the book to give you practice in listening comprehension. You may have used *Barron's Practice Exercises for the TOEFL* before using this book.

Barron's How to Prepare for the TOEFL. A book for learners at high intermediate and advanced levels who need review and practice for the TOEFL. It includes questions and answers about the TOEFL examination, a detailed review for each section of the examination, practice exercises, and eight model tests similar to the actual TOEFL examination. Audiocassettes are available separately.

Barron's Pass Key to the TOEFL. A pocket-sized edition of *Barron's How to Prepare for the TOEFL.* It is for high intermediate and advanced learners who need review and practice for the TOEFL and want to be able to carry a smaller book with them. It includes questions and answers about the TOEFL examination, basic tips on how to prepare for the TOEFL, and five model tests from *Barron's How to Prepare for the TOEFL.* Two cassette tapes accompany the book to give you practice in listening comprehension.

More About This Book

In preparing to take the TOEFL or any other language examination, it is very important to review the language skills for each section of the examination and to have an opportunity to take model tests that are similar to the actual examination.

Reviewing will help you recall some of the language skills you have studied in previous classes and other books. Taking model tests will give you the experience of taking a TOEFL before you take the actual examination.

Remember, the purpose of this book is to provide you with a detailed review of the language skills for each section of the TOEFL examination and to provide you with eight opportunities to take a model test similar to the actual TOEFL examination.

By studying this book, you should renew and sharpen your skills, increase your speed, and improve your score.

Planning to Take the TOEFL

Most learners who use Barron's *How to Prepare for the TOEFL* take the test *after* they have finished studying this book.

Study Plan I—For Intermediate Level Learners

- First, use *Barron's Practice Exercises for the TOEFL.*
- Then use this book, *Barron's How to Prepare for the TOEFL.*

Study Plan II—For High Intermediate Level or Advanced Learners

• Use this book, *Barron's How to Prepare for the TOEFL.*

A Twelve-Week Calendar

Week One. First, read the second part of this chapter, "Questions and Answers Concerning the TOEFL." Then, following the instructions there, write the TOEFL Office for a copy of the *Bulletin of Information for the TOEFL.* Research shows that when you know what to expect in an examination, your score will be better. After you have read the *Bulletin,* arrange your test date.

Week Two. Study Chapter 2, "Review of Listening Comprehension," and test yourself by taking Section 1, Listening Comprehension, of Model Test 1. Be sure to time yourself. Then, refer to the Answer Key in Chapter 6 and the Explanatory Answers in Chapter 7. Review your errors by returning to the audiocassette and listening to it again. Finally, refer to the "Transcript for the Listening Comprehension Sections" in the Appendix of this book.

Week Three. Study the *patterns* in Chapter 3, "Review of Structure and Written Expression." Skim those problems that are familiar to you and concentrate on the unfamiliar ones. Spend two days reviewing verbs, then five days reviewing pronouns, nouns, adjectives, comparatives, prepositions, conjunctions, and adverbs. At the end of each day, complete the practice exercises and mark those problems that you are still unsure of so that you can return to them easily at a later time.

Week Four. Study the *style problems* in Chapter 3, "Review of Structure and Written Expression." At the end of each day, complete the practice exercises and mark those problems that you are still unsure of so that you can return to them easily at a later time. Test yourself by taking Section 2, Structure and Written Expression, of Model Test 1. Be sure to time yourself. Then, refer to the Answer Key in Chapter 6 and the Explanatory Answers in Chapter 7. Review your errors by returning to the problems keyed in the "Review of Structure and Written Expression." Study those problems again.

Week Five. Study Chapter 4, "Review of Reading Comprehension," and test yourself by taking Section 3, Reading Comprehension, of Model Test 1. Be sure to time yourself. Then, refer to the Answer Key in Chapter 6 and the Explanatory Answers in Chapter 7. Review your errors by returning to the passages and reading them again.

Week Six. First, test yourself by taking all three sections of Model Test 2. Be sure to time yourself. Then, refer to the Answer Key in Chapter 6 and the Explanatory Answers in Chapter 7. Review your errors.

Week Seven. Test yourself by taking all three sections of Model Test 3. Then, refer to the Answer Key in Chapter 6 and the Explanatory Answers in Chapter 7. Review your errors.

Week Eight. Test yourself by taking all three sections of Model Tests 4 and 5. Then, refer to the Answer Key in Chapter 6 and the Explanatory Answers in Chapter 7. Review your errors.

Week Nine. Test yourself by taking all three sections of Model Tests 6 and 7. Then, refer to the Answer Key in Chapter 6 and the Explanatory Answers in Chapter 7. Review your errors.

Week Ten. Study all of the problems that you have marked in the review chapters, and all of the errors that you have made on Model Tests 1 through 7.

Week Eleven. Test yourself by taking all three sections of Model Test 8. Then, refer to the Answer Key in Chapter 6 and the Explanatory Answers in Chapter 7. Review your errors.

Week Twelve. Study all of the problems and errors that you have marked in the review chapters and model tests.

Adjusting the Calendar

Ideally, you will have twelve weeks to prepare for the TOEFL. But, if you have a shorter time to prepare, follow the plan in the same order, adjusting the time to meet your needs.

If you have taken the TOEFL before, you already know which section or sections are difficult for you. Look at the part scores on your score report. If your lowest score is on Section 1, Listening Comprehension, then you should spend more time reviewing Section 1. If your lowest score is on Section 2 or Section 3, then you should spend more time reviewing them.

If you are participating in a TOEFL administration that includes the Test of Written English (TWE), you should plan time early in your study calendar to read Chapter 8, "Test of Written English (TWE)." Then, test yourself by taking one of the TWE model tests included in Chapter 8 every week.

Suggestions for Preparation

To improve your scores most, follow three suggestions:

- *First,* concentrate on listening, structure, writing ability, and reading, instead of on vocabulary. Your score will improve, because when you are engaged in listening and reading, you are practicing skills that you can apply during the examination regardless of the content of the material. When you are reviewing structure, you are studying a system that is smaller than that of vocabulary, and, like the skills of listening and reading, has the potential for application on the TOEFL that you take. Many of the structures that you study will probably appear on the examination.
  But when you review lists of vocabulary, even very good lists, you may study hundreds of words and not find any of them on the examination. This is so because the system is very large. There are thousands of possible words that may be tested.

- *Second,* spend time preparing every day for at least an hour instead of sitting down to review once a week for seven hours. Even though you are studying for the same amount of time, research shows that daily shorter sessions produce better results on the test.

- *Finally,* do not try to memorize questions from this or any other book. The questions on the test that you take will be very similar to the questions in this book, but they will not be exactly the same.

What you should try to do as you use this and your other books is to learn how to apply your knowledge. Do not hurry through the practice exercises. While you are checking your answers to the model tests, *think* about the correct answer. Why is it correct? Can you explain the answer to yourself before you check the explanatory answer? Is the question similar to others that you have seen before?

Suggestions for Additional Preparation

Although this book should provide you with enough review material, some of you will want to do more in order to prepare for the TOEFL. Suggestions for each section follow.

To prepare for Section 1, Listening Comprehension, listen to radio and television newscasts and weather reports, television documentaries, lectures on educational television stations, and free lectures sponsored by clubs and universities. Attend movies in English. Try to make friends with speakers of American English and participate in conversations.

To prepare for Section 2, Structure and Written Expression, use an advanced grammar review book. If you are attending an English course, do not stop attending.

To prepare for Section 3, Reading Comprehension, read articles in English newspapers and magazines, college catalogs and admissions materials, travel brochures, and entries that interest you from American and English encyclopedias. Try to read a variety of topics—American history, culture, social science, and natural science.

Suggestions for Success

Your attitude will influence your success on the TOEFL examination. You must develop patterns of positive thinking. To help in developing a positive attitude, memorize the following sentences and bring them to mind after each study session. Bring them to mind when you begin to have negative thoughts.

I know more today than I did yesterday.
I am preparing.
I will succeed.

Remember, some tension is normal and good. Accept it. Use it constructively. It will motivate you to study. But don't panic or worry. Panic will cause loss of concentration and poor performance. Avoid people who panic and worry. Don't listen to them. They will encourage negative thoughts.

You know more today than you did yesterday.
You are preparing.
You will succeed.

Questions and Answers Concerning the TOEFL

Approximately 835,000 students from 180 countries register to take the Test of English as a Foreign Language (TOEFL) every year at 1,275 test centers in the United States and in their home countries. Some of them do not pass the TOEFL because they do not understand enough English. Others do not pass it because they do not understand the examination.

The following questions are commonly asked by students as they prepare for the TOEFL. To help you, they have been answered here.

What Is the Purpose of the TOEFL?

Since 1963 the TOEFL has been used by scholarship selection committees of governments, universities, and agencies such as Fulbright, the Agency for International Development, AMIDEAST, Latin American Scholarship Program, and others as a standard measure of the English proficiency of their candidates. Now some professional licensing and certification agencies also use TOEFL scores to evaluate English proficiency.

The majority of admissions committees of colleges and universities in the United States require foreign applicants to submit TOEFL scores along with transcripts and recommendations in order to be considered for admission. Some colleges and universities in Canada and other English-speaking countries also require the TOEFL for admissions purposes.

Many universities use TOEFL scores to fulfill the foreign language requirement for doctoral candidates whose first language is not English.

What Is an International TOEFL Testing?

The TOEFL is offered once a month on regularly scheduled Fridays and Saturdays at designated test centers in 180 countries throughout the world, including all of the states of the United States. This is called an International TOEFL Testing or an "official" administration. A list of test centers established for the purpose of administering the International TOEFL Testing appears in the free *Bulletin of Information* available from the TOEFL Office.

In order to receive a copy of the *Bulletin of Information,* write:

TOEFL Office
P.O. 6151
Princeton, NJ 08541-6151
U.S.A.

It is correct to limit your letter to two sentences. For example:

A LETTER OF REQUEST FOR THE
BULLETIN OF INFORMATION

(write your address here)
(write the date here)

TOEFL Office
P.O. 6151
Princeton, NJ 08541-6151
U.S.A.

Dear TOEFL Representative:

Please send a copy of the *TOEFL Bulletin of Information* to the address above.

Thank you for your earliest attention.

Sincerely yours,

(write your name here)

The TOEFL *Bulletin* is also available overseas in U.S. embassies and offices of the United States Information Service (USIS), binational centers, as well as IIE and AMIDEAST Counseling Centers. A partial list of centers is printed on pages 8–9.

What Is the Difference Between a Friday and Saturday TOEFL Test?

The format and length of the tests on Friday and on Saturday are the same. The registration fees are different. The Friday test costs $45 US and the Saturday test costs $38 US. The Friday test costs more because there are fewer test centers available.

The dates for the Friday and Saturday tests are also different. The Friday tests are offered in July, September, December, March, and June. The Saturday tests are offered in August, October, November, January, February, April, and May.

What Is an Institutional TOEFL Testing?

More than 1,200 schools, colleges, universities, and private agencies administer the Institutional TOEFL. The Institutional TOEFL is the same length, format, and difficulty as the International TOEFL, but the dates and the purposes of the Institutional TOEFL are different from those of the International TOEFL.

The dates for the Institutional TOEFL usually correspond to the beginning of an academic session on a college or university calendar.

The Institutional TOEFL is used for admission, placement, eligibility, or employment only at the school or agency that offers the test.

If you plan to use your scores for a different college, university, or agency, you should take the International TOEFL.

Are Scores Considered the Same for All Testings?

There is no difference in the scores from an International TOEFL Testing administered on Friday or Saturday, or an Institutional TOEFL Testing. They are both calculated using the same scale.

WHERE TO OBTAIN A TOEFL *BULLETIN*

ALGERIA, OMAN, QATAR, SAUDI ARABIA, SUDAN, UNITED ARAB EMIRATES
AMIDEAST
Testing Programs, Suite 1100
1730 M Street, NW
Washington, DC 20036-4601, USA
Telephone: 202-785-0022

AUSTRALIA, NEW ZEALAND, PAPUA NEW GUINEA
Australian Council for Educational Research
ACER-ETS
Test Administration Office
Private Bag 55
Camberwell, Victoria 3124
Australia
Telephone: (03) 277 5555

BAHRAIN
AMIDEAST
P.O. Box 10410
Manama
Bahrain
Telephone: 973 729-011

BRAZIL
Instituto Brasil-Estados Unidos
Av. Nossa Senhora de Copacabana
690-9° Andar
22050-000 Rio de Janeiro, RJ, Brasil
Telephone: (021) 2555830

CANADA
TOEFL/TSE
Trans-Canada Educational
Evaluation Service
1712 Avenue Road
P.O. Box 54502
North York, ON M5M 4N5
Canada
Telephone: 416-789-2331

EGYPT
AMIDEAST
6 Kamel El Shennawy Street
Second Floor, Apartment 5
Garden City, Cairo, Egypt
Telephone: 202-3553170

or

AMIDEAST
American Cultural Center
3 Pharaana Street
Azarita, Alexandria
Egypt
Telephone: 203 4829091

EUROPE, East/West
CITO-TOEFL
P.O. Box 1203
6801 BE Arnhem
Netherlands
Telephone: ••/3185521427

HONG KONG
Hong Kong Examinations Authority
San Po Kong Sub-Office
17 Tseuk Luk Street
San Po Kong
Kowloon, Hong Kong
Telephone: 23-280061, ext. 365

INDIA/BHUTAN
Institute of Psychological and
Educational Measurement
119/25-A Mahatma Gandhi Marg
Allahabad, U.P. 211 001, India
Telephone: 532-624881

INDONESIA
The International Education
Foundation
P.O. Box 8515 JKSCO
Jakarta 12085, Indonesia
Telephone: 5200364

JAPAN
Council on International
Educational Exchange (CIEE)
Hirakawa-cho Kaisaka Bldg. 1F
1-6-8 Hirakawa-cho, Chiyoda-ku
Tokyo 102, Japan
Telephone: (03) 3239-1830

JORDAN
AMIDEAST
P.O. Box 1249
Amman, Jordan
Telephone: 962-6-624495

KOREA
Korean-American Educational
Commission
K.P.O. Box 643
Seoul 110-606, Korea
Telephone: 2-732-7928

KUWAIT
AMIDEAST
P.O. Box 44818
Hawalli 32063
Kuwait
Telephone: 965-5327794

LEBANON
AMIDEAST
P.O. Box 135-155
Ras Beirut, Lebanon
Telephone: 961-1-345-341

or

AMIDEAST
P.O. Box 70-744
Antelias, Beirut, Lebanon
Telephone: 961-1-411-676

MALAYSIA/SINGAPORE
MACEE
TOEFL/TSE Services
191, Jalan Tun Razak
50400 Kuala Lumpur, Malaysia
Telephone: 60-3-242-4539

MEXICO
Institute of International Education
Londres No. 16, 2nd Floor
Apartado Postal 61-115
Mexico 06600 D.F., Mexico
Telephone: 525 • 211-00-42

MOROCCO
AMIDEAST
25 bis Patrice Lumumba
Apt. No. 8
Rabat, Morocco
Telephone: 212-7-724000

PAKISTAN
World Learning Inc.
P.O. Box 13042
Karachi, Pakistan 75350

Telephone: (92-21) 455-7166

PEOPLE'S REPUBLIC OF CHINA
China International Examinations
Coordination Bureau
#30 Yu Quan Road
Beijing 100039
People's Republic of China
Telephone: 1-821-7122

**NEWLY INDEPENDENT STATES OF
THE FORMER SOVIET UNION***
ASPRIAL/AKSELS
a/ya 1, V-49
117049 Moscow, Russia

SYRIA
AMIDEAST
P.O. Box 2313
Damascus, Syria
Telephone: 963-11-3334-801

TAIWAN
The Language Training & Testing
Center
P.O. Box 23-41
Taipei, Taiwan 100
Telephone: (02) 362-6045

THAILAND
Institute of International Education
G.P.O. Box 2050
Bangkok 10501, Thailand
Telephone: 66-2-652-0726

TUNISIA
AMIDEAST
BP 351 Tunis-Belvedere 1002
Tunis, Tunisia
Telephone: 216-1-790559

YEMEN
AMIDEAST
P.O. Box 22347
Sana´a, Yemen
Telephone: 967-1-216975

ALL OTHER COUNTRIES AND AREAS
TOEFL/TSE Publications
P.O. Box 6154
Princeton, NJ 08541-6154, USA
Telephone: 609-771-7100

---

*Applicants from this area will be given the European edition of the *Bulletin,* which can also be obtained from CITO.
 See the address listed under Europe.

Which Language Skills Are Tested on the TOEFL?

Five language skills—listening, structure, written expression, vocabulary, and reading—are tested on the TOEFL. They are tested in three separate sections.

Section 1   Listening Comprehension
Section 2   Structure and Written Expression
Section 3   Reading Comprehension

Does the TOEFL Examination Have a Composition Section?

The TOEFL does not have a composition section, but if you take the TOEFL in August, October, December, February, or May, you will also take the TWE (Test of Written English).

On the TWE, you have an opportunity to write a short essay on an assigned topic. The essay should be about 300 words long. The topic is typical of academic writing requirements at colleges and universities in North America. You have 30 minutes to finish writing. The Test of Written English is described in greater detail in Chapter 8 of this book.

Is the Same TOEFL Used for All Testings?

In general, the same TOEFL format is used for all International Testings administered on Friday or Saturday, and all Institutional Testings in the United States and around the world.

Beginning in July, 1995, some minor differences in question types were introduced in Sections I and III of the international tests. This is called the revised format. It is the most recent version of the TOEFL.

By 1996, the institutional TOEFL will also use the revised format. This book contains the most recent version of the TOEFL format, the revised version.

COMPARISONS OF FORMATS

TOEFL	Institutional Test Old Format	International Test Revised Format
Section I Part A Part B Part C	Statements Short Conversations Mini-talks with Longer Conversations and Short Talks	Short Conversations Longer Conversations Short Talks and Short Lectures
Section II Part A Part B	Incomplete Sentences Sentence Correction	Incomplete Sentences Sentence Correction
Section III Part A Part B	Vocabulary Reading Comprehension	Reading Comprehension

What Is the Short Form of the TOEFL?

The short form of the TOEFL has 140 questions, including 50 questions for the Listening Comprehension Section, 40 questions for the Structure and Written Expression Section, and 50 questions for the Vocabulary and Reading Comprehension Section.

In the short form of the TOEFL, all questions are used to compute your score.

What Is the Long Form of the TOEFL?

The long form of the TOEFL has approximately 210 questions, including 80 questions for the Listening Comprehension Section, 60 questions for the Structure and Written Expression Section, and 70 questions for the Reading Comprehension Section. In the long form of the TOEFL, some of the questions are experimental. The experimental questions may be used in the short form of future tests.

In the long form of the TOEFL, the experimental questions are not used to compute your score.

May I Choose to Take a Short Form?

The form of the TOEFL is selected by Educational Testing Service for each date and test center. You will find both forms of the TOEFL in the model tests in this book so that you will have practice in taking both the short form and the long form of the test.

How Do I Register for an International Testing?

A registration form is included in the free *Bulletin of Information.*

Return the registration form along with the registration fee to TOEFL Office, P.O. 6151, Princeton, NJ 08541-6151 USA. The registration fee for a Friday Test is $45 US. The registration fee for a Saturday Test is $38 US.

All fees must be paid in U.S. dollars. Pay by check, bank draft, or money order.

If you are living in a country where it is difficult to comply with this regulation, mail your completed registration form to a friend or relative living in the United States, Canada, or a country where checks, bank drafts, or money orders may be drawn on banks in the United States. Your friend or relative may mail the registration form and fee directly to the TOEFL Office.

The check, bank draft, or money order must be made out to TOEFL, and your TOEFL registration number must appear on it.

Or you can have your friend purchase a TOEFL certificate for you. The cost of the certificate is $55 US and it can be used as payment to register for one TOEFL test at test locations in every country except Japan, Taiwan, or the People's Republic of China. It is valid for fourteen months from the date of purchase. To purchase a TOEFL certificate, use the fee certificate service form in the *Bulletin of Information.*

How Do I Register for an Institutional Testing?

You will need to fill out the registration form that is used in an International Testing, but it will probably not be necessary for you to write to the TOEFL Office in order to secure one. The school, college, university, or agency that administers the Institutional Testing should have registration forms available. Fees vary.

The school, college, university, or agency will return your registration form and the registration fee to the TOEFL Office along with the forms and fees of all of the other applicants for the Institutional Testing.

Will Educational Testing Service Confirm My Registration?

Two weeks before your test date, the TOEFL Office will mail you an Admission Ticket. You must complete the ticket and take it with you to the test center on the day of the test. You will also receive a Photo File Record to which you must attach a passport-sized photograph. Your photograph will be made available to the institutions that receive your scores.

If you have not received your Admission Ticket and Photo File Record five days before the test date, call the TOEFL Office. The telephone number is (609) 771-7100. Or, send a FAX to (609) 771-7500.

May I Change the Date or Cancel My Registration?

Test date changes are not permitted. If you want to take the test on another date, you must send in a new application form with another check or money order.

If you do not take the test, you can send your Admission Ticket to the TOEFL Office in Princeton, New Jersey. If they receive your request within sixty days of your test date, you will receive part of your money, usually $10, as a credit toward the new test date fee.

May I Register on the Day of the TOEFL Examination?

Registration of candidates on the day of the TOEFL examination is not permitted under any circumstances at test centers in the United States or abroad.

How Should I Prepare the Night Before the TOEFL Examination?

Don't go to a party the night before you take your TOEFL examination. But don't try to review everything that you have studied in this book either. By going to a party, you will lose the opportunity to review a few problems that may add valuable points to your TOEFL score. But by trying to review everything, you will probably get confused, and you may even panic.

Select a *limited* amount of material to review the night before you take the TOEFL.

And remember, you are not trying to score 100 percent on the TOEFL examination. No one knows everything. If you answer 75 percent of the questions correctly, you will receive an excellent score.

What Can I Do If I Do Not Appear to Take the Test?

If you do not appear to take the test, you have a right to request a partial refund. All refunds are in the form of a credit voucher that you can use as partial payment toward the fee for a future test. If you enter the examination room, you cannot request a partial refund. You must make your request within sixty days of the date of the TOEFL test. Ask for "absentee credit" when you write to the TOEFL Office.

What Should I Take with Me to the Examination Room?

Take three sharpened number two pencils with erasers on them, your Admission Ticket, and Photo Identification Form. In addition to your photo identification, you must have official identification with you. Only your valid passport will be accepted as official identification. Be sure that your photo identification and passport picture look like you do on the day of the examination. If not, you may not be admitted to the examination room. If you do not have a valid passport, follow the special directions for identification requirements on your Admission Ticket.

It would be helpful to take a watch, although most examination rooms will have clocks. Books, dictionaries, tape recorders, and notes are not permitted in the examination room.

Where Should I Sit?

You will be assigned a seat. You may not select your own seat.

It is usually better not to sit with friends anyway. You may find yourself looking at friends instead of concentrating on your test materials. You may even be accused of cheating if it appears that you are communicating in some way.

It is the responsibility of the supervisor to assure that everyone is able to hear the tape. If you can't hear well, ask the supervisor to adjust the volume.

What If I Am Late?

Report to the test center no later than the time on your admission ticket. No one will be admitted after the test materials have been distributed.

How Long Is the Testing Session of the TOEFL?

The total time for the testing session of the TOEFL is two hours. Since the instructions are not included as part of the timed sections, the actual time that you will spend in the examination room will be about three hours. When the TWE is given with the TOEFL, the total time will be about three and one half hours.

How Much Time Do I Have to Complete Each of the Sections?

It is wise to work as rapidly as possible without compromising accuracy. Check the Timetable for the TOEFL on page viii.

How Do I Answer the Test Questions?

Read the four possible answers in your test book and mark the corresponding space on the answer sheet, which will be provided for you at the test center.

There are two versions of the answer sheet—a horizontal and a vertical version. We have included both versions of answer sheets with the model examinations included in this book. Because it takes a little longer to finish an examination when you mark the answers on a separate sheet, always use the answer sheets when you take the timed model examinations in this book.

How Do I Mark the Answer Sheet?

Before the examination begins, the supervisor will explain how to mark the answer sheet. Be sure to fill in the space completely.

MARKING THE ANSWER SHEET

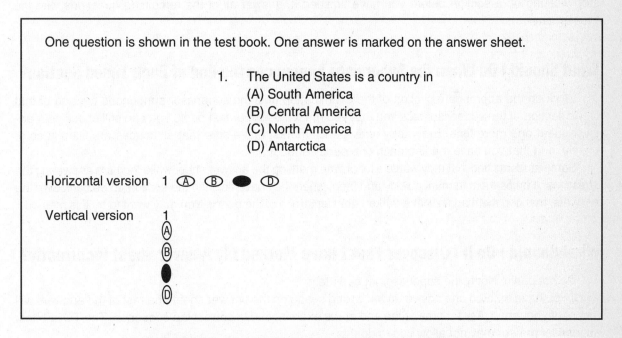

May I Make Marks in the Test Book?

You are not allowed to make marks in your test book. You may not underline words or write notes in the margins of the test book. It is considered cheating.

May I Erase an Answer?

You may erase an answer if you do so carefully and completely. Stray pencil marks may cause inaccurate scoring by the test-scoring machine.

If I Am Not Sure of an Answer, Should I Guess?

If you are not sure of an answer, you should guess. The number of incorrect answers is not subtracted from your score. Your score is based upon the number of correct answers only.

Do not mark more than one answer for each question. Do not leave any questions blank on your answer sheet.

How Should I Guess?

First, eliminate all of the possibilities which you know are NOT correct. Then, if you are almost sure of an answer, guess that one.

If you have no idea of the correct answer for a question, choose one letter and use it for your "guess" answer throughout the entire examination.

By using the same letter each time that you guess, you will probably answer correctly 25 percent of the time.

The "guess" answer is especially useful for finishing a section quickly. If the supervisor tells you to stop working on a section before you have finished it, answer all of the remaining questions with the "guess" answer.

What Should I Do When the Supervisor Announces the End of Each Timed Section?

Work on the appropriate section of the examination until the supervisor announces the end of that timed section. If the supervisor tells you that you must close your test book, you can still check your answer sheet one more time. Erase any stray pencil marks. Make sure that all spaces are filled in completely, and that you have marked each one darkly enough.

Some students find that they waste a lot of time marking the answer sheet while they are answering the questions. It helps them to mark quickly and then, when they have finished the section, to go back over the answers, marking them again with a darker, heavier stroke of the pencil. You may want to try this method.

What Should I Do If I Discover That I Have Marked My Answer Sheet Incorrectly?

Do not panic. Notify the supervisor immediately.

If you have marked one answer in the wrong space on the answer sheet, the rest of the answers will be out of sequence. Ask for time at the end of the examination to correct the sequence. The TOEFL test supervisor may or may not allow you to do this.

If you have marked the answers in the test book instead of on the answer sheet, ask for your test book to be attached to your answer sheet and included in the supervisor's "Irregularities Report."

To save time finding the number on the answer sheet that corresponds to the problem you are reading, to avoid mismarking, and to save space on your desk, use your test book as a marker on your answer sheet. As you advance, slide the book down underneath the number of the question that you are marking on the answer sheet.

USING THE TEST BOOK AS A MARKER

May I Keep My Test Book?

The TOEFL Office makes copies of test books available for tests taken on specific dates listed in the *Bulletin of Information.* They are called "disclosed" tests. If you take the TOEFL on one of the specified dates, you must bring a 15.3cm x 22.8cm self-addressed envelope with enough stamps attached to mail forty-three grams. Your test book will then be mailed to you by the test supervisor the week after the test. This service is free. If you do not have a self-addressed stamped envelope, you may not request your test later.

The TOEFL Office will also mail you a copy of your answer sheet, a list of the correct answers, and a cassette tape recording of the Listening Comprehension Section. To receive these materials, complete the order form on the inside cover of your test book and mail it along with a fee of $18 to the TOEFL Office.

If you try to take your test book without the permission of your test supervisor, your test will not be scored. In addition, the TOEFL Office may take legal action against you.

How Can I Complain About a Test Administration?

If you feel that the test situation was not fair, you have a right to register a complaint. Within three days of the date of the test, write a letter to the TOEFL Office. Include the date of your test, the city, and the country. Explain why you feel that the test was not fair.

If I Score Very Poorly on One Part of the Examination, Is It Still Possible to Receive a Good Total Score?

If you have mismarked an entire part of a section, or if you feel that you have done very poorly on one part of a section, do not despair. You may receive a low score on one part of a section and still score well on the total examination if your scores on the other parts of that section and the other sections are good.

How Is My TOEFL Test Scored?

Total TOEFL scores range from 200 to 677.

First, each of the three sections of the TOEFL is graded on a scale from 20 to 68. Then the scores from the three sections are added together. Finally, the sum is multiplied by 10 and divided by 3.

For example, the following scores were received on the three sections.

Listening Comprehension	52
Structure and Written Expression	48
Vocabulary and Reading Comprehension	50
	150

150 x 10 = 1500 ÷ 3 = 500 Total TOEFL Score

How Do I Interpret My Score?

There are no passing or failing scores on the TOEFL. Each agency or university will evaluate the scores according to its own requirements. Even at the same university, the requirements may vary for different programs of study, levels of study (graduate or undergraduate), and degrees of responsibility (student or teaching assistant).

The admissions policies summarized below are typical of U.S. universities, assuming of course, that the applicant's documents other than English proficiency are acceptable.

**TYPICAL ADMISSIONS POLICIES
OF AMERICAN UNIVERSITIES**

TOEFL Score	Policy
600 or more	admission assured for graduate students
550–599	admission assured for undergraduate students; admission probable for graduate students
500–549	admission probable for undergraduate students
450–499	individual cases reviewed
449 or less	admission doubtful to university; admission possible to two-year college

Refer to the *Bulletin of Information* for a detailed chart of percentile ranks for total TOEFL scores. This will help you interpret your score relative to the scores of others taking the examination.

How Can a Score Report Be Canceled?

The TOEFL Office reserves the right to cancel your test score if there is evidence from the test supervisor that there has been cheating.

If you do not want your scores to be reported, you have a right to cancel them. To cancel your test scores, you must complete the score cancellation section of your TOEFL answer sheet, you must write, call, or FAX the TOEFL Office. If your request is received at the TOEFL Office within seven days of the date of the test, your scores will not be reported.

When Will I Receive My Score Report?

You are entitled to four copies of your test results, including one personal copy for yourself and three Official Score Reports.

You will receive your copy about five weeks after you take the test.

How Will the Agencies or Universities of My Choice Be Informed of My Score?

Five weeks after the testing, your Official Score Reports will be forwarded directly to the agencies and/or universities that you designated on an information section at the top of the TOEFL answer sheet on the day of the examination.

You may send your personal copy to an institution or agency, but the score will probably have to be confirmed by an official at the TOEFL Office before you can be admitted. Scores more than two years old cannot be reported or verified.

How Can I Send Additional Reports?

Your scores will be sent to the three institutions or agencies that you mark on your answer sheet when you take your exam. There are two reporting services that will send additional reports as well. One service is the Regular Reporting Service. The Regular Reporting Service costs $11 for each additional report, and the reports are mailed two weeks after the request arrives at the TOEFL Office. The other service is the Rush Reporting Service. The Rush Reporting Service costs $31 for the first report, plus $11 for each additional report you request. The reports are mailed two days after the request is received.

To use either the Regular or the Rush Reporting Service, complete the Score Report Request Form in the *Bulletin of Information.* Only scores achieved within the last two years will be reported.

What Can I Do If I Question My Score Report?

Occasionally, the computer will score an answer sheet incorrectly because of the way you have marked it. If you feel your score is much, much lower than you expected, you have a right to request that your answer sheet be hand scored.

Two people will score your answer sheet independently. If their results are different from that of the computer, your score will be changed. The cost of this service is $20 for the TOEFL and $40 for the TWE. You must make your request within six months of the date of the test.

To make a request, write a letter to the TOEFL Office.

May I Take the TOEFL More Than One Time?

You may take the TOEFL as many times as you wish in order to score to your satisfaction.

If I Have Already Taken the TOEFL, How Will the First Score or Scores Affect My New Score?

TOEFL scores are considered to be valid for two years. If you have taken the TOEFL more than once, but your first score report is dated more than two years ago, the TOEFL Office will not report your score.

If you have taken the TOEFL more than once in the past two years, the TOEFL Office will report the score for the test date you request on your Score Request Form.

How Difficult Is the TOEFL?

The level of difficulty of the TOEFL is directly related to the average level of proficiency in English of the candidates who take the examination.

This means that each question will probably be answered correctly by 50 percent of the candidates.

Is There a Direct Correspondence Between Proficiency in English and a Good Score on the TOEFL?

There is not always a direct correspondence between proficiency in English and a good score on the TOEFL. Many students who are proficient in English are not proficient in how to approach the examination. That is why it is important to prepare by using this book.

What Is the Relationship Between My Score on Model Tests and My Score on the TOEFL Examination?

It is not possible to calculate a TOEFL score from a score that you might receive on a model test in this book. This is so because the actual TOEFL examination has a wider variety of problems.

The model tests in this book have been especially designed to help you improve your total TOEFL score by improving your knowledge of the types of problems that most often appear on the TOEFL. These problem types are repeated throughout the eight model tests so that you will have practice in recognizing and answering them.

By improving your ability to recognize and correctly answer those types of problems that most often appear on the TOEFL, you will improve your total TOEFL score.

Thousands of other students have succeeded by using this book. You can be successful, too.

2

REVIEW OF
LISTENING
COMPREHENSION

Getting a Good Start

The Listening Comprehension Section of the TOEFL is the first section tested. If you do well on this section, you will feel confident about the rest of the test.

Learn to relax. If you start to panic in the examination room, close your eyes and say "no" in your mind. Tell yourself, "I will not panic. I am prepared." Then take several slow, deep breaths, letting your shoulders drop in a relaxed manner as you exhale.

Concentrate while listening. Do not talk. Concentrate your attention. Do not look at anything in the test room except the answers that correspond to the problem you are hearing.

Do not think about your situation, the test in general, your score, or your future. If you do, force yourself to return to the problem you are hearing.

If you do not understand a problem and you do not have a good answer, use your "guess" answer. Then stop thinking about it. Be ready to hear the next problem.

Use the test book for selective listening. Sometimes the four possible answers in the test book will have something in common. For example, you may find four places, four names, four dates, or four amounts of money. In problems like these, you know what the question will be. You can prepare to listen selectively for one piece of information.

Do not cheat. In spite of opportunity, knowledge that others are doing it, desire to help a friend, or fear that you will not make a good score, do not cheat.

On the TOEFL, cheating is a very serious matter. If you are discovered, your answer sheet will not be scored. Legal action may be taken by the TOEFL Office.

OVERVIEW

Section 1: Listening Comprehension

**50 QUESTIONS
40 MINUTES**

Part A   Short Conversations

Thirty short conversations between two speakers with one question spoken on tape after each conversation.

You must choose from four possible answers in your test book the answer that would be the best response to the question you have heard.

Part B   Longer Conversations

Two longer conversations between two speakers with four questions spoken on tape after each conversation.

You must choose from four possible answers for each question the answer that would be the best response to each question you have heard.

Part C   Talks and Lectures

Three short talks and lectures with several questions spoken on tape after each talk.

You must choose from four possible answers for each question the answer that would be the best response to each question you have heard.

TYPES OF PROBLEMS IN THE LISTENING COMPREHENSION SECTION

Problems like those in this Review of Listening Comprehension frequently appear on Parts A, B, and C of the Listening Comprehension Section of the TOEFL.

Part A   Short Conversations

1   Details

2   Idiomatic Expressions

3   Suggestions

4   Assumptions

5   Predictions

6   Implications

7   Problems

8   Topics

Part B   Longer Conversations

9   Informal Conversations

10   Academic Conversations

11   Class Discussions

Part C   Talks and Lectures

12   Radio Programs

13   Tours

14   Academic Talks

15   Lectures

Types of Problems in Part A (Short Conversations)

 Details

Details are specific facts stated in a conversation.

In some conversations on Part A, you will hear all of the information that you need to answer the problem correctly. You will NOT need to draw conclusions.

When you hear a conversation between two speakers, you must remember the details that were stated.

EXAMPLE

Man:	Front desk. How may I help you?
Woman:	I'd like to arrange a wake-up call for tomorrow morning at seven o'clock, please.
Narrator:	When does the woman want to get up tomorrow?
Answer:	Seven o'clock in the morning.

 Idiomatic expressions

Idiomatic expressions are words and phrases that are characteristic of a particular language with meanings that are usually different from the meanings of each of the words used alone.

In some conversations on Part A, you will hear idiomatic expressions, such as "to kill time," which means to wait.

When you hear a conversation between two speakers, you must listen for the idiomatic expressions. You will be expected to recognize them and restate the idiom or identify the feelings or attitudes of the speaker.

It will help you if you study a list of common idioms as part of your TOEFL preparation.

EXAMPLE

Man:	I'm single. In fact, I've never been married.
Woman:	No kidding!
Narrator:	What does the woman mean?
Answer:	She is surprised by the man's statement.

 Suggestions

A *suggestion* is a recommendation.

In some conversations on Part A, you will hear words and phrases that make a suggestion, such as "you should," "why don't you," or "why not."

When you hear the words and phrases that introduce a suggestion, you must be able to recognize and remember what the speaker suggested, and who made the suggestion.

EXAMPLE

Woman:	Do you know if there is a Lost and Found on campus? I left my book bag in this room earlier, and it's gone.
Man:	Too bad. Look, why don't you check with your teacher first? Maybe someone in your class turned it in.
Narrator:	What does the man suggest that the woman do?
Answer:	Ask her teacher about the book bag.

4   Assumptions

An *assumption* is a statement accepted as true without proof or demonstration.

In some conversations on Part A, an assumption is proven false, and the speaker or speakers who had made the assumption express surprise.

When you hear a conversation between two speakers, you must be able to recognize remarks that register surprise, and draw conclusions about the assumptions that the speaker may have made.

EXAMPLE

Woman:	Let's just e-mail our response to Larry instead of calling.
Man:	*Larry* has an e-mail address?
Narrator:	What had the man assumed about Larry?
Answer:	He would not have an e-mail address.

5   Predictions

A *prediction* is a guess about the future based on evidence from the present.

In some short conversations on Part A, you will be asked to make predictions about the future activities of the speakers involved.

When you hear a conversation between two speakers, you must listen for evidence from which you may draw a logical conclusion about their future activities.

EXAMPLE

Man:	Could you please book me on the next flight out to Los Angeles?
Woman:	I'm sorry, sir. Continental doesn't fly into Los Angeles. Why don't you try Northern or Worldwide?

Narrator: What will the man probably do?
Answer: He will probably get a ticket for a flight on Northern or Worldwide Airlines.

6   Implications

Implied means suggested, but not stated. In many ways, implied conversations are like prediction conversations.

In some conversations on Part A, you will hear words and phrases or intonations that will suggest how the speakers felt, what kind of work or activity they were involved in, or where the conversation may have taken place.

When you hear a conversation between two speakers, you must listen for information that will help you draw a conclusion about the situation.

EXAMPLE

Woman: Where's Anita? We were supposed to go to the library to study.
Man: Well, here is her coat, and her books are over there on the chair.

Narrator: What does the woman imply about Anita?
Answer: Anita has not left for the library yet.

7   Problems

A *problem* is a situation that requires discussion or solution.

In some conversations on Part A, you will hear the speakers discuss a problem.

When you hear a discussion between two speakers, you must be able to identify what the problem is. This may be more difficult because different aspects of the problem will also be included in the conversation.

EXAMPLE

Woman: It only takes two hours to get to New York, but you'll have a six-hour layover between
                   flights.
Man: Maybe you could try routing me through Philadelphia or Boston instead.

Narrator: What is the man's problem?
Answer: His flight connections are not very convenient.

8   Topics

A *topic* is a main theme in a conversation or in a piece of writing.

In some conversations on Part A, the speakers will discuss a particular topic.

When you hear a conversation, you must be able to identify the main topic from among several secondary themes that support the topic.

EXAMPLE

Man:	Tell me about your trip to New York.
Woman:	It was great! We saw the Statue of Liberty and the Empire State Building and all of the tourist attractions the first day, then we saw the museums the second day and spent the rest of the time shopping and seeing shows.
Narrator:	What are the man and woman talking about?
Answer:	The woman's trip.

Types of Problems in Part B (Longer Conversations)

9   Informal Conversations

Informal conversations are conversations between friends or with service personnel in stores or restaurants.

In some conversations on Part B, you will hear an informal conversation between two speakers.

When you hear a conversation, you must be able to summarize the important ideas. You will usually NOT be required to remember small details.

It will help you to review the conversations in Part A.

EXAMPLE

Ted Parker:	Are you Mrs. Williams?
Mrs. Williams:	Why, yes!
Ted Parker:	I'm Ted Parker. I talked with you on the telephone earlier today.
Mrs. Williams:	Oh, good.
Ted Parker:	Let me show you what we have in a new Oldsmobile Cutlass.
Mrs. Williams:	I want to look at last year's model, too, if you have any.
Ted Parker:	I have one. A red Delta 88, with 2,000 miles on it. It was a demonstrator.
Mrs. Williams:	A demonstrator?
Ted Parker:	That means that only the sales staff have driven it.
Mrs. Williams:	Oh, well, let's just look at the new ones then.

Ted Parker:	Okay. Everything on this side of the lot is the Cutlass model. You said on the phone that you are looking for automatic. Did you have any idea of other options that you'd like to have on the car? Air conditioning, power windows, maybe cruise control?
Mrs. Williams:	Just air conditioning…and an FM radio.
Ted Parker:	Then I suggest that you just spend some time looking at the cars in the last row there. Those six. They have the options and the prices on the sticker on the window, and if you have any questions, I'll be glad to help you.
Mrs. Williams:	Thank you.
Ted Parker:	Let me just say that the best way to know whether you want a car is to drive it. So, when you find something you think you may be interested in, we can take it out for a test drive and let you get the feel of it.
Mrs. Williams:	Okay. That sounds like a good idea.
Question:	Who is the man?
Answer:	A car salesman.
Question:	What is the woman looking for?
Answer:	A new Oldsmobile.
Question:	Besides automatic shift, what options does the woman want?
Answer:	Only air conditioning and a radio.
Question:	What will the woman probably do?
Answer:	Take the car for a test drive.

10   Academic Conversations

Academic conversations are conversations between students and professors or other academic personnel on a college or university campus.

In some conversations on Part B, you will hear an academic conversation between two speakers.

When you hear a conversation, you must be able to summarize the main ideas. You may also be asked to recall important details.

EXAMPLE

Marcy:	Do you have a minute, Dr. Peterson?
Dr. Peterson:	Sure. Come on in, Marcy. What's the problem?
Marcy:	Well, I'm not sure. I got this letter, and I don't understand it very well.
Dr. Peterson:	Let's see it.
Marcy:	It's from the Financial Aid Office. Are they going to cancel my student aid?
Dr. Peterson:	I would hope not. Hmmmn. Oh, I see. Here's what happened. You are only registered for three hours next semester.

Marcy:	That's true, but I plan to register for another class during open registration. I heard about a new environmental science course, and I'm waiting for it to be assigned a sequence number.
Dr. Peterson:	Well, then, you don't have a problem. You see, the terms of your grant require that you take at least six hours per semester.
Marcy:	I know, but I've never gotten a letter before.
Dr. Peterson:	I think it's a new procedure. Don't worry about it. Just be sure to sign up for at least three more hours before the beginning of the semester.
Marcy:	Thanks, Dr. Peterson. I'm really glad you were in your office today.
Question:	What is Marcy's problem?
Answer:	She has received a letter from the Financial Aid Office.
Question:	Why did Marcy receive a letter?
Answer:	She did not register for six hours this semester.
Question:	What had Marcy planned to do?
Answer:	Register for three more hours during open registration.
Question:	How does Marcy feel when she leaves Dr. Peterson's office?
Answer:	Relieved.

11   Class Discussions

Class discussions are conversations that occur in classrooms.

In some talks on Part B, you will hear a class discussion between two, three, or more speakers.

When you hear a discussion, you must be able to summarize the important ideas. You will usually NOT be required to remember small details.

It will help you to audit some college classes.

EXAMPLE

Miss Richards:	Good morning. My name is Miss Richards, and I'll be your instructor for Career Education 100. Before we get started, I'd appreciate it if you would introduce yourselves and tell us a little bit about why you decided to take this class. Let's start here....
Bill:	I'm Bill Jensen, and I'm a sophomore this term, but I still haven't decided what to major in. I hope that this class will help me.
Miss Richards:	Good, I hope so, too. Next.
Patty:	I'm Patty Davis, and I'm majoring in foreign languages, but I'm not sure what kind of job I can get after I graduate.
Miss Richards:	Are you a sophomore, too, Patty?
Patty:	No. I'm a senior. I wish I'd taken this class sooner, but I didn't know about it until this term.

| Miss Richards: | Didn't your advisor tell you about it? |
| Patty: | No. A friend of mine took it last year, and it helped her a lot. |

| Miss Richards: | How did you find out about the course, Bill? |
| Bill: | The same way Patty did. A friend of mine told me about it. |

| Question: | In what class does this discussion take place? |
| Answer: | Career Education. |

| Question: | What are the two students talking about? |
| Answer: | They are introducing themselves. |

| Question: | Why is the woman taking the course? |
| Answer: | To help her find a job after graduation. |

| Question: | How did the students find out about the course? |
| Answer: | From friends who had taken it. |

Types of Problems in Part C (Talks and Lectures)

12   Radio Programs

Radio programs are short talks that provide information about the news.
In some talks on Part C, you will hear information about the news.
When you hear a talk, you must be able to summarize the information. You will usually NOT be required to remember small details.
It will help you to listen to feature news programs on radio and television. Listen carefully. Ask yourself questions to test your ability to remember the information.

EXAMPLE

This is Morning News Magazine, and I'm Jack Stevens. I'll be your host while Mark Watkins is on assignment in the Middle East.

Today's story is about the flight from the cities. Everyone knows that it's happening, but only recently have we been able to determine where the people are going. To the suburbs? To the fringes of the city? Surprisingly not. In a marked reversal of U.S. migration patterns, nonmetropolitan areas have started growing faster than metropolitan areas. City dwellers are leaving to settle in small-town America.

Census figures confirm both the shrinkage of many urban areas and the revival of small towns, a trend that began to become apparent in the last two decades. For example, while the national population increased by 4.8 percent from 1970–1975, towns of 2,500 to 25,000 persons rose 7.5 percent, and the smallest towns with populations of less than 2,500 rose 8.7 percent, or nearly double the national rate.

Recent surveys consistently show that a majority of people, including four out of ten big-city dwellers, prefer life outside the urban environment. They associate small towns with a feeling of community and a sense of security.

Tomorrow's report will focus on crime control. Till then, this is Jack Stevens wishing you a good morning.

Question: What is the topic of this talk?
Answer: Migration out of the cities.

Question: Where are many people moving?
Answer: To small towns.

Question: Which areas have experienced the most growth?
Answer: The towns with a population of 2,500 or fewer people.

Question: According to surveys, why are people moving?
Answer: Because people feel secure in small towns.

13   Tours

Tours are short talks that provide factual information about a tourist attraction.

In some talks on Part C, you will hear a talk by a tour guide.

When you hear a talk, you must be able to summarize the important ideas. You must also be able to answer questions that begin with the following words: *who, what, when, where, why?*

It will help you to listen to travel programs on radio and television. Listen carefully. Ask yourself questions to test your ability to remember the information.

EXAMPLE

Welcome to the Lincoln Memorial, located, as you can see, on the west bank of the Potomac River, on the axis of the Capitol Building and the Washington Monument.

The structure itself was designed by Henry Bacon in 1912 and completed ten years later at a cost of 2.9 million dollars.

The outer walls of the memorial are white Colorado marble, 189 feet long and 118 feet 8 inches wide. The thirty-six outer columns are also of marble, representing the thirty-six states that were in the Union at the time of Lincoln's death. The name of each state is cut into stone above the column.

Inside the memorial, the walls are Indiana limestone and the floor is pink Tennessee marble. Three commemorative features include the huge seated statue of Lincoln and two inscribed stone tablets.

The marble statue occupies the place of honor, centrally located, as you will note, and facing the Washington Monument and the Capitol Building. The statue is 19 feet high and 19 feet wide, made of twenty-eight blocks of Georgia white marble. Because of the immense size, it took two men four years to complete the carving.

On the north wall, inscribed in stone, is Lincoln's Second Inaugural Address; on the south wall, similarly inscribed, is the Gettysburg Address.

There is a mural above each inscription, representing the two greatest accomplishments of Lincoln's presidency—the emancipation of the slaves and the unification of the North and South after the Civil War.

This memorial is open daily from eight o'clock in the morning to midnight. Stay as long as you like, and be sure to ask one of the park service employees if you have any questions.

Question: What material was used in the construction of most of the Lincoln Memorial?
Answer: Marble.

Question: Why are there thirty-six columns?
Answer: There is one for each state in the Union at the time of Lincoln's death.

Question: What other buildings can be seen from the memorial?
Answer: The Capitol Building and the Washington Monument.

Question: When is the memorial open?
Answer: Every day from 8 a.m. to midnight.

14   Academic Talks

Academic talks are short talks that provide orientation to academic courses and procedures. In some talks on Part C, you will hear academic talks on a variety of college and university topics. When you hear a talk, you must be able to summarize the main ideas. You must also be able to answer questions about important details. You will usually not be asked to remember minor details.

EXAMPLE

Since we'll be having our midterm exam next week, I thought I'd spend a few minutes talking with you about it. I realize that none of you has ever taken a class with me before, so you really don't know what to expect on one of my exams.

First, let me remind you that I have included a very short description of the midterm on the syllabus that you received at the beginning of the semester. So you should read that. I also recommend that you organize and review your notes from all of our class sessions. I'm not saying that the book is unimportant, but the notes should help you to identify those topics that we covered in greatest detail. Then, you can go back to your book and reread the sections that deal with those topics. I also suggest that you take another look at the articles on reserve in the library. They have information in them that is not in the book, and although we didn't talk much about them in class, I do feel that they are important, so you can expect to see a few questions from the articles on the exam. Oh, yes, I almost forgot. Besides the twenty-five objective questions, there will be five essay questions, and you must choose three.

EXAMPLE

Question: What does the speaker mainly discuss?
Answer: The midterm exam.

Question: When will the students take the exam?
Answer: Next week.

Question: According to the professor, what should the students do to prepare?
Answer: Study their notes, the articles on reserve, and appropriate sections of the book.

Question: What is the format of the exam?
Answer: Twenty-five objective questions and five essay questions.

15   Lectures

Lectures are short talks that provide information about academic subjects. They are like short lectures that might be heard in a college classroom.

In some talks on Part C, you will hear academic information in a short lecture.

When you hear a lecture, you must be able to summarize the important ideas. You must also be able to answer questions that begin with the following words: *who, what, when, where, why?*

It will help you to listen to documentary programs on radio and television. Programs on educational broadcasting networks are especially helpful. Listen carefully. Ask yourself questions to test your ability to remember the information.

EXAMPLE

Ernest Hemingway began his writing career as an ambitious young American newspaperman in Paris after the first World War. His early books, including *The Sun Also Rises*, were published in Europe before they were released in the United States.

Hemingway always wrote from experience rather than from imagination. In *Farewell to Arms*, published in 1929, he recounted his adventures as an ambulance driver in Italy during the war. In *For Whom the Bell Tolls*, published in 1940, he retold his memories of the Spanish Civil War.

Perhaps more than any other twentieth-century American writer, he was responsible for creating a style of literature. The Hemingway style was hard, economical, and powerful. It lured the reader into using imagination in order to fill in the details.

In 1952, Hemingway published *The Old Man and the Sea*, a short, compelling tale of an old fisherman's struggle to haul in a giant marlin that he had caught in the Gulf of Mexico. Some critics interpreted it as the allegory of man's struggle against old age; others interpreted it as man against the forces of nature. This book was the climax of Hemingway's career. Two years later he was awarded the Nobel prize for literature.

Question: What theme did Hemingway use for many of his books?
Answer: War.

Question: What was the Hemingway style?
Answer: Short and powerful.

Question: What prize did Hemingway win after he wrote *The Old Man and the Sea?*
Answer: The Nobel prize for literature.

Question: What advice would Hemingway probably give to other writers?
Answer: Write from experience about things you have seen and people you have known.

REVIEW OF
STRUCTURE
AND WRITTEN
EXPRESSION

OVERVIEW

Section 2: Structure and Written Expression

40 QUESTIONS
25 MINUTES

Part A   Incomplete sentences

Fifteen incomplete sentences with four words or phrases listed beneath each sentence.

You must choose the one word or phrase that best completes the sentence.

Part B   Incorrect sentences

Twenty-five incorrect sentences with four underlined words or phrases in each sentence.

You must choose the one word or phrase that is not correct in the sentence.

Strategies and Symbols for Review

Strategies

How will this Review of Structure and Written Expression help you?

It won't teach you every rule of English grammar, but it will provide you with a review of the problems in structure and written expression that are most commonly tested on the TOEFL.

Use this review to study and to check your progress. Follow three easy steps for each problem.

1. *Review the generalization.* First, read the explanation and study the word order in the chart. Then, close your eyes, and try to see the chart in your mind.
2. *Study the examples.* Focus on the examples. First, read them silently, noting the difference between the correct and incorrect sentences. Then, read the underlined parts of the correct sentences aloud.
3. *Check your progress.* First, complete the exercise. Each exercise has two questions—one similar to Part A and the other similar to Part B on the Structure and Written Expression section of the TOEFL. Then, check your answers, using the answer key in Chapter 6 of this book.

If you are studying in an English program, use this review with your grammar book. After your teacher presents a grammar rule in class, find it in the table of contents of this review (see pages 37–40). Refer to the generalization, study the examples, and check your progress by completing the exercise.

When you go to your next grammar class, you will be more prepared. When you go to your TOEFL examination, you will be more confident. With preparation, you can succeed in school and on the TOEFL.

Symbols

In order for you to use the patterns and rules of style in this review, you must understand five kinds of symbols.

Abbreviations. An abbreviation is a shortened form. In the patterns, five abbreviations, or shortened forms, are used: *S* is an abbreviation for *Subject, V* for *Verb, V Ph* for *Verb Phrase, C* for *Complement,* and *M* for *Modifier.*

Small Letters. Small letters are lowercase letters. In the patterns, a verb written in small (lowercase) letters may not change form. For example, the verb *have* may not change to *has* or *had* when it is written in small letters.

Capital Letters. Capital letters are uppercase letters. In the patterns, a verb written in capital (uppercase) letters may change form. For example, the verb *HAVE* may remain as *have,* or may change to *has* or *had,* depending upon agreement with the subject and choice of tense.

Parentheses. Parentheses are curved lines used as punctuation marks. The following punctuation marks are parentheses: (   ). In the patterns, the words in parentheses give specific information about the abbreviation or word which precedes them. For example, *V (present)* means that the verb in the pattern must be a present tense verb. *N (count)* means that the noun in the pattern must be a countable noun.

Alternatives. Alternatives are different ways to express the same idea. In the patterns, alternatives are written in a column. For example, in the following pattern, there are three alternatives:

had would have could have	participle

The alternatives are *had, would have,* and *could have.* Any one of the alternatives may be used with the participle. All three alternatives are correct.

TYPES OF PROBLEMS IN THE STRUCTURE AND WRITTEN EXPRESSION SECTION

Patterns and rules of style like those in this Review of Structure and Written Expression frequently appear on Parts A and B of the Structure and Written Expression Section of the TOEFL.

The emphasis that is placed on various patterns and style problems changes from year to year on the TOEFL examination. Research indicates that those problems shown in bold print in the reference list below are most frequently tested on current examinations.

To prepare for Section 2 of the TOEFL, study the problems in this chapter. Give special attention to the problems in bold print.

PATTERNS

Problems with Verbs

Problems with Main Verbs

1 Missing Main Verb

2 Verbs that Require an Infinitive in the Complement

3 Verbs that Require an -ing Form in the Complement

4 Verb Phrases that Require an -ing Form in the Complement

Problems with Tense

5 Irregular Past Forms

Problems with Modals

6 Modal + Verb Word

7 Logical Conclusions — Events in the Past

8 Logical Conclusions — Events in the Present

9 Logical Conclusions — Events that Repeat

10 Knowledge and Ability — *Know* and *Know How*

11 Past Custom — *Used to* and BE *Used to*

12 Advisability — *Had Better*

13 Preference — *Would Rather*

14 Preference for Another — *Would Rather That*

15 Negative Imperatives

Problems with Causatives

16 Causative MAKE

17 Causative GET

18 Causative HAVE

19 Causative LET

20 Causative HELP

Problems with Conditionals

21 **Factual Conditionals — Absolute, Scientific Results**

22 Factual Conditionals — Probable Results for the Future

23 Factual Conditionals — Possible Results

24 Factual Conditionals — Probable Changes in Past Results

25 Contrary-to-Fact Conditionals — Impossible Results *Were*

26 Contrary-to-Fact Conditionals — Change in Conditions *Unless*

Problems with Subjunctives

27 Importance — Subjunctive Verbs

28 Importance — Nouns Derived from Subjunctive Verbs

29 Importance — Impersonal Expressions

Problems with Infinitives

30   Purpose — Infinitives

Problems with Passives

31   **Passives — Word Order**

32   Passives — Agent

33   Passives—Infinitives

34   Necessity for Repair or Improvement — NEED

35   **Belief and Knowledge — Anticipatory *It***

Problems with HAVE + Participle

36   Duration — HAVE + Participle

37   Duration — HAVE + *Been* + Participle

38   Predictions — *Will Have* + Participle

39   Unfulfilled Desires in the Past — *Had Hoped*

Problems with Auxiliary Verbs

40   **Missing Auxiliary Verb—Active**

41   **Missing Auxiliary Verb—Passive**

Problems with Pronouns

42   Subject Pronouns

43   Subject Pronouns in Complement Position

44   Object Pronouns

45   Object Pronouns after Prepositions

46   Possessive Pronouns before *-ing* Forms

47   Possessive Pronouns before Parts of the Body

48   Relative Pronouns that Refer to Persons and Things

49   Relative Pronouns that Refer to Persons

50   Reflexive Pronouns

51   Reciprocal Pronouns

Problems with Nouns

52   Count Nouns

53   Noncount Nouns

54   Nouns with Count and Noncount Meanings

55   Count and Noncount Nouns with Similar Meanings

56   Noncount Nouns that are Count Nouns in Other Languages

57   Singular and Plural Expressions of Noncount Nouns

58   Classifications — *Kind* and *Type*

59   Infinitive and *-ing* Subjects

60   Qualifying Phrases with *-ing* Nouns

61   Nominal *That* Clause

Problems with Adjectives

Problems with Determiners

62   Determiners — *A* and *An*

63   Noncount Nouns with Qualifying Phrases — *The*

64   Ø meaning *All*

65   *No* Meaning *Not Any*

66   *One of the* and *Some of the*

67   *Few* and *Little*

68   *Much* and *Many*

69   *A Little* and *Little*; *A Few* and *Few*

70   *Only a Few* and *Only a Little*

71   *A Large (Small) Number of* and *a Large (Small) Amount of*

72   ***Almost All of the* and *Most of the***

Problems with Other Adjectives

73   Sufficiency — *Enough* with Nouns

74   Sufficiency — *Enough* with Adjectives

75   Consecutive Order — *One, Another, the Other*

76   Consecutive Order — *Some, Other, the Other; Some, Others, the Others (the Rest)*

77   Numerical Order

78   Nouns that Function as Adjectives

79 Hyphenated Adjectives

80 Adjectives Ending in *-ed* and *-ing*

81 Cause-and-Result — *So*

82 Cause-and-Result — *Such*

83 Excess — *Too*

84 Emphasis — *Very*

85 Adjectives with Verbs of the Senses

Problems with Comparatives

86 Exact Similarity — *the Same as* and *the Same*

87 General Similarity — *Similar to* and *Similar*

88 General Similarity — *Like* and *Alike*

89 Specific Similarity — Quality Nouns

90 Specific Similarity — Quality Adjectives

91 General Difference — *Different from* and *Different*

92 General Difference — *to Differ from*

93 Comparative Estimates — Multiple Numbers

94 Comparative Estimates — *More Than* and *Less Than*

95 Comparative Estimates — *As Many As*

96 Degrees of Comparison — Comparative Adjectives

97 Degrees of Comparison — Superlative Adjectives

98 Degrees of Comparison — Irregular Adjectives

99 Degrees of Comparison — Comparative Adverbs

100 Double Comparatives

101 Illogical Comparatives — General Similarity and Difference

102 Illogical Comparatives — Degrees

Problems with Prepositions

103 Place — *Between* and *Among*

104 Place — *In, On, At*

105 Time — *In, On, At*

106 Addition — *Besides*

107 Exception — *But* and *Except*

108 Replacement — *Instead of* and *Instead*

109 Example — *Such As*

110 Condition and Unexpected Result — *Despite* and *in Spite of*

111 **Cause — *Because of* and *Because***

112 Cause — *From*

113 Purpose — *For*

114 Means — *By*

115 Time Limit — *From, To*

Problems with Conjunctions

Problems with Correlative Conjunctions

116 Correlative Conjunctions — Inclusives *both ...and*

117 Correlative Conjunctions — Inclusives *both...and...as well as*

118 **Correlative Conjunctions — Inclusives *not only ...but also***

119 Correlative Conjunctions — Exclusives *not...but*

Problems with Other Conjunctions

120 Affirmative Agreement — *So* and *Too*

121 Negative Agreement — *Neither* and *Either*

122 Planned Result — *So That*

123 Future Result — *When*

124 **Indirect Questions**

125 Question Words with *-ever*

Problems with Adverbs

126 Adverbs of Manner

127 Adverbs of Manner — *Fast, Late, Hard*

128 *Sometime* and *Sometimes*

129 **Negative Emphasis**

130 Introductory Adverbial Modifiers — *Once*

131 Introductory Adverbial Modifiers — *While*

132 *No Longer*

133 **Duration — *For* and *Since***

134 Dates

135 Pseudocomparatives

136 Generalization — *As a Whole* and *Wholly*

Problems with Sentences and Clauses

137 Sentences and Clauses

138 Clause-Marker Subjects

139 Verbs in Dependent Clauses

140 Adjective Clauses

STYLE

Problems with Point of View

1 Point of View — Verbs

2 Point of View — Reported Speech

3 Point of View — Verbs and Adverbs

4 Point of View — Activities of the Dead

Problems with Agreement

5 **Agreement — Modified Subject and Verb**

6 Agreement — Subject with Accompaniment and Verb

7 **Agreement — Subject with Appositive and Verb**

8 Agreement — Verb-Subject Order

9 Agreement — Indefinite Subject and Verb

10 Agreement — Collective Subject and Verb

11 Agreement — Noun and Pronoun

12 Agreement — Subject and Possessive Pronouns

13 Agreement — Impersonal Pronouns

14 Agreement — Subject and Appositive

Problems with Introductory Verbal Modifiers

15 Verbal Modifiers — *-ing* and *-ed* Forms

16 Verbal Modifiers — Infinitives of Purpose to Introduce Instructions

Problems with Parallel Structure

17 **Parallel Structure — In a Series**

18 **Parallel Structure — After Correlative Conjunctions**

Problems with Redundancy

19 Redundancy — Unnecessary Phrases

20 Redundancy — Repetition of Words with the Same Meaning

21 Redundancy — Repetition of Noun by Pronoun

Problems with Word Choice

22 Transitive and Intransitive Verbs — *Raise* and *Rise*

23 Transitive and Intransitive Verbs — *Lay* and *Lie*

24 Transitive and Intransitive Verbs — *Set* and *Sit*

25 Similar Verbs — *Tell* and *Say*

26 Similar Verbs — *Let* and *Leave*

27 Similar Verbs — *Borrow* and *Lend*

28   Similar Verbs — *Make* and *Do*   30   **Parts of Speech**

29   **Prepositional Idioms**

PATTERNS

Patterns are the parts of a sentence. In some books, *patterns* are called *structures*. In *patterns,* the words have the same order most of the time.

Some of the most important patterns are summarized in this review section. Remember, the generalizations in the charts and explanations for each pattern refer to the structure in the examples. There may be similar structures for which these generalizations are not appropriate.

Problems with Verbs

A *verb* is a word or phrase that expresses existence, action, or experience.

There are two kinds of verbs in English. They are the *main verb* and the *auxiliary verb.* In some grammar books, the *auxiliary verb* is called a *helping verb* because it is used with a *main verb.*

Every verb in English can be described by the following formula:

$$\text{VERB} = \text{tense} + (\text{modal}) + (\text{have} + \text{participle}) + (\text{be} + \text{-ing}) + \text{verb word}$$

Each of the parts of this formula will be summarized in one or more of the problems in this review. Don't spend time studying it now. Just refer to it as you progress through this review section.

PROBLEMS WITH MAIN VERBS

In English, a sentence must have a main verb. A sentence may or may not have an auxiliary verb.

1   Missing Main Verb

Remember that every English sentence must have a subject and a main verb.

S	V	
The sound of the dryer	bothers	my concentration

Avoid using an *-ing* form, an infinitive, an auxiliary verb, or another part of speech instead of a main verb.

EXAMPLES

INCORRECT: The prettiest girl in our class with long brown hair and brown eyes.
CORRECT: The prettiest girl in our class <u>has</u> long brown hair and brown eyes.

INCORRECT: In my opinion, too soon to make a decision.
CORRECT: In my opinion, <u>it is</u> too soon to make a decision.

INCORRECT: Do you know whether the movie that starts at seven?
CORRECT: Do you know whether the movie that starts at seven <u>is</u> good?
or
Do you know whether the movie <u>starts</u> at seven?

INCORRECT: Sam almost always a lot of fun.
CORRECT: Sam <u>is</u> almost always a lot of fun.

INCORRECT: The book that I lent you having a good bibliography.
CORRECT: The book that I lent you <u>has</u> a good bibliography.

EXERCISES

Part A: Choose the correct answer.

Arizona _____ a very dry climate.
(A) has
(B) being
(C) having
(D) with

Part B: Choose the incorrect word or phrase and correct it.

Venomous snakes <u>with</u> modified teeth connected to <u>poison glands</u> <u>in which</u> the venom <u>is secreted</u> and
               (A)   (B)   (C)   (D)
stored.

Verbs that Require an Infinitive in the Complement

Remember that the following verbs require an infinitive for a verb in the complement.

agree	decide	hesitate	need	refuse
appear	demand	hope	offer	seem
arrange	deserve	intend	plan	tend
ask	expect	learn	prepare	threaten
claim	fail	manage	pretend	wait
consent	forget	mean	promise	want

S	V	C (infinitive)	M
We	had planned	to leave	day before yesterday

Avoid using an *-ing* form after the verbs listed. Avoid using a verb word after *want*.

EXAMPLES

INCORRECT: He wanted speak with Mr. Brown.
  CORRECT: He <u>wanted to speak</u> with Mr. Brown.

INCORRECT: We demand knowing our status.
  CORRECT: We <u>demand to know</u> our status.

INCORRECT: I intend the inform you that we cannot approve your application.
  CORRECT: I <u>intend to inform</u> you that we cannot approve your application.

INCORRECT: They didn't plan buying a car.
  CORRECT: They didn't <u>plan to buy</u> a car.

INCORRECT: The weather tends improving in May.
  CORRECT: The weather <u>tends to improve</u> in May.

EXERCISES

Part A: Choose the correct answer.

One of the least effective ways of storing information is learning _____ it.
  (A) how repeat
  (B) repeating
  (C) to repeat
  (D) repeat

Part B: Choose the incorrect word or phrase and correct it.

Representative democracy seemed <u>evolve</u> <u>simultaneously</u> <u>during</u> the eighteenth and nineteenth cen-
                                            (A)   (B)   (C)
turies in Britain, Europe, and <u>the United States</u>.
                                              (D)

3   Verbs that Require an *-ing* Form in the Complement

Remember that the following verbs require an *-ing* form for a verb in the complement:

admit	complete	deny
appreciate	consider	discuss
avoid	delay	enjoy

finish	practice	risk
keep	quit	stop
mention	recall	suggest
miss	recommend	tolerate
postpone	regret	understand

S	V	C (-ing)	M
He	enjoys	traveling	by plane

Avoid using an infinitive after the verbs listed.

Forbid may be used with either an infinitive or an *-ing* complement, but *forbid from* is not idiomatic.

EXAMPLES

INCORRECT: She is considering not to go.
  CORRECT: She is considering not going.

INCORRECT: We enjoyed talk with your friend.
  CORRECT: We enjoyed talking with your friend.

INCORRECT: Hank completed the writing his thesis this summer.
  CORRECT: Hank completed writing his thesis this summer.

INCORRECT: I miss to watch the news when I am traveling.
  CORRECT: I miss watching the news when I am traveling.

INCORRECT: She mentions stop at El Paso in her letter.
  CORRECT: She mentions stopping at El Paso in her letter.

EXERCISES

Part A: Choose the correct answer.

Strauss finished _____ two of his published compositions before his tenth birthday.
  (A) written
  (B) write
  (C) to write
  (D) writing

Part B: Choose the incorrect word or phrase and correct it.

Many people have stopped to smoke because they are afraid that it may be harmful to their health.
  (A)   (B)   (C)   (D)

4   Verb Phrases that Require an *-ing* Form in the Complement

Remember that the following verb phrases require an *-ing* form for a verb in the complement:

approve of	*do not mind*	*keep on*
be better off	*forget about*	*look forward to*
can't help	*get through*	*object to*
count on	*insist on*	*think about*
		think of

S	V Ph	C (-ing)	M
She	forgot about	canceling	her appointment

Avoid using an infinitive after the verb phrases listed. Avoid using a verb word after *look forward to* and *object to*. (Refer to page 48 for more on verb words.)

Remember that the verb phrase *BE likely* does not require an *-ing* form but requires an infinitive in the complement.

EXAMPLES

INCORRECT: She is likely knowing.
 CORRECT: She is likely to know.

INCORRECT: Let's go to the movie when you get through to study.
 CORRECT: Let's go to the movie when you get through studying.

INCORRECT: We can't help to wonder why she left.
 CORRECT: We can't help wondering why she left.

INCORRECT: I have been looking forward to meet you.
 CORRECT: I have been looking forward to meeting you.

INCORRECT: We wouldn't mind to wait.
 CORRECT: We wouldn't mind waiting.

EXERCISES

Part A: Choose the correct answer.

Many modern architects insist on _____ materials native to the region that will blend into the surrounding landscape.
 (A) use
 (B) to use
 (C) the use
 (D) using

Part B: Choose the incorrect word or phrase and correct it.

During Jackson's administration, those <u>who</u> did not approve of <u>permit</u> common people in the White
            (A)   (B)

House <u>were shocked</u> by the president's insistence that they <u>be invited</u> into the mansion.
        (C)   (D)

PROBLEMS WITH TENSE

Many grammar books list a large number of *tenses* in English, but the two basic tenses are present and past.

Auxiliary verbs are used with main verbs to express future and other special times.

PROBLEM 5

Irregular Past Forms

Remember that past forms of the following irregular verbs are not the same as the participles:

Verb Word	Past Form	Participle
be	was/were	been
beat	beat	beaten
become	became	become
begin	began	begun
bite	bit	bitten
blow	blew	blown
break	broke	broken
choose	chose	chosen
come	came	come
do	did	done
draw	drew	drawn
drink	drank	drunk
drive	drove	driven
eat	ate	eaten
fall	fell	fallen
fly	flew	flown
forget	forgot	forgotten
forgive	forgave	forgiven
freeze	froze	frozen
get	got	gotten or got
give	gave	given
go	went	gone
grow	grew	grown
hide	hid	hidden
know	knew	known
ride	rode	ridden
run	ran	run

Verb Word	Past Form	Participle
see	saw	seen
shake	shook	shaken
show	showed	shown
shrink	shrank	shrunk
sing	sang	sung
speak	spoke	spoken
steal	stole	stolen
swear	swore	sworn
swim	swam	swum
take	took	taken
tear	tore	torn
throw	threw	thrown
wear	wore	worn
weave	wove	woven
withdraw	withdrew	withdrawn
write	wrote	written

S	V (past)	M
The concert	began	at eight o'clock

Avoid using a participle instead of a past for simple past statements.

EXAMPLES

INCORRECT: They done it very well after they had practiced.
  CORRECT: They <u>did</u> it very well after they had practiced.

INCORRECT: Before she run the computer program, she had checked it out with her supervisor.
  CORRECT: Before she <u>ran</u> the computer program, she had checked it out with her supervisor.

INCORRECT: We eat dinner in Albuquerque on our vacation last year.
  CORRECT: We <u>ate</u> dinner in Albuquerque on our vacation last year.

INCORRECT: My nephew begun working for me about ten years ago.
  CORRECT: My nephew <u>began</u> working for me about ten years ago.

INCORRECT: I know that you been forty on your last birthday.
  CORRECT: I know that you <u>were</u> forty on your last birthday.

EXERCISES

Part A: Choose the correct answer.

Before the Angles and the Saxons _____ to England, the Iberians had lived there.
   (A) coming
   (B) come
 ∨ (C) came
   (D) did come

Part B: Choose the incorrect word or phrase and correct it.

When Columbus <u>seen</u> the New World, he <u>thought</u> that he <u>had reached</u> the East Indies <u>by way of</u> a
                (A)   (B)   (C)   (D)
Western route.

PROBLEMS WITH MODALS AND MODAL-RELATED PATTERNS

Modals are auxiliary verbs. They are used with main verbs to give additional meaning to main verbs. The most common modals are listed below, along with some of the additional meanings that they add to main verbs.

can	possibility, ability, permission
could	possibility, ability in the past
may	probability, permission
might	probability
must	necessity, logical conclusion
shall	future with emphasis
should	advice, obligation, prediction
will	future
would	condition

6 Modal + Verb Word

Remember that a *modal* is used with a *verb word*. A *verb word* is the dictionary form of the verb. In some grammar books, the *verb word* is called the bare infinitive because it appears without the word *to*. Verb words are very important in many patterns, but they are used most often with modals.

S	modal	verb word	
They	might	visit	us

Avoid using an infinitive or an *-ing* form instead of a verb word after a modal.

EXAMPLES

INCORRECT: After you show me the way, I can to go by myself.
  CORRECT: After you show me the way, I <u>can go</u> by myself.

INCORRECT: Our friends might stopping to see us on their way to California.
  CORRECT: Our friends <u>might stop</u> to see us on their way to California.

INCORRECT: I would, if there is time, liking to make a phone call.
  CORRECT: I <u>would</u>, if there is time, <u>like</u> to make a phone call.

INCORRECT: Beth may, with effort, to pass this course.
  CORRECT: Beth <u>may</u>, with effort, <u>pass</u> this course.

INCORRECT: The flight should to be on time.
  CORRECT: The flight <u>should</u> <u>be</u> on time.

EXERCISES

Part A: Choose the correct answer.

By the time a baby has reached his first birthday, he should, without the help of an adult, _____ sit up or even stand up.
   (A) to be able to
   (B) able to
   (C) to be able
✓ (D) be able to

Part B: Choose the incorrect word or phrase and correct it.

Many birds will, in the normal course of <u>their</u> migrations, <u>flying</u> more than three thousand miles
                                            (A)   (B)   (C)

<u>to reach</u> their winter homes.
   (D)

7   Logical Conclusions—Events in the Past

Remember that *must* is a modal. *Must* followed by the verb word <u>have</u> and a <u>participle</u> expresses a logical conclusion based on evidence. The conclusion is about an event that happened in the past.

Remember that an observation in the present may serve as the basis for a conclusion about something that happened in the past. For example, "here is a message on my desk." It may be concluded that "my friend must have called last night."

S	must have	participle	past time
My friend	must have	called	last night

Avoid using *should* or *can* instead of *must*. Avoid using a verb word instead of *have* and a participle when referring to events in the past.

EXAMPLES

INCORRECT: The streets are wet; it should have rained last night.
  CORRECT: The streets are wet; it <u>must have rained</u> last night.

INCORRECT: This pen won't write; it can have run out of ink (in the past).
  CORRECT: This pen won't write; it <u>must have run out</u> of ink (in the past).

INCORRECT: The ring that I was looking at is gone; someone else must buy it.
  CORRECT: The ring that I was looking at is gone; someone else <u>must have bought</u> it.

INCORRECT: He doesn't have his keys; he must locked them in his car.
  CORRECT: He doesn't have his keys; he <u>must have locked</u> them in his car.

INCORRECT: I don't see Martha anywhere; she must be left early.
  CORRECT: I don't see Martha anywhere; she <u>must have left</u> early.

EXERCISES

Part A: Choose the correct answer.

The theory of Continental Drift assumes that there _____ long-term climatic changes in many areas during the past.
   (A) must have been
   (B) must be
   (C) must have
   (D) must

Part B: Choose the incorrect word or phrase and correct it.

When the weather <u>becomes</u> <u>colder</u> we know that the air mass <u>must originated</u> in the Arctic
                    (A)   (B)   (C)
<u>rather than</u> over the Gulf of Mexico.
   (D)

√

8   Logical Conclusions—Events in the Present

Remember that *must* is a modal. *Must* followed by *be* and an *-ing* form or an adjective expresses a logical conclusion based on evidence. The conclusion is about an event that is happening now.

S	must be	*-ing*	present tense
My friend	must be	calling	now

S	must be	adjective	present time
He	must be	upset	now

Avoid using a verb word instead of an *-ing* form after *must be*.

EXAMPLES

INCORRECT: The line is busy; someone should be using the telephone now.
  CORRECT: The line is busy; someone <u>must be using</u> the telephone now.

INCORRECT: Bob is absent; he must have been sick again (now).
CORRECT: Bob is absent; he <u>must be sick</u> again (now).

INCORRECT: He is taking a walk; he must have felt better now.
CORRECT: He is taking a walk; he <u>must be feeling</u> better now.

INCORRECT: She must be study at the library now because all of her books are gone.
CORRECT: She <u>must be studying</u> at the library now because all of her books are gone.

INCORRECT: Sarah must get a divorce (now) because her husband is living in an apartment.
CORRECT: Sarah <u>must be getting</u> a divorce (now) because her husband is living in an apartment.

EXERCISES

Part A: Choose the correct answer.

The general public _____ a large number of computers now, because prices are beginning to decrease.
   (A) must buy
   (B) must have bought
   (C) must be buying
   (D) must buying

Part B: Choose the incorrect word or phrase and correct it.

The American buffalo must be <u>reproduce</u> <u>itself</u> again <u>because</u> <u>it</u> has been removed from the endan-
                          (A)   (B)   (C)   (D)
gered species list.

9   Logical Conclusions—Events that Repeat

Remember that *must* is a modal. *Must* followed by a verb word expresses a logical conclusion based on evidence. The conclusion is about an event that happens repeatedly.

S	must	verb word	repeated time
My friend	must	call	often

Avoid using an infinitive or an *-ing* form instead of a verb word after *must*.

EXAMPLES

INCORRECT: The light is always out in her room at ten o'clock; she must have go to bed early every night.
CORRECT: The light is always out in her room at ten o'clock; she <u>must go</u> to bed early every night.

INCORRECT: Our neighbors must having a lot of money because they are always taking expensive trips.

CORRECT: Our neighbors <u>must have</u> a lot of money because they are always taking expensive trips.

INCORRECT: He can like his job because he seems very happy.

CORRECT: He <u>must like</u> his job because he seems very happy.

INCORRECT: Her English is very good; she must spoken it often.

CORRECT: Her English is very good; she <u>must speak</u> it often.

INCORRECT: Carol always gets good grades; she should study a lot.

CORRECT: Carol always gets good grades; she <u>must study</u> a lot.

EXERCISES

Part A: Choose the correct answer.

Since more than 50 percent of all marriages in the United States end in divorce, about half of the children in America must _____ in single-parent homes.

(A) grow up
(B) to grow up
(C) growing up
(D) have grow up

Part B: Choose the incorrect word or phrase and correct it.

<u>Sheep</u> <u>must have mate</u> in fall <u>since</u> the young <u>are born</u> in early spring every year.
 (A)   (B)   (C)   (D)

PROBLEM 10   Knowledge and Ability—*Know* and *Know How*

Remember that *know* followed by a noun expresses knowledge.

S	KNOW	noun
I	know	the answer

Avoid using an infinitive after *know*.
Remember that *know how* followed by an infinitive expresses ability.

S	KNOW	how	infinitive	
I	know	how	to answer	the question

EXAMPLES

INCORRECT: If she knew to drive, he would lend her his car.
CORRECT: If she <u>knew how</u> <u>to drive</u>, he would lend her his car.

INCORRECT: I don't know to use the card catalog in the library.
CORRECT: I don't <u>know how</u> <u>to use</u> the card catalog in the library.

INCORRECT: Until he came to the United States to study, he didn't know to cook.
CORRECT: Until he came to the United States to study, he didn't <u>know how</u> <u>to cook</u>.

INCORRECT: Do you know to type?
CORRECT: Do you <u>know how</u> <u>to type</u>?

INCORRECT: You'll have to help her because she doesn't know to do it.
CORRECT: You'll have to help her because she doesn't <u>know how</u> <u>to do</u> it.

EXERCISES

Part A: Choose the correct answer.

In a liberal arts curriculum, it is assumed that graduates will _____ about English, languages, literature, history, and the other social sciences.
(A) know
(B) know how
(C) knowledge
(D) knowing

Part B: Choose the incorrect word or phrase and correct it.

The Impressionists <u>like</u> Monet and Manet <u>knew</u> to use color in order <u>to create</u> an image of reality
        (A)   (B)   (C)
rather than reality <u>itself</u>.
              (D)

11 Past Custom—*Used to* and BE *Used to*

Remember that *used to* is similar to a modal. *Used to* with a verb word means that a custom in the past has not continued.

S	used to	verb word	
He	used to	live	in the country

Avoid using a form of *be* after the subject. Avoid using the incorrect form *use to*.

Remember that *BE used to* with an *-ing* form means to be accustomed to.

S	BE	used to	*-ing* form	
He	was	used to	living	in the country

Avoid using a form of *be* after *used to*. Avoid using a verb word instead of an *-ing* form. Avoid using the incorrect form *use to*.

EXAMPLES

INCORRECT: I used to was studying at the University of Southern California before I transferred here.
CORRECT: I used to study at the University of Southern California before I transferred here.
          or
I was used to studying at the University of Southern California before I transferred here.

INCORRECT: We use to go to the movies quite frequently.
CORRECT: We used to go to the movies quite frequently.
          or
We were used to going to the movies quite frequently.

INCORRECT: She was used to get up early.
CORRECT: She used to get up early.
          or
She was used to getting up early.

INCORRECT: He was used to drink too much.
CORRECT: He used to drink too much.
          or
He was used to drinking too much.

INCORRECT: She used to speaking in public.
CORRECT: She used to speak in public.
          or
She was used to speaking in public.

EXERCISES

Part A: Choose the correct answer.

Harvard _____ a school for men, but now it is coeducational, serving as many women as men.
   (A) was used
 √(B) used to be
   (C) was used to
   (D) was used to be

Part B: Choose the incorrect word or phrase and correct it.

As television images of the astronauts showed, even for trained professionals <u>who are</u> <u>used to move</u>
(A)   (B)   (C)
about in a lessened gravitational field, <u>there are</u> still problems.
                                          (D)

Advisability—*Had Better*

Remember that *had better* is similar to a modal. Although *had* appears to be a past, *had better* expresses advice for the future.

S	had better	verb word	
You	had better	take	Chemistry 600 this semester

S	had better	not	verb word	
You	had better	not	take	Chemistry 600 this semester

Avoid using an infinitive or a past form of a verb instead of a verb word. Avoid using *don't* instead of *not*.

EXAMPLES

INCORRECT: You had better to hurry if you don't want to miss the bus.
  CORRECT: You <u>had better hurry</u> if you don't want to miss the bus.

INCORRECT: We had better made reservations so that we will be sure of getting a good table.
  CORRECT: We <u>had better make</u> reservations so that we will be sure of getting a good table.

INCORRECT: We had better to check the schedule.
  CORRECT: We <u>had better check</u> the schedule.

INCORRECT: You had better don't quit your job until you find another one.
  CORRECT: You <u>had better not quit</u> your job until you find another one.

INCORRECT: You had better don't go alone.
  CORRECT: You <u>had better not go</u> alone.

EXERCISES

Part A: Choose the correct answer.

To check for acidity, one had better _____ litmus paper.
  √ (A) use
   (B) using
   (C) to use
   (D) useful

Part B: Choose the incorrect word or phrase and correct it.

In today's competitive markets, even small businesses had better to advertise on TV and radio in
   (A)   (B)   (C)

order to gain a share of the market.
   (D)

13   Preference—*Would Rather*

Remember that the phrase *would rather* is similar to a modal. Although *would rather* appears to be a past, it expresses preference in present and future time.

S	would rather	verb word
I	would rather	drive

S	would rather	not	verb word
I	would rather	not	drive

Avoid using an infinitive or an *-ing* form instead of a verb word.

EXAMPLES

INCORRECT: She told me that she'd rather not to serve on the committee.
CORRECT: She told me that she'd rather not serve on the committee.

INCORRECT: If you don't mind, I'd rather not going.
CORRECT: If you don't mind, I'd rather not go.

INCORRECT: He said that he'd rather went to a small college instead of to a large university.
CORRECT: He said that he'd rather go to a small college instead of to a large university.

INCORRECT: I'd rather writing this than print it because I don't print well.
CORRECT: I'd rather write this than print it because I don't print well.

INCORRECT: Greg would rather has a Pepsi than a beer.
CORRECT: Greg would rather have a Pepsi than a beer.

EXERCISES

Part A: Choose the correct answer.

Rhododendrons would rather _____ in shady places, and so would azaleas.
   (A) to grow
   (B) growing
   (C) grown
   (D) grow

Part B: Choose the incorrect word or phrase and correct it.

The Amish people, descended from the Germans and Swiss, would rather <u>using</u> horses <u>than</u>
                                                                        (A)   (B)

machines for transportation and <u>farm work</u> because they believe that a simple life keeps them
                                  (C)

<u>closer</u> to God.
  (D)

14 Preference for Another—*Would Rather That*

Remember that when the preference is for another person or thing, *would rather that* introduces a
clause. The other person or thing is the subject of the clause.
    Although the verb is past tense, the preference is for present or future time.

S	would rather	that	S	V (past)
I	would rather	that	you	drove

Avoid using a present verb or a verb word instead of a past verb. Avoid using *should* and a verb
word instead of a past verb.

S	would rather	that	S	didn't	verb word
I	would rather	that	you	didn't	drive

Avoid using *don't* or *doesn't* instead of *didn't*.

EXAMPLES

INCORRECT: I'd rather that you don't do that.
  CORRECT: I'd <u>rather</u> that <u>you</u> <u>didn't</u> do that.

INCORRECT: Diane would rather that her husband doesn't working so hard.
  CORRECT: Diane <u>would rather</u> that <u>her husband</u> <u>didn't work</u> so hard.

INCORRECT: The dean would rather that students make appointments instead of dropping by.
  CORRECT: The dean <u>would rather</u> that <u>students</u> <u>made</u> appointments instead of dropping by.

INCORRECT: My roommate would rather that I don't keep the light on after ten o'clock.
  CORRECT: My roommate <u>would rather</u> that <u>I</u> <u>didn't keep</u> the light on after ten o'clock.

INCORRECT: We'd rather that you should come tomorrow.
  CORRECT: We'd <u>rather</u> that <u>you</u> <u>came</u> tomorrow.

EXERCISES

Part A: Choose the correct answer.

A good counselor would rather that the patient _____ his or her own decisions after being helped to arrive at a general understanding of the alternatives.

(A) makes
(B) making
(C) will make
(D) made

Part B: Choose the incorrect word or phrase and correct it.

It is said that the American flag has five-pointed stars because Betsy Ross told General Washington
‾‾‾‾
(A)   (B)
she would rather that he changing the six-pointed ones.
(C)   ‾‾‾‾‾‾‾‾
                             (D)

15   Negative Imperatives

Remember that an imperative is expressed by a verb word.

Please don't	verb word	
Please don't	tell	anyone

Avoid using an infinitive instead of a verb word.

Would you please not	verb word	
Would you please not	tell	anyone

Avoid using an infinitive instead of a verb word. Avoid using *don't* after *would you please.*

EXAMPLES

INCORRECT: Would you please don't smoke.
 CORRECT: Please don't smoke.
                      or
             Would you please not smoke.

INCORRECT: Please don't to park here.
 CORRECT: Please don't park here.
                      or
             Would you please not park here.

INCORRECT: Would you please not to be late.
  CORRECT: Please don't be late.
              or
             Would you please not be late.

INCORRECT: Please don't to go yet.
  CORRECT: Please don't go yet.
              or
             Would you please not go yet.

INCORRECT: Would you please don't worry.
  CORRECT: Please don't worry.
              or
             Would you please not worry.

EXERCISES

Part A: Choose the correct answer.

Please _____ photocopies of copyrighted material without the permission of the publisher.
   (A) no make
   (B) don't make
   (C) not make
   (D) not to make

Part B: Choose the incorrect word or phrase and correct it.

Please don't parking in those spaces that have signs reserving them for the handicapped.
         (A)   (B)   (C)   (D)

REVIEW EXERCISE: PROBLEMS 1–15

Part A: Choose the correct answer.

1. After her famous husband's death, Eleanor Roosevelt continued _____ for peace.
   (A) working
   (B) work
   (C) the working
   (D) to working

2. The Palo Verde tree _____ in spring.
   (A) has beautiful yellow blossoms
   (B) beautiful yellow blossoms
   (C) having beautiful yellow blossoms
   (D) with beautiful yellow blossoms

3. The great apes, a generally peaceful species, _____ in groups.
   (A) would rather living
   (B) would rather live
   (C) would rather they live
   (D) would rather lived

Part B: Choose the incorrect word or phrase and correct it.

4. Insurance rates are not the same for different people <u>because</u> <u>they</u> are not likely <u>have</u> the same <u>risk</u>.
                                             (A) (B)   (C)   (D)

5. Many people with spinal cord <u>injuries</u> can, with the <u>help</u> of computer implants, <u>recovering</u> some of
                                 (A)   (B)   (C)

    <u>their</u> mobility.
    (D)

6. <u>Although</u> thousands of grizzly bears <u>used to roaming</u> the Western Plains of the United States,
      (A)   (B)

    today <u>only a few thousand</u> <u>exist</u>.
               (C)   (D)

7. Although fraternal twins <u>are born</u> at the same time, they do not tend <u>resembling</u> <u>each other</u> any
                                (A)   (B)   (C)

    more <u>than</u> do other siblings.
         (D)

8. Some astronomers <u>contend</u> that in ancient times, the Big Horn Medicine Wheel, an arrangement of
                      (A)

    stones <u>in</u> Wyoming, must <u>have serve</u> as <u>sighting</u> points for observations of the sun.
           (B)   (C)   (D)

9. Because doctors <u>are treating</u> more people for skin cancer, it is widely <u>believed</u> that <u>changes</u> in the
                   (A)   (B)   (C)

    protective layers of the earth's atmosphere <u>must be produce</u> harmful effects now.
                                         (D)

10. Secretariat <u>run</u> the Kentucky Derby in 1.59 minutes, <u>setting</u> a record that <u>has remained</u> unbroken
              (A)   (B)   (C)

    <u>since 1973</u>.
       (D)

PROBLEMS WITH CAUSATIVES

Causatives are main verbs that cause people or machines to do things or cause things to change. They are listed below in order of the most forceful to the least forceful:

make
get
have
let
help

16 Causative MAKE

Remember that MAKE can be used as a causative. In a causative, a person does not perform an action directly. The person causes it to happen by forcing another person to do it.

S	MAKE	someone	verb word	
His mother	made	him	take	his medicine

S	MAKE	something	verb word
I	made	the machine	work

Avoid using an infinitive or an *-ing* form instead of a verb word after a person or thing in a causative with MAKE.

EXAMPLES

INCORRECT: She made the baby to take a nap.
CORRECT: She <u>made</u> the baby <u>take</u> a nap.

INCORRECT: Professor Rogers didn't make us typed up our lab reports.
CORRECT: Professor Rogers didn't <u>make</u> us <u>type</u> up our lab reports.

INCORRECT: Are you going to make your daughter to work part time in the store this summer?
CORRECT: Are you going to <u>make</u> your daughter <u>work</u> part time in the store this summer?

INCORRECT: I can't seem to make this dishwasher running.
CORRECT: I can't seem to <u>make</u> this dishwasher <u>run.</u>

INCORRECT: Patsy makes everyone doing his share around the house.
CORRECT: Patsy <u>makes</u> everyone <u>do</u> his share around the house.

EXERCISES

Part A: Choose the correct answer.

Psychologists believe that incentives _____ increase our productivity.
   (A) make us want
   (B) make us to want
   (C) making us want
   (D) makes us wanting

Part B: Choose the incorrect word or phrase and correct it.

Too much water <u>makes</u> plants <u>turning</u> brown on the edges of <u>their</u> leaves.
(A)   (B)   (C)   (D)

PROBLEM 17 Causative GET

Remember that GET can be used as a causative. In a causative, a person does not perform an action directly.

GET has less force and authority than MAKE.

S	GET	someone	infinitive	
Let's	get	Ralph	to go	with us

S	GET	something	participle	
Let's	get	our car	fixed	first

Avoid using a verb word instead of an infinitive after a person in a causative with GET. Avoid using a verb word instead of a participle after things in a causative with GET.

EXAMPLES

INCORRECT: Do you think we can get Karen takes us to San Diego?
  CORRECT: Do you think that we can <u>get</u> <u>Karen</u> <u>to take</u> us to San Diego?

INCORRECT: I want to get the house paint before winter.
  CORRECT: I want to <u>get</u> the <u>house</u> <u>painted</u> before winter.

INCORRECT: Let's get some of our money exchange for dollars.
  CORRECT: Let's get some of <u>our</u> <u>money</u> <u>exchanged</u> for dollars.

INCORRECT: Nora got her mother's wedding dress to alter so that it fit perfectly.
  CORRECT: Nora <u>got</u> <u>her mother's wedding dress</u> <u>altered</u> so that it fit perfectly.

INCORRECT: We will have to get someone fixing the phone right away.
  CORRECT: We will have to <u>get</u> <u>someone</u> <u>to fix</u> the phone right away.

EXERCISES

Part A: Choose the correct answer.

Lobbyists who represent special interest groups get _____ that benefits their groups.
    (A) Congress to pass the legislation
    (B) Congress passed the legislation
    (C) the legislation to pass by Congress
    (D) the legislation that Congress passing

Part B: Choose the incorrect word or phrase and correct it.

In order to <u>receive</u> full reimbursement for jewelry that might <u>be stolen,</u> the owner must get
        (A)   (B)

<u>all pieces</u> <u>appraise.</u>
    (C)   (D)

18   Causative HAVE

Remember that HAVE can be used as a causative. In a causative, a person does not perform an action directly.

HAVE has even less force and authority than GET.

S	HAVE	someone	verb word	
My English teacher	had	us	give	oral reports

S	HAVE	something	participle	
I	want to have	this book	renewed,	please

Avoid using an infinitive or an *-ing* form instead of a verb word after a person in a causative with HAVE. Avoid using a verb word or an infinitive instead of a participle after a thing in a causative with HAVE.

EXAMPLES

INCORRECT: Tom had a tooth fill.
 CORRECT: Tom <u>had</u> a tooth <u>filled</u>.

INCORRECT: Have you had your temperature taking yet?
 CORRECT: Have you <u>had</u> your temperature <u>taken</u> yet?

INCORRECT: They had their lawyer to change their will.
 CORRECT: They <u>had</u> their lawyer <u>change</u> their will.

INCORRECT: I like the way you had the beautician done your hair.
 CORRECT: I like the way you <u>had</u> the beautician <u>do</u> your hair.

INCORRECT: We are going to have our car fix before we go to Toronto.
 CORRECT: We are going to <u>have</u> <u>our car</u> <u>fixed</u> before we go to Toronto.

EXERCISES

Part A: Choose the correct answer.

Like humans, zoo animals must have a dentist _____ their teeth.
  (A) fill
  (B) filled
  (C) filling
  (D) to be filled

Part B: Choose the incorrect word or phrase and correct it.

Most presidential candidates have their names <u>print</u> on the ballot in the New Hampshire primary
                                                     (A)

election because <u>it is</u> <u>customarily</u> <u>the first one</u> in the nation, and winning it can give them a good
                    (B)   (C)   (D)

chance to be nominated by their parties.

19   Causative LET

Remember that LET can be used as a causative. In a causative, a person does not perform an action directly. With LET, a person gives permission for another person to do it.

S	LET	someone	verb word	
His mother	let	him	go	to school

S	LET	something	verb word
I	am letting	this machine	cool

Avoid using an infinitive or an *-ing* form instead of a verb word after a person or thing in a causative with LET.

EXAMPLES

INCORRECT: Professor Baker let us to write a paper instead of taking a final exam.
 CORRECT: Professor Baker <u>let us write</u> a paper instead of taking a final exam.

INCORRECT: When I was learning to drive, my Dad let me using his car.
 CORRECT: When I was learning to drive, my Dad <u>let me use</u> his car.

INCORRECT: Would you let us the borrow your notes?
 CORRECT: Would you <u>let us borrow</u> your notes?

INCORRECT: Larry is so good-hearted, he lets people took advantage of him.
 CORRECT: Larry is so good-hearted, he <u>lets</u> <u>people</u> <u>take</u> advantage of him.

INCORRECT: Don't let that bothers you.
 CORRECT: Don't <u>let</u> <u>that</u> <u>bother</u> <u>you</u>.

EXERCISES

Part A: Choose the correct answer.

The Immigration and Naturalization Service often _____ their visas if they fill out the appropriate papers.
(A) lets students extend
(B) lets students for extend
(C) letting students to extend
(D) let students extending

Part B: Choose the incorrect word or phrase and correct it.

The National Basketball Association will not let any athlete <u>to continue</u> <u>playing</u> in the league unless
                                                     (A)   (B)

he submits <u>voluntarily</u> to treatment for <u>drug addiction</u>.
          (C)   (D)

Causative HELP

Remember that HELP can be used as a causative. In a causative, a person does not perform an action directly. With HELP, a person assists another person to do it.

S	HELP	someone	verb word infinitive	
He	is helping	me	type	my paper
He	is helping	me	to type	my paper

Avoid using an *-ing* form instead of a verb word or an infinitive after a person in a causative with HELP.

EXAMPLES

INCORRECT: Her husband always helps her that she does the laundry.
 CORRECT: Her husband always <u>helps</u> <u>her</u> <u>do</u> the laundry.

                    or

          Her husband always <u>helps</u> <u>her</u> <u>to do</u> the laundry.

INCORRECT: Don't you help each other the study for tests?
  CORRECT: Don't you <u>help</u> <u>each other</u> <u>study</u> for tests?
             or
             Don't you <u>help</u> <u>each other</u> to study for tests?

INCORRECT: My teacher helped me getting this job.
  CORRECT: My teacher <u>helped</u> <u>me</u> <u>get</u> this job.
             or
             My teacher <u>helped</u> <u>me</u> to get this job.

INCORRECT: Bob said that he would help our finding the place.
  CORRECT: Bob said that he would help us <u>find</u> the place.
             or
             Bob said that he would <u>help</u> us to find the place.

INCORRECT: This book should help you understanding the lecture.
  CORRECT: This book should <u>help</u> <u>you</u> <u>understand</u> the lecture.
             or
             This book should <u>help</u> <u>you</u> to understand the lecture.

EXERCISES

Part A: Choose the correct answer.

In partnership with John D. Rockefeller, Henry Flager _____ the Standard Oil Company.
  (A) helped forming
  (B) helped form
  (C) he helped form
  (D) helping to form

Part B: Choose the incorrect word or phrase and correct it.

<u>Doctors</u> <u>agree</u> that <u>the fluid</u> around the spinal cord helps <u>the nourish</u> the brain.
  (A)   (B)   (C)   (D)

PROBLEMS WITH CONDITIONALS

Conditionals are statements with *if* or *unless.* They are opinions about the conditions (circumstances) that influence results, and opinions about the results.

There are two kinds of conditionals. In most grammar books, they are called *real* or *factual* conditionals and *unreal* or *contrary-to-fact* conditionals. *Factual conditionals* express absolute, scientific facts, probable results, or possible results. *Contrary-to-fact* conditionals express improbable or impossible results.

21   Factual Conditionals—Absolute, Scientific Results

Remember that *absolute conditionals* express scientific facts. *Will* and a verb word expresses the opinion that the result is absolutely certain.

CONDITION			RESULT		
If	S	V (present) ,	S	V (present)	
If	a catalyst	is used ,	the reaction	occurs	more rapidly

or

CONDITION			RESULT		
If	S	V (present) ,	S	will	verb word	
If	a catalyst	is used ,	the reaction	will	occur	more rapidly

Avoid using *will* and a verb word instead of the present verb in the clause beginning with *if*. Avoid using the auxiliary verbs *have*, *has*, *do*, and *does* with main verbs in the clause of result.

EXAMPLES

INCORRECT: If water freezes, it has become a solid.
   CORRECT: If water freezes, it becomes a solid.
         or
   If water freezes, it will become a solid.

INCORRECT: If children be healthy, they learn to walk at about eighteen months old.
   CORRECT: If children are healthy, they learn to walk at about eighteen months old.
         or
   If children are healthy, they will learn to walk at about eighteen months old.

INCORRECT: If orange blossoms are exposed to very cold temperatures, they withered and died.
   CORRECT: If orange blossoms are exposed to very cold temperatures, they wither and die.
         or
   If orange blossoms are exposed to very cold temperatures, they will wither and die.

INCORRECT: If the trajectory of a satellite will be slightly off at launch, it will get worse as the flight progresses.
   CORRECT: If the trajectory of a satellite is slightly off at launch, it gets worse as the flight progresses.
         or
   If the trajectory of a satellite is slightly off at launch, it will get worse as the flight progresses.

INCORRECT: If light strikes a rough surface, it diffused.

CORRECT: If <u>light</u> <u>strikes</u> a rough surface, <u>it</u> <u>diffuses</u>.

or

If <u>light</u> <u>strikes</u> a rough surface, <u>it</u> <u>will diffuse</u>.

EXERCISES

Part A: Choose the correct answer.

If water is heated to 212 degrees F. _____ as steam.

(A) it will boil and escape

(B) it is boiling and escaping

(C) it boil and escape

(D) it would boil and escape

Part B: Choose the incorrect word or phrase and correct it.

If a live sponge is <u>broken</u> into pieces, each piece <u>would turn</u> into a new sponge <u>like</u>
               (A)   (B)   (C)

the original one.
    (D)

22   Factual Conditionals—Probable Results for the Future

Remember that *will* and a verb word expresses the opinion that the results are absolutely certain. In order of more to less probable, use the following modals: *will, can, may.*

If	S	V (present)		,	S	will can may	verb word	
If	we	find	her address	,	we	will	write	her

S	will can may	verb word		if	S	V (present)	
We	will	write	her	if	we	find	her address

Avoid using the present tense verb instead of a modal and a verb word in the clause of result.

EXAMPLES

INCORRECT: If you put too much water in rice when you cook it, it got sticky.
  CORRECT: If you put too much water in rice when you cook it, it will get sticky.
               or
           It will get sticky, if you put too much water in rice when you cook it.

INCORRECT: If they have a good sale, I would have stopped by on my way home.
  CORRECT: If they have a good sale, I will stop by on my way home.
               or
           I will stop by on my way home, if they have a good sale.

INCORRECT: We will wait if you wanted to go.
  CORRECT: We will wait if you want to go.
               or
           If you want to go, we will wait.

INCORRECT: If you listen to the questions carefully, you answer them easily.
  CORRECT: If you listen to the questions carefully, you will answer them easily.
               or
           You will answer them easily if you listen to the questions carefully.

INCORRECT: If we finished our work a little early today, we'll attend the lecture at the art museum.
  CORRECT: If we finish our work a little early today, we'll attend the lecture at the art museum.
               or
           We'll attend the lecture at the art museum if we finish our work a little early today.

EXERCISES

Part A: Choose the correct answer.

    If services are increased, taxes _____.
      (A) will probably go up
      (B) probably go up
      (C) probably up
      (D) going up probably

Part B: Choose the incorrect word or phrase and correct it.

    If you don't register before the last day of regular registration, you paying a late fee.
           (A)   (B)   (C) (D)

23   Factual Conditionals—Possible Results

    Remember that although a past verb is used, the opinion is for future time. In order of most possible to least possible, use the following modals: *would, could, might.*

If	S	V (past)		,	S	would could might	verb word	
If	we	found	her address,		we	would	write	her
If	we	found	her address,		we	could	write	her
If	we	found	her address,		we	might	write	her

or

S	would could might	verb word			if	S	V (past)	
We	would	write	her		if	we	found	her address
We	could	write	her		if	we	found	her address
We	might	write	her		if	we	found	her address

Avoid using *would* and a verb word instead of a past tense verb in an "if" clause.

EXAMPLES

INCORRECT: If Jim's family meet Karen, I am sure that they would like her.
CORRECT: If Jim's family met Karen, I am sure that they would like her.
        or
I am sure that they would like her if Jim's family met Karen.

INCORRECT: If you made your bed in the morning, your room looks better when you got back in the afternoon.
CORRECT: If you made your bed in the morning, your room would look better when you got back in the afternoon.
        or
Your room would look better when you got back in the afternoon if you made your bed in the morning.

INCORRECT: If Judy didn't drink so much coffee, she wouldn't have been so nervous.
CORRECT: If Judy didn't drink so much coffee, she wouldn't be so nervous.
        or
Judy wouldn't be so nervous if she didn't drink so much coffee.

INCORRECT: If you would go to bed earlier, you wouldn't be so sleepy in the morning.
CORRECT: If you went to bed earlier, you wouldn't be so sleepy in the morning.
        or
You wouldn't be so sleepy in the morning if you went to bed earlier.

INCORRECT: If she would eat fewer sweets, she would lose weight.
CORRECT: If she ate fewer sweets, she would lose weight.
        or
She would lose weight if she ate fewer sweets.

EXERCISES

Part A: Choose the correct answer.

If Americans ate fewer foods with sugar and salt, their general health _____ better.
(A) be
(B) will be
(C) is
(D) would be

Part B: Choose the incorrect word or phrase and correct it.

If <u>drivers</u> obeyed the <u>speed limit</u>, <u>fewer</u> accidents <u>occur</u>.
    (A)   (B)   (C)   (D)

24   Factual Conditionals—Probable Changes in Past Results

Remember that the speaker or writer is expressing an opinion about the results of the past under different conditions or circumstances. In order of the most to the least probable, use the following modals: *would, could, might.*

If	S	had	participle		,	S	would have could have might have	participle	
If	we	had	found	her address,		we	would have	written	her
If	we	had	found	her address,		we	could have	written	her
If	we	had	found	her address,		we	might have	written	her

Avoid using *would have* and a participle instead of *had* and a participle in the clause beginning with *if*. Avoid using *have* as a participle.

EXAMPLES

INCORRECT: If we had the money, we would have bought a new stereo system.
  CORRECT: If <u>we had had</u> the money, <u>we would have bought</u> a new stereo system.
                or
          <u>We would have bought</u> a new stereo system if <u>we had had</u> the money.

INCORRECT: If the neighbors hadn't quieted down, I would have have to call the police.
  CORRECT: If <u>the neighbors hadn't quieted down</u>, <u>I would have had</u> to call the police.
                or
          <u>I would have had</u> to call the police if <u>the neighbors hadn't quieted down</u>.

INCORRECT: If her mother let her, Anne would have stayed longer.

CORRECT: Anne <u>would have stayed</u> longer, <u>if</u> her mother <u>had let</u> her.

or

If her mother <u>had let</u> her, Anne <u>would have stayed</u> longer.

INCORRECT: If we would have known that she had planned to arrive today, we could have met her at the bus station.

CORRECT: <u>If we had known</u> that she had planned to arrive today, <u>we could have met</u> her at the bus station.

or

<u>We could have met</u> her at the bus station, <u>if we had known</u> that she had planned to arrive today.

INCORRECT: If I had more time, I would have checked my paper again.

CORRECT: <u>If I had had</u> more time, <u>I would have checked</u> my paper again.

or

<u>I would have checked</u> my paper again <u>if I had had</u> more time.

EXERCISES

Part A: Choose the correct answer.

According to some historians, if Napoleon had not invaded Russia, he _____ the rest of Europe.

   (A) had conquered

   (B) would conquer

   (C) would have conquered

   (D) conquered

Part B: Choose the incorrect word or phrase and correct it.

If dinosaurs <u>would have</u> continued <u>roaming</u> the earth, <u>man</u> would have evolved quite <u>differently</u>.
           (A)   (B)   (C)   (D)

25   Contrary-to-Fact Conditionals—Impossible Results *Were*

Remember that the verb *BE* is always *were* in contrary-to-fact conditionals.

If	S	were	
If	the party	were	on Friday, we could go

Avoid changing *were* to agree with the subject in contrary-to-fact statements.

EXAMPLES

INCORRECT: If Barbara was really my friend, she would call me once in a while.
 CORRECT: If <u>Barbara were</u> really my friend, she would call me once in a while.
              (Barbara is not my friend.)

                          or

              She would call me once in a while <u>if Barbara were</u> really my friend.
              (Barbara is not my friend.)

INCORRECT: If Mr. Harris is single, I could introduce him to my sister.
 CORRECT: If <u>Mr. Harris were</u> single, I could introduce him to my sister.
              (Mr. Harris is not single.)

                          or

              I could introduce him to my sister <u>if Mr. Harris were</u> single.
              (Mr. Harris is not single.)

INCORRECT: If the meat was a little more done, this would be an excellent meal.
 CORRECT: If <u>the meat were</u> a little more done, this would be an excellent meal.
              (The meat is not done.)

                          or

              This would be an excellent meal <u>if the meat were</u> a little more done.
              (The meat is not done.)

INCORRECT: If my daughter is here, I would be very happy.
 CORRECT: If <u>my daughter were</u> here, I would be very happy.
              (My daughter is not here.)

                          or

              I would be very happy <u>if my daughter were</u> here.
              (My daughter is not here.)

INCORRECT: This apartment be perfect if it were a little larger.
 CORRECT: This apartment would be perfect <u>if it were</u> a little larger.
              (The apartment is not larger.)

                          or

              If <u>it were</u> a little larger, this apartment would be perfect.
              (The apartment is not larger.)

EXERCISES

Part A: Choose the correct answer.

If humans were totally deprived of sleep, they _____ hallucinations, anxiety, coma, and eventually, death.

   (A) would experience
   (B) experience
   (C) would have experienced
   (D) had experienced

Part B: Choose the incorrect word or phrase and correct it.

If we were to consider all of the <u>different kinds</u> of motion in discussing the movement of an object,
                                 (A)

it <u>is</u> <u>very</u> confusing, because even an object at rest is moving <u>as the earth turns.</u>
 (B)(C)   (D)

26 Contrary-to-Fact Conditionals—Change in Conditions *Unless*

Remember that there is a subject and verb that determines the change in conditions after the connector *unless*.

S	V	unless	S	V	
Luisa	won't return	unless	she	gets	a scholarship

Avoid deleting *unless* from the sentence; avoid deleting either the subject or the verb from the clause after *unless*.

EXAMPLES

INCORRECT: I can't go I don't get my work finished.
  CORRECT: I can't go <u>unless</u> I <u>get</u> my work finished.

INCORRECT: They are going to get a divorce unless he stopping drugs.
  CORRECT: They are going to get a divorce <u>unless</u> he <u>stops</u> taking drugs.

INCORRECT: You won't get well unless you are taking your medicine.
  CORRECT: You won't get well <u>unless</u> you <u>take</u> your medicine.

INCORRECT: Dean never calls his father unless needs money.
  CORRECT: Dean never calls his father <u>unless</u> he <u>needs</u> money.

INCORRECT: We can't pay the rent unless the scholarship check.
  CORRECT: We can't pay the rent <u>unless</u> the <u>scholarship check</u> comes.

EXERCISES

Part A: Choose the correct answer.

Football teams don't play in the Super Bowl championship _____ either the National or the American Conference.
  (A) unless they win
  (B) but they win
  (C) unless they will win
  (D) but to have won

Part B: Choose the incorrect word or phrase and correct it.

Boys cannot become Cub Scouts unless completed the first grade.
(A)   (B)   (C)   (D)

REVIEW EXERCISE: PROBLEMS 16–26

Part A: Choose the correct answer.

1. If the Normans had not invaded England in the tenth century, the English language _____ in a very different way.
   (A) develop
   (B) developed
   (C) would develop
   (D) would have developed

2. In *The Wizard of Oz*, the wizard could not help Dorothy _____ .
   (A) that she return to Kansas
   (B) return to Kansas
   (C) returning to Kansas
   (D) returned Kansas

3. If teaching _____ more, fewer teachers would leave the profession.
   (A) pays
   (B) is paying
   (C) paid
   (D) had paid

Part B: Choose the incorrect word or phrase and correct it.

4. The Food and Drug Administration, <u>known as</u> the FDA, <u>makes</u> grocers and restaurant owners
                                       (A)   (B)
   <u>pasteurized</u> all milk before <u>selling</u> it.
     (C)   (D)

5. Besides <u>his</u> contributions to the field of science, Franklin <u>helped</u> the people of Philadelphia <u>founded</u>
       (A)   (B)   (C)
   an insurance company, a hospital, a public library, and a night watch, <u>as well as</u> a city militia.
                                                             (D)

6. If baby geese are hatched in the absence of <u>their</u> mother, they <u>following</u> the first <u>moving</u> object they
                                               (A)   (B)   (C)
   see.
   (D)

7. The Rural Free Delivery Act <u>was passed</u> so that people on farms <u>could</u> have <u>their</u> mail <u>deliver</u>
                                     (A)   (B)   (C)   (D)
   cheaper and faster.

8. A temporary driver's permit lets the learner <u>drives</u> with <u>another</u> <u>licensed</u> <u>driver</u> in the car.
                                                        (A)   (B)   (C)   (D)

9. <u>Unless complications</u> from the anesthetic, operations <u>to remove</u> the appendix <u>are not</u>
         (A)   (B)   (C)
   considered serious.
       (D)

10. If the cerebellum of a pigeon <u>was destroyed</u>, the bird <u>would not be able</u> <u>to fly</u>.
                               (A)   (B)   (C)   (D)

PROBLEMS WITH SUBJUNCTIVES

Some verbs, nouns, and expressions require a subjunctive. A subjunctive is a change in the usual form of the verb. A subjunctive is often a verb word in English.

27 Importance—Subjunctive Verbs

Remember that the following verbs are used before *that* and the verb word clause to express importance.

ask	propose
demand	recommend
desire	request
insist	require
prefer	suggest
	urge

S	V	that	S	verb word	
Mr. Johnson	prefers	that	she	speak	with him personally

Avoid using a present or past tense verb instead of a verb word. Avoid using a modal before the verb word.

Note: The verb *insist* may be used in non-subjunctive patterns in the past tense. For example: *He insisted that I was wrong.*

EXAMPLES

INCORRECT: The doctor suggested that she will not smoke.
CORRECT: The doctor <u>suggested</u> that she not <u>smoke</u>.

INCORRECT: I propose that the vote is secret ballot.
CORRECT: I <u>propose</u> that the vote <u>be</u> secret ballot.

INCORRECT: The foreign student advisor recommended that she studied more English before enrolling at the university.
CORRECT: The foreign student advisor <u>recommended</u> that she <u>study</u> more English before enrolling at the university.

INCORRECT: The law requires that everyone has his car checked at least once a year.
CORRECT: The law <u>requires</u> that everyone <u>have</u> his car checked at least once a year.

INCORRECT: She insisted that they would give her a receipt.
CORRECT: She <u>insisted</u> that they <u>give</u> her a receipt.

EXERCISES

Part A: Choose the correct answer.

Less moderate members of Congress are insisting that changes in the social security system _____ made.
 (A) will
 (B) are
 (C) being
 (D) be

Part B: Choose the incorrect word or phrase and correct it.

<u>Many</u> architects prefer that a dome <u>is used</u> to roof buildings that need <u>to conserve</u> <u>floor space</u>.
 (A)   (B)   (C) (D)

28 Importance—Nouns Derived from Subjunctive Verbs

Remember that the following nouns are used in this pattern:

demand	*recommendation*
insistence	*request*
preference	*requirement*
proposal	*suggestion*

noun	that	S	verb word	
The recommendation	that	we	be	evaluated was approved

Avoid using a present or past tense verb instead of a verb word. Avoid using a modal before the verb word.

EXAMPLES

INCORRECT: He complied with the requirement that all graduate students in education should write a thesis.
CORRECT: He complied with the <u>requirement</u> <u>that</u> <u>all</u> graduate students in education <u>write</u> a thesis.

INCORRECT: The committee refused the request that the prerequisite shall be waived.
CORRECT: The committee refused the <u>request</u> <u>that</u> <u>the prerequisite</u> <u>be</u> waived.

INCORRECT: She ignored the suggestion that she gets more exercise.
CORRECT: She ignored the <u>suggestion</u> <u>that</u> <u>she</u> <u>get</u> more exercise.

INCORRECT: The terrorist's demand that the airline provides a plane will not be met by the deadline.
CORRECT: The terrorist's <u>demand</u> <u>that</u> the airline <u>provide</u> a plane will not be met by the deadline.

INCORRECT: He regretted not having followed his advisor's recommendation that he dropping the class.
CORRECT: He regretted not having followed his advisor's <u>recommendation</u> <u>that</u> <u>he</u> <u>drop</u> the class.

EXERCISES

Part A: Choose the correct answer.

It is the recommendation of many psychologists _____ to associate words and remember names.

(A) that a learner uses mental images
(B) a learner to use mental images
(C) mental images are used
(D) that a learner use mental images

Part B: Choose the incorrect word or phrase and correct it.

<u>Despite</u> their insistence that he <u>will appear</u> when <u>there is</u> an important event, the president <u>schedules</u>
  (A)   (B)   (C)   (D)
press conferences with the news media at his discretion.

PROBLEM 29   Importance—Impersonal Expressions

Remember that the following adjectives are used in impersonal expressions.

essential
imperative
important
necessary

it is	adjective	infinitive	
It is	important	to verify	the data

or

it is	adjective	that	S	verb word	
It is	important	that	the data	be	verified

Avoid using a present tense verb instead of a verb word. Avoid using a modal before the verb word.

EXAMPLES

INCORRECT: It is not necessary that you must take an entrance examination to be admitted to an American university.

CORRECT: It is not necessary to take an entrance examination to be admitted to an American university.

or

It is not necessary that you take an entrance examination to be admitted to an American university.

INCORRECT: It is imperative that you are on time.

CORRECT: It is imperative to be on time.

or

It is imperative that you be on time.

INCORRECT: It is important that I will speak with Mr. Williams immediately.

CORRECT: It is important to speak with Mr. Williams immediately.

or

It is important that I speak with Mr. Williams immediately.

INCORRECT: It is imperative that your signature appears on your identification card.

CORRECT: It is imperative to sign your identification card.

or

It is imperative that your signature appear on your identification card.

INCORRECT: It is essential that all applications and transcripts are filed no later than July 1.

CORRECT: It is essential to file all applications and transcripts no later than July 1.

or

It is essential that all applications and transcripts be filed no later than July 1.

EXERCISES

Part A: Choose the correct answer.

It is necessary _____ the approaches to a bridge, the road design, and the alignment in such a way as to best accommodate the expected traffic flow over and under it.

(A) plan

(B) to plan

(C) planning

(D) the plan

Part B: Choose the incorrect word or phrase and correct it.

It is essential that vitamins are supplied either by foods or by supplementary tablets for normal
                        (A)   (B)   (C)

growth to occur.
      (D)

PROBLEMS WITH INFINITIVES

An infinitive is *to* + the verb word.

30 Purpose—Infinitives

Remember that an infinitive can express purpose. It is a short form of *in order to*.

S	V	C	infinitive (purpose)	
Laura She	jogs takes	vitamins	to stay to feel	fit better

Avoid expressing purpose without the word *to* in the infinitive. Avoid using *for* instead of *to*.

EXAMPLES

INCORRECT: Wear several layers of clothing for keep warm.
  CORRECT: Wear several layers of clothing to keep warm.

INCORRECT: David has studied hard the succeed.
  CORRECT: David has studied hard to succeed.

INCORRECT: Don't move your feet when you swing for play golf well.
  CORRECT: Don't move your feet when you swing to play golf well.

INCORRECT: Virginia always boils the water twice make tea.
  CORRECT: Virginia always boils the water twice to make tea.

INCORRECT: Wait until June plant those bulbs.
  CORRECT: Wait until June to plant those bulbs.

EXERCISES

Part A: Choose the correct answer.

In the Morrill Act, Congress granted federal lands to the states _____ agricultural and mechanical arts colleges.
  (A) for establish
  (B) to establish
  (C) establish
  (D) establishment

Part B: Choose the incorrect word or phrase and correct it.

Papyrus <u>was used</u> <u>for to make</u> not only paper <u>but also</u> sails, baskets, <u>and</u> clothing.
      (A)   (B)   (C)   (D)

PROBLEMS WITH PASSIVES

A passive changes the emphasis of a sentence. Usually in a passive, the event or result is more important than the person who causes it to happen.

For example, *born, known as,* and *left* are participles. They are commonly used with BE in passive sentences. Why? Because the person born, the person known, and the person or thing left are the important parts of the sentences.

Passives—Word Order

Remember that in a passive sentence the actor is unknown or not important. The subject is not the actor.

Passive sentences are also common in certain styles of scientific writing.

S	BE	participle	
State University	is	located	at the corner of College and Third

Avoid using a participle without a form of the verb BE.

EXAMPLES

INCORRECT: My wedding ring made of yellow and white gold.
  CORRECT: My wedding ring <u>is made</u> of yellow and white gold.
                  (It is the *ring*, not the person who made the ring, that is important.)

INCORRECT: If your brother invited, he would come.
  CORRECT: If your brother <u>were invited,</u> he would come.
                  (It is your *brother*, not the person who invited him, that is important.)

INCORRECT: Mr. Wilson known as Willie to his friends.
  CORRECT: Mr. Wilson <u>is known</u> as Willie to his friends.
                  (It is *Mr. Wilson*, not his friends, that is important.)

INCORRECT: References not used in the examination room.
  CORRECT: References <u>are not used</u> in the examination room.
                  (It is *references*, not the persons using them, that are important.)

INCORRECT: Laura born in Iowa.
CORRECT: Laura <u>was born</u> in Iowa.
            (It is *Laura*, not her mother who bore her, that is important.)

EXERCISES

Part A: Choose the correct answer.

In the stringed instruments, the tones _____ by playing a bow across a set of strings that may be made of wire or gut.

(A) they produce
(B) producing
(C) are produced
(D) that are producing

Part B: Choose the incorrect word or phrase and correct it.

Work is often measure in units called foot pounds.
　(A) (B)　　(C)　　　　　(D)

32　Passives—Agent

Remember that in a passive sentence, the actor is unknown or not important. The subject is not the actor.

The actor in a passive sentence is called the agent.

	by	person machine
This report was written	by	Phil
It was printed	by	computer

Avoid using *for* or *from* instead of *by*.

EXAMPLES

INCORRECT: The decisions on cases like this are made from Dean White.
CORRECT: The decisions on cases like this are made <u>by</u> <u>Dean White</u>.

INCORRECT: Most of us are sponsored from our parents.
CORRECT: Most of us are sponsored <u>by</u> <u>our parents</u>.

INCORRECT: The car was inspected for customs.
CORRECT: The car was inspected <u>by</u> <u>customs</u>.

INCORRECT: The bill has already been paid Mr. Adams.
CORRECT: The bill has already been paid <u>by</u> <u>Mr. Adams</u>.

INCORRECT: State University is governed from the Board of Regents.
CORRECT: State University is governed <u>by</u> the Board of Regents.

EXERCISES

Part A: Choose the correct answer.

The famous architect, Frank Lloyd Wright, was greatly _____ , who wanted him to study architecture.
   (A) influenced by his mother
   (B) from his mother's influence
   (C) his mother influenced him
   (D) influencing for his mother

Part B: Choose the incorrect word or phrase and correct it.

In the ionosphere, gases have been <u>partly</u> ionized <u>for high frequency</u> radiation from the sun and
    (A)   (B)   (C)
<u>other sources</u>.
    (D)

33   Passives—Infinitives

Remember that a passive infinitive can be used with a present form of the BE verb to express a future intention, and with the past form of the BE verb to express an intention that was not realized in the past.

S	BE (pres)	to be	participle	future time
The project	is	to be	completed	by 1999

S	BE (past)	to be	participle	past time
The project	was	to be	completed	by 1995

Avoid using a participle without *to* or *be* to express intention. Avoid using a verb word instead of a participle with *to be*.

EXAMPLES

INCORRECT: The play was to be cancel, but it was only postponed.
CORRECT: The play <u>was</u> to be <u>canceled</u>, but it was only postponed.

INCORRECT: The finalists are to named at the next meeting.
CORRECT: The finalists <u>are</u> <u>to be</u> <u>named</u> at the next meeting.

INCORRECT: The results of the exam are be announced tomorrow.
 CORRECT: The results of the exam <u>are</u> <u>to be</u> <u>announced</u> tomorrow.

INCORRECT: We were to be notify if there was a problem.
 CORRECT: We <u>were</u> <u>to be</u> <u>notified</u> if there was a problem.

INCORRECT: The game is to rescheduled.
 CORRECT: The game <u>is</u> <u>to be</u> <u>rescheduled</u>.

EXERCISES

Part A: Choose the correct answer.

The TOEFL examination_____by the year 2000.
  (A) completely revised
  (B) is revised completely
  (C) is to be revised completely
  (D) completely is to revise

Part B: Choose the incorrect word or phrase and correct it.

<u>From now on</u>, new buildings in level one earthquake zones in the United States are <u>to constructed</u>
        (A)   (B)
<u>to withstand</u> a tremor without <u>suffering</u> structural damage.
        (C)   (D)

34   Necessity for Repair or Improvement—NEED

Remember that NEED may express necessity for repair or improvement.

S	NEED	*-ing* form
This paragraph	needs	revising

Avoid using an infinitive or a participle instead of an *-ing* form.

S	NEED	to be	participle
This paragraph	needs	to be	revised

Avoid using an *-ing* form instead of a participle.

EXAMPLES

INCORRECT:	His car needs to fix.
CORRECT:	His car needs <u>fixing</u>.
	or
	His car needs <u>to be fixed</u>.

INCORRECT:	The rug needs cleaned before we move in.
CORRECT:	The rug needs <u>cleaning</u> before we move in.
	or
	The rug needs <u>to be cleaned</u> before we move in.

INCORRECT:	The house needs to paint, but we plan to wait until next summer to do it.
CORRECT:	The house needs <u>painting</u>, but we plan to wait until next summer to do it.
	or
	The house needs <u>to be painted</u>, but we plan to wait until next summer to do it.

INCORRECT:	Her watch needed repaired.
CORRECT:	Her watch needed <u>repairing</u>.
	or
	Her watch needed <u>to be repaired</u>.

INCORRECT:	The hem of this dress needs mended before I wear it again.
CORRECT:	The hem of this dress needs <u>mending</u> before I wear it again.
	or
	The hem of this dress needs <u>to be mended</u> before I wear it again.

EXERCISES

Part A: Choose the correct answer.

If more than five thousand dollars in monetary instruments is transported into the United States, a report needs _____ with the customs office.
(A) file
(B) filing
(C) to file
(D) to be filed

Part B: Choose the incorrect word or phrase and correct it.

<u>Because</u> the interstate highway system linking roads across the country <u>was built</u> about thirty-five
  (A)   (B)

years <u>ago</u>, most of the roads in the system now need <u>repaired</u>.
  (C)   (D)

35   Belief and Knowledge—Anticipatory *It*

Remember that an anticipatory *it* clause expresses belief or knowledge. Anticipatory means before. Some *it* clauses that go before main clauses are listed on the next page:

It is believed
It is hypothesized
It is known
It is said
It is thought
It is true
It is written

Anticipatory *it*	that	S	V	
It is believed	that	all mammals	experience	dreams

Avoid using an *-ing* form, a noun, or an infinitive instead of a subject and verb after an anticipatory *it* clause.

EXAMPLES

INCORRECT: It is hypothesized that the subjects in the control group not to score as well.
  CORRECT: It is hypothesized that the subjects in the control group will not score as well.

INCORRECT: It is generally known that she leaving at the end of the year.
  CORRECT: It is generally known that she is leaving at the end of the year.

INCORRECT: It is said that a buried treasure near here.
  CORRECT: It is said that a buried treasure was hidden near here.

INCORRECT: It is believed that a horseshoe bringing good luck.
  CORRECT: It is believed that a horseshoe brings good luck.

INCORRECT: It is thought that our ancestors building this city.
  CORRECT: It is thought that our ancestors built this city.

EXERCISES

Part A: Choose the correct answer.

_____ Giant Ape Man, our biggest and probably one of our first human ancestors, was just about the size of a male gorilla.
  (A) It is believed that
  (B) That it is
  (C) That is believed
  (D) That believing

Part B: Choose the incorrect word or phrase and correct it.

That it is believed that most of the earthquakes in the world occur near the youngest mountain
     (A)   (B)   (C)   (D)
ranges—the Himalayas, the Andes, and the Sierra Nevadas.

PROBLEMS WITH HAVE + PARTICIPLE

Have, *has*, or *had* + participle express duration of time.

36 Duration—HAVE + Participle

Remember HAVE + participle means that the activity is extended over a period of time. HAVE + participle is especially common with adverbs of duration such as *since* and *for*.

S	HAVE	participle	(duration)
The English language	has	changed	since Shakespeare's time

Avoid using the participle instead of HAVE + participle. Avoid using a verb word or a past form instead of a participle.

EXAMPLES

INCORRECT: We have live in Seattle for five years.
  CORRECT: We <u>have lived</u> in Seattle for five years.

INCORRECT: Have you wrote your mother a letter?
  CORRECT: <u>Have</u> you <u>written</u> your mother a letter?

INCORRECT: Ray given us a lot of help since we arrived.
  CORRECT: Ray <u>has given</u> us a lot of help since we arrived.

INCORRECT: I have took this medication since 1985.
  CORRECT: I <u>have taken</u> this medication since 1985.

INCORRECT: We been friends since we were children.
  CORRECT: We <u>have been</u> friends since we were children.

EXERCISES

Part A: Choose the correct answer.

People who have very little technical background have _____ to understand computer language.
  (A) learn
  (B) learning
  (C) learned
  (D) learns

Part B: Choose the incorrect word or phrase and correct it.

Arlington National Cemetery, a memorial area that <u>includes</u> the mast of the battleship Maine, the
    (A)

Tomb of the Unknown Soldier, and the eternal flame at the grave of John F. Kennedy, <u>is</u> the site
    (B)

where the families of <u>more than</u> 160,000 American veterans <u>have bury</u> their loved ones.
    (C)   (D)

37   Duration—HAVE + *Been* + Participle

Remember that HAVE + *been* + participle means that a recently completed activity was extended over a period of time.

Remember that it is a passive. The actor is not known or not important.

	HAVE	been	participle	
She	has	been	accepted	to State University

Avoid using HAVE + participle instead of HAVE + *been* + participle in a passive pattern. Avoid using *been* + participle.

EXAMPLES

INCORRECT: The party has planned for two weeks.
CORRECT: The party <u>has</u> <u>been</u> <u>planned</u> for two weeks.
        (It is the party, not the people who planned it, that is important.)

INCORRECT: Your typewriter been fixed and you can pick it up any time.
CORRECT: Your typewriter <u>has</u> <u>been</u> <u>fixed</u> and you can pick it up any time.
        (It is your typewriter, not the person who fixed it, that is important.)

INCORRECT: Wayne has elected to the student government.
CORRECT: Wayne <u>has</u> <u>been</u> <u>elected</u> to the student government.
        (It is Wayne, not the people who elected him, who is important.)

INCORRECT: We been taught how to cook.
CORRECT: We <u>have</u> <u>been</u> <u>taught</u> how to cook.
        (It is we, not the people who taught us, who are important.)

INCORRECT: The class been changed to room 10.
CORRECT: The class <u>has</u> <u>been</u> <u>changed</u> to room 10.
        (It is the class, not the person who changed it, that is important.)

EXERCISES

Part A: Choose the correct answer.

Many books _____, but one of the best is *How to Win Friends and Influence People* by Dale Carnegie.
    (A) have written about success
    (B) written about success
    (C) have been written about success
    (D) about successful

Part B: Choose the incorrect word or phrase and correct it.

Gettysburg has been <u>preserve</u> as a national historic monument <u>because</u> it was the site of a major
                (A)   (B)
Civil War battle in which <u>many lives</u> <u>were lost</u>.
                          (C)   (D)

PROBLEM 38   Predictions—*Will Have* + Participle

Remember that *will have* followed by a participle and a future adverb expresses a prediction for a future activity or event.

adverb (future)	S	will	have	participle	
By the year 2000,	researchers	will	have	discovered	a cure for cancer

Avoid using *will* instead of *will have*.

EXAMPLES

INCORRECT: You will finished your homework by the time the movie starts.
  CORRECT: You <u>will</u> <u>have</u> <u>finished</u> your homework <u>by the time the movie starts</u>.

INCORRECT: Jan will left by five o'clock.
  CORRECT: Jan <u>will</u> <u>have</u> <u>left</u> by five o'clock.

INCORRECT: Before school is out, I have returned all of my library books.
  CORRECT: <u>Before school is out</u>, I <u>will</u> <u>have</u> <u>returned</u> all of my library books.

INCORRECT: We have gotten an answer to our letter by the time we have to make a decision.
  CORRECT: We <u>will</u> <u>have</u> <u>gotten</u> an answer to our letter <u>by the time we have to make a decision</u>.

INCORRECT: Before we can tell them about the discount, they will bought the tickets.
  CORRECT: <u>Before we can tell them</u> about the discount, they <u>will</u> <u>have</u> <u>bought</u> the tickets.

EXERCISES

Part A: Choose the correct answer.

By the twenty-first century, the computer _____ a necessity in every home.
(A) became
(B) becoming
(C) has become
(D) will have become

Part B: Choose the incorrect word or phrase and correct it.

It is believed that by 1990 immunotherapy have succeeded in curing a number of serious illnesses.
    (A)   (B)   (C)   (D)

39 Unfulfilled Desires in the Past—*Had Hoped*

Remember that *had hoped* expresses a hope in the past that did not happen.

S	had hoped	that	S	would	verb word	
We	had hoped	that	she	would	change	her mind

Avoid using a verb word instead of *would* and a verb word.

Avoid using the incorrect pattern:

S	had hoped	object pronoun	*-ing* form	
We	had hoped	her	changing	her mind

EXAMPLES

INCORRECT: He had hoped that he graduate this semester, but he couldn't finish his thesis in time.
CORRECT: He had hoped <u>that he would graduate</u> this semester, but he couldn't finish his thesis in time.

INCORRECT: We had hoped him staying longer.
CORRECT: We had hoped <u>that he would stay</u> longer.

INCORRECT: They had hoped that she not find out about it.
CORRECT: They had hoped <u>that she would not find out</u> about it.

INCORRECT: I had hoped she coming to the party.
CORRECT: I had hoped <u>that she would come</u> to the party.

INCORRECT: His father had hoped that he go into business with him.
CORRECT: His father had hoped <u>that he would go</u> into business with him.

EXERCISES

Part A: Choose the correct answer.

Although research scientists had hoped that the new drug interferon _____ to be a cure for cancer, its applications now appear to be more limited.
- (A) prove
- (B) had proven
- (C) would prove
- (D) will prove

Part B: Choose the incorrect word or phrase and correct it.

President Wilson had hoped that World War I <u>be</u> the last great war, but only two decades <u>later</u>,
                                            (A)   (B)

<u>the Second World War</u> <u>was erupting</u>.
      (C)   (D)

PROBLEMS WITH AUXILIARY VERBS

Auxiliary verbs are additional verbs that may be used with main verbs to add meaning. For example, all of the forms of BE, HAVE, DO, and all modals are auxiliary verbs.

40 Missing Auxiliary Verb—Active

Remember that some main verbs require auxiliary verbs.

	BE	*-ing*	
Mom	is	watering	her plants

	HAVE	participle	
Mom	has	watered	her plants

	MODAL	verb word	
Mom	should	water	her plants

Avoid using *-ing* forms without BE, participles without HAVE, and verb words without modals when *-ing*, a participle, or a verb word function as a main verb.

EXAMPLES

INCORRECT:	The party is a surprise, but all of her friends coming.
CORRECT:	The party is a surprise but all of her friends <u>are coming</u>.

INCORRECT:	She read it to you later tonight.
CORRECT:	She <u>will read</u> it to you later tonight.

INCORRECT:	The sun shining when we left this morning.
CORRECT:	The sun <u>was shining</u> when we left this morning.

INCORRECT:	We gone there before.
CORRECT:	We <u>have gone</u> there before.

INCORRECT:	I can't talk with you right now because the doorbell ringing.
CORRECT:	I can't talk with you right now because the doorbell <u>is ringing</u>.

EXERCISES

Part A: Choose the correct answer.

The giraffe survives in part because it _____ the vegetation in the high branches of trees where other animals have not grazed.
(A) to reach
(B) can reach
(C) reaching
(D) reach

Part B: Choose the incorrect word or phrase and correct it.

According to some scientists, the earth losing its outer atmosphere because of pollutants.
    (A)   (B) (C)   (D)

PROBLEM 41   Missing Auxiliary Verb—Passive

Remember that the passive requires an auxiliary BE verb.

S		BE	participle
The plants		are	watered
The plants	have	been	watered
The plants	should	be	watered

Avoid using a passive without a form of BE.

EXAMPLES

INCORRECT:	The phone answered automatically.
CORRECT:	The phone <u>is</u> <u>answered</u> automatically.

INCORRECT: They have informed already.
CORRECT: They <u>have been</u> <u>informed</u> already.

INCORRECT: These books should returned today.
CORRECT: These books <u>should be</u> <u>returned</u> today.

INCORRECT: The plane delayed by bad weather.
CORRECT: The plane <u>was</u> <u>delayed</u> by bad weather.

INCORRECT: My paper has not typed.
CORRECT: My paper <u>has</u> not <u>been</u> <u>typed</u>.

EXERCISES

Part A: Choose the correct answer.

Hydrogen peroxide_____as a bleaching agent because it effectively whitens a variety of fibers and surfaces.
(A) used
(B) is used
(C) is using
(D) that it uses

Part B: Choose the incorrect word or phrase and correct it.

If a rash <u>occurs</u> within twenty-four hours <u>after taking</u> a new <u>medication</u>, the treatment
      (A)   (B)   (C)
<u>should discontinued</u>.
      (D)

REVIEW EXERCISE: PROBLEMS 27–41

Part A: Choose the correct answer.

1. There are still many examples of Cro-Magnon murals _____ in the caves of France and Spain.
(A) they are left
(B) leaving them
(C) left
(D) leave

2. _____ that Lee Harvey Oswald may not have acted alone in the assassination of John Kennedy.
(A) Thinking
(B) To think
(C) It is thought
(D) The thought

3. Phosphates _____ to most farm land in America.
(A) need added
(B) need to add
(C) need to adding
(D) need to be added

Part B: Choose the incorrect word or phrase and correct it.

4. The states require that every citizen registers before voting in an election.
                            (A)   (B)   (C)   (D)

5. The money needed to start and continue operating a business known as capital.
      (A)   (B)   (C)   (D)

6. The purpose of hibernation is maintain animals in winter climates where food supplies are reduced.
                (A) (B)   (C)   (D)

7. It is believed that, by the year 2000, a space station will been constructed between the earth and
     (A)   (B)   (C)   (D)
   the moon.

8. It is essential the practice a foreign language in order to retain a high level of proficiency.
             (A)   (B)   (C)   (D)

9. Fewer babies born with birth defects because of advances in prenatal care during this decade.
    (A)   (B)   (C)   (D)

10. Although the sculptor had hoped that he be able to finish the large stone faces at Mount Rushmore,
                                 (A)   (B)
    the work was left for his son to complete.
      (C)   (D)

CUMULATIVE REVIEW EXERCISE FOR VERBS

DIRECTIONS: Some of the sentences in this exercise are correct. Some are incorrect. First, find the correct sentences, and mark them with a check (√). Then find the incorrect sentences, and correct them. Check your answers using the key on pages 445–446.

1. In the entire history of the solar system, thirty billion planets may has been lost or destroyed.

2. A victim of the influenza virus usually with headache, fever, chills, and body ache.

3. Rubber is a good insulator of electricity, and so does glass.

4. Light rays can make the desert appears to be a lake.

5. It is essential that nitrogen is present in the soil for plants to grow.

6. A great many athletes have managed to overcome serious physical handicaps.

7. If the eucalyptus tree was to become extinct, the koala bear would also die.

8. Various species must begin their development in similar ways, since the embryos of a fish and a cat appear to be very similar during the early stages of life.

9. Some teachers argue that students who used to using a calculator may forget how to do mental calculations.

10. Last year Americans spent six times as much money for pet food as they did for baby food.

11. Secretaries are usually eligible for higher salaries when they know how shorthand.

12. A new automobile needs to tuned up after the first five thousand miles.

13. Financial planners usually recommend that an individual save two to six months' income for emergencies.

14. If a baby is held up so that the sole of the foot touches a flat surface, well-coordinated walking movements will be triggered.

15. Generally, the use of one building material in preference to another indicates that it found in large quantities in the construction area and does an adequate job of protecting the inhabitants from the weather.

Problems with Pronouns

You probably remember learning that "pronouns take the place of nouns." What this means is that pronouns often are used instead of nouns to avoid repetition of nouns.

A pronoun usually has a reference noun that has been mentioned before in conversation or in writing. The pronoun is used instead of repeating the reference noun. In some grammar books, the reference noun is called the "antecedent of the pronoun" because it has been mentioned before. "Ante" means "before." For example, in the following sentence, the word *them* is a pronoun that refers to the noun *secretaries*.

Many *secretaries* are using computers to help *them* work faster and more efficiently.

There are several different kinds of pronouns in English. Some of them are *personal* pronouns, which can be either subject or object pronouns; *possessive* pronouns; *relative* pronouns; *reflexive* pronouns; and *reciprocal* pronouns.

42   Subject Pronouns

Remember that personal pronouns used as the subject of a sentence or clause should be subject case pronouns.

	pronoun (subject)	V	
If the weather is good,	Ellen and I	will go	to the beach

Remember that the following pronouns are subject pronouns:

I	*we*
you	*you*
he/she	*they*
it	

Avoid using an object pronoun as a subject.

EXAMPLES

INCORRECT: When he comes back from vacation, Bob and me plan to look for another apartment.
CORRECT: When he comes back from vacation, Bob and I plan to look for another apartment.

INCORRECT: Betty studied business, and after she graduated, her and her best friend opened a book store.
CORRECT: Betty studied business, and after she graduated, she and her best friend opened a book store.

INCORRECT: After Sandy talked them into buying bikes, she and them never drove to school.
CORRECT: After Sandy talked them into buying bikes, she and they never drove to school.

INCORRECT: Frank and us are going to join the same fraternity.
CORRECT: Frank and we are going to join the same fraternity.

INCORRECT: When they have enough money, Pat and her will probably go back to school.
CORRECT: When they have enough money, Pat and she will probably go back to school.

EXERCISES

Part A: Choose the correct answer.

When Franklin Roosevelt became very ill, his wife began to take a more active role in politics, and many people believed that _____ and the president shared his responsibilities.

(A) she
(B) her
(C) herself
(D) hers

Part B: Choose the incorrect word or phrase and correct it.

We know that in 1000 A.D. Leif Eriksson landed on the North American coast, and that him and his
          (A)   (B)
Norwegian companions were the first white men to see the New World.
                  (C)   (D)

43   Subject Pronouns in Complement Position

Remember that in complement position after the verb BE, a subject pronoun must be used.

it	BE	pronoun (subject)	
It	is	he	whom the committee has named

Avoid using an object pronoun instead of a subject pronoun after the verb *BE*.

EXAMPLES

INCORRECT: It was her whom everyone wanted to win.
  CORRECT: It <u>was she</u> whom everyone wanted to win.

INCORRECT: Is it them at the door again?
  CORRECT: Is it <u>they</u> at the door again?

INCORRECT: This is him speaking.
  CORRECT: This <u>is he</u> speaking.

INCORRECT: Didn't you know that it was us who played the joke?
  CORRECT: Didn't you know that it <u>was we</u> who played the joke?

INCORRECT: I have to admit that it was me who wanted to go.
  CORRECT: I have to admit that it <u>was I</u> who wanted to go.

EXERCISES

Part A: Choose the correct answer.

According to the Christian Bible, when the disciples saw Jesus after he had risen from the dead, they said, _____ .
  (A) it is him
  (B) it is he
  (C) it is his
  (D) it is himself

Part B: Choose the incorrect word or phrase and correct it.

It was <u>her</u>, Elizabeth I, not <u>her father</u>, King Henry, <u>who</u> <u>led</u> England into the Age of Empire.
        (A)   (B)   (C) (D)

44   Object Pronouns

Remember that personal pronouns used as the complement of a sentence or clause should be object case pronouns.

S	V	pronoun (object)	
They	asked	us, Jane and me,	whether we were satisfied

Remember that the following pronouns are object pronouns:

me	*us*
you	*you*
her	*them*
him	
it	

Avoid using a subject pronoun as an object.

Let	pronoun (object)	V	
Let	us (you and me)	try	to reach an agreement

Avoid using a subject pronoun after *let*.

EXAMPLES

INCORRECT: He always helps my wife and I with our tax returns.
CORRECT: He always <u>helps</u> my wife and <u>me</u> with our tax returns.

INCORRECT: Do you really believe that she has blamed us for the accident, especially you and l?
CORRECT: Do you really believe that <u>she has blamed</u> us for the accident, especially <u>you and me</u>?

INCORRECT: Let you and I promise not to quarrel about such unimportant matters anymore.
CORRECT: (You) <u>Let</u> <u>you and me</u> promise not to quarrel about such unimportant matters anymore.

INCORRECT: The bus leaves Ted and she at the corner.
CORRECT: The bus <u>leaves</u> Ted and <u>her</u> at the corner.

INCORRECT: The results of the test surprised they because everyone scored much better than expected.
CORRECT: The <u>results</u> of the test <u>surprised</u> <u>them</u> because everyone scored much better than expected.

EXERCISES

Part A: Choose the correct answer.

Moby Dick is a mythical account of evil and revenge as shown by Captain Ahab's pursuit of the whale that had wounded _____ earlier in life.
   (A) he
   (B) his
   (C) him
   (D) to him

Part B: Choose the incorrect word or phrase and correct it.

<u>According to</u> legend, <u>because</u> the Indian Princess Pocahontas said that she loved <u>he</u>, Captain John
   (A)   (B)   (C)
Smith <u>was</u> set free.
   (D)

45 Object Pronouns after Prepositions

Remember that personal pronouns used as the object of a preposition should be object case pronouns.

	preposition	pronoun (object)
I would be glad to take a message	for	her

Remember that the following prepositions are commonly used with object pronouns:

among	of
between	to
for	with
from	

Avoid using a subject pronoun instead of an object pronoun after a preposition.

EXAMPLES

INCORRECT: The experiment proved to my lab partner and I that prejudices about the results of an investigation are often unfounded.

CORRECT: The experiment proved <u>to</u> my lab partner and <u>me</u> that prejudice about the results of an investigation are often unfounded.

INCORRECT: Of those who graduated with Betty and he, Ellen is the only one who has found a good job.

CORRECT: Of those who graduated <u>with</u> Betty and <u>him</u>, Ellen is the only one who has found a good job.

INCORRECT: Among we men, it was he who always acted as the interpreter.

CORRECT: <u>Among us</u> men, it was he who always acted as the interpreter.

INCORRECT: The cake is from Jan and the flowers are from Larry and we.

CORRECT: The cake is from Jan and the flowers are <u>from</u> Larry and <u>us</u>.

INCORRECT: Just between you and I, this isn't a very good price.

CORRECT: Just <u>between</u> you and <u>me</u>, this isn't a very good price.

EXERCISES

Part A: Choose the correct answer.

Since the earth's crust is much thicker under the continents, equipment would have to be capable of drilling through 100,000 feet of rock to investigate the mantle _____ .

    (A) beneath them
    (B) beneath their
    (C) beneath its
    (D) beneath they

Part B: Choose the incorrect word or phrase and correct it.

According to Amazon legends, men <u>were forced</u> <u>to do</u> all of the household tasks for the women war-
                             (A)   (B)

riors <u>who</u> governed and protected the cities <u>for they</u>.
   (C)   (D)

46   Possessive Pronouns Before *-ing* Forms

Remember that when possessive pronouns are used before *-ing* forms that are used as nouns.

The following are possessive pronouns:

my	our
your	your
her	their
his	
its	

S	V Ph V	pronoun (possessive)	*-ing* form	
We	can count on	her	helping	us
He	regretted	their	misunderstanding	him

Avoid using subject or object pronouns between the verb and the *-ing* form.

EXAMPLES

INCORRECT: We don't understand why you object to him coming with us.
  CORRECT: We don't understand why you object to <u>his coming</u> with us.

INCORRECT: I would appreciate you letting me know as soon as possible.
  CORRECT: I would appreciate <u>your letting</u> me know as soon as possible.

INCORRECT: The doctor insisted on she taking a leave of absence.
  CORRECT: The doctor insisted on <u>her taking</u> a leave of absence.

INCORRECT: He is surprised by you having to pay for the accident.
  CORRECT: He is surprised by <u>your having</u> to pay for the accident.

INCORRECT: My father approves of me studying in the United States.
  CORRECT: My father approves of <u>my studying</u> in the United States.

EXERCISES

Part A: Choose the correct answer.

One property of radioisotopes is that _____ decaying occurs in half-lives over a long period of time.
- (A) they
- (B) them
- (C) they're
- (D) their

Part B: Choose the incorrect word or phrase and correct it.

Although Barney Clark lived only <u>a few months</u> with the artificial heart, doctors were able <u>to learn</u>
                                (A)   (B)

a great deal from <u>him</u> having <u>used</u> it.
                  (C)   (D)

47 Possessive Pronouns Before Parts of the Body

Remember that possessive pronouns are used before nouns that identify a part of the body.

		pronoun (possessive)	noun (part of body)
He	hurt	his	arm

Avoid using *the* instead of a possessive pronoun.

EXAMPLES

INCORRECT: How did you twist the ankle?
 CORRECT: How did you twist <u>your</u> ankle?

INCORRECT: Kevin jammed the finger while he was fixing his car.
 CORRECT: Kevin jammed <u>his</u> <u>finger</u> while he was fixing his car.

INCORRECT: Does Alice color the hair?
 CORRECT: Does Alice color <u>her</u> <u>hair</u>?

INCORRECT: The arms are so long that he can't find shirts to fit him.
 CORRECT: <u>His</u> <u>arms</u> are so long that he can't find shirts to fit him.

INCORRECT: She broke the wrist in the accident.
 CORRECT: She broke <u>her</u> <u>wrist</u> in the accident.

EXERCISES

Part A: Choose the correct answer.

Sports medicine experts agree that ice should be applied immediately when an athlete suffers an injury to _____ leg.

(A) its
(B) an
(C) the
(D) his

Part B: Choose the incorrect word or phrase and correct it.

According to the theory of natural selection, the man who was able to use the hands and feet most
                                                                                            (A)

freely to walk and grasp was the one who survived and evolved.
  (B)   (C)   (D)

48   Relative Pronouns That Refer to Persons and Things

Remember that *who* is used to refer to persons, and *which* is used to refer to things.

	someone	who	
She is	the secretary	who	works in the international office

Avoid using *which* instead of *who* in reference to a person.

	something	which	
This is	the new typewriter	which	you ordered

Avoid using *who* instead of *which* in reference to a thing.

EXAMPLES

INCORRECT: The people which cheated on the examination had to leave the room.
CORRECT: The people who cheated on the examination had to leave the room.

INCORRECT: There is someone on line two which would like to speak with you.
CORRECT: There is someone on line two who would like to speak with you.

INCORRECT: Who is the man which asked the question?
CORRECT: Who is the man who asked the question?

INCORRECT: The person which was recommended for the position did not fulfill the minimum requirements.
CORRECT: The person who was recommended for the position did not fulfill the minimum requirements.

INCORRECT: The student which receives the highest score will be awarded a scholarship.
CORRECT: The student <u>who</u> receives the highest score will be awarded a scholarship.

EXERCISES

Part A: Choose the correct answer.

Charlie Chaplin was a comedian _____ was best known for his work in silent movies.
(A) who
(B) which
(C) whose
(D) what

Part B: Choose the incorrect word or phrase and correct it.

Absolute zero, the temperature at <u>whom</u> <u>all substances</u> have zero thermal energy and thus,
                                         (A)   (B)

<u>the lowest</u> possible temperatures, <u>is</u> unattainable in practice.
  (C)   (D)

49   Relative Pronouns That Refer to Persons

Remember that both *who* and *whom* are used to refer to persons. *Who* is used as the subject of a sentence or a clause. *Whom* is used as the complement of a sentence or a clause. *Whom* is often used after a preposition as the object of the preposition.

	who	V	
Everyone	who	took	the tour was impressed by the paintings

Avoid using *whom* as the subject of a verb.

	whom	S	V	
He was the only American	whom	I	saw	at the conference

Avoid using *who* instead of *whom* before a subject and a verb.

EXAMPLES

INCORRECT: I asked him who he was calling.
CORRECT: I asked him <u>whom</u> he was calling.

INCORRECT: Did you meet the girl whom was chosen Homecoming Queen?
CORRECT: Did you meet the girl <u>who was chosen</u> Homecoming Queen?

INCORRECT: He didn't know who he would take to the party.
 CORRECT: He didn't know <u>whom</u> he would take to the party.

INCORRECT: I know the candidate whom was elected.
 CORRECT: I know the candidate <u>who</u> was elected.

INCORRECT: There is often disagreement as to whom is the better student, Bob or Ellen.
 CORRECT: There is often disagreement as to <u>who is</u> the better student, Bob or Ellen.

EXERCISES

Part A: Choose the correct answer.

In a parliamentary system, it is not the monarch but the prime minister _____ .
  (A) whom the real power
  (B) who has the real power
  (C) whom has the real power
  (D) who the real power

Part B: Choose the incorrect word or phrase and correct it.

The Pilgrims were 102 English emigrants <u>whom</u>, after <u>arriving</u> on the Mayflower, <u>became</u> <u>the first</u>
                                          (A)   (B)   (C)   (D)
European settlers in New England.

50   Reflexive Pronouns

Remember that reflexive pronouns may be used when both the subject and the complement refer to
the same person or thing. Reflexive pronouns are used as the complement of a sentence or a clause or
as the object of a preposition.

S	V	pronoun (reflexive)
Some language learners	can correct	themselves

Avoid using object pronouns or possessive pronouns instead of reflexive pronouns.

EXAMPLES

INCORRECT: Be careful or you will hurt to you.
 CORRECT: Be careful or you will hurt <u>yourself</u>.

INCORRECT: A child can usually feed self by the age of six months.
 CORRECT: A child can usually feed <u>himself</u> by the age of six months.

INCORRECT: I had to teach me to swim.
 CORRECT: I had to teach <u>myself</u> to swim.

INCORRECT: Help you to whatever you like.
 CORRECT: Help <u>yourself</u> to whatever you like.

INCORRECT: An oven that cleans its is very handy.
CORRECT: An oven that cleans <u>itself</u> is very handy.

EXERCISES

Part A: Choose the correct answer.

The jaw structure of a snake permits it to eat and digest animals much larger than _____.
(A) it
(B) itself
(C) its
(D) it has

Part B: Choose the incorrect word or phrase and correct it.

<u>According to</u> the Fifth Amendment to the U.S. Constitution, <u>no</u> person <u>should be compelled</u> to be a
     (A)   (B)   (C)
witness against <u>him own</u>.
                (D)

51   Reciprocal Pronouns

Remember that the reciprocal pronoun phrase *each other* may be used when the plural subject and complement refer to the same persons or things, and they are performing a reciprocal (mutual) act.

S	V	pronoun (reciprocal)	
My sister and I	visit	each other	about once a week

Remember that *each other* is used to express mutual acts for all persons. *One another* is also correct.

EXAMPLES

INCORRECT: Family members love to each other.
CORRECT: Family members love <u>each other</u>.

INCORRECT: Let's meet each to the other after class.
CORRECT: Let's meet <u>each other</u> after class.

INCORRECT: It is considered cheating when students help each the other one on tests or quizzes.
CORRECT: It is considered cheating when students help <u>each other</u> on tests or quizzes.

INCORRECT: Jack and Sandra aren't dating one to the other any more.
CORRECT: Jack and Sandra aren't dating <u>each other</u> any more.

INCORRECT: They will never find each another at this crowded airport.
CORRECT: They will never find <u>each other</u> at this crowded airport.

<u>**EXERCISES**</u>

Part A: Choose the correct answer.

Business partners can usually sell their mutually owned property without consulting _____ unless they have agreed to a separate contract.

(A) other
(B) other one
(C) one the other
(D) each other

Part B: Choose the incorrect word or phrase and correct it.

The twinkling lights of the firefly <u>are</u> signals <u>so that</u> the male and female of the species can <u>find</u>
                  (A)   (B)   (C)

<u>each to the other.</u>
     (D)

CUMULATIVE REVIEW EXERCISE FOR PRONOUNS

<u>DIRECTIONS</u>: Some of the sentences in this exercise are correct. Some are incorrect. First, find the correct sentences, and mark them with a check (√). Then find the incorrect sentences, and correct them. Check your answers using the key on pages 446–447.

1. College students like to entertain themselves by playing Frisbee, a game of catch played with a plastic disk instead of a ball.

2. The final member of the Bach family, Dr. Otto Bach, died in 1893, taking with he the musical genius that had entertained Germany for two centuries.

3. When recessive genes combine with each the other one, a child with blue eyes can be born to parents both of whom have brown eyes.

4. Almost all of the people who ultimately commit suicide have made a previous unsuccessful attempt to kill themselves or have threatened to do so.

5. Officials at a college or university must see a student's transcripts and financial guarantees prior to them issuing him or her a form I-20.

6. Through elected officials, a representative democracy includes citizens like you and I in the decision-making process.

7. It was her, Anne Sullivan, who stayed with Helen Keller for fifty years, teaching and encouraging her student.

8. To appreciate what the hybrid corn breeder does, it is necessary to understand how corn reproduces its.

9. Most foreign students realize that it is important for they to buy health insurance while they are living in the United States, because hospital costs are very high.

10. Top management in a firm is usually interpreted to mean the president and the vice-presidents that report to him or her.

11. The barnacle produces glue and attaches itself to ship bottoms and other places.

12. Peers are people of the same general age and educational level with whom an individual associates.

13. When an acid and a base neutralize one the other, the hydrogen from the acid and the oxygen from the base join to form water.

14. About two thirds of the world is inhabited by people which are severely undernourished.

15. In order for a caller to charge a call from another location to his home telephone number, the operator insists on him using a credit card or waiting until someone at the home number can verify that charges will be paid.

Problems with Nouns

You have probably learned that "a noun is the name of a person, place, or thing." Nouns perform several functions in English, but "naming" is clearly the most important.

There are two basic classifications of nouns in English. In some grammar books, they are called *count nouns* and *noncount nouns.* In other grammar books, they are called *count nouns* and *mass nouns.* In still other grammar books, they are called *countable* and *uncountable* nouns.

All of these names are very confusing because, of course, everything can be counted. The problem is *how* to count it. And, in that respect, the two classifications of nouns are very different.

Count or countable nouns have both singular and plural forms. They are used in agreement with singular or plural verbs. In contrast, mass or noncount, uncountable nouns have only one form. They are used in agreement with singular verbs.

Often count or countable nouns are individual persons, places, or things that can be seen and counted individually. Often mass, noncount, or uncountable nouns are substances and ideas that are shapeless by nature and cannot be seen and counted individually.

But it is not always logic that determines whether a noun is count or noncount. Sometimes it is simply a grammatical convention—that is, a category that people agree to use in their language. Both beans and rice have small parts that would be difficult but not impossible to count. But beans is considered a count noun and rice is considered a noncount noun. Why? Because it is a grammatical convention.

52   Count Nouns

Remember that *count nouns* have both singular and plural forms. Plural numbers can precede *count nouns* but not *noncount* nouns.

There are several categories of *count nouns* that can help you organize your study. Some of them are listed here.

1. Names of persons, their relationships, and their occupations:
   one boy   two boys
   one friend   two friends
   one student   two students

2. Names of animals, plants, insects:
   one dog   two dogs
   one flower   two flowers
   one bee   two bees

3. Names of things with a definite, individual shape:
   one car   two cars
   one house   two houses
   one room   two rooms

4. Units of measurement:
   one inch   two inches
   one pound   two pounds
   one degree   two degrees

5. Units of classification in society:
   one family   two families
   one country   two countries
   one language   two languages

6. Containers of noncount solids, liquids, pastes, and gases:
   one bottle   two bottles
   one jar   two jars
   one tube   two tubes

7. A limited number of abstract concepts:
   one idea   two ideas
   one invention two inventions
   one plan   two plans

Number (plural)	Noun (count-plural)
sixty	years

Avoid using a singular *count noun* with a plural number.

EXAMPLES

INCORRECT: We have twenty dollar left.
 CORRECT: We have twenty dollars left.

INCORRECT: I hope that I can lose about five pound before summer.
 CORRECT: I hope that I can lose about five pounds before summer.

INCORRECT: Several of the people in this class speak three or four language.
 CORRECT: Several of the people in this class speak three or four languages.

INCORRECT: The temperature has risen ten degree in two hours.
 CORRECT: The temperature has risen ten degrees in two hours.

INCORRECT: The teacher has ordered two book, but they aren't in at the bookstore.
CORRECT: The teacher has ordered two books, but they aren't in at the bookstore.

EXERCISES

Part A: Choose the correct answer.

A desert receives less than twenty-five _____ of rainfall every year.
   (A) centimeter
   (B) a centimeter
   (C) centimeters
   (D) of centimeters

Part B: Choose the incorrect word or phrase and correct it.

In 1950 it was naively predicted that eight or ten computer would be sufficient to handle all of the
   (A)   (B)   (C)   (D)
scientific and business needs in the United States.

53 Noncount Nouns

Remember that *noncount* nouns have only one form. They are used in agreement with singular verbs. The word *the* does not precede them.

There are categories of *noncount* nouns that can help you organize your study. Some of them are listed here.

1. Food staples that can be purchased in various forms:
   bread
   meat
   butter

2. Construction materials that can change shape, depending on what is made:
   wood
   iron
   glass

3. Liquids that can change shape, depending on the shape of the container:
   oil
   tea
   milk

4. Natural substances that can change shape, depending on natural laws:
   steam, water, ice
   smoke, ashes
   oxygen

5. Substances with many small parts:
   rice
   sand
   sugar

6. Groups of things that have different sizes and shapes:

clothing	(a coat, a shirt, a sock)
furniture	(a table, a chair, a bed)
luggage	(a suitcase, a trunk, a box)

7. Languages:
   Arabic
   Japanese
   Spanish

8. Abstract concepts, often with endings *-ness, -ance, -ence, -ity:*
   beauty
   ignorance
   peace

9. Most *-ing* forms:
   learning
   shopping
   working

noun (noncount)	verb (singular)	
Friendship	is	important

Avoid using *the* before a *noncount* noun. Avoid using a plural verb with a noncount noun.

EXAMPLES

INCORRECT: The happiness means different things to different people.
CORRECT: Happiness means different things to different people.

INCORRECT: Toshi speaks the Japanese at home.
CORRECT: Toshi speaks Japanese at home.

INCORRECT: Bread are expensive in the grocery store on the corner.
CORRECT: Bread is expensive in the grocery store on the corner.

INCORRECT: I like my tea with the milk.
CORRECT: I like my tea with milk.

INCORRECT: If you open the door, airs will circulate better.
CORRECT: If you open the door, air will circulate better.

EXERCISES

Part A: Choose the correct answer.

_____ at 212 degrees F. and freezes at 32 degrees F.
(A) Waters boils
(B) The water boils
(C) Water boils
(D) Waters boil

Part B: Choose the incorrect word or phrase and correct it.

The religion attempts to clarify man's relationship with a superhuman power.
 (A)   (B) (C)   (D)

54 Nouns with Count and Noncount Meanings

Remember that some nouns may be used as *count* or as *noncount* nouns depending on their meanings. Materials and abstract concepts are *noncount* nouns, but they may be used as *count* nouns to express specific meanings.

Count noun	Specific meaning	Noncount noun	General meaning
an agreement agreements	an occasion or a document	agreement	abstract concept all agreements
a bone bones	a part of a skeleton	bone	construction material
a business businesses	a company	business	abstract concept all business transactions
a cloth cloths	a piece of cloth	cloth	construction material
a decision decisions	an occasion	decision	abstract concept all decisions
an education educations	a specific person's	education	abstract concept all education
a fire fires	an event	fire	material
a glass glasses	a container	glass	construction material
a history histories	a historical account	history	abstract concept all history
an honor honors	an occasion or an award	honor	abstract concept all honor
a language languages	a specific variety	language	abstract concept all languages

a life lives	a specific person's	life	abstract concept all life
a light lights	a lamp	light	the absence of darkness
a noise noises	a specific sound	noise	abstract concept all sounds
a pain pains	a specific occasion	pain	abstract concept all pain
a paper papers	a document or sheet	paper	construction material
a pleasure pleasures	a specific occasion	pleasure	abstract concept all pleasure
a silence silences	a specific occasion	silence	abstract concept all silence
a space spaces	a blank	space	the universe
a stone stones	a small rock	stone	construction material
a success successes	an achievement	success	abstract concept all success
a thought thoughts	an idea	thought	abstract concept all thought
a time times	a historical period or moment	time	abstract concept all time
a war wars	a specific war	war	the general act of war all wars
a work works	an artistic creation	work	employment abstract concept all work

	a document	
I have	a paper	due Monday

	construction material	
Let's use	paper	to make the present

Avoid using *count* nouns with specific meanings to express the general meanings of *noncount* nouns.

EXAMPLES

INCORRECT: Dr. Bradley will receive special honor at the graduation.
  CORRECT: Dr. Bradley will receive a special honor at the graduation.
        (an award)

INCORRECT: She needs to find a work.
  CORRECT: She needs to find work.
        (employment)

INCORRECT: My neighbor dislikes a noise.
  CORRECT: My neighbor dislikes noise.
        (all sounds)

INCORRECT: We need glass for the juice.
  CORRECT: We need a glass for the juice.
            or
        We need glasses for the juice.
        (containers)

INCORRECT: A war is as old as mankind.
  CORRECT: War is as old as mankind.
        (the act of war)

EXERCISES

Part A: Choose the correct answer.

It is generally believed that an M.B.A. degree is good preparation for a career in _____ .
   (A) a business
   (B) business
   (C) businesses
   (D) one business

Part B: Choose the incorrect word or phrase and correct it.

A space is the last frontier for man to conquer.
   (A)   (B)   (C)   (D)

PROBLEM 55

Count and Noncount Nouns with Similar Meanings

Remember that there are pairs of nouns with similar meanings, but one is a *count* noun and the other is a *noncount* noun.

Count noun	Noncount noun
a climate climates	weather
a laugh laughs	laughter
a human being human beings	humanity
a job jobs	work
a machine machines	machinery
a person persons	people
a snowflake snowflakes	snow
a sunbeam sunbeams	sunlight; sunshine
a traffic jam traffic jams	traffic

	a	noun (count)	
The shape of	a	snowflake	is unique

Avoid using *a* with a *noncount* noun instead of a singular *count* noun.

EXAMPLES

INCORRECT:	California has a good weather.
CORRECT:	California has good <u>weather</u>.
	or
	California has <u>a</u> good <u>climate</u>.

INCORRECT:	A laughter is the best medicine.
CORRECT:	<u>Laughter</u> is the best medicine.
	or
	A <u>laugh</u> is the best medicine.

INCORRECT:	We are late because we got stuck in a traffic.
CORRECT:	We are late because we got stuck in <u>traffic</u>.
	or
	We are late because we got stuck in <u>a</u> traffic jam.

INCORRECT:	A machinery in the factory needs to be fixed.
CORRECT:	<u>Machinery</u> in the factory needs to be fixed.
	or
	A <u>machine</u> in the factory needs to be fixed.

INCORRECT:	We are supposed to have a sunshine this weekend.
CORRECT:	We are supposed to have <u>sunshine</u> this weekend.

EXERCISES

Part A: Choose the correct answer.

Unemployment compensation is money to support an unemployed person while he or she is looking for _____ .
- (A) job
- (B) a job
- (C) works
- (D) a work

Part B: Choose the incorrect word or phrase and correct it.

It is believed that a <u>people</u> could <u>live</u> on <u>Mars</u> with little life support because the atmosphere is sim-
               (A)   (B)   (C)
ilar to <u>that</u> of Earth.
   (D)

56   Noncount Nouns that Are Count Nouns in Other Languages

Remember that many nouns which are *count* nouns in other languages may be *noncount* nouns in English. Some of the most troublesome have been listed for you on the following page.

advice	homework	money	poetry
anger	ignorance	music	poverty
courage	information	news	progress
damage	knowledge	patience	
equipment	leisure	permission	
fun	luck		

	Ø	Noun (noncount)
Did you do your		homework?

Avoid using *a* or *an* before *noncount* nouns.

EXAMPLES

INCORRECT: Do you have an information about it?
CORRECT: Do you have <u>information</u> about it?

INCORRECT: Counselors are available to give you an advice before you register for your classes.
CORRECT: Counselors are available to give you <u>advice</u> before you register for your classes.

INCORRECT: George had a good luck when he first came to State University.
CORRECT: George had good <u>luck</u> when he first came to State University.

INCORRECT: A news was released about the hostages.
CORRECT: <u>News</u> was released about the hostages.

INCORRECT: Did you get a permission to take the placement test?
CORRECT: Did you get <u>permission</u> to take the placement test?

EXERCISES

Part A: Choose the correct answer.

Fire-resistant materials are used to retard _____ of modern aircraft in case of accidents.
   (A) a damage to the passenger cabin
   (B) that damages to the passenger cabin
   (C) damage to the passenger cabin
   (D) passenger cabin's damages

Part B: Choose the incorrect word or phrase and correct it.

A <u>progress</u> <u>has been made</u> toward <u>finding</u> <u>a cure</u> for AIDS.
   (A)   (B)   (C)   (D)

57   Singular and Plural Expressions of Noncount Nouns

Remember that the following singular and plural expressions are idiomatic:

a piece of advice	two pieces of advice
a piece of bread	two pieces of bread
a piece of equipment	two pieces of equipment
a piece of furniture	two pieces of furniture
a piece of information	two pieces of information
a piece of jewelry	two pieces of jewelry
a piece of luggage	two pieces of luggage
a piece of mail	two pieces of mail
a piece of music	two pieces of music
a piece of news	two pieces of news
a piece of toast	two pieces of toast
a loaf of bread	two loaves of bread
a slice of bread	two slices of bread
an ear of corn	two ears of corn
a bar of soap	two bars of soap
a bolt of lightning	two bolts of lightning
a clap of thunder	two claps of thunder
a gust of wind	two gusts of wind

	a	singular	of	noun (noncount)
A folk song is	a	piece	of	popular music

	number	plural	of	noun (noncount)
I ordered	twelve	bars	of	soap

Avoid using the noncount noun without the singular or plural idiom to express a singular or plural.

EXAMPLES

INCORRECT: A mail travels faster when the zip code is indicated on the envelope.
CORRECT: A piece of mail travels faster when the zip code is indicated on the envelope.

INCORRECT: There is a limit of two carry-on luggages for each passenger.
CORRECT: There is a limit of two pieces of carry-on luggage for each passenger.

INCORRECT: Each furniture in this display is on sale for half price.
CORRECT: Each piece of furniture in this display is on sale for half price.

INCORRECT: I'd like a steak, a salad, and a corn's ear with butter.
CORRECT: I'd like a steak, a salad, and an ear of corn with butter.

INCORRECT: The Engineering Department purchased a new equipment to simulate conditions in outer space.

CORRECT: The Engineering Department purchased <u>a new piece of equipment</u> to simulate conditions in outer space.

EXERCISES

Part A: Choose the correct answer.

Hybrids have one more _____ per plant than the other varieties.
(A) corns
(B) ear of corn
(C) corn ears
(D) corn's ears

Part B: Choose the incorrect word or phrase and correct it.

<u>A few</u> tiles on Skylab <u>were</u> the only <u>equipments</u> that failed <u>to perform</u> well in outer space.
   (A)   (B)   (C)   (D)

58   Classifications—*Kind* and *Type*

Remember that *kind* and *type* express classification.

	kinds types	of	noun (plural count) (noncount)
Cable TV has many different Dr. Parker gives several	kinds types	of of	shows homework

one	kind type	of	noun (singular count) (noncount)	
One One	kind type	of of	show homework	is news is a lab report

Avoid using *kind of* and *type of* with a plural count noun. Avoid using *kind* and *type* without *of*.

EXAMPLES

INCORRECT: There are four kind of Coke now.
CORRECT: There are <u>four kinds of Coke</u> now.

INCORRECT: We saw several kind of birds at the wildlife preserve.
CORRECT: We saw <u>several kinds of birds</u> at the wildlife preserve.

INCORRECT: This exam has two types problems.
  CORRECT: This exam has <u>two types of problems</u>.

INCORRECT: Are you looking for a special kinds of car?
  CORRECT: Are you looking for <u>a special kind of car</u>?

INCORRECT: I only know how to run one type a computer program.
  CORRECT: I only know how to run <u>one type of computer program</u>.

EXERCISES

Part A: Choose the correct answer.

According to estimates by some botanists, there are _____ of plants.
(A) seven thousand type
(B) seven thousand types
(C) type of seven thousand
(D) types seven thousand

Part B: Choose the incorrect word or phrase and correct it.

One <u>kinds of tool</u> that <u>was</u> popular during the Stone Age <u>was</u> a flake, used <u>for cutting</u> and scraping.
          (A)   (B)   (C)   (D)

59 Infinitive and -*ing* Subjects

Remember that either an infinitive or an -*ing* form may be used as the subject of a sentence or a clause.

S (infinitive)	V	
To read a foreign language	is	even more difficult

S (-*ing*)	V	
Reading quickly and well	requires	practice

Avoid using a verb word instead of an infinitive or an -*ing* form in the subject. Avoid using *to* with an -*ing* form.

EXAMPLES

INCORRECT: To working provides people with personal satisfaction as well as money.
  CORRECT: <u>To work</u> provides people with personal satisfaction as well as money.
                        or
                   <u>Working</u> provides people with personal satisfaction as well as money.

INCORRECT: The sneeze spreads germs.
  CORRECT: To sneeze spreads germs.
                        or
             Sneezing spreads germs.

INCORRECT: Shoplift is considered a serious crime.
  CORRECT: To shoplift is considered a serious crime.
                        or
             Shoplifting is considered a serious crime.

INCORRECT: The rest in the afternoon is a custom in many countries.
  CORRECT: To rest in the afternoon is a custom in many countries.
                        or
             Resting in the afternoon is a custom in many countries.

INCORRECT: To exercising makes most people feel better.
  CORRECT: To exercise makes most people feel better.
                        or
             Exercising makes most people feel better.

EXERCISES

Part A: Choose the correct answer.

_____ trees is a custom that many people engage in to celebrate Arbor Day.
   (A) The plant
   (B) Plant
   (C) Planting
   (D) To planting

Part B: Choose the incorrect word or phrase and correct it.

Spell correctly is easy with the aid of a number of word processing programs for personal computers.
(A)   (B)   (C)   (D)

60 Qualifying Phrases with *-ing* Nouns

Remember that an *-ing* form may be used as a noun. In some grammar books, this *-ing* form is called a gerund. Remember that *-ing* forms are usually noncount nouns and that noncount nouns are not preceded by *the* unless followed by a qualifying phrase.

We have already classified most *-ing* forms as *noncount* nouns, but there is one pattern in which *the* is used with a *noncount -ing* noun. When a prepositional phrase qualifies the noun, that is, adds specific information, *the* may be used with an *-ing* noun subject.

| the | *-ing* | qualifying phrase | |
		of noun	
The	reading	of technical material	requires knowledge of technical terms

EXAMPLES

INCORRECT: Correcting of errors in a language class can be embarrassing.
CORRECT: The correcting of errors in a language class can be embarrassing.

INCORRECT: Writing of letters is an art.
CORRECT: The writing of letters is an art.

INCORRECT: Winning of prizes is not as important as playing well.
CORRECT: The winning of prizes is not as important as playing well.

INCORRECT: Sending of electronic mail (E-mail) is now common.
CORRECT: The sending of electronic mail (E-mail) is now common.

INCORRECT: Singing of Christmas carols is an old tradition.
CORRECT: The singing of Christmas carols is an old tradition.

EXERCISES

Part A: Choose the correct answer.

_____ is not a new idea.
(A) The planning of cities
(B) Cities to plan them
(C) Plan cities
(D) To planning cities

Part B: Choose the incorrect word or phrase and correct it.

Writing of instructions for computers is called computer programming.
  (A)   (B)   (C)   (D)

61   Nominal *That* Clause

Remember that sometimes the subject of a verb is a single noun. Other times it is a long noun phrase or a long noun clause.

One example of a long noun clause is the *nominal that* clause. Like all clauses, the *nominal that* clause has a subject and verb. The *nominal that* clause functions as the main subject of the main verb which follows it.

Nominal *that* clause S	V	
That vitamin C prevents colds	is	well known

EXAMPLES

INCORRECT:	That it is that she has known him for a long time influenced her decision.
CORRECT:	That she has known him for a long time influenced her decision.

INCORRECT:	It is that we need to move is sure.
CORRECT:	That we need to move is sure.

INCORRECT:	Is likely that the library is closed.
CORRECT:	That the library is closed is likely.

INCORRECT:	She will win is almost certain.
CORRECT:	That she will win is almost certain.

INCORRECT:	That is not fair seems obvious.
CORRECT:	That it is not fair seems obvious.

EXERCISES

Part A: Choose the correct answer.

_____ migrate long distances is well documented.
  (A) That it is birds
  (B) That birds
  (C) Birds that
  (D) It is that birds

Part B: Choose the incorrect word or phrase and correct it.

That it is the moon influences only one kind of tide is not generally known.
  (A)   (B)   (C)   (D)

CUMULATIVE REVIEW EXERCISE FOR NOUNS

DIRECTIONS: Some of the sentences in this exercise are correct. Some are incorrect. First, find the correct sentences, and mark them with a check (√). Then find the incorrect sentences, and correct them. Check your answers using the key on pages 447–448.

1. Tuition at state universities has risen by one hundred fifty dollar.

2. Although polyester was very popular and is still used in making clothing, cloths made of natural fibers is more fashionable today.

3. The peace in the world is the goal of the United Nations.

4. Dam is a wall constructed across a valley to enclose an area in which water is stored.

5. The light travels in a straight line.

6. To hitchhike in the United States is very dangerous.

7. The ptarmigan, like a large number of Arctic animal, is white in winter and brown in summer.

8. Even children in elementary school are assigned homeworks.

9. Spirituals were influenced by a music from the African coast.

10. The stare at a computer screen for long periods of time can cause severe eyestrain.

11. There are two kind of major joints in the body of a vertebrate, called the hinge joint and the ball and socket joint.

12. That an earthquake of magnitude eight on the Richter Scale occurs once every five or ten years.

13. Art of colonial America was very functional, consisting mainly of useful objects such as furniture and household utensils.

14. To producing one ton of coal it may be necessary to strip as much as thirty tons of rock.

15. A mail that is postmarked on Monday before noon and sent express can be delivered the next day anywhere in the United States.

Problems with Adjectives

Adjectives and adjective phrases describe nouns. They may be used to describe *quantity* (number or amount); *sufficiency* (number or amount needed); *consecutive order* (order in a sequence); *quality* (appearance); and *emphasis* (importance or force.)

Most adjectives and adjective phrases have only one form in English. They do not change forms to agree with the nouns they describe.

PROBLEMS WITH DETERMINERS

Determiners are a special kind of adjective. Like other adjectives, determiners describe nouns. But unlike other adjectives, determiners must agree with the nouns they describe. In other words, you must know whether the noun is a singular count noun, a plural count noun, or a noncount noun before you can choose the correct determiner. The noun *determines* which adjective form you use.

62 Determiners—*A* and *An*

Remember that both *a* and *an* mean *one*. They are used before singular count nouns. *A* is used before words that begin with a consonant sound. *An* is used before words that begin with a vowel sound.

A	consonant sound	
A	*f*oreign student	must have an I-20 form

An	vowel sound	
An	*i*nternational student	must have an I-20 form

Avoid confusing vowel and consonant spellings with vowel and consonant sounds. *U* is a vowel spelling, but it has the consonant sound *Y* in words like *use, universal, usual*, etc. *H* is a consonant spelling, that has a vowel sound in words like *hour* and *honor*, but not in words like *history* and *horror*.

EXAMPLES

INCORRECT: It is a big decision to choose an university.
CORRECT: It is a big decision to choose a university.

INCORRECT: Do you have an use for this empty box?
CORRECT: Do you have a use for this empty box?

INCORRECT: Chemistry 100H is a honors section.
CORRECT: Chemistry 100H is an honors section.

INCORRECT: Let's just wait an year or two before we get married.
CORRECT: Let's just wait a year or two before we get married.

INCORRECT: I'll call you back in a hour.
CORRECT: I'll call you back in an hour.

EXERCISES

Part A: Choose the correct answer.

Sunspots are known to cause _____ enormous increase in the intensity of the sun's electro-magnetic radiation.

(A) an
(B) a
(C) some
(D) one

Part B: Choose the incorrect word or phrase and correct it.

Although <u>almost all</u> insects <u>have</u> six legs a immature insect <u>may not have any</u>.
          (A)   (B)   (C)   (D)

63 Noncount Nouns with Qualifying Phrases—*The*

Remember *the* is used with count nouns. You have also learned that *the* can be used before an *-ing* noun that is followed by a qualifying phrase.

In addition, *the* can be used before a noncount noun with a qualifying phrase.

The	noncount noun	Qualifying Phrase	
The	art	of the Middle Ages	is on display

EXAMPLES

INCORRECT: Poetry of Carl Sandburg is being read at the student union on Friday.
CORRECT: The poetry of Carl Sandburg is being read at the student union on Friday.

INCORRECT: Poverty of people in the rural areas is not as visible as that of people in the city.
CORRECT: The poverty of people in the rural areas is not as visible as that of people in the city.

INCORRECT: Science of genetic engineering is not very old.
CORRECT: The science of genetic engineering is not very old.

INCORRECT: History of this area is interesting.
CORRECT: The history of this area is interesting.

INCORRECT: Work of many people made the project a success.
CORRECT: The work of many people made the project a success.

EXERCISES

Part A: Choose the correct answer.

_____ of Country-Western singers may be related to old English ballads.
(A) The music
(B) Music
(C) Their music
(D) Musics

Part B: Choose the incorrect word or phrase and correct it.

Philosophy of the ancient Greeks has been preserved in the scholarly writing of Western civilization.
   (A)   (B)   (C)   (D)

64   Ø Meaning *All*

Remember that no article (Ø) before a noncount or a plural count noun has the same meaning as *all*.

all Ø	noun (noncount)	verb (singular)	
All	art Art	is is	interesting interesting

all Ø	noun (count-plural)	verb (plural)	
All	trees Trees	prevent prevent	erosion erosion

Avoid using *the* before the noun to express *all*.

EXAMPLES

INCORRECT: The dormitories are noisy.
 · CORRECT: <u>Dormitories</u> are noisy.
                 (all dormitories)

INCORRECT: The convenience stores have high prices.
   CORRECT: <u>Convenience stores</u> have high prices.
                 (all convenience stores)

INCORRECT: I like the music.
   CORRECT: I like <u>music</u>.
                 (all music)

INCORRECT: The mathematics is easy for me.
   CORRECT: <u>Mathematics</u> is easy for me.
                 (all mathematics)

INCORRECT: Professor Collins is an expert in the microbiology.
   CORRECT: Professor Collins is an expert in <u>microbiology</u>.
                 (all microbiology)

EXERCISES

Part A: Choose the correct answer.

_____ is an ancient source of energy.
(A) The wind
(B) Winds
(C) Wind
(D) A wind

Part B: Choose the incorrect word or phrase and correct it.

The soil is composed of a mixture of organic matter called humus and inorganic matter derived from
  (A) (B)   (C)   (D)
rocks.

65   *No* Meaning *Not Any*

Remember that *no* means *not any*. It may be used with a singular or plural count noun or with a non-count noun.

no	noun (count singular) noun (count plural)	verb (singular) verb (plural)
No No	tree trees	grows above the tree line grow above the tree line

no	noun (noncount)	verb (singular)	
No	art	is	on display today

Avoid using the negatives *not* or *none* instead of *no*. Avoid using a singular verb with a plural count noun.

EXAMPLES

INCORRECT: There is not reason to worry.
  CORRECT: There is <u>no reason</u> to worry.

INCORRECT: None news is good news.
  CORRECT: <u>No news</u> is good news.

INCORRECT: We have not a file under the name Wagner.
  CORRECT: We have <u>no file</u> under the name Wagner.

INCORRECT: None of cheating will be tolerated.
  CORRECT: <u>No cheating</u> will be tolerated.

INCORRECT: Bill told me that he has none friends.
  CORRECT: Bill told me that he has <u>no friends</u>.

EXERCISES

Part A: Choose the correct answer.

At Woolworth's first five-and-ten-cent store, _____ more than a dime.
  (A) neither items cost
  (B) items not cost
  (C) items none costing
  (D) no item cost

Part B: Choose the incorrect word or phrase and correct it.

Some religions <u>have</u> <u>none</u> deity but <u>are</u> philosophies that function <u>instead of religions</u>.
          (A) (B)   (C)   (D)

66   *One of the* and *Some of the*

Remember that *one* means one of a group. *Some* means several of a group.

one of the	noun (count plural)	verb (singular)	
One of the	trees	is	dead

some of the	noun (count plural)	verb (plural)	
Some of the	trees	are	dead

some of the	noun (noncount)	verb (singular)	
Some of the	art	is	in the museum

Avoid using *one of the* or *some of the* with a singular count noun or *one of the* with a noncount noun. Avoid using a plural verb with *one of the*.

EXAMPLES

INCORRECT: Some of the parking space at the back are empty.
  CORRECT: Some of the <u>parking spaces</u> at the back <u>are</u> empty.

INCORRECT: One of the major field of study that Laura is considering is nursing.
  CORRECT: One of the <u>major fields</u> of study that Laura is considering <u>is</u> nursing.

INCORRECT: One of my friends are in the hospital.
  CORRECT: One of my <u>friends</u> <u>is</u> in the hospital.

INCORRECT: You should save some of the moneys.
  CORRECT: You should save <u>some of the money</u>.

INCORRECT: One of the best reason to eat vegetables is to add fiber to your diet.
CORRECT: One of the best <u>reasons</u> to eat vegetables <u>is</u> to add fiber to your diet.

EXERCISES

Part A: Choose the correct answer.

One of _____ of the late Middle Ages was Saint Thomas Aquinas, a scholar who studied under Albertus Magnus.
   (A) the thinkers who was great
   (B) the great thinker
   (C) the greatest thinkers
   (D) who thought greatly

Part B: Choose the incorrect word or phrase and correct it.

One of the primary <u>cause</u> of accidents in <u>coal mines</u> <u>is</u> the accumulation of <u>gas</u>.
                        (A)   (B)   (C)   (D)

Few and *Little*

Remember that *few* and *little* have the same meaning, but *few* is used before plural count nouns and *little* is used before noncount nouns.

few	noun (count)	
Few	reference books	may be checked out

Avoid using a noncount noun instead of a count noun after *few*.

	little	noun (noncount)
Before he came to the U.S., he had done	little	traveling

Avoid using a count noun instead of a noncount noun after *little*.

EXAMPLES

INCORRECT: Professor Stone keeps little chairs in his office because he doesn't have room for many.
CORRECT: Professor Stone keeps <u>few chairs</u> in his office because he doesn't have room for many.

INCORRECT: John has very little friends.
CORRECT: John has very <u>few friends</u>.

INCORRECT: There is few time to waste.
CORRECT: There is <u>little time</u> to waste.

INCORRECT: My brother used to help me a lot, but now he gives me few advice.
CORRECT: My brother used to help me a lot, but now he gives me <u>little</u> <u>advice</u>.

INCORRECT: He had to balance his account very carefully because he had few money.
CORRECT: He had to balance his account very carefully because he had <u>little</u> <u>money</u>.

EXERCISES

Part A: Choose the correct answer.

Although southern California is densely populated, _____ live in the northern part of the state.
   (A) a little people
   (B) a few the people
   (C) few people
   (D) a little of people

Part B: Choose the incorrect word or phrase and correct it.

Unless <u>one</u> subscribes to a large metropolitan newspaper <u>such as</u> the *Wall Street Journal,* or the
         (A)   (B)
Washington Post, <u>one</u> will find very <u>few news</u> from abroad.
                 (C)   (D)

68   *Much* and *Many*

Remember that *many* and *much* have the same meaning, but *many* is used before plural count nouns and *much* is used before noncount nouns.

	many	noun (count—plural)	
There are	many	television programs	for children on Saturday

Avoid using a noncount noun instead of a plural count noun after *many*.

	much	noun (noncount)
We don't have	much	information

Avoid using a count noun instead of a noncount noun after *much*.

EXAMPLES

INCORRECT: The letter was short because there wasn't many news.
CORRECT: The letter was short because there wasn't <u>much</u> <u>news</u>.

INCORRECT: Peter and Carol don't have much children.
CORRECT: Peter and Carol don't have <u>many</u> <u>children</u>.

INCORRECT: How much years have you been living in Texas?
 CORRECT: How <u>many</u> <u>years</u> have you been living in Texas?

INCORRECT: He always has much problems with his teeth.
 CORRECT: He always has <u>many</u> <u>problems</u> with his teeth.

INCORRECT: I think that there is too many violence on TV.
 CORRECT: I think that there is too <u>much</u> <u>violence</u> on TV.

EXERCISES

Part A: Choose the correct answer.

Although the Ojibwa Indians fought frequently with the Sioux, they didn't have _____ with early white settlers.
   (A) much contact
   (B) lots contact
   (C) many contact
   (D) large contact

Part B: Choose the incorrect word or phrase and correct it.

<u>Many</u> heavy work that was once <u>done</u> <u>by hand</u> can now be done more <u>easily</u> with the help of com-
  (A)   (B)   (C)   (D)
pressed air.

69   *A Little* and *Little*
A Few and *Few*

Remember this story in English:
There were two men. Each man had half a cup of happiness. One man said, "How sad! I have *little* happiness." The other man said, "How wonderful! I have *a little* happiness." The difference between *little* and *a little* is the point of view. *Little* or *few* means not a lot. *A little* or *a few* means some.

	a little little	noun (noncount)
We have We have	a little little	time time

	a few few	noun (count—plural)
We made We made	a few few	mistakes mistakes

EXAMPLES

INCORRECT: Give me little butter, please.
  CORRECT: Give me a <u>little</u> <u>butter</u>, please.
          (some)

INCORRECT: We have a little news about the plane crash.
  CORRECT: We have <u>little</u> <u>news</u> about the plane crash.
          (not much)

INCORRECT: There are few tickets left for the concert.
  CORRECT: There are a <u>few</u> <u>tickets</u> left for the concert.
          (some)

INCORRECT: A few people in my apartment building are friendly.
  CORRECT: <u>Few</u> <u>people</u> in my apartment building are friendly.
          (not many)

INCORRECT: She speaks a little French.
  CORRECT: She speaks <u>little</u> <u>French</u>.
          (not much)

Note: All of the sentences in this problem are grammatically correct, but only the sentences marked correct express the meanings in parentheses.

EXERCISES

Part A: Choose the correct answer.

_____ is currently available to researchers and physicians who study and treat acromegaly, a glandular disorder characterized by enlargement and obesity.

(A) The little information
(B) Few information
(C) Little information
(D) A few information

Part B: Choose the incorrect word or phrase and correct it.

When <u>there is</u> <u>a few</u> money remaining after all expenses <u>have been paid</u>, we say that a small eco-
     (A)   (B)   (C)
nomic surplus or profit <u>has been created</u>.
               (D)

70   *Only a Few* and *Only a Little*

Remember that *only a few* and *only a little* have the same meaning, but *only a few* is used before a plural count noun and *only a little* is used before a noncount noun.

only	a few	noun (count—plural)	
Only	a few	dollars	have been budgeted for supplies

Avoid using *few* instead of *a few* after *only*.

	only	a little	noun (noncount)	
We have	only	a little	homework	for Monday

Avoid using *little* instead of *a little* after *only*.

EXAMPLES

INCORRECT: Only a little students are lazy.
  CORRECT: Only a few students are lazy.

INCORRECT: Tom took only few pictures.
  CORRECT: Tom took only a few pictures.

INCORRECT: We will need only a few food for the picnic.
  CORRECT: We will need only a little food for the picnic.

INCORRECT: Only few people were at the reception.
  CORRECT: Only a few people were at the reception.

INCORRECT: The advisor makes only few exceptions to the rules regarding prerequisites.
  CORRECT: The advisor makes only a few exceptions to the rules regarding prerequisites.

EXERCISES

Part A: Choose the correct answer.

_____ can be grown on arid land.
  (A) Only a few crops
  (B) Only few crop
  (C) Only a little crops
  (D) Only little crop

Part B: Choose the incorrect word or phrase and correct it.

Only a little early scientists, among them Bacon, Copernicus, and Bruno, believed that the principles
          (A)   (B)   (C)   (D)
underlying the physical world could be discovered and understood through careful observation and
analysis.

71   A Large (Small) Number of and a Large (Small) Amount of

Remember that *a large (small) number of* and *a large (small) amount of* have the same meaning, but *a large (small) number of* is used before a plural count noun and *a large (small) amount of* is used before a noncount noun.

A large number of small	noun (count—plural)	
A large number of	students	from other countries attend State University

A large amount of small	noun (noncount)	
A small amount of	rain	is expected tomorrow

Avoid using *number* with noncount nouns and *amount* with count nouns.

EXAMPLES

INCORRECT: You will just need a small number of clothing to go to college because the lifestyle is very informal.

CORRECT: You will just need a small amount of clothing to go to college because the lifestyle is very informal.

INCORRECT: There are a small amount of Chinese restaurants in the city.
CORRECT: There are a small number of Chinese restaurants in the city.

INCORRECT: We don't have time for a large amount of interruptions.
CORRECT: We don't have time for a large number of interruptions.

INCORRECT: The lab has a large number of equipment.
CORRECT: The lab has a large amount of equipment.

INCORRECT: A small amount of families own most of the land here.
CORRECT: A small number of families own most of the land here.

EXERCISES

Part A: Choose the correct answer.

Only _____ of the breeds of cattle have been brought to the United States.
  (A) a small amount
  (B) a little amount
  (C) a small number
  (D) a little number

Part B: Choose the incorrect word or phrase and correct it.

The amount of books in the Library of Congress is more than 58 million volumes.
    (A)   (B)   (C)   (D)

72 *Almost All of the* and *Most of the*

Remember that *almost all of the* and *most of the* mean all except a few, but *almost all of the* includes more.

almost all (of the) most (of the)	noun (count—plural)	verb (plural)	
Almost all (of the) Most (of the)	trees in our yard trees	are are	oaks oaks

almost all (of the) most (of the)	noun (noncount)	verb (singular)
Almost all (of the) Most (of the)	art by R. C. Gorman art by R. C. Gorman	is expensive is expensive

Avoid using *almost* without *all* or *all of the*. Avoid using *most of* without *the*.

EXAMPLES

INCORRECT: Almost the states have a sales tax.
  CORRECT: Almost all of the states have a sales tax.
                    or
             Almost all states have a sales tax.
                    or
             Most of the states have a sales tax.
                    or
             Most states have a sales tax.

INCORRECT: Most of teachers at State University care about their students' progress.
  CORRECT: Almost all of the teachers at State University care about their students' progress.
                    or
             Almost all teachers at State University care about their students' progress.
                    or
             Most of the teachers at State University care about their students' progress.
                    or
             Most teachers at State University care about their students' progress.

INCORRECT: My cousin told me that most of people who won the lottery got only a few dollars, not the grand prize.

CORRECT: My cousin told me that <u>almost all of the people</u> who won the lottery got only a few dollars, not the grand prize.

> *or*

My cousin told me that <u>almost all people</u> who won the lottery got only a few dollars, not the grand prize.

> *or*

My cousin told me that <u>most of the people</u> who won the lottery got only a few dollars, not the grand prize.

> *or*

My cousin told me that <u>most people</u> who won the lottery got only a few dollars, not the grand prize.

INCORRECT: Most the dictionaries have information about pronunciation.

CORRECT: <u>Almost all of the dictionaries</u> have information about pronunciation.

> *or*

<u>Almost all dictionaries</u> have information about pronunciation.

> *or*

<u>Most of the dictionaries</u> have information about pronunciation.

> *or*

<u>Most dictionaries</u> have information about pronunciation.

INCORRECT: Is it true that most Americans watches TV every night?

CORRECT: It is true that <u>almost all of the Americans</u> watch TV every night?

> *or*

Is it true that <u>almost all Americans</u> watch TV every night?

> *or*

Is it true that <u>most of the Americans</u> watch TV every night?

> *or*

Is it true that <u>most Americans</u> <u>watch</u> TV every night?

EXERCISES

Part A: Choose the correct answer.

_____ fuel that is used today is a chemical form of solar energy.

(A) Most of
(B) The most
(C) Most
(D) Almost the

Part B: Choose the incorrect word or phrase and correct it.

<u>Almost</u> the plants <u>known to us</u> are made up of <u>a great many cells,</u> specialized <u>to perform</u> different
 (A)   (B)   (C)   (D)
tasks.

PROBLEMS WITH OTHER ADJECTIVES

Besides determiners that express number and amount, there are adjectives and adjective-related structures that express *sufficiency*, *consecutive order*, *quality*, and *emphasis*.
Adjectives usually do not change to agree with the noun that they modify.

Sufficiency—*Enough* with Nouns

Remember that *enough* means sufficient. It can be used before or after a plural count noun or a noncount noun.

			noun (count—plural) noun (noncount)
We	have	enough	tickets
We	have	enough	time

		noun (count—plural) noun (noncount)	enough
We	have	tickets	enough
We	have	time	enough

Avoid using *as* and *the* with *enough*. Avoid using a singular count noun instead of a plural count noun.

EXAMPLES

INCORRECT:	There aren't enough car for all of us to go.
CORRECT:	There aren't <u>enough</u> <u>cars</u> for all of us to go.
	or
	There aren't <u>cars</u> <u>enough</u> for all of us to go.
INCORRECT:	Without enough the sleep, you won't be able to do well on the examination.
CORRECT:	Without <u>enough</u> <u>sleep</u>, you won't be able to do well on the examination.
	or
	Without <u>sleep</u> <u>enough</u>, you won't be able to do well on the examination.
INCORRECT:	Do we have hamburgers enough as for the party?
CORRECT:	Do we have <u>enough</u> <u>hamburgers</u> for the party?
	or
	Do we have <u>hamburgers</u> <u>enough</u> for the party?

INCORRECT: Virginia doesn't have the enough information to make a decision.
  CORRECT: Virginia doesn't have <u>enough</u> <u>information</u> to make a decision.
                    or
                Virginia doesn't have <u>information</u> <u>enough</u> to make a decision.

INCORRECT: I need to buy a lamp because I don't have enough the light in my room.
  CORRECT: I need to buy a lamp because I don't have <u>enough</u> <u>light</u> in my room.
                    or
                I need to buy a lamp because I don't have <u>light</u> <u>enough</u> in my room.

EXERCISES

Part A: Choose the correct answer.

When your body does not get _____ , it cannot make the glucose it needs.
  (A) enough food
  (B) food as enough
  (C) food enoughly
  (D) enough the food

Part B: Choose the incorrect word or phrase and correct it.

<u>As soon</u> as the company has <u>as enough earnings</u> <u>to make up for</u> a bad year, the stockholders of cu-
    (A)   (B)   (C)
mulative preferred stock receive dividends for the bad year <u>as well</u> as for the good year.
                                                              (D)

74   Sufficiency—*Enough* with Adjectives

Remember that *enough* with adjectives means sufficiently.

S	V	adjective	enough	infinitive	
It	is	warm	enough	to go	swimming

S	V	not	adjective	enough	infinitive	
It	is	not	warm	enough	to go	swimming

Avoid using *enough* before the adjective instead of after it. Avoid using *as* between *enough* and the infinitive.

EXAMPLES

INCORRECT: Her little car isn't big enough as to seat more than two people comfortably.
  CORRECT: Her little car isn't <u>big enough</u> to seat more than two people comfortably.

INCORRECT: That excuse isn't enough good.
  CORRECT: That excuse isn't <u>good enough</u>.

INCORRECT: He should be as strong enough to get out of bed in a few days.
  CORRECT: He should be <u>strong enough</u> to get out of bed in a few days.

INCORRECT: Billy isn't enough old to enlist in the army.
  CORRECT: Billy isn't <u>old enough</u> to enlist in the army.

INCORRECT: His score on the exam was enough good to qualify him for a graduate program.
  CORRECT: His score on the exam was <u>good enough</u> to qualify him for a graduate program.

EXERCISES

Part A: Choose the correct answer.

The definitions for "gram calories" or "calories" are _____ for most engineering work.
   (A) accurate as enough
   (B) enough accurate
   (C) accurate enough
   (D) as accurate enough

Part B: Choose the incorrect word or phrase and correct it.

Most large corporations provide pension plans for their employees <u>so that</u> they will be
                                                   (A)

<u>secure enough than</u> <u>to live</u> <u>comfortably</u> during their retirement.
    (B)   (C)   (D)

75   Consecutive Order—*One, Another, the Other*

Remember that *one*, *another*, and *the other* are used before or instead of singular count nouns. When they are used before singular count nouns, they are adjectives. When they are used instead of singular count nouns, they are pronouns.

One, *another*, and *the other* organize three nouns consecutively. *One* and *the other* organize two nouns consecutively. *One* means the first one mentioned. *Another* means one more in addition to the first one mentioned. *The other* means the one remaining.

1 one	count noun (singular)		2 another	count noun (singular)	
One	movie	starts at five,	another	movie	starts at seven, and
3 the other	count noun (singular)				
the other	movie				starts at nine

1			2		3	
one	count noun (singular)		another		the other	
One	bus	leaves at two,	another	at six, and	the other	at ten

EXAMPLES

INCORRECT: One of my roommates studies engineering, another studies business, and the another studies computer science.

CORRECT: One of my roommates studies engineering, <u>another</u> (roommate) studies business, and <u>the other</u> (roommate) studies computer science.

INCORRECT: One problem is finding an apartment, another is furnishing it, and other is getting the utilities turned on.

CORRECT: One problem is finding an apartment, <u>another</u> (problem) is furnishing it, and <u>the other</u> (problem) is getting the utilities turned on.

INCORRECT: Of the three busiest vacation areas in the United States, one is Disney World, one another is New York City, and the other is Washington, D.C.

CORRECT: Of the three busiest vacation areas in the United States, <u>one</u> (area) is Disney World, <u>another</u> (area) is New York City, and <u>the other</u> (area) is Washington, D.C.

INCORRECT: There are three major restaurant chains near the campus that specialize in fast-food hamburgers: one is MacDonald's, another is Wendy's, and the another one is Burger King.

CORRECT: There are three major restaurant chains near the campus that specialize in fast-food hamburgers: <u>one</u> (restaurant) is MacDonald's, <u>another</u> (restaurant) is Wendy's, and <u>the other</u> (restaurant) is Burger King.

INCORRECT: One English proficiency test is the TOEFL and other is the Michigan Test of English Language Proficiency.

CORRECT: One English proficiency test is the TOEFL and <u>the other</u> (test) is the Michigan Test of English Language Proficiency.

EXERCISES

Part A: Choose the correct answer.

There are three kinds of solar eclipses: one is total, another is annular, and _____ .
   (A) the another is partial
   (B) the partial is other
   (C) other is partial
   (D) the other is partial

Part B: Choose the incorrect word or phrase and correct it.

One of the most popular major fields of study for <u>foreign scholars</u> <u>in the United States</u> <u>is</u> business
                                                          (A)   (B)   (C)

and <u>the another</u> is engineering.
        (D)

76   Consecutive Order—*Some, Other, the Other*
Some, Others, the Others (the Rest)

Remember that *some*, *other*, and *the other* are used before plural count nouns. They are adjectives.

1 Some	count noun (plural)		2 other	count noun (plural)	
Some	houses	are for rent,	other	houses	are for sale, and
3 the other the rest of the			count noun (plural)		
the other the rest of the			houses		are empty

Some, *others*, and *the others* (*the rest*) are used instead of plural count nouns. They are pronouns.

1 Some	count noun (plural)		2 others	
Some Some	schools schools	are universities, are universities,	others others	are colleges, and are colleges, and
3 the others the rest				
the others the rest			are junior colleges arc junior colleges	

Avoid using *another* instead of *other*. Avoid using *rest of* or *rest* instead of *the rest of the* or *the rest*.

EXAMPLES

INCORRECT: Some of these T-shirts are red, others are blue, and rest are white.
CORRECT: Some of these T-shirts are red, others are blue, and the rest are white.

INCORRECT: Some of our friends are from the Middle East, the others are from the Far East, and the
             rest are from Latin America.
CORRECT: Some of our friends are from the Middle East, others are from the Far East, and the rest
             are from Latin America.

INCORRECT: Some people finish a bachelor's degree in four years and other take five years.
CORRECT: Some people finish a bachelor's degree in four years and other people take five years.

INCORRECT: Some of the home computer models on sale have 2MB, other models have 4MB, and the rest of models have 8MB.

CORRECT: Some of the home computer <u>models</u> on sale have 2MB, <u>other models</u> have 4MB, and <u>the rest of the models</u> have 8MB.

INCORRECT: Some applicants want student visas, other applicants want resident visas, and the others applicants want tourist visas.

CORRECT: Some <u>applicants</u> want student visas, <u>other applicants</u> want resident visas, and <u>the other applicants</u> want tourist visas.

EXERCISES

Part A: Choose the correct answer.

Some plants are annuals; _____ are biennials; the rest are perennials.
   (A) some another
   (B) another
   (C) others
   (D) other

Part B: Choose the incorrect word or phrase and correct it.

In experiments with <u>large numbers</u> of animals crowded in small cages, some have not been affected,
                    (A)

but <u>the rest of</u> <u>have shown</u> <u>all of the symptoms</u> associated with stress and mental illness.
      (B)   (C)   (D)

77   Numerical Order.

Remember that *the* is used with an ordinal number before a singular count noun to express numerical order. A cardinal number is used after a singular count noun to express numerical order.
Remember that the following are ordinal numbers:

first	*sixth*	*eleventh*	*sixteenth*
second	*seventh*	*twelfth*	*seventeenth*
third	*eighth*	*thirteenth*	*eighteenth*
fourth	*ninth*	*fourteenth*	*nineteenth*
fifth	*tenth*	*fifteenth*	*twentieth*

	the	ordinal number	count noun (singular)	
I am outlining	the	sixth	chapter	in my notebook

Avoid using *the* before the noun instead of before the ordinal number. Avoid using a cardinal instead of an ordinal number.

Remember that the following are cardinal numbers:

one	six	eleven	sixteen
two	seven	twelve	seventeen
three	eight	thirteen	eighteen
four	nine	fourteen	nineteen
five	ten	fifteen	twenty

	count noun (singular)	cardinal number	
I am outlining	chapter	six	in my notebook

Avoid using *the* before the cardinal number or before the noun. Avoid using an ordinal number instead of a cardinal number.

EXAMPLES

INCORRECT: Flight 656 for Los Angeles is now ready for boarding at the concourse seven.
CORRECT: Flight 656 for Los Angeles is now ready for boarding at <u>concourse seven</u>.

INCORRECT: We left before the beginning of act third.
CORRECT: We left before the beginning of <u>the third act</u>.
or
We left before the beginning of <u>act three</u>.

INCORRECT: Your tickets are for gate the tenth, section B.
CORRECT: Your tickets are for <u>gate ten</u>, section B.

INCORRECT: Look in volume second of the *Modern Medical Dictionary*.
CORRECT: Look in <u>the second volume</u> of the *Modern Medical Dictionary*.
or
Look in <u>volume two</u> of the *Modern Medical Dictionary*.

INCORRECT: The New York–Washington train is arriving on track the fourth.
CORRECT: The New York–Washington train is arriving on <u>track four</u>.

EXERCISES

Part A: Choose the correct answer.

_____ planet from the sun, Mars, has a year of 687 days.
(A) The fourth
(B) The four
(C) Four
(D) Fourth

Part B: Choose the incorrect word or phrase and correct it.

<u>Labor Day</u> is always <u>celebrated</u> on <u>first</u> Monday in <u>September</u>.
    (A)   (B)   (C)   (D)

78   Nouns That Function as Adjectives

Remember that when two nouns occur together, the first noun describes the second noun; that is, the first noun functions as an adjective. Adjectives do not change form, singular or plural.

	noun	noun
All of us are foreign	language	teachers

Avoid using a plural form for the first noun even when the second noun is plural. Avoid using a possessive form for the first noun.

EXAMPLES

INCORRECT: May I borrow some notebooks paper?
CORRECT: May I borrow some notebook paper?

INCORRECT: All business' students must take the Graduate Management Admission Test.
CORRECT: All business students must take the Graduate Management Admission Test.

INCORRECT: I forgot their telephone's number.
CORRECT: I forgot their telephone number.

INCORRECT: There is a sale at the shoes store.
CORRECT: There is a sale at the shoe store.

INCORRECT: Put the mail on the hall's table.
CORRECT: Put the mail on the hall table.

EXERCISES

Part A: Choose the correct answer.

_____ is cheaper for students who maintain a B average because they are a better risk than average or below-average students.
   (A) Automobile's insurance
   (B) Insurance of automobiles
   (C) Automobile insurance
   (D) Insurance automobile

Part B: Choose the incorrect word or phrase and correct it.

Sex's education is instituted to help the student understand the process of maturation,
   ‾‾‾‾‾‾‾‾‾‾‾‾‾   ‾‾‾‾‾‾‾‾‾‾
        (A)   (B)

to eliminate anxieties related to development, to learn values, and to prevent disease.
‾‾‾‾‾‾‾‾‾‾‾‾‾‾‾‾‾‾‾‾‾ ‾‾‾‾‾‾‾
        (C)   (D)

79 Hyphenated Adjectives

Remember that it is common for a number to appear as the first in a series of hyphenated adjectives. Each word in a hyphenated adjective is an adjective and does not change form, singular or plural.

	a	adjective	—	adjective	noun
Agriculture 420 is	a	five	—	hour	class

	a	adjective	—	adjective	—	adjective	noun	
	A	sixty	—	year	—	old	employee	may retire

Avoid using a plural form for any of the adjectives joined by hyphens even when the noun that follows is plural.

EXAMPLES

INCORRECT: A three-minutes call anywhere in the United States costs less than a dollar when you dial it yourself.

CORRECT: A three-minute call anywhere in the United States costs less than a dollar when you dial it yourself.

INCORRECT: They have a four-months-old baby.

CORRECT: They have a four-month-old baby.

INCORRECT: Can you make change for a twenty-dollars bill?

CORRECT: Can you make change for a twenty-dollar bill?

INCORRECT: A two-doors car is cheaper than a four-doors model.

CORRECT: A two-door car is cheaper than a four-door model.

INCORRECT: I have to write a one-thousand-words paper this weekend.

CORRECT: I have to write a one-thousand-word paper this weekend.

EXERCISES

Part A: Choose the correct answer.

The evolution of vertebrates suggests development from a very simple heart in fish to a _____ in man.

(A) four-chamber heart
(B) four-chambers heart
(C) four-chamber hearts
(D) four-chamber's heart

Part B: Choose the incorrect word or phrase and correct it.

The MX <u>is a four-stages</u> rocket with <u>an 8,000-mile range</u>, <u>larger than</u> that of the Minuteman.
      (A)   (B)   (C)   (D)

PROBLEM 80   Adjectives Ending in *-ed* and *-ing*

Remember that an *-ing* noun that functions as an adjective usually expresses cause. It is derived from an active verb. An *-ed* adjective usually expresses result. It is derived from a passive verb.

	-ed adjective	(by someone or something)
The audience is	thrilled	(by the concert)

	-ing adjective	(to someone or something)
The concert is	thrilling	(the audience)

EXAMPLES

INCORRECT: We were surprising by the results of the test.
  CORRECT: We were <u>surprised</u> by the results of the test.
               (The results were surprising.)

INCORRECT: This desk is disorganizing.
  CORRECT: This desk is <u>disorganized</u>.

INCORRECT: What an interested idea!
  CORRECT: What an <u>interesting</u> idea!
               (We are interested.)

INCORRECT: Drug abuse is increasing at an alarmed rate.
  CORRECT: Drug abuse is increasing at an <u>alarming</u> rate.
               (We are alarmed.)

INCORRECT: The petition has been signed by concerning citizens.
  CORRECT: The petition has been signed by <u>concerned</u> citizens.

EXERCISES

Part A: Choose the correct answer.

The *Canterbury Tales*, written about 1386, is as alive and _____ today as it was nearly 600 years ago.
    (A) appealed
    (B) appeal
    (C) appealing
    (D) the appeal of

Part B: Choose the incorrect word or phrase and correct it.

It is not <u>surprised</u> that the Arabs, <u>who</u> <u>possessed</u> a remarkable gift for astronomy, mathematics, and
        (A)   (B)   (C)

geometry, <u>were</u> also skillful mapmakers.
         (D)

81   Cause-and-Result—*So*

Remember that *so* is used before an adjective or an adverb followed by *that*. The *so* clause expresses cause. The *that* clause expresses result.

CAUSE				RESULT			
S	V	so	adverb adjective	that	S	V	
She The music	got up was	so so	late loud	that that	she we	missed couldn't talk	her bus

Avoid using *as* or *too* instead of *so* in clauses of cause. Avoid using *as* instead of *that* in clauses of result.

EXAMPLES

INCORRECT: He is so slow as he never gets to class on time.
  CORRECT: He is <u>so slow that</u> he never gets to class on time.

INCORRECT: This suitcase is as heavy that I can hardly carry it.
  CORRECT: This suitcase is <u>so heavy that</u> I can hardly carry it.

INCORRECT: We arrived so late as Professor Baker had already called the roll.
  CORRECT: We arrived <u>so late that</u> Professor Baker had already called the roll.

INCORRECT: He drives so fast as no one likes to ride with him.
  CORRECT: He drives <u>so fast that</u> no one likes to ride with him.

INCORRECT: Preparing frozen foods is too easy that anyone can do it.
  CORRECT: Preparing frozen foods is <u>so easy that</u> anyone can do it.

EXERCISES

Part A: Choose the correct answer.

Oil paints are _____ they have become the most popular painter's colors.
  (A) so versatile and durable that
  (B) so versatile and durable than
  (C) such versatile and durable as
  (D) such versatile and durable

Part B: Choose the incorrect word or phrase and correct it.

By the mid-nineteenth century, land was such expensive in large cities that architects began to
   (A)   (B)

conserve space by designing skyscrapers.
  (C)   (D)

82   Cause-and-Result—*Such*

Remember that the *such* clause expresses cause and the *that* clause expresses result.

CAUSE						RESULT		
S	V	such	a	adjective	count noun (singular)	that	S	V
It	was	such	a	hot	day	that	we	went out

or

CAUSE						RESULT		
S	V	so	adjective	a	count noun (singular)	that	S	V
It	was	so	hot	a	day	that	we	went out

Avoid using *so* instead of *such* before *a*. Avoid omitting *a* from the patterns.

CAUSE					RESULT			
S	V	such	adjective	count noun (plural) noun (noncount)	that	S	V	
These	are	such	long	assignments	that	I	can't finish	them
This	is	such	good	news	that	I	will call	them

Avoid using *so* instead of *such*.

EXAMPLES

INCORRECT: It was so interesting book that he couldn't put it down.
  CORRECT: It was such an interesting book that he couldn't put it down.

                   or

    It was so interesting a book that he couldn't put it down.

INCORRECT:	She is such nice girl that everyone likes her.
CORRECT:	She is <u>such a nice girl</u> that everyone likes her.
	or
	She is <u>so nice a girl</u> that everyone likes her.

INCORRECT:	We had so a small lunch that I am hungry already.
CORRECT:	We had <u>such a small lunch</u> that I am hungry already.
	or
	We had <u>so small a lunch</u> that I am hungry already.

INCORRECT:	That so many advances have been made in so short time is the most valid argument for retaining the research unit.
CORRECT:	That so many advances have been made in <u>such a short time</u> is the most valid argument for retaining the research unit.
	or
	That so many advances have been made in <u>so short a time</u> is the most valid argument for retaining the research unit.

| INCORRECT: | It is so nice weather that I would like to go to the beach. |
| CORRECT: | It is <u>such nice weather</u> that I would like to go to the beach. |

EXERCISES

Part A: Choose the correct answer.

Water is _____ that it generally contains dissolved materials in greater or lesser amounts.
(A) such an excellent solvent
(B) such excellent a solvent
(C) such a excellent solvents
(D) a such excellent solvent

Part B: Choose the incorrect word or phrase and correct it.

Albert Einstein was <u>such brilliant a scientist</u> that <u>many of his colleagues</u> had to <u>study</u> for
                               (A)   (B)   (C)
<u>several years</u> in order to form opinions about his theories.
   (D)

83 Excess—*Too*

Remember that *too* means excessively. The *too* clause expresses cause. The infinitive expresses result.

	CAUSE		RESULT
	too	adjective	infinitive
This tea is	too	hot	to drink

Avoid using *so* or *such a* instead of *too* before an adjective when an infinitive follows.

EXAMPLES

INCORRECT: The top shelf in the cupboard is so high for me to reach.
CORRECT: The top shelf in the cupboard is <u>too high</u> for me <u>to reach</u>.

INCORRECT: Ralph is such a young to retire.
CORRECT: Ralph is <u>too young to retire</u>.

INCORRECT: This brand is too expensive for buy.
CORRECT: This brand is <u>too expensive to buy</u>.

INCORRECT: He always plays his stereo so loud (to enjoy).
CORRECT: He always plays his stereo <u>too loud</u> (to enjoy).

INCORRECT: It is too cold go swimming.
CORRECT: It is <u>too cold to go</u> swimming.

EXERCISES

Part A: Choose the correct answer.

The tiny pictures on microfilm are _____ small to be read with the naked eye.
   (A) so
   (B) too
   (C) much
   (D) such

Part B: Choose the incorrect word or phrase and correct it.

<u>Mercury</u> is not often visible <u>because</u> it is <u>so</u> <u>near the sun</u> to be seen.
   (A)   (B)   (C)   (D)

84 Emphasis—*Very*

Remember that *very* is used for emphasis. *Very* does not usually introduce a clause or infinitive that expresses result.

			very	adjective	Ø
This	tea	is	very	hot	

Avoid using *too* or *so* instead of *very* when there is no clause of result.
Note: In conversational English, you will often hear *so* instead of *very*, but this is not correct in the kind of formal, written English found on the TOEFL.

EXAMPLES

INCORRECT: We went out to eat because we were too hungry.
CORRECT: We went out to eat because we were <u>very hungry</u>.

INCORRECT: This dorm has too small rooms.
 CORRECT: This dorm has <u>very small</u> rooms.

INCORRECT: New York is so big, and I am not used to it.
 CORRECT: New York is <u>very big</u>, and I am not used to it.

INCORRECT: Last month we had a too high electric bill.
 CORRECT: Last month we had a <u>very high</u> electric bill.

INCORRECT: Darlene says that the courts are so lenient.
 CORRECT: Darlene says that the courts are <u>very lenient</u>.

EXERCISES

Part A: Choose the correct answer.

Young rivers have no flood plains and their valleys are _____ .
 (A) very narrow
 (B) too narrow
 (C) so narrow
 (D) narrowly

Part B: Choose the incorrect word or phrase and correct it.

<u>The smallest</u> of the apes, the gibbon, is distinguished <u>by</u> <u>its</u> <u>too long</u> arms.
    (A)   (B)(C)   (D)

85 Adjectives with Verbs of the Senses

Remember that an adjective, not an adverb, is used after verbs of the senses. The following verbs are examples of verbs of the senses:

feel	*sound*
look	*taste*
smell	

S	V (senses)	adjective	
I	felt	bad	about the mistake

Avoid using an adverb instead of an adjective after verbs of the senses.

EXAMPLES

INCORRECT: We love to go to the country in the spring because the wild flowers smell so sweetly.
 CORRECT: We love to go to the country in the spring because the wild flowers <u>smell</u> so <u>sweet</u>.

INCORRECT: Although the medicine tastes badly, it seems to help my condition.
 CORRECT: Although the medicine <u>tastes bad</u>, it seems to help my condition.

INCORRECT: The meal tasted well.
 CORRECT: The meal <u>tasted</u> <u>good</u>.

INCORRECT: The music sounds sweetly and soothing.
 CORRECT: The music <u>sounds</u> <u>sweet</u> and soothing.

INCORRECT: When he complained that the food tasted badly, the waiter took it back to the kitchen
              and brought him something else.
 CORRECT: When he complained that the food <u>tasted</u> <u>bad</u>, the waiter took it back to the kitchen and
              brought him something else.

EXERCISES

Part A: Choose the correct answer.

If one is suffering from a psychosomatic illness, that is, a disease contributed to by mental anxiety,
one may still feel very _____ .
   (A) badly
   (B) bad
   (C) worsely
   (D) worser

Part B: Choose the incorrect word or phrase and correct it.

<u>It has been proven</u> that when a subject identifies a substance as tasting <u>well</u>, <u>he</u> is often <u>associating</u>
      (A)   (B) (C)   (D)
the taste with the smell.

CUMULATIVE REVIEW EXERCISE FOR ADJECTIVES
AND ADJECTIVE-RELATED STRUCTURES

<u>DIRECTIONS</u>: Some of the sentences in this exercise are correct. Some are incorrect. First, find the correct
sentences, and mark them with a check (√). Then find the incorrect sentences, and correct them. Check
your answers using the key on page 448.

1. Today's modern TV cameras require only a few light as compared with earlier models.

2. Diamonds that are not good enough to be made into gems are used in industry for cutting and
   drilling.

3. Cane sugar contains not vitamins.

4. Humorist Will Rogers was brought up on a cattle ranch in the Oklahoma Indian territory, but the life
   of a cowboy was not excited enough for him.

5. One of the most distinctive features of Islamic architecture is the arch.

6. It is impossible to view Picasso's *Guernica* without feeling badly about the fate of the people portrayed.

7. The Erie was so large a canal that more than eighty locks and twenty aqueducts were required.

8. An usual treatment for the flu is to drink plenty of liquids.

9. The United States did not issue any stamps until 1847 when one was printed for use east of the Mississippi and one another for use west of the Mississippi.

10. Red corpuscles are so numerous that a thimbleful of human's blood would contain almost ten thousand million of them.

11. The Malay Archipelago is the world's largest group of islands, forming a ten-thousand islands chain.

12. Some property of lead are its softness and its resistance.

13. Aristotle is considered the father of the logic.

14. Metals such as iron and magnesium are quite common, but are mostly found in silicates, making them so expensive to extract.

15. History of the war in Vietnam is just being written.

Problems with Comparatives

Nouns may be compared for exact or general *similarity* or *difference*. They may also be compared for similar or different *qualities* or *degrees,* more or less, of specific qualities. In addition, they may be compared to *estimates.*

86   Exact Similarity—*the Same as* and *the Same*

Remember that *the same as* and *the same* have the same meaning, but *the same as* is used between the two nouns compared, and *the same* is used after the two nouns or a plural noun.

noun			the same as		noun
This coat	is		the same as		that one

noun		noun		the same
This coat	and	that one	are	the same

noun (plural)		the same
These coats	are	the same

Avoid using *to* and *like* instead of *as.* Avoid using *the same* between the two nouns compared.

EXAMPLES

INCORRECT:	That car is almost the same like mine.
CORRECT:	That car is almost <u>the same as</u> <u>mine</u>.
	or
	That car and mine are almost <u>the same</u>.

INCORRECT:	My briefcase is exactly the same that yours.
CORRECT:	My briefcase is exactly <u>the same as</u> <u>yours</u>.
	or
	My briefcase and yours are exactly <u>the same</u>.

INCORRECT:	Is your book the same to mine?
CORRECT:	Is your book <u>the same as</u> <u>mine</u>?
	or
	Are your book and mine <u>the same</u>?

INCORRECT:	Are this picture and the one on your desk same?
CORRECT:	Are this picture and the one on your desk <u>the same</u>?
	or
	Is this picture <u>the same as</u> <u>the one</u> on your desk?

INCORRECT:	The teacher gave Martha a failing grade on her composition because it was the same a composition he had already read.
CORRECT:	The teacher gave Martha a failing grade on her composition because it was <u>the same as</u> <u>a</u> <u>composition</u> he had already read.
	or
	The teacher gave Martha a failing grade on her composition because it and a composition he had already read were <u>the same</u>.

EXERCISES

Part A: Choose the correct answer.

Although we often use "speed" and "velocity" interchangeably, in a technical sense, "speed" is not always _____ "velocity."
(A) alike
(B) the same as
(C) similar
(D) as

Part B: Choose the incorrect word or phrase and correct it.

When two products are <u>basically</u> <u>the same as</u>, <u>advertising</u> can <u>influence</u> the public's choice.
                         (A)   (B)   (C)   (D)

PROBLEM 87   General Similarity—*Similar to* and *Similar*

Remember that *similar to* and *similar* have the same meaning, but *similar to* is used between the two nouns compared, and *similar* is used after the two nouns or a plural noun.

noun		similar to	noun
This coat	is	similar to	that one

noun		noun		similar
This coat	and	that one	are	similar

noun (plural)		similar
These coats	are	similar

Avoid using *as* instead of *to.* Avoid using *similar to* after the two nouns or a plural noun.

EXAMPLES

INCORRECT: I would really like to have a stereo that is similar the one on display.
CORRECT: I would really like to have a stereo that is <u>similar to the one</u> on display.
> *or*
The stereo that I would like to have and the one on display are <u>similar.</u>

INCORRECT: My roommate's values and mine are similar to in spite of our being from different countries.
CORRECT: My roommate's values are <u>similar to mine</u> in spite of our being from different countries.
> *or*
My roommate's values and mine are <u>similar</u> in spite of our being from different countries.

INCORRECT: Cliff's glasses are similar like yours, but his cost a lot less.
CORRECT: Cliff's glasses are <u>similar to yours</u>, but his cost a lot less.
> *or*
Cliff's glasses and yours are <u>similar</u>, but his cost a lot less.

INCORRECT: That joke is similar as a joke that I heard.
CORRECT: That joke is <u>similar to a joke</u> that I heard.
> *or*
That joke and a joke that I heard are <u>similar.</u>

INCORRECT: All of the other departments are similar this one.
CORRECT: All of the other departments are <u>similar to this one.</u>
> *or*
All of the other departments and this one are <u>similar.</u>

EXERCISES

Part A: Choose the correct answer.

The vegetation in temperate zones all around the world is _____ .
(A) similar
(B) like
(C) same
(D) as

Part B: Choose the incorrect word or phrase and correct it.

The medical problems of parents and their children tend to be very similar to because of the heredi-
                              (A)   (B)   (C)   (D)

tary nature of many diseases.

88   General Similarity—*Like* and *Alike*

Remember that *like* and *alike* have the same meaning, but *like* is used between the two nouns compared, and *alike* is used after the two nouns or a plural noun.

noun		like	noun
This coat	is	like	that one

noun		noun		alike
This coat	and	that one	are	alike

noun (plural)		alike
These coats	are	alike

Avoid using *as* instead of *like*. Avoid using *like* after the two nouns compared.

EXAMPLES

INCORRECT: The weather feels as spring.
  CORRECT: The weather feels like spring.

INCORRECT: These suits are like.
  CORRECT: This suit is like that suit.
                    or
           These suits are alike.

INCORRECT: Your recipe for chicken is like to a recipe that my mother has.
  CORRECT: Your recipe for chicken is <u>like a recipe</u> that my mother has.

or

Your recipe for chicken and a recipe that my mother has are <u>alike</u>.

INCORRECT: I want to buy some shoes same like the ones I have on.
  CORRECT: I want to buy some shoes <u>like the ones</u> I have on.

or

The shoes I want to buy and the shoes I have on are <u>alike</u>.

INCORRECT: Anthony and his brother don't look like.
  CORRECT: Anthony doesn't look <u>like his brother</u>.

or

Anthony and his brother don't look <u>alike</u>.

EXERCISES

Part A: Choose the correct answer.

Although they are smaller, chipmunks are _____ most other ground squirrels.
   (A) like to
   (B) like as
   (C) like
   (D) alike

Part B: Choose the incorrect word or phrase and correct it.

<u>The first</u> living structures <u>to appear</u> on earth thousands of years <u>ago</u> were <u>alike</u> viruses.
     (A)   (B)   (C)   (D)

89   Specific Similarity—Quality Nouns

Remember that a quality noun is used in comparisons of a specific characteristic.

The following are examples of quality nouns:

age	height	price	style
color	length	size	weight

noun	V	the same	noun (quality)	as	noun
She	is	the same	age	as	John

Avoid using *to, than,* or *like* instead of *as.* Avoid using a quality adjective instead of a quality noun after *the same.*

EXAMPLES

INCORRECT: I want to buy a pair of shoes the same style like these I'm wearing.
CORRECT: I want to buy a pair of shoes <u>the same</u> style <u>as</u> these I'm wearing.

INCORRECT: This is not the same big as the rest of the apartments.
CORRECT: This is not <u>the same</u> size <u>as</u> the rest of the apartments.

INCORRECT: The gold chain that Edith saw is same weight as yours.
CORRECT: The gold chain that Edith saw is <u>the same</u> weight <u>as</u> yours.

INCORRECT: Please cut my hair the same length like the style in this magazine.
CORRECT: Please cut my hair <u>the same</u> length <u>as</u> the style in this magazine.

INCORRECT: Is this thread the same color the cloth?
CORRECT: Is this thread <u>the same</u> color <u>as</u> the cloth?

EXERCISES

Part A: Choose the correct answer.

Some retirement communities will not sell property to new residents unless they are about _____ the rest of the residents.
   (A) the same age
   (B) the same old
   (C) the same age as
   (D) the same old as

Part B: Choose the incorrect word or phrase and correct it.

The bodies of <u>cold-blooded animals</u> <u>have</u> <u>the same temperature</u> their surroundings, but those of
　　　　　　　　　　(A)　　　　　　(B)　　　　　　(C)
warm-blooded animals <u>do not</u>.
　　　　　　　　　　(D)

90   Specific Similarity—Quality Adjectives

Remember that a quality adjective is used in comparisons of a specific characteristic.

The following are examples of quality adjectives:

big	expensive	light	small
cheap	hard	little	tall
clear	heavy	long	young
cold	hot	old	
easy	large	short	

noun	V	as	adjective (quality)	as	noun
She	is	as	old	as	John

Avoid using *to*, *than*, or *like* instead of *as*. Avoid using a quality noun instead of a quality adjective after *as*.

EXAMPLES

INCORRECT: Mary's job is as hard than Bill's.
 CORRECT: Mary's job is <u>as hard as</u> Bill's.

INCORRECT: Miss Jones' English is not as clear than Dr. Baker's.
 CORRECT: Miss Jones' English is not <u>as clear as</u> Dr. Baker's.

INCORRECT: He is not as tall like his brother.
 CORRECT: He is not <u>as tall as</u> his brother.

INCORRECT: The meat at the supermarket is not as expensive that the meat at a butcher shop.
 CORRECT: The meat at the supermarket is not <u>as expensive as</u> the meat at a butcher shop.

INCORRECT: College Station is not as big Austin.
 CORRECT: College Station is not <u>as big as</u> Austin.

EXERCISES

Part A: Choose the correct answer.

Although the name was not popularized until the Middle Ages, engineering _____ civilization.
   (A) as old as
   (B) is as old as
   (C) that is old as
   (D) as old as that

Part B: Choose the incorrect word or phrase and correct it.

<u>Despite</u> its <u>smaller</u> size, the Indian Ocean is <u>as deep</u> the Atlantic Ocean.
   (A)   (B)   (C)   (D)

91   General Difference—*Different from* and *Different*

Remember that *different from* and *different* have the same meaning, but *different from* is used between the two nouns compared, and *different* is used after the two nouns or a plural noun.

noun		different from	noun
This coat	is	different from	that one

noun		noun		different
This coat	and	that one	are	different

noun (plural)		different
These coats	are	different

Avoid using *to* and *than* instead of *from*. Avoid using *different* between the two nouns compared.

EXAMPLES

INCORRECT: Although they are both weekly news magazines, *Time* and *Newsweek* are different from in several ways.

CORRECT: Although they are both weekly news magazines, *Time is* <u>different from</u> *Newsweek* in several ways.

or

Although they are both weekly news magazines, *Time* and *Newsweek* are <u>different</u> in several ways.

INCORRECT: The watch in the window is a little different this one.

CORRECT: The watch in the window is a little <u>different from</u> this one.

or

The watch in the window and this one are a little <u>different</u>.

INCORRECT: Long distance telephone rates for daytime hours are different than rates for nighttime hours.

CORRECT: Long distance telephone rates for daytime hours are <u>different from</u> <u>rates</u> for nighttime hours.

or

Long distance telephone rates for daytime hours and rates for nighttime hours are <u>different</u>.

INCORRECT: A nursery school is different a day care center.

CORRECT: A nursery school is <u>different from</u> a day care center.

or

A nursery school and a day care center are <u>different</u>.

INCORRECT: The tour packages that we offer are different than most tours.

CORRECT: The tour packages that we offer are <u>different from</u> <u>most tours</u>.

or

The tour packages that we offer and most tours are <u>different</u>.

EXERCISES

Part A: Choose the correct answer.

The works of Picasso were quite _____ during various periods of his artistic life.
    (A) differ
    (B) different
    (C) different from
    (D) different than

Part B: Choose the incorrect word or phrase and correct it.

Although business practices have been <u>applied</u> <u>successfully</u> to agriculture, <u>farming</u> is <u>different</u> other
                               (A)   (B)   (C)   (D)
industries.

92 General Difference—*to Differ from*

Remember that *differ* is a verb and must change forms to agree with the subject.

	DIFFER	from	
This one	differs	from	the rest

Avoid using BE with *differ*. Avoid using *than*, *of*, or *to* after *differ*.

EXAMPLES

INCORRECT: Sharon is different of other women I know.
  CORRECT: Sharon is <u>different from</u> other women I know.
                  or
           Sharon <u>differs from</u> other women I know.

INCORRECT: Do you have anything a little different to these?
  CORRECT: Do you have anything a little <u>different from</u> these?
                  or
           Do you have anything that <u>differs</u> a little <u>from</u> these?

INCORRECT: The campus at State University different from that of City College.
  CORRECT: The campus at State University <u>differs from</u> that of City College.
                  or
           The campus at State University is <u>different from</u> that of City College.

INCORRECT: Jayne's apartment is very differs from Bill's even though they are in the same building.
  CORRECT: Jayne's apartment is very <u>different from</u> Bill's even though they are in the same building.
                  or
           Jayne's apartment <u>differs from</u> Bill's even though they are in the same building.

INCORRECT: Customs differ one region of the country to another.
  CORRECT: Customs <u>differ from</u> one region of the country to another.
                  or
           Customs are <u>different from</u> one region of the country to another.

EXERCISES

Part A: Choose the correct answer.

Modern blimps like the famous Goodyear blimps _____ the first ones in that they are filled with helium instead of hydrogen.
   (A) differ from
   (B) different from
   (C) is different from
   (D) different

Part B: Choose the incorrect word or phrase and correct it.

Crocodiles <u>different from</u> alligators in that they have <u>pointed snouts</u> and long lower teeth that stick
    (A)   (B)   (C)

out when their mouths <u>are closed</u>.
                          (D)

93 Comparative Estimates—Multiple Numbers

Remember that the following are examples of multiple numbers:

half	four times
twice	five times
three times	ten times

	multiple	as	much many	as	
Fresh fruit costs	twice	as	much	as	canned fruit
We have	half	as	many	as	we need

Avoid using *so* instead of *as* after a multiple. Avoid using *more than* instead of *as much as* or *as many as*. Avoid using the multiple after *as much* and *as many*.

EXAMPLES

INCORRECT: This one is prettier, but it costs twice more than the other one.
 CORRECT: This one is prettier, but it costs <u>twice as much as</u> the other one.

INCORRECT: The rent at College Apartments is only half so much as you pay here.
 CORRECT: The rent at College Apartments is only <u>half as much as</u> you pay here.

INCORRECT: Bob found a job that paid as much twice as he made working at the library.
 CORRECT: Bob found a job that paid <u>twice as much as</u> he made working at the library.

INCORRECT: The price was very reasonable; I would gladly have paid three times more than he asked.
 CORRECT: The price was very reasonable; I would gladly have paid <u>three times as much as</u> he asked.

INCORRECT: We didn't buy the car because they wanted as much twice as it was worth.
  CORRECT: We didn't buy the car because they wanted <u>twice as much as</u> it was worth.

EXERCISES

Part A: Choose the correct answer.

After the purchase of the Louisiana Territory, the United States had _____ it had previously owned.
    (A) twice more land than
    (B) two times more land than
    (C) twice as much land as
    (D) two times much land than

Part B: Choose the incorrect word or phrase and correct it.

With American prices for sugar at three times <u>as much</u> the world price, manufacturers <u>are</u> beginning
                                        (A)   (B)

<u>to use</u> fructose blended with pure sugar, <u>or</u> sucrose.
 (C)   (D)

94   Comparative Estimates—*More Than* and *Less Than*

Remember that *more than* or *less than* is used before a specific number to express an estimate that may be a little more or a little less than the number.

	more than	number	
Steve has	more than	a thousand	coins in his collection

	less than	number	
Andy has	less than	a dozen	coins in his pocket

Avoid using *more* or *less* without *than* in estimates. Avoid using *as* instead of *than*.

EXAMPLES

INCORRECT: More one hundred people came to the meeting.
  CORRECT: <u>More than one hundred</u> people came to the meeting.

INCORRECT: We have lived in the United States for as less than seven years.
  CORRECT: We have lived in the United States for <u>less than seven</u> years.

INCORRECT: The main library has more as one million volumes.
  CORRECT: The main library has <u>more than one million</u> volumes.

INCORRECT: A new shopping center on the north side will have five hundred shops more than.
CORRECT: A new shopping center on the north side will have <u>more than five hundred</u> shops.

INCORRECT: There are most than fifty students in the lab, but only two computers.
CORRECT: There are <u>more than fifty</u> students in the lab, but only two computers.

EXERCISES

Part A: Choose the correct answer.

In the Great Smoky Mountains, one can see _____ 150 different kinds of trees.
(A) more than
(B) as much as
(C) up as
(D) as many to

Part B: Choose the incorrect word or phrase and correct it.

Pelé scored <u>more as</u> 1,280 goals <u>during his career,</u> <u>gaining</u> a reputation as <u>the best</u> soccer player of
       (A)   (B)   (C)   (D)
all time.

95 Comparative Estimates—*As Many As*

Remember that *as many as* is used before a specific number to express an estimate that does not exceed the number.

	as many as	number	
We should have	as many as	five hundred	applications

Avoid using *as many* instead of *as many as*. Avoid using *much* instead of *many* before a specific number.

Note: Comparative estimates with *as much as* are also used before a specific number that refers to weight, distance, or money. For example, *as much as* ten pounds, *as much as* two miles, or *as much as* twenty dollars.

EXAMPLES

INCORRECT: We expect as much as thirty people to come.
CORRECT: We expect <u>as many as</u> <u>thirty</u> people to come.

INCORRECT: There are as many fifteen thousand students attending summer school.
CORRECT: There are <u>as many as</u> <u>fifteen thousand</u> students attending summer school.

INCORRECT: The children can see as much as twenty-five baby animals in the nursery at the zoo.
CORRECT: The children can see <u>as many as</u> <u>twenty-five</u> baby animals in the nursery at the zoo.

INCORRECT: Many as ten planes have sat in line waiting to take off.
   CORRECT:.   <u>As many as</u> <u>ten</u> planes have sat in line waiting to take off.

INCORRECT: State University offers as much as two hundred major fields of study.
   CORRECT: State University offers <u>as many as</u> <u>two hundred</u> major fields of study.

EXERCISES

Part A: Choose the correct answer.

It has been estimated that _____ one hundred thousand men participated in the gold rush of 1898.
   (A) approximate
   (B) until
   (C) as many as
   (D) more

Part B: Choose the incorrect word or phrase and correct it.

It is generally accepted that the common cold <u>is caused</u> <u>by</u> as <u>much as</u> forty strains of viruses <u>that</u>
                                               (A)   (B)   (C)   (D)

may be present in the air at all times.

96   Degrees of Comparison—Comparative Adjectives

Remember that two- and three-syllable adjectives form the comparative by using *more* or *less* before the adjective form. One-syllable adjectives form the comparative by using *-er* after the form. Two-syllable adjectives which end in *y* form the comparative by changing the *y* to *i* and adding *-er*.

	more (less) adjective (two syllables) adjective *-er* (one syllable) adjective *-er* (two syllables ending in *-y*)	than	
An essay test is	more difficult	than	an objective test
An essay test is	harder	than	an objective test
An essay test is	easier	than	an objective test

Avoid using *as* or *that* instead of *than*. Avoid using both *more* and an *-er* form.

EXAMPLES

INCORRECT: This room is more spacious as the other one.
   CORRECT: This room is <u>more spacious than</u> the other one.

INCORRECT: The bill which we received was more higher than the estimate.
   CORRECT: The bill which we received was <u>higher than</u> the estimate.

INCORRECT: Eileen has been more happy lately than she was when she first came.
CORRECT: Eileen has been <u>happier</u> lately <u>than</u> she was when she first came.

INCORRECT: The books for my engineering course are expensive the books for my other courses.
CORRECT: The books for my engineering course are <u>more expensive than</u> the books for my other courses.

INCORRECT: The climate here is more milder than that of New England.
CORRECT: The climate here is <u>milder than</u> that of New England.

EXERCISES

Part A: Choose the correct answer.

The Disney amusement park in Japan is _____ Florida or California.
    (A) the largest than the ones in
    (B) larger than the ones in
    (C) larger the ones in
    (D) the largest of the ones

Part B: Choose the incorrect word or phrase and correct it.

The diesel engine <u>that</u> runs on oil <u>is efficient</u> than most other engines <u>because</u> it converts more of the
           (A)   (B) (C)   (D)
useful energy stored up in the fuel.

97   Degrees of Comparison—Superlative Adjectives

Remember that superlatives are used to compare more than two.

		most (least) adjective (two syllables) adjective -*est* (one syllable) adjective -*est* (two syllables ending in -*er*)
An essay test is	the	most difficult
An essay test is	the	hardest
An essay test is	the	trickiest

Avoid using a comparative -*er* form when three or more are compared.

EXAMPLES

INCORRECT: She is more prettier than all of the girls in our class.
CORRECT: She is <u>the prettiest</u> of all of the girls in our class.

INCORRECT: New York is the larger of all American cities.
CORRECT: New York is <u>the largest</u> of all American cities.

INCORRECT: Of all of the candidates, Alex is probably the less qualified.
CORRECT: Of all of the candidates, Alex is probably <u>the least</u> qualified.

INCORRECT: Although there are a number of interesting findings, a most significant results are in the abstract.

CORRECT: Although there are a number of interesting findings, <u>the</u> <u>most</u> <u>significant</u> results are in the abstract.

INCORRECT: In my opinion, the more beautiful place in Oregon is Mount Hood.

CORRECT: In my opinion, <u>the</u> <u>most</u> <u>beautiful</u> place in Oregon is Mount Hood.

EXERCISES

Part A: Choose the correct answer.

The blue whale is _____ known animal, reaching a length of more than one hundred feet.
  (A) the large
  (B) the larger
  (C) the largest
  (D) most largest

Part B: Choose the incorrect answer and correct it.

The <u>more</u> important theorem of all in plane geometry <u>is</u> <u>the</u> Pythagorean Theorem.
<u>(A)</u> <u>(B)</u>   <u>(C)(D)</u>

PROBLEM 98   Degrees of Comparison—Irregular Adjectives

Remember that some very common adjectives have irregular forms. Some of them are listed here for you.

Adjective	Comparative— to compare two	Superlative— to compare three or more
bad	worse	the worst
far	farther	the farthest
	further	the furthest
good	better	the best
little	less	the least
many	more	the most
much	more	the most

	irregular comparative	than	
This ice cream is	better	than	the other brands

	irregular superlative		
This ice cream is	the best		of all

Avoid using a regular form instead of an irregular form for these adjectives.

EXAMPLES

INCORRECT: The lab is more far from the bus stop than the library.
  CORRECT: The lab is <u>farther from</u> the bus stop than the library.
                    or
              The lab is <u>further from</u> the bus stop than the library.

INCORRECT: The badest accident in the history of the city occurred last night on the North Freeway.
  CORRECT: The <u>worst</u> accident in the history of the city occurred last night on the North Freeway.

INCORRECT: These photographs are very good, but that one is the better of all.
  CORRECT: These photographs are very good, but that one is <u>the best</u> of all.

INCORRECT: Please give me much sugar than you did last time.
  CORRECT: Please give me <u>more</u> sugar than you did last time.

INCORRECT: This composition is more good than your last one.
  CORRECT: This composition is <u>better</u> than your last one.

EXERCISES

Part A: Choose the correct answer.

_____ apples are grown in Washington State.
  (A) Best
  (B) The most good
  (C) The best
  (D) The better

Part B: Choose the incorrect word or phrase and correct it.

<u>Because</u> a felony is <u>more bad</u> than a misdemeanor, the punishment is <u>more severe</u>, and often in-
  (A)   (B)   (C)
cludes a jail sentence <u>as well as</u> a fine.
                          (D)

99   Degrees of Comparison—Comparative Adverbs

Remember that adverbs also have a comparative form to compare two verb actions and a superlative form to compare three or more verb actions.

	more adverb (two + syllables) less adverb (two + syllables) adverb -*er* (one syllable)		
		than	
We finished the test	more rapidly	than	Mark
We finished the test	less rapidly	than	Mark
We finished the test	faster	than	Mark

	the most adverb (two + syllables) the least adverb (two+ syllables) adverb *-est* (one syllable)	
We finished the test	the most rapidly	of all
We finished the test	the least rapidly	of all
We finished the test	the fastest	of all

Avoid using *-er* with adverbs of more than one syllable even when they end in *-ly*.

EXAMPLES

INCORRECT: Professor Tucker was pleased because our group approached the project more scientifi-
cally the others.

CORRECT: Professor Tucker was pleased because our group approached the project <u>more</u> <u>scientifi-</u>
<u>cally</u> <u>than</u> the others.

INCORRECT: This train always leaves late than the time on the schedule.

CORRECT: This train always leaves <u>later</u> <u>than</u> the time on the schedule.

INCORRECT: The students in Dr. Neal's class complained the most bitter about the grading system.

CORRECT: The students in Dr. Neal's class complained <u>the</u> <u>most</u> bitterly about the grading system.

INCORRECT: I wish we could see each other more frequenter.

CORRECT: I wish we could see each other <u>more</u> <u>frequently</u>.

INCORRECT: He drives more fast than she does.

CORRECT: He drives <u>faster</u> <u>than</u> she does.

EXERCISES

Part A: Choose the correct answer.

Many chemicals react _____ in acid solutions.
   (A) more quick
   (B) more quickly
   (C) quicklier
   (D) as quickly more

Part B: Choose the incorrect word or phrase and correct it.

Quality control studies show that employees work the most <u>efficient</u> when they are <u>involved in</u> the
                                                          (A)   (B)

total operation rather than <u>in</u> only one part of <u>it</u>.
                            (C)   (D)

100   Double Comparatives

Remember that when two comparatives are used together, the first comparative expresses cause and the second comparative expresses result. A comparative is *more* or *less* with an adjective, or an adjective with *-er*.

CAUSE				RESULT			
The	comparative	S	V,	the	comparative	S	V
The	more	you	review,	the	easier	the patterns	will be

Avoid using *as* instead of *the*. Avoid using the **incorrect** form *lesser* Avoid omitting *the*. Avoid omitting *-er* from the adjective.

EXAMPLES

INCORRECT: The more you study during the semester, the lesser you have to study the week before exams.

CORRECT: The more you study during the semester, the less you have to study the week before exams.

INCORRECT: The faster we finish, the soon we can leave.
CORRECT: The faster we finish, the sooner we can leave.

INCORRECT: The less one earns, the lesser one must pay in income taxes.
CORRECT: The less one earns, the less one must pay in income taxes.

INCORRECT: The louder he shouted, less he convinced anyone.
CORRECT: The louder he shouted, the less he convinced anyone.

INCORRECT: The more you practice speaking, the well you will do it.
CORRECT: The more you practice speaking, the better you will do it.

EXERCISES

Part A: Choose the correct answer.

It is generally true that the lower the stock market falls, _____ .
(A) higher the price of gold rises
(B) the price of gold rises high
(C) the higher the price of gold rises
(D) rises high the price of gold

Part B: Choose the incorrect word or phrase and correct it.

The higher the solar activity, the intense the auroras or polar light displays in the skies near
                              (A)   (B)   (C)
the earth's geomagnetic poles.
      (D)

101   Illogical Comparatives—General Similarity and Difference

Remember that comparisons must be made with logically comparable nouns. You can't compare *the climate* in the north with *the south*. You must compare *the climate* in the north with *the climate* in the south.

Remember that *that of* and *those of* are used instead of repeating a noun to express a logical comparative. An example with *different from* appears below.

noun (singular)		different	from	that	
Football in the U.S.	is	different	from	that	in other countries

noun (plural)		different	from	those	
The rules	are	different	from	those	of soccer

Avoid omitting *that* and *those*. Avoid using *than* instead of *from* with *different*.

EXAMPLES

INCORRECT: The food in my country is very different than that in the United States.
  CORRECT: The food in my country is very <u>different from</u> <u>that</u> in the United States.

INCORRECT: The classes at my university are very different from State University.
  CORRECT: The classes at my university are very <u>different from</u> <u>those</u> at State University.

INCORRECT: The English that is spoken in Canada is similar to the United States.
  CORRECT: The English that is spoken in Canada is <u>similar to</u> <u>that</u> of the United States.

INCORRECT: Drugstores here are not like at home.
  CORRECT: Drugstores here are not <u>like</u> <u>those</u> at home.

INCORRECT: The time in New York City differs three hours from Los Angeles.
  CORRECT: The time in New York City <u>differs</u> three hours <u>from</u> <u>that</u> of Los Angeles.

EXERCISES

Part A: Choose the correct answer.

One's fingerprints are _____ .
   (A) different from those of any other person
   (B) different from any other person
   (C) different any other person
   (D) differs from another person

Part B: Choose the incorrect word or phrase and correct it.

Perhaps the colonists were <u>looking for</u> a climate <u>like England</u>, when they decided <u>to settle</u> the North
                                        (A)   (B)   (C)
American continent <u>instead of</u> the South American continent.
                              (D)

102   Illogical Comparatives—Degrees

Remember that comparisons must be made with logically comparable nouns.

noun (singular)		more + adjective adjective -er	than	that	
The climate in the north	is	more severe	than	that	of the south
The climate in the north	is	colder	than	that	of the south

noun (plural)		more + adjective adjective -er	than	those	
The prices	are	more expensive	than	those	at a discount store
The prices	are	higher	than	those	at a discount store

Avoid omitting *that* and *those*.

EXAMPLES

INCORRECT: Her qualifications are better than any other candidate.
CORRECT: Her qualifications are <u>better</u> <u>than</u> <u>those</u> of any other candidate.

INCORRECT: Professor Baker's class is more interesting than Professor Williams.
CORRECT: Professor Baker's class is <u>more</u> <u>interesting</u> <u>than</u> <u>that</u> of Professor Williams.

INCORRECT: The audience is much larger than last year's concert.
CORRECT: The audience is much <u>larger</u> <u>than</u> <u>that</u> of last year's concert.

INCORRECT: The rooms in the front are much noisier than the back.
CORRECT: The rooms in the front are much <u>noisier</u> <u>than</u> <u>those</u> in the back.

INCORRECT: The interest on savings accounts at City Bank are higher than Bank Plus.
CORRECT: The interest on savings accounts at City Bank are <u>higher</u> <u>than</u> <u>that</u> of Bank Plus.

EXERCISES

Part A: Choose the correct answer.

The total production of bushels of corn in the United States is _____ all other cereal crops combined.
  (A) more as
  (B) more than that of
  (C) more of
  (D) more that

Part B: Choose the incorrect word or phrase and correct it.

Because there were so few women in the early Western states, the freedom and rights of Western
 (A)   (B)

women were more extensive than Eastern ladies.
                    (C)   (D)

CUMULATIVE REVIEW EXERCISE FOR COMPARATIVES

DIRECTIONS: Some of the sentences in this exercise are correct. Some are incorrect. First, find the correct sentences, and mark them with a check (√). Then find the incorrect sentences, and correct them. Check your answers using the key on page 449.

1. One object will not be the same weight than another object because the gravitational attraction differs from place to place on the earth's surface.

2. An identical twin is always the same sex as his or her twin because they develop from the same zygote.

3. As many l00 billion stars are in the Milky Way.

4. Compared with numbers fifty years ago, there are twice more students in college today.

5. The valuablest information we currently have on the ocean floors is that which was obtained by oceanographic satellites such as Seasat.

6. The oxygen concentration in the lungs is higher than the blood.

7. Since the earth is spherical, the larger the area, the worser the distortion on a flat map.

8. The eyes of an octopus are remarkably similar to those of a human being.

9. The terms used in one textbook may be different another text.

10. In 1980, residential utility bills were as high sixteen hundred dollars a month in New England.

11. When the ratio of gear teeth is five: one, the small gear rotates five times as fast as the large gear.

12. Although lacking in calcium and vitamin A, grains have most carbohydrates than any other food.

13. The more narrow the lens diameter, the more great the depth of field.

14. No fingerprint is exactly alike another.

15. There is disagreement among industrialists as to whether the products of this decade are inferior to the past.

Problems with Prepositions

Prepositions are words or phrases that clarify relationships. Prepositions are usually followed by nouns and pronouns. Sometimes the nouns are *-ing* form nouns.

Prepositions are also used in idioms.

103 Place—*Between* and *Among*

Remember that *between* and *among* have the same meaning, but *between* is used with two nouns and *among* is used with three or more nouns or a plural noun.

	between	noun 1		noun 2
The work is distributed	between	the secretary	and	the receptionist

	among	noun 1	noun 2		noun 3
The rent payments are divided	among	Don,	Bill,	and	Gene

Avoid using *between* with three or more nouns or a plural noun.

EXAMPLES

INCORRECT: The choice is between a vanilla, chocolate, and strawberry ice cream cone.
CORRECT: The choice is among a vanilla, chocolate, and strawberry ice cream cone.

INCORRECT: Rick and his wife can usually solve their problems among them.
CORRECT: Rick and his wife can usually solve their problems between them.

INCORRECT: Profits are divided between the stockholders of the corporation.
CORRECT: Profits are divided among the stockholders of the corporation.

INCORRECT: The votes were evenly divided among the Democratic candidate and the Republican candidate.
CORRECT: The votes were evenly divided between the Democratic candidate and the Republican candidate.

INCORRECT: The property was divided equally among his son and daughter.
CORRECT: The property was divided equally between his son and daughter.

EXERCISES

Part A: Choose the correct answer.

Although it is difficult _____ , a frog is more likely to be smooth and wet, and a toad rough and dry.
(A) distinguishing among a frog and a toad
(B) distinguish a frog and a toad
(C) between a frog and a toad distinguish
(D) to distinguish between a frog and a toad

Part B: Choose the incorrect word or phrase and correct it.

In a federal form of government <u>like</u> <u>that of the United States</u>, power <u>is divided</u> <u>between</u> the legisla-

          (A)   (B)   (C) (D)

tive, executive, and judicial branches.

104 Place—*In, On, At*

Remember that *in*, *on*, and *at* have similar meanings, but they are used with different kinds of places. In general, *in* is used before large places; *on* is used before middle-sized places; and *at* is used before numbers in addresses. Finally, *in* is used again before very small places.

in COUNTRY	*on* STREET	*at* NUMBER	*in* a corner
STATE	STREET CORNER		(of a room)
PROVINCE	COAST		a room
COUNTY	RIVER		a building
CITY	a ship		a park
	a train		a car
	a plane		a boat

	in	COUNTRY	in	STATE	in	CITY
We live	in	the United States	in	North Carolina	in	Jacksonville

on	COAST	on	RIVER	at	NUMBER
on	the East Coast	on	New River	at	2600 River Road

Avoid using *in* instead of *on* for streets and other middle-sized places.

EXAMPLES

INCORRECT: Cliff can live on Yellowstone National Park because he is a park ranger.
CORRECT: Cliff can live <u>in</u> <u>Yellowstone National Park</u> because he is a park ranger.

INCORRECT: Is Domino's Pizza in Tenth Street?
CORRECT: Is Domino's Pizza <u>on</u> <u>Tenth Street</u>?

INCORRECT: The apartments at the Hudson River are more expensive than the ones across the street.
CORRECT: The apartments on the Hudson River are more expensive than the ones across the street.

INCORRECT: We are going to stay overnight on Chicago.
CORRECT: We are going to stay overnight in Chicago.

INCORRECT: Let's take our vacation in the coast instead of in the mountains.
CORRECT: Let's take our vacation on the coast instead of in the mountains.

EXERCISES

Part A: Choose the correct answer.

_____ of the United States from southern New Hampshire in the north to Virginia in the south, a vast urban region has been defined as a megalopolis, that is, a cluster of cities.
 (A) On the northeastern seaboard
 (B) It is in the northeastern seaboard
 (C) That the northeastern seaboard
 (D) At the northeastern seaboard

Part B: Choose the incorrect word or phrase and correct it.

Many of the famous advertising offices are located in Madison Avenue.
 (A)   (B)   (C) (D)

105   Time—*In, On, At*

Remember that *in, on*, and *at* have similar meanings, but they are used with different times. In general, *in* is used before large units of time; *on* is used before middle-sized units of time; and *at* is used before numbers in clock time.

Idiomatic phrases such as *in the morning, in the afternoon, in the evening, at night, at noon*, must be learned individually like vocabulary.

in YEAR	*on* DAY	*at* TIME
MONTH	DATE	

	in	YEAR	in	MONTH	on	DAY	at	TIME
Lilly was born	in	1919	in	December	on	Sunday	at	7:00

Avoid using *in* before days and dates.

EXAMPLES

INCORRECT: I would rather take classes on the afternoon.
CORRECT: I would rather take classes in the afternoon.

INCORRECT: Gloria has a part-time job in the night.
CORRECT: Gloria has a part-time job at night.

INCORRECT: The rainy season begins on July.
 CORRECT: The rainy season begins <u>in</u> July.

INCORRECT: The graduation is in May 20.
 CORRECT: The graduation is <u>on</u> May 20.

INCORRECT: We came to the United States on 1987.
 CORRECT: We came to the United States <u>in</u> 1987.

EXERCISES

Part A: Choose the correct answer.

Most stores in large American cities close _____ five or six o'clock on weekdays, but the malls in the suburbs stay open much later.
   (A) at
   (B) in
   (C) on
   (D) until

Part B: Choose the incorrect word or phrase and correct it.

<u>Accountants</u> are always busiest <u>on April</u> because both federal <u>and</u> state taxes are due
     (A)   (B)   (C)
<u>on the fifteenth.</u>
     (D)

106   Addition—*Besides*

Remember that *besides* means *in addition to. Beside* means *near.*

besides	noun adjective	
Besides	our dog,	we have two cats and a canary
Besides	white,	we stock green and blue

	beside	noun
We sat	beside	the teacher

Avoid using *beside* instead of *besides* to mean *in addition.*

EXAMPLES

INCORRECT: Beside Marge, three couples are invited.
 CORRECT: <u>Besides</u> Marge, three couples are invited.

INCORRECT:	Beside Domino's, four other pizza places deliver.
CORRECT:	Besides Domino's, four other pizza places deliver.

INCORRECT:	To lead a well-balanced life, you need to have other interests beside studying.
CORRECT:	To lead a well balanced life, you need to have other interests besides studying.

INCORRECT:	Beside taxi service, there isn't any public transportation in town.
CORRECT:	Besides taxi service, there isn't any public transportation in town.

INCORRECT:	Janice has lots of friends beside her roommate.
CORRECT:	Janice has lots of friends besides her roommate.

EXERCISES

Part A: Choose the correct answer.

_____ a mayor, many city governments employ a city manager.
- (A) Beside
- (B) Besides
- (C) And
- (D) Also

Part B: Choose the incorrect word or phrase and correct it.

To receive a degree from an American university, one must take many courses beside those in one's
  (A)   (B) (C)   (D)
major field.

PROBLEM 107   Exception—*But* and *Except*

Remember that when it is used as a preposition, *but* means *except*.

	but except	noun	
All of the students All of the students	but except	the seniors the seniors	will receive their grades will receive their grades

Avoid using *exception, except to,* or *excepting* instead of *except*.

EXAMPLES

INCORRECT:	All of the group exception Barbara went to the lake.
CORRECT:	All of the group but Barbara went to the lake.
	or
	All of the group except Barbara went to the lake.

INCORRECT: You can put everything but for those silk blouses in the washer.
  CORRECT: You can put everything <u>but</u> those silk blouses in the washer.
or
You can put everything <u>except</u> those silk blouses in the washer.

INCORRECT: Everyone except to Larry wants sugar in the tea.
  CORRECT: Everyone <u>but</u> Larry wants sugar in the tea.
or
Everyone <u>except</u> Larry wants sugar in the tea.

INCORRECT: No one excepting Kathy knows very much about it.
  CORRECT: No one <u>but</u> Kathy knows very much about it.
or
No one <u>except</u> Kathy knows very much about it.

INCORRECT: The mail comes at ten o'clock every day not Saturday.
  CORRECT: The mail comes at ten o'clock every day <u>but</u> Saturday.
or
The mail comes at ten o'clock every day <u>except</u> Saturday.

EXERCISES

Part A: Choose the correct answer.

Everyone _____ albinos has a certain amount of pigment in the skin to add color.
(A) but
(B) that
(C) without
(D) not

Part B: Choose the incorrect word or phrase and correct it.

There are <u>no</u> pouched animals <u>in the United States</u> <u>but only</u> the opossum.
  (A) (B)   (C)   (D)

108   Replacement—*Instead of* and *Instead*

Remember that *instead of* and *instead* both mean *in place of*, but *instead of* is used before a noun, adjective, or adverb, and *instead* is used at the end of a sentence or a clause to refer to a noun, adjective, or adverb that has already been mentioned.

	noun adjective adverb	instead of	noun adjective adverb	
We went to	Colorado	instead of	abroad	on our vacation this year
You should be	firm	instead of	patient	in this case
Treat the dog	gently	instead of	roughly	

Avoid using *instead* without *of*.

	noun adjective adverb	instead
We went to You should be Treat the dog	Colorado firm gently	instead instead instead

Avoid using *instead* before a noun.

EXAMPLES

INCORRECT: Bob's father wanted him to be an engineer instead a geologist.
CORRECT: Bob's father wanted him to be an engineer <u>instead of</u> a geologist.
          or
          Bob's father wanted him to be an engineer <u>instead</u>.

INCORRECT: Could I have rice instead potatoes, please?
CORRECT: Could I have rice <u>instead of</u> potatoes, please?
          or
          Could I have rice <u>instead</u>, please?

INCORRECT: Paula's problem is that she likes to go to movies stead of to class.
CORRECT: Paula's problem is that she likes to go to movies <u>instead of</u> to class.
          or
          Paula's problem is that she likes to go to movies <u>instead</u>.

INCORRECT: We chose Terry instead from Gene as our representative.
CORRECT: We chose Terry <u>instead of</u> Gene as our representative.
          or
          We chose Terry <u>instead</u>.

INCORRECT: It is important to eat well at lunchtime in place buying snacks from vending machines.
CORRECT: It is important to eat well at lunchtime <u>instead of</u> buying snacks from vending machines.
          or
          It is important to eat well at lunchtime <u>instead</u>.

EXERCISES

Part A: Choose the correct answer.

John Dewey advocated teaching methods that provided teaching experiences for students to partici-
pate in _____ material to memorize.
   (A) instead of
   (B) not only
   (C) although
   (D) contrasting

Part B: Choose the incorrect word or phrase and correct it.

Sharks <u>differ from</u> <u>other fish</u> in that their skeletons <u>are made</u> of cartilage <u>instead</u> bone.
       (A)   (B)   (C)   (D)

109   Example—Such as

Remember that *such as* means for example.

	such as	noun (example)	
Some birds	such as	robins and cardinals	spend the winter in the North

Avoid using *such* or *as such* instead of *such as*.

EXAMPLES

INCORRECT: By using coupons, you can get a discount on a lot of things, such groceries, toiletries, and household items.

CORRECT: By using coupons, you can get a discount on a lot of things, <u>such as</u> groceries, toiletries, and household items.

INCORRECT: Taking care of pets as such dogs and cats can teach children lessons in responsibility.

CORRECT: Taking care of pets <u>such as</u> dogs and cats can teach children lessons in responsibility.

INCORRECT: Magazines such *Time, Newsweek,* and *U.S. News and World Report* provide the reader with a pictorial report of the week's events.

CORRECT: Magazines <u>such as</u> *Time, Newsweek,* and *U.S. News and World Report* provide the reader with a pictorial report of the week's events.

INCORRECT: Jobs at fast-food restaurants for such as McDonald's or Taco Bell are often filled by students.

CORRECT: Jobs at fast-food restaurants <u>such as</u> McDonald's or Taco Bell are often filled by students.

INCORRECT: A metal detector buzzes not only when firearms are located but also when smaller metal objects as keys and belt buckles are found.

CORRECT: A metal detector buzzes not only when firearms are located, but also when smaller metal objects <u>such as</u> keys and belt buckles are found.

EXERCISES

Part A: Choose the correct answer.

Some forms of mollusks are extremely useful as food, especially the bivalves _____ oysters, clams, and scallops.

(A) such

(B) such as

(C) as

(D) so

Part B: Choose the incorrect word or phrase and correct it.

Urban consumers <u>have formed</u> co-operatives to <u>provide</u> <u>themselves</u> with necessities <u>such</u> groceries,
(A)   (B)   (C)   (D)

household appliances, and gasoline at a lower cost.

PROBLEM 110 Condition and Unexpected Result—*Despite* and *in Spite of*

Remember that *despite* and *in spite of* have the same meaning. They introduce a contradiction in a sentence or clause of cause-and-result.

Despite	noun,	
Despite	his denial,	we knew that he was guilty

or

In spite of	noun,	
In spite of	his denial,	we knew that he was guilty

Avoid using *of* with *despite*. Avoid omitting *of* after *in spite*.

EXAMPLES

INCORRECT: Despite of the light rain, the baseball game was not canceled.
CORRECT: <u>Despite</u> the light rain, the baseball game was not canceled.
or
<u>In spite of</u> the light rain, the baseball game was not canceled.

INCORRECT: Dick and Sarah are still planning to get married despite of their disagreement.
CORRECT: Dick and Sarah are still planning to get married <u>despite</u> their disagreement.
or
Dick and Sarah are still planning to get married <u>in spite of</u> their disagreement.

INCORRECT: In spite the interruption, she was still able to finish her assignment before class.
CORRECT: <u>Despite</u> the interruption, she was still able to finish her assignment before class.
or
<u>In spite of</u> the interruption, she was still able to finish her assignment before class.

INCORRECT: Despite of their quarrel, they are very good friends.
CORRECT: <u>Despite</u> their quarrel, they are very good friends.
or
<u>In spite of</u> their quarrel, they are very good friends.

INCORRECT: In spite the delay, they arrived on time.
CORRECT: <u>Despite</u> the delay, they arrived on time.
or
<u>In spite of</u> the delay, they arrived on time.

EXERCISES

Part A: Choose the correct answer.

_____ under Chief Tecumseh, the Shawnees lost most of their lands to whites and were moved into territories.

(A) In spite of resistance
(B) In spite resistance
(C) Spite of resistance
(D) Spite resistance

Part B: Choose the incorrect word or phrase and correct it.

<u>Despite of</u> the fact that backgammon is easy to learn, it is as difficult <u>to play</u> as chess.
    (A)   (B)   (C)   (D)

111   Cause—*Because of* and *Because*

Remember that *because of* is a prepositional phrase. It introduces a noun or a noun phrase. *Because* is a conjunction. It introduces a clause with a subject and a verb.

	because	S	V
They decided to stay at home	because	the weather	was bad

or

	because of	noun
They decided to stay at home	because of	the weather

Avoid using *because of* before a subject and verb. Avoid using *because* before a noun which is not followed by a verb.

EXAMPLES

INCORRECT: Classes will be canceled tomorrow because a national holiday.
  CORRECT: Classes will be canceled tomorrow <u>because it is</u> a national holiday.
                or
          Classes will be canceled tomorrow <u>because of a national holiday</u>.

INCORRECT: She was absent because of her cold was worse.
  CORRECT: She was absent <u>because her cold was</u> worse.
                or
          She was absent <u>because of her cold</u>.

INCORRECT: John's family is very happy because his being awarded a scholarship.

CORRECT: John's family is very happy because <u>he has been awarded</u> a scholarship.

        or

  John's family is very happy because <u>of his being awarded</u> a scholarship.

INCORRECT: She didn't buy it because of the price was too high.

CORRECT: She didn't buy it because <u>the price was</u> too high.

        or

  She didn't buy it <u>because of the price.</u>

INCORRECT: It was difficult to see the road clearly because the rain.

CORRECT: It was difficult to see the road clearly because <u>it was raining.</u>

        or

  It was difficult to see the road clearly <u>because of the rain.</u>

EXERCISES

Part A: Choose the correct answer.

_____ in the cultivation of a forest, trees need more careful planning than any other crop does.

(A) Because the time and area involved

(B) For the time and area involving

(C) Because of the time and area involved

(D) As a cause of the time and area involved

Part B: Choose the incorrect word or phrase and correct it.

Many roads and railroads <u>were built</u> <u>in the 1880s</u> <u>because of</u> the industrial cities needed a network
                  (A)   (B)   (C)

<u>to link</u> them with sources of supply.
 (D)

112   Cause—*From*

Remember that *from* means caused by. It is usually used after adjectives.

	adjective	from	noun -*ing* noun	
The chairs are	wet	from	the rain	
The chairs are	wet	from	sitting	out in the rain

Avoid using *for* before the -*ing* noun.

EXAMPLES

INCORRECT: Be careful not to get sunburned from stay out on the beach too long.
  CORRECT: Be careful not to get sunburned <u>from</u> <u>staying</u> out on the beach too long.

INCORRECT: We felt sleepy all day for watching television so late last night.
  CORRECT: We felt sleepy all day <u>from</u> <u>watching</u> television so late last night.

INCORRECT: Joe is going to get sick to study too much.
  CORRECT: Joe is going to get sick <u>from</u> <u>studying</u> too much.

INCORRECT: If you go early, you will just get nervous to waiting.
  CORRECT: If you go early, you will just get nervous <u>from</u> <u>waiting</u>.

INCORRECT: The car is really hot from to sit in the sun all day.
  CORRECT: The car is really hot <u>from</u> <u>sitting</u> in the sun all day.

EXERCISES

Part A: Choose the correct answer.

It is now believed that some damage to tissues may result _____ them to frequent X-rays.
(A) the exposing
(B) from exposure
(C) from exposing
(D) expose

Part B: Choose the incorrect word or phrase and correct it.

<u>Many</u> of the problems associated with aging <u>such as</u> disorientation and irritability <u>may result</u>
  (A)   (B)   (C)
<u>from to eat</u> an unbalanced diet.
  (D)

113   Purpose—*For*

Remember that *for* is used before a noun to express purpose for a tool or instrument. Some nouns are *-ing* forms.

	noun (instrument)	for	noun *-ing* noun	
This is a good	book	for	research	
This is a good	book	for	researching	the topic

Avoid using *for to* before the *-ing* noun.

Note: The infinitive is the most common way to express purpose. The infinitive can be used in all situations. *For* with an *-ing* form is usually limited to situations in which there is an instrument named.

EXAMPLES

INCORRECT: I bought a trunk for to store my winter clothes.
  CORRECT: I bought a <u>trunk</u> <u>for</u> <u>storing</u> my winter clothes.
             or
             I bought a trunk <u>to store</u> my winter clothes.

INCORRECT: She has a CB radio in her car to emergencies.
  CORRECT: She has a <u>CB radio</u> in her car <u>for</u> <u>emergencies</u>.
             or
             She has a CB radio in her car <u>to help</u> in emergencies.

INCORRECT: Each room has its own thermostat for to control the temperature.
  CORRECT: Each room has its own <u>thermostat</u> <u>for</u> <u>controlling</u> the temperature.
             or
             Each room has its own thermostat <u>to control</u> the temperature.

INCORRECT: Sam needs another VCR for copy videotapes.
  CORRECT: Sam needs another <u>VCR</u> <u>for</u> <u>copying</u> videotapes.
             or
             Sam needs another VCR <u>to copy</u> videotapes.

INCORRECT: Why don't you use the microscope in the lab for to examine the specimen?
  CORRECT: Why don't you use the <u>microscope</u> in the lab <u>for</u> <u>examining</u> the specimen?
             or
             Why don't you use the microscope in the lab <u>to examine</u> the specimen?

EXERCISES

Part A: Choose the correct answer.

The most exact way known to science _____ the age of artifacts is based on the radioactivity of certain minerals.
  (A) for to determine
  (B) for determine
  (C) for determining
  (D) to determining

Part B: Choose the incorrect word or phrase and correct it.

George Ellery Hale and <u>his</u> colleagues designed the <u>two-hundred-inch</u> telescope <u>on Mount Palomar</u>
                            (A)   (B)   (C)

<u>study</u> the structure of the universe.
 (D)

114   Means—*By*

Remember that *by* expresses means. *By* answers the question *how*?
Remember that a phrase with *by* answers the question *how*?

Avoid using an infinitive instead of an *-ing* form.

	by	*-ing*	
This report was written	by	programming	a computer

EXAMPLES

INCORRECT: You can win by to practice.
 CORRECT: You can win <u>by practicing</u>.

INCORRECT: Make a reservation for calling our 800 number.
 CORRECT: Make a reservation <u>by calling</u> our 800 number.

INCORRECT: Beverly lost weight for hiking.
 CORRECT: Beverly lost weight <u>by hiking</u>.

INCORRECT: Gloria made a lot of friends to working in the cafeteria.
 CORRECT: Gloria made a lot of friends <u>by working</u> in the cafeteria.

INCORRECT: Choose the correct answer for marking the letter that corresponds to it on the answer
                    sheet.
 CORRECT: Choose the correct answer <u>by marking</u> the letter that corresponds to it on the answer
                    sheet.

EXERCISES

Part A: Choose the correct answer.

Ladybugs are brightly colored beetles that help farmers by _____.
(A) eat other insects
(B) to eat other insects
(C) eating other insects
(D) other insect's eating

Part B: Choose the incorrect word or phrase and correct it.

The government <u>raises</u> money <u>to operate</u> by tax cigarettes, liquor, gasoline, tires, and <u>telephone calls</u>.
          (A)   (B)   (C)   (D)

115   Time Limit—From, To

Remember that *from* introduces a time and *to* sets a limit.

	from	time	to	limit
The group was popular	from	the 1960s	to	the 1980s

Avoid using *for* instead of *from* and instead of *to*.

EXAMPLES

INCORRECT:	I need you to baby-sit from six o'clock and ten-thirty.
CORRECT:	I need you to baby-sit <u>from six o'clock to ten-thirty</u>.
INCORRECT:	The class is scheduled for January 15 to May 7.
CORRECT:	The class is scheduled <u>from January 15 to May 7</u>.
INCORRECT:	You could have a room from Monday and Friday, but we are booked over the weekend.
CORRECT:	You could have a room <u>from Monday to Friday</u>, but we are booked over the weekend.
INCORRECT:	She was a student here to 1990 to 1995.
CORRECT:	She was a student here <u>from 1990 to 1995</u>.
INCORRECT:	The ticket is valid from June and September.
CORRECT:	The ticket is valid <u>from June to September</u>.

EXERCISES

Part A: Choose the correct answer.

The Copper Age lasted_____, after which bronze was introduced.
(A) from about 5000 BC to about 3700 BC
(B) about from 5000 BC and about 3700 BC
(C) for about 5000 BC to 3700 BC about
(D) about 5000 BC to about 3700 BC

Part B: Choose the incorrect word or phrase and correct it.

Led by <u>Daniel Webster</u>, the Whig party was <u>one of</u> the two major <u>political powers</u> in the United
      (A)   (B)   (C)
States from 1834 <u>and 1852</u>.
                 (D)

CUMULATIVE REVIEW EXERCISE FOR PREPOSITIONS

DIRECTIONS: Some of the sentences in this exercise are correct. Some are incorrect. First, find the correct sentences, and mark them with a check (√). Then find the incorrect sentences, and correct them. Check your answers using the key on pages 449–450.

1. It is possible to find the weight of anything that floats for weighing the water that it displaces.

2. Metals such copper, silver, iron, and aluminum are good conductors of electricity.

3. The Mother Goose nursery rhymes have been traced back to a collection that appeared in England on 1760.

4. In making a distinction between butterflies and moths, it is best to examine the antennae.

5. None of the states but for Hawaii is an island.

6. Beside copper, which is the principal metal produced, gold, silver, lead, zinc, iron, and uranium are mined in Utah.

7. This year, beside figuring standard income tax, taxpayers might also have to compute alternative minimum tax.

8. Jet engines are used instead piston engines for almost all but the smallest aircraft.

9. Trained athletes have slower heart rates because of their hearts can pump more blood with every beat.

10. Tools as such axes, hammerstones, sickles, and awls were made by Paleolithic man using a method called pressure flaking.

11. Despite of some opposition, many city authorities still fluoridate water to prevent tooth decay.

12. The White House is on 1700 Pennsylvania Avenue.

13. Ice skating surfaces can be made of interlocking plastic squares instead of ice.

14. In supply side economics, a balanced budget results from to reduce government spending.

15. All of the Native Americans but the Sioux were defeated by the European settlers.

Problems with Conjunctions

Conjunctions are words or phrases that clarify relationships between clauses. "Conjoin" means "to join together."

PROBLEMS WITH CORRELATIVE CONJUNCTIONS

Correlative conjunctions are pairs that are used together. They often express inclusion or exclusion. Correlative conjunctions must be followed by the same grammatical structures; in other words, you must use parallel structures after correlative conjunctions.

116 Correlative Conjunctions—Inclusives *both . . . and*

Remember that *both . . . and* are correlative conjunctions. They are used together to include two parallel structures (two nouns, adjectives, verbs, adverbs).

	both	noun adjective	and	noun adjective	
	Both	Dr. Jones	and	Miss Smith	spoke
The lecture was	both	interesting	and	instructive	

Avoid using *as well as* instead of *and* with *both.* Avoid using *both . . . and* for more than two nouns or adjectives.

EXAMPLES

INCORRECT: She speaks both English as well as Spanish at home.
  CORRECT: She speaks both English and Spanish at home.

INCORRECT: Virginia opened and a savings account and a checking account.
  CORRECT: Virginia opened both a savings account and a checking account.

INCORRECT: The weather on Sunday will be both sunny, warmer also.
  CORRECT: The weather on Sunday will be both sunny and warmer.

INCORRECT: We can use the bike both to ride to school also go to the grocery store.
  CORRECT: We can use the bike both to ride to school and to go to the grocery store.

INCORRECT: The party will celebrate both our finishing the term as well your getting a new job.
  CORRECT: The party will celebrate both our finishing the term and your getting a new job.

EXERCISES

Part A: Choose the correct answer.

The belief in life after death is prevalent in both primitive societies _____ advanced cultures.
  (A) and
  (B) and in
  (C) and also
  (D) also

Part B: Choose the incorrect word or phrase and correct it.

Both viruses also genes are made from nucleoproteins, the essential chemicals with which living
      (A)   (B)   (C)
matter duplicates itself.
       (D)

117   Correlative Conjunctions—Inclusives *and . . . as well as*

Remember that *both . . . and . . . as well as* are correlative conjunctions. They must be used in sequence to include two or three parallel structures (nouns, adjectives, verbs, adverbs).

	noun adjective	as well as	noun adjective
He enjoys playing He is	basketball intelligent	as well as as well as	football athletic

	(both)	noun adjective	and	noun adjective	as well as	noun adjective
He enjoys playing He is	both both	soccer intelligent	and and	baseball artistic	as well as as well as	tennis athletic

Avoid using *as well* instead of *as well as*.

EXAMPLES

INCORRECT: Both Mary, Ellen, and Jean are going on the tour.
  CORRECT: Both Mary and Ellen as well as Jean are going on the tour.

INCORRECT: My fiancé is both attractive and intelligent as well considerate.
  CORRECT: My fiancé is both attractive and intelligent as well as considerate.

INCORRECT: There are snacks both in the refrigerator and in the oven as well on the table.
  CORRECT: There are snacks both in the refrigerator and in the oven as well as on the table.

INCORRECT: To reach your goal, you must plan and work as well dream.
  CORRECT: To reach your goal, you must plan and work as well as dream.

INCORRECT: We will keep in touch by both writing both calling and visiting each other.
  CORRECT: We will keep in touch by both writing and calling as well as visiting each other.

EXERCISES

Part A: Choose the correct answer.

The terrain in North Carolina includes both the Highlands and the Coastal Plain, _____ the Piedmont Plateau between them.
  (A) as well as
  (B) also
  (C) and too
  (D) and so

Part B: Choose the incorrect word or phrase and correct it.

Agronomists study crop disease, selective breeding, crop rotation, and climatic factors, as well soil
         (A)   (B)   (C)
content and erosion.
    (D)

118   Correlative Conjunctions—Inclusives *not only . . . but also*

Remember that *not only . . . but also* are correlative conjunctions. They are used together to include two parallel structures (two nouns, adjectives, verbs, adverbs).

	not only	noun adjective	but also	noun adjective
One should take	not only	cash	but also	traveler's checks
Checks are	not only	safer	but also	more convenient

Avoid using *only not* instead of *not only*. Avoid using *but* instead of *but also*.
Avoid using the incorrect pattern:

not only	noun adjective	but	noun adjective	also
not only	cash safer	but but	traveler's checks more convenient	also also

EXAMPLES

INCORRECT: The program provides only not theoretical classes but also practical training.
  CORRECT: The program provides <u>not only</u> theoretical classes but also practical training.

INCORRECT: The new models are not only less expensive but more efficient also.
  CORRECT: The new models are <u>not only</u> less expensive but also more efficient.

INCORRECT: The objective is not to identify the problem but also to solve it.
  CORRECT: The objective is <u>not only</u> to identify the problem but also to solve it.

INCORRECT: Not only her parents but her brothers and sisters also live in Wisconsin.
  CORRECT: <u>Not only</u> her parents but also her brothers and sisters live in Wisconsin.

INCORRECT: To complete his physical education credits, John took not only swimming also golf.
  CORRECT: To complete his physical education credits, John took <u>not only</u> swimming but also golf.

EXERCISES

Part A: Choose the correct answer.

Amniocentesis can be used not only to diagnose fetal disorders _____ the sex of the unborn child with 95 percent accuracy.
   (A) but determining
   (B) but also determining
   (C) but to determine
   (D) but also to determine

Part B: Choose the incorrect word or phrase and correct it.

The deadbolt is <u>the best lock</u> for entry doors <u>because</u> it is <u>not only</u> inexpensive but <u>installation is easy.</u>
　　　　　　　(A)　　　　　　　　　　　　　(B)　　　　(C)　　　　　　　　　　　(D)

119 Correlative Conjunctions—Exclusives *not. . . but*

Remember that *not. . . but* are correlative conjunctions. They are used together to exclude the structure that follows *not* (noun, adjective, verb, adverb) and include the structure that follows *but.*

	not	noun adjective	but	noun adjective
The largest university is	not	Minnesota	but	Ohio State
The school color is	not	blue	but	red

Avoid using *only* instead *of but.*

EXAMPLES

INCORRECT: According to the coroner, she died not of injuries sustained in the accident, only of a heart attack.

CORRECT: According to the coroner, she died <u>not</u> of injuries sustained in the accident <u>but</u> of a heart attack.

INCORRECT: The office that I was assigned was not large and cheerful but only small and dark.

CORRECT: The office that I was assigned was <u>not</u> large and cheerful <u>but</u> small and dark.

INCORRECT: To judge your friends, you should not listen to what they say only observe what they do.

CORRECT: To judge your friends, you should <u>not</u> listen to what they say <u>but</u> observe what they do.

INCORRECT: Jill could make herself understood if she spoke not louder but only more slowly.

CORRECT: Jill could make herself understood if she spoke <u>not</u> louder <u>but</u> more slowly.

INCORRECT: It is not the money only the principle that makes me angry.

CORRECT: It is <u>not</u> the money <u>but</u> the principle that makes me angry.

EXERCISES

Part A: Choose the correct answer.

It is usually _____ lava but gas that kills people during volcanic eruptions.
(A) not only
(B) not
(C) neither
(D) no

Part B: Choose the incorrect word or phrase and correct it.

<u>Before</u> the invention of the musical staff, people passed musical compositions on to <u>each other</u> not
  (A)   (B)

by writing them down <u>but also</u> by remembering <u>them</u>.
                     (C)   (D)

PROBLEMS WITH OTHER CONJUNCTIONS

PROBLEM 120

Affirmative Agreement—*So* and *Too*

Remember that *so, too,* and *also* have the same meaning, but *so* is used before auxiliary verbs and *too* and *also* are used after auxiliary verbs.

S	MODAL HAVE V Be	verb word participle -ing			and	so	MODAL HAVE DO BE	S
My wife	will	talk	to him		and	so	will	I
My wife	has	talked	about it,		and	so	have	I
My wife	talked				and	so	did	I
My wife	is	talking			and	so	am	I

S	MODAL HAVE V Be	verb word participle -ing			and	S	MODAL HAVE DO BE	also too
My wife	will	talk	to him		and	I	will	too
My wife	has	talked	about it,		and	I	have	too.
My wife	talked				and	I	did	too
My wife	is	talking			and	I	am	too

Avoid using *also* instead of *so.*

EXAMPLES

INCORRECT: We are going to the concert, and so do they.
CORRECT: We are <u>going</u> to the concert, and <u>so are they</u>.
                or
        We are <u>going</u> to the concert, and <u>they are too</u>.
                or
        We are <u>going</u> to the concert, and <u>they are also</u>.

INCORRECT:	He likes to travel, and so is she.
CORRECT:	He likes to travel, and so does she.
	or
	He likes to travel, and she does too.
	or
	He likes to travel, and she does also.

INCORRECT:	I am worried about it, and also is he.
CORRECT:	I am worried about it, and so is he.
	or
	I am worried about it, and he is too.
	or
	I am worried about it, and he is also.

INCORRECT:	Mary wants to go home, and so want we.
CORRECT:	Mary wants to go home, and so do we.
	or
	Mary wants to go home, and we do too.
	or
	Mary wants to go home, and we do also.

INCORRECT:	She took pictures, and I did so.
CORRECT:	She took pictures, and so did I.
	or
	She took pictures, and I did too.
	or
	She took pictures, and I did also.

EXERCISES

Part A: Choose the correct answer.

Technically, glass is a mineral and _____.
- (A) water so
- (B) water is so
- (C) so is water
- (D) so water is

Part B: Choose the incorrect word or phrase and correct it.

Some birds can travel at speeds approaching one hundred miles an hour, and a few land animals can so.
   (A)   (B)   (C)   (D)

121   Negative Agreement—*Neither* and *Either*

Remember that *neither* and *either* have the same meaning, but *neither* is used before auxiliary verbs and *either* is used after auxiliary verbs and *not*.

S	MODAL HAVE DO BE not	verb word participle verb word -ing form,	and	neither	MODAL HAVE DO BE	S
My roommate	won't	go,	and	neither	will	I
My roommate	hasn't	gone,	and	neither	have	I
My roommate	doesn't	go,	and	neither	do	I
My roommate	isn't	going,	and	neither	am	I

Avoid using *either* instead of *neither*. Avoid using the subject before *BE, DO, HAVE,* or the modal in a clause with *neither*.

S	MODAL HAVE DO BE not	verb word participle verb word -ing form	and	S	MODAL HAVE DO BE not	either
My roommate	won't	go,	and	I	won't	either
My roommate	hasn't	gone,	and	I	haven't	either
My roommate	doesn't	go,	and	I	don't	either
My roommate	isn't	going,	and	I	'm not	either

Avoid using *neither* instead of *either*.

EXAMPLES

INCORRECT: She hasn't finished the assignment yet, and neither I have.
CORRECT: She hasn't finished the assignment yet, and <u>neither have I</u>.
> *or*
She hasn't finished the assignment yet, and <u>I haven't either</u>.

INCORRECT: I didn't know the answer, and he didn't neither.
CORRECT: I didn't know the answer, and <u>neither did he</u>.
> *or*
I didn't know the answer, and <u>he didn't either</u>.

INCORRECT: If Jane won't go to the party, either will he.
CORRECT: If <u>Jane won't go</u> to the party, <u>neither will he</u>.
> *or*
If Jane won't go to the party, <u>he won't either</u>.

INCORRECT: She is not in agreement, and neither do I.
CORRECT: She is not in agreement, and <u>neither am I</u>.
> *or*
She is not in agreement, and <u>I'm not either</u>.

INCORRECT: He won't be here today, and either his sister will.
CORRECT: He won't be here today, and <u>neither will his sister</u>.
> *or*
He won't be here today, and <u>his sister won't either</u>.

EXERCISES

Part A: Choose the correct answer.

Although they are both grown in the United States and exported abroad, corn is not native to America and winter wheat _____.

(A) is neither
(B) isn't either
(C) isn't neither
(D) is either

Part B: Choose the incorrect word or phrase and correct it.

<u>According</u> to <u>many educators</u>, television should not <u>become</u> a replacement for good teachers, and
  (A)   (B)   (C)

neither <u>are</u> computers.
     (D)

122   Planned Result—*So That*

Remember that *so that* introduces a clause of planned result.

S	V		so that	S	V	
He	is studying	hard	so that	he	can pass	his exams

Avoid using *so* instead of *so that* as a purpose connector in written English.
Note: In spoken English, *so* instead of *so that* is often used. In written English, *so that* is preferred.

EXAMPLES

INCORRECT: He borrowed the money so he could finish his education.
CORRECT: He borrowed the money <u>so that</u> he could finish his education.

INCORRECT: Larry took a bus from New York to California so he could see the country.
CORRECT: Larry took a bus from New York to California <u>so that</u> he could see the country.

INCORRECT: Many men join fraternities so they will be assured of group support.
CORRECT: Many men join fraternities <u>so that</u> they will be assured of group support.

INCORRECT: Don't forget to register this week so you can vote in the election.
CORRECT: Don't forget to register this week <u>so that</u> you can vote in the election.

INCORRECT: Every student needs a social security number so he can get a university identification card made.
CORRECT: Every student needs a social security number <u>so that</u> he can get a university identification card made.

EXERCISES

Part A: Choose the correct answer.

A communications satellite orbits the earth at the same rate that the earth revolves _____ over a fixed point on the surface.
(A) so it can remain
(B) so that it can remain
(C) it can remain
(D) so can remain

Part B: Choose the incorrect word or phrase and correct it.

The function of pain is to warn the individual of danger so he can take action to avoid more serious
                        (A)   (B)(C)   (D)
damage.

123   Future Result—*When*

Remember that *when* introduces a clause of condition for future result.

RESULT		CONDITION		
S	V (present) V (will + verb word)	when	S	V (present)
The temperature The temperature	drops will drop	when when	the sun the sun	sets sets

Avoid using *will* instead of a present verb after *when*.

EXAMPLES

INCORRECT: I will call you when I will return from my country.
 CORRECT: I will call you <u>when I return</u> from my country.

INCORRECT: Marilyn plans to work in her family's store when she will get her M.B.A.
 CORRECT: Marilyn plans to work in her family's store <u>when she gets</u> her M.B.A.

INCORRECT: He will probably buy some more computer software when he will get paid.
 CORRECT: He will probably buy some more computer software <u>when he gets</u> paid.

INCORRECT: She will feel a lot better when she will stop smoking.
 CORRECT: She will feel a lot better <u>when she stops</u> smoking.

INCORRECT: When Gary will go to State University, he will be a teaching assistant.
 CORRECT: <u>When Gary goes</u> to State University, he will be a teaching assistant.

EXERCISES

Part A: Choose the correct answer.

Bacterial spores germinate and sprout _____ favorable conditions of temperature and food supply.
- (A) when encountering of
- (B) when they encounter
- (C) when they will encounter
- (D) when the encounter of

Part B: Choose the incorrect word or phrase and correct it.

In <u>most states</u> insurance agents <u>must pass</u> an examination <u>to be licensed</u> when they <u>will complete</u>
       (A)   (B)   (C)   (D)
their training.

124   Indirect Questions

Remember that question words can be used as conjunctions. Question words introduce a clause of indirect question.

Question words include the following:

who	*why*
what	*how*
what time	*how long*
when	*how many*
where	*how much*

S	V	question word	S	V
I	don't remember	what	her name	is

V	S		question word	S	V
Do	you	remember	what	her name	is?

Avoid using *do, does,* or *did* after the question word. Avoid using the verb before the subject after the question word.

EXAMPLES

INCORRECT: I didn't understood what did he say.
CORRECT: I didn't understand <u>what</u> <u>he said</u>.

INCORRECT: Do you know how much do they cost?
CORRECT: Do you know <u>how much</u> <u>they cost</u>?

INCORRECT: I wonder when is her birthday.
CORRECT: I wonder <u>when</u> her birthday <u>is</u>.

INCORRECT: Could you please tell me where is the post office?
CORRECT: Could you please tell me <u>where</u> the post office <u>is</u>?

INCORRECT: Can they tell you what time does the movie start?
CORRECT: Can they tell you <u>what time</u> the movie <u>starts</u>?

EXERCISES

Part A: Choose the correct answer.

Recently, there have been several outbreaks of disease like legionnaire's syndrome, and doctors don't know _____.
(A) what is the cause
(B) the cause is what
(C) is what the cause
(D) what the cause is

Part B: Choose the incorrect word or phrase and correct it.

In Ground Control Approach, <u>the air traffic controller</u> <u>informs</u> the pilot how far <u>is the plane</u> from
                      (A)   (B)   (C)
<u>the touchdown point</u>.
  (D)

PROBLEM 125   Question Words with *-ever*

Remember that *-ever* means *any*. *Whoever* and *whomever* mean anyone; *whatever* means anything; *wherever* means anywhere; *whenever* means any time; *however* means any way.
The *-ever* words may be used as conjunctions to introduce clauses.

S	V		-ever	S	V
I	agree	with	whatever	you	decide

Avoid using *any* instead of *-ever*. Avoid using *-ever* before instead of after the question word.

EXAMPLES

INCORRECT: We can leave ever when Donna is ready.
CORRECT: We can leave <u>whenever</u> <u>Donna</u> <u>is</u> ready.

INCORRECT: Order any what you like.
CORRECT: Order <u>whatever</u> <u>you</u> <u>like</u>.

INCORRECT: The representative will vote for whom the membership supports.
CORRECT: The representative will vote for <u>whomever</u> <u>the</u> <u>membership</u> <u>supports</u>.

INCORRECT: Feel free to present your projects ever how you wish.
  CORRECT: Feel free to present your projects <u>however</u> <u>you</u> <u>wish</u>.

INCORRECT: I can meet with you ever you have the time.
  CORRECT: I can meet with you <u>whenever</u> <u>you</u> <u>have</u> the time.

EXERCISES

Part A: Choose the correct answer.

Blue-green algae are found _____ there is ample moisture.
(A) wherever
(B) ever where
(C) ever
(D) there ever

Part B: Choose the incorrect word or phrase and correct it.

<u>Ever</u> the Senate <u>passes</u> a bill, a messenger takes it to the House of Representatives, delivers it to the
  (A)   (B)
Speaker of the House, and <u>bows</u> <u>deeply</u> from the waist.
                          (C)   (D)

CUMULATIVE REVIEW EXERCISE FOR CONJUNCTIONS

DIRECTIONS: Some of the sentences in this exercise are correct. Some are incorrect. First, find the correct sentences, and mark them with a (√). Then find the incorrect sentences, and correct them. Check your answers using the key on pages 450–451.

1. Foreign students who are making a decision about which school to attend may not know exactly where the choices are located.

2. In the future, classes taught by television will be equipped with boom microphones in the classrooms so students can stop the action, ask their questions, and receive immediate answers.

3. The Colosseum received its name not for its size but for a colossally large statue of Nero near it.

4. A wind instrument is really just a pipe arranged so air can be blown into it at one end.

5. It is very difficult to compute how much does an item cost in dollars when one is accustomed to calculating in another monetary system.

6. Adolescence, or the transitional period between childhood and adulthood, is not only a biological concept but a social concept.

7. Light is diffused when it will strike a rough surface.

8. The koala bear is not a bear at all, but a marsupial.

9. Ferns will grow wherever the soil is moist and the air is humid.

10. Although most rocks contain several minerals, limestone contains only one and marble is too.

11. Learners use both visual and auditory as well that analytical means to understand a new language.

12. In a recent study, many high school students did not know where were important geographical entities on the map of the United States.

13. It is not only lava but poisonous gases also that cause destruction and death during the eruption of a volcano.

14. Until recently West Point did not admit women and neither Annapolis.

15. The Federal Trade Commission may intervene whenever unfair business practices, particularly monopolies, are suspected.

Problems with Adverbs and Adverb-Related Structures

Adverbs and adverb phrases add information to sentences. They add information about *manner*, that is, how something is done; *frequency* or how often; *time* and *date* or when; and *duration* of time or how long.

126   Adverbs of Manner

Remember that adverbs of manner describe the manner in which something is done. They answer the question, *how?* Adverbs of manner usually end in *-ly*.

S	V	adverb (manner)	
The class	listened	attentively	to the lecture

Avoid using an adjective instead of an adverb of manner. Avoid using an adverb of manner between the two words of an infinitive.

EXAMPLES

INCORRECT: After only six months in the United States, Jack understood everyone perfect.
 CORRECT: After only six months in the United States, Jack understood everyone <u>perfectly</u>.

INCORRECT: Please do exact as your doctor says.
 CORRECT: Please do <u>exactly</u> as your doctor says.

INCORRECT: From the top of the Empire State Building, tourists are able to clearly see New York.

CORRECT: From the top of the Empire State Building, tourists are able to see New York <u>clearly</u>.

INCORRECT: Broad speaking, curriculum includes all experiences which the student may have within the environment of the school.

CORRECT: <u>Broadly</u> speaking, curriculum includes all experiences which the student may have within the environment of the school.

INCORRECT: Passengers travel comfortable and safely in the new jumbo jets.

CORRECT: Passengers travel <u>comfortably</u> and safely in the new jumbo jets.

EXERCISES

Part A: Choose the correct answer.

A symbol of the ancient competition, the Olympic flame burns _____throughout the games.
(A) in a continuous way
(B) continuous
(C) continuously
(D) continual

Part B: Choose the incorrect word or phrase and correct it.

Although the "Lake Poets" Wordsworth, Coleridge, and Southey were friends, <u>they</u> did not really
                                                                              (A)

form a group since Southey's style differed <u>wide</u> <u>from</u> that of <u>the other two</u>.
                                              (B)   (C)   (D)

127 Adverbs of Manner—*Fast, Late,* and *Hard*

Remember that although most adverbs of manner end in -ly, *fast, late,* and *hard* do not have *-ly* endings.

S	V		fast
This medication	relieves	headaches	fast

S	V		late	
My roommate	returned	home	late	last night

S	V	hard
The team	played	hard

Avoid using the **incorrect** forms ~~fastly~~ and ~~lately~~ and ~~hardly~~.

Note: *Lately* and *hardly* are not adverb forms of *late* and *hard*. *Lately* means recently. *Hardly* means almost not at all.

EXAMPLES

INCORRECT: Helen types fastly and efficiently.
  CORRECT: Helen types <u>fast</u> and efficiently.

INCORRECT: The plane is scheduled to arrive lately because of bad weather.
  CORRECT: The plane is scheduled to arrive <u>late</u> because of bad weather.

INCORRECT: Although he tried as hardly as he could, he did not win the race.
  CORRECT: Although he tried as <u>hard</u> as he could, he did not win the race.

INCORRECT: When students register lately for classes, they must pay an additional fee.
  CORRECT: When students register <u>late</u> for classes, they must pay an additional fee.

INCORRECT: First class mail travels as fastly as airmail now.
  CORRECT: First class mail travels as <u>fast</u> as airmail now.

EXERCISES

Part A: Choose the correct answer.

When a woman becomes pregnant _____ in life, she encounters additional risks in delivering a healthy baby.
  (A) lately
  (B) lateness
  (C) latest
  (D) late

Part B: Choose the incorrect word or phrase and correct it.

Overseas telephone service has been <u>expanding</u> <u>fastly</u> since its inauguration <u>in 1927</u> when a radio
                                      (A)   (B)   (C)
circuit <u>was established</u> between New York and London.
           (D)

128

Sometime and *Sometimes*

Remember that *sometime* means at some time in the indefinite future. *Sometimes* means occasionally.

Sometime is usually used after a verb. *Sometimes* is usually used at the beginning or end of a sentence or a clause.

Sometime answers the question, *when? Sometimes* answers the question, *how often?*

S	V		no specific date in the future sometime
My family	will call	me long distance	sometime

occasionally sometimes	S	V	
Sometimes	my family	calls	me long distance

Avoid using *sometimes* instead of *sometime* to express an indefinite time in the future.

EXAMPLES

INCORRECT:	Let's have lunch sometimes.
CORRECT:	Let's have lunch <u>sometime</u>. (no specific date in the future)
INCORRECT:	It is cool now, but sometime it gets very warm here.
CORRECT:	It is cool now, but <u>sometimes</u> it gets very warm here. (occasionally)
INCORRECT:	Janet would like to travel sometimes, but right now she has to finish her degree.
CORRECT:	Janet would like to travel <u>sometime</u>, but right now she has to finish her degree. (no specific date in the future)
INCORRECT:	Why don't you call me sometimes?
CORRECT:	Why don't you call me <u>sometime</u>? (no specific date in the future)
INCORRECT:	Sometime car manufacturers must recall certain models because of defects in design.
CORRECT:	<u>Sometimes</u> car manufacturers must recall certain models because of defects in design. (occasionally)

EXERCISES

Part A: Choose the correct answer.

_____ on clear days one can see the snowcap of Mount Rainier from Seattle.
(A) Sometime
(B) Some
(C) Sometimes
(D) Somestime

Part B: Choose the incorrect word or phrase and correct it.

<u>Sometime</u> <u>several nations</u> <u>become</u> partners in a larger political state, <u>as for example,</u> the four nations
  (A)   (B)   (C)   (D)
joined in the United Kingdom of Great Britain and Northern Ireland.

129 Negative Emphasis

Remember that negatives include phrases like *not one, not once, not until, never, never again, only rarely,* and *very seldom.* Negatives answer the question, *how often?* They are used at the beginning of a statement to express emphasis. Auxiliaries must agree with verbs and subjects.

negative	auxiliary	S	V	
Never	have	I	seen	so much snow

Avoid using a subject before the auxiliary in this pattern.

EXAMPLES

INCORRECT: Never again they will stay in that hotel.
CORRECT: Never again will they stay in that hotel.

INCORRECT: Only rarely an accident has occurred.
CORRECT: Only rarely has an accident occurred.

INCORRECT: Very seldom a movie can hold my attention like this one.
CORRECT: Very seldom can a movie hold my attention like this one.

INCORRECT: Not one paper she has finished on time.
CORRECT: Not one paper has she finished on time.

INCORRECT: Not once Steve and Jan have invited us to their house.
CORRECT: Not once have Steve and Jan invited us to their house.

EXERCISES

Part A: Choose the correct answer.

Not until the Triassic Period _____ .
    (A) the first primitive mammals did develop
    (B) did the first primitive mammals develop
    (C) did develop the first primitive mammals
    (D) the first primitive mammals develop

Part B: Chose the incorrect word or phrase and correct it.

Only rarely wins the same major league baseball team the World Series two years in a row.
 (A)   (B)   (C)   (D)

130   Introductory Adverbial Modifiers—*Once*

Remember that *once* means at one time in the past. *Once* answers the question, *when? Once* is often used as an introductory adverbial modifier. It modifies the main subject that follows the clause.

once	noun	,	S	V	
Once	a salesman	,	Pete	has been promoted	to district manager

Avoid using *that* before *once*.

EXAMPLES

INCORRECT: That once a student at State University, he is now an engineer for an American company.
  CORRECT: Once a student at State University, he is now an engineer for an American company.

INCORRECT: Once that a clerk in a grocery store, Helen is now a policewoman.
  CORRECT: Once a clerk in a grocery store, Helen is now a policewoman.

INCORRECT: That once a citizen of Ireland, he is now applying for permanent residency in Canada.
  CORRECT: Once a citizen of Ireland, he is now applying for permanent residency in Canada.

INCORRECT: It was once Republicans, we usually vote for Democratic candidates now.
  CORRECT: Once Republicans, we usually vote for Democratic candidates now.

INCORRECT: That once an avid soccer fan, he is now becoming more interested in American football.
  CORRECT: Once an avid soccer fan, he is now becoming more interested in American football.

EXERCISES

Part A: Choose the correct answer.

_____ a novelty in American retailing, fixed prices are now universal in sales.
  (A) It was once
  (B) Once it was
  (C) That once
  (D) Once

Part B: Choose the incorrect word or phrase and correct it.

That once a talented child actress, Shirley Temple Black has established herself as a career diplomat,
  (A)   (B)
serving both as a representative in the United Nations and as an ambassador abroad.
  (C)   (D)

PROBLEM 131 Introductory Adverbial Modifiers—*While*

Remember that *while* means at the same time. *While* answers the question *when?* It is often used as an introductory adverbial modifier. It modifies the main subject that follows the clause.

When can also mean at the same time, but *when* must be used before a subject and a verb in the same clause.

while	noun	,	S	V	
While	a salesman	,	Pete	traveled	a lot

while when	S	V		,	S	V	
While	he	was	a salesman	,	Pete	traveled	a lot
When	he	was	a salesman	,	Pete	traveled	a lot

Avoid using *when* instead of *while* without a subject and verb in the same clause.

EXAMPLES

INCORRECT: When in Washington, D.C., they saw the Capitol Building where Congress meets.

CORRECT: While (tourists) in Washington, D.C., they saw the Capitol Building where Congress meets.

or

While they were (tourists) in Washington, D.C., they saw the Capitol Building where Congress meets.

or

When they were (tourists) in Washington, D.C., they saw the Capitol Building where Congress meets.

INCORRECT: I was very homesick when a student abroad.

CORRECT: I was very homesick while a student abroad.

or

I was very homesick while I was a student abroad

or

I was very homesick when I was a student abroad.

INCORRECT: When still a teaching assistant, he was doing important research.

CORRECT: While still a teaching assistant, he was doing important research.

or

While he was still a teaching assistant, he was doing important research.

or

When he was still a teaching assistant, he was doing important research.

INCORRECT: According to the newspapers he accepted bribes when a high official of the government.
CORRECT: According to the newspaper, he accepted bribes <u>while</u> <u>a high official</u> of the government.

or

According to the newspaper, he accepted bribes <u>while</u> <u>he</u> <u>was</u> a high official of the government.

or

According to the newspaper, he accepted bribes <u>when</u> <u>he</u> <u>was</u> a high official of the government.

INCORRECT: While she on vacation, she bought gifts for her family.
CORRECT: <u>While</u> <u>(a visitor)</u> on vacation, she bought gifts for her family.

or

<u>While</u> she <u>was</u> (a visitor) on vacation, she bought gifts for her family.

or

<u>When</u> she <u>was</u> (a visitor) on vacation, she bought gifts for her family.

EXERCISES

Part A: Choose the correct answer.

_____ a bridge builder, Gustav Eiffel designed the Eiffel Tower for the Paris Exposition of 1889.

(A) While
(B) When
(C) It was when
(D) It while was

Part B: Choose the incorrect word or phrase and correct it.

<u>When</u> a child, Barbara Mandrell <u>played</u> the guitar, banjo, and saxophone in her family's band, but
  (A)   (B)

<u>in 1981</u> she <u>was named</u> Entertainer of the Year for her singing.
   (C)   (D)

132 *No Longer*

Remember that *no longer* means not any more. *No longer* is often used between the auxiliary verb and the main verb.

No longer answers the question, *when?*

S	V (auxiliary)	no longer	V (main)	
I	can	no longer	see	without my glasses

Avoid using *not* and *none* instead of *no*.

EXAMPLES

INCORRECT: We can not longer tolerate living with Terry.
CORRECT: We can <u>no longer</u> tolerate living with Terry.

INCORRECT: Brad none longer works here.
CORRECT: Brad <u>no longer</u> works here.

INCORRECT: Since she talked with her advisor, she is not longer interested in majoring in political science.
CORRECT: Since she talked with her advisor, she is <u>no longer</u> interested in majoring in political science.

INCORRECT: The person you are trying to reach is no long at this telephone number.
CORRECT: The person you are trying to reach is <u>no longer</u> at this telephone number.

INCORRECT: Although they used to write each other every day, they are not longer exchanging letters.
CORRECT: Although they used to write each other every day, they are <u>no longer</u> exchanging letters.

EXERCISES

Part A: Choose the correct answer.

According to communications theory, after the message leaves the sender, he _____ controls it.
(A) not longer
(B) none longer
(C) longer doesn't
(D) no longer

Part B: Choose the incorrect word or phrase and correct it.

Ghost towns <u>like</u> Rhyolite, Nevada are communities that are <u>not longer</u> inhabited <u>because</u> changes
       (A)   (B)   (C)

in economic conditions have caused the people <u>to move</u> elsewhere.
                                             (D)

133 Duration—*For* and *Since*

Remember that *for* is used before a quantity of time. *For* expresses duration. *For* answers the question, *how long? Since* is used before a specific time. *Since* expresses duration too, but *since* answers the question, *beginning when?*

Remember that a quantity of time may be several days—a month, two years, etc. A specific time may be Wednesday, July, 1960, etc. You will notice that the structure *HAVE* and *a* participle is often used with adverbs of duration.

S	HAVE	participle		for	quantity of time
She	has	been	in the U.S.	for	six months

S	HAVE	participle		since	specific time
She	has	been	in the U.S.	since	June

Avoid using *for* before specific times. Avoid using *before* after HAVE and a participle.

EXAMPLES

INCORRECT: Mary has been on a diet since three weeks.
  CORRECT: Mary has been on a diet <u>for three weeks.</u>

INCORRECT: She has been living here before April.
  CORRECT: She has been living here <u>since April.</u>

INCORRECT: We haven't seen him since almost a year.
  CORRECT: We haven't seen him <u>for almost a year.</u>

INCORRECT: We have known each other before 1974.
  CORRECT: We have known each other <u>since 1974.</u>

INCORRECT: He has studied English since five years.
  CORRECT: He has studied English <u>for five years.</u>

EXERCISES

Part A: Choose the correct answer.

Penguins, the most highly specialized of all aquatic birds, may live _____ twenty years.
(A) before
(B) since
(C) for
(D) from

Part B: Choose the incorrect word or phrase and correct it.

Because national statistics on crime have only been kept for 1930, it is not possible <u>to make</u> judg-
                                                    (A)   (B)   (C)

ments about crime <u>during the early years</u> of the nation.
                         (D)

134 Dates

Remember that there is an expected pattern for dates of the month. Dates answer the question, *when?*

	the	ordinal number	of	month
Valentine's Day is on	the	fourteenth	of	February

	Ø	month	ordinal number
Valentine's Day is on		February	fourteenth

Avoid using a cardinal number instead of an ordinal number.

EXAMPLES

INCORRECT: I have an appointment on the five of June at three o'clock.
CORRECT: I have an appointment on the fifth of June at three o'clock.
>   *or*
>   I have an appointment on June fifth at three o'clock.

INCORRECT: School starts on sixteen September this year.
CORRECT: School starts on the sixteenth of September this year.
>   *or*
>   School starts on September sixteenth this year.

INCORRECT: Her birthday is second December.
CORRECT: Her birthday is the second of December.
>   *or*
>   Her birthday is December second.

INCORRECT: Please change my reservation to the ten of November.
CORRECT: Please change my reservation to the tenth of November.
>   *or*
>   Please change my reservation to November tenth.

INCORRECT: Independence Day in the United States is the four of July.
CORRECT: Independence Day in the United States is the fourth of July.
>   *or*
>   Independence Day in the United States is July fourth.

EXERCISES

Part A: Choose the correct answer.

Memorial Day, a holiday set aside to remember those who have died, is usually celebrated on

_____ .

    (A) thirtieth May
    (B) the thirtieth May
    (C) May thirty
    (D) the thirtieth of May

Part B: Choose the incorrect word or phrase and correct it.

On the fourth July in 1884, the Statue of Liberty was presented formally by the people of France to
      (A)   (B)   (C)   (D)
the people of the United States.

135 Pseudocomparatives

Remember that although *as high as* and *as soon as* appear to be comparatives, they are adverbial idioms. *As high as* introduces a limit of height or cost. It answers the question, *how high* or *how much* (money)? *As soon as* introduces a limit of time. It answers the question, *when?*

	as high as	
The price of a haircut runs	as high as	fifty dollars

S	will	verb word		as soon as when	S	V (present)
He	will	go	home	as soon as	he	graduates

Avoid using *to* instead of *as*. Avoid using *will* and a verb word instead of a present verb after *as soon as*.

EXAMPLES

INCORRECT: I plan to move as soon as I will find another apartment.
CORRECT: I plan to move <u>as soon as</u> <u>I find</u> another apartment.

INCORRECT: Since taxi fare from the airport may run as high to twenty dollars, I suggest that you take a limousine.
CORRECT: Since taxi fare from the airport may run <u>as high as</u> <u>twenty dollars</u>, I suggest that you take a limousine.

INCORRECT: She will call you back as soon as she will finish dinner.
CORRECT: She will call you back <u>as soon as</u> <u>she finishes</u> dinner.

INCORRECT: The cost of one day in an average hospital can run as high to $2,000.
CORRECT: The cost of one day in an average hospital can run <u>as high as</u> $2,000.

INCORRECT: Your application will be considered as soon as your file will be complete.
CORRECT: Your application will be considered <u>as soon as</u> <u>your file is</u> complete.

EXERCISES

Part A: Choose the correct answer.

In xerox printing, the ink becomes fused to the paper as soon as _____.
    (A) the paper heated
    (B) the paper is heated
    (C) heats the paper
    (D) heating the paper

Part B: Choose the incorrect word or phrase and correct it.

Alcoholic beverages vary <u>widely</u> in content, ranging <u>from</u> only 2 or 3 percent for some light beers to
              (A)   (B)

<u>as high to</u> 60 percent <u>for</u> some vodkas and brandies.
   (C)   (D)

136   Generalization—*As a Whole* and *Wholly*

Remember that *as a whole* means generally. *Wholly* means completely. *As a whole* is often used at the beginning of a sentence or a clause. *Wholly* is often used after the auxiliary or main verb.

generally as a whole	S	V	
As a whole	the news	is	correct

S	V	completely wholly	
The news	is	wholly	correct

Avoid using *wholly* instead of *as a whole* at the beginning of a sentence or clause to mean generally. Avoid using *as whole* instead of *as a whole*.

EXAMPLES

INCORRECT:	Wholly, we are in agreement.
CORRECT:	<u>As a whole</u>, we are in agreement. (generally)
INCORRECT:	The house and all of its contents was as a whole consumed by the fire.
CORRECT:	The house and all of its contents was <u>wholly</u> consumed by the fire. (completely)
INCORRECT:	The teams are not rated equally, but, wholly, they are evenly matched.
CORRECT:	The teams are not rated equally, but, <u>as a whole</u>, they are evenly matched. (generally)
INCORRECT:	Wholly, Dan's operation proved to be successful.
CORRECT:	<u>As a whole</u>, Dan's operation proved to be successful. (generally)
INCORRECT:	As whole, people try to be helpful to tourists.
CORRECT:	<u>As a whole</u>, people try to be helpful to tourists. (generally)

EXERCISES

Part A: Choose the correct answer.

_____ the Gulf Stream is warmer than the ocean water surrounding it.
- (A) Wholly
- (B) Whole
- (C) As a whole
- (D) A whole as

Part B: Choose the incorrect word or phrase and correct it.

Although <u>there are</u> exceptions, <u>as whole</u>, the male of the bird species is <u>more</u> <u>brilliantly</u> colored.
      (A)   (B)   (C)   (D)

CUMULATIVE REVIEW EXERCISE FOR ADVERBS AND ADVERB-RELATED STRUCTURES

<u>DIRECTIONS</u>: Some of the sentences in this exercise are correct. Some are incorrect. First, find the correct sentences and mark them with a (√). Then find the incorrect sentences, and correct them. Check your answers using the key on page 451.

1. Not once Lincoln has been painted smiling.

2. The first Skylab crew was launched on twenty-fifth May, 1973.

3. Wholly, artificial insemination has contributed to the quality of maintaining dairy herds.

4. Thor Heyerdahl worked diligent to prove his theory of cultural diffusion.

5. The Navajos have lived in Arizona for almost one thousand years.

6. That once a serious problem, measles can now be prevented by a vaccine.

7. Because the British fleet arrived lately off the Yorktown Peninsula, the French were able to control the seas, thereby aiding the United States during the Revolution.

8. When the chemicals inside a cell not longer produce ions, the cell stops functioning.

9. The common goldfish may live as long twenty-five years.

10. When a mechanic working at odd jobs, Elisha Otis invented the elevator.

11. Sometimes students fail to score well on examinations because they are too nervous to concentrate.

12. Alligators are no longer on the endangered species list.

13. The standard for atomic weight has been provided by the carbon isotope C12 since 1961.

14. That it was once a busy mining settlement, Virginia City is now a small town with a population of one thousand people.

15. Not until the late Middle Ages glass did become a major construction material.

Problems with Sentences and Clauses

137   Sentences and Clauses

Remember that a main clause, also called an independent clause, can function as a separate sentence. A subordinate clause, also called a dependent clause, must be attached to a main clause. A dependent clause is often marked with the clause marker *that*.

SENTENCE		
Main Clause (Sentence)	Clause Marker - - - - - - - - - - Dependent Clause	
We were glad	that	the box came

Avoid using the clause marker with dependent clauses as sentences. Avoid using the clause marker *that* with a sentence that has no dependent clause following it.

EXAMPLES

INCORRECT: Utensils and condiments that are found on the table by the door.
CORRECT: Utensils and condiments are found on the table by the door.

INCORRECT: During final exam week, that the library when opening all night.
CORRECT: During final exam week, the library is open all night.

INCORRECT: The weather that is very rainy this time of year.
CORRECT: The weather is very rainy this time of year.

INCORRECT: All of the dorms that are located on East Campus.
CORRECT: All of the dorms are located on East Campus.

INCORRECT: During our vacation, that we suspended the newspaper delivery.
CORRECT: During our vacation, we suspended the newspaper delivery.

EXERCISES

Part A: Choose the correct answer.

Of all the cities in Texas,_____.
   (A) that San Antonio is probably the most picturesque
   (B) San Antonio is probably the most picturesque
   (C) probably San Antonio the most picturesque
   (D) the most picturesque probably that San Antonio

Part B: Choose the incorrect word or phrase and correct it.

Thunder that is audible from distances as far away as ten miles.
   (A)   (B)   (C)   (D)

138 Clause Marker Subjects

Remember that some dependent clauses may come in the middle of a main clause. In many of these dependent clauses, the clause marker is the subject of the dependent clause. For example, the clause marker *which*.

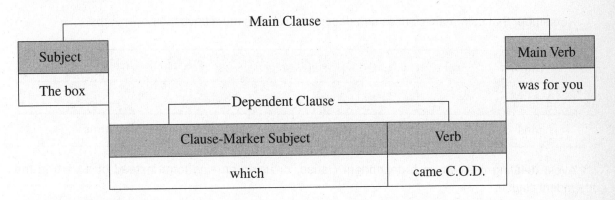

Avoid using a clause marker subject without a verb or a verb without a clause marker subject in dependent clauses of this type.

EXAMPLES

INCORRECT: The concert, is scheduled for Friday, has been canceled.
CORRECT: The concert, <u>which is scheduled</u> for Friday, has been canceled.

INCORRECT: Asking questions, which essential in learning a language, can be difficult for beginners.
CORRECT: Asking questions, <u>which is</u> essential in learning a language, can be difficult for beginners.

INCORRECT: My suitcases, which they are now at the city airport, have been located.
CORRECT: My suitcases, <u>which are</u> now at the city airport, have been located.

INCORRECT: The telephone number, which number I wrote down, is for the hotel.
CORRECT: The telephone number, <u>which is written down</u>, is for the hotel.

INCORRECT: The flowers, which were just delivering, are from Steve.
CORRECT: The flowers, which <u>were</u> just <u>delivered</u>, are from Steve.

EXERCISES

Part A: Choose the correct answer.

The Good Earth, _____, is a novel set in China.
   (A) which by Pearl Buck
   (B) which was written by Pearl Buck
   (C) was written by Pearl Buck
   (D) Pearl Buck being the one who wrote it

Part B: Choose the incorrect word or phrase and correct it.

Quasars, which *are* relatively small objects, emit an enormous amount of energy.
  (A)   (B)   (C)   (D)

Verbs in Dependent Clauses

Remember that both main clauses and dependent clauses must have their own verbs.

Main Clause	Clause Marker - - - - - - - - - Dependent Clause		
S V	that	S	V
It is good	that	the box arrived on time	

Avoid deleting the verb in a dependent clause, or using an *-ing* form instead of a verb in the dependent clause.

EXAMPLES

INCORRECT: It is a shame that you missing the movie.
  CORRECT: It is a shame <u>that</u> <u>you</u> <u>missed</u> the movie.

INCORRECT: She knows that mistakes in grammar occasionally.
  CORRECT: She knows <u>that</u> <u>she</u> <u>makes</u> mistakes in grammar occasionally.

INCORRECT: He said that going was he wanted.
  CORRECT: He said <u>that</u> <u>he</u> <u>wanted</u> to go.

INCORRECT: I noticed that Mary's absence today.
  CORRECT: I noticed <u>that</u> <u>Mary</u> <u>was</u> absent today.

INCORRECT: The experiment proved that less water for the plants.
  CORRECT: The experiment proved <u>that</u> <u>the plants</u> <u>needed</u> less water.

EXERCISES

Part A: Choose the correct answer.

Most beekeepers have observed_____at the approach of a thunderstorm.
  (A) enraging the bees
  (B) that bees become enraged
  (C) that bees enraging
  (D) become enraged the bees

Part B: Choose the incorrect word or phrase and correct it.

Most modern observatories contain telescopes that scientists using as cameras to take photographs
(A)   (B)   (C)   (D)
of remote galaxies.

140   Adjective Clauses

Remember that in some dependent clauses, called adjective clauses, the clause marker refers to and modifies the object of the main clause.

Main Clause			Clause Marker - - - Dependent Clause		
S	V		O	that	S V
These boxes	are	the ones	that	we	ordered

Avoid adjective clauses without a subject or without a verb.

EXAMPLES

INCORRECT: This is the way that coming the last time.
  CORRECT: This is <u>the way</u> <u>that</u> <u>we came</u> the last time.

INCORRECT: These are the ones that bought.
  CORRECT: These are <u>the ones</u> <u>that</u> <u>I bought</u>.

INCORRECT: This book is the one that our class.
  CORRECT: This book is <u>the one</u> <u>that</u> <u>our class</u> <u>used</u>.

INCORRECT: These are the assignments that our teacher giving us.
  CORRECT: These are <u>the assignments</u> <u>that</u> <u>our teacher</u> <u>gave</u> us.

INCORRECT: There are some things that don't understand about living in the United States.
  CORRECT: There are <u>some things</u> <u>that</u> <u>I</u> don't <u>understand</u> about living in the United States.

EXERCISES

Part A: Choose the correct answer.

Culture influences the way_____.
  (A) viewing the world
  (B) that we view the world
  (C) the world view
  (D) is the view of the world

Part B: Choose the incorrect word or phrase and correct it.

Of all the reference materials, <u>the encyclopedia</u> is the one that <u>most</u> people <u>using</u>.
                                          (A)   (B)   (C)   (D)

CUMULATIVE REVIEW EXERCISE FOR
SENTENCES AND CLAUSES

<u>DIRECTIONS</u>: Some of the sentences in this exercise are correct. Some are incorrect. First, find the correct sentences and mark them with a check (√). Then find the incorrect sentences, and correct them. Check your answers using the key on page 452.

1. Since 1927, that the Academy Awards have been given for outstanding contributions to the film industry.

2. The Guggenheim Museum is cast in concrete with a smooth finish and curving walls that offer a unique backdrop for the art exhibited there.

3. Solar panels that convert sunlight into electricity are still not being exploited fully.

4. During a total eclipse of the Sun that the Earth moving into the shadow of the Moon.

5. Founded by John Smith, that Jamestown became the first successful English colony in America.

6. A chameleon is a tree lizard that can change colors in order to conceal itself in the vegetation.

7. Many of the names of cities in California that are adapted from the Spanish language because of the influence of early missionaries and settlers from Spain.

8. The oceans, which cover two-thirds of the Earth's surface, are the object of study for oceanographers.

9. Sports heroes in the United States earn salaries that they are extraordinarily high in comparison with those of most other occupations.

10. The atoms of elements that joining together to form compounds or molecules.

11. Rafts made from the trunks of trees may have been the earliest vehicles.

12. The idea of a set which is the most fundamental concept in mathematics.

13. Water that has had the minerals removed is called "soft" water.

14. Feelings of superiority based on pride in cultural achievements and characteristics that calling ethnocentrism.

15. Skeletal muscles are voluntary muscles which are controlled directly by the nervous system.

STYLE

Style is a general term that includes elements larger than a single grammatical pattern or structure. In most grammar books, *style* means *sentence structure*— that is, how the parts of a sentence relate to each other.

Some of the most important elements of style are summarized in this review section.

Problems with Point of View

Point of view means maintaining the correct sequence of verb tenses and time phrases in a sentence.

Point of View—Verbs

In all patterns, maintain a point of view, either present or past.
Avoid changing from present to past tense, or from past to present tense in the same sentence.

EXAMPLES

INCORRECT: He was among the few who want to continue working on the project.
CORRECT: He <u>is</u> among the few who <u>want</u> to continue working on the project.
> *or*

He <u>was</u> among the few who <u>wanted</u> to continue working on the project.

INCORRECT: It is an accepted custom for a man to open the door when he accompanied a woman.
CORRECT: It <u>is</u> an accepted custom for a man to open the door when he <u>accompanies</u> a woman.
> *or*

It <u>was</u> an accepted custom for a man to open the door when he <u>accompanied</u> a woman.

INCORRECT: She closed the door and hurries away to class.
CORRECT: She <u>closes</u> the door and <u>hurries</u> away to class.
> *or*

She <u>closed</u> the door and <u>hurried</u> away to class.

INCORRECT: We receive several applications a day and with them had been copies of transcripts and degrees.
CORRECT: We <u>receive</u> several applications a day and with them <u>are</u> copies of transcripts and degrees.
> *or*

We <u>received</u> several applications a day and with them <u>were</u> copies of transcripts and degrees.

INCORRECT: Mr. Davis tried to finish his research, but he found only part of the information that he needs.

CORRECT: Mr. Davis <u>tries</u> to finish his research, but he <u>finds</u> only part of the information that he <u>needs</u>.

or

Mr. Davis <u>tried</u> to finish his research, but he <u>found</u> only part of the information that he <u>needed</u>.

EXERCISES

Part A: Choose the correct answer.

The first transistor was basically a small chip made of germanium onto one surface of which two pointed wire contacts _____ side by side.

(A) are made
(B) made
(C) were made
(D) making

Part B: Choose the incorrect word or phrase and correct it.

<u>Because</u> early balloons were at the mercy of <u>shifting</u> winds, they <u>are</u> not considered a practical
(A)   (B)   (C)

means of transportation <u>until the 1850s</u>.
(D)

2 Point of View—Reported Speech

Some verbs are used to report past events.
Remember that the following verbs are used as the first past verb in the pattern below:

asked	*knew*	*said*
believed	*remembered*	*thought*
forgot	*reported*	*told*

S	V (past)	that	S	V (past)	
He	said	that	he	was	sorry

Avoid using a present verb after *that* in the pattern.

Note: When the reported sentence deals with a general truth, then a present verb may be used after *that* in the pattern. For example, *in the early 1500s, some sailors believed that the world* is *round*. If current knowledge supersedes a formerly accepted truth, then the past verb is retained. For example, *in the early 1500s, many sailors believed that the world* was *flat*.

EXAMPLES

INCORRECT: I thought that he is coming today.
CORRECT: I <u>thought</u> that he <u>was</u> coming today.

INCORRECT: A research scientist at State University reported that he finds a blood test to diagnose cancer.

CORRECT: A research scientist at State University <u>reported</u> that he <u>found</u> a blood test to diagnose cancer.

INCORRECT: When she told us that everything is ready, we went into the dining room and seated ourselves.

CORRECT: When she <u>told</u> us that everything <u>was</u> ready, we <u>went</u> into the dining room and <u>seated</u> ourselves.

INCORRECT: They asked him if he will help us.

CORRECT: They <u>asked</u> him if he <u>would</u> help us.

INCORRECT: Professor Baker told his class that there 10,000 species of ferns.

CORRECT: Professor Baker <u>told</u> his class that there <u>are</u> 10,000 species of ferns.
        (A general truth by current scientific standards.)

EXERCISES

Part A: Choose the correct answer.

Ancient people believed that _____ with a sun and a moon rotating around it.
(A) the earth was the center of the universe
(B) the earth is the center of the universe
(C) the center of the universe is earth
(D) the universe has earth at the center

Part B: Choose the incorrect word or phrase and correct it.

William Faulkner, a famous novelist from Mississippi, said that it <u>is</u> not possible <u>to understand</u>
                                              (A)   (B)

<u>the South</u> unless <u>you</u> were born there.
  (C)   (D)

3   Point of View—Verbs and Adverbs

In all patterns, avoid using past adverbs with verbs in the present tense.

EXAMPLES

INCORRECT: Between one thing and another, Charles does not finish typing his paper last night.
CORRECT: Between one thing and another, Charles <u>did</u> not finish typing his paper <u>last night</u>.

INCORRECT: In 1990, according to statistics from the Bureau of Census, the population of the United States is 250,000,000.
CORRECT: In <u>1990</u>, according to statistics from the Bureau of Census, the population of the United States <u>was</u> 250,000,000.

INCORRECT: We do not receive mail yesterday because it was a holiday.
CORRECT: We <u>did</u> not receive mail <u>yesterday</u> because it <u>was</u> a holiday.

INCORRECT: Mary does not finish her homework in time to go with us to the football game yesterday afternoon.

CORRECT: Mary <u>did</u> not finish her homework in time to go with us to the football game <u>yesterday afternoon</u>.

INCORRECT: Although there are only two hundred foreign students studying at State University in 1970, there are more than five hundred now.

CORRECT: Although there <u>were</u> only two hundred foreign students studying at State University <u>in 1970</u>, there are more than five hundred now.

EXERCISES

Part A: Choose the correct answer.

Iron_____ for weapons and tools in the Bronze Age following the Stone Age.
  (A) is generally used
  (B) generally used
  (C) was generally used
  (D) used generally

Part B: Choose the incorrect word or phrase and correct it.

<u>The Nineteenth Amendment</u> to the Constitution <u>gives</u> women the right <u>to vote</u> in <u>the elections</u> of
                    (A)   (B)   (C)   (D)
1920.

PROBLEM 4

Point of View—Activities of the Dead

In all patterns, avoid using present verbs to refer to activities of the dead.

EXAMPLES

INCORRECT: Just before he died, my friend who writes poetry published his first book.
CORRECT: Just before he died, my friend who <u>wrote</u> poetry published his first book.

INCORRECT: Professor Ayers was so punctual that until the day he died, he always arrives in class just as the bell rings.

CORRECT: Professor Ayers was so punctual that <u>until the day he died,</u> he always <u>arrived</u> in class just as the bell <u>rang</u>.

INCORRECT: Before he died, the man who lives across the street used to help me with my English.
CORRECT: <u>Before he died,</u> the man who <u>lived</u> across the street used to help me with my English.

INCORRECT: A short time before he died, the old man has written a will, leaving his entire estate to his brother.

CORRECT: <u>A short time before he died,</u> the old man <u>had written</u> a will, leaving his entire estate to his brother.

INCORRECT: Until the day she died, the lady who lives next door visited me every evening.
CORRECT: <u>Until the day she died,</u> the lady who <u>lived</u> next door visited me every evening.

EXERCISES

Part A: Choose the correct answer.

From 1926 until her death, Margaret Mead_____ New York's American Museum of Natural History.
- (A) was associated with
- (B) associates with
- (C) is associated with
- (D) associated

Part B: Choose the incorrect word or phrase and correct it.

Before dinosaurs <u>became</u> extinct, plant life <u>is</u> <u>very</u> <u>different</u> on Earth.
                  (A)   (B) (C)   (D)

CUMULATIVE REVIEW EXERCISE FOR POINT OF VIEW

DIRECTIONS: Some of the sentences in this exercise are correct. Some are incorrect. First, find the correct sentences, and mark them with a check (√). Then find the incorrect sentences and correct them. Check your answers using the key on pages 452–453.

1. Until she died at the age of forty, Marilyn Monroe is the most glamorous star in Hollywood.

2. American colleges do not have very many foreign students learning English full time before 1970.

3. Ted Kennedy told the American people that he could not run for president for personal reasons.

4. George Washington Carver was one of the first educators who try to establish schools of higher education for blacks.

5. Before the 1920s, no women will have voted in national elections in the United States.

6. Styles that have been popular in the 1940s have recently reappeared in high-fashion boutiques.

7. Since his murder, John Lennon has become a legend among those who had been his fans.

8. When Lyndon Johnson became president in 1963, he had already served in politics for thirty-two years.

9. Early TV programs like the "Arthur Godfrey Show" are beginning as radio programs.

10. Dr. Howard Evans of Colorado State University reported that insects solve the food shortage if we could adjust to eating them.

11. The year that James Smithson died, he was leaving a half million dollars to the United States government to found the Smithsonian Institute.

12. Mary Decker said that she ran every day to train for the Olympics.

13. A liquid crystal is among the few unstable molecular arrangements that are on the borderline between solids and liquids and whose molecules were easily changed from one to the other.

14. The chestnut tree used to be an important species in the Eastern forests of the United States until a blight kills a large number of trees.

15. The Cincinnati Reds win the championship several years ago.

Problems with Agreement

Agreement means selecting subjects that agree in person and number with verbs, and selecting pronouns that agree in person and number with reference nouns and other pronouns.

Agreement—Modified Subject and Verb

In all patterns, there must be agreement of subject and verb.
Avoid using a verb that agrees with the modifier of a subject instead of with the subject itself.

EXAMPLES

INCORRECT: His knowledge of languages and international relations aid him in his work.
CORRECT: His <u>knowledge</u> of languages and international relations <u>aids</u> him in his work.

INCORRECT: The facilities at the new research library, including an excellent microfilm file, is a among the best in the country.
CORRECT: The <u>facilities</u> at the new research library, including an excellent microfilm file, <u>are</u> among the best in the country.

INCORRECT: All trade between the two countries were suspended pending negotiation of a new agreement.
CORRECT: All <u>trade</u> between the two countries <u>was</u> suspended pending negotiation of a new agreement.

INCORRECT: The production of different kinds of artificial materials are essential to the conservation of our natural resources.
CORRECT: The <u>production</u> of different kinds of artificial materials <u>is</u> essential to the conservation of our natural resources.

INCORRECT: Since the shipment of supplies for our experiments were delayed, we will have to reschedule our work.
CORRECT: Since the <u>shipment</u> of supplies for our experiments <u>was</u> delayed, we will have to reschedule our work.

EXERCISES

Part A: Choose the correct answer.

Groups of tissues, each with its own function, _____ in the human body.
   (A) it makes up the organs
   (B) make up the organs
   (C) they make up the organs
   (D) makes up the organs

Part B: Choose the incorrect word or phrase and correct it.

The Zoning Improvement Plan, better known as zip codes, enable postal clerks to speed the routing
                           (A)   (B)   (C)
of an ever-increasing volume of mail.
   (D)

6   Agreement—Subject with Accompaniment and Verb

Remember that there must be agreement of subject and verb. In all patterns, avoid using a verb that agrees with a phrase of accompaniment instead of with the subject itself.

EXAMPLES

INCORRECT: The guest of honor, along with his wife and two sons, were seated at the first table.
  CORRECT: The guest of honor, along with his wife and two sons, was seated at the first table.

INCORRECT: The ambassador, with his family and staff, invite you to a reception at the embassy on Tuesday afternoon at five o'clock.
  CORRECT: The ambassador, with his family and staff, invites you to a reception at the embassy on Tuesday afternoon at five o'clock.

INCORRECT: Mary, accompanied by her brother on the piano, were very well received at the talent show.
  CORRECT: Mary, accompanied by her brother on the piano, was very well received at the talent show.

INCORRECT: Senator Davis, with his assistant and his press secretary, are scheduled to arrive in New York today.
  CORRECT: Senator Davis, with his assistant and his press secretary, is scheduled to arrive in New York today.

INCORRECT: Folk singer Neil Young, accompanied by the musical group Stray Gators, are appearing in concert at the Student Center on Saturday night.
  CORRECT: Folk singer Neil Young, accompanied by the musical group Stray Gators, is appearing in concert at the Student Center on Saturday night.

EXERCISES

Part A: Choose the correct answer.

Thor Heyerdahl, accompanied by the crew of the *Kon Tiki*, _____ in order to prove
his theories of cultural diffusion.
   (A) have sailed specifically charted courses
   (B) sailing specifically charted courses
   (C) has sailed specifically charted courses
   (D) they sail specifically charted courses

Part B: Choose the incorrect word or phrase and correct it.

The high protein content of various strains of alfalfa plants, along with the <u>characteristically</u> long
                                                                                (A)
root system that <u>enables</u> them to survive long droughts, <u>make</u> them <u>particularly</u> valuable in arid
                  (B)   (C)   (D)
countries.

7   Agreement—Subject with Appositive and Verb

Remember that there must be agreement of subject and verb. An appositive is a word or phrase
that follows a noun and defines it. An appositive usually has a comma before it and a comma after it.
   In all patterns, avoid using a verb that agrees with words in the appositive after a subject instead of
with the subject itself.

EXAMPLES

INCORRECT: The books, an English dictionary and a chemistry text, was on the shelf yesterday.
  CORRECT: <u>The books,</u> an English dictionary and a chemistry text, <u>were</u> on the shelf yesterday.

INCORRECT: Three swimmers from our team, Paul, Ed, and Jim, is in competition for medals.
  CORRECT: <u>Three swimmers</u> from our team, Paul, Ed, and Jim, <u>are</u> in competition for medals.

INCORRECT: Several pets, two dogs and a cat, needs to be taken care of while we are gone.
  CORRECT: <u>Several pets,</u> two dogs and a cat, <u>need</u> to be taken care of while we are gone.

INCORRECT: State University, the largest of the state-supported schools, have more than 50,000 stu-
             dents on main campus.
  CORRECT: <u>State University,</u> the largest of the state-supported schools, <u>has</u> more than 50,000 stu-
             dents on main campus.

INCORRECT: This recipe, an old family secret, are an especially important part of our holiday celebra-
             tions.
  CORRECT: <u>This recipe,</u> an old family secret, <u>is</u> an especially important part of our holiday celebra-
             tions.

EXERCISES

Part A: Choose the correct answer.

Cupid, one of the ancient Roman gods, _____.
(A) were a little winged child
(B) representing as a little winged child
(C) was represented as a little winged child
(D) a little winged child

Part B: Choose the incorrect word or phrase and correct it.

Columbus, Ohio, the capital of the state, are not only the largest city in Ohio but also a typical met-
                                          (A)   (B)   (C)
ropolitan area, often used in market research.
                  (D)

8   Agreement—Verb-Subject Order

There and *here* introduce verb-subject order. The verb agrees with the subject following it.

there	V	S
There	are	the results of the election

here	V	S
Here	is	the result of the election

Avoid using a verb that does not agree with the subject.

EXAMPLES

INCORRECT:	There was ten people in line already when we arrived.
CORRECT:	There were ten people in line already when we arrived.

INCORRECT:	There have been very little rain this summer.
CORRECT:	There has been very little rain this summer.

INCORRECT:	Here are their house.
CORRECT:	Here is their house.

INCORRECT:	There has been several objections to the new policy.
CORRECT:	There have been several objections to the new policy.

INCORRECT:	I think that there were a problem.
CORRECT:	I think that there was a problem.

EXERCISES

Part A: Choose the correct answer.

In a suspension bridge_____ that carry one or more flexible cables firmly attached at each end.
 (A) there is two towers on it
 (B) there are two towers
 (C) two towers there are
 (D) towers there are two

Part B: Choose the incorrect word or phrase and correct it.

There is about 600 schools in the United States that use the Montessori method to encourage indi-
   (A)   (B)   (C)   (D)
vidual initiative.

Agreement—Indefinite Subject and Verb

Remember that the following subjects require a singular verb:

anyone	either	neither	what
anything	everyone	no one	whatever
each	everything	nothing	whoever

The following subjects require either a singular or a plural verb depending on a qualifying phrase or other context from the sentence:

all
any
some
the rest

Avoid using plural verbs with singular subjects, and singular verbs with plural subjects.

EXAMPLES

INCORRECT: Everyone who majors in architecture and fine arts study History of Art 450.
 CORRECT: Everyone who majors in architecture and fine arts studies History of Art 450.

INCORRECT: Either of these buses go past the university.
 CORRECT: Either of these buses goes past the university.

INCORRECT: Anyone who wish to participate in the state lottery may do so by purchasing a ticket at a store that displays the official lottery seal.
 CORRECT: Anyone who wishes to participate in the state lottery may do so by purchasing a ticket at a store that displays the official lottery seal.

INCORRECT: Neither Canada nor Mexico require that citizens of the United States have passports.
 CORRECT: Neither Canada nor Mexico requires that citizens of the United States have passports.

INCORRECT: The first two problems are very difficult, but the rest is easy.
 CORRECT: The first two problems are very difficult, but the rest (of the problems) are easy.

EXERCISES

Part A: Choose the correct answer.

Each of the radioisotopes produced artificially _____ its own distinct structure.
(A) have
(B) has
(C) having
(D) have had

Part B: Choose the incorrect word or phrase and correct it.

Everyone who has traveled across the United States by car, train, or bus are surprised to see
          (A)   (B)   (C)
such a large expanse of territory with such variation among the life-styles of the people.
          (D)

10   Agreement—Collective Subject and Verb

Remember that the following collective subjects agree with singular verbs:

audience	faculty	police	variety
band	family	public	2, 3, 4, . . . dollars
chorus	group	series	2, 3, 4, . . . miles
class	majority	staff	
committee	orchestra	team	

Remember that the following subject agrees with a plural verb:

people

Avoid using plural verbs with singular subjects and singular verbs with plural subjects.

Note: In certain cases, to express the separate nature of individuals in a group, the writer may use a plural verb with the collective subjects.

EXAMPLES

INCORRECT: Twenty dollars are the price.
 CORRECT: Twenty dollars is the price.

INCORRECT: Many people is coming to the graduation.
 CORRECT: Many people are coming to the graduation.

INCORRECT: An audience usually do not applaud in a church.
 CORRECT: An audience usually does not applaud in a church.

INCORRECT: Four miles are the distance to the office.
 CORRECT: Four miles is the distance to the office.

INCORRECT: The staff are meeting in the conference room.
 CORRECT: The staff is meeting in the conference room.

EXERCISES

Part A: Choose the correct answer.

A good team_____ of both recruiting and coaching as well as performing.
    (A) are a result
    (B) it is a result
    (C) resulting
    (D) result it

Part B: Choose the incorrect word or phrase and correct it.

Because entertaining is such a competitive business, a group of singers or musicians needing a
    (A)   (B)   (C)
manager to help market the music.
                (D)

11   Agreement—Noun and Pronoun

In all patterns, there must be agreement of noun and pronoun.
Avoid using a pronoun that does not agree in number with the noun to which it refers.

EXAMPLES

INCORRECT: If you want to leave a message for Mr. and Mrs. Carlson, I will be glad to take them.
  CORRECT: If you want to leave a message for Mr. and Mrs. Carlson, I will be glad to take it.

INCORRECT: Al is interested in mathematics and their applications.
  CORRECT: Al is interested in mathematics and its applications.

INCORRECT: It is easier to talk about a problem than to resolve them.
  CORRECT: It is easier to talk about a problem than to resolve it.

INCORRECT: Although their visas will expire in June, they can have it extended for three months.
  CORRECT: Although their visas will expire in June, they can have them extended for three months.

INCORRECT: In spite of its small size, these cameras take very good pictures.
  CORRECT: In spite of their small size, these cameras take very good pictures.

EXERCISES

Part A: Choose the correct answer.

A college bookstore that sells used textbooks stocks _____ along with the new ones on the shelf under the course title.
    (A) its
    (B) their
    (C) a
    (D) them

Part B: Choose the incorrect word or phrase and correct it.

Magnesium, the lightest of our structural metals, has an important place among common
        (A)   (B)

engineering materials because of their weight.
                   (C)   (D)

12   Agreement—Subject and Possessive Pronouns

In all patterns, there must be agreement of subject pronoun and possessive pronouns that refer to the subject.

Subject Pronouns	Possessive Pronouns
I	my
you	your
he	his
she	her
it	its
we	our
you	your
they	their

Avoid using *it's* instead of *its* as a possessive pronoun. *It's* means *it is*.

EXAMPLES

INCORRECT: Those of us who are over fifty years old should get their blood pressure checked regularly.
CORRECT: Those of us who are over fifty years old should get our blood pressure checked regularly.

INCORRECT: Our neighbors know that when they go on vacation, we will get its mail for them.
CORRECT: Our neighbors know that when they go on vacation, we will get their mail for them.

INCORRECT: A mother who works outside of the home has to prepare for emergencies when she cannot be there to take care of your sick child.
CORRECT: A mother who works outside of the home has to prepare for emergencies when she cannot be there to take care of her sick child.

INCORRECT: Wine tends to lose their flavor when it has not been properly sealed.
CORRECT: Wine tends to lose its flavor when it has not been properly sealed.

INCORRECT: Optional equipment on a car can add several hundred dollars to it's resale value when you trade it in.
CORRECT: Optional equipment on a car can add several hundred dollars to its resale value when you trade it in.

EXERCISES

Part A: Choose the correct answer.

The television programs we allow _____ to watch influence their learning.
(A) a children
(B) our children
(C) our child
(D) their childs

Part B: Choose the incorrect word or phrase and correct it.

Although maple trees are <u>among</u> the most colorful varieties <u>in the fall</u>, they lose <u>its</u> leaves
                          (A)   (B)   (C)

<u>sooner than</u> oak trees.
   (D)

13   Agreement—Impersonal Pronouns

In all patterns, there must be agreement of impersonal pronouns in a sentence.

Remember that for formal writing, it is necessary to continue using the impersonal pronoun *one* throughout a sentence. For more informal writing, *he* or *his* may be used instead of *one* or *one's* to refer to a previous use of the pronoun *one*.

Avoid using *you, your, they,* or *their* to refer to the impersonal pronoun *one*.

EXAMPLES

INCORRECT: At a large university, one will almost always be able to find a friend who speaks your language.

CORRECT: At a large university, <u>one</u> will almost always be able to find a friend who speaks <u>one's</u> language.

        or

At a large university, <u>one</u> will almost always be able to find a friend who speaks <u>his</u> language.

INCORRECT: If one knew the facts, you would not be so quick to criticize.

CORRECT: If <u>one</u> knew the facts, <u>one</u> would not be so quick to criticize.

        or

If <u>one</u> knew the facts, <u>he</u> would not be so quick to criticize.

INCORRECT: In order to graduate, one must present their thesis thirty days prior to the last day of classes.

CORRECT: In order to graduate, <u>one</u> must present <u>one's</u> thesis thirty days prior to the last day of classes.

        or

In order to graduate, <u>one</u> must present <u>his</u> thesis thirty days prior to the last day of classes.

INCORRECT: Regardless of one's personal beliefs, you have the responsibility to report the facts as impartially as possible.

CORRECT: Regardless of one's personal beliefs, one has the responsibility to report the facts as impartially as possible.

or

Regardless of one's personal beliefs, he has the responsibility to report the facts as impartially as possible.

INCORRECT: If one does not work hard, you cannot expect to succeed.

CORRECT: If one does not work hard, one cannot expect to succeed.

or

If one does not work hard, he cannot expect to succeed.

EXERCISES

Part A: Choose the correct answer.

The more hemoglobin one has, the more oxygen is carried to _____ cells.
(A) one
(B) its
(C) their
(D) one's

Part B: Choose the incorrect word or phrase and correct it.

One can only live without water for about ten days because almost 60 percent of their body is water.
                            (A)   (B)   (C)   (D)

14   Agreement —Subject and Appositive

In all patterns, there must be agreement of the subject and the appositive, an explanatory phrase that follows the subject.

Avoid using a noun or pronoun in the appositive that does not agree in number with the subject to which it refers.

EXAMPLES

INCORRECT: The people in my class, mostly international student, are very friendly.

CORRECT: The people in my class, mostly international students, are very friendly.

INCORRECT: The final exam, essay tests, will be given during the last week of classes.

CORRECT: The final exam, an essay test, will be given during the last week of classes.

INCORRECT: We didn't sleep because of Jan's dog, a little poodle puppy that missed their mother.

CORRECT: We didn't sleep because of Jan's dog, a little poodle puppy that missed its mother.

INCORRECT: I haven't seen my cousins, now a young woman, for many years.

CORRECT: I haven't seen my cousins, now young women, for many years.

INCORRECT: The notes that I took, some of it with extensive drawings, are missing from my folder.

CORRECT: The notes that I took, some of them with extensive drawings, are missing from my folder.

<u>EXERCISES</u>

Part A: Choose the correct answer.

Clones,_____, are genetically homogeneous.
(A) plant growing from a single specimen
(B) that a plant grown from a single specimen
(C) plants grown from a single specimen
(D) from a single specimen, plants

Part B: Choose the incorrect word or phrase and correct it.

The Gray Wolf, a species <u>reintroduced</u> into <u>their native habitat</u> in Yellowstone National Park,
                                    (A)   (B)

<u>has begun</u> to breed <u>naturally</u> there.
   (C)   (D)

CUMULATIVE REVIEW EXERCISE FOR AGREEMENT

<u>DIRECTIONS</u>: Some of the sentences in this exercise are correct. Some are incorrect. First, find the correct sentences, and mark them with a check (√). Then find the incorrect sentences, and correct them. Check your answers using the key on pages 453–454.

1. Thirty-five thousand dollars are the average income for a four-person family living in a medium-sized community in the United States.

2. Mary Ovington, along with a number of journalists and social workers, were instrumental in establishing the Negro National Committee, now called the NAACP.

3. Fossils show that early people was only four feet six inches tall on the average.

4. Each of the Medic Alert bracelets worn by millions of Americans who suffer from diabetes and drug allergic reactions is individually engraved with the wearer's name.

5. The Yon Ho, which is still in use today and is recognized as one of the world's great canals, date from the sixth century.

6. Since the Federal Deposit Insurance Corporation started guaranteeing bank accounts of $100,000 or less, there is no reason for small investors to fear losing their savings.

7. One hundred eighty-six thousand miles per second are the speed of light.

8. It is believed that dodo birds forgot how to fly and eventually became extinct because there was no natural enemies on the island of Mauritius, where they lived.

9. Several arid areas in Arizona has been irrigated and reclaimed for cultivation.

10. The nucleus of a human cell except those of eggs and sperm contain forty-six thread-like structures called chromosomes.

11. In spite of its fragile appearance, a newborn infant is extremely sturdy.

12. The ozone layer, eight to thirty miles above the earth, protect us from too many ultraviolet rays.

13. Although amendments have been added, not once has the American Constitution been changed.

14. Michael Jackson, with members of his band, travel to key cities to give concerts and make public appearances.

15. Over 90 percent of the world's population now uses the metric system.

Problems with Introductory Verbal Modifiers

Introductory verbal modifiers introduce and modify the subject and verb in the main clause of the sentence. They can be *-ing* forms, *-ed* forms, or infinitives. They are usually separated from the main clause by a comma.

Verbal Modifiers— *-ing* and *-ed* Forms

-ing forms and *-ed* forms may be used as verbals. Verbals function as modifiers.

An introductory verbal modifier with *-ing* or *-ed* should immediately precede the noun it modifies. Otherwise, the relationship between the noun and the modifier is unclear and the sentence is illogical.

Avoid using a noun immediately after an introductory verbal phrase which may not be logically modified by the phrase. Avoid using a passive construction after an introductory verbal modifier.

EXAMPLES

INCORRECT: After graduating from City College, Professor Baker's studies were continued at State University, where he received his Ph.D. in English.

CORRECT: After graduating from City College, Professor Baker continued his studies at State University, where he received his Ph.D. in English.

INCORRECT: Returning to her room, several pieces of jewelry were missing.

CORRECT: Returning to her room, she found that several pieces of jewelry were missing.

INCORRECT: Having been delayed by heavy traffic, it was not possible for her to arrive on time.

CORRECT: Having been delayed by heavy traffic, she arrived late.

INCORRECT: Accustomed to getting up early, the new schedule was not difficult for him to adjust to.

CORRECT: Accustomed to getting up early, he had no difficulty adjusting to the new schedule.

INCORRECT: After finishing his speech, the audience was invited to ask questions.

CORRECT: After finishing his speech, he invited the audience to ask questions.

EXERCISES

Part A: Choose the correct answer.

_____ air traffic controllers guide planes through conditions of near zero visibility.
(A) They talk with pilots and watch their approach on radar,
(B) Talking with pilots and watching their approach on radar,
(C) Talk with pilots and watch their approach on radar,
(D) When they talked with pilots and watched their approach on radar,

Part B: Choose the incorrect word or phrase and correct it.

Have designed his own plane, *The Spirit of St. Louis,* Lindbergh flew from Roosevelt Field in New
  (A)   (B)
York across the ocean to Le Bourget Field outside Paris.
                 (C)   (D)

PROBLEM 16

Verbal Modifiers—Infinitives of Purpose to Introduce Instructions

An infinitive that expresses purpose may be used as an introductory verbal modifier. Remember that a verb word follows the infinitive. The verb word expresses a manner to accomplish the purpose.

Avoid using a noun or *to* with an *-ing* form instead of the infinitive of purpose. Avoid using an *-ing* form or a passive construction after an introductory verbal modifier.

EXAMPLES

INCORRECT: To protect yourself from dangerous exposure to the sun's rays, using a sun screen.
CORRECT: To protect yourself from dangerous exposure to the sun's rays, use a sun screen.

INCORRECT: Prepare for the TOEFL, study thirty minutes every day for several months.
CORRECT: To prepare for the TOEFL, study thirty minutes every day for several months.

INCORRECT: In order to take advantage of low air fares, to buy your tickets well in advance.
CORRECT: In order to take advantage of low air fares, buy your tickets well in advance.

INCORRECT: To taking action pictures, always use a high-speed film.
CORRECT: To take action pictures, always use a high-speed film.

INCORRECT: The send letters and packages from the United States overseas, use Express Mail or DHL Delivery.
CORRECT: To send letters and packages from the United States overseas, use Express Mail or DHL Delivery.

EXERCISES

Part A: Choose the correct answer.

To relieve pressure in the skull,_____ into the blood.
(A) you will inject a strong solution of pure glucose
(B) to inject a strong solution of pure glucose
(C) a strong solution of glucose will inject purely
(D) inject a strong solution of pure glucose

Part B: Choose the incorrect word or phrase and correct it.

To estimate how much it will cost to build a home, finding the total square footage of the house and
                      (A)   (B)   (C)

multiply by cost per square foot.
      (D)

CUMULATIVE REVIEW EXERCISE FOR INTRODUCTORY VERBAL MODIFIERS

DIRECTIONS: Some of the sentences in this exercise are correct. Some are incorrect. First, find the correct sentences, and mark them with a check (√). Then find the incorrect sentences, and correct them. Check your answers using the key on pages 454–455.

1. Having ruled since the sixth century, the present emperor of Japan has a long and noble tradition.

2. Built on 230 acres, the palace of Versailles is one of the showplaces of France.

3. Believing that true emeralds could not be broken, Spanish soldiers in Pizarro's expedition to Peru tested the jewels they found by pounding them with hammers.

4. Adopted as the laws of the former British colonies after the Revolutionary War, Canada was invited to become a member of the Confederation under the Articles of Confederation.

5. After surrendering in 1886 and being imprisoned in Florida and Alabama, the Apache chief Geronimo became a farmer and lived out his life on a military reservation in Oklahoma.

6. While hibernating, the respiration of animals decreases.

7. To improve the study of chemical reactions, the introduction of effective quantitative methods by Lavoisier.

8. Migrating in a wedge formation, a goose conserves energy by flying in the air currents created by the goose ahead of it.

9. Invented in China about 105 A.D., paper was manufactured in Baghdad and later in Spain four hundred years before the first English paper mill was founded.

10. After lasting for six centuries, it has never been explained why the Mayan culture collapsed.

11. Wounded by an assassin's bullet while he was watching a play at the Ford Theater, death came to Lincoln a few hours after being shot.

12. While viewing objects under a microscope, Robert Hooke discovered that all living things were made up of cells.

13. Located in San Francisco Bay and nicknamed the "Rock," dangerous criminals were once incarcerated in Alcatraz.

14. Having calculated the length of time for the first voyages to the moon, Kepler wrote that passengers would have to be drugged.

15. To prepare the fields for planting and irrigation, farmers use laser beams.

Problems with Parallel Structure

Parallel structure means expressing ideas of equal importance with the same grammatical structures.

17   Parallel Structure—In a Series

In all patterns, ideas of equal importance should be expressed by the same grammatical structure. Avoid expressing ideas in a series by different structures.

EXAMPLES

INCORRECT: Jane is young, enthusiastic, and she has talent.
 CORRECT: Jane is <u>young</u>, <u>enthusiastic</u>, and <u>talented</u>.

INCORRECT: We learned to read the passages carefully and underlining the main ideas.
 CORRECT: We learned <u>to read</u> the passages carefully and <u>to underline</u> the main ideas.

INCORRECT: The duties of the new secretary are to answer the telephone, to type letters, and book keeping.
 CORRECT: The duties of the new secretary are <u>to answer</u> the telephone, <u>to type</u> letters, and <u>to do</u> the bookkeeping.

INCORRECT: The patient's symptoms were fever, dizziness, and his head hurt.
 CORRECT: The patient's symptoms were <u>fever</u>, <u>dizziness</u>, and <u>headaches</u>.

INCORRECT: Professor Williams enjoys teaching and to write.
 CORRECT: Professor Williams enjoys <u>teaching</u> and <u>writing</u>.

EXERCISES

Part A: Choose the correct answer.

In a hot, sunny climate, man acclimatizes by eating less, drinking more liquids, wearing lighter clothing, and _____.
   (A) skin changes that darken
   (B) his skin may darken
   (C) experiencing a darkening of the skin
   (D) darkens his skin

Part B: Choose the incorrect word or phrase and correct it.

The aims of the European Economic Community are to eliminate tariffs between member countries;
                                                                        (A)

developing common policies for agriculture, labor, welfare, trade, and transportation; and to abolish
    (B)   (C)   (D)

trusts and cartels.

18   Parallel Structure—After Correlative Conjunctions

Remember that ideas of equal importance are introduced by correlative conjunctions:

both...and
not only...but also

Avoid expressing ideas after correlative conjunctions by different structures.

EXAMPLES

INCORRECT: She is not only famous in the United States, but also abroad.
 CORRECT: She is famous not only in the United States, but also abroad.

INCORRECT: The exam tested both listening and to read.
 CORRECT: The exam tested both listening and reading.

INCORRECT: He is not only intelligent but also he is creative.
 CORRECT: He is not only intelligent but also creative.

INCORRECT: Flying is not only faster but also it is safer than traveling by car.
 CORRECT: Flying is not only faster but also safer than traveling by car.

INCORRECT: John registered for both Electrical Engineering 500 and to study Mathematics 390.
 CORRECT: John registered for both Electrical Engineering 500 and Mathematics 390.

EXERCISES

Part A: Choose the correct answer.

Both historically and _____, Ontario is the heartland of Canada.
   (A) in its geography
 √ (B) geographically
   (C) also its geography
   (D) geography

Part B: Choose the incorrect word or phrase and correct it.

The cacao bean was cultivated by the Aztecs not only to drink but also currency.
                    (A)   (B)   (C)   (D)

CUMULATIVE REVIEW EXERCISE FOR PARALLEL STRUCTURE

DIRECTIONS: Some of the sentences in this exercise are correct. Some are incorrect. First, find the correct sentences, and mark them with a check (√). Then find the incorrect sentences, and correct them. Check your answers using the key on page 455.

1. We are indebted to the Arabs not only for reviving Greek works but also they introduced useful ideas from India.

2. A century ago in America, all postal rates were determined not by weighing the mail but measuring the distance that the mail had to travel.

3. The four basic elements that make up all but 1 percent of terrestrial matter include carbon, hydrogen, nitrogen, and oxygen is also.

4. The three thousand stars visible to the naked eye can be seen because they are either extremely bright or they are relatively close to the earth.

5. George Kaufman distinguished himself as a newspaperman, a drama critic, and he was a successful playwright.

6. To apply for a passport, fill out the application form, attach two recent photographs, and taking it to your local post office or passport office.

7. Shakespeare was both a writer and he acted.

8. To save on heating and finding cheaper labor are two of the most common reasons that companies give for moving from the Midwest to the South.

9. Both plants and animals have digestive systems, respiratory systems, and reproduce.

10. Pollution control involves identifying the sources of contamination, development improved or alternative technologies and sources of raw material, and persuading industries and citizens to adopt them either voluntarily or legally.

11. Tobacco was considered a sacred plant, and it was used to indicate friendship and concluded peace negotiations between Indians and whites.

12. The kidneys both eliminate water and salt.

13. A person who purchases a gun for protection is six times more likely to kill a friend or relative than killing an intruder.

14. The Brooklyn Bridge was remarkable not only for the early use of the pneumatic caisson but also for the introduction of steel wire.

15. Microwaves are used for cooking, for telecommunications, and also medical diagnosis is made from them.

Problems with Redundancy

Redundancy means using more words than necessary.

Redundancy—Unnecessary Phrases

In all patterns, prefer simple, direct sentences to complicated, indirect sentences. Find the Subject-Verb-Complement-Modifier, and determine whether the other words are useful or unnecessary.

S	V	C	M
Lee	learned	English	quickly

Avoid using an adjective with such phrases as *in character* or *in nature*.

Avoid using the redundant pattern instead of an adverb such as *quickly*.

in a	adjective	manner
in a	quick	manner

EXAMPLES

INCORRECT: The key officials who testified before the Senate committee responded in a manner that was evasive.

CORRECT: The key officials who testified before the Senate committee responded evasively.

INCORRECT: Mr. Davis knows a great deal in terms of the condition of the situation.

CORRECT: Mr. Davis knows a great deal about the situation.

INCORRECT: It was a problem which was very difficult in character and very delicate in nature.

CORRECT: The problem was difficult and delicate.

INCORRECT: The disease was very serious in the nature of it.

CORRECT: The disease was very serious.

INCORRECT: Mary had always behaved in a responsible manner.

CORRECT: Mary had always behaved responsibly.

EXERCISES

Part A: Choose the correct answer.

Waitresses and waiters who serve _____ deserve at least a 20 percent tip.
    (A) in a courteous manner
    (B) courteously
    (C) with courtesy in their manner
    (D) courteous

Part B: Choose the incorrect word or phrase and correct it.

Hummingbirds move <u>their</u> wings so <u>rapid a way</u> that they appear <u>to be hanging</u> <u>in the air</u>.
                 (A)   (B)   (C)   (D)

20   Redundancy—Repetition of Words with the Same Meaning

In all patterns, avoid using words with the same meaning consecutively in a sentence.

EXAMPLES

INCORRECT: The money that I have is sufficient enough for my needs.
CORRECT: The money that I have is <u>sufficient</u> for my needs.

INCORRECT: Bill asked the speaker to repeat again because he had not heard him the first time.
CORRECT: Bill asked the speaker <u>to repeat</u> because he had not heard him the first time.

INCORRECT: The class advanced forward rapidly.
CORRECT: The class <u>advanced</u> rapidly.

INCORRECT: She returned back to her hometown after she had finished her degree.
CORRECT: She <u>returned</u> to her hometown after she had finished her degree.

INCORRECT: I am nearly almost finished with this chapter.
CORRECT: I am <u>nearly</u> finished with this chapter.
                  or
          I am <u>almost</u> finished with this chapter.

EXERCISES

Part A: Choose the correct answer.

Famous for his _____ punctuation, typography, and language, Edward Estlin Cummings published his collected poems in 1954.

    (A) new innovations for
    (B) innovations in
    (C) newly approached
    (D) innovations newly approached in

Part B: Choose the incorrect word or phrase and correct it.

The idea of a submarine is <u>an old ancient one,</u> dating from <u>as early as</u> <u>the fifteenth century</u> when
                            (A)   (B)   (C)
Drebbel and Da Vinci <u>made</u> preliminary drawings.
          (D)

21   Redundancy—Repetition of Noun by Pronoun

In all patterns, avoid using a noun and the pronoun that refers to it consecutively in a sentence. Avoid using a pronoun after the noun it refers to, and *that*.

EXAMPLES

INCORRECT: My teacher he said to listen to the news on the radio in order to practice listening comprehension.

CORRECT: My teacher said to listen to the news on the radio in order to practice listening comprehension.

INCORRECT: Steve he plans to go into business with his father.

CORRECT: Steve plans to go into business with his father.

INCORRECT: My sister she found a store that imported food from our country.

CORRECT: My sister found a store that imported food from our country.

INCORRECT: Hospitalization that it covers room, meals, nursing, and additional hospital expenses such as lab tests, X-rays, and medicine.

CORRECT: Hospitalization covers room, meals, nursing, and additional hospital expenses such as lab tests, X-rays, and medicine.

INCORRECT: Anne she wants to visit Washington, D.C., before she goes home.

CORRECT: Anne wants to visit Washington, D.C., before she goes home.

EXERCISES

Part A: Choose the correct answer.

A perennial is_____ for more than two years, such as trees and shrubs.
    (A) any plant that it continues to grow
    (B) any plant it continuing to grow
    (C) any plant that continues to grow
    (D) any plant continuing growth

Part B: Choose the incorrect word or phrase and correct it.

Advertising it provides most of the income for magazines, newspapers, radio, and television
               (A)   (B)   (C)
    in the United States today.
        (D)

CUMULATIVE REVIEW EXERCISE FOR REDUNDANCY

<u>DIRECTIONS</u>: Some of the sentences in this exercise are correct. Some are incorrect. First, find the correct sentences, and mark them with a check (√). Then find the incorrect sentences, and correct them. Check your answers using the key on page 456.

1. Many dentists now say that plaque can cause damage of a more serious nature and degree to teeth than cavities.

2. The most common name in the world it is Mohammad.

3. The idea for the Monroe Doctrine was originally first proposed not by Monroe but by the British Secretary for Foreign Affairs, George Canning.

4. That comets' tails are caused by solar wind it is generally accepted.

5. One hundred thousand earthquakes are felt every year, one thousand of which cause severe serious damage.

6. Irving Berlin, America's most prolific songwriter, he never learned to read or write music.

7. The corporation, which is by far the most influential form of business ownership, is a comparatively new innovation.

8. That the earth and the moon formed simultaneously at the same time is a theory that accounts for the heat of the early atmosphere surrounding the earth.

9. The longest mountain range, the Mid-Atlantic Range, is not hardly visible because most of it lies under the ocean.

10. The Navajo language was used in a successful manner as a code by the United States in World War II.

11. One of the magnificent Seven Wonders of the Ancient World was the enormous large statue known as the Colossus of Rhodes.

12. It is the first digit that appears on any zip code that it refers to one of ten geographical areas in the United States.

13. Limestone formations growing downward from the roofs of caves that they are stalactites.

14. All matter is composed of molecules or atoms that are in motion in a constant way.

15. The fact that the earth rotates wasn't known until the years of the 1850s.

Problems with Word Choice

Word choice means choosing between similar words to express precise meanings.

22   Transitive and Intransitive Verbs—*Raise* and *Rise*

A transitive verb is a verb that takes a complement. An intransitive verb is a verb that does not take a complement.

The following pairs of verbs can be confusing. Remember that *raise* is a transitive verb; it takes a complement. *Rise* is an intransitive verb; it does not take a complement.

Transitive			Intransitive		
Verb word	*Past*	*Participle*	*Verb word*	*Past*	*Participle*
raise	raised	raised	rise	rose	risen

Remember that *to raise* means to move to a higher place or to cause to rise. *To rise* means to go up or to increase.

Raise and rise are also used as nouns. A *raise* means an increase in salary. A *rise* means an increase in price, worth, quantity, or degree.

S	RAISE	C	M
Heavy rain	raises	the water level of the reservoir	every spring
Heavy rain	raised	the water level of the reservoir	last week

S	RISE	C	M
The water level	rises		when it rains every spring
The water level	rose		when it rained last week

EXAMPLES

INCORRECT:	The cost of living has raised 3 percent in the past year.
CORRECT:	The cost of living <u>has risen</u> 3 percent in the past year.

INCORRECT:	The flag is risen at dawn by an honor guard.
CORRECT:	<u>The flag</u> is raised at dawn <u>by an honor guard.</u>
	(An honor guard <u>raises</u> <u>the flag</u>.)

INCORRECT:	Kay needs to rise her grades if she wants to get into graduate school.
CORRECT:	Kay <u>needs</u> <u>to raise</u> <u>her grades</u> if she wants to get into graduate school.

INCORRECT: The landlord has risen the rent.
CORRECT: The landlord has raised the rent.

INCORRECT: The smoke that is raising from that oil refinery is black.
CORRECT: The smoke that is rising from that oil refinery is black.

EXERCISES

Part A: Choose the correct answer.

The average elevation of the Himalayas is twenty thousand feet, and Mount Everest _____ to more than twenty-nine thousand feet at its apex.

(A) raises
(B) rises
(C) roses
(D) arises

Part B: Choose the incorrect word or phrase and correct it.

When the temperature is risen to the burning point without a source of escape for the heat, sponta-
　　　　　　　　　　　(A)　　　　　(B)　　　　　　　　　　　　　　　　　　　　(C)
neous combustion occurs.
　　　　　　　　(D)

23 Transitive and Intransitive Verbs—*Lay* and *Lie*

Remember that *lay* is a transitive verb; it takes a complement. *Lie* is an intransitive verb; it does not take a complement.

Transitive			Intransitive		
Verb word	*Past*	*Participle*	*Verb word*	*Past*	*Participle*
lay	*laid*	*laid*	*lie*	*lay*	*lain*

Remember that *to lay* means to put, to place or to cause to lie. *To lie* means to recline or to occupy a place.

The past form of the verb *to lie* is *lay*.

S	LAY	C	M
The postman	lays	the mail	on the table every day
The postman	laid	the mail	on the table yesterday

S	LIE	C	M
He	lies		on the sofa to rest every day after work
He	lay		on the sofa to rest yesterday after work

EXAMPLES

INCORRECT:	Her coat was laying on the chair.
CORRECT:	Her coat was lying on the chair.
INCORRECT:	I have lain your notebook on the table by the door so that you won't forget it.
CORRECT:	I have laid your notebook on the table by the door so that you won't forget it.
INCORRECT:	Key West lays off the coast of Florida.
CORRECT:	Key West lies off the coast of Florida.
INCORRECT:	Why don't you lay down for awhile?
CORRECT:	Why don't you lie down for awhile?
INCORRECT:	Linda always forgets where she lies her glasses.
CORRECT:	Linda always forgets where she lays her glasses.

EXERCISES

Part A: Choose the correct answer.

The geographic position of North America, _____ in the early days of the European settlement.

    (A) laying between the Atlantic and the Pacific Oceans, isolating it

    (B) isolating it as it laid between the Atlantic and the Pacific Oceans

    (C) lying between the Atlantic and the Pacific Oceans, isolated it

    (D) isolating it between the Atlantic and the Pacific Oceans as it was layed

Part B: Choose the incorrect word or phrase and correct it.

Melanin, a pigment that lays under the skin, is responsible for skin color, including the varia-
                         (A)   (B)

tions that occur among different races.
          (C)   (D)

Transitive and Intransitive Verbs—*Set* and *Sit*

Remember that *set* is a transitive verb; it takes a complement. *Sit* is an intransitive verb; it does not take a complement.

Transitive			Intransitive		
Verb word	*Past*	*Participle*	*Verb word*	*Past*	*Participle*
set	set	set	sit	sat	sat

Remember that *to set* means to put, to place, or to cause to sit. *To sit* means to occupy a place on a chair or a flat surface.

S	SET	C	M
The students	set	the lab equipment	on the table every class
The students	set	the lab equipment	on the table last class period

S	SIT	C	M
The equipment	sits		on the table every class
The equipment	sat		on the table last class period

EXAMPLES

INCORRECT: Please sit the telephone on the table by the bed.
CORRECT: Please <u>set</u> the <u>telephone</u> on the table by the bed.

INCORRECT: Won't you set down?
CORRECT: Won't <u>you</u> <u>sit</u> down?

INCORRECT: Their house sets on a hill overlooking a lake.
CORRECT: Their <u>house</u> <u>sits</u> on a hill overlooking a lake.

INCORRECT: Let's sit your suitcases out of the way.
CORRECT: Let's <u>set</u> <u>your</u> <u>suitcases</u> out of the way.

INCORRECT: Terry has set there waiting for us for almost an hour.
CORRECT: <u>Terry</u> <u>has</u> <u>sat</u> there waiting for us for almost an hour.

EXERCISES

Part A: Choose the correct answer.

When Jacqueline Kennedy was first lady, she collected many beautiful antiques and _____ them among the original pieces in the White House.

(A) sat
(B) set
(C) sit
(D) sits

Part B: Choose the incorrect word or phrase and correct it.

Hyde Park, the family estate <u>of Franklin D. Roosevelt,</u> <u>sets</u> on top of a bluff <u>overlooking</u>
                               (A)   (B)   (C)

<u>the Hudson River.</u>
   (D)

25 Similar Verbs—*Tell* and *Say*

Verb word	Past	Participle	Verb word	Past	Participle
tell	*told*	*told*	*say*	*said*	*said*

Remember that *to tell* and *to say* have similar meanings, but *tell* is often used before complements, especially persons. *To say* is not used before complements that are persons. *To say* is usually followed by a clause introduced by *that*.

S	TELL	C	M
The teacher	tells	us	how to do it
The teacher	told	us	how to do it

S	SAY	C	M
The teacher	says		that we were making progress
The teacher	said		that we were making progress

EXAMPLES

INCORRECT: Jayne said him that she would meet us here.
  CORRECT: Jayne <u>told</u> <u>him</u> that she would meet us here.

INCORRECT: Margaret told that she would call before she came.
  CORRECT: Margaret <u>said</u> <u>that</u> she would call before she came.

INCORRECT: Randy says a lot of jokes and funny stories.
  CORRECT: Randy <u>tells</u> a lot of <u>jokes</u> and funny stories.

INCORRECT: I have said the truth.
  CORRECT: I have <u>told</u> <u>the truth</u>.

INCORRECT: The girls told (that) they were hungry.
  CORRECT: The girls <u>said</u> <u>that</u> they were hungry.

EXERCISES

Part A: Choose the correct answer.

In his inaugural speech, John Kennedy _____ that we should not ask what our country could do for us but what we could do for our country.
    (A) said
    (B) told
    (C) did
    (D) got

Part B: Choose the incorrect word or phrase and correct it.

Before television became <u>so popular</u>, Americans used <u>to entertain</u> <u>each other</u> in the evening by play-
                (A)   (B)   (C)

ing games, <u>saying</u> stories, and singing songs.
           (D)

Similar Verbs—*Let* and *Leave*

Verb word	Past	Participle	Verb word	Past	Participle
let	*let*	*let*	*leave*	*left*	*left*

Remember that *to let* and *to leave* have similar sounds, but not similar meanings. *To let* means to allow or to permit. *To leave* means to let someone or something remain. *To leave* also means to depart or to go.

S	LET	C	M
Their mother	lets	them	stay up late every night
Their mother	let	them	stay up late last night

S	LEAVE	C	M
She	leaves	her briefcase	at the office every day
She	left	her briefcase	at the office yesterday

EXAMPLES

INCORRECT: Although her doctor allowed her family to visit her, he wouldn't leave anyone else go into her room.

CORRECT: Although her doctor allowed her family to visit her, he wouldn't <u>let</u> anyone else go into her room.

INCORRECT: You can let your car in long-term parking until you come back.
CORRECT: You can <u>leave</u> your car in long-term parking until you come back.

INCORRECT: Professor Baker wouldn't leave us use our dictionaries during the test.
CORRECT: Professor Baker wouldn't <u>let</u> us use our dictionaries during the test.

INCORRECT: Just let the paper in my mailbox.
CORRECT: Just <u>leave</u> the paper in my mailbox.

INCORRECT: Just let your coats on the racks in the hall.
CORRECT: Just <u>leave</u> your coats on the racks in the hall.

EXERCISES

Part A: Choose the correct answer.

Although blood_____ a residue in urine and stool samples, it cannot always be detected without the aid of a microscope.
- (A) let
- (B) leave
- (C) leaves
- (D) lets

Part B: Choose the incorrect word or phrase and correct it.

To assure the safety of those workers who must handle radioactive material, the employer should
    (A)   (B)
not leave them enter contaminated areas without protective clothing.
    (C)   (D)

Similar Verbs—*Borrow* and *Lend*

Verb word	Past	Participle	Verb word	Past	Participle
borrow	*borrowed*	*borrowed*	*lend*	*lent*	*lent*

Remember that *to borrow* and *to lend* have related meanings. *To borrow* means to take and give back. It is often followed by the word *from*. *To lend* means to give and take back. It is often followed by the word *to*.

S	BORROW	C	M
Karen's father	borrows	money	from the bank every term
Karen's father	borrowed	money	from the bank last term

S	LEND	C	M
The bank	lends	money	to Karen's father every term
The bank	lent	money	to Karen's father last term

EXAMPLES

INCORRECT: Stan had an accident while he was driving the car that his cousin had borrowed him.
  CORRECT: Stan had an accident while he was driving the car that his cousin had lent him.

INCORRECT: Would you please borrow me your pen?
  CORRECT: Would you please lend me your pen?

INCORRECT: Can I lend this dictionary for a few minutes while I check my composition?
CORRECT: Can I <u>borrow</u> this dictionary for a few minutes while I check my composition?

INCORRECT: She lent my key to get into the apartment, and lost it.
CORRECT: She <u>borrowed</u> my key to get into the apartment, and lost it.

INCORRECT: Thank you for borrowing me your umbrella.
CORRECT: Thank you for <u>lending</u> me your umbrella.

EXERCISES

Part A: Choose the correct answer.

Countries may _____ the World Bank for development projects.
(A) borrow large sums of money from
(B) lend large sums of money from
(C) borrow large sums of money
(D) lend large sums of money

Part B: Choose the incorrect word or phrase and correct it.

Either a savings and loan company or a bank can <u>borrow</u> money to those people <u>who</u> want <u>to buy</u> a
          (A)   (B)   (C)   (D)

home.

Similar Verbs—*Make* and *Do*

Verb word	Past	Participle	Verb word	Past	Participle
do	did	done	make	made	made

Remember that *to do* and *to make* have similar meanings, but *do* is often used before complements that describe work and chores. *To make* is often used before complements that are derived from verbs.

DO an assignment	MAKE an agreement	(to agree)
the dishes	an announcement	(to announce)
a favor	an attempt	(to attempt)
homework	a decision	(to decide)
the laundry	a discovery	(to discover)
a paper	an offer	(to offer)
research	a profit	(to profit)
work	a promise	(to promise)

S	DO	C	M
We	do	our homework	before class every day
We	did	our homework	before class yesterday

S	MAKE	C	M
We	make	an agreement	with each other every semester
We	made	an agreement	with each other last semester

EXAMPLES

INCORRECT:	I really don't mind making the homework for this class.
CORRECT:	I really don't mind <u>doing the homework</u> for this class.

INCORRECT:	Did you do a mistake?
CORRECT:	Did you <u>make a mistake</u>?

INCORRECT:	Please make me a favor.
CORRECT:	Please <u>do me a favor</u>.

INCORRECT:	Are they doing progress on the new road?
CORRECT:	Are they <u>making progress</u> on the new road?

INCORRECT:	Have you done any interesting discoveries while you were doing your research?
CORRECT:	Have you <u>made</u> any interesting <u>discoveries</u> while you were <u>doing</u> your <u>research</u>?

EXERCISES

Part A: Choose the correct answer.

The president usually _____ unless his press secretary approves it.
   (A) doesn't do a statement
   (B) doesn't make a statement
   (C) doesn't statement
   (D) no statement

Part B: Choose the incorrect word or phrase and correct it.

A <u>one hundred-horsepower tractor</u> <u>can</u> <u>make</u> the work of <u>a large number</u> of horses.
    (A)   (B) (C)   (D)

29 Prepositional Idioms

Prefer these idioms	Avoid these errors
accede to	accede on, by
according to	according
approve of	approve for
ashamed of	ashamed with
bored with	bored of

capable of	capable to
compete with	compete together
composed of	composed from
concerned with	concerned of
conscious of	conscious for
depend on	depend in, to
effects on	effects in
equal to	equal as
except for	excepting for
from now on	after now on
from time to time	for, when time to time
frown on	frown to
glance at, through	glance
incapable of	incapable to
in conflict	on conflict
inferior to	inferior with
in the habit of	in the habit to
in the near future	at the near future
knowledge of	knowledge on
near; next to	near to
of the opinion	in opinion
on top of	on top
opposite	opposite over
prior to	prior
regard to	regard of
related to	related with
respect for	respect of
responsible for	responsible
similar to	similar as
since	ever since
until	up until
with regard to	with regard of

EXAMPLES

INCORRECT: Excepting for the Gulf Coast region, most of the nation will have very pleasant weather tonight and tomorrow.

CORRECT: Except for the Gulf Coast region, most of the nation will have very pleasant weather tonight and tomorrow.

INCORRECT:	In recent years, educators have become more concerned of bilingualism.
CORRECT:	In recent years, educators have become more <u>concerned with</u> bilingualism.

INCORRECT:	He always does what he pleases, without regard of the rules and regulations.
CORRECT:	He always does what he pleases, without <u>regard to</u> the rules and regulations.

INCORRECT:	The bank opposite over the university isn't open on Saturdays.
CORRECT:	The bank <u>opposite</u> the university isn't open on Saturdays.

INCORRECT:	The customs of other countries are not inferior with those of our own country.
CORRECT:	The customs of other countries are not <u>inferior to</u> those of our own country.

EXERCISES

Part A: Choose the correct answer.

_____ discovery of insulin, it was not possible to treat diabetes.
- (A) Prior to the
- (B) Prior
- (C) The prior
- (D) To prior

Part B: Choose the incorrect word or phrase and correct it.

The price of gold depends in several factors, including supply and demand in relation to the value of
  (A)   (B)   (C)   (D)
the dollar.

30 Parts of Speech

Although it is usually very easy to identify the parts of speech, word families can be confusing. Word families are groups of words with similar meanings and spellings. Each word in the family is a different part of speech. For example, *agreement* is a noun; *agreeable* is an adjective; to *agree* is a verb.

The endings of words can help you identify the part of speech.

Nouns Derived from Verbs

Verb	Ending	Noun
store	*-age*	*storage*
accept	*-ance*	*acceptance*
insist	*-ence*	*insistence*
agree	*-ment*	*agreement*
authorize	*-sion/-tion*	*authorization*

Nouns Derived from Adjectives

Adjective	Ending	Noun
convenient	*-ce*	*convenience*
redundant	*-cy*	*redundancy*
opposite	*-tion*	*opposition*
soft	*-ness*	*softness*
durable	*-ty*	*durability*

Adjectives Derived from Nouns

Noun	Ending	Adjective
possibility	-able/-ible	possible
intention	-al	intentional
distance	-ant	distant
frequency	-ent	frequent
juice	-y	juicy

Adverbs Derived from Adjectives

Adjective	Ending	Adverb
efficient	-ly	efficiently

EXAMPLES

INCORRECT:	The agreeing is not legal unless everyone signs his name.
CORRECT:	The agreement is not legal unless everyone signs his name.

INCORRECT:	Even young children begin to show able in mathematics.
CORRECT:	Even young children begin to show ability in mathematics.

INCORRECT:	Arranging have been made for the funeral.
CORRECT:	Arrangements have been made for the funeral.

INCORRECT:	A free educating is guaranteed to every citizen.
CORRECT:	A free education is guaranteed to every citizen.

INCORRECT:	The develop of hybrids has increased yields.
CORRECT:	The development of hybrids has increased yields.

EXERCISES

Part A: Choose the correct answer.

Unless protected areas are established, the Bengal tiger, the blue whale, and the California condor face_____ of extinction.

(A) possible
(B) the possibility
(C) to be possible
(D) possibly

Part B: Choose the incorrect word or phrase and correct it.

Because blood from different individuals may different in the type of antigen on the surface of the
(A)   (B)

red cells and the type of antibody in the plasma, a dangerous reaction can occur between the donor
                                                                                 (C)

and recipient in a blood transfusion.
(D)

CUMULATIVE REVIEW EXERCISE FOR WORD CHOICE

DIRECTIONS: Some of the sentences in this exercise are correct. Some are incorrect. First, find the correct sentences, and mark them with a check (√). Then find the incorrect sentences, and correct them. Check your answers using the key on pages 456–457.

1. The manage of a small business requires either education or experience in sales and accounting.

2. Because of the traffic in ancient Rome, Julius Caesar would not let anyone use a wheeled vehicle on the streets during the day.

3. Occasionally dolphins need to raise to the surface of the water to take in oxygen.

4. Thomas Jefferson's home, which he designed and built, sets on a hill overlooking the Virginia countryside.

5. Once, the gold reserve of the United States Treasury was saved when J.P. Morgan, then the richest man in America, borrowed more than fifty million dollars' worth of gold to the federal government.

6. Dreams may be the expression of fears and desires that we are not conscious of during our waking hours.

7. Ice has the same hard as concrete.

8. We might never have heard about Daniel Boone had he not told a schoolmaster his stories about the frontier.

9. Terrorists are capable to hijacking planes and taking hostages in spite of security at international airports.

10. It is not the TOEFL but the academic preparation of a student that is the best indicator of his successfully.

11. Some business analysts argue that the U.S. automobile industry is suffering because Congress will not impose heavier import duties, but others say that the cars themselves are inferior with the foreign competition.

12. Lotteries are used to rise money for the states that sponsor them.

13. When a human being gets hurt, the brain excretes a chemical called enkaphalin to numb the painful.

14. Benjamin Franklin told that the turkey should be our national bird.

15. The prime rate is the rate of interest that a bank will charge when it lends money to its best clients.

REVIEW OF
READING
COMPREHENSION

OVERVIEW

Section 3: Reading Comprehension   **50 QUESTIONS**
                                                        55 MINUTES

Reading Passages

Five reading passages with an average of ten questions after each passage.

You must choose from four possible answers the answer that would be the best response to each question.

TYPES OF PROBLEMS IN THE READING COMPREHENSION SECTION

Problems like those in this Review of Reading Comprehension frequently appear on Section 3 of the TOEFL.

To prepare for Section 3 of the TOEFL, study the problems in this chapter.

Reading Comprehension

1	Previewing
2	Reading for Main Ideas
3	Using Contexts for Vocabulary

4	Scanning for Details
5	Making Inferences
6	Identifying Exceptions
7	Locating References
8	Referring to the Passage

1 Previewing

Research shows that it is easier to understand what you are reading if you begin with a general idea of what the passage is about. Previewing helps you form a general idea of the topic in your mind.

To preview, read the title, if there is one; the first sentence of each paragraph; and the last sentence of the passage. You should do this as quickly as possible. Remember, you are not reading for specific information, but for an impression of the *topic.*

EXERCISE

<u>DIRECTIONS:</u> Preview the following passage. Focus on the first sentence in each paragraph and the last sentence of the passage. Can you identify the topic? Check your answer using the key on page 458.

A black hole is a region of space created by the total gravitational collapse of matter. It is so intense that nothing, not even light or radiation, can escape. In other words, it is a one-way surface through which matter can fall inward but cannot emerge.

Some astronomers believe that a black hole may be formed when a large star collapses inward from its own weight. So long as they are emitting heat and light into space, stars support themselves against their own gravitational pull with the outward thermal pressure generated by heat from nuclear reactions deep in their interiors. But if a star eventually exhausts its nuclear fuel, then its unbalanced gravitational attraction could cause it to contract and collapse. Furthermore, it could begin to pull in surrounding matter, including nearby comets and planets, creating a black hole.

2 Reading for Main Ideas

By previewing, you can form a general idea of what a reading passage is about; that is, you identify the *topic.* By reading for main ideas, you identify the point of view of the author—that is, what the writer's *thesis* is. Specifically, what does the author propose to write about the topic? If you could reduce the reading to one sentence, what would it be?

Questions about the main idea can be worded in many ways. For example, the following questions are all asking for the same information: (l) What is the main idea? (2) What is the subject? (3) What is the topic? (4) What would be a good title?

EXERCISE

<u>DIRECTIONS:</u> The main idea usually occurs at the beginning of a reading passage. Look at the first two sentences in the following passage. Can you identify the main idea? What would be a good title for this passage? Check your answers using the key on page 458.

For more than a century, despite attacks by a few opposing scientists, Charles Darwin's theory of evolution by natural selection has stood firm. Now, however, some respected biologists are beginning to question whether the theory accounts for major developments such as the shift from water to land habitation. Clearly, evolution has not proceeded steadily but has progressed by radical advances. Recent research in molecular biology, particularly in the study of DNA, provides us with a new possibility. Not only environmental change but also genetic codes in the underlying structure of DNA could govern evolution.

3   Using Contexts for Vocabulary

Before you can use a context, you must understand what a context is. In English, a context is the combination of vocabulary and grammar that surrounds a word. Context can be a sentence or a paragraph or a passage. Context helps you make a general *prediction* about meaning. If you know the general meaning of a sentence, you also know the general meaning of the words in the sentence.

Making predictions from contexts is very important when you are reading a foreign language. In this way, you can read and understand the meaning of a passage without stopping to look up every new word in a dictionary. On an examination like the TOEFL, dictionaries are not permitted in the room.

EXERCISE

DIRECTIONS: Read the following passage, paying close attention to the underlined words. Can you understand their meanings from the context without using a dictionary? Check your answers using the key on page 458.

At the age of sixty-six, Harland Sanders had to <u>auction</u> off everything he owned in order to pay his debts. Once the successful <u>proprietor</u> of a large restaurant, Sanders saw his business suffer from the construction of a new freeway that bypassed his establishment and rerouted the traffic that had <u>formerly</u> passed.

With an income of only $105 a month in Social Security, he packed his car with a pressure cooker, some chickens, and sixty pounds of the seasoning that he had developed for frying chicken. He stopped at restaurants, where he cooked chicken for owners to <u>sample</u>. If they liked it, he offered to show them how to cook it. Then he sold them the seasoning and collected a <u>royalty</u> of four cents on each chicken they cooked. The rest is history. Eight years later, there were 638 Kentucky Fried Chicken franchises, and Colonel Sanders had sold his business again—this time for over two million dollars.

4   Scanning for Details

After reading a passage on the TOEFL, you will be expected to answer eight to ten multiple-choice questions. First, read a question and find the important content words. Content words are usually nouns, verbs, or adjectives. They are called content words because they contain the content or meaning of a sentence.

Next, let your eyes travel quickly over the passage for the same content words or synonyms of the words. This is called *scanning*. By scanning, you can find a place in the reading passage where the answer to a question is found. Finally, read those specific sentences carefully and choose the answer that corresponds to the meaning of the sentences you have read.

EXERCISE

DIRECTIONS: First, read the following passage. Then, read the questions after the reading passage, and look for the content words. Finally, scan the passage for the same words or synonyms. Can you answer the questions? Check your answers using the key on pages 458–459.

To prepare for a career in engineering, a student must begin planning in high school. Mathematics and science should form the core curriculum. For example, in a school where sixteen credit hours are required for high school graduation, four should be in mathematics, one each in chemistry, biology, and physics. The remaining credits should include four in English and at least three in the humanities and social sciences. The average entering freshman in engineering should have achieved at least a 2.5 grade point average on a 4.0 scale in his or her high school. Although deficiencies can be corrected during the first year, the student who needs additional work should expect to spend five instead of four years to complete a degree.

1. What is the average grade point for an entering freshman in engineering?

2. When should a student begin planning for a career in engineering?

3. How can a student correct deficiencies in preparation?

4. How many credits should a student have in English?

5. How many credits are required for a high school diploma?

5   Making Inferences

Sometimes, in a reading passage, you will find a direct statement of fact. That is called evidence. But other times, you will not find a direct statement. Then you will need to use the evidence you have to make an inference. An *inference* is a logical conclusion based on evidence. It can be about the passage itself or about the author's viewpoint.

EXERCISE

DIRECTIONS: First, read the following passage. Then, read the questions after the passage, and make inferences. Can you find the evidence for your inference in the reading passage? Check your answers using the key on page 458.

When an acid is dissolved in water, the acid molecule divides into two parts, a hydrogen ion and another ion. An ion is an atom or a group of atoms that has an electrical charge. The charge can be either positive or negative. If hydrochloric acid is mixed with water, for example, it divides into hydrogen ions and chlorine ions.

A strong acid ionizes to a great extent, but a weak acid does not ionize so much. The strength of an acid, therefore, depends on how much it ionizes, not on how many hydrogen ions are produced. It is interesting that nitric acid and sulfuric acid become greatly ionized whereas boric acid and carbonic acid do not.

1. What kind of acid is sulfuric acid?

2. What kind of acid is boric acid?

6   Identifying Exceptions

After reading a passage on the TOEFL, you will be asked to select from four possible answers the one that is NOT mentioned in the reading.

Use your scanning skills to locate related words and phrases in the passage and the answer choices.

EXERCISE

DIRECTIONS: First, read the following passage. Then, read the question after the reading passage. Last, scan the passage again for related words and phrases. Try to eliminate three of the choices. Check your answer using the key on pages 459–460.

All music consists of two elements—expression and design. Expression is inexact and subjective, and may be enjoyed in a personal or instinctive way. Design, on the other hand is exact and must be analyzed objectively in order to be understood and appreciated. The folk song, for example, has a definite musical design which relies on simple repetition with a definite beginning and ending. A folk song generally consists of one stanza of music repeated for each stanza of verse.

Because of their communal, and usually uncertain origin, folk songs are often popular verse set to music. They are not always recorded, and tend to be passed on in a kind of musical version of oral history. Each singer revises and perfects the song. In part as a consequence of this continuous revision process, most folk songs are almost perfect in their construction and design. A particular singer's interpretation of the folk song may provide an interesting expression, but the simple design that underlies the song itself is stable and enduring.

1. All of the following is true of a folk song EXCEPT
   (A) there is a clear start and finish
   (B) the origin is often not known
   (C) the design may change in the interpretation
   (D) simple repetition is characteristic of its design

7 Locating References

After reading a passage on the TOEFL, you will be asked to find the antecedent of a pronoun. An antecedent is a word or phrase to which a pronoun refers. Usually, you will be given a pronoun such as "it," "its," "them," or "their," and you will be asked to locate the reference word or phrase in the passage.

First, find the pronoun in the passage. Then read the sentence using the four answer choices in place of the pronoun. The meaning of the sentence in the context of the passage will not change when you substitute the correct antecedent.

EXERCISE

DIRECTIONS: First find the pronoun in the following passage. Next, start reading several sentences before the sentence in which the pronoun is found, and continue reading several sentences after it. Then, substitute the words or phrases in the answer choices. Which one does not change the meaning of the sentence? Check your answer using the key on page 460.

The National Road, also known as the Cumberland Road, was constructed in the early 1800s to provide transportation between the established commercial areas of the East and Northwest Territory. By 1818, the road had reached Wheeling, West Virginia, 130 miles from
Line its point of origin in Cumberland, Maryland. The cost was a monumental thirteen thousand
(5) dollars per mile.

Upon reaching the Ohio River, the National Road became one of the major trade routes to the western states and territories, providing Baltimore with a trade advantage over neighboring cities. In order to compete, New York state authorized the construction of the Erie Canal, and Philadelphia initiated a transportation plan to link it with Pittsburgh. Towns along the
(10) rivers, canals, and the new National Road became important trade centers.

1. The word "its" in line 4 refers to
   (A) the Northwest Territory
   (B) 1818
   (C) the road
   (D) Wheeling, West Virginia

8 Referring to the Passage

After reading the passage on the TOEFL, you will be asked to find certain information in the passage, and identify it by line number.

First, read the question. Then refer to the line numbers in the answer choices to scan for the information in the question.

EXERCISE

DIRECTIONS: First, read the following passage. Then, refer to the passage using the line numbers in the answer choices. Can you find the correct reference? Check your answer using the key on page 460.

In September of 1929, traders experienced a lack of confidence in the stock market's ability to continue its phenomenal rise. Prices fell. For many inexperienced investors, the drop produced a panic. They had all their money tied up in the market, and they were pressed to sell

Line before the prices fell even lower. Sell orders were coming in so fast that the ticker tape at the

(5) New York Stock Exchange could not accommodate all the transactions.

To try to reestablish confidence in the market, a powerful group of New York bankers agreed to pool their funds and purchase stock above current market values. Although the buy orders were minimal, they were counting on their reputations to restore confidence on the part of the smaller investors, thereby affecting the number of sell orders. On Thursday, October 24,

(10) Richard Whitney, the Vice President of the New York Stock Exchange and a broker for the J.P. Morgan Company, made the effort on their behalf. Initially, it appeared to have been successful, then, on the following Tuesday, the crash began again and accelerated. By 1932, stocks were worth only twenty percent of their value at the 1929 high. The results of the crash had extended into every aspect of the economy, causing a long and painful depression, referred to

(15) in American history as the Great Depression.

1. Where in the passage does the author refer to the reason for the stock market crash?

2. Where in the passage does the author suggest that there was a temporary recovery in the stock market?

CUMULATIVE REVIEW EXERCISE
FOR READING COMPREHENSION

DIRECTIONS: Read the following passage, using the skills you have learned. Preview, read for main ideas, and use contexts for vocabulary. To read faster, read phrases instead of words. Then, answer the questions that follow the passage. Scan for details and evidence. Make inferences. Check your answers using the key on page 461.

Although each baby has an individual schedule of development, general patterns of growth have been observed. Three periods of development have been identified, including early infancy, which extends from the first to the sixth month; middle infancy, from the sixth to the

Line ninth month; and late infancy, from the ninth to the fifteenth month. Whereas the newborn is

(5) concerned with his or her inner world and responds primarily to hunger and pain, in early infancy the baby is already aware of the surrounding world. During the second month, many infants are awake more and can raise their heads to look at things. They also begin to smile at people. By four months, the baby is searching for things but not yet grasping them with its hands. It is also beginning to be wary of strangers and may scream when a visiting relative

(10) tries to pick it up. By five months, the baby is grabbing objects and putting them into its mouth. Some babies are trying to feed themselves with their hands.

In middle infancy, the baby concentrates on practicing a great many speech sounds. It loves to imitate actions and examine interesting objects. At about seven months, it begins to crawl, a skill that it masters at the end of middle infancy.

(15)   In late infancy, the baby takes an interest in games, songs, and even books. Progress toward walking moves through standing, balancing, bouncing in place, and walking with others. As soon as the baby walks well alone, it has passed from infancy into the active toddler stage.

1. What does this passage mainly discuss?
   (A) Growth in early infancy
   (B) The active toddler stage
   (C) How a baby learns to walk
   (D) The developmental stages of infancy

2. Where in the passage does the author mention the characteristics of newborns?
   (A) Lines 4–5
   (B) Lines 5–7
   (C) Lines 8–10
   (D) Lines 10–11

3. The word "primarily" in line 5 could best be repaced by
   (A) often
   (B) naturally
   (C) for the most part
   (D) in a loud way

4. When does a baby become frightened of unfamiliar people?
   (A) In early infancy
   (B) In middle infancy
   (C) In late infancy
   (D) In the toddler stage

5. The word "grasping" in line 8 is the closest in meaning to
   (A) watching
   (B) liking
   (C) holding
   (D) fearing

6. The word "it" in line 12 refers to
   (A) the baby
   (B) speech
   (C) skill
   (D) to imitate

7. According to this reading passage, what would a six-month-old baby like to do?
   (A) Smile at people
   (B) Crawl on the floor
   (C) Imitate actions
   (D) Play simple games

8. According to the passage, what can be inferred about babies that are standing and balancing?
   (A) They can walk.
   (B) They are about seven months old.
   (C) They are in the late infancy stage.
   (D) They are developing on schedule.

9. A baby in late infancy would be able to do all of the following EXCEPT
   (A) make many speech sounds
   (B) walk well alone
   (C) show interest in games
   (D) imitate actions

10. The next paragraph will probably discuss
    (A) speech
    (B) school
    (C) toddlers
    (D) activities

TOEFL
MODEL TESTS

MODEL TEST 1—ANSWER SHEET

Section 1

1. Ⓐ Ⓑ Ⓒ Ⓓ
2. Ⓐ Ⓑ Ⓒ Ⓓ
3. Ⓐ Ⓑ Ⓒ Ⓓ
4. Ⓐ Ⓑ Ⓒ Ⓓ
5. Ⓐ Ⓑ Ⓒ Ⓓ
6. Ⓐ Ⓑ Ⓒ Ⓓ
7. Ⓐ Ⓑ Ⓒ Ⓓ
8. Ⓐ Ⓑ Ⓒ Ⓓ
9. Ⓐ Ⓑ Ⓒ Ⓓ
10. Ⓐ Ⓑ Ⓒ Ⓓ
11. Ⓐ Ⓑ Ⓒ Ⓓ
12. Ⓐ Ⓑ Ⓒ Ⓓ
13. Ⓐ Ⓑ Ⓒ Ⓓ
14. Ⓐ Ⓑ Ⓒ Ⓓ
15. Ⓐ Ⓑ Ⓒ Ⓓ
16. Ⓐ Ⓑ Ⓒ Ⓓ
17. Ⓐ Ⓑ Ⓒ Ⓓ
18. Ⓐ Ⓑ Ⓒ Ⓓ
19. Ⓐ Ⓑ Ⓒ Ⓓ
20. Ⓐ Ⓑ Ⓒ Ⓓ
21. Ⓐ Ⓑ Ⓒ Ⓓ
22. Ⓐ Ⓑ Ⓒ Ⓓ
23. Ⓐ Ⓑ Ⓒ Ⓓ
24. Ⓐ Ⓑ Ⓒ Ⓓ
25. Ⓐ Ⓑ Ⓒ Ⓓ
26. Ⓐ Ⓑ Ⓒ Ⓓ
27. Ⓐ Ⓑ Ⓒ Ⓓ
28. Ⓐ Ⓑ Ⓒ Ⓓ
29. Ⓐ Ⓑ Ⓒ Ⓓ
30. Ⓐ Ⓑ Ⓒ Ⓓ
31. Ⓐ Ⓑ Ⓒ Ⓓ
32. Ⓐ Ⓑ Ⓒ Ⓓ
33. Ⓐ Ⓑ Ⓒ Ⓓ
34. Ⓐ Ⓑ Ⓒ Ⓓ
35. Ⓐ Ⓑ Ⓒ Ⓓ
36. Ⓐ Ⓑ Ⓒ Ⓓ
37. Ⓐ Ⓑ Ⓒ Ⓓ
38. Ⓐ Ⓑ Ⓒ Ⓓ
39. Ⓐ Ⓑ Ⓒ Ⓓ
40. Ⓐ Ⓑ Ⓒ Ⓓ
41. Ⓐ Ⓑ Ⓒ Ⓓ
42. Ⓐ Ⓑ Ⓒ Ⓓ
43. Ⓐ Ⓑ Ⓒ Ⓓ
44. Ⓐ Ⓑ Ⓒ Ⓓ
45. Ⓐ Ⓑ Ⓒ Ⓓ
46. Ⓐ Ⓑ Ⓒ Ⓓ
47. Ⓐ Ⓑ Ⓒ Ⓓ
48. Ⓐ Ⓑ Ⓒ Ⓓ
49. Ⓐ Ⓑ Ⓒ Ⓓ
50. Ⓐ Ⓑ Ⓒ Ⓓ

Section 2

1. Ⓐ Ⓑ Ⓒ Ⓓ
2. Ⓐ Ⓑ Ⓒ Ⓓ
3. Ⓐ Ⓑ Ⓒ Ⓓ
4. Ⓐ Ⓑ Ⓒ Ⓓ
5. Ⓐ Ⓑ Ⓒ Ⓓ
6. Ⓐ Ⓑ Ⓒ Ⓓ
7. Ⓐ Ⓑ Ⓒ Ⓓ
8. Ⓐ Ⓑ Ⓒ Ⓓ
9. Ⓐ Ⓑ Ⓒ Ⓓ
10. Ⓐ Ⓑ Ⓒ Ⓓ
11. Ⓐ Ⓑ Ⓒ Ⓓ
12. Ⓐ Ⓑ Ⓒ Ⓓ
13. Ⓐ Ⓑ Ⓒ Ⓓ
14. Ⓐ Ⓑ Ⓒ Ⓓ
15. Ⓐ Ⓑ Ⓒ Ⓓ
16. Ⓐ Ⓑ Ⓒ Ⓓ
17. Ⓐ Ⓑ Ⓒ Ⓓ
18. Ⓐ Ⓑ Ⓒ Ⓓ
19. Ⓐ Ⓑ Ⓒ Ⓓ
20. Ⓐ Ⓑ Ⓒ Ⓓ
21. Ⓐ Ⓑ Ⓒ Ⓓ
22. Ⓐ Ⓑ Ⓒ Ⓓ
23. Ⓐ Ⓑ Ⓒ Ⓓ
24. Ⓐ Ⓑ Ⓒ Ⓓ
25. Ⓐ Ⓑ Ⓒ Ⓓ
26. Ⓐ Ⓑ Ⓒ Ⓓ
27. Ⓐ Ⓑ Ⓒ Ⓓ
28. Ⓐ Ⓑ Ⓒ Ⓓ
29. Ⓐ Ⓑ Ⓒ Ⓓ
30. Ⓐ Ⓑ Ⓒ Ⓓ
31. Ⓐ Ⓑ Ⓒ Ⓓ
32. Ⓐ Ⓑ Ⓒ Ⓓ
33. Ⓐ Ⓑ Ⓒ Ⓓ
34. Ⓐ Ⓑ Ⓒ Ⓓ
35. Ⓐ Ⓑ Ⓒ Ⓓ
36. Ⓐ Ⓑ Ⓒ Ⓓ
37. Ⓐ Ⓑ Ⓒ Ⓓ
38. Ⓐ Ⓑ Ⓒ Ⓓ
39. Ⓐ Ⓑ Ⓒ Ⓓ
40. Ⓐ Ⓑ Ⓒ Ⓓ

Section 3

1. Ⓐ Ⓑ Ⓒ Ⓓ
2. Ⓐ Ⓑ Ⓒ Ⓓ
3. Ⓐ Ⓑ Ⓒ Ⓓ
4. Ⓐ Ⓑ Ⓒ Ⓓ
5. Ⓐ Ⓑ Ⓒ Ⓓ
6. Ⓐ Ⓑ Ⓒ Ⓓ
7. Ⓐ Ⓑ Ⓒ Ⓓ
8. Ⓐ Ⓑ Ⓒ Ⓓ
9. Ⓐ Ⓑ Ⓒ Ⓓ
10. Ⓐ Ⓑ Ⓒ Ⓓ
11. Ⓐ Ⓑ Ⓒ Ⓓ
12. Ⓐ Ⓑ Ⓒ Ⓓ
13. Ⓐ Ⓑ Ⓒ Ⓓ
14. Ⓐ Ⓑ Ⓒ Ⓓ
15. Ⓐ Ⓑ Ⓒ Ⓓ
16. Ⓐ Ⓑ Ⓒ Ⓓ
17. Ⓐ Ⓑ Ⓒ Ⓓ
18. Ⓐ Ⓑ Ⓒ Ⓓ
19. Ⓐ Ⓑ Ⓒ Ⓓ
20. Ⓐ Ⓑ Ⓒ Ⓓ
21. Ⓐ Ⓑ Ⓒ Ⓓ
22. Ⓐ Ⓑ Ⓒ Ⓓ
23. Ⓐ Ⓑ Ⓒ Ⓓ
24. Ⓐ Ⓑ Ⓒ Ⓓ
25. Ⓐ Ⓑ Ⓒ Ⓓ
26. Ⓐ Ⓑ Ⓒ Ⓓ
27. Ⓐ Ⓑ Ⓒ Ⓓ
28. Ⓐ Ⓑ Ⓒ Ⓓ
29. Ⓐ Ⓑ Ⓒ Ⓓ
30. Ⓐ Ⓑ Ⓒ Ⓓ
31. Ⓐ Ⓑ Ⓒ Ⓓ
32. Ⓐ Ⓑ Ⓒ Ⓓ
33. Ⓐ Ⓑ Ⓒ Ⓓ
34. Ⓐ Ⓑ Ⓒ Ⓓ
35. Ⓐ Ⓑ Ⓒ Ⓓ
36. Ⓐ Ⓑ Ⓒ Ⓓ
37. Ⓐ Ⓑ Ⓒ Ⓓ
38. Ⓐ Ⓑ Ⓒ Ⓓ
39. Ⓐ Ⓑ Ⓒ Ⓓ
40. Ⓐ Ⓑ Ⓒ Ⓓ
41. Ⓐ Ⓑ Ⓒ Ⓓ
42. Ⓐ Ⓑ Ⓒ Ⓓ
43. Ⓐ Ⓑ Ⓒ Ⓓ
44. Ⓐ Ⓑ Ⓒ Ⓓ
45. Ⓐ Ⓑ Ⓒ Ⓓ
46. Ⓐ Ⓑ Ⓒ Ⓓ
47. Ⓐ Ⓑ Ⓒ Ⓓ
48. Ⓐ Ⓑ Ⓒ Ⓓ
49. Ⓐ Ⓑ Ⓒ Ⓓ
50. Ⓐ Ⓑ Ⓒ Ⓓ

1 1 1 1 1 1 1 1 1 1 1 1

Model Test 1
Short Form

Section 1:
Listening Comprehension

50 QUESTIONS 40 MINUTES

In this section of the test, you will have an opportunity to demonstrate your ability to understand conversations and talks in English. There are three parts to this section with special directions for each part. Answer all the questions on the basis of what is stated or implied by the speakers in this test. When you take the actual TOEFL test, you will not be allowed to take notes or write in your test book. Try to work on this Model Test in the same way.

Part A

Directions: In Part A, you will hear short conversations between two people. After each conversation, you will hear a question about the conversation. The conversations and questions will not be repeated. After you hear a question, read the four possible answers in your book and choose the best answer. Then, on your answer sheet, find the number of the question and fill in the space that corresponds to the letter of the answer you have chosen.

1. (A) Wait at a drugstore.
   (B) Go to a doctor's office.
   (C) Find a hospital.
   (D) Look for some aspirin.

2. (A) He doesn't mind the traffic.
   (B) He takes the bus to work.
   (C) He has to stand on the bus if he takes it to work.
   (D) He wants to ride to work with the woman.

3. (A) She is flattered.
   (B) She is not interested.
   (C) She is not busy.
   (D) She will support the man's nomination.

4. (A) The woman should not consider her advisor in the decision.
   (B) The woman should not take Dr. Sullivan's section.
   (C) The woman's advisor will not be offended.
   (D) The woman should not take a physics course.

5. (A) It was too far from work.
   (B) It was very old.
   (C) The school was far away.
   (D) The area was not nice.

6. (A) She is not interested in the man.
   (B) She does not like lectures.
   (C) She would go out with the man on another occasion.
   (D) She would rather stay at home.

7. (A) The bike is in good condition.
   (B) The man needs to replace the bike.
   (C) The bike is missing.
   (D) It is a new bike.

8. (A) The books were more expensive than two hundred dollars.
   (B) She would like to buy the books.
   (C) She cannot afford the price of the books.
   (D) She has not purchased her books yet.

GO ON TO THE NEXT PAGE

1 1 1 1 1 1 1 1 1 1 1

9. (A) She wants to fix supper.
   (B) She wants to stay at home.
   (C) She is not hungry.
   (D) She wants to go out.

10. (A) He is at his office.
    (B) He is at lunch.
    (C) He is at the travel agency.
    (D) He is at the bakery.

11. (A) See a lawyer.
    (B) Come to an agreement.
    (C) Sue the company.
    (D) Go to court.

12. (A) Something cold.
    (B) Coffee.
    (C) Tea.
    (D) Both coffee and tea.

13. (A) Ask directions.
    (B) Walk to the shopping center.
    (C) Take a taxi.
    (D) Wait for the bus.

14. (A) He does not plan to study.
    (B) He has a very busy schedule.
    (C) He is lost.
    (D) He has not registered yet.

15. (A) He does not want to listen to the radio.
    (B) He has changed his opinion about turn-
        ing on the radio.
    (C) The radio will not bother him.
    (D) The radio is not working very well.

16. (A) Stop worrying.
    (B) Go out more.
    (C) Talk to a friend.
    (D) Get counseling.

17. (A) A telephone call.
    (B) A visit from friends.
    (C) A mistake on a bill.
    (D) A letter they have written.

18. (A) He prefers to talk another time.
    (B) He wants the woman to go away.
    (C) He would like the woman to continue.
    (D) He doesn't know what to think.

19. (A) Accept the woman's apology.
    (B) Allow the woman to go ahead of him.
    (C) Apologize to the woman.
    (D) Go to the front of the line.

20. (A) The neighbors have parties often.
    (B) She does not like her neighbors.
    (C) The neighbors' party is disturbing her.
    (D) She will not be invited to the neighbors'
        party.

21. (A) Dr. Franklin is not very understanding.
    (B) The extension was a very bad idea.
    (C) She is sorry that the man was denied his
        request.
    (D) The professor's answer is not surprising.

22. (A) The computer needs to be replaced.
    (B) The man should check the plug.
    (C) The man should use the printer at work.
    (D) The man doesn't know how to use the
        printer.

23. (A) She was not capable of making such a
        long trip.
    (B) She did not know about the reception.
    (C) She was sorry that she could not attend.
    (D) She was not able to go because she was
        tired.

24. (A) They do not have a telephone.
    (B) They are late.
    (C) They have been left.
    (D) They got lost.

25. (A) Pay the rent for half a month.
    (B) Help the man move.
    (C) Stay where she is living until the 15th.
    (D) Move out of the apartment.

GO ON TO THE NEXT PAGE ➤

1 1 1 1 1 1 1 1 1 1 1 1

26. (A) She had already taken the test.
    (B) She did not want to take classes.
    (C) She had not taken the placement test.
    (D) She would take the math classes later.

27. (A) The man bought his car at Discount Automotive.
    (B) The woman has probably made a mistake.
    (C) The cars at Discount Automotive are not very reliable.
    (D) The prices are very competitive.

28. (A) He may not be able to come.
    (B) He would rather go to Miami.
    (C) He is not an honest person.
    (D) He doesn't know that the woman is having a birthday.

29. (A) The plan is to remain in the class.
    (B) It is not comfortable in the classroom.
    (C) He has been absent because he was sick.
    (D) The weather has been very bad.

30. (A) She thinks the pizza place is closed.
    (B) She does not like the man.
    (C) She is very busy now.
    (D) She is not hungry for a pizza.

Part B

Directions: In this part of the test, you will hear longer conversations. After each conversation, you will hear several questions. The conversations and questions will not be repeated.

After you hear a question, read the four possible answers in your book and choose the best answer. Then, on your answer sheet, find the number of the question and fill in the space that corresponds to the letter of the answer you have chosen.

Remember, you are **not** allowed to take notes or write on your test pages.

31. (A) The speakers wanted coffee.
    (B) The man lost money.
    (C) The Student Center was crowded.
    (D) The woman needed to make a phone call.

32. (A) The time.
    (B) The money.
    (C) The coffee.
    (D) The test.

33. (A) They decided that they did not want any coffee.
    (B) They thought that the Student Center would be closed.
    (C) They thought that the Student Center would be crowded.
    (D) The man lost his money in the vending machine.

34. (A) To study for a test.
    (B) To use the telephone.
    (C) To complain about the vending machine.
    (D) To get a cup of coffee from the vending machine.

35. (A) He was late arriving at registration.
    (B) He needs an advisor's signature on a course request form.
    (C) He is not doing well in the class because it is so large.
    (D) He must have the permission of the instructor to enroll in a class.

GO ON TO THE NEXT PAGE

1 1 1 1 1 1 1 1 1 1 1

36. (A) Help him with the class.
    (B) Explain some technical vocabulary.
    (C) Give him special permission to take the class.
    (D) Take a form to the registration area.

37. (A) He has planned to graduate in the fall.
    (B) He has to take Professor Day's class in order to graduate.
    (C) He needs the professor to sign his application for graduation.
    (D) He does not have enough credits for graduation.

38. (A) Enroll Mike in the class next year.
    (B) Allow Mike to take the class this term.
    (C) Give Mike permission to graduate without the class.
    (D) Register Mike for another class.

Part C

Directions: In this part of the test, you will hear several short talks. After each talk, you will hear some questions. The talks and questions will not be repeated.

After you hear a question, read the four possible answers in your book and choose the best answer. Then, on your answer sheet, find the number of the question and fill in the space that corresponds to the letter of the answer you have chosen.

39. (A) A slow, soft song.
    (B) Music in restaurants.
    (C) Background music.
    (D) A pleasant addition to the environment.

40. (A) Thirteen percent.
    (B) Five to ten percent.
    (C) One hundred percent.
    (D) Thirty percent.

41. (A) Background music that is low in stimulus value.
    (B) Upbeat music that stimulates sales.
    (C) Music engineered to reduce stress.
    (D) Music that starts slow and gets faster at times of the day when people get tired.

42. (A) It can cause shoppers to go through the line faster.
    (B) It can cause shoppers to buy thirty percent more or less.
    (C) It can cause shoppers to walk slower and buy more.
    (D) It does not influence sales.

43. (A) The "Sun-Up Semester" program.
    (B) The Community College campus.
    (C) Video telecourses.
    (D) Technology for distance learning.

44. (A) To clarify how to register.
    (B) To advertise the college.
    (C) To provide a listing of courses.
    (D) To give students an alternative to video tapes.

45. (A) They should come to campus.
    (B) They can call the Community College.
    (C) They must contact the instructor.
    (D) They can use computers.

46. (A) By using e-mail.
    (B) By calling KCC-TV.
    (C) By writing letters.
    (D) By making video tapes.

GO ON TO THE NEXT PAGE

1 1 1 1 1 1 1 1 1 1 1

47. (A) The relationship between language and
culture.
(B) The culture of Hopi society.
(C) American Indian cultures.
(D) The life of Benjamin Lee Whorf.

48. (A) European languages.
(B) South American languages.
(C) American Indian languages.
(D) Computer languages.

49. (A) All languages are related.
(B) All American Indian languages are
related.
(C) Language influences the manner in
which an individual understands
reality.
(D) Language and culture are not related.

50. (A) The Sapir Hypothesis.
(B) The Sapir-Whorf Hypothesis.
(C) The Sapir-Whorf-Boas Hypothesis.
(D) The American Indian Model of the
Universe.

**THIS IS THE END OF THE LISTENING COMPREHENSION SECTION
OF TOEFL MODEL TEST 1.**

DO NOT READ OR WORK ON ANY OTHER SECTION OF THE TEST.

2 2 2 2 2 2 2 2 2 2 2

Section 2:
Structure and Written Expression

40 QUESTIONS 25 MINUTES

This section is designed to measure your ability to recognize language that is appropriate for standard written English. There are two types of questions in this section, with special directions for each type.

Structure

Directions: Questions 1–15 are incomplete sentences. Beneath each sentence you will see four words or phrases, marked (A), (B), (C), and (D). Choose the **one** word or phrase that best completes the sentence. Then, on your answer sheet, find the number of the question and fill in the space that corresponds to the letter of the answer you have chosen. Fill in the space so that the letter inside the oval cannot be seen.

1. Political demonstrations on American campuses have abated -------- .

   (A) after 1970
   (B) in 1970
   (C) for 1970
   (D) since 1970

2. Ancient civilizations such as those of the Phoenicians and the Mesopotamians -------- goods rather than use money.

   (A) use to trade
   (B) is used to trade
   (C) used to trade
   (D) was used to trade

3. Justice Sandra Day O'Connor was ------- to serve on the U.S. Supreme Court.

   (A) the woman who first
   (B) the first woman
   (C) who the first woman
   (D) the first and a woman

4. North Carolina is well known not only for the Great Smoky Mountains National Park -------- for the Cherokee Indian settlements.

   (A) also
   (B) and
   (C) but also
   (D) because of

5. General Grant had General Lee -------- him at Appomattox to sign the official surrender of the Confederate forces.

   (A) to meet
   (B) met
   (C) meet
   (D) meeting

6. If a ruby is heated it -------- temporarily lose its color.

   (A) would
   (B) will
   (C) does
   (D) has

7. -------- small specimen of the embryonic fluid is removed from a fetus, it will be possible to determine whether the baby will be born with birth defects.

   (A) A
   (B) That a
   (C) If a
   (D) When it is a

GO ON TO THE NEXT PAGE

2 2 2 2 2 2 2 2 2 2 2

8. All of the people at the AAME conference are -------- .

   (A) mathematic teachers
   (B) mathematics teachers
   (C) mathematics teacher
   (D) mathematic's teachers

9. To generate income, magazine publishers must decide whether to increase the subscription price or -------- .

   (A) to sell advertising
   (B) if they should sell advertising
   (C) selling advertising
   (D) sold advertising

10. If it -------- more humid in the desert of the Southwest, the hot temperatures would be unbearable.

    (A) be
    (B) is
    (C) was
    (D) were

11. -------- Java Man, who lived before the first Ice Age, is the first manlike animal.

    (A) It is generally believed that
    (B) Generally believed it is
    (C) Believed generally is
    (D) That is generally believed

12. For the investor who -------- money, silver or bonds are good options.

    (A) has so little a
    (B) has very little
    (C) has so few
    (D) has very few

13. -------- both men and women have often achieved their career ambitions by midlife, many people are afflicted by at least a temporary period of dissatisfaction and depression.

    (A) Because
    (B) So
    (C) A
    (D) Who

14. Of all the cereals, rice is the one -------- food for more people than any of the other grain crops.

    (A) it provides
    (B) that providing
    (C) provides
    (D) that provides

15. Travelers -------- their reservations well in advance if they want to fly during the Christmas holidays.

    (A) had better to get
    (B) had to get better
    (C) had better get
    (D) had better got

Written Expression

Directions: In questions 16–40, each sentence has four underlined words or phrases. The four underlined parts of the sentence are marked (A), (B), (C), and (D). Identify the **one** underlined word or phrase that must be changed in order for the sentence to be correct. Then, on your answer sheet, find the number of the question and fill in the space that corresponds to the letter of the answer you have chosen.

16. The duties of the secretary are to take the minutes, mailing the correspondence, and calling the
                              (A) (B)   (C)
    members before meetings.
                  (D)

GO ON TO THE NEXT PAGE ➤

2 2 2 2 2 2 2 2 2 2 2

17. If biennials were planted this year, they will be likely to bloom next year.
                                            (A)   (B)   (C)   (D)

18. The value of the dollar declines as the rate of inflation raises.
                   (A)   (B) (C)   (D)

19. Even though a member has drank too much the night before, the counselors at Alcoholics
                            (A)   (B)   (C)
Anonymous will try to convince him or her to sober up and stop drinking again.
                      (D)

20. Anthropologists assert that many of the early American Plains Indians did not engage in planting

crops but to hunt, living primarily on buffalo meat.
       (A) (B)   (C)   (D)

21. The neutron bomb provides the capable of a limited nuclear war in which buildings
                                  (A)   (B)   (C)
would be preserved, but people would be destroyed.
        (D)

22. The differential attractions of the sun and the moon have a direct effect in the rising and falling of the
                                                         (A)   (B)   (C)   (D)
tides.

23. With special enzymes that are call restriction enzymes, it is possible to split off segments of DNA
                                (A)   (B)
from the donor organism.
 (C)   (D)

24. Before TV, the common man seldom never had the opportunity to see and hear his leaders express
                              (A)   (B)   (C)
their views.
 (D)

25. If it receives enough rain at the proper time, hay will grow quickly, as grass.
 (A)   (B)   (C)   (D)

26. *Psychology Today* is interesting, informative, and it is easy to read.
                      (A)   (B)   (C)   (D)

27. Before she died, Andrew Jackson's daughter, who lives in the family mansion, used to take tourists
 (A)   (B) (C)   (D)
through her home.

GO ON TO THE NEXT PAGE

2   2   2   2   2   2   2   2   2   2   2

28. It is essential that the temperature is not elevated to a point where the substance formed
                                        (A)   (B)
    may become unstable and decompose into its constituent elements.
       (C)   (D)

29. Two of the players from the Yankees has been chosen to participate in the All Star game.
          (A)   (B)   (C) (D)

30. John Philip Sousa, who many people consider the greatest composer of marches, wrote his music
                       (A) (B)   (C)
    during the era known as the Gay 90s.
                    (D)

31. Although it can be derived from oil, coal, and tar, kerosene is usually produced by refine it from
              (A)   (B)   (C)   (D)
    petroleum.

32. Aeronomy is the study of the earth's upper atmosphere, which includes their composition,
             (A) (B)   (C)   (D)
    temperature, density, and chemical reactions.

33. The new model costs twice more than last year's model.
                   (A)   (B)   (C) (D)

34. The purpose of the United Nations, broad speaking, is to maintain peace and security and
               (A)   (B)   (C)
    to encourage respect for human rights.
       (D)

35. Aging in most animals can be readily modified when they will limit caloric intake.
    (A)   (B)   (C)   (D)

36. Even though Miss Alabama lost the beauty contest, she was still more prettier than the other girls
    (A)   (B)   (C)   (D)
    in the Miss America pageant.

37. Although Congressional representatives and senators may serve an unlimited number of term, the
                                                                                          (A)
    president is limited to two, for a total of eight years.
             (B)   (C)   (D)

GO ON TO THE NEXT PAGE

2 2   2   2 2 **2**

38. Although we are concerned about the problem of energy sources, we must not fail recognizing the need
                        (A)   (B)   (C)
    for environmental protection.
    (D)

39. Because of the movement of a glacier, the form of the Great Lakes was very slow.
       (A)   (B)   (C)   (D)

40. In 1776 to 1800, the population of the U.S. continued to rise, reaching five million citizens by the
     (A)   (B)   (C)   (D)
    turn of the century.

        THIS IS THE END OF THE STRUCTURE AND WRITTEN EXPRESSION SECTION OF TOEFL MODEL TEST 1.

        IF YOU FINISH BEFORE 25 MINUTES HAS ENDED, CHECK YOUR WORK ON SECTION 2 ONLY.

        DO NOT READ OR WORK ON ANY OTHER SECTION OF THE TEST.

STOP   STOP   STOP   **STOP**   STOP   STOP   STOP

3 3 3 3 3 3 3 3 3 3 | 3

Section 3:
Reading Comprehension

50 Questions 55 Minutes

Directions: In this section you will read several passages. Each one is followed by a number of questions about it. For questions 1–50, you are to choose the **one** best answer, (A), (B), (C), or (D), to each question. Then, on your answer sheet, find the number of the question and fill in the space that corresponds to the letter of the answer you have chosen.

Answer all questions about the information in a passage on the basis of what is **stated** or **implied** in that passage.

Questions 1–10

It has long been known that when exposed to light under suitable conditions of temperature and moisture, the green parts of plants use carbon dioxide from the atmosphere and release oxygen to it. These exchanges are the opposite of those that occur in respiration. The
Line process is called photosynthesis. In photosynthesis, carbohydrates are synthesized from car-
(5) bon dioxide and water by the chloroplasts of plant cells in the presence of light. In most plants, the water used in photosynthesis is absorbed from the soil by the roots and translocated through the xylem of the root and stem to the leaves. Except for the usually small percentage used in respiration, the oxygen released in the process diffuses out of the leaf into the atmosphere through the stomates. Oxygen is the product of the reaction. For each molecule of car-
(10) bon dioxide used, one molecule of oxygen is released. A summary chemical equation for photosynthesis is:

$$6CO_2 + 6H_2O \rightarrow C_6H_{12}O_6 + 6O_2$$

As a result of this process, radiant energy from the sun is stored as chemical energy. In turn, the chemical energy is used to decompose carbon dioxide and water. The products of
(15) their decomposition are recombined into a new compound, which is successively built up into more and more complex substances. After many intermediate steps, sugar is produced. At the same time, a balance of gases is preserved in the atmosphere.

1. Which title best expresses the ideas in this passage?

   (A) A Chemical Equation
   (B) The Process of Photosynthesis
   (C) The Parts of Vascular Plants
   (D) The Production of Sugar

2. In photosynthesis, water

   (A) must be present
   (B) is produced in carbohydrates
   (C) is stored as chemical energy
   (D) interrupts the chemical reaction

3. Which process is the opposite of photosynthesis?

   (A) Decomposition
   (B) Synthesization
   (C) Diffusion
   (D) Respiration

GO ON TO THE NEXT PAGE

3 3 3 3 3 3 3 3 3 3 3

4. The combination of carbon dioxide and water to form sugar results in an excess of

(A) water
(B) oxygen
(C) carbon
(D) chlorophyll

5. The word "stored" in line 13 is closest in meaning to

(A) retained
(B) converted
(C) discovered
(D) specified

6. In photosynthesis, energy from the sun is

(A) changed to chemical energy
(B) conducted from the xylem to the leaves of green plants
(C) not necessary to the process
(D) released one to one for each molecule of carbon dioxide used

7. The word "their" in line 15 refers to

(A) radiant energy and chemical energy
(B) carbon dioxide and water
(C) products
(D) complex substances

8. The word "successively" in line 15 is closest in meaning to

(A) with effort
(B) in a sequence
(C) slowly
(D) carefully

9. Besides the manufacture of food for plants, what is another benefit of photosynthesis?

(A) It produces solar energy.
(B) It diffuses additional carbon dioxide into the air.
(C) It maintains a balance of gases in the atmosphere.
(D) It removes harmful gases from the air.

10. Which of the following is NOT true of the oxygen used in photosynthesis?

(A) Oxygen is absorbed by the roots.
(B) Oxygen is the product of photosynthesis.
(C) Oxygen is used in respiration.
(D) Oxygen is released into the atmosphere through the leaves.

Questions 11–20

   Alfred Bernhard Nobel, a Swedish inventor and philanthropist, bequeathed most of his vast fortune in trust as a fund from which annual prizes could be awarded to individuals and organizations who had achieved the greatest benefit to humanity in a particular year. Origi-
Line nally, there were six classifications for outstanding contributions designated in Nobel's will
 (5) including chemistry, physics, physiology or medicine, literature, and international peace.
   The prizes are administered by the Nobel Foundation in Stockholm. In 1969, a prize for economics endowed by the Central Bank of Sweden was added. Candidates for the prizes must be nominated in writing by a qualified authority in the field of competition. Recipients in physics, chemistry, and economics are selected by the Royal Swedish Academy of Sciences; in
(10) physiology or medicine by the Caroline Institute; in literature by the Swedish Academy; and in peace by the Norwegian Nobel Committee appointed by Norway's parliament. The prizes are usually presented in Stockholm on December 10, with the King of Sweden officiating, an appropriate tribute to Alfred Nobel on the anniversary of his death. Each one includes a gold medal, a diploma, and a cash award of about one million dollars.

GO ON TO THE NEXT PAGE

3 3 3 3 3 3 3 3 3 3 3

11. What does this passage mainly discuss?

(A) Alfred Bernhard Nobel
(B) The Nobel prizes
(C) Great contributions to mankind
(D) Swedish philanthropy

12. Why were the prizes named for Alfred Bernhard Nobel?

(A) He left money in his will to establish a fund for the prizes.
(B) He won the first Nobel prize for his work in philanthropy.
(C) He is now living in Sweden.
(D) He serves as chairman of the committee to choose the recipients of the prizes.

13. How often are the Nobel prizes awarded?

(A) Five times a year
(B) Once a year
(C) Twice a year
(D) Once every two years

14. The word "outstanding" in line 4 could best be replaced by

(A) recent
(B) unusual
(C) established
(D) exceptional

15. The word "will" in line 4 refers to
(A) Nobel's wishes
(B) a legal document
(C) a future intention
(D) a free choice

16. A Nobel prize would NOT be given to

(A) an author who wrote a novel
(B) a doctor who discovered a vaccine
(C) a composer who wrote a symphony
(D) a diplomat who negotiated a peace settlement

17. The word "one" in line 13 refers to

(A) tribute
(B) anniversary
(C) prize
(D) candidate

18. Which individual or organization serves as administrator for the trust?

(A) The King of Sweden
(B) The Nobel Foundation
(C) The Central Bank of Sweden
(D) Swedish and Norwegian academies and institutes

19. The word "appropriate" in line 13 is closest in meaning to

(A) prestigious
(B) customary
(C) suitable
(D) transitory

20. Why are the awards presented on December 10?

(A) It is a tribute to the King of Sweden.
(B) Alfred Bernhard Nobel died on that day.
(C) That date was established in Alfred Nobel's will.
(D) The Central Bank of Sweden administers the trust.

GO ON TO THE NEXT PAGE

3 3 3 3 3 3 3 3 3 3 3

Questions 21–30

Although stage plays have been set to music since the era of the ancient Greeks, when the dramas of Sophocles and Aeschylus were accompanied by lyres and flutes, the usually accepted date for the beginning of opera as we know it is 1600. As part of the celebration of
Line the marriage of King Henry IV of France to the Italian aristocrat Maria de Medici, the Flo-
(5) rentine composer Jacopo Perí produced his famous *Euridice,* generally considered to be the first opera. Following his example, a group of Italian musicians, poets, and noblemen called the Camerata began to revive the style of musical story that had been used in Greek tragedy. The Camerata took most of the plots for their operas from Greek and Roman history and mythology, writing librettos or dramas for music. They called their compositions *opera in*
(10) *musica* or musical works. It is from this phrase that the word "opera" is borrowed.

For several years, the center of opera was Florence, but gradually, during the baroque period, it spread throughout Italy. By the late 1600s, operas were being written and performed in Europe, especially in England, France, and Germany. But, for many years, the Italian opera was considered the ideal, and many non-Italian composers continued to use Italian librettos.
(15) The European form de-emphasized the dramatic aspect. New orchestral effects and even ballet were introduced under the guise of opera. Composers gave in to the demands of singers, writing many operas that were nothing more than a succession of brilliant tricks for the voice. Complicated arias, recitatives, and duets evolved. The aria, which is a long solo, may be compared to a song in which the characters express their thoughts and feelings. The recitative,
(20) which is also a solo, is a recitation set to music whose purpose is to continue the story line. The duet is a musical piece written for two voices which may serve the function of either an aria or a recitative.

21. This passage is a summary of

   (A) opera in Italy
   (B) the Camerata
   (C) the development of opera
   (D) *Euridice*

22. According to this passage, when did modern opera begin?

   (A) In the time of the ancient Greeks
   (B) In the fifteenth century
   (C) At the beginning of the sixteenth century
   (D) At the beginning of the seventeenth century

23. The word "it" in line 3 refers to

   (A) opera
   (B) date
   (C) era
   (D) music

24. According to the author, what did Jacopo Perí write?

   (A) Greek tragedy
   (B) The first opera
   (C) The opera *Maria de Medici*
   (D) The opera *The Camerata*

25. The author suggests that *Euridice* was produced

   (A) in France
   (B) originally by Sophocles and Aeschylus
   (C) without much success
   (D) for the wedding of King Henry IV

GO ON TO THE NEXT PAGE ➤

3 3 3 3 3 3 3 3 3 3 3

26. What was the Camerata?

   (A) A group of Greek musicians
   (B) Musicians who developed a new musi-
       cal drama based upon Greek drama
   (C) A style of music not known in Italy
   (D) The name given to the court of King
       Henry IV

27. The word "revive" in line 7 could best be
    replaced by

   (A) appreciate
   (B) resume
   (C) modify
   (D) investigate

28. The word "plots" in line 8 is closest in
    meaning to

   (A) locations
   (B) instruments
   (C) stories
   (D) inspiration

29. From what did the term "opera" derive?

   (A) Greek and Roman history and
       mythology
   (B) Non-Italian composers
   (C) The Italian phrase the means "musical
       works"
   (D) The ideas of composer Jacopo Peri

30. Which of the following is an example of a
    solo?

   (A) A recitative
   (B) A duet
   (C) An opera
   (D) A lyre

Questions 31–40

         According to the controversial sunspot theory, great storms on the surface of the sun hurl
    streams of solar particles into the atmosphere, causing a shift in the weather on earth.
         A typical sunspot consists of a dark central umbra surrounded by a lighter penumbra of
Line light and dark threads extending out from the center like the spokes of a wheel. Actually, the
  (5) sunspots are cooler than the rest of the photosphere, which may account for their color. Typi-
    cally, the temperature in a sunspot umbra is about 4000 K, whereas the temperature in a
    penumbra registers 5500 K, and the granules outside the spot are 6000 K.
         Sunspots range in size from tiny granules to complex structures with areas stretching for
    billions of square miles. About 5 percent of the spots are large enough so that they can be seen
 (10) without instruments; consequently, observations of sunspots have been recorded for several
    thousand years.
         Sunspots have been observed in arrangements of one to more than one hundred spots, but
    they tend to occur in pairs. There is also a marked tendency for the two spots of a pair to have
    opposite magnetic polarities. Furthermore, the strength of the magnetic field associated with
 (15) any given sunspot is closely related to the spot's size.
         Although there is no theory that completely explains the nature and function of sunspots,
    several models attempt to relate the phenomenon to magnetic fields along the lines of longi-
    tude from the north and south poles of the sun.

GO ON TO THE NEXT PAGE ➤

31. What is the author's main purpose in the passage?

   (A) To propose a theory to explain sunspots
   (B) To describe the nature of sunspots
   (C) To compare the umbra and the penumbra in sunspots
   (D) To argue for the existence of magnetic fields in sunspots

32. The word "controversial" in line 1 is closest in meaning to

   (A) widely accepted
   (B) open to debate
   (C) just introduced
   (D) very complicated

33. Solar particles are hurled into space by

   (A) undetermined causes
   (B) disturbances of wind
   (C) small rivers on the surface of the sun
   (D) changes in the earth's atmosphere

34. The word "particles" in line 2 refers to

   (A) gas explosions in the atmosphere
   (B) light rays from the sun
   (C) liquid streams on the sun
   (D) small pieces of matter from the sun

35. How can we describe matter from the sun that enters the earth's atmosphere?

   (A) Very small
   (B) Very hot
   (C) Very bright
   (D) Very hard

36. The sunspot theory is

   (A) not considered very important
   (B) widely accepted
   (C) subject to disagreement
   (D) relatively new

37. The word "they" in line 9 refers to

   (A) structures
   (B) spots
   (C) miles
   (D) granules

38. The word "consequently" in line 10 could best be replaced by

   (A) as a result
   (B) nevertheless
   (C) without doubt
   (D) in this way

39. In which configuration do sunspots usually occur?

   (A) In one spot of varying size
   (B) In a configuration of two spots
   (C) In arrangements of one hundred or more spots
   (D) In groups of several thousand spots

40. How are sunspots explained?

   (A) Sunspots appear to be related to magnetic fields on the earth.
   (B) Sunspots may be related to magnetic fields that follow longitudinal lines on the sun.
   (C) Sunspots are explained by storms that occur on the earth.
   (D) Sunspots have no theory or model to explain them.

GO ON TO THE NEXT PAGE

3   3   3   3   3   3   3   3   3   3   **3**

Questions 41–50

Recent technological advances in manned and unmanned undersea vehicles along with breakthroughs in satellite technology and computer equipment have overcome some of the limitations of divers and diving equipment. Without a vehicle, divers often became sluggish
Line and their mental concentration was limited. Because of undersea pressure that affected their
(5) speech organs, communication among divers was difficult or impossible. But today, most oceanographers make direct observations by means of instruments that are lowered into the ocean, from samples taken from the water, or from photographs made by orbiting satellites. Direct observations of the ocean floor are made not only by divers but also by deep-diving submarines and aerial photography. Some of the submarines can dive to depths of more than
(10) seven miles and cruise at depths of fifteen thousand feet. In addition, radio-equipped buoys can be operated by remote control in order to transmit information back to land-based laboratories, often via satellite. Particularly important are data about water temperature, currents and weather. Satellite photographs can show the distribution of sea ice, oil slicks, and cloud formations over the ocean. Maps created from satellite pictures can represent the temperature
(15) and the color of the ocean's surface, enabling researchers to study the ocean currents. Furthermore, computers help oceanographers to collect and analyze data from submarines and satellites. By creating a model of the ocean's movement and characteristics, scientists can predict the patterns and possible effects of the ocean on the environment.

Recently, many oceanographers have been relying more on satellites and computers than
(20) on research ships or even submarine vehicles because they can supply a greater range of information more quickly and more efficiently. Some of mankind's most serious problems, especially those concerning energy and food, may be solved with the help of observations made possible by this new technology.

41. With what topic is the passage primarily concerned?

(A) Technological advances in oceanography
(B) Communication among divers
(C) Direct observation of the ocean floor
(D) Undersea vehicles

42. The word "sluggish" in line 3 is closest in meaning to

(A) nervous
(B) confused
(C) slow moving
(D) very weak

43. Divers have had problems in communicating underwater because

(A) the pressure affected their speech organs
(B) the vehicles they used have not been perfected
(C) they did not pronounce clearly
(D) the water destroyed their speech organs

44. This passage suggests that the successful exploration of the ocean depends upon

(A) vehicles as well as divers
(B) radios that divers use to communicate
(C) controlling currents and the weather
(D) the limitations of diving equipment

45. Undersea vehicles

(A) are too small for a man to fit inside
(B) are very slow to respond
(C) have the same limitations that divers have
(D) make direct observations of the ocean floor

GO ON TO THE NEXT PAGE

3 3 3 3 3 3 3 3 3 3 3

46. The word "cruise" in line 10 could best be replaced by

    (A) travel at a constant speed
    (B) function without problems
    (C) stay in communication
    (D) remain still

47. How is a radio-equipped buoy operated?

    (A) By operators inside the vehicle in the part underwater
    (B) By operators outside the vehicle on a ship
    (C) By operators outside the vehicle on a diving platform
    (D) By operators outside the vehicle in a laboratory on shore

48. Which of the following are NOT shown in satellite photographs?

    (A) The temperature of the ocean's surface
    (B) Cloud formations over the ocean
    (C) A model of the ocean's movements
    (D) The location of sea ice

49. The word "those" in line 22 refers to

    (A) energy and food
    (B) problems
    (C) observations
    (D) vehicles

50. According to the author, what are some of the problems the underwater studies may eventually resolve?

    (A) Weather and temperature control
    (B) Food and energy shortages
    (C) Transportation and communication problems
    (D) Overcrowding and housing problems

THIS IS THE END OF THE READING COMPREHENSION SECTION OF TOEFL MODEL TEST 1.

IF YOU FINISH BEFORE 55 MINUTES HAS ENDED, CHECK YOUR WORK ON SECTION 3 ONLY.

DO NOT READ OR WORK ON ANY OTHER SECTION OF THE TEST.

END OF TOEFL MODEL TEST 1.

To check your answers for Model Test 1, refer to the Answer Key on page 462. For an explanation of the answers, refer to the Explanatory Answers for Model Test 1 on pages 469–476.

MODEL TEST 2—ANSWER SHEET

Section 1

1	2	3	4	5	6	7	8	9	10	11	12	13	14	15	16	17	18	19	20	21	22	23	24	25	26	27	28	29	30
A	A	A	A	A	A	A	A	A	A	A	A	A	A	A	A	A	A	A	A	A	A	A	A	A	A	A	A	A	A
B	B	B	B	B	B	B	B	B	B	B	B	B	B	B	B	B	B	B	B	B	B	B	B	B	B	B	B	B	B
C	C	C	C	C	C	C	C	C	C	C	C	C	C	C	C	C	C	C	C	C	C	C	C	C	C	C	C	C	C
D	D	D	D	D	D	D	D	D	D	D	D	D	D	D	D	D	D	D	D	D	D	D	D	D	D	D	D	D	D

31	32	33	34	35	36	37	38	39	40	41	42	43	44	45	46	47	48	49	50
A	A	A	A	A	A	A	A	A	A	A	A	A	A	A	A	A	A	A	A
B	B	B	B	B	B	B	B	B	B	B	B	B	B	B	B	B	B	B	B
C	C	C	C	C	C	C	C	C	C	C	C	C	C	C	C	C	C	C	C
D	D	D	D	D	D	D	D	D	D	D	D	D	D	D	D	D	D	D	D

Section 2

1	2	3	4	5	6	7	8	9	10	11	12	13	14	15	16	17	18	19	20	21	22	23	24	25	26	27	28	29	30
A	A	A	A	A	A	A	A	A	A	A	A	A	A	A	A	A	A	A	A	A	A	A	A	A	A	A	A	A	A
B	B	B	B	B	B	B	B	B	B	B	B	B	B	B	B	B	B	B	B	B	B	B	B	B	B	B	B	B	B
C	C	C	C	C	C	C	C	C	C	C	C	C	C	C	C	C	C	C	C	C	C	C	C	C	C	C	C	C	C
D	D	D	D	D	D	D	D	D	D	D	D	D	D	D	D	D	D	D	D	D	D	D	D	D	D	D	D	D	D

31	32	33	34	35	36	37	38	39	40
A	A	A	A	A	A	A	A	A	A
B	B	B	B	B	B	B	B	B	B
C	C	C	C	C	C	C	C	C	C
D	D	D	D	D	D	D	D	D	D

Section 3

1	2	3	4	5	6	7	8	9	10	11	12	13	14	15	16	17	18	19	20	21	22	23	24	25	26	27	28	29	30
A	A	A	A	A	A	A	A	A	A	A	A	A	A	A	A	A	A	A	A	A	A	A	A	A	A	A	A	A	A
B	B	B	B	B	B	B	B	B	B	B	B	B	B	B	B	B	B	B	B	B	B	B	B	B	B	B	B	B	B
C	C	C	C	C	C	C	C	C	C	C	C	C	C	C	C	C	C	C	C	C	C	C	C	C	C	C	C	C	C
D	D	D	D	D	D	D	D	D	D	D	D	D	D	D	D	D	D	D	D	D	D	D	D	D	D	D	D	D	D

31	32	33	34	35	36	37	38	39	40	41	42	43	44	45	46	47	48	49	50
A	A	A	A	A	A	A	A	A	A	A	A	A	A	A	A	A	A	A	A
B	B	B	B	B	B	B	B	B	B	B	B	B	B	B	B	B	B	B	B
C	C	C	C	C	C	C	C	C	C	C	C	C	C	C	C	C	C	C	C
D	D	D	D	D	D	D	D	D	D	D	D	D	D	D	D	D	D	D	D

Cut here to remove answer sheet.

1 1 1 1 1 1 1 1 1 1 1

Model Test 2
Short Form

Section 1:
Listening Comprehension

50 QUESTIONS 40 MINUTES

In this section of the test, you will have an opportunity to demonstrate your ability to understand conversations and talks in English. There are three parts to this section with special directions for each part. Answer all the questions on the basis of what is stated or implied by the speakers in this test. When you take the actual TOEFL test, you will not be allowed to take notes or write in your test book. Try to work on this Model Test in the same way.

Part A

Directions: In Part A, you will hear short conversations between two people. After each conversation, you will hear a question about the conversation. The conversations and questions will not be repeated. After you hear a question, read the four possible answers in your book and choose the best answer. Then, on your answer sheet, find the number of the question and fill in the space that corresponds to the letter of the answer you have chosen.

1. (A) That it looks exactly like Susan.
   (B) That it makes Susan look younger than she really is.
   (C) That it makes Susan look older than she really is.
   (D) That it makes Susan look better than she looks in person.

2. (A) The woman was not truthful.
   (B) Fewer students would attend.
   (C) There would be a large group.
   (D) Only foreign students would come.

3. (A) Knock on the door.
   (B) Come back later.
   (C) See Dr. Smith.
   (D) Look at the sign.

4. (A) The time.
   (B) A flight.
   (C) A class.
   (D) A city.

5. (A) Take a class from Professor Wilson.
   (B) Help the man with his class.
   (C) Take an extra class.
   (D) Do a project for her class.

6. (A) That he wants something to eat.
   (B) That he will tell them if there is a problem.
   (C) That he is not hungry.
   (D) That he is angry.

7. (A) Miss Brown does not know how to paint.
   (B) Miss Brown will teach art.
   (C) Miss Brown will teach English.
   (D) Miss Brown will not go to the high school.

8. (A) At a post office.
   (B) At a bank.
   (C) At an airport.
   (D) At a drugstore.

GO ON TO THE NEXT PAGE

1 1 1 1 1 1 1 1 1 1 1

9. (A) She is late.
   (B) She made a mistake.
   (C) She is afraid.
   (D) She feels ill.

10. (A) His briefcase is exactly like the
        woman's.
    (B) His briefcase has a lock.
    (C) His briefcase is smaller than the other
        briefcase.
    (D) He doesn't have a briefcase.

11. (A) The appointment has been cancelled.
    (B) The appointment is inconvenient.
    (C) Mr. Smith will see Mr. Jacobs today.
    (D) Mr. Jacobs is too busy to see Mr. Smith.

12. (A) Go to Grove City another day.
    (B) Take Route 18 to Grove City.
    (C) Ask directions to Grove City.
    (D) Get lost on the way to Grove City.

13. (A) Good grades are not that important to
        her.
    (B) She did not get an A on the exam either.
    (C) Two students got higher grades than she
        did.
    (D) Besides hers, there were several other A
        grades.

14. (A) There is still time to finish.
    (B) She cannot do it quickly.
    (C) He needs the letters tomorrow.
    (D) He doesn't know what time it is.

15. (A) She does not agree with the man.
    (B) She thinks that it is better to wait.
    (C) She thinks that it is better to drive at
        night.
    (D) She does not think that the man made a
        wise decision.

16. (A) Go to class.
    (B) See a movie.
    (C) Study at the library.
    (D) Make an appointment.

17. (A) The message was not clear.
    (B) There was no message on the machine.
    (C) It was his intention to return the
        woman's call.
    (D) He did not hear the woman's message.

18. (A) They do not have as many people work-
        ing as usual.
    (B) The machine is broken.
    (C) The man is next to be served.
    (D) There is usually a long line.

19. (A) He thought that there were too many
        questions.
    (B) He is glad that the interview is over.
    (C) He believes that he did well.
    (D) He is looking forward to it.

20. (A) Get directions to the Math Department.
    (B) Speak with the secretary.
    (C) Go into Dr. Davis's office.
    (D) Take the elevator to the fourth floor.

21. (A) Make a dessert.
    (B) Stay at home.
    (C) Stop worrying.
    (D) Buy a cake.

22. (A) He has finished the class.
    (B) He has been sick.
    (C) He does not have to take the final exam.
    (D) He is not very responsible.

23. (A) He cannot find the woman's house.
    (B) He has to change their plans.
    (C) He will be happy to see the woman.
    (D) He wants to know whether they have a
        date.

24. (A) She does not like the apartment.
    (B) She is concerned about the rent for the
        apartment.
    (C) She wants to live in the apartment.
    (D) She agrees with the man.

GO ON TO THE NEXT PAGE ➤

1 1 1 1 1 1 1 1 1 1 1

25. (A) Register for Dr. Collin's class.
    (B) Graduate at a later date.
    (C) Enroll in the section marked "staff."
    (D) Find out who is teaching the other
         section of the class.

26. (A) It is the final call for boarding the flight.
    (B) It is not for the flight to San Antonio.
    (C) It is a mistake and should be disregarded.
    (D) It is a special opportunity for people
         who may have difficulty boarding the
         flight.

27. (A) Wait for the results to be mailed.
    (B) Call about the score.
    (C) Take the test.
    (D) Show more concern.

.28. (A) He does not enjoy arguing with the
         woman.
    (B) He cannot use his coupon at this store.
    (C) He wants the woman to wait for him to
         return.
    (D) They don't have his size.

29. (A) Wash his car.
    (B) Drive through the car wash.
    (C) Tip the guys at the car wash.
    (D) Get in his car and leave.

30. (A) They have more time to travel.
    (B) They are taking advantage of travel
         opportunities.
    (C) They travel more than the man does.
    (D) They spend most of their time traveling.

Part B

Directions: In this part of the test, you will hear longer conversations. After each conversation, you will hear several questions. The conversations and questions will not be repeated.

After you hear a question, read the four possible answers in your book and choose the best answer. Then, on your answer sheet, find the number of the question and fill in the space that corresponds to the letter of the answer you have chosen.

Remember, you are **not** allowed to take notes or write on your test pages.

31. (A) To invite her to go to Florida with him.
    (B) To ask her to watch his house while he
         is gone.
    (C) To make a date for that evening.
    (D) To talk about his vacation.

32. (A) She is Brian's neighbor.
    (B) She goes to school with Brian.
    (C) She does not know Brian very well.
    (D) She does not have a job.

33. (A) Feed the cats.
    (B) Collect the mail.
    (C) Water the plants.
    (D) Watch the house.

34. (A) Go to work.
    (B) Take the keys to Melissa.
    (C) Leave for Florida.
    (D) Call Melissa.

35. (A) The national health.
    (B) Stress.
    (C) Heart attacks.
    (D) Health care for women.

GO ON TO THE NEXT PAGE

1 1 1 1 1 1 1 1 1 1 1

36. (A) They are under more stress than men.
    (B) They have more heart attacks than men.
    (C) They do not get the same level of care as men.
    (D) They have less serious heart attacks than men.

37. (A) He did not see it.
    (B) He thought it was interesting.
    (C) He would not recommend it.
    (D) He was not surprised by it.

38. (A) Discuss the video with the man.
    (B) Go to the library to see the video.
    (C) Check the video out of the library.
    (D) Get ready for class.

Part C

Directions: In this part of the test, you will hear several short talks. After each talk, you will hear some questions. The talks and questions will not be repeated.

After you hear a question, read the four possible answers in your book and choose the best answer. Then, on your answer sheet, find the number of the question and fill in the space that corresponds to the letter of the answer you have chosen.

39. (A) Poet laureates.
    (B) The Victorian Period.
    (C) Love poems in the English language.
    (D) Elizabeth Barrett Browning.

40. (A) Because her husband was a famous poet.
    (B) Because of her publication, *Sonnets from the Portuguese*.
    (C) Because the monarch was a woman.
    (D) Because of her friendship with William Wordsworth.

41. (A) In Spain.
    (B) In Italy.
    (C) In Portugal.
    (D) In England.

42. (A) In 1843.
    (B) In 1849.
    (C) In 1856.
    (D) In 1861.

43. (A) To provide general information about the trip.
    (B) To thank the passengers.
    (C) To state federal regulations.
    (D) To advertise for Scenic Cruiser Bus Lines.

44. (A) Bloomington.
    (B) Springfield.
    (C) Saint Louis.
    (D) New Orleans.

45. (A) 4118.
    (B) 4180.
    (C) 4108.
    (D) 4811.

46. (A) He will say good-bye to the passengers.
    (B) He will start the bus and begin the trip.
    (C) He will smoke.
    (D) He will eat dinner.

GO ON TO THE NEXT PAGE

1   1   1   1   1   1   1   1   1   1   1

47. (A) The history of medicine in Greece.
    (B) The contributions of biology to medi-
        cine.
    (C) The scientific method.
    (D) Medical advances in the twentieth
        century.

48. (A) The classification of plants on the basis
        of body structure.
    (B) The sterilization of surgical instruments.
    (C) The scientific recording of symptoms
        and treatments.
    (D) The theory that disease was caused by
        the gods.

49. (A) Hippocrates.
    (B) Aristotle.
    (C) Dioscorides.
    (D) Edward Jenner.

50. (A) The theory of germs and bacteria.
    (B) The discovery of a vaccine against
        smallpox.
    (C) The discovery of a mechanism for the
        circulation of the blood.
    (D) The *Materia Medica*.

**THIS IS THE END OF THE LISTENING COMPREHENSION SECTION
OF TOEFL MODEL TEST 2.**

DO NOT READ OR WORK ON ANY OTHER SECTION OF THE TEST.

2 2 2 2 2 2 2 2 2 2 2

Section 2:
Structure and Written Expression

40 QUESTIONS 25 MINUTES

This section is designed to measure your ability to recognize language that is appropriate for standard written English. There are two types of questions in this section, with special directions for each type.

Structure

Directions: Questions 1–15 are incomplete sentences. Beneath each sentence you will see four words or phrases, marked (A), (B), (C), and (D). Choose the **one** word or phrase that best completes the sentence. Then, on your answer sheet, find the number of the question and fill in the space that corresponds to the letter of the answer you have chosen. Fill in the space so that the letter inside the oval cannot be seen.

1. One of the most effective vegetable protein substitutes is the soybean -------- used to manufacture imitation meat products.

   (A) which can be
   (B) it can be
   (C) who can be
   (D) can be

2. -------- 1,000 species of finch have been identified.

   (A) As many as
   (B) As many
   (C) As much as
   (D) Much as

3. The greater the demand, -------- the price.

   (A) higher
   (B) high
   (C) the higher
   (D) the high

4. The Continental United States is -------- that there are four time zones.

   (A) much big
   (B) too big
   (C) so big
   (D) very big

5. Benjamin West contributed a great deal to American art: -------- .

   (A) painting, teaching, and lecturing
   (B) painting, as a teacher and lecturer
   (C) painting, teaching, and as a lecturer
   (D) painting, a teacher, and a lecturer

6. Most insurance agents would rather you -------- anything about collecting claims until they investigate the situation.

   (A) do
   (B) not do
   (C) don't
   (D) did not

7. Upon hatching, -------- .

   (A) young ducks know how to swim
   (B) swimming is known by young ducks
   (C) the knowledge of swimming is in young ducks
   (D) how to swim is known in young ducks

8. The observation deck at the World Trade Center -------- in New York.

   (A) is highest than any other one
   (B) is higher than any other one
   (C) is highest that any other one
   (D) is higher that any other one

GO ON TO THE NEXT PAGE ➤

2 2 2 2 2 2 2 2 2 2 2

9. A seventeen-year-old is not -------- to vote in an election.

(A) old enough
(B) as old enough
(C) enough old
(D) enough old as

10. -------- is necessary for the development of strong bones and teeth.

(A) It is calcium
(B) That calcium
(C) Calcium
(D) Although calcium

11. -------- withstands testing, we may not conclude that it is true, but we may retain it.

(A) If a hypothesis
(B) That a hypothesis
(C) A hypothesis
(D) Hypothesis

12. Only after food has been dried or canned -------- .

(A) that it should be stored for later consumption
(B) should be stored for later consumption
(C) should it be stored for later consumption
(D) it should be stored for later consumption

13. Not until a monkey is several years old -------- to exhibit signs of independence from its mother.

(A) it begins
(B) does it begin
(C) and begin
(D) beginning

14. Almost everyone fails -------- on the first try.

(A) in passing the driver's test
(B) to pass the driver's test
(C) to have passed the driver's test
(D) pass the driver's test

15. Since Elizabeth Barrett Browning's father never approved of -------- Robert Browning, the couple eloped to Italy, where they lived and wrote.

(A) her to marry
(B) her marrying
(C) she marrying
(D) she to marry

Written Expression

Directions: In questions 16–40 each sentence has four underlined words or phrases. The four underlined parts of the sentence are marked (A), (B), (C), and (D). Identify the **one** underlined word or phrase that must be changed in order for the sentence to be correct. Then, on your answer sheet, find the number of the question and fill in the space that corresponds to the letter of the answer you have chosen.

16. The information officer at the bank told his customers that there was several different kinds of
                            (A)   (B)   (C)   (D)
checking accounts available.

17. The first electric lamp had two carbon rods from which vapor serves to conduct the current across
    (A)   (B)   (C)   (D)
the gap.

GO ON TO THE NEXT PAGE

18. The Department of Fine Arts and Architecture <u>has</u> been criticized for <u>not having</u> <u>much</u> required
                                (A)   (B)   (C)

    courses scheduled <u>for</u> this semester.
                      (D)

19. A thunderhead, dense clouds that <u>rise</u> <u>high</u> into the sky in huge columns, <u>produce</u> hail,
    (A)   (B) (C)   (D)
    rain, or snow.

20. Although <u>no country</u> has exactly the same folk music <u>like</u> <u>that</u> of any other, it is significant that
                   (A)   (B) (C)

    similar songs exist among <u>widely</u> separated people.
                                (D)

21. <u>Despite of</u> the Taft-Hartley Act which <u>forbids</u> unfair union practices, some unions <u>such as</u> the air
       (A)   (B)   (C)

    traffic controllers have voted <u>to strike</u> even though this action might endanger the national security.
                                (D)

22. Never before <u>has</u> <u>so many</u> people <u>in</u> the United States been <u>interested in</u> soccer.
                 (A)   (B)   (C)   (D)

23. Operant conditioning involves rewarding or punishing certain <u>behave</u> to <u>reinforce</u> or <u>extinguish</u>
                                                     (A)   (B)   (C)

    its occurrence.
       (D)

24. <u>Not one</u> in one hundred children exposed to the disease <u>are</u> <u>likely</u> to <u>develop</u> symptoms of it.
      (A)   (B) (C)   (D)

25. <u>There is</u> an unresolved controversy as to <u>whom</u> <u>is</u> the real author of the Elizabethan plays <u>commonly</u>
       (A)   (B) (C)   (D)

    credited to William Shakespeare.

26. A catalytic agent <u>such as</u> platinum may be used <u>so</u> the chemical reaction <u>advances</u> more <u>rapidly</u>.
                   (A)   (B)   (C)   (D)

27. <u>From space</u>, astronauts are <u>able</u> to <u>clearly see</u> the outline <u>of</u> the whole earth.
        (A)   (B)   (C)   (D)

28. When a patient's blood pressure is <u>much</u> higher <u>than</u> it <u>should</u> be, a doctor usually insists that
                                         (A)   (B)   (C)

    he <u>will not</u> smoke.
        (D)

GO ON TO THE NEXT PAGE ➡

2 **2** **2** **2** **2** **2** **2** **2** **2** **2** **2**

29. Excavations in several mounds and villages on the east bank of the Euphrates River have revealed
                                                       (A)   (B)

    the city of Nebuchadnezzar, an ancient community that had been laying under later reconstructions
                                                           (C)   (D)

    of the city of Babylon.

30. It was the invent of the hand-held electronic calculator that provided the original technology for
    (A)(B)   (C)

    the present generation of small but powerful computers.
         (D)

31. Located in the cranial cavity in the skull, the brain is the larger mass of nerve tissue in the
              (A)   (B)   (C)

    human body.
         (D)

32. The examination will test your ability to understand spoken English, to read non-technical
                      (A)   (B)

    language, and writing correctly.
                (C)   (D)

33. Alike other forms of energy, natural gas may be used to heat homes, cook food, and even run
     (A)   (B)   (C)   (D)

    automobiles.

34. An organ is a group of tissues capable to perform some special function, as, for example, the
              (A)   (B)   (C)   (D)

    heart, the liver, or the lungs.

35. Insulin, it is used to treat diabetes and is secured chiefly from the pancreas of cattle and hogs.
        (A)   (B)   (C)   (D)

36. One of the world's best-selling authors, Louis L'Amour said to have written 101 books,
              (A)   (B)   (C)

    mostly westerns.
      (D)

37. Dairying is concerned not only with the production of milk, but with the manufacture of milk
              (A)   (B)   (C)

    products such as butter and cheese.
              (D)

GO ON TO THE NEXT PAGE

2   2   2   2   2   2   2   2   2   2   2

38. In autumn, brilliant yellow, orange, and red leaves are <u>commonly</u> to both the Sweet Gum tree <u>and</u>
    <u>(A)</u>   (B)   (C)   (D)
    the Maple.

39. When he <u>was</u> a little boy, Mark Twain <u>would walk</u> along the piers, <u>watch</u> the river boats, <u>swimming</u>
             (A)   (B)   (C)   (D)
    and fish in the Mississippi, much like his famous character, Tom Sawyer.

40. <u>Almost all</u> books have a few errors in them <u>in spite of</u> the care <u>taken</u> to check <u>its</u> proof pages
        (A)   (B)   (C)   (D)
    before the final printing.

**THIS IS THE END OF THE STRUCTURE AND WRITTEN EXPRESSION
SECTION OF TOEFL MODEL TEST 2.**

**IF YOU FINISH BEFORE 25 MINUTES HAS ENDED, CHECK YOUR
WORK ON SECTION 2 ONLY.**

DO NOT READ OR WORK ON ANY OTHER SECTION OF THE TEST.

3 3 3 3 3 3 3 3 3 3 3 3

Section 3:
Reading Comprehension

50 QUESTIONS 55 MINUTES

Directions: In this section you will read several passages. Each one is followed by a number of questions about it. For questions 1–50, you are to choose the **one** best answer, (A), (B), (C), or (D), to each question. Then, on your answer sheet, find the number of the question and fill in the space that corresponds to the letter of the answer you have chosen.

Answer all questions about the information in a passage on the basis of what is **stated** or **implied** in that passage.

Questions 1–10

Although speech is the most advanced form of communication, there are many ways of communicating without using speech. Signals, signs, symbols, and gestures may be found in every known culture. The basic function of a signal is to impinge upon the environment in
Line such a way that it attracts attention, as, for example, the dots and dashes of a telegraph circuit.
(5) Coded to refer to speech, the potential for communication is very great. Less adaptable to the codification of words, signs also contain meaning in and of themselves. A stop sign or a barber pole conveys meaning quickly and conveniently. Symbols are more difficult to describe than either signals or signs because of their intricate relationship with the receiver's cultural perceptions. In some cultures, applauding in a theater provides performers with an auditory
(10) symbol of approval. Gestures such as waving and handshaking also communicate certain cultural messages.
    Although signals, signs, symbols, and gestures are very useful, they do have a major disadvantage. They usually do not allow ideas to be shared without the sender being directly adjacent to the receiver. As a result, means of communication intended to be used for long dis-
(15) tances and extended periods are based upon speech. Radio, television, and the telephone are only a few.

1. Which of the following would be the best title for the passage?

   (A) Signs and Signals
   (B) Gestures
   (C) Communication
   (D) Speech

2. What does the author say about speech?

   (A) It is the only true form of communication.
   (B) It is dependent upon the advances made by inventors.
   (C) It is necessary for communication to occur.
   (D) It is the most advanced form of communication.

3. According to the passage, what is a signal?

   (A) The most difficult form of communication to describe
   (B) A form of communication which may be used across long distances
   (C) A form of communication that interrupts the environment
   (D) The form of communication most related to cultural perceptions

GO ON TO THE NEXT PAGE →

4. The phrase "impinge on" in line 3 is closest in meaning to

   (A) intrude
   (B) improve
   (C) vary
   (D) prohibit

5. The word "it" in line 4 refers to

   (A) function
   (B) signal
   (C) environment
   (D) way

6. The word "potential" in line 5 could best be replaced by

   (A) range
   (B) advantage
   (C) organization
   (D) possibility

7. The word "intricate" in line 8 could best be replaced by which of the following?

   (A) inefficient
   (B) complicated
   (C) historical
   (D) uncertain

8. Applauding was cited as an example of

   (A) a signal
   (B) a sign
   (C) a symbol
   (D) a gesture

9. Why were the telephone, radio, and TV invented?

   (A) People were unable to understand signs, symbols, and signals.
   (B) People wanted to communicate across long distances.
   (C) People believed that signs, signals, and symbols were obsolete.
   (D) People wanted new forms of entertainment.

10. It may be concluded from this passage that

   (A) signals, signs, symbols, and gestures are forms of communication
   (B) symbols are very easy to define and interpret
   (C) only some cultures have signals, signs, and symbols
   (D) waving and handshaking are not related to culture

Questions 11–20

   Application for admission to the Graduate School at this university must be made on forms provided by the Director of Admissions. An applicant whose undergraduate work was done at another institution should request that two copies of undergraduate transcripts and degrees be
Line   sent directly to the Dean of the Graduate School. Both the application and the transcripts must
(5)   be on file at least one month prior to the registration date, and must be accompanied by a nonrefundable ten-dollar check or money order to cover the cost of processing the application.
   Students who have already been admitted to the Graduate School but were not enrolled during the previous semester should reapply for admission using a special short form available in the office of the Graduate School. It is not necessary for students who have previously been de-
(10)   nied admission to resubmit transcripts; however, new application forms must accompany all requests for reconsideration. Applications should be submitted at least eight weeks in advance of the session in which the student wishes to enroll. Students whose applications are received after the deadline may be considered for admission as non-degree students, and may enroll for six credit hours. Non-degree status must be changed prior to the completion of the first se-
(15)   mester of study however.

GO ON TO THE NEXT PAGE ➡

3   3   3   3   3   3   3   3   3   3   3

An undergraduate student of this university who has senior status and is within ten credit hours of completing all requirements for graduation may register for graduate work with the recommendation of the chairperson of the department and the approval of the Dean of the Graduate School.

11. What is the author's main point?

(A) How to apply to the Graduate School
(B) How to obtain senior status
(C) How to register for graduate coursework
(D) How to make application for graduation

12. Where would this passage most probably be found?

(A) In a university catalog
(B) In a travel folder
(C) In a newspaper
(D) In a textbook

13. According to this passage, where would a student secure application forms for admission to the university?

(A) From the chairperson of the department
(B) From the Dean of the Graduate School
(C) From the institution where the undergraduate work was done
(D) From the Director of Admissions

14. Which of the following documents must be on file thirty days before the registration date?

(A) Two copies of recommendations from former professors
(B) A written approval of the Dean of the Graduate School
(C) One set of transcripts and an English proficiency score
(D) Two copies of undergraduate courses and grades, an application form, and an application fee

15. The author uses the word "nonrefundable" in line 6 to refer to

(A) a process
(B) an application
(C) a check
(D) a date

16. The phrase "in advance of" in line 11 is closest in meaning to

(A) into
(B) on either side of
(C) after the end of
(D) prior to

17. The author makes all of the following observations about non-degree students EXCEPT

(A) they may be admitted after the deadline
(B) they may enroll for six credit hours
(C) they must change their status during the first semester
(D) they need not submit transcripts

18. The word "status" in line 14 could best be replaced by which of the following?

(A) information
(B) classification
(C) payment
(D) agreement

19. Students who have already been admitted to the Graduate School

(A) never need to apply for readmission
(B) must reapply if they have not been registered at the university during the previous semester
(C) must reapply every semester
(D) must reapply when they are within ten credit hours of graduation

GO ON TO THE NEXT PAGE

3 3 3 3 3 3 3 3 3 3 | 3

20. What special rule applies to undergraduate
students?

(A) They may not register for graduate
work.
(B) They must pass an examination in order
to register for graduate work.
(C) They may receive special permission to
register for graduate work.
(D) They may register for graduate work at
any time.

Questions 21–30

Fertilizer is any substance that can be added to the soil to provide chemical elements
essential for plant nutrition. Natural substances such as animal droppings and straw have been
used as fertilizers for thousands of years, and lime has been used since the Romans introduced
Line it during the Empire. It was not until the nineteenth century, in fact, that chemical fertilizers
(5) became popular. Today, both natural and synthetic fertilizers are available in a variety of
forms.

A complete fertilizer is usually marked with a formula consisting of three numbers, such
as 4-8-2 or 3-6-4, which designate the percentage content of nitrogen, phosphoric acid, and
potash in the order stated.
(10) Synthetic fertilizers are available in either solid or liquid form. Solids, in the shape of
chemical granules are popular because they are easy to store and apply. Recently, liquids have
shown an increase in popularity, accounting for about 20 percent of the nitrogen fertilizer used
throughout the world. Formerly, powders were also used, but these were found to be less
convenient than either solids or liquids.
(15) Fertilizers have no harmful effects on the soil, the crop, or the consumer as long as they are
used according to recommendations based on the results of local research. Occasionally, however, farmers may use more fertilizer than necessary, damaging not only the crop but also the animals or humans that eat it. Accumulations of fertilizer in the water supply accelerate the growth
of algae and, consequently, may disturb the natural cycle of life, contributing to the death of
(20) fish. Too much fertilizer on grass can cause digestive disorders in cattle and in infants who drink
cow's milk.

21. With which of the following topics is the
passage primarily concerned?

(A) Local research and harmful effects of
fertilizer
(B) Advantages and disadvantages of liquid
fertilizer
(C) A formula for the production of
fertilizer
(D) Content, form, and effects of fertilizer

22. The word "essential" in line 2 could best be
replaced by which of the following?

(A) limited
(B) preferred
(C) anticipated
(D) required

GO ON TO THE NEXT PAGE

3   3   3   3   3   3   3   3   3   3 | 3

23. In the formula 3-6-4

   (A) the content of nitrogen is greater than
       that of potash
   (B) the content of potash is greater than that
       of phosphoric acid
   (C) the content of phosphoric acid is less
       than that of nitrogen
   (D) the content of nitrogen is less than that
       of phosphoric acid

24. Which of the following has the smallest per-
    centage content in the formula 4-8-2?

   (A) Nitrogen
   (B) Phosphorus
   (C) Acid
   (D) Potash

25. What is the percentage of nitrogen in a 5-8-
    7 formula fertilizer?

   (A) 3 percent
   (B) 5 percent
   (C) 7 percent
   (D) 8 percent

26. The word "designate" in line 8 could be re-
    placed by

   (A) modify
   (B) specify
   (C) limit
   (D) increase

27. Which of the following statements about
    fertilizer is true?

   (A) Powders are more popular than ever.
   (B) Solids are difficult to store.
   (C) Liquids are increasing in popularity.
   (D) Chemical granules are difficult to apply.

28. The word "these" in line 13 refers to

   (A) powders
   (B) solids
   (C) liquids
   (D) fertilizer

29. The word "convenient" in line 14 is closest
    in meaning to

   (A) effective
   (B) plentiful
   (C) easy to use
   (D) cheap to produce

30. What happens when too much fertilizer is
    used?

   (A) Local research teams provide recom-
       mendations.
   (B) Algae in the water supplies begin to die.
   (C) Animals and humans may become ill.
   (D) Crops have no harmful effects.

Questions 31–40

        The development of the horse has been recorded from the beginning through all of its evo-
    lutionary stages to the modern form. It is, in fact, one of the most complete and well-docu-
    mented chapters in paleontological history. Fossil finds provide us not only with detailed in-
Line formation about the horse itself, but also with valuable insights into the migration of herds and
 (5) even evidence for speculation about the climatic conditions that could have instigated such
    migratory behavior.
        It has been documented that, almost twelve million years ago at the beginning of the
    Pliocene Age, a horse, about midway through its evolutionary development, crossed a land
    bridge where the Bering Straits are now located, from Alaska into the grasslands of Europe.
(10) The horse was the hipparion, about the size of a modern-day pony with three toes and special-
    ized cheek teeth for grazing. In Europe the hipparion encountered another less advanced horse

GO ON TO THE NEXT PAGE

3 3 3 3 3 3 3 3 3 3 3

called the anchitheres, which had previously invaded Europe by the same route, probably during the Miocene Period. Less developed and smaller than the hipparion, the anchitheres was
completely replaced by it. By the end of the Pleistocene Age both the anchitheres and the hip-
(15) parion had become extinct in North America, where they had originated. In Europe they had
evolved into an animal very similar to the horse as we know it today. It was the descendant of
this horse that was brought by the European colonists to the Americas.

31. What is this passage mainly about?

(A) The evolution of the horse
(B) The migration of horses
(C) The modern-day pony
(D) The replacement of the anchitheres by
the hipparion

32. According to the author, fossils are considered valuable for all of the following reasons
EXCEPT

(A) they suggest how the climate may have
been
(B) they provide information about migration
(C) they document the evolution of the
horse
(D) they maintain a record of life prior to
the Miocene Age

33. The word "instigated" in line 5 could best be
replaced by

(A) explained
(B) caused
(C) improved
(D) influenced

34. The author suggests that the hipparion and
the anchitheres migrated to Europe

(A) by means of a land route that is now
nonexistent
(B) on the ships of European colonists
(C) because of a very cold climate in North
America
(D) during the Miocene Period

35. Which of the following conclusions may be
made on the basis of information in the passage?

(A) The hipparions migrated to Europe to
feed in developing grasslands.
(B) There are no fossil remains of either the
anchitheres or the hipparion.
(C) There were horses in North America
when the first European colonists arrived.
(D) Very little is known about the evolution
of the horse.

36. According to this passage, the hipparions
were

(A) five-toed animals
(B) not as highly developed as the anchitheres
(C) larger than the anchitheres
(D) about the size of a small dog

37. The word "it" in line 14 refers to

(A) anchitheres
(B) hipparion
(C) Miocene Period
(D) route

38. The word "extinct" in line 15 is closest in
meaning to

(A) familiar
(B) widespread
(C) nonexistent
(D) tame

GO ON TO THE NEXT PAGE

3 3 3 3 3 3 3 3 3 3 3

39. Both the hipparion and the anchitheres

    (A) were the size of a modern pony
    (B) were native to North America
    (C) migrated to Europe in the Pliocene
        Period
    (D) had unspecialized teeth

40. It can be concluded from this passage that the

    (A) Miocene Period was prior to the
        Pliocene
    (B) Pleistocene Period was prior to the
        Miocene
    (C) Pleistocene Period was prior to the
        Pliocene
    (D) Pliocene Period was prior to the
        Miocene

Questions 41–50

    It was the first photograph that I had ever seen, and it fascinated me. I can remember holding it at every angle in order to catch the flickering light from the oil lamp on the dresser. The man in the photograph was unsmiling, but his eyes were kind. I had never met him, but I felt
Line that I knew him. One evening when I was looking at the photograph, as I always did before I
(5) went to sleep, I noticed a shadow across the man's thin face. I moved the photograph so that the shadow lay perfectly around his hollow cheeks. How different he looked!

    That night I could not sleep, thinking about the letter that I would write. First, I would tell him that I was eleven years old, and that if he had a little girl my age, she could write to me instead of him. I knew that he was a very busy man. Then I would explain to him the real pur-
(10) pose of my letter. I would tell him how wonderful he looked with the shadow that I had seen across his photograph, and I would most carefully suggest that he grow whiskers.

    Four months later when I met him at the train station near my home in Westfield, New York, he was wearing a full beard. He was so much taller than I had imagined from my tiny photograph.

    "Ladies and gentlemen," he said, "I have no speech to make and no time to make it in. I ap-
(15) pear before you that I may see you and that you may see me." Then he picked me right up and kissed me on both cheeks. The whiskers scratched. "Do you think I look better, my little friend?" he asked me.

    My name is Grace Bedell, and the man in the photograph was Abraham Lincoln.

41. What is the author's main purpose in the passage?

    (A) To explain how Grace Bedell took a
        photograph of Abraham Lincoln
    (B) To explain why Abraham Lincoln wore
        a beard
    (C) To explain why the first photographs
        were significant in American life
    (D) To explain why Westfield is an impor-
        tant city

42. The word "fascinated" in line 1 could best be replaced by

    (A) interested
    (B) frightened
    (C) confused
    (D) disgusted

GO ON TO THE NEXT PAGE ▶

3 3 3 3 3 3 3 3 3 3 3

43. The word "flickering" in line 2 is closest in meaning to

(A) burning constantly
(B) burning unsteadily
(C) burning very dimly
(D) burning brightly

44. The man in the photograph

(A) was smiling
(B) had a beard
(C) had a round, fat face
(D) looked kind

45. What did Grace Bedell do every night before she went to sleep?

(A) She wrote letters.
(B) She looked at the photograph.
(C) She made shadow figures on the wall.
(D) She read stories.

46. The little girl could not sleep because she was

(A) sick
(B) excited
(C) lonely
(D) sad

47. Why did the little girl write the man a letter?

(A) She was lonely.
(B) She wanted his daughter to write to her.
(C) She wanted him to grow a beard.
(D) She wanted him to visit her.

48. The word "it" in line 14 refers to

(A) time
(B) speech
(C) photograph
(D) station

49. From this passage, it may be inferred that

(A) Grace Bedell was the only one at the train station when Lincoln stopped at Westfield
(B) There were many people waiting for Lincoln to arrive on the train
(C) Lincoln made a long speech at the station in Westfield
(D) Lincoln was offended by the letter

50. Why did the author wait until the last line to reveal the identity of the man in the photograph?

(A) The author did not know it.
(B) The author wanted to make the reader feel foolish.
(C) The author wanted to build the interest and curiosity of the reader.
(D) The author was just a little girl.

THIS IS THE END OF THE READING COMPREHENSION SECTION OF TOEFL MODEL TEST 2.

IF YOU FINISH BEFORE 55 MINUTES HAS ENDED, CHECK YOUR WORK ON SECTION 3 ONLY.

DO NOT READ OR WORK ON ANY OTHER SECTION OF THE TEST.

END OF TOEFL MODEL TEST 2.

To check your answers for Model Test 2, refer to the Answer Key on page 462. For an explanation of the answers, refer to the Explanatory Answers for Model Test 2 on page 478.

MODEL TEST 3—ANSWER SHEET

Section 1

1. Ⓐ Ⓑ Ⓒ Ⓓ
2. Ⓐ Ⓑ Ⓒ Ⓓ
3. Ⓐ Ⓑ Ⓒ Ⓓ
4. Ⓐ Ⓑ Ⓒ Ⓓ
5. Ⓐ Ⓑ Ⓒ Ⓓ
6. Ⓐ Ⓑ Ⓒ Ⓓ
7. Ⓐ Ⓑ Ⓒ Ⓓ
8. Ⓐ Ⓑ Ⓒ Ⓓ
9. Ⓐ Ⓑ Ⓒ Ⓓ
10. Ⓐ Ⓑ Ⓒ Ⓓ
11. Ⓐ Ⓑ Ⓒ Ⓓ
12. Ⓐ Ⓑ Ⓒ Ⓓ
13. Ⓐ Ⓑ Ⓒ Ⓓ
14. Ⓐ Ⓑ Ⓒ Ⓓ
15. Ⓐ Ⓑ Ⓒ Ⓓ
16. Ⓐ Ⓑ Ⓒ Ⓓ
17. Ⓐ Ⓑ Ⓒ Ⓓ
18. Ⓐ Ⓑ Ⓒ Ⓓ
19. Ⓐ Ⓑ Ⓒ Ⓓ
20. Ⓐ Ⓑ Ⓒ Ⓓ
21. Ⓐ Ⓑ Ⓒ Ⓓ
22. Ⓐ Ⓑ Ⓒ Ⓓ
23. Ⓐ Ⓑ Ⓒ Ⓓ
24. Ⓐ Ⓑ Ⓒ Ⓓ
25. Ⓐ Ⓑ Ⓒ Ⓓ
26. Ⓐ Ⓑ Ⓒ Ⓓ
27. Ⓐ Ⓑ Ⓒ Ⓓ
28. Ⓐ Ⓑ Ⓒ Ⓓ
29. Ⓐ Ⓑ Ⓒ Ⓓ
30. Ⓐ Ⓑ Ⓒ Ⓓ
31. Ⓐ Ⓑ Ⓒ Ⓓ
32. Ⓐ Ⓑ Ⓒ Ⓓ
33. Ⓐ Ⓑ Ⓒ Ⓓ
34. Ⓐ Ⓑ Ⓒ Ⓓ
35. Ⓐ Ⓑ Ⓒ Ⓓ
36. Ⓐ Ⓑ Ⓒ Ⓓ
37. Ⓐ Ⓑ Ⓒ Ⓓ
38. Ⓐ Ⓑ Ⓒ Ⓓ
39. Ⓐ Ⓑ Ⓒ Ⓓ
40. Ⓐ Ⓑ Ⓒ Ⓓ
41. Ⓐ Ⓑ Ⓒ Ⓓ
42. Ⓐ Ⓑ Ⓒ Ⓓ
43. Ⓐ Ⓑ Ⓒ Ⓓ
44. Ⓐ Ⓑ Ⓒ Ⓓ
45. Ⓐ Ⓑ Ⓒ Ⓓ
46. Ⓐ Ⓑ Ⓒ Ⓓ
47. Ⓐ Ⓑ Ⓒ Ⓓ
48. Ⓐ Ⓑ Ⓒ Ⓓ
49. Ⓐ Ⓑ Ⓒ Ⓓ
50. Ⓐ Ⓑ Ⓒ Ⓓ

Section 2

1. Ⓐ Ⓑ Ⓒ Ⓓ
2. Ⓐ Ⓑ Ⓒ Ⓓ
3. Ⓐ Ⓑ Ⓒ Ⓓ
4. Ⓐ Ⓑ Ⓒ Ⓓ
5. Ⓐ Ⓑ Ⓒ Ⓓ
6. Ⓐ Ⓑ Ⓒ Ⓓ
7. Ⓐ Ⓑ Ⓒ Ⓓ
8. Ⓐ Ⓑ Ⓒ Ⓓ
9. Ⓐ Ⓑ Ⓒ Ⓓ
10. Ⓐ Ⓑ Ⓒ Ⓓ
11. Ⓐ Ⓑ Ⓒ Ⓓ
12. Ⓐ Ⓑ Ⓒ Ⓓ
13. Ⓐ Ⓑ Ⓒ Ⓓ
14. Ⓐ Ⓑ Ⓒ Ⓓ
15. Ⓐ Ⓑ Ⓒ Ⓓ
16. Ⓐ Ⓑ Ⓒ Ⓓ
17. Ⓐ Ⓑ Ⓒ Ⓓ
18. Ⓐ Ⓑ Ⓒ Ⓓ
19. Ⓐ Ⓑ Ⓒ Ⓓ
20. Ⓐ Ⓑ Ⓒ Ⓓ
21. Ⓐ Ⓑ Ⓒ Ⓓ
22. Ⓐ Ⓑ Ⓒ Ⓓ
23. Ⓐ Ⓑ Ⓒ Ⓓ
24. Ⓐ Ⓑ Ⓒ Ⓓ
25. Ⓐ Ⓑ Ⓒ Ⓓ
26. Ⓐ Ⓑ Ⓒ Ⓓ
27. Ⓐ Ⓑ Ⓒ Ⓓ
28. Ⓐ Ⓑ Ⓒ Ⓓ
29. Ⓐ Ⓑ Ⓒ Ⓓ
30. Ⓐ Ⓑ Ⓒ Ⓓ
31. Ⓐ Ⓑ Ⓒ Ⓓ
32. Ⓐ Ⓑ Ⓒ Ⓓ
33. Ⓐ Ⓑ Ⓒ Ⓓ
34. Ⓐ Ⓑ Ⓒ Ⓓ
35. Ⓐ Ⓑ Ⓒ Ⓓ
36. Ⓐ Ⓑ Ⓒ Ⓓ
37. Ⓐ Ⓑ Ⓒ Ⓓ
38. Ⓐ Ⓑ Ⓒ Ⓓ
39. Ⓐ Ⓑ Ⓒ Ⓓ
40. Ⓐ Ⓑ Ⓒ Ⓓ

Section 3

1. Ⓐ Ⓑ Ⓒ Ⓓ
2. Ⓐ Ⓑ Ⓒ Ⓓ
3. Ⓐ Ⓑ Ⓒ Ⓓ
4. Ⓐ Ⓑ Ⓒ Ⓓ
5. Ⓐ Ⓑ Ⓒ Ⓓ
6. Ⓐ Ⓑ Ⓒ Ⓓ
7. Ⓐ Ⓑ Ⓒ Ⓓ
8. Ⓐ Ⓑ Ⓒ Ⓓ
9. Ⓐ Ⓑ Ⓒ Ⓓ
10. Ⓐ Ⓑ Ⓒ Ⓓ
11. Ⓐ Ⓑ Ⓒ Ⓓ
12. Ⓐ Ⓑ Ⓒ Ⓓ
13. Ⓐ Ⓑ Ⓒ Ⓓ
14. Ⓐ Ⓑ Ⓒ Ⓓ
15. Ⓐ Ⓑ Ⓒ Ⓓ
16. Ⓐ Ⓑ Ⓒ Ⓓ
17. Ⓐ Ⓑ Ⓒ Ⓓ
18. Ⓐ Ⓑ Ⓒ Ⓓ
19. Ⓐ Ⓑ Ⓒ Ⓓ
20. Ⓐ Ⓑ Ⓒ Ⓓ
21. Ⓐ Ⓑ Ⓒ Ⓓ
22. Ⓐ Ⓑ Ⓒ Ⓓ
23. Ⓐ Ⓑ Ⓒ Ⓓ
24. Ⓐ Ⓑ Ⓒ Ⓓ
25. Ⓐ Ⓑ Ⓒ Ⓓ
26. Ⓐ Ⓑ Ⓒ Ⓓ
27. Ⓐ Ⓑ Ⓒ Ⓓ
28. Ⓐ Ⓑ Ⓒ Ⓓ
29. Ⓐ Ⓑ Ⓒ Ⓓ
30. Ⓐ Ⓑ Ⓒ Ⓓ
31. Ⓐ Ⓑ Ⓒ Ⓓ
32. Ⓐ Ⓑ Ⓒ Ⓓ
33. Ⓐ Ⓑ Ⓒ Ⓓ
34. Ⓐ Ⓑ Ⓒ Ⓓ
35. Ⓐ Ⓑ Ⓒ Ⓓ
36. Ⓐ Ⓑ Ⓒ Ⓓ
37. Ⓐ Ⓑ Ⓒ Ⓓ
38. Ⓐ Ⓑ Ⓒ Ⓓ
39. Ⓐ Ⓑ Ⓒ Ⓓ
40. Ⓐ Ⓑ Ⓒ Ⓓ
41. Ⓐ Ⓑ Ⓒ Ⓓ
42. Ⓐ Ⓑ Ⓒ Ⓓ
43. Ⓐ Ⓑ Ⓒ Ⓓ
44. Ⓐ Ⓑ Ⓒ Ⓓ
45. Ⓐ Ⓑ Ⓒ Ⓓ
46. Ⓐ Ⓑ Ⓒ Ⓓ
47. Ⓐ Ⓑ Ⓒ Ⓓ
48. Ⓐ Ⓑ Ⓒ Ⓓ
49. Ⓐ Ⓑ Ⓒ Ⓓ
50. Ⓐ Ⓑ Ⓒ Ⓓ

1 1 1 1 1 1 1 1 1 1 1 1

Model Test 3
Short Form

Section 1:
Listening Comprehension

50 QUESTIONS 40 MINUTES

In this section of the test, you will have an opportunity to demonstrate your ability to understand conversations and talks in English. There are three parts to this section with special directions for each part. Answer all the questions on the basis of what is stated or implied by the speakers in this test. When you take the actual TOEFL test, you will not be allowed to take notes or write in your test book. Try to work on this Model Test in the same way.

Part A

Directions: In Part A, you will hear short conversations between two people. After each conversation, you will hear a question about the conversation. The conversations and questions will not be repeated. After you hear a question, read the four possible answers in your book and choose the best answer. Then, on your answer sheet, find the number of the question and fill in the space that corresponds to the letter of the answer you have chosen.

1. (A) She will not go home for spring vacation.
   (B) She has not taken a vacation for a long time.
   (C) She does not plan to graduate.
   (D) She does not want to go home after graduation in May.

2. (A) At a butcher shop.
   (B) At a restaurant.
   (C) At a bookstore.
   (D) At a grocery store.

3. (A) The class.
   (B) The weekend.
   (C) Homework.
   (D) Books.

4. (A) That the man will not be able to sleep.
   (B) That someone will enter the back door while the man is sleeping.
   (C) That the lock on the door will break.
   (D) That the man will not be able to come back.

5. (A) She forgot her brother's birthday.
   (B) She does not have very much money.
   (C) She needs a gift for her brother.
   (D) Her brother did not like the present.

6. (A) He should have prepared more.
   (B) He is very worried.
   (C) He has been studying a lot.
   (D) He needs a few more days.

7. (A) She works at Sun Valley.
   (B) She does not like Mr. Miller.
   (C) Her husband is not well today.
   (D) She is Mrs. Adams.

8. (A) He believes that Jack will not be able to sell his house.
   (B) He believes that Jack was joking.
   (C) He agrees with the woman.
   (D) He believes that Jack will quit his job.

GO ON TO THE NEXT PAGE

1 1 1 1 1 1 1 1 1 1 1

9. (A) Buy a textbook.
   (B) Come back later.
   (C) Go to the bookstore.
   (D) Drop his English class.

10. (A) She likes the weather.
    (B) She needs a new dress.
    (C) She wants to please the man.
    (D) She will wear the more comfortable dress.

11. (A) She does not like the class.
    (B) Her classmates are really great.
    (C) The professor is not very nice.
    (D) The class is interesting.

12. (A) She went to Atlanta.
    (B) She went to a convention.
    (C) She went to a hospital.
    (D) She stayed home.

13. (A) Make an appointment with a dentist.
    (B) Cancel her appointment with the dentist.
    (C) Postpone her appointment with the dentist.
    (D) See the dentist more often.

14. (A) He would rather have American food.
    (B) He has always liked American food.
    (C) He is accustomed to eating American food.
    (D) He ate American food more in the past.

15. (A) He should go to bed.
    (B) He did not know the time.
    (C) He is trying to bring his work up to date.
    (D) He is not sleepy yet.

16. (A) He intends to invite the woman to their home.
    (B) He does not want to see the woman.
    (C) He is not very polite to the woman.
    (D) He prefers seeing Connie.

17. (A) Spend some time with the man.
    (B) Make a list of the names.
    (C) Pass out the names.
    (D) Let someone else call the names.

18. (A) The woman has missed the deadline.
    (B) He will investigate the situation.
    (C) The deadline has been canceled.
    (D) An exception might be possible.

19. (A) The tickets are lost.
    (B) Judy was responsible for getting the tickets.
    (C) There were no tickets available.
    (D) He does not have his tickets yet.

20. (A) He is often wrong.
    (B) He usually recommends the freeway.
    (C) He is not a local radio personality.
    (D) He is a popular announcer.

21. (A) The book is confusing.
    (B) He is doing well in the class.
    (C) The teacher is not very clear.
    (D) The lectures are from the book.

22. (A) Randy is a confident person.
    (B) Randy is very fortunate.
    (C) She does not know Randy.
    (D) She is not sure whether she knows Randy.

23. (A) She wants to submit her paper early.
    (B) The answers on the paper are all correct.
    (C) The deadline has passed for the paper.
    (D) The paper is not quite finished.

24. (A) She prefers singing a solo.
    (B) She does not want to help the men.
    (C) She is not a good singer.
    (D) She does not like music.

25. (A) She does not like the class.
    (B) It is not a required class.
    (C) She has already taken the class.
    (D) The man will have to take the class.

GO ON TO THE NEXT PAGE ➡

1 1 1 1 1 1 1 1 1 1 1

26. (A) Get his car repaired.
    (B) Buy a different car.
    (C) Borrow a car.
    (D) Bring the car in.

27. (A) Study together.
    (B) Prepare for an oral final.
    (C) Review the quizzes.
    (D) Take the professor's advice.

28. (A) Make an appointment.
    (B) Give the man a pen.
    (C) Sign the form for the man.
    (D) Wait for the man.

29. (A) Revise her work.
    (B) Close the window.
    (C) Copy from the man.
    (D) Hand in the work.

30. (A) The computer made an error.
    (B) The payment is due on the fifth of every month.
    (C) The loan must be paid by the first of the month.
    (D) The loan had already been paid in full.

Part B

Directions: In this part of the test, you will hear longer conversations. After each conversation, you will hear several questions. The conversations and questions will not be repeated.

After you hear a question, read the four possible answers in your book and choose the best answer. Then, on your answer sheet, find the number of the question and fill in the space that corresponds to the letter of the answer you have chosen.

Remember, you are **not** allowed to take notes or write on your test pages.

31. (A) She is waiting for the man.
    (B) She is waiting for her mother.
    (C) She is waiting for a bus.
    (D) She is waiting for it to stop raining.

32. (A) Cold.
    (B) Very hot.
    (C) Cooler than the weather on the day of this conversation.
    (D) Drier than the weather on the day of this conversation.

33. (A) Florida.
    (B) New York.
    (C) California.
    (D) Indiana.

34. (A) Every ten minutes.
    (B) At twenty to one.
    (C) Every half-hour.
    (D) Once a day.

35. (A) To enroll in a class.
    (B) To ask his opinion about a university.
    (C) To find out who is chair of the selection committee.
    (D) To get a letter for graduate school.

36. (A) She might need to take his seminar.
    (B) She should do well in graduate school.
    (C) She had better go to another university.
    (D) She needs to apply before the end of April.

37. (A) The chair of the selection committee.
    (B) The entire selection committee.
    (C) Professor Hayes.
    (D) Dr. Warren.

GO ON TO THE NEXT PAGE ▶

1   1   1   1   1   1   1   1   1   1   1

38. (A) On May 1.
    (B) In three days.
    (C) Before the April 30th deadline.
    (D) Today.

Part C

Directions: In this part of the test, you will hear several short talks. After each talk, you will hear some questions. The talks and questions will not be repeated.

After you hear a question, read the four possible answers in your book and choose the best answer. Then, on your answer sheet, find the number of the question and fill in the space that corresponds to the letter of the answer you have chosen.

39. (A) A professor of religion.
    (B) A professor of business.
    (C) A guest lecturer in a drama class.
    (D) A guest lecturer in a writing class.

40. (A) By threatening to go to war.
    (B) By competing with farmers.
    (C) By keeping manufacturing processes secret.
    (D) By stealing plans from the colonies.

41. (A) He kept designs for English machinery from being used in the colonies.
    (B) He prevented Moses Brown from opening a mill.
    (C) He committed designs for English machinery to memory.
    (D) He smuggled drawings for English machines into the United States.

42. (A) A change from agriculture to industry began to occur in the United States.
    (B) A rise in prices for English goods was evidenced.
    (C) Many small farmers began to send their products to England.
    (D) Americans had to keep their manufacturing processes secret.

43. (A) The term "essay."
    (B) Prose writing.
    (C) Personal viewpoint.
    (D) Brainstorming.

44. (A) The work of Alexander Pope.
    (B) The difference between prose and poetry.
    (C) The general characteristics of essays.
    (D) The reason that the phrase "personal essay" is redundant.

45. (A) It is usually short.
    (B) It can be either prose or poetry.
    (C) It expresses a personal point of view.
    (D) It discusses one topic.

46. (A) They will prepare for a quiz.
    (B) They will write their first essay.
    (C) They will read works by Pope.
    (D) They will review their notes.

47. (A) To provide an overview of U.S. history from 1743 to 1826.
    (B) To discuss Jefferson's contribution to the American Revolution.
    (C) To analyze Jefferson's presidency.
    (D) To summarize Jefferson's life.

GO ON TO THE NEXT PAGE ➡

1   1   1   1   1   1   1   1   1   1   1   1

48. (A) Monarchist.
    (B) Federalist.
    (C) Republican.
    (D) Democrat.

49. (A) He received the most votes.
    (B) Congress approved him.
    (C) Aaron Burr withdrew from the race.
    (D) As vice president, he automatically
        became president.

50. (A) An effective public speaker.
    (B) An architect.
    (C) A literary draftsman.
    (D) A diplomat.

**THIS IS THE END OF THE LISTENING COMPREHENSION SECTION
OF TOEFL MODEL TEST 3.**

DO NOT READ OR WORK ON ANY OTHER SECTION OF THE TEST.

2 2 2 2 2 2 2 2 2 2 2

Section 2:
Structure and Written Expression

40 QUESTIONS 25 MINUTES

This section is designed to measure your ability to recognize language that is appropriate for standard written English. There are two types of questions in this section, with special directions for each type.

Structure

Directions: Questions 1–15 are incomplete sentences. Beneath each sentence you will see four words or phrases, marked (A), (B), (C), and (D). Choose the **one** word or phrase that best completes the sentence. Then, on your answer sheet, find the number of the question and fill in the space that corresponds to the letter of the answer you have chosen. Fill in the space so that the letter inside the oval cannot be seen.

1. In simple animals, --------- reflex movement or involuntary response to stimuli.

   (A) behavior mostly
   (B) most is behavior
   (C) most behavior is
   (D) the most behavior

2. Although the weather in Martha's Vineyard isn't ----------- to have a year-round tourist session, it has become a favorite summer resort.

   (A) goodly enough
   (B) good enough
   (C) good as enough
   (D) enough good

3. According to the wave theory, --------- population of the Americas may have been the result of a number of separate migrations.

   (A) the
   (B) their
   (C) that
   (D) whose

4. It is presumed that rules governing the sharing of food influenced ----------- that the earliest cultures evolved.

   (A) that the way
   (B) is the way
   (C) the way
   (D) which way

5. Calculus, ----------- elegant and economical symbolic system, can reduce complex problems to simple terms.

   (A) it is an
   (B) that an
   (C) an
   (D) is an

6. Canada does not require that U.S. citizens obtain passports to enter the country, and -----------

   (A) Mexico does neither
   (B) Mexico doesn't either
   (C) neither Mexico does
   (D) either does Mexico

7. The poet ----------- just beginning to be recognized as an important influence at the time of his death.

   (A) being Walt Whitman
   (B) who was Walt Whitman
   (C) Walt Whitman
   (D) Walt Whitman was

GO ON TO THE NEXT PAGE

2   2   2   2   2   2   2   2   2   2   2

8. ----------- the formation of the sun, the planets, and other stars began with the condensation of an interstellar cloud.

(A) It accepted that
(B) Accepted that
(C) It is accepted that
(D) That is accepted

9. As a general rule, the standard of living ----------- by the average output of each person in society.

(A) is fixed
(B) fixed
(C) has fixed
(D) fixes

10. The *Consumer Price Index* lists ------- .

(A) how much costs every car
(B) how much does every car cost
(C) how much every car costs
(D) how much are every car cost

11. The Ford Theater where Lincoln was shot ----------- .

(A) must restore
(B) must be restoring
(C) must have been restored
(D) must restored

12. Fast-food restaurants have become popular because many working people want -------- .

(A) to eat quickly and cheaply
(B) eating quickly and cheaply
(C) eat quickly and cheaply
(D) the eat quickly and cheaply

13. After seeing the movie *Centennial,* ----------- .

(A) the book was read by many people
(B) the book made many people want to read it
(C) many people wanted to read the book
(D) the reading of the book interested many people

14. -----------, Carl Sandburg is also well known for his multivolume biography of Lincoln.

(A) An eminent American poet
(B) He is an eminent American poet
(C) An eminent American poet who is
(D) Despite an eminent American poet

15. The examiner made us ----------- our identification in order to be admitted to the test center.

(A) showing
(B) show
(C) showed
(D) to show

Written Expression

Directions: In questions 16–40, each sentence has four underlined words or phrases. The four underlined parts of the sentence are marked (A), (B), (C), and (D). Identify the **one** underlined word or phrase that must be changed in order for the sentence to be correct. Then, on your answer sheet, find the number of the question and fill in the space that corresponds to the letter of the answer you have chosen.

16. A swarm of locusts is responsible the consumption of enough plant material to feed a million
                       (A)   (B)   (C)
    and a half people.
    (D)

GO ON TO THE NEXT PAGE

17. Oyster farming has been practice in most parts of the world for many years.
          (A)   (B)   (C)   (D)

18. Those of us who smoke should have their lungs X-rayed regularly.
     (A)   (B)   (C)   (D)

19. After the team of geologists had drawn diagrams in their notebooks and wrote explanations of
                                                  (A)   (B)

    the formations which they had observed, they returned to their campsite to compare notes.
                (C)   (D)

20. If Robert Kennedy would have lived a little longer, he probably would have won the election.
                    (A)   (B)   (C)   (D)

21. It was Shirley Temple Black which represented her country in the United Nations and later
    (A)   (B)   (C)   (D)

    became an ambassador.

22. The prices at chain stores are as reasonable, if not more reasonable, as those at discount stores.
             (A)   (B)   (C)   (D)

23. It is extremely important for an engineer to know to use a computer.
    (A)   (B)   (C)   (D)

24. Historically there has been only two major factions in the Republican Party—the liberals and the
       (A)   (B)   (C)   (D)

    conservatives.

25. Whitman wrote *Leaves of Grass* as a tribute to the Civil War soldiers who had laid on the
                                                           (A)

    battlefields and whom he had seen while serving as an army nurse.
             (B)   (C)   (D)

26. One of the first and ultimately the most important purposeful of a reservoir was to control
                    (A)   (B)   (C)

    flooding.
     (D)

27. The Chinese were the first and large ethnic group to work on the construction of the
        (A)   (B)   (C)   (D)

    transcontinental railroad system.

GO ON TO THE NEXT PAGE

2 **2** **2** **2** **2** **2** **2** **2** **2** **2** **2**

28. The range of plant life on a mountainside is a results of differences in temperature and
                                          (A)   (B)   (C)

    precipitation at varying altitudes.
                     (D)

29. Even a professional psychologist may have difficulty talking calm and logically about his own
     (A)   (B)   (C)   (D)
    problems.

30. The more the relative humidity reading rises, the worst the heat affects us.
                                          (A)   (B)   (C) (D)

31. Because correlations are not causes, statistical data which are extremely easy to misuse.
                                  (A)   (B)   (C)   (D)

32. Lectures for the week of March 22–26 will include the following: The Causes of the Civil War,
             (A)   (B)   (C)

    The Economy of the South, Battle Strategies, and The Assassinate Lincoln.
                                                         (D)

33. Despite of many attempts to introduce a universal language, notably Esperanto and Idiom Neutral,
     (A)   (B)   (C)

    the effort has met with very little success.
                              (D)

34. As every other nation, the United States used to define its unit of currency, the dollar, in terms of
    (A)   (B)   (C)   (D)
    the gold standard.

35. It is necessary that one met with a judge before signing the final papers for a divorce.
                        (A)   (B)   (C)   (D)

36. Until recently, women were forbidden by law from owning property.
         (A)   (B)   (C)   (D)

37. According to the graduate catalog, student housing is more cheaper than housing off campus.
     (A)   (B)   (C)   (D)

38. John Dewey thought that children will learn better through participating in experiences
                                    (A)   (B)

    rather than through listening to lectures.
        (C)   (D)

GO ON TO THE NEXT PAGE

3 **3** **3** **3** **3** **3** **3** **3** **3** **3** **3**

39. In England as early as the twelfth century, young boys enjoyed to play football.
    (A)   (B)   (C)   (D)

40. Some methods to prevent soil erosion are plowing parallel with the slopes of hills, to plant trees
    (A)   (B)   (C)   (D)
    on unproductive land, and rotating crops.

**THIS IS THE END OF THE STRUCTURE AND WRITTEN EXPRESSION
SECTION OF TOEFL MODEL TEST 3.**

**IF YOU FINISH BEFORE 25 MINUTES HAS ENDED, CHECK YOUR
WORK ON SECTION 2 ONLY.**

DO NOT READ OR WORK ON ANY OTHER SECTION OF THE TEST.

3 3 3 3 3 3 3 3 3 3 3

Section 3:
Reading Comprehension

50 QUESTIONS 55 MINUTES

Directions: In this section you will read several passages. Each one is followed by a number of questions about it. For questions 1–50, you are to choose the **one** best answer, (A), (B), (C), or (D), to each question. Then, on your answer sheet, find the number of the question and fill in the space that corresponds to the letter of the answer you have chosen.

Answer all questions about the information in a passage on the basis of what is **stated** or **implied** in that passage.

Questions 1–10

Few men have influenced the development of American English to the extent that Noah Webster did. Born in West Hartford, Connecticut, in 1758, his name has become synonymous with American dictionaries. Graduated from Yale in 1778, he was admitted to the bar
Line in 1781 and thereafter began to practice law in Hartford. Later, when he turned to teaching,
(5) he discovered how inadequate the available schoolbooks were for the children of a new and independent nation.

In response to the need for truly American textbooks, Webster published *A Grammatical Institute of the English Language*, a three-volume work that consisted of a speller, a grammar, and a reader. The first volume, which was generally known as *The American Spelling Book*,
(10) was so popular that eventually it sold more than 80 million copies and provided him with a considerable income for the rest of his life. While teaching, Webster began work on the *Compendious Dictionary of the English Language*, which was published in 1806.

In 1807 Noah Webster began his greatest work, *An American Dictionary of the English Language*. In preparing the manuscript, he devoted ten years to the study of English and its
(15) relationship to other languages, and seven more years to the writing itself. Published in two volumes in 1828, *An American Dictionary of the English Language* has become the recognized authority for usage in the United States. Webster's purpose in writing it was to demonstrate that the American language was developing distinct meanings, pronunciations, and spellings from those of British English. He is responsible for advancing simplified spelling
(20) forms: *develop* instead of the British form *develope*; *theater* and *center* instead of *theatre* and *centre*; *color* and *honor* instead of *colour* and *honour*.

In 1840 Webster brought out a second edition of his dictionary, which included 70,000 entries instead of the original 38,000. This edition has served as the basis for the many revisions that have been produced under the Webster name.

1. Which of the following would be the best
   title for the passage?

   (A) Webster's Work
   (B) Webster's Dictionaries
   (C) Webster's School
   (D) Webster's Life

GO ON TO THE NEXT PAGE

2. The word "inadequate" in line 5 could best be replaced by

(A) unavailable
(B) expensive
(C) difficult
(D) unsatisfactory

3. Why did Webster write *A Grammatical Institute of the English Language*?

(A) He wanted to supplement his income.
(B) There were no books available after the Revolutionary War.
(C) He felt that British books were not appropriate for American children.
(D) The children did not know how to spell.

4. From which publication did Webster earn a lifetime income?

(A) *Compendious Dictionary of the English Language*
(B) *An American Dictionary of the English Language*
(C) *An American Dictionary of the English Language: Second Edition*
(D) *The American Spelling Book*

5. In how many volumes was *An American Dictionary of the English Language* published?

(A) One volume
(B) Two volumes
(C) Three volumes
(D) Four volumes

6. When was *An American Dictionary of the English Language* published?

(A) 1817
(B) 1807
(C) 1828
(D) 1824

7. According to the author, what was Webster's purpose in writing *An American Dictionary of the English Language*?

(A) To respond to the need for new school-books
(B) To demonstrate the distinct development of the English language in America
(C) To promote spelling forms based upon British models
(D) To influence the pronunciation of the English language

8. The word "it" in line 17 refers to

(A) language
(B) usage
(C) authority
(D) dictionary

9. The word "distinct" in line 18 is closest in meaning to

(A) new
(B) simple
(C) different
(D) exact

10. According to this passage, which one of the following spellings would Webster have approved in his dictionaries?

(A) *Develope*
(B) *Theatre*
(C) *Color*
(D) *Honour*

GO ON TO THE NEXT PAGE

3 3 3 3 3 3 3 3 3 3 3

Questions 11–20

      The San Andreas Fault is a fracture at the congruence of two major plates of the earth's crust, one of which supports most of the North American continent, and the other of which underlies the coast of California and the ocean floor of the Pacific. The fault originates about
Line six hundred miles from the Gulf of California and runs north in an irregular line along the
(5) west coast to San Francisco, where it continues north for about two hundred more miles before angling into the ocean. In places, the trace of the fault is marked by a trench, or, in geological terms, a rift, and small ponds called sag ponds that dot the landscape. Its western side always moves north in relation to its eastern side. The total net slip along the San Andreas Fault and the length of time it has been active are matters of conjecture, but it has been esti-
(10) mated that, during the past fifteen million years, coastal California along the San Andreas Fault has moved about 190 miles in a northwesterly direction with respect to North America. Although the movement along the fault averages only a few inches a year, it is intermittent and variable. Some segments of the fault do not move at all for long periods of time, building up tremendous pressure that must be released. For this reason, tremors are not unusual along
(15) the San Andreas Fault, and some of them are classified as major earthquakes.
      It is worth noting that the San Andreas Fault passes uncomfortably close to several major metropolitan areas, including Los Angeles and San Francisco. In addition, the San Andreas Fault has created smaller fault systems, many of which underlie the smaller towns and cities along the California Coast. For this reason, Californians have long anticipated the recurrence
(20) of what they refer to as the "Big One," a destructive earthquake that would measure near 8 on the Richter scale, similar in intensity to those that occurred in 1857 and 1906. The effects of such a quake would wreak devastating effects on the life and property in the region. Unfortunately, as pressure continues to build along the fault, the likelihood of such an earthquake increases substantially.

11. What is the author's main purpose in the passage?

   (A) To describe the San Andreas Fault
   (B) To give a definition of a fault
   (C) To explain the reason for tremors and earthquakes
   (D) To classify different kinds of faults

12. The word "originates" in line 3 could best be replaced by

   (A) gets wider
   (B) changes direction
   (C) begins
   (D) disappears

13. Where does the fault lie?

   (A) East of the Gulf of California
   (B) West of the Gulf of California
   (C) North of the Gulf of California
   (D) South of the Gulf of California

14. Which of the following words best describes the San Andreas Fault?

   (A) Straight
   (B) Deep
   (C) Wide
   (D) Rough

15. In which direction does the western side of the fault move?

   (A) West
   (B) East
   (C) North
   (D) South

GO ON TO THE NEXT PAGE

3 3 3 3 3 3 3 3 3 3 3

16. The word "it" in line 5 refers to

(A) San Francisco
(B) ocean
(C) coast
(D) fault

17. The word "intermittent" in line 12 could best be replaced by which of the following?

(A) dangerous
(B) predictable
(C) uncommon
(D) occasional

18. The phrase "the Big One" refers to which of the following?

(A) A serious earthquake
(B) The San Andreas Fault
(C) The Richter Scale
(D) California

19. Along the San Andreas Fault, tremors are

(A) small and insignificant
(B) rare, but disastrous
(C) frequent events
(D) very unpredictable

20. How does the author define the San Andreas Fault?

(A) A plate that underlies the North American continent
(B) A crack in the earth's crust between two plates
(C) Occasional tremors and earthquakes
(D) Intense pressure that builds up

Questions 21–30

The body of an adult insect is subdivided into a head, a thorax of three segments, and a segmented abdomen. Ordinarily, the thorax bears three pairs of legs. One or two pairs of wings may be attached to the thorax. Most adult insects have two large compound eyes, and
Line two or three small simple eyes.
(5) Features of the mouth parts are very helpful in classifying the many kinds of insects. A majority of insects have biting mouth parts or mandibles as in grasshoppers and beetles. Behind the mandibles are the maxillae, which serve to direct food into the mouth between the jaws. A labrum above and a labium below are similar to an upper and lower lip. In insects with sucking mouth parts, the mandibles, maxillae, labrum, and labium are modified to provide a
(10) tube through which liquid can be drawn. In a butterfly or moth, the coiled drinking tube is called the proboscis. Composed chiefly of modified maxillae fitted together, the proboscis can be extended to reach nectar deep in a flower. In a mosquito or an aphid, mandibles and maxillae are modified to sharp stylets with which the insect can drill through surfaces to reach juice. In a housefly, the expanding labium forms a spongelike mouth pad that it can use to stamp
(15) over the surface of food.

21. What is the best title for this passage?

(A) An Insect's Environment
(B) The Structure of an Insect
(C) Grasshoppers and Beetles
(D) The Stages of Life of an Insect

22. What is the purpose of this passage?

(A) To complain
(B) To persuade
(C) To entertain
(D) To inform

GO ON TO THE NEXT PAGE

3   3   3   3   3   3   3   3   3   3   3

23. How are insects classified?

    (A) By the environment in which they live
    (B) By the food they eat
    (C) By the structure of the mouth
    (D) By the number and type of wings

24. The word "majority" in line 6 is closest in meaning to

    (A) more than half
    (B) more than twelve
    (C) more than three
    (D) more than one

25. What is the purpose of the maxillae?

    (A) To bite or sting
    (B) To drill through surfaces to find nourishment
    (C) To put food between the jaws
    (D) To soak up nourishment like a sponge

26. The author compares labrum and labium to

    (A) an upper and lower lip
    (B) mandibles
    (C) maxillae
    (D) jaws

27. What is the proboscis?

    (A) Nectar
    (B) A tube constructed of modified maxillae
    (C) A kind of butterfly
    (D) A kind of flower

28. Which of the following have mandibles and maxillae that have been modified to sharp stylets?

    (A) Grasshoppers
    (B) Butterflies
    (C) Mosquitoes
    (D) Houseflies

29. The phrase "drill through" in line 13 could best be replaced by

    (A) penetrate
    (B) saturate
    (C) explore
    (D) distinguish

30. The word "it" in line 14 refers to

    (A) pad
    (B) food
    (C) housefly
    (D) mouth

Questions 31–40

Interest is the sum charged for borrowing money for a fixed period of time. Principal is the term used for the money that is borrowed, and the rate of interest is the percent per year of the principal charged for its use. Most of the profits for a bank are derived from the interest that
Line they charge for the use of their own or their depositors' money.
(5)   All problems in interest may be solved by using one general equation that may be stated as follows:

$$\text{Interest} = \text{Principal} \times \text{Rate} \times \text{Time}$$

Any one of the four quantities—that is, interest, principal, rate, or time—may be found when the other three are known. The time is expressed in years. The rate is expressed as a dec-
(10) imal fraction. Thus, 6 percent interest means six cents charged for the use of $1 of principal borrowed for one year. Although the time may be less than, equal to, or greater than one year, most applications for loans are for periods of less than one year. For purposes of computing interest for short periods, the commercial year or 360 days is commonly used, but when large sums of money are involved, exact interest is computed on the basis of 365 days.

GO ON TO THE NEXT PAGE ➤

3 3 3 3 3 3 3 3 3 3 3

31. With what topic is this passage primarily concerned?

    (A) Profits
    (B) Rate
    (C) Interest
    (D) Principal

32. The word "sum" in line 1 could best be replaced by

    (A) amount
    (B) institution
    (C) customer
    (D) formula

33. The word "fixed" in line 1 is closest in meaning to

    (A) definite
    (B) short
    (C) repeated
    (D) trial

34. The word "its" in line 3 refers to

    (A) principal
    (B) percent
    (C) rate
    (D) interest

35. At 4 percent interest for the use of $1 principal, how much would one pay?

    (A) Six cents per year
    (B) Twenty-five cents per year
    (C) Four cents per year
    (D) One cent per year

36. Which of the following would be a correct expression of an interest rate as stated in the equation for computing interest?

    (A) Four
    (B) .04
    (C) 4
    (D) 4/100

37. Most applications for loans are for

    (A) one year
    (B) less than one year
    (C) more than one year
    (D) 360 days

38. The word "periods" in line 12 refers to

    (A) time
    (B) loans
    (C) applications
    (D) interest

39. A commercial year is used to compute

    (A) exact interest
    (B) interest on large sums of money
    (C) interest on a large principal
    (D) interest for short periods of time

40. Which of the following is the best definition of interest?

    (A) Money borrowed
    (B) Rate × Time
    (C) A fee paid for the use of money
    (D) The number of years a bank allows a borrower in order to repay a loan

Questions 41–50

    The protozoans, minute, aquatic creatures each of which consists of a single cell of protoplasm, constitute a classification of the most primitive forms of animal life. They are fantastically diverse, but three major groups may be identified on the basis of their motility. The
Line Mastigophora have one or more long tails, which they use to project themselves forward. The
(5) Ciliata, which use the same basic means for locomotion as the Mastigophora, have a larger number of short tails. The Sarcodina, which include amoebae, float or row themselves about on their crusted bodies.

GO ON TO THE NEXT PAGE

In addition to their form of movement, several other features discriminate among the three groups of protozoans. For example, at least two nuclei per cell have been identified in the Cil-

(10) iata, usually a large nucleus that regulates growth but decomposes during reproduction, and a smaller one that contains the genetic code necessary to generate the large nucleus.

Protozoans are considered animals because, unlike pigmented plants to which some protozoans are otherwise almost identical, they do not live on simple organic compounds. Their cell demonstrates all of the major characteristics of the cells of higher animals.

(15)   Many species of protozoans collect into colonies, physically connected to each other and responding uniformly to outside stimulae. Current research into this phenomenon along with investigations carried out with advanced microscopes may necessitate a redefinition of what constitutes protozoans, even calling into question the basic premise that they have only one cell. Nevertheless, with the current data available, almost 40,000 species of protozoans have

(20) been identified. No doubt, as the technology improves our methods of observation, better models of classification will be proposed.

41. With what topic is the passage primarily concerned?

(A) Colonies of protozoans
(B) Mastigophora
(C) Motility in protozoans
(D) Characteristics of protozoans

42. The word "minute" in line 1 could best be replaced by

(A) very common
(B) very fast
(C) very old
(D) very small

43. Where do protozoans probably live?

(A) Water
(B) Sand
(C) Grass
(D) Wood

44. What is protoplasm?

(A) A class of protozoan
(B) The substance that forms the cell of a protozoan
(C) A primitive animal similar to a protozoan
(D) An animal that developed from a protozoan

45. To which class of protozoans do the amoebae belong?

(A) Mastigophora
(B) Ciliata
(C) Sarcodina
(D) Motility

46. What is the purpose of the large nucleus in the Ciliata?

(A) It generates the other nucleus.
(B) It contains the genetic code for the small nucleus.
(C) It regulates growth.
(D) It reproduces itself.

47. Why are protozoans classified as animals?

(A) They do not live on simple organic compounds.
(B) They collect in colonies.
(C) They respond uniformly to outside stimulae.
(D) They may have more than one cell.

48. The word "uniformly" in line 16 is closest in meaning to

(A) in the same way
(B) once in a while
(C) all of a sudden
(D) in the long run

GO ON TO THE NEXT PAGE

3   3   3   3   3   3   3   3   3   3   **3**

49. The word "they" in line 13 refers to

(A) protozoans
(B) microscopes
(C) investigations
(D) colonies

50. Which of the following statements are NOT true of protozoans?

(A) There are approximately 40,000 species.
(B) They are the most primitive forms of animal life.
(C) They have a large cell and a smaller cell.
(D) They are difficult to observe.

THIS IS THE END OF THE READING COMPREHENSION SECTION OF TOEFL MODEL TEST 3.

IF YOU FINISH BEFORE 55 MINUTES HAS ENDED, CHECK YOUR WORK ON SECTION 3 ONLY.

DO NOT READ OR WORK ON ANY OTHER SECTION OF THE TEST.

END OF TOEFL MODEL TEST 3.

To check your answers for Model Test 3, refer to the Answer Key on page 463. For an explanation of the answers, refer to the Explanatory Answers for Model Test 3 on page 487.

MODEL TEST 4—ANSWER SHEET

Section 1

1	2	3	4	5	6	7	8	9	10	11	12	13	14	15	16	17	18	19	20	21	22	23	24	25	26	27	28	29	30
Ⓐ	Ⓐ	Ⓐ	Ⓐ	Ⓐ	Ⓐ	Ⓐ	Ⓐ	Ⓐ	Ⓐ	Ⓐ	Ⓐ	Ⓐ	Ⓐ	Ⓐ	Ⓐ	Ⓐ	Ⓐ	Ⓐ	Ⓐ	Ⓐ	Ⓐ	Ⓐ	Ⓐ	Ⓐ	Ⓐ	Ⓐ	Ⓐ	Ⓐ	Ⓐ
Ⓑ	Ⓑ	Ⓑ	Ⓑ	Ⓑ	Ⓑ	Ⓑ	Ⓑ	Ⓑ	Ⓑ	Ⓑ	Ⓑ	Ⓑ	Ⓑ	Ⓑ	Ⓑ	Ⓑ	Ⓑ	Ⓑ	Ⓑ	Ⓑ	Ⓑ	Ⓑ	Ⓑ	Ⓑ	Ⓑ	Ⓑ	Ⓑ	Ⓑ	Ⓑ
Ⓒ	Ⓒ	Ⓒ	Ⓒ	Ⓒ	Ⓒ	Ⓒ	Ⓒ	Ⓒ	Ⓒ	Ⓒ	Ⓒ	Ⓒ	Ⓒ	Ⓒ	Ⓒ	Ⓒ	Ⓒ	Ⓒ	Ⓒ	Ⓒ	Ⓒ	Ⓒ	Ⓒ	Ⓒ	Ⓒ	Ⓒ	Ⓒ	Ⓒ	Ⓒ
Ⓓ	Ⓓ	Ⓓ	Ⓓ	Ⓓ	Ⓓ	Ⓓ	Ⓓ	Ⓓ	Ⓓ	Ⓓ	Ⓓ	Ⓓ	Ⓓ	Ⓓ	Ⓓ	Ⓓ	Ⓓ	Ⓓ	Ⓓ	Ⓓ	Ⓓ	Ⓓ	Ⓓ	Ⓓ	Ⓓ	Ⓓ	Ⓓ	Ⓓ	Ⓓ

31	32	33	34	35	36	37	38	39	40	41	42	43	44	45	46	47	48	49	50
Ⓐ	Ⓐ	Ⓐ	Ⓐ	Ⓐ	Ⓐ	Ⓐ	Ⓐ	Ⓐ	Ⓐ	Ⓐ	Ⓐ	Ⓐ	Ⓐ	Ⓐ	Ⓐ	Ⓐ	Ⓐ	Ⓐ	Ⓐ
Ⓑ	Ⓑ	Ⓑ	Ⓑ	Ⓑ	Ⓑ	Ⓑ	Ⓑ	Ⓑ	Ⓑ	Ⓑ	Ⓑ	Ⓑ	Ⓑ	Ⓑ	Ⓑ	Ⓑ	Ⓑ	Ⓑ	Ⓑ
Ⓒ	Ⓒ	Ⓒ	Ⓒ	Ⓒ	Ⓒ	Ⓒ	Ⓒ	Ⓒ	Ⓒ	Ⓒ	Ⓒ	Ⓒ	Ⓒ	Ⓒ	Ⓒ	Ⓒ	Ⓒ	Ⓒ	Ⓒ
Ⓓ	Ⓓ	Ⓓ	Ⓓ	Ⓓ	Ⓓ	Ⓓ	Ⓓ	Ⓓ	Ⓓ	Ⓓ	Ⓓ	Ⓓ	Ⓓ	Ⓓ	Ⓓ	Ⓓ	Ⓓ	Ⓓ	Ⓓ

Section 2

1	2	3	4	5	6	7	8	9	10	11	12	13	14	15	16	17	18	19	20	21	22	23	24	25	26	27	28	29	30
Ⓐ	Ⓐ	Ⓐ	Ⓐ	Ⓐ	Ⓐ	Ⓐ	Ⓐ	Ⓐ	Ⓐ	Ⓐ	Ⓐ	Ⓐ	Ⓐ	Ⓐ	Ⓐ	Ⓐ	Ⓐ	Ⓐ	Ⓐ	Ⓐ	Ⓐ	Ⓐ	Ⓐ	Ⓐ	Ⓐ	Ⓐ	Ⓐ	Ⓐ	Ⓐ
Ⓑ	Ⓑ	Ⓑ	Ⓑ	Ⓑ	Ⓑ	Ⓑ	Ⓑ	Ⓑ	Ⓑ	Ⓑ	Ⓑ	Ⓑ	Ⓑ	Ⓑ	Ⓑ	Ⓑ	Ⓑ	Ⓑ	Ⓑ	Ⓑ	Ⓑ	Ⓑ	Ⓑ	Ⓑ	Ⓑ	Ⓑ	Ⓑ	Ⓑ	Ⓑ
Ⓒ	Ⓒ	Ⓒ	Ⓒ	Ⓒ	Ⓒ	Ⓒ	Ⓒ	Ⓒ	Ⓒ	Ⓒ	Ⓒ	Ⓒ	Ⓒ	Ⓒ	Ⓒ	Ⓒ	Ⓒ	Ⓒ	Ⓒ	Ⓒ	Ⓒ	Ⓒ	Ⓒ	Ⓒ	Ⓒ	Ⓒ	Ⓒ	Ⓒ	Ⓒ
Ⓓ	Ⓓ	Ⓓ	Ⓓ	Ⓓ	Ⓓ	Ⓓ	Ⓓ	Ⓓ	Ⓓ	Ⓓ	Ⓓ	Ⓓ	Ⓓ	Ⓓ	Ⓓ	Ⓓ	Ⓓ	Ⓓ	Ⓓ	Ⓓ	Ⓓ	Ⓓ	Ⓓ	Ⓓ	Ⓓ	Ⓓ	Ⓓ	Ⓓ	Ⓓ

31	32	33	34	35	36	37	38	39	40
Ⓐ	Ⓐ	Ⓐ	Ⓐ	Ⓐ	Ⓐ	Ⓐ	Ⓐ	Ⓐ	Ⓐ
Ⓑ	Ⓑ	Ⓑ	Ⓑ	Ⓑ	Ⓑ	Ⓑ	Ⓑ	Ⓑ	Ⓑ
Ⓒ	Ⓒ	Ⓒ	Ⓒ	Ⓒ	Ⓒ	Ⓒ	Ⓒ	Ⓒ	Ⓒ
Ⓓ	Ⓓ	Ⓓ	Ⓓ	Ⓓ	Ⓓ	Ⓓ	Ⓓ	Ⓓ	Ⓓ

Section 3

1	2	3	4	5	6	7	8	9	10	11	12	13	14	15	16	17	18	19	20	21	22	23	24	25	26	27	28	29	30
Ⓐ	Ⓐ	Ⓐ	Ⓐ	Ⓐ	Ⓐ	Ⓐ	Ⓐ	Ⓐ	Ⓐ	Ⓐ	Ⓐ	Ⓐ	Ⓐ	Ⓐ	Ⓐ	Ⓐ	Ⓐ	Ⓐ	Ⓐ	Ⓐ	Ⓐ	Ⓐ	Ⓐ	Ⓐ	Ⓐ	Ⓐ	Ⓐ	Ⓐ	Ⓐ
Ⓑ	Ⓑ	Ⓑ	Ⓑ	Ⓑ	Ⓑ	Ⓑ	Ⓑ	Ⓑ	Ⓑ	Ⓑ	Ⓑ	Ⓑ	Ⓑ	Ⓑ	Ⓑ	Ⓑ	Ⓑ	Ⓑ	Ⓑ	Ⓑ	Ⓑ	Ⓑ	Ⓑ	Ⓑ	Ⓑ	Ⓑ	Ⓑ	Ⓑ	Ⓑ
Ⓒ	Ⓒ	Ⓒ	Ⓒ	Ⓒ	Ⓒ	Ⓒ	Ⓒ	Ⓒ	Ⓒ	Ⓒ	Ⓒ	Ⓒ	Ⓒ	Ⓒ	Ⓒ	Ⓒ	Ⓒ	Ⓒ	Ⓒ	Ⓒ	Ⓒ	Ⓒ	Ⓒ	Ⓒ	Ⓒ	Ⓒ	Ⓒ	Ⓒ	Ⓒ
Ⓓ	Ⓓ	Ⓓ	Ⓓ	Ⓓ	Ⓓ	Ⓓ	Ⓓ	Ⓓ	Ⓓ	Ⓓ	Ⓓ	Ⓓ	Ⓓ	Ⓓ	Ⓓ	Ⓓ	Ⓓ	Ⓓ	Ⓓ	Ⓓ	Ⓓ	Ⓓ	Ⓓ	Ⓓ	Ⓓ	Ⓓ	Ⓓ	Ⓓ	Ⓓ

31	32	33	34	35	36	37	38	39	40	41	42	43	44	45	46	47	48	49	50
Ⓐ	Ⓐ	Ⓐ	Ⓐ	Ⓐ	Ⓐ	Ⓐ	Ⓐ	Ⓐ	Ⓐ	Ⓐ	Ⓐ	Ⓐ	Ⓐ	Ⓐ	Ⓐ	Ⓐ	Ⓐ	Ⓐ	Ⓐ
Ⓑ	Ⓑ	Ⓑ	Ⓑ	Ⓑ	Ⓑ	Ⓑ	Ⓑ	Ⓑ	Ⓑ	Ⓑ	Ⓑ	Ⓑ	Ⓑ	Ⓑ	Ⓑ	Ⓑ	Ⓑ	Ⓑ	Ⓑ
Ⓒ	Ⓒ	Ⓒ	Ⓒ	Ⓒ	Ⓒ	Ⓒ	Ⓒ	Ⓒ	Ⓒ	Ⓒ	Ⓒ	Ⓒ	Ⓒ	Ⓒ	Ⓒ	Ⓒ	Ⓒ	Ⓒ	Ⓒ
Ⓓ	Ⓓ	Ⓓ	Ⓓ	Ⓓ	Ⓓ	Ⓓ	Ⓓ	Ⓓ	Ⓓ	Ⓓ	Ⓓ	Ⓓ	Ⓓ	Ⓓ	Ⓓ	Ⓓ	Ⓓ	Ⓓ	Ⓓ

Cut here to remove answer sheet.

1 1 1 1 1 1 1 1 1 1 1

Model Test 4
Short Form

Section 1:
Listening Comprehension

50 QUESTIONS 40 MINUTES

In this section of the test, you will have an opportunity to demonstrate your ability to understand conversations and talks in English. There are three parts to this section with special directions for each part. Answer all the questions on the basis of what is stated or implied by the speakers in this test. When you take the actual TOEFL test, you will not be allowed to take notes or write in your test book. Try to work on this Model Test in the same way.

Part A

Directions: In Part A you will hear short conversations between two people. After each conversation, you will hear a question about the conversation. The conversations and questions will not be repeated. After you hear a question, read the four possible answers in your book and choose the best answer. Then, on your answer sheet, find the number of the question and fill in the space that corresponds to the letter of the answer you have chosen.

1. (A) Car repairs should be done at a garage.
   (B) The price was not too high.
   (C) The garage took advantage of the woman.
   (D) The car had serious problems.

2. (A) Have a party.
   (B) Attend the International Students' Association.
   (C) Go to work.
   (D) Get some rest.

3. (A) Leave immediately.
   (B) Watch the game on TV.
   (C) Start to play.
   (D) Eat a sandwich.

4. (A) He went to see the foreign student advisor.
   (B) He went to Washington.
   (C) He wrote to the Passport Office.
   (D) He reported it to the Passport Office.

5. (A) It is the policy of the bank.
   (B) The man was not helpful at all.
   (C) Her account at the bank is in order.
   (D) The check should be cashed.

6. (A) Ask Dr. Tyler to clarify the assignment.
   (B) Show a preliminary version to Dr. Tyler.
   (C) Let her see the first draft before Dr. Tyler sees it.
   (D) Talk to some of the other students in Dr. Tyler's class.

7. (A) Dr. Clark is a good teacher.
   (B) Statistics is a boring class.
   (C) Two semesters of statistics are required.
   (D) The students do not like Dr. Clark.

8. (A) He cannot do them.
   (B) They are finished.
   (C) It will be a difficult job.
   (D) They will be ready Saturday afternoon.

GO ON TO THE NEXT PAGE

1 1 1 1 1 1 1 1 1 1

9. (A) A concert.
   (B) An art museum.
   (C) A flower shop.
   (D) A restaurant.

10. (A) He is at lunch.
    (B) He is at the office.
    (C) He is in class.
    (D) He is at home.

11. (A) Take the ten o'clock bus.
    (B) Come back in five minutes.
    (C) Go to New York another day.
    (D) Call the airport.

12. (A) A teacher.
    (B) A textbook.
    (C) An assignment.
    (D) A movie.

13. (A) Make corrections on the original.
    (B) Make copies.
    (C) Deliver the copies to Mr. Brown.
    (D) Find the original.

14. (A) She was Sally Harrison's cousin.
    (B) She was Sally Harrison's sister.
    (C) She was Sally Harrison's friend.
    (D) She was Sally Harrison.

15. (A) The desk drawer won't open.
    (B) The pen is out of ink.
    (C) She cannot find her pen.
    (D) She is angry with the man.

16. (A) John is usually late.
    (B) John will be there at eight-thirty.
    (C) John will not show up.
    (D) John is usually on time.

17. (A) She does not agree with the man.
    (B) She needs a larger home.
    (C) She regrets the cost of their vacation.
    (D) She thinks that houses are very expensive.

18. (A) He did not make a presentation.
    (B) He got confused during the presentation.
    (C) He should have spoken more loudly.
    (D) He did a very complete job.

19. (A) He has decided not to mail the invitations.
    (B) He wants to get Janet's opinion.
    (C) He is waiting for Janet to answer the phone.
    (D) He does not want to invite Janet.

20. (A) The baby is asleep.
    (B) The baby is very active.
    (C) The baby is not staying with the woman.
    (D) The baby is just about to start walking.

21. (A) The results of the tests are not available.
    (B) The experiment had unexpected results.
    (C) He has not completed the experiment yet.
    (D) It is taking a lot of time to do the experiment.

22. (A) She does not put much effort in her studies.
    (B) She is very likable.
    (C) She prefers talking to the woman.
    (D) She has a telephone.

23. (A) See the doctor.
    (B) Get another job.
    (C) Go to the counter.
    (D) Buy some medicine.

24. (A) She will try her best.
    (B) She has to save her money.
    (C) She is still undecided.
    (D) She needs an application.

GO ON TO THE NEXT PAGE

1 1 1 1 1 1 1 1 1 1 1

25. (A) She is glad to meet Robert.
    (B) She is surprised to hear from Robert.
    (C) She does not enjoy talking with Robert.
    (D) She was ready to call Robert.

26. (A) The man must stop working.
    (B) There is a little more time.
    (C) The test is important.
    (D) It is time for the test.

27. (A) The woman's roommate took a different class.
    (B) The book is very expensive.
    (C) The textbook may have been changed.
    (D) The course is not offered this semester.

28. (A) Sally may get a bike for Christmas.
    (B) Sally already has a bike like that one.
    (C) Sally likes riding a bike.
    (D) Sally may prefer a different gift.

29. (A) He does not want to give Carol a ride.
    (B) He does not have a car.
    (C) He cannot hear well.
    (D) He does not know Carol.

30. (A) Take a break.
    (B) Go to work.
    (C) Do the other problems.
    (D) Keep trying.

Part B

Directions: In this part of the test, you will hear longer conversations. After each conversation, you will hear several questions. The conversations and questions will not be repeated.

After you hear a question, read the four possible answers in your book and choose the best answer. Then, on your answer sheet, find the number of the question and fill in the space that corresponds to the letter of the answer you have chosen.

Remember, you are **not** allowed to take notes or write on your test pages.

31. (A) Whether to introduce the metric system in the United States.
    (B) How the metric system should be introduced in the United States.
    (C) Which system is better—the English system or the metric system.
    (D) How to convert measurements from the English system to the metric system.

32. (A) Now the weather on radio and TV is reported exclusively in metrics.
    (B) Road signs have miles marked on them, but not kilometers.
    (C) Both the English system and the metric system are being used on signs, packages, and weather reports.
    (D) Grocery stores use only metrics for their packaging.

33. (A) He thought that a gradual adoption would be better for everyone.
    (B) He thought that only metrics should be used.
    (C) He thought that only the English system should be used.
    (D) He thought that adults should use both systems, but that children should be taught only the metric system.

34. (A) Unfriendly.
    (B) Patronizing.
    (C) Uninterested.
    (D) Cooperative.

35. (A) To change his travel plans.
    (B) To arrange a time to pick up his tickets.
    (C) To reserve a hotel room.
    (D) To make a plane reservation.

GO ON TO THE NEXT PAGE ▶

1 1 1 1 1 1 1 1 1 1 1

36. (A) The man can save money by staying an extra night.
    (B) The man should have called earlier.
    (C) She needs the man to come into the office.
    (D) She will mail the tickets to the man.

37. (A) Travel on May 19 as planned.
    (B) Wait for a cheaper fare.
    (C) Stay an extra day in Atlanta.
    (D) Return on Sunday.

38. (A) Go back to his hotel.
    (B) Pack his suitcase.
    (C) Call a different travel agent.
    (D) Go to the travel agent's office in the afternoon.

Part C

Directions: In this part of the test, you will hear several short talks. After each talk, you will hear some questions. The talks and questions will not be repeated.

After you hear a question, read the four possible answers in your book and choose the best answer. Then, on your answer sheet, find the number of the question and fill in the space that corresponds to the letter of the answer you have chosen.

39. (A) Private industry.
    (B) Advances in medicine.
    (C) Space missions.
    (D) Technological developments.

40. (A) Contact lenses.
    (B) Cordless tools.
    (C) Food packaging.
    (D) Ultrasound.

41. (A) To monitor the condition of astronauts in spacecraft.
    (B) To evaluate candidates who wanted to join the space program.
    (C) To check the health of astronauts when they returned from space.
    (D) To test spacecraft and equipment for imperfections.

42. (A) Archaeologists and astronauts were compared.
    (B) Astronauts made photographs of the earth later used by archaeologists.
    (C) Archaeologists have used advances in medical technology developed for astronauts.
    (D) Space missions and underwater missions are very similar.

43. (A) Transportation on the Pacific Coast.
    (B) History of California.
    (C) Orientation to San Francisco.
    (D) Specifications of the Golden Gate Bridge.

44. (A) Golden Gate.
    (B) San Francisco de Asis Mission.
    (C) Military Post Seventy-six.
    (D) Yerba Buena.

GO ON TO THE NEXT PAGE

1 1 1 1 1 1 1 1 1 1 **1**

45. (A) Gold was discovered.
    (B) The Transcontinental Railroad was completed.
    (C) The Golden Gate Bridge was constructed.
    (D) Telegraph communications were established with the East.

46. (A) Eighteen miles.
    (B) 938 feet.
    (C) One mile.
    (D) Between five and six miles.

47. (A) Transcendentalism.
    (B) Puritanism.
    (C) Ralph Waldo Emerson.
    (D) Nature.

48. (A) Seventeenth century.
    (B) Eighteenth century.
    (C) Nineteenth century.
    (D) Twentieth century.

49. (A) They stressed the importance of the individual.
    (B) They supported the ideals of the Transcendental Club.
    (C) They believed that society was more important than the individual.
    (D) They established a commune at Brook Farm.

50. (A) A book by Emerson.
    (B) A history of Puritanism.
    (C) A novel by Nathaniel Hawthorne.
    (D) A book by Thoreau.

THIS IS THE END OF THE LISTENING COMPREHENSION SECTION OF TOEFL MODEL TEST 4.

DO NOT READ OR WORK ON ANY OTHER SECTION OF THE TEST.

2 2 2 2 2 2 2 2 2 2 2

Section 2:
Structure and Written Expression

40 QUESTIONS 25 MINUTES

This section is designed to measure your ability to recognize language that is appropriate for standard written English. There are two types of questions in this section, with special directions for each type.

Structure

Directions: Questions 1–15 are incomplete sentences. Beneath each sentence you will see four words or phrases, marked (A), (B), (C), and (D). Choose the **one** word or phrase that best completes the sentence. Then, on your answer sheet, find the number of the question and fill in the space that corresponds to the letter of the answer you have chosen. Fill in the space so that the letter inside the oval cannot be seen.

1. Based on the premise that light was composed of color, the Impressionists came to the conclusion ---------- not really black.

   (A) which was that shadows
   (B) was shadows which
   (C) were shadows
   (D) that shadows were

2. ---------- a parliamentary system, the prime minister must be appointed on the basis of the distribution of power in the parliament.

   (A) The considered
   (B) To be considered
   (C) Considering
   (D) Considers

3. ---------- of the play *Mourning Becomes Electra* introduces the cast of characters and hints at the plot.

   (A) The act first
   (B) Act one
   (C) Act first
   (D) First act

4. As soon as -------- with an acid, salt, and sometimes water, is formed.

   (A) a base will react
   (B) a base reacts
   (C) a base is reacting
   (D) the reaction of a base

5. The Internal Revenue Service ------- their tax forms by April 15 every year.

   (A) makes all Americans file
   (B) makes all Americans to file
   (C) makes the filing of all Americans
   (D) makes all Americans filing

6. Although one of his ships succeeded in sailing all the way back to Spain past the Cape of Good Hope, Magellan never completed the first circumnavigation of the world, and ---------- .

   (A) most of his crew didn't too
   (B) neither most of his crew did
   (C) neither did most of his crew
   (D) most of his crew didn't also

7. To answer accurately is more important than ---------- .

   (A) a quick finish
   (B) to finish quickly
   (C) finishing quickly
   (D) you finish quickly

GO ON TO THE NEXT PAGE

2 2 2 2 2 2 2 2 2 2 2

8. Weathering ---------- the action whereby surface rock is disintegrated or decomposed.

(A) it is
(B) is that
(C) is
(D) being

9. A telephone recording tells callers ---------.

(A) what time the movie starts
(B) what time starts the movie
(C) what time does the movie start
(D) the movie starts what time

10. The people of Western Canada have been considering ---------- themselves from the rest of the provinces.

(A) to separate
(B) separated
(C) separate
(D) separating

11. It costs about sixty dollars to have a tooth ---------- .

(A) filling
(B) to fill
(C) filled
(D) fill

12. Not until a student has mastered algebra ---------- the principles of geometry, trigonometry, and physics.

(A) he can begin to understand
(B) can he begin to understand
(C) he begins to understand
(D) begins to understand

13. Although Margaret Mead had several assistants during her long investigations of Samoa, the bulk of the research was done by ---------- alone.

(A) herself
(B) she
(C) her
(D) hers

14. ---------- war correspondent, Hemingway used his experiences for some of his most powerful novels.

(A) But a
(B) It is a
(C) While
(D) A

15. Thirty-eight national sites are known as parks, another eighty-two as monuments, and ---------- .

(A) the another one hundred seventy-eight as historical sites
(B) the other one hundred seventy-eight as historical sites
(C) seventy-eight plus one hundred more as historical sites
(D) as historical sites one hundred seventy-eight

Written Expression

Directions: In questions 16–40, each sentence has four underlined words or phrases. The four underlined parts of the sentence are marked (A), (B), (C), and (D). Identify the **one** underlined word or phrase that must be changed in order for the sentence to be correct. Then, on your answer sheet, find the number of the question and fill in the space that corresponds to the letter of the answer you have chosen.

GO ON TO THE NEXT PAGE

2   2   2   2   2   2   2   2   2   2   **2**

16. Interest in automatic data processing has grown rapid since the first large calculators were
          (A)   (B)   (C)   (D)
    introduced in 1950.

17. Vaslav Nijinsky achieved world recognition as both a dancer as well as a choreographer.
                      (A)   (B)   (C)   (D)

18. Airports must be located near to major population centers for the advantage of air transportation
                     (A)   (B)   (C)
    to be retained.
        (D)

19. It is said that Einstein felt very badly about the application of his theories to the creation of
         (A)   (B) (C)   (D)
    weapons of war.

20. The plants that they belong to the family of ferns are quite varied in their size and structure.
                    (A)   (B)   (C)   (D)

21. Despite of the increase in air fares, most people still prefer to travel by plane.
        (A)   (B)   (C)   (D)

22. All of we students must have an identification card in order to check books out of the library.
            (A)   (B)   (C)(D)

23. Columbus Day is celebrated on the twelve of October because on that day in 1492, Christopher
                              (A)   (B)   (C)   (D)
    Columbus first landed in the Americas.

24. One of the most influence newspapers in the U.S. is *The New York Times* which is widely distributed
            (A)   (B)   (C)   (D)
    throughout the world.

25. An unexpected raise in the cost of living as well as a decline in employment opportunities has
                   (A)   (B)
    resulted in the rapid creation by Congress of new government programs for the unemployed.
        (C)   (D)

26. It is imperative that a graduate student maintains a grade point average of "B" in his major field.
    (A)   (B)   (C)   (D)

GO ON TO THE NEXT PAGE

2   2   2   2   2   2   2   2   2   2   2

27. Coastal and inland waters <u>are inhabited</u> <u>not only</u> by fish but also by <u>such</u> <u>sea creature</u> as shrimps
                                      (A)   (B)   (C)   (D)
    and clams.

28. Economists have tried <u>to discourage</u> <u>the use</u> of the phrase "underdeveloped nation" and
                                  (A)   (B)
    <u>encouraging</u> <u>the more</u> accurate phrase "developing nation" in order to suggest an ongoing process.
        (C)   (D)

29. A gas <u>like</u> propane will <u>combination</u> with water molecules in a saline solution <u>to form</u> a solid
              (A)   (B)   (C)
    <u>called</u> a hydrate.
        (D)

30. Although it cannot <u>be proven</u>, <u>presumable</u> the expansion of the universe will slow down as
                            (A)   (B)   (C)
    <u>it approaches</u> a critical radius.
          (D)

31. <u>Regardless of</u> your teaching method, the objective of any conversation class <u>should be</u> for the
          (A)   (B)
    students <u>to practice</u> <u>speaking words</u>.
                (C)   (D)

32. A City University professor reported that he <u>discovers</u> a vaccine <u>that</u> has been 80 percent effective
                                                      (A)   (B)
    <u>in reducing</u> the instances of tooth decay <u>among</u> small children.
          (C)   (D)

33. American baseball teams, <u>once</u> the only contenders for the world championship, are now <u>being</u>
                                  (A)   (B)
    challenged <u>by</u> <u>either</u> Japanese teams and Venezuelan teams.
                  (C) (D)

34. When they <u>have been</u> <u>frightened</u>, as, for example, <u>by</u> an electrical storm, dairy cows may refuse
                  (A)   (B)   (C)
    <u>giving</u> milk.
        (D)

35. Miami, Florida is <u>among</u> the few cities in the United States <u>that</u> <u>has been awarded</u> official status
                          (A)   (B)   (C)
    <u>as</u> bilingual municipalities.
    (D)

GO ON TO THE NEXT PAGE

2　　2　　2　　2　　2　　2　　2　　2　　2　　2　　2

36. No other quality is more important for a scientist to acquire as to observe carefully.
　　　(A)　　　　　　　　　　　　(B)　　　　　　　　　(C)　　　　(D)

37. After the police had tried unsuccessfully to determine to who the car belonged, they towed it into
　　　　　　(A)　　　　　　　(B)　　　　　　　　　(C)　　　　　　　　　　　　(D)
　　the station.

38. Fertilizers are used primarily to enrich soil and increasing yield.
　　　　　　　(A)　　　(B)　　　　　　(C)　　　　(D)

39. If the ozone gases of the atmosphere did not filter out the ultraviolet rays of the sun, life as we
　　　　　　　　　　　　　　　　　　(A)　　　　　　　　　　　　　　　　　　　　(B)
　　know it would not have evolved on earth.
　　　(C)　　　　　　　　　　(D)

40. The regulation requires that everyone who holds a nonimmigrant visa reports an address to the
　　　　　　　　　　　　　　　　　(A)　(B)　　　　　　　　　　　　(C) (D)
　　federal government in January of each year.

**THIS IS THE END OF THE STRUCTURE AND WRITTEN EXPRESSION
SECTION OF TOEFL MODEL TEST 4.**

**IF YOU FINISH BEFORE 25 MINUTES HAS ENDED, CHECK YOUR
WORK ON SECTION 2 ONLY.**

DO NOT READ OR WORK ON ANY OTHER SECTION OF THE TEST.

3 3 3 3 3 3 3 3 3 3 | 3

Section 3:
Reading Comprehension

50 QUESTIONS 55 MINUTES

Directions: In this section you will read several passages. Each one is followed by a number of questions about it. For questions 1–50, you are to choose the **one** best answer, (A), (B), (C), or (D), to each question. Then, on your answer sheet, find the number of the question and fill in the space that corresponds to the letter of the answer you have chosen.

Answer all questions about the information in a passage on the basis of what is **stated** or **implied** in that passage.

Questions 1–10

Precipitation, commonly referred to as rainfall, is a measure of the quantity of water in the form of either rain, hail, or snow which reaches the ground. The average annual precipitation over the whole of the United States is thirty-six inches. It should be understood however, that
Line a foot of snow is not equal to a foot of precipitation. A general formula for computing the pre-
 (5) cipitation of snowfall is that ten inches of snow is equal to one inch of precipitation. In New York State, for example, twenty inches of snow in one year would be recorded as only two inches of precipitation. Forty inches of rain would be recorded as forty inches of precipitation. The total annual precipitation would be recorded as forty-two inches.

The amount of precipitation is a combined result of several factors, including location, al-
 (10) titude, proximity to the sea, and the direction of prevailing winds. Most of the precipitation in the United States is brought originally by prevailing winds from the Pacific Ocean, the Gulf of Mexico, the Atlantic Ocean, and the Great Lakes. Because these prevailing winds generally come from the West, the Pacific Coast receives more annual precipitation than the Atlantic Coast. Along the Pacific Coast itself, however, altitude causes some diversity in rainfall. The
 (15) mountain ranges of the United States, especially the Rocky Mountain Range and the Appalachian Mountain Range, influence the amount of precipitation in their areas. East of the Rocky Mountains, the annual precipitation decreases substantially from that west of the Rocky Mountains. The precipitation north of the Appalachian Mountains is about 40 percent less than that south of the Appalachian Mountains.

1. What does this passage mainly discuss?

   (A) Precipitation
   (B) Snowfall
   (C) New York State
   (D) A general formula

2. Which of the following is another word that is often used in place of precipitation?

   (A) Humidity
   (B) Wetness
   (C) Rainfall
   (D) Rain-snow

3. The term *precipitation* includes

   (A) only rainfall
   (B) rain, hail, and snow
   (C) rain, snow, and humidity
   (D) rain, hail, and humidity

GO ON TO THE NEXT PAGE

3 3 3 3 3 3 3 3 3 3 3

4. What is the average annual rainfall in inches in the United States?

(A) Thirty-six inches
(B) Thirty-eight inches
(C) Forty inches
(D) Forty-two inches

5. If a state has 40 inches of snow in a year, by how much does this increase the annual precipitation?

(A) By two feet
(B) By four inches
(C) By four feet
(D) By 40 inches

6. The phrase "proximity to" in line 10 is closest in meaning to

(A) communication with
(B) dependence on
(C) nearness to
(D) similarity to

7. Where is the annual precipitation highest?

(A) The Atlantic Coast
(B) The Great Lakes
(C) The Gulf of Mexico
(D) The Pacific Coast

8. Which of the following was NOT mentioned as a factor in determining the amount of precipitation that an area will receive?

(A) Mountains
(B) Latitude
(C) The sea
(D) Wind

9. The word "substantially" in line 17 could best be replaced by

(A) fundamentally
(B) slightly
(C) completely
(D) apparently

10. The word "that" in line 19 refers to

(A) decreases
(B) precipitation
(C) areas
(D) mountain ranges

Questions 11–20

    Course numbers are an indication of which courses are open to various categories of students at the University. Undergraduate courses with the numbers 100 or 200 are generally introducto-ry courses appropriate for freshmen or sophomores, whereas courses with the numbers 300 or
Line 400 often have prerequisites and are open to juniors and seniors only. Courses with the numbers
(5) 800 or above are open only to graduate students. Certain graduate courses, generally those de-voted to introductory material, are numbered 400 for undergraduate students who qualify to take them and 600 for graduate students. Courses designed for students seeking a profession-al degree carry a 500 number for undergraduate students and a 700 number for graduate stu-dents. Courses numbered 99 or below are special interest courses that do not carry academic
(10) credit. If students elect to take a special interest course, it will not count toward the number of hours needed to complete graduation requirements.

    A full-time undergraduate student is expected to take courses that total twelve to eighteen credit hours. A full-time graduate student is expected to take courses that total ten to sixteen credit hours. Students holding assistantships are expected to enroll for proportionately fewer
(15) hours. A part-time graduate student may register for a minimum of three credit hours.

GO ON TO THE NEXT PAGE ➡

3 3 3 3 3 3 3 3 3 3 3

An overload, that is, more than the maximum number of hours, may be taken with the approval of an academic advisor. To register for an overload, students must submit the appropriate approval form when registering. Overloads above 24 hours will not be approved under any circumstances.

11. Where would this passage most likely be found?

(A) In a syllabus
(B) In a college catalog
(C) In an undergraduate course
(D) In a graduate course

12. What is the purpose of the passage?

(A) To inform
(B) To persuade
(C) To criticize
(D) To apologize

13. The word "prerequisites" in line 4 is closest in meaning to

(A) courses required before enrolling
(B) courses needed for graduation
(C) courses that include additional charges
(D) courses that do not carry academic credit

14. The word "those" in line 5 refers to

(A) graduate students
(B) graduate courses
(C) introductory courses
(D) course numbers

15. Which classification of students would be eligible to enroll in Mechanical Engineering 850?

(A) A graduate student
(B) A part-time student
(C) A full-time student
(D) An undergraduate student

16. If an undergraduate student uses the number 520 to register for an accounting course, what number would a graduate student probably use to register for the same course?

(A) Accounting 520
(B) Accounting 620
(C) Accounting 720
(D) Accounting 820

17. How is a student who registers for eight credit hours classified?

(A) Full-time student
(B) Graduate student
(C) Part-time student
(D) Non-degree student

18. Which of the following courses would not be included in the list of courses for graduation?

(A) English 90
(B) English 100
(C) English 300
(D) English 400

19. A graduate student may NOT

(A) enroll in a course numbered 610
(B) register for only one one-hour course
(C) register for courses if he has an assistantship
(D) enroll in an introductory course

GO ON TO THE NEXT PAGE

3 3 3 3 3 3 3 3 3 3 3

20. The phrase "under any circumstances" in lines 18–19 is closest in meaning to

   (A) without cause
   (B) without permission
   (C) without exception
   (D) without a good reason

Questions 21–30

   During the nineteenth century, women in the United States organized and participated in a large number of reform movements, including movements to reorganize the prison system, improve education, ban the sale of alcohol, and, most importantly, to free the slaves. Some
Line women saw similarities in the social status of women and slaves. Women like Elizabeth Cady
 (5) Stanton and Lucy Stone were feminists and abolitionists who supported the rights of both women and blacks. A number of male abolitionists, including William Lloyd Garrison and Wendell Philips, also supported the rights of women to speak and participate equally with men in antislavery activities. Probably more than any other movement, abolitionism offered women a previously denied entry into politics. They became involved primarily in order to
(10) better their living conditions and the conditions of others.
   When the Civil War ended in 1865, the Fourteenth and Fifteenth Amendments to the Constitution adopted in 1868 and 1870 granted citizenship and suffrage to blacks but not to women. Discouraged but resolved, feminists influenced more and more women to demand the right to vote. In 1869 the Wyoming Territory had yielded to demands by feminists, but eastern
(15) states resisted more stubbornly than before. A women's suffrage bill had been presented to every Congress since 1878 but it continually failed to pass until 1920, when the Nineteenth Amendment granted women the right to vote.

21. With what topic is the passage primarily concerned?

   (A) The Wyoming Territory
   (B) The Fourteenth and Fifteenth Amendments
   (C) Abolitionists
   (D) Women's suffrage

22. The word "ban" in line 3 most nearly means to

   (A) encourage
   (B) publish
   (C) prohibit
   (D) limit

23. The word "supported" in line 5 could best be replaced by

   (A) disregarded
   (B) acknowledged
   (C) contested
   (D) promoted

24. According to the passage, why did women become active in politics?

   (A) To improve the conditions of life that existed at the time
   (B) To support Elizabeth Cady Stanton for president
   (C) To be elected to public office
   (D) To amend the Declaration of Independence

25. The word "primarily" in line 9 is closest in meaning to

   (A) above all
   (B) somewhat
   (C) finally
   (D) always

GO ON TO THE NEXT PAGE

3   3   3   3   3   3   3   3   3   3 | 3

26. What had occurred shortly after the Civil War?

    (A) The Wyoming Territory was admitted to the Union.
    (B) A women's suffrage bill was introduced in Congress.
    (C) The eastern states resisted the end of the war.
    (D) Black people were granted the right to vote.

27. The word "suffrage" in line 12 could best be replaced by which of the following?

    (A) pain
    (B) citizenship
    (C) freedom from bondage
    (D) the right to vote

28. What does the Nineteenth Amendment guarantee?

    (A) Voting rights for blacks
    (B) Citizenship for blacks
    (C) Voting rights for women
    (D) Citizenship for women

29. The word "it" in line 16 refers to

    (A) bill
    (B) Congress
    (C) Nineteenth Amendment
    (D) vote

30. When were women allowed to vote throughout the United States?

    (A) After 1866
    (B) After 1870
    (C) After 1878
    (D) After 1920

Questions 31–40

The *Acacia* is a genus of trees and shrubs of the Mimosa family. Although nearly five hundred species of *Acacia* have been identified, only about a dozen of the three hundred Australian varieties grow well in the southern United States, and of these, only three are flower-
Line ing. The *Bailey Acacia* has fernlike silver leaves and small, fragrant flowers arranged in
(5) rounded clusters. The *Silver Wattle*, although very similar to the *Bailey Acacia*, grows twice as high. The *Sydney Golden Wattle* is squat and bushy with broad, flat leaves and sharp spined twigs. Named for its bright, yellow flowers, the *Golden Wattle* is the most showy and fragrant of the Acacias. Another variety, the *Black Acacia* or *Blackwood*, has dark green leaves and unobtrusive blossoms. Besides being a popular tree for ornamental purposes, the *Black Acacia* is
(10) valuable for its dark wood, which is used in making cabinets and furniture, including highly prized pianos.

The *Acacia's* unusual custom of blossoming in February has been commonly attributed to its Australian origins. In the Southern Hemisphere, of course, the seasons are reversed, and February, which is wintertime in the United States, is summertime in Australia. Actually,
(15) however, the pale, yellow blossoms appear in August in Australia. Whether growing in the Northern or Southern Hemisphere, the *Acacia* will bloom in winter.

GO ON TO THE NEXT PAGE

3 3 3 3 3 3 3 3 3 3 3

31. With which of the following topics is the passage primarily concerned?

   (A) The *Black Acacia*
   (B) Characteristics and varieties of the *Acacia*
   (C) Australian varieties of the *Acacia*
   (D) The use of *Acacia* wood in ornamental furniture

32. How many species of *Acacia* grow well in the southern United States?

   (A) Five hundred
   (B) Three hundred
   (C) Twelve
   (D) Three

33. The word "these" in line 3 refers to

   (A) United States
   (B) varieties
   (C) species
   (D) trees and shrubs

34. According to this passage, the *Silver Wattle*

   (A) is squat and bushy
   (B) has unobtrusive blossoms
   (C) is taller than the *Bailey Acacia*
   (D) is used for making furniture

35. In line 6, the word "flat" most nearly means

   (A) smooth
   (B) pretty
   (C) pointed
   (D) short

36. The word "showy" in line 7 could best be replaced by

   (A) strange
   (B) elaborate
   (C) huge
   (D) fragile

37. Which of the following *Acacias* has the least colorful blossoms?

   (A) *Bailey Acacia*
   (B) *Sydney Golden Wattle*
   (C) *Silver Wattle*
   (D) *Black Acacia*

38. Which of the following would most probably be made from a *Black Acacia* tree?

   (A) A flower arrangement
   (B) A table
   (C) A pie
   (D) Paper

39. The phrase "highly prized" in lines 10–11 is closest in meaning to

   (A) valuable
   (B) unique
   (C) stylish
   (D) attractive

40. When do *Acacia* trees bloom in Australia?

   (A) February
   (B) Summer
   (C) August
   (D) Spring

Questions 41–50

   In 1626, Peter Minuit, governor of the Dutch settlements in North America known as New Amsterdam, negotiated with Canarsee Indian chiefs for the purchase of Manhattan Island for merchandise valued at sixty guilders or about $24.12. He purchased the island for the Dutch
Line West India Company.
(5)   The next year, Fort Amsterdam was built by the company at the extreme southern tip of the island. Because attempts to encourage Dutch immigration were not immediately successful, offers, generous by the standards of the era, were extended throughout Europe. Consequently, the

GO ON TO THE NEXT PAGE

3   3   3   3   3   3   3   3   3   3   3

settlement became the most heterogeneous of the North American colonies. By 1637, the fort
had expanded into the village of New Amsterdam, and other small communities had grown
(10) up around it, including New Haarlem and Stuyvesant's Bouwery, and New Amsterdam began
to prosper, developing characteristics of religious and linguistic tolerance unusual for the
times. By 1643, it was reported that eighteen different languages were heard in New Amsterdam alone.

Among the multilingual settlers was a large group of English colonists from Connecticut
(15) and Massachusetts who supported the English King's claim to all of New Netherlands set out
in a charter that gave the territory to his brother James, the Duke of York. In 1664, when the
English sent a formidable fleet of warships into the New Amsterdam harbor, Dutch governor
Peter Stuyvesant surrendered without resistance.

When the English acquired the island, the village of New Amsterdam was renamed New
(20) York in honor of the Duke. By the onset of the Revolution, New York City was already a
bustling commercial center. After the war, it was selected as the first capital of the United
States. Although the government was eventually moved, first to Philadelphia and then to
Washington, D.C., New York City has remained the unofficial commercial capital.

During the 1690s, New York became a haven for pirates who conspired with leading mer-
(25) chants to exchange supplies for their ships in return for a share in the plunder. As a colony,
New York exchanged many agricultural products for English manufactured goods. In addition,
trade with the West Indies prospered. Three centuries after his initial trade with the Indians,
Minuit's tiny investment was worth more than seven billion dollars.

41. Which of the following would be the best
title for this passage?

(A) A History of New York City
(B) An Account of the Dutch Colonies
(C) A Biography of Peter Minuit
(D) The First Capital of the United States

42. What did the Indians receive in exchange for
their island?

(A) Sixty Dutch guilders
(B) $24.12 U.S.
(C) Goods and supplies
(D) Land in New Amsterdam

43. Where was New Amsterdam located?

(A) In Holland
(B) In North America
(C) On the island of Manhattan
(D) In India

44. The word "heterogeneous" in line 8 could
best be replaced by

(A) liberal
(B) renowned
(C) diverse
(D) prosperous

45. Why were so many languages spoken in
New Amsterdam?

(A) The Dutch West India Company
was owned by England.
(B) The Dutch West India Company
allowed freedom of speech.
(C) The Dutch West India Company
recruited settlers from many different
countries in Europe.
(D) The Indians who lived there
before the Dutch West India Company
purchase spoke many languages.

GO ON TO THE NEXT PAGE

46. The word "formidible" in line 17 is closest in meaning to

   (A) powerful
   (B) modern
   (C) expensive
   (D) unexpected

47. The name of New Amsterdam was changed

   (A) to avoid a war with England
   (B) to honor the Duke of York
   (C) to attract more English colonists from
        Connecticut and Massachusetts
   (D) to encourage trade during the 1690s

48. The word "it" in line 21 refers to
   (A) Revolution
   (B) New York City
   (C) the island
   (D) the first capital

49. Which city was the first capital of the new United States?

   (A) New Amsterdam
   (B) New York
   (C) Philadelphia
   (D) Washington

50. On what date was Manhattan valued at $7 billion?

   (A) 1626
   (B) 1726
   (C) 1656
   (D) 1926

THIS IS THE END OF THE READING COMPREHENSION SECTION OF TOEFL MODEL TEST 4.

IF YOU FINISH BEFORE 55 MINUTES HAS ENDED, CHECK YOUR WORK ON SECTION 3 ONLY.

DO NOT READ OR WORK ON ANY OTHER SECTION OF THE TEST.

END OF TOEFL MODEL TEST 4.

To check your answers for Model Test 4, refer to the Answer Key on page 463. For an explanation of the answers, refer to the Explanatory Answers for Model Test 4 on page 496.

MODEL TEST 5—ANSWER SHEET

Section 1

1. Ⓐ Ⓑ Ⓒ Ⓓ
2. Ⓐ Ⓑ Ⓒ Ⓓ
3. Ⓐ Ⓑ Ⓒ Ⓓ
4. Ⓐ Ⓑ Ⓒ Ⓓ
5. Ⓐ Ⓑ Ⓒ Ⓓ
6. Ⓐ Ⓑ Ⓒ Ⓓ
7. Ⓐ Ⓑ Ⓒ Ⓓ
8. Ⓐ Ⓑ Ⓒ Ⓓ
9. Ⓐ Ⓑ Ⓒ Ⓓ
10. Ⓐ Ⓑ Ⓒ Ⓓ
11. Ⓐ Ⓑ Ⓒ Ⓓ
12. Ⓐ Ⓑ Ⓒ Ⓓ
13. Ⓐ Ⓑ Ⓒ Ⓓ
14. Ⓐ Ⓑ Ⓒ Ⓓ
15. Ⓐ Ⓑ Ⓒ Ⓓ
16. Ⓐ Ⓑ Ⓒ Ⓓ
17. Ⓐ Ⓑ Ⓒ Ⓓ
18. Ⓐ Ⓑ Ⓒ Ⓓ
19. Ⓐ Ⓑ Ⓒ Ⓓ
20. Ⓐ Ⓑ Ⓒ Ⓓ
21. Ⓐ Ⓑ Ⓒ Ⓓ
22. Ⓐ Ⓑ Ⓒ Ⓓ
23. Ⓐ Ⓑ Ⓒ Ⓓ
24. Ⓐ Ⓑ Ⓒ Ⓓ
25. Ⓐ Ⓑ Ⓒ Ⓓ
26. Ⓐ Ⓑ Ⓒ Ⓓ
27. Ⓐ Ⓑ Ⓒ Ⓓ
28. Ⓐ Ⓑ Ⓒ Ⓓ
29. Ⓐ Ⓑ Ⓒ Ⓓ
30. Ⓐ Ⓑ Ⓒ Ⓓ
31. Ⓐ Ⓑ Ⓒ Ⓓ
32. Ⓐ Ⓑ Ⓒ Ⓓ
33. Ⓐ Ⓑ Ⓒ Ⓓ
34. Ⓐ Ⓑ Ⓒ Ⓓ
35. Ⓐ Ⓑ Ⓒ Ⓓ
36. Ⓐ Ⓑ Ⓒ Ⓓ
37. Ⓐ Ⓑ Ⓒ Ⓓ
38. Ⓐ Ⓑ Ⓒ Ⓓ
39. Ⓐ Ⓑ Ⓒ Ⓓ
40. Ⓐ Ⓑ Ⓒ Ⓓ
41. Ⓐ Ⓑ Ⓒ Ⓓ
42. Ⓐ Ⓑ Ⓒ Ⓓ
43. Ⓐ Ⓑ Ⓒ Ⓓ
44. Ⓐ Ⓑ Ⓒ Ⓓ
45. Ⓐ Ⓑ Ⓒ Ⓓ
46. Ⓐ Ⓑ Ⓒ Ⓓ
47. Ⓐ Ⓑ Ⓒ Ⓓ
48. Ⓐ Ⓑ Ⓒ Ⓓ
49. Ⓐ Ⓑ Ⓒ Ⓓ
50. Ⓐ Ⓑ Ⓒ Ⓓ

Section 2

1. Ⓐ Ⓑ Ⓒ Ⓓ
2. Ⓐ Ⓑ Ⓒ Ⓓ
3. Ⓐ Ⓑ Ⓒ Ⓓ
4. Ⓐ Ⓑ Ⓒ Ⓓ
5. Ⓐ Ⓑ Ⓒ Ⓓ
6. Ⓐ Ⓑ Ⓒ Ⓓ
7. Ⓐ Ⓑ Ⓒ Ⓓ
8. Ⓐ Ⓑ Ⓒ Ⓓ
9. Ⓐ Ⓑ Ⓒ Ⓓ
10. Ⓐ Ⓑ Ⓒ Ⓓ
11. Ⓐ Ⓑ Ⓒ Ⓓ
12. Ⓐ Ⓑ Ⓒ Ⓓ
13. Ⓐ Ⓑ Ⓒ Ⓓ
14. Ⓐ Ⓑ Ⓒ Ⓓ
15. Ⓐ Ⓑ Ⓒ Ⓓ
16. Ⓐ Ⓑ Ⓒ Ⓓ
17. Ⓐ Ⓑ Ⓒ Ⓓ
18. Ⓐ Ⓑ Ⓒ Ⓓ
19. Ⓐ Ⓑ Ⓒ Ⓓ
20. Ⓐ Ⓑ Ⓒ Ⓓ
21. Ⓐ Ⓑ Ⓒ Ⓓ
22. Ⓐ Ⓑ Ⓒ Ⓓ
23. Ⓐ Ⓑ Ⓒ Ⓓ
24. Ⓐ Ⓑ Ⓒ Ⓓ
25. Ⓐ Ⓑ Ⓒ Ⓓ
26. Ⓐ Ⓑ Ⓒ Ⓓ
27. Ⓐ Ⓑ Ⓒ Ⓓ
28. Ⓐ Ⓑ Ⓒ Ⓓ
29. Ⓐ Ⓑ Ⓒ Ⓓ
30. Ⓐ Ⓑ Ⓒ Ⓓ
31. Ⓐ Ⓑ Ⓒ Ⓓ
32. Ⓐ Ⓑ Ⓒ Ⓓ
33. Ⓐ Ⓑ Ⓒ Ⓓ
34. Ⓐ Ⓑ Ⓒ Ⓓ
35. Ⓐ Ⓑ Ⓒ Ⓓ
36. Ⓐ Ⓑ Ⓒ Ⓓ
37. Ⓐ Ⓑ Ⓒ Ⓓ
38. Ⓐ Ⓑ Ⓒ Ⓓ
39. Ⓐ Ⓑ Ⓒ Ⓓ
40. Ⓐ Ⓑ Ⓒ Ⓓ

Section 3

1. Ⓐ Ⓑ Ⓒ Ⓓ
2. Ⓐ Ⓑ Ⓒ Ⓓ
3. Ⓐ Ⓑ Ⓒ Ⓓ
4. Ⓐ Ⓑ Ⓒ Ⓓ
5. Ⓐ Ⓑ Ⓒ Ⓓ
6. Ⓐ Ⓑ Ⓒ Ⓓ
7. Ⓐ Ⓑ Ⓒ Ⓓ
8. Ⓐ Ⓑ Ⓒ Ⓓ
9. Ⓐ Ⓑ Ⓒ Ⓓ
10. Ⓐ Ⓑ Ⓒ Ⓓ
11. Ⓐ Ⓑ Ⓒ Ⓓ
12. Ⓐ Ⓑ Ⓒ Ⓓ
13. Ⓐ Ⓑ Ⓒ Ⓓ
14. Ⓐ Ⓑ Ⓒ Ⓓ
15. Ⓐ Ⓑ Ⓒ Ⓓ
16. Ⓐ Ⓑ Ⓒ Ⓓ
17. Ⓐ Ⓑ Ⓒ Ⓓ
18. Ⓐ Ⓑ Ⓒ Ⓓ
19. Ⓐ Ⓑ Ⓒ Ⓓ
20. Ⓐ Ⓑ Ⓒ Ⓓ
21. Ⓐ Ⓑ Ⓒ Ⓓ
22. Ⓐ Ⓑ Ⓒ Ⓓ
23. Ⓐ Ⓑ Ⓒ Ⓓ
24. Ⓐ Ⓑ Ⓒ Ⓓ
25. Ⓐ Ⓑ Ⓒ Ⓓ
26. Ⓐ Ⓑ Ⓒ Ⓓ
27. Ⓐ Ⓑ Ⓒ Ⓓ
28. Ⓐ Ⓑ Ⓒ Ⓓ
29. Ⓐ Ⓑ Ⓒ Ⓓ
30. Ⓐ Ⓑ Ⓒ Ⓓ
31. Ⓐ Ⓑ Ⓒ Ⓓ
32. Ⓐ Ⓑ Ⓒ Ⓓ
33. Ⓐ Ⓑ Ⓒ Ⓓ
34. Ⓐ Ⓑ Ⓒ Ⓓ
35. Ⓐ Ⓑ Ⓒ Ⓓ
36. Ⓐ Ⓑ Ⓒ Ⓓ
37. Ⓐ Ⓑ Ⓒ Ⓓ
38. Ⓐ Ⓑ Ⓒ Ⓓ
39. Ⓐ Ⓑ Ⓒ Ⓓ
40. Ⓐ Ⓑ Ⓒ Ⓓ
41. Ⓐ Ⓑ Ⓒ Ⓓ
42. Ⓐ Ⓑ Ⓒ Ⓓ
43. Ⓐ Ⓑ Ⓒ Ⓓ
44. Ⓐ Ⓑ Ⓒ Ⓓ
45. Ⓐ Ⓑ Ⓒ Ⓓ
46. Ⓐ Ⓑ Ⓒ Ⓓ
47. Ⓐ Ⓑ Ⓒ Ⓓ
48. Ⓐ Ⓑ Ⓒ Ⓓ
49. Ⓐ Ⓑ Ⓒ Ⓓ
50. Ⓐ Ⓑ Ⓒ Ⓓ

1 1 1 1 1 1 1 1 1 1 1 1

Model Test 5
Short Form

Section 1:
Listening Comprehension

50 QUESTIONS 40 MINUTES

In this section of the test, you will have an opportunity to demonstrate your ability to understand conversations and talks in English. There are three parts to this section with special directions for each part. Answer all the questions on the basis of what is stated or implied by the speakers in this test. When you take the actual TOEFL test, you will not be allowed to take notes or write in your test book. Try to work on this Model Test in the same way.

Part A

Directions: In Part A, you will hear short conversations between two people. After each conversation, you will hear a question about the conversation. The conversations and questions will not be repeated. After you hear a question, read the four possible answers in your book and choose the best answer. Then, on your answer sheet, find the number of the question and fill in the space that corresponds to the letter of the answer you have chosen.

1. (A) The cable is not working.
   (B) All of them but Channel 17 have a good picture.
   (C) Channel 17 is on a different cable system.
   (D) All of the channels have good programs.

2. (A) Mr. Davis wants to confer with Mr. Ward.
   (B) Mr. Davis is talking with the Office of Immigration.
   (C) Mr. Davis cannot talk with Mr. Ward now.
   (D) Mr. Ward should hold for a minute.

3. (A) She thinks the man is too tired to go to the movie.
   (B) She really wants to go to the movie.
   (C) She wants to go out to dinner.
   (D) She does not want to go to the movie.

4. (A) He will borrow some typing paper from the woman.
   (B) He will lend the woman some typing paper.
   (C) He will type the woman's paper.
   (D) He will buy some typing paper for the woman.

5. (A) He is a student at the university.
   (B) He is not driving a car.
   (C) He knows the woman.
   (D) He needs to go to the drug store.

6. (A) The man's father did not go.
   (B) The man thought that the game was excellent.
   (C) The man and his father thought that the game was unsatisfactory.
   (D) The man thought that the game was excellent, but his father thought that it was unsatisfactory.

GO ON TO THE NEXT PAGE

1 1 1 1 1 1 1 1 1 1 1

7. (A) He could not stay with his parents.
   (B) He did not want to change his plans.
   (C) He will not go to summer school.
   (D) He has completed all the courses.

8. (A) A library.
   (B) A hotel.
   (C) A hospital.
   (D) An elevator.

9. (A) The telephone.
   (B) An apartment.
   (C) Utilities.
   (D) Furniture.

10. (A) She likes Dr. Taylor's class.
    (B) She is not sure how Dr. Taylor feels.
    (C) She did not get an A on the paper.
    (D) She is not doing very well in the class.

11. (A) Look at the menu.
    (B) Order lunch.
    (C) Talk to the waitress.
    (D) Eat one of the special lunches.

12. (A) Pay ten dollars an hour.
    (B) Be a subject in an experiment.
    (C) Ask Sandy to participate.
    (D) Go to a psychologist.

13. (A) That the speakers did not go to the meeting.
    (B) That the woman went to the meeting, but the man did not.
    (C) That the man went to the meeting, but the woman did not.
    (D) That both speakers went to the meeting.

14. (A) He will need to renew the books.
    (B) He does not plan to check the books out.
    (C) He only wants one book.
    (D) He will return the books by the due date.

15. (A) The operator.
    (B) The person receiving the call.
    (C) The person making the call.
    (D) No one. The call is free.

16. (A) The woman can borrow his pen.
    (B) A pen might be a good gift.
    (C) Her advisor would probably like a card.
    (D) A gift is not necessary.

17. (A) She does not want to leave.
    (B) She must stay.
    (C) She did not like the dorm.
    (D) She is undecided.

18. (A) She is not going home now.
    (B) She has already had some exercise.
    (C) She does not like to go to the gym.
    (D) She does not want to spend time with the man.

19. (A) The man may be taking on too much.
    (B) The job is more important than school.
    (C) The opportunity is very good.
    (D) The contract may not be valid.

20. (A) Call his family.
    (B) Write a letter.
    (C) Send postcards.
    (D) Buy presents.

21. (A) The length of time that it takes to get an answer from a university.
    (B) Where the woman will go to school.
    (C) States in the Midwest.
    (D) The University of Minnesota.

22. (A) The CD was very expensive.
    (B) He would like to have a CD like it.
    (C) Steve knows a lot about CD systems.
    (D) CD systems are not easy to operate.

GO ON TO THE NEXT PAGE ➤

1 1 1 1 1 1 1 1 1 1 1

23. (A) Buy a ticket.
    (B) Go to room 27.
    (C) Take a test in room 32.
    (D) Show the man her ticket.

24. (A) She wasn't able to attend the reception.
    (B) She is an honors student.
    (C) She likes flowers very much.
    (D) She is a teacher.

25. (A) Try to be in class more often.
    (B) Try to get the work done.
    (C) Take the class twice.
    (D) Take the class next term.

26. (A) She is staying at a motel.
    (B) She is not working now.
    (C) She is saving her money for school.
    (D) She is studying very hard.

27. (A) There is no seat belt law in her state.
    (B) Passengers in the back seat do not have
        to use seat belts.
    (C) The man should buckle his seat belt.
    (D) She feels the fifty-dollar fine is too high.

28. (A) He does not like English.
    (B) Graduate school is easier than teaching.
    (C) It is not surprising that the woman is
        doing well.
    (D) The course is very interesting.

29. (A) They are going to make a group presen-
        tation.
    (B) They don't want to have Jane in their
        group.
    (C) Carl does not want to be in their group.
    (D) They are not good presenters.

30. (A) Get in line.
    (B) Take a number.
    (C) Ask someone else for help.
    (D) Count the number of people in line.

Part B

Directions: In this part of the test, you will hear longer conversations. After each conversation, you will hear several questions. The conversations and questions will not be repeated.

After you hear a question, read the four possible answers in your book and choose the best answer. Then, on your answer sheet, find the number of the question and fill in the space that corresponds to the letter of the answer you have chosen.

Remember, you are **not** allowed to take notes or write on your test pages.

31. (A) To sell the woman magazine subscrip-
        tions.
    (B) To give the woman free magazines.
    (C) To ask the woman's opinion about mag-
        azines.
    (D) To find out what kind of magazines the
        woman likes to read.

32. (A) She likes to read news magazines.
    (B) She does not read magazines.
    (C) She is not very assertive.
    (D) She lives alone.

33. (A) The magazines were not interesting.
    (B) She thought she would have to pay later.
    (C) The man was very rude.
    (D) The subscription rate was too high.

GO ON TO THE NEXT PAGE

1 1 1 1 1 1 1 1 1 1 1

34. (A) By placing an order.
    (B) By apologizing to the man.
    (C) By thanking the man.
    (D) By agreeing to think about it.

35. (A) British English pronunciation.
    (B) Spelling patterns.
    (C) British and American English.
    (D) Movies.

36. (A) *Center*.
    (B) *Centre*.
    (C) *Centr*.
    (D) *Centere*.

37. (A) A smooth surface.
    (B) An actor.
    (C) An apartment.
    (D) A movie.

38. (A) That British English and American English are the same.
    (B) That British English and American English are so different that Americans cannot understand Englishmen when they speak.
    (C) That British English and American English have different spelling and vocabulary but the same pronunciation.
    (D) That British English and American English have slightly different spelling, vocabulary, and pronunciation, but Americans and Englishmen still understand each other.

Part C

Directions: In this part of the test, you will hear several short talks. After each talk, you will hear some questions. The talks and questions will not be repeated.

After you hear a question, read the four possible answers in your book and choose the best answer. Then, on your answer sheet, find the number of the question and fill in the space that corresponds to the letter of the answer you have chosen.

39. (A) Captain Cook's life.
    (B) History of Hawaii.
    (C) Captain Cook's exploration of Hawaii.
    (D) Hawaiian culture.

40. (A) *Third Voyage* and the *Discovery*.
    (B) *Resolution* and the *Discovery*.
    (C) *Revolution* and the *Third Voyage*.
    (D) *England* and the *Discovery*.

41. (A) They fished and raised crops.
    (B) They cared for the children and raised crops.
    (C) They cared for the children and made clothing.
    (D) They made clothing and raised animals.

42. (A) Cook offended the god Launo.
    (B) Cook's men became very ill.
    (C) Cook took the king prisoner.
    (D) Cook stole a boat from the islanders.

43. (A) Impure metals that occur accidentally.
    (B) Metals melted into liquid form.
    (C) A planned combination of metals for a specific purpose.
    (D) Industrial metals that do not have to be very pure.

GO ON TO THE NEXT PAGE

1 1 1 1 1 1 1 1 1 1 1

44. (A) They are chosen for a particular pur-
pose.
(B) They are heavy and strong.
(C) They are difficult to determine because
there is more than one metal involved.
(D) They occur accidentally in nature.

45. (A) To demonstrate how alloys can be used
to solve industrial problems.
(B) To emphasize the importance of the avi-
ation industry.
(C) To compare alloys and other mixtures.
(D) To illustrate how metals can be used
without alloying them.

46. (A) Mixtures of metals in nature are very
pure.
(B) Combinations of metals do not occur in
nature.
(C) Metals combined in nature are mixed in
random proportion.
(D) Alloys are mixtures, but metals that
occur in nature are not.

47. (A) The national department of education.
(B) School boards.
(C) Public schools in the United States.
(D) Local control of schools.

48. (A) The school board approves the recommendations of the superintendent.
(B) The superintendent selects the school
board.
(C) The superintendent serves on the school
board.
(D) The school board carries out the policies
of the superintendent.

49. (A) Professional educators.
(B) Community leaders.
(C) Officials in city government.
(D) Representatives of the Department of
Education.

50. (A) To establish policies for local districts.
(B) To organize a national curriculum.
(C) To monitor national legislation for
schools.
(D) To appoint local school boards.

**THIS IS THE END OF THE LISTENING COMPREHENSION SECTION
OF TOEFL MODEL TEST 5.**

DO NOT READ OR WORK ON ANY OTHER SECTION OF THE TEST.

2 **2** **2** **2** **2** **2** **2** **2** **2** **2** **2**

Section 2:
Structure and Written Expression

40 QUESTIONS 25 MINUTES

This section is designed to measure your ability to recognize language that is appropriate for standard written English. There are two types of questions in this section, with special directions for each type.

Structure

Directions: Questions 1–15 are incomplete sentences. Beneath each sentence you will see four words or phrases, marked (A), (B), (C), and (D). Choose the **one** word or phrase that best completes the sentence. Then, on your answer sheet, find the number of the question and fill in the space that corresponds to the letter of the answer you have chosen. Fill in the space so that the letter inside the oval cannot be seen.

1. When a body enters the earth's atmosphere, it travels -------- .

   (A) very rapidly
   (B) in a rapid manner
   (C) fastly
   (D) with great speed

2. Put plants -------- a window so that they will get enough light.

   (A) near to
   (B) near of
   (C) next to
   (D) nearly

3. Employers often require that candidates have not only a degree -------- .

   (A) but two years experience
   (B) also two years experience
   (C) but also two years experience
   (D) but more two years experience

4. Richard Nixon had been a lawyer and -------- before he entered politics.

   (A) served in the Navy as an officer
   (B) an officer in the Navy
   (C) the Navy had him as an officer
   (D) did service in the Navy as an officer

5. If one of the participants in a conversation wonders -------- no real communication has taken place.

   (A) what said the other person
   (B) what the other person said
   (C) what did the other person say
   (D) what was the other person saying

6. The salary of a bus driver is much higher -------- .

   (A) in comparison with the salary of a teacher
   (B) than a teacher
   (C) than that of a teacher
   (D) to compare as a teacher

7. Professional people expect -------- when it is necessary to cancel an appointment.

   (A) you to call them
   (B) that you would call them
   (C) your calling them
   (D) that you are calling them

GO ON TO THE NEXT PAGE ➤

2 2 2 2 2 2 2 2 2 2 2

8. Sedimentary rocks are formed below the surface of the earth ------- very high temperatures and pressures.

(A) where there are
(B) there are
(C) where are there
(D) there are where

9. Farmers look forward to -------- every summer.

(A) participating in the county fairs
(B) participate in the county fairs
(C) be participating in the county fairs
(D) have participated in the county fairs

10. A computer is usually chosen because of its simplicity of operation and ease of maintenance -------- its capacity to store information.

(A) the same as
(B) the same
(C) as well as
(D) as well

11. In a new culture, many embarrassing situations occur -------- a misunderstanding.

(A) for
(B) of
(C) because of
(D) because

12. Neptune is an extremely cold planet, and -------- .

(A) so does Uranus
(B) so has Uranus
(C) so is Uranus
(D) Uranus so

13. -------- that gold was discovered at Sutter's Mill and that the California Gold Rush began.

(A) Because in 1848
(B) That in 1848
(C) In 1848 that it was
(D) It was in 1848

14. The crime rate has continued to rise in American cities despite efforts on the part of both government and private citizens to curb --------

(A) them
(B) him
(C) its
(D) it

15. Frost occurs in valleys and on low grounds -------- on adjacent hills.

(A) more frequently as
(B) as frequently than
(C) more frequently than
(D) frequently than

Written Expression

Directions: In questions 16–40, each sentence has four underlined words or phrases. The four underlined parts of the sentence are marked (A), (B), (C), and (D). Identify the **one** underlined word or phrase that must be changed in order for the sentence to be correct. Then, on your answer sheet, find the number of the question and fill in the space that corresponds to the letter of the answer you have chosen.

16. The statement will be spoken just one time; therefore, you must listen very careful in order
                    (A)   (B)
    to understand what the speaker has said.
       (C)   (D)

GO ON TO THE NEXT PAGE

2   2   2   2   2   2   2   2   2   2   2

17. Gunpowder, in some ways the most effective of all the explosive materials, were a mixture of
             (A)   (B)   (C)   (D)
    potassium nitrate, charcoal, and sulfur.

18. In the relatively short history of industrial developing in the United States, New York City
         (A)   (B)   (C)
    has played a vital role.
      (D)

19. As the demand increases, manufacturers who previously produced only a large, luxury car is
                                       (A)   (B)
    compelled to make a smaller model in order to compete in the market.
          (C)   (D)

20. For the first time in the history of the country, the person which was recommended by the president
                                            (A)   (B)
    to replace a retiring justice on the Supreme Court is a woman.
     (C)   (D)

21. A prism is used to refract white light so it spreads out in a continuous spectrum
                (A)   (B)(C)
    of colors.
      (D)

22. Despite of rain or snow there are always more than fifty thousand fans at the OSU football games.
       (A)   (B)   (C)   (D)

23. The prices of homes are as high in urban areas that most young people cannot afford to buy them.
              (A)(B)   (C)   (D)

24. To see the Statue of Liberty and taking pictures from the top of the Empire State Building are two
                            (A)   (B)   (C)
    reasons for visiting New York City.
        (D)

25. There are twenty species of wild roses in North America, all of which have prickly stems, pinnate
     (A)   (B)
    leaves, and large flowers, which usually smell sweetly.
                 (C)   (D)

26. Having chose the topics for their essays, the students were instructed to make either a preliminary
       (A)   (B)   (C)   (D)
    outline or a rough draft.

GO ON TO THE NEXT PAGE

2 2 2 2 2 2 2 2 2 2 2

27. Factoring is the process of finding two or more expressions whose product is equal as the given
        (A)   (B)   (C)   (D)
    expression.

28. If Grandma Moses having been able to continue farming, she might never have begun to paint.
                        (A)   (B)   (C)   (D)

29. Since infection can cause both fever as well as pain, it is a good idea to check a patient's temperature.
                     (A)   (B)   (C)   (D)

30. Schizophrenia, a behavioral disorder typified by a fundamental break with reality, may be triggered
                                            (A)   (B)   (C)
    by genetic predisposition, stressful, drugs, or infections.
                                (D)

31. They asked us, Henry and I, whether we thought that the statistics had been presented fairly and
                              (A)   (B)   (C)   (D)
    accurately.

32. In purchasing a winter coat, it is very important for trying it on with heavy clothing underneath.
        (A)   (B)   (C)   (D)

33. What happened in New York were a reaction from city workers, including firemen and policemen
        (A)   (B)   (C)
    who had been laid off from their jobs.
                                (D)

34. A number of novels submitted their manuscripts under pseudonyms to conceal the fact that
        (A)   (B)   (C)
    they were women.
        (D)

35. Some executives require that the secretary is responsible for writing all reports as well as for
                            (A)   (B)   (C)   (D)
    balancing the books.

36. Although a doctor may be able to diagnose a problem perfect, he still may not be able to find a
                                    (A)   (B)   (C)
    drug to which the patient will respond.
        (D)

GO ON TO THE NEXT PAGE

2 2 2 2 2 2 2 2 2 2 2

37. Although the Red Cross <u>accepts</u> blood from most donors, the nurses will not <u>leave</u> you <u>give</u> blood
    (A)   (B)   (C)

    if you have just <u>had</u> a cold.
    (D)

38. A turtle differs <u>from</u> all <u>other</u> reptiles in that its body is encased in a protective shell of <u>their</u> <u>own</u>.
    (A)   (B)   (C) (D)

39. Benjamin Franklin <u>was</u> the editor of <u>the largest</u> newspaper in the colonies, a diplomatic
    (A)   (B)

    representative to France and later to England, and <u>he invented</u> <u>many</u> useful devices.
    (C)   (D)

40. The native people of the Americans <u>are called</u> Indians <u>because</u> when Columbus landed in the
    (A)   (B)

    Bahamas in <u>1492</u>, he thought that he <u>has reached</u> the East Indies.
    (C)   (D)

**THIS IS THE END OF THE STRUCTURE AND WRITTEN EXPRESSION
SECTION OF TOEFL MODEL TEST 5.**

**IF YOU FINISH BEFORE 25 MINUTES HAS ENDED, CHECK YOUR
WORK ON SECTION 2 ONLY.**

DO NOT READ OR WORK ON ANY OTHER SECTION OF THE TEST.

3 3 3 3 3 3 3 3 3 3   3

Section 3:
Reading Comprehension

50 QUESTIONS 55 MINUTES

Directions: In this section you will read several passages. Each one is followed by a number of questions about it. For questions 1–50, you are to choose the **one** best answer, (A), (B), (C), or (D), to each question. Then, on your answer sheet, find the number of the question and fill in the space that corresponds to the letter of the answer you have chosen.

Answer all questions about the information in a passage on the basis of what is **stated** or **implied** in that passage.

Questions 1–10

    The general principles of dynamics are rules that demonstrate a relationship between the motions of bodies and the forces that produce those motions. Based in large part on the work of his predecessors, Sir Isaac Newton deduced three laws of dynamics, which he published in
Line 1687 in his famous *Principia*.
(5)   Prior to Newton, Aristotle had established that the natural state of a body was a state of rest, and that unless a force acted upon it to maintain motion, a moving body would come to rest. Galileo had succeeded in correctly describing the behavior of falling objects and in recording that no force was required to maintain a body in motion. He noted that the effect of force was to change motion. Huygens recognized that a change in the direction of motion in-
(10) volved acceleration, just as did a change in speed, and further, that the action of a force was required. Kepler deduced the laws describing the motion of planets around the sun. It was primarily from Galileo and Kepler that Newton borrowed.
    In short, Newton's Laws of Motion are (1) a body at rest remains at rest, and a body in motion remains in motion along a straight line, unless acted upon by an unbalanced force; (2)
(15) if an unbalanced force acts upon a body, the momentum of the body changes in proportion to the force and in the same direction as the force; (3) to every action or force, there is an equal and opposite reaction.

1. What was the main purpose of this passage?

    (A) To demonstrate the development of
        Newton's laws
    (B) To establish Newton as the authority in
        the field of physics
    (C) To discredit Newton's laws of motion
    (D) To describe the motion of planets
        around the sun

2. The word "predecessors" in line 3 refers to

    (A) those who came before
    (B) those who provided help
    (C) those who published their work
    (D) those who agreed with the ideas

3. The phrase "prior to" in line 5 could best be replaced by which of the following?

    (A) before
    (B) after
    (C) with
    (D) simultaneously

GO ON TO THE NEXT PAGE

4. Which of the following scientists established that the natural state of a body was a state of rest?

(A) Galileo
(B) Kepler
(C) Aristotle
(D) Newton

5. The word "it" in line 6 refers to

(A) rest
(B) body
(C) state
(D) motion

6. Who was the first scientist to correctly describe the behavior of falling objects?

(A) Aristotle
(B) Newton
(C) Kepler
(D) Galileo

7. According to Huygen, when was acceleration required?

(A) For either a change in direction or a change in speed
(B) Only for a change in speed
(C) Only for a change in direction
(D) Neither for a change in direction nor for a change in speed

8. According to this passage, Newton based his laws primarily upon the work of

(A) Galileo and Copernicus
(B) Ptolemy and Copernicus
(C) Huygens and Kepler
(D) Galileo and Kepler

9. The word "momentum" in line 15 is closest in meaning to

(A) weight
(B) speed
(C) shape
(D) size

10. Which of the following describes inertia, or the principles of bodies at rest?

(A) Newton's first law
(B) Newton's third law
(C) Newton's law of motion
(D) Newton's law of dynamics

Questions 11–20

Perhaps it was his own lack of adequate schooling that inspired Horace Mann to work so hard for the important reforms in education that he accomplished. While he was still a boy, his father and older brother died, and he became responsible for supporting his family. Like most
Line of the children in his town, he attended school only two or three months a year. Later, with the
(5) help of several teachers, he was able to study law and become a member of the Massachusetts bar, but he never forgot those early struggles.

While serving in the Massachusetts legislature, he signed a historic education bill that set up a state board of education. Without regret, he gave up his successful legal practice and political career to become the first secretary of the board. There he exercised an enormous influ-
(10) ence during the critical period of reconstruction that brought into existence the American graded elementary school as a substitute for the older district school system. Under his leadership,

GO ON TO THE NEXT PAGE

3 3 3 3 3 3 3 3 3 3

the curriculum was restructured, the school year was increased to a minimum of six months, and mandatory schooling was extended to age sixteen. Other important reforms included the establishment of state normal schools for teacher training, institutes for inservice teacher edu-

(15) cation, and lyceums for adult education. He was also instrumental in improving salaries for teachers and creating school libraries.

Mann's ideas about school reform were developed and distributed in twelve annual reports to the state of Massachusetts that he wrote during his tenure as secretary of education. Considered quite radical at the time, the Massachusetts reforms later served as a model for the

(20) nation. Mann was recognized as the father of public education.

During his lifetime, Horace Mann worked tirelessly to extend educational opportunities to agrarian families and the children of poor laborers. In one of his last speeches he summed up his philosophy of education and life: "Be ashamed to die until you have won some victory for humanity." Surely, his own life was an example of that philosophy.

11. Which of the following titles would best express the main topic of the passage?

(A) The Father of American Public Education
(B) Philosophy of Education
(C) The Massachusetts State Board of Education
(D) Politics of Educational Institutions

12. Which of the following describes Horace Mann's early life?

(A) He attended school six months a year.
(B) He supported his family after his father died.
(C) He was an only child.
(D) He had to study alone, without help.

13. The word "struggles" in line 6 could best be replaced by

(A) valuable experiences
(B) happy situations
(C) influential people
(D) difficult times

14. The word "regret" in line 8 could best be replaced by which of the following?

(A) finances
(B) diappointment
(C) consideration
(D) limitations

15. Horace Mann's influence on American education was

(A) very great
(B) small, but important
(C) misunderstood
(D) not accepted

16. What did Horace Mann advocate?

(A) The state board school system
(B) The district school system
(C) The substitute school system
(D) The graded school system

17. The word "mandatory" in line 13 is closest in meaning to

(A) required
(B) equal
(C) excellent
(D) basic

18. How were Mann's educational reforms distributed?

(A) In twelve annual reports to the state of Massachusetts
(B) In reports that he wrote for national distribution
(C) In speeches that he made throughout the country
(D) In books that could be found in school libraries

GO ON TO THE NEXT PAGE

19. The reforms that Horace Mann achieved

   (A) were not very radical for the time
   (B) were used only by the state of Massa-
       chusetts
   (C) were later adopted by the nation as a
       model
   (D) were enforced by the Massachusetts bar

20. Which of the following statements best rep-
    resents Mann's philosophy?

   (A) Think in new ways.
   (B) Help others.
   (C) Study as much as possible.
   (D) Work hard.

Questions 21–30

   The population of the world has increased more in modern times than in all other ages of
history combined. World population totaled about 500 million in 1650. It doubled in the period from 1650–1850. Today the population is more than five billion. Estimates based on re-
Line search by the United Nations indicate that it will more than double in the twenty-five years be-
(5) tween 1975 and the year 2000, reaching seven billion by the turn of the century.

   No one knows the limits of population that the earth can support. Thomas Malthus, an
English economist, developed a theory that became widely accepted in the nineteenth century.
He suggested that because world population tended to increase more rapidly than the food
supply, a continual strain was exerted upon available resources. Malthus cited wars, famines,
(10) epidemics, and other disasters as the usual limitations of population growth.

   With recent advances in science and technology, including improved agricultural methods
and great strides in medicine, some of the limiting factors in population growth have been
lessened, with obvious results. International organizations have put forward several recommendations to alleviate the problem of overpopulation, including an increase in food produc-
(15) tion, general economic development in target areas, and a decrease in birth rates. Most experts
agree that it will be necessary to combine all three recommendations in an effort to effect a
lasting solution.

21. The title below that best expresses the ideas
    in this passage is

   (A) Thomas Malthus' Theory
   (B) The United Nations' Estimate
   (C) Limiting Factors in Population Growth
   (D) A Brief History of Population and Over-
       population

22. By 1850, approximately what was the world
    population?

   (A) 500 million
   (B) One billion
   (C) Five billion
   (D) Seven billion

23. World population doubled in the years be-
    tween

   (A) 500–1650
   (B) 1650–1850
   (C) 1650–today
   (D) 1850–2000

24. According to this passage, by the year 2000
    the earth's population should exceed the
    present figure by how much?

   (A) 500 million
   (B) Five billion
   (C) Two billion
   (D) Seven billion

GO ON TO THE NEXT PAGE

3 3 3 3 3 3 3 3 3 3

25. Who was Thomas Malthus?

(A) A scientist
(B) A doctor of medicine
(C) An economist
(D) A United Nations representative

26. The word "resources" in line 9 refers to

(A) the people who already occupy the earth
(B) war, famine, and epidemic
(C) natural supplies of energy, food, and other raw materials
(D) agricultural and medical advances

27. According to the passage, why has overpopulation been caused?

(A) Improved technology
(B) Disasters
(C) Scarcity
(D) Precaution

28. The word "obvious" in line 13 could best be replaced by

(A) clear
(B) negative
(C) several
(D) significant

29. The word "lasting" in line 17 is closest in meaning to

(A) complete
(B) important
(C) permanent
(D) expected

30. What do most experts recommend in order to solve problems of overpopulation?

(A) Famine and epidemic
(B) Medical advances and improved agricultural methods
(C) Economic development and a decline in the birth rate
(D) Conservation of available resources

Questions 31–40

Organic architecture—that is, natural architecture—may be varied in concept and form, but it is always faithful to natural principles. Organic architecture rejects rules imposed by individual preference or mere aesthetics in order to remain true to the nature of the site, the ma-
Line terials, the purpose of the structure, and the people who will ultimately use it. If these natural
(5) principles are upheld, then a bank cannot be built to look like a Greek temple. Form does not follow function; form is inseparable from function. In other words, a building should be inspired by nature's forms and constructed with materials that retain and respect the natural characteristics of the setting to create harmony with its natural environment. It should maximize people's contact with and utilization of the outdoors.
(10)   Natural principles then, are principles of design, not style, expressed by construction that reflects unity, balance, proportion, rhythm, and scale. Like a sculptor, the organic architect views the site and materials as an innate form that shapes and develops organically from within. Truth in architecture results in a natural, spontaneous structure in total harmony with the setting. For the most part, these structures find their geometric themes in the contours of the
(15) land and their colors in the surrounding palette of nature.

GO ON TO THE NEXT PAGE

3 3 3 3 3 3 3 3 3 3 3

From the outside, an organic structure is so much a part of nature that it is often obscured by it. In other words, it may not be possible for the eye to easily separate the man-made structure from the natural terrain. From the inside, rooms open into each other. Natural light, air, and view permeate the whole structure, providing a sense of communication with the out-
(20) doors.

31. What is another name for organic architecture?

    (A) Natural architecture
    (B) Aesthetic architecture
    (C) Principle architecture
    (D) Varied architecture

32. The word "ultimately" in line 4 could best be replaced by

    (A) fortunately
    (B) eventually
    (C) supposedly
    (D) obviously

33. The word "it" in line 2 refers to

    (A) architecture
    (B) site
    (C) purpose
    (D) structure

34. The word "upheld" in line 5 is closest in meaning to

    (A) invalidated
    (B) disputed
    (C) promoted
    (D) perceived

35. In organic architecture, which of the following is true?

    (A) Form follows function.
    (B) Function follows form.
    (C) Function is not important to form.
    (D) Form and function are one.

36. A good example of natural principles is a

    (A) bank that is built to look like a Greek temple
    (B) bank built so that the location is unimportant to the structure
    (C) bank that is built to conform to the natural surroundings
    (D) bank that is built to be beautiful rather than functional

37. Why does the author compare an organic architect to a sculptor?

    (A) To emphasize aesthetics
    (B) To give an example of natural principles
    (C) To make a point about the development of geometry
    (D) To demonstrate the importance of style

38. Where in the passage does the author mention the source of geometric themes?

    (A) Lines 14–15
    (B) Lines 16–17
    (C) Lines 17–18
    (D) Lines 19–20

39. The word "obscured" in line 16 is closest in meaning to

    (A) difficult to see
    (B) in high demand
    (C) not very attractive
    (D) mutually beneficial

GO ON TO THE NEXT PAGE ➡

3 3 3 3 3 3 3 3 3 3 3

40. Which of the following statements best describes the architect's view of nature?

(A) Nature should be conquered.
(B) Nature should not be considered.
(C) Nature should be respected.
(D) Nature should be improved.

Questions 41–50

   The earliest authentic works on European alchemy are those of the English monk Roger Bacon and the German philosopher St. Albertus Magnus. In their treatises they maintained that gold was the perfect metal and that inferior metals such as lead and mercury were re-
Line moved by various degrees of imperfection from gold. They further asserted that these base
(5) metals could be transmuted to gold by blending them with a substance even more perfect than gold. This elusive substance was referred to as the "philosopher's stone."
   Most of the early alchemists were artisans who were accustomed to keeping trade secrets and often resorted to cryptic terminology to record the progress of their work. The term *sun* was used for gold, *moon* for silver, and the five known planets for base metals. This convention
(10) of substituting symbolic language attracted a group of mystical philosophers who compared the search for the perfect metal with the struggle of mankind for the perfection of the soul. The philosophers began to use the artisan's terms in the mystical literature that they produced. Thus, by the fourteenth century, alchemy had developed two distinct groups of practitioners— the laboratory alchemist and the literary alchemist. Both groups of alchemists continued
(15) to work throughout the history of alchemy, but, of course, it was the literary alchemist who was most likely to produce a written record; therefore, much of what is known about the science of alchemy is derived from philosophers rather than from the alchemists who labored in laboratories.

41. What is the author's main point?

(A) There were both laboratory and literary alchemists.
(B) The philosopher's stone was essential to alchemy.
(C) Roger Bacon and St. Albertus Magnus wrote about alchemy.
(D) Base metals can be transmuted to gold by blending them with a substance more perfect than gold.

42. The word "authentic" in line 1 could best be replaced by

(A) valuable
(B) genuine
(C) complete
(D) comprehensible

43. The word "those" in line 1 refers to

(A) metals
(B) treatises
(C) alchemy
(D) works

44. Roger Bacon and St. Albertus Magnus had the same

(A) nationality
(B) premise
(C) profession
(D) education

GO ON TO THE NEXT PAGE

3 3 3 3 3 3 3 3 3 3 3

45. According to the alchemists, what was the difference between base metals and gold?

(A) Perfection
(B) Chemical content
(C) Temperature
(D) Weight

46. What was the "philosopher's stone?"

(A) Lead that was mixed with gold
(B) An element that was never found
(C) Another name for alchemy
(D) A base metal

47. It is probable that Roger Bacon's work

(A) was not genuine
(B) disproved that of St. Albertus Magnus
(C) was written after St. Albertus Magnus
(D) contained references to the conversion of base metals to gold

48. Who were the first alchemists?

(A) Chemists
(B) Writers
(C) Artisans
(D) Linguists

49. The word "cryptic" in line 8 could be replaced by which of the following?

(A) scholarly
(B) secret
(C) foreign
(D) precise

50. How do we know about the history of alchemy?

(A) The laboratory alchemists kept secret notes.
(B) The literary alchemists recorded it in writing.
(C) The mystical philosophers were not able to hide the secrets of alchemy.
(D) The historians were able to interpret the secret writings of the alchemists.

THIS IS THE END OF THE READING COMPREHENSION SECTION OF TOEFL MODEL TEST 5.

IF YOU FINISH BEFORE 55 MINUTES HAS ENDED, CHECK YOUR WORK ON SECTION 3 ONLY.

DO NOT READ OR WORK ON ANY OTHER SECTION OF THE TEST.

END OF TOEFL MODEL TEST 5.

To check your answers for Model Test 5, refer to the Answer Key on page 464. For an explanation of the answers, refer to the Explanatory Answers for Model Test 5 on page 504.

MODEL TEST 6—ANSWER SHEET

Section 1

1 2 3 4 5 6 7 8 9 10 11 12 13 14 15 16 17 18 19 20 21 22 23 24 25 26 27 28 29 30
A A A A A A A A A A A A A A A A A A A A A A A A A A A A A A
B B B B B B B B B B B B B B B B B B B B B B B B B B B B B B
C C C C C C C C C C C C C C C C C C C C C C C C C C C C C C
D D D D D D D D D D D D D D D D D D D D D D D D D D D D D D

31 32 33 34 35 36 37 38 39 40 41 42 43 44 45 46 47 48 49 50
A A A A A A A A A A A A A A A A A A A A
B B B B B B B B B B B B B B B B B B B B
C C C C C C C C C C C C C C C C C C C C
D D D D D D D D D D D D D D D D D D D D

Section 2

1 2 3 4 5 6 7 8 9 10 11 12 13 14 15 16 17 18 19 20 21 22 23 24 25 26 27 28 29 30
A A A A A A A A A A A A A A A A A A A A A A A A A A A A A A
B B B B B B B B B B B B B B B B B B B B B B B B B B B B B B
C C C C C C C C C C C C C C C C C C C C C C C C C C C C C C
D D D D D D D D D D D D D D D D D D D D D D D D D D D D D D

31 32 33 34 35 36 37 38 39 40
A A A A A A A A A A
B B B B B B B B B B
C C C C C C C C C C
D D D D D D D D D D

Section 3

1 2 3 4 5 6 7 8 9 10 11 12 13 14 15 16 17 18 19 20 21 22 23 24 25 26 27 28 29 30
A A A A A A A A A A A A A A A A A A A A A A A A A A A A A A
B B B B B B B B B B B B B B B B B B B B B B B B B B B B B B
C C C C C C C C C C C C C C C C C C C C C C C C C C C C C C
D D D D D D D D D D D D D D D D D D D D D D D D D D D D D D

31 32 33 34 35 36 37 38 39 40 41 42 43 44 45 46 47 48 49 50
A A A A A A A A A A A A A A A A A A A A
B B B B B B B B B B B B B B B B B B B B
C C C C C C C C C C C C C C C C C C C C
D D D D D D D D D D D D D D D D D D D D

Cut here to remove answer sheet.

$$\boxed{1 \quad 1 \quad 1 \quad 1 \quad 1 \quad 1 \quad 1 \quad 1 \quad 1 \quad 1 \quad 1 \quad 1}$$

Model Test 6
Short Form

Section 1:
Listening Comprehension

50 QUESTIONS 40 MINUTES

In this section of the test, you will have an opportunity to demonstrate your ability to understand conversations and talks in English. There are three parts to this section with special directions for each part. Answer all the questions on the basis of what is stated or implied by the speakers in this test. When you take the actual TOEFL test, you will not be allowed to take notes or write in your test book. Try to work on this Model Test in the same way.

Part A

Directions: In Part A, you will hear short conversations between two people. After each conversation, you will hear a question about the conversation. The conversations and questions will not be repeated. After you hear a question, read the four possible answers in your book and choose the best answer. Then, on your answer sheet, find the number of the question and fill in the space that corresponds to the letter of the answer you have chosen.

1. (A) It has reached a high, and will start to go down.
   (B) It is going to increase.
   (C) It is very expensive.
   (D) It is not very surprising.

2. (A) She is going to spend the summer in Zimbabwe.
   (B) She is from Africa.
   (C) She and Ellen are sisters.
   (D) Both women are interested in art.

3. (A) She does not know how to play tennis.
   (B) She has to study.
   (C) She does not like the man.
   (D) She does not qualify to play.

4. (A) She has no attendance policy.
   (B) The attendance policy is not the same for undergraduates and graduate students.
   (C) The grade will be affected by absences.
   (D) This class is not for graduate students.

5. (A) Make a cake.
   (B) Go to the bakery.
   (C) Visit her mother.
   (D) Eat at the Dutch Oven.

6. (A) He is a librarian.
   (B) He is a professor.
   (C) He is an accountant.
   (D) He is a reporter.

7. (A) He is studying only at the American Language Institute.
   (B) He is taking three classes at the university.
   (C) He is a part-time student.
   (D) He is surprised.

GO ON TO THE NEXT PAGE ➤

1   1   1   1   1   1   1   1   1   1   1

8. (A) She will help the man.
   (B) She is not Miss Evans.
   (C) The man's wife has already gone.
   (D) The man should wait for his wife to answer the call.

9. (A) Sweets.
   (B) The woman's teeth.
   (C) X-rays.
   (D) An appointment.

10. (A) Mr. Adams is the new foreign student advisor.
    (B) The foreign student advisor is a man.
    (C) The foreign student advisor is married.
    (D) The foreign student advisor is not here.

11. (A) She did not get a letter from her family today.
    (B) She is worried about the letter that she got from her family.
    (C) She is worried about the money that she owes.
    (D) She does not expect to get any letters from her family.

12. (A) Return home.
    (B) Ask someone else about the flight.
    (C) Make a telephone call.
    (D) Board the plane.

13. (A) She will go to the bookstore.
    (B) The books were too expensive.
    (C) There weren't any math and English books left.
    (D) She does not need any books.

14. (A) Take a different route.
    (B) Leave earlier than planned.
    (C) Wait until seven to leave.
    (D) Stay at home.

15. (A) The class with the graduate assistant is very enjoyable.
    (B) The students make a lot of errors in the class.
    (C) The graduate assistant ridicules his students.
    (D) She is sorry that she took the class with the graduate assistant.

16. (A) He did not mean to insult the woman.
    (B) What he said to Susan was true.
    (C) The woman does not have an accent.
    (D) Susan did not report the conversation accurately.

17. (A) Tell him the time.
    (B) Take care of his bag.
    (C) Help him find his books.
    (D) Go with him.

18. (A) He has heard the woman talk about this often.
    (B) He understands the woman's point of view.
    (C) He is too tired to talk about it.
    (D) He can hear the woman very well.

19. (A) Mike does not have a car.
    (B) Mike's brother is taking a break.
    (C) Mike is in Florida.
    (D) Mike is visiting his brother.

20. (A) Get a job.
    (B) Finish the assignment.
    (C) Begin his project.
    (D) Pay his bills.

21. (A) He wants to arrive at a permanent solution to the problem.
    (B) The problem has been resolved.
    (C) The woman should call customer service.
    (D) They need to call information for the number.

GO ON TO THE NEXT PAGE ➡

22. (A) She is not sure about going.
    (B) She does not want to go to the show.
    (C) She wants to know why the man asked her.
    (D) She would like to go with the man.

23. (A) They would not get married.
    (B) They were still away on their honeymoon.
    (C) They didn't go on a honeymoon.
    (D) They had not planned a large wedding.

24. (A) She has already reviewed for the test.
    (B) The test is important to her.
    (C) The review session will not be helpful.
    (D) The man does not understand her.

25. (A) Telephone his sponsor.
    (B) Collect his check.
    (C) Help the woman look for his check.
    (D) Ask the woman to look again.

26. (A) The university has been slow to respond.
    (B) There are other universities.
    (C) The situation is not that bad.
    (D) The woman should keep trying.

27. (A) He could have used help to find his books.
    (B) He found everything that he was looking for.
    (C) He had a stack of books to check out.
    (D) He enjoyed using the library.

28. (A) His insurance rates.
    (B) His citation.
    (C) His injuries.
    (D) His guilty conscience.

29. (A) She was planning to go to Yale.
    (B) She could not score in the 600s on the TOEFL.
    (C) She would be accepted at Yale.
    (D) She didn't want to go to Yale.

30. (A) Take the seat away.
    (B) Sit down beside the woman.
    (C) Help the woman be seated.
    (D) Invite the woman to sit with him.

Part B

Directions: In this part of the test, you will hear longer conversations. After each conversation, you will hear several questions. The conversations and questions will not be repeated.

After you hear a question, read the four possible answers in your book and choose the best answer. Then, on your answer sheet, find the number of the question and fill in the space that corresponds to the letter of the answer you have chosen.

Remember, you are **not** allowed to take notes or write on your test pages.

31. (A) He is sick with the flu.
    (B) He is in the hospital.
    (C) He has missed some quizzes.
    (D) He is behind in lab.

32. (A) Go to lab for him.
    (B) Let him copy her notes.
    (C) Help him study.
    (D) Be his lab partner.

33. (A) Meet with him to clarify her notes.
    (B) Make a copy of the quizzes for him.
    (C) Read his notes before the next lab.
    (D) Show him how to do the lab experiments.

GO ON TO THE NEXT PAGE

1 1 1 1 1 1 1 1 1 1 1

34. (A) Helpful.
    (B) Worried.
    (C) Apologetic.
    (D) Unfriendly.

35. (A) To make an appointment.
    (B) To cancel his appointment.
    (C) To change his appointment time.
    (D) To rearrange his schedule so that he could keep his appointment.

36. (A) He is busy on Wednesday.
    (B) He will not be in on Wednesday.
    (C) He does not schedule appointments on Wednesday.
    (D) He will be moving his Wednesday appointment to Thursday this week.

37. (A) Give him an appointment at three o'clock on Wednesday.
    (B) Give him an appointment at either four-thirty on Wednesday or ten o'clock on Thursday.
    (C) Give him an appointment at lunch time.
    (D) Give him a new appointment earlier on the same day as his original appointment.

38. (A) Make a new appointment later.
    (B) Cancel his regular appointment.
    (C) Rearrange his schedule to keep his original appointment.
    (D) Call back later when Dr. Benjamin is in.

Part C

Directions: In this part of the test, you will hear several short talks. After each talk, you will hear some questions. The talks and questions will not be repeated.

After you hear a question, read the four possible answers in your book and choose the best answer. Then, on your answer sheet, find the number of the question and fill in the space that corresponds to the letter of the answer you have chosen.

39. (A) Novelists of this century.
    (B) F. Scott Fitzgerald's work.
    (C) First novels by young authors.
    (D) Film versions of F. Scott Fitzgerald's novels.

40. (A) He had little natural talent.
    (B) He was a compulsive drinker.
    (C) He improved his work as a mature writer.
    (D) He adjusted to a changing world.

41. (A) They described the Jazz Age.
    (B) They described the Deep South.
    (C) They were based upon war experiences.
    (D) They were written in stream-of-consciousness style.

42. (A) Write a book report.
    (B) Read one of Fitzgerald's books.
    (C) Watch and discuss a video.
    (D) Research Fitzgerald's life.

43. (A) To explain chamber music.
    (B) To give examples of composers.
    (C) To congratulate the University Quartet.
    (D) To introduce madrigal singing.

44. (A) Recorders used to be the most important instrument.
    (B) Piano must be used in all chamber music.
    (C) Any combination of instruments may be used.
    (D) Strings and harpsichord are the most popular instruments.

GO ON TO THE NEXT PAGE ➡

1 1 1 1 1 1 1 1 1 1 1 1

45. (A) He was a famous composer.
    (B) He composed the pieces that will be performed.
    (C) He wrote vocal chamber music.
    (D) He wrote trio sonatas.

46. (A) A discussion of music from the eighteenth century.
    (B) A concert by the University Quartet.
    (C) An introduction to religious music.
    (D) A history of music from the Elizabethan Period.

47. (A) Health food.
    (B) The processing of bread.
    (C) Organic gardens.
    (D) Poisons.

48. (A) Refined foods.
    (B) Natural foods.
    (C) Organic foods.
    (D) Unprocessed foods.

49. (A) The ultimate content remains the same.
    (B) Vitamin information is not available after processing.
    (C) Vitamins are added to the food.
    (D) The vitamin content is reduced.

50. (A) Uninformed.
    (B) Convinced.
    (C) Uncertain.
    (D) Humorous.

THIS IS THE END OF THE LISTENING COMPREHENSION SECTION OF TOEFL MODEL TEST 6.

DO NOT READ OR WORK ON ANY OTHER SECTION OF THE TEST.

2   2   2   2   2   2   2   2   2   2   2

Section 2:
Structure and Written Expression

40 QUESTIONS 25 MINUTES

This section is designed to measure your ability to recognize language that is appropriate for standard written English. There are two types of questions in this section, with special directions for each type.

Structure

Directions: Questions 1–15 are incomplete sentences. Beneath each sentence you will see four words or phrases, marked (A), (B), (C), and (D). Choose the **one** word or phrase that best completes the sentence. Then, on your answer sheet, find the number of the question and fill in the space that corresponds to the letter of the answer you have chosen. Fill in the space so that the letter inside the oval cannot be seen.

1. It is important that the TOEFL Office ------- an applicant's registration.

   (A) will confirm
   (B) confirm
   (C) confirms
   (D) must confirm

2. Deserts are often formed ------- they are cut off from rain-bearing winds by the surrounding mountain ranges.

   (A) because
   (B) in spite of
   (C) so
   (D) due to

3. ------- that the English settled in Jamestown.

   (A) In 1607 that it was
   (B) That in 1607
   (C) Because in 1607
   (D) It was in 1607

4. Staying in a hotel costs ------- renting a room in a dormitory for a week.

   (A) twice more than
   (B) twice as much as
   (C) as much twice as
   (D) as much as twice

5. When friends insist on ------- expensive gifts, it makes most Americans uncomfortable.

   (A) them to accept
   (B) their accepting
   (C) they accepting
   (D) they accept

6. Gilbert Stuart is considered by most art critics ------- greatest portrait painter in the North American colonies.

   (A) that he was
   (B) as he was
   (C) who was the
   (D) the

7. As a safety measure, the detonator for a nuclear device may be made of ---------, each of which is controlled by a different employee.

   (A) two equipments
   (B) two pieces of equipments
   (C) two pieces of equipment
   (D) two equipment pieces

GO ON TO THE NEXT PAGE ➡

2   2   2   2   2   2   2   2   2   2   2

8. An equilateral triangle is a triangle ------ and three angles of equal size.
   - (A) that have three sides of equal length
   - (B) it has three sides equally long
   - (C) that has three sides of equal length
   - (D) having three equal length sides in it

9. ------ are found on the surface of the moon.
   - (A) Craters and waterless seas that
   - (B) When craters and waterless seas
   - (C) Craters and waterless seas
   - (D) Since craters and waterless seas

10. ------ two waves pass a given point simultaneously, they will have no effect on each other's subsequent motion.
    - (A) So that
    - (B) They are
    - (C) That
    - (D) If

11. A child in the first grade tends to be -------- all of the other children in the class.
    - (A) the same old to
    - (B) the same age than
    - (C) as old like
    - (D) the same age as

12. The bird's egg is such an efficient structure for protecting the embryo inside -------- difficult for the hatchling to break.
    - (A) that is
    - (B) that
    - (C) and is
    - (D) that it is

13. We had hoped ------- the game, but the other team played very well.
    - (A) State University to win
    - (B) that State University win
    - (C) that State University would win
    - (D) State University's winning

14. The artistic medium of clay is ------- that images have been found near the remains of fires from the last Ice Age.
    - (A) so old
    - (B) such an old
    - (C) oldest
    - (D) old

15. Unlike most Europeans, many Americans ------- a bowl of cereal for breakfast every day.
    - (A) used to eating
    - (B) are used to eat
    - (C) are used to eating
    - (D) use to eat

Written Expression

Directions: In questions 16–40, each sentence has four underlined words or phrases. The four underlined parts of the sentence are marked (A), (B), (C), and (D). Identify the **one** underlined word or phrase that must be changed in order for the sentence to be correct. Then, on your answer sheet, find the number of the question and fill in the space that corresponds to the letter of the answer you have chosen.

GO ON TO THE NEXT PAGE

2   2   2   2   2   2   2   2   2   2   2

16. The Pickerel Frog, native to Southern Canada and the Eastern United States, should be avoided
    (A)   (B)
    because their skin secretions are lethal to small animals and irritating to humans.
             (C)   (D)

17. The most common form of treatment it is mass inoculation and chlorination of water sources.
        (A)   (B)   (C)   (D)

18. People with exceptionally high intelligence quotients may not be the best employees since they
                  (A)   (B)
    become bored of their work unless the job is constantly changing.
           (C)   (D)

19. Neither the mathematics department nor the biology department at State University requires that
                                       (A)
    the students must write a thesis in order to graduate with a master's degree.
                (B)   (C)   (D)

20. The oxygen content of Mars is not sufficient enough to support life as we know it.
                                       (A)   (B)   (C) (D)

21. Students in the United States often support themselves by babysitting, working in restaurants, or
                                  (A)   (B)   (C)
    they drive taxicabs.
        (D)

22. Those of us who have a family history of heart disease should make yearly appointments with
                 (A)   (B)   (C)
    their doctors.
    (D)

23. Although federal support for basic research programs are much less than it was ten years ago,
                            (A)   (B) (C)   (D)
    more funds are now available from the National Science Foundation.

24. Living in New York, apartments cost more to rent than they do in other, smaller cities.
    (A)   (B)   (C)   (D)

25. This new model not only saves time but also energy by operating on two batteries instead of four.
    (A)   (B)   (C)   (D)

26. The government requires that a census be taken every ten years so accurate statistics
                                       (A)   (B)   (C)
    may be compiled.
        (D)

GO ON TO THE NEXT PAGE ➡

2 2 2 2 2 2 2 2 2 2 2

27. In 1975, according to the National Center for Health Statistics, the average life expectancy for
                    (A)
    people born during that year is 72.4 years.
          (B)   (C)   (D)

28. Traditionally, the flag is risen in the morning and taken down at night.
                        (A)   (B)   (C)   (D)

29. When the silkworm gets through to lay its eggs, it dies.
              (A)   (B) (C)   (D)

30. Frank Lloyd Wright has been acclaimed by colleagues as the greater of all modern architects.
                      (A)   (B)   (C)   (D)

31. Scientists had previously estimated that the Grand Canyon in Arizona is ten million years old;
                    (A)   (B)
    but now, by using a more modern dating method, they agree that the age is closer to
              (C)
    six million years.
          (D)

32. The corals can be divided into three groups, two of which is extinct.
                (A)   (B)   (C) (D)

33. Without alphabetical order, dictionaries would be impossibility to use.
                                (A)   (B)   (C)   (D)

34. Jane Addams had already established Hull House in Chicago and began her work in the Women's
                      (A)   (B)   (C)
    Suffrage Movement when she was awarded the Nobel prize for peace.
                                      (D)

35. The extent to which an individual is a product of either heredity or environment cannot proven,
                 (A)   (B)
    but several theories have been proposed.
        (C)   (D)

36. Although jogging is a good way to lose weight and improve one's physical condition, most doctors
              (A)   (B)
    recommend that the potential jogger begin in a correct manner by getting a complete checkup.
                                            (C)   (D)

37. The flag of the original first colonies may or may not have been made by Betsy Ross
                    (A)   (B)   (C)
    during the Revolution.
          (D)

GO ON TO THE NEXT PAGE

2 **2** **2** **2** **2** **2** **2**

38. Some conifers, that is, tree that have cones, are able to thrive on poor, thin soil.
    (A)   (B) (C)   (D)

39. The Indians of the southwestern United States are famous for their beautiful art work, especially
                                              (A)   (B)   (C)

    handmade jewelry cast from silver, carved from stones, or decorations with beads and feathers.
                                                               (D)

40. Because the solar tiles were very secure fastened, only a few became detached when the Space
                                    (A)   (B)   (C)

    Shuttle reentered the earth's atmosphere.
                       (D)

**THIS IS THE END OF THE STRUCTURE AND WRITTEN EXPRESSION
SECTION OF TOEFL MODEL TEST 6.**

**IF YOU FINISH BEFORE 25 MINUTES HAS ENDED, CHECK YOUR
WORK ON SECTION 2 ONLY.**

DO NOT READ OR WORK ON ANY OTHER SECTION OF THE TEST.

STOP   STOP   STOP   **STOP**   STOP   STOP   STOP

3 3 3 3 3 3 3 3 3 3 3

Section 3:
Reading Comprehension

50 QUESTIONS 55 MINUTES

Directions: In this section you will read several passages. Each one is followed by a number of questions about it. For questions 1–50, you are to choose the **one** best answer, (A), (B), (C), or (D), to each question. Then, on your answer sheet, find the number of the question and fill in the space that corresponds to the letter of the answer you have chosen.

Answer all questions about the information in a passage on the basis of what is **stated** or **implied** in that passage.

Questions 1–10

A geyser is the result of underground water under the combined conditions of high temperatures and increased pressure beneath the surface of the earth. Since temperature rises approximately 1°F for every sixty feet under the earth's surface, and pressure increases with
Line depth, water that seeps down in cracks and fissures until it reaches very hot rocks in the
(5) earth's interior becomes heated to a temperature in excess of 290°F. Because of the greater pressure, it shoots out of the surface in the form of steam and hot water. The result is a geyser.

In order to function, then, a geyser must have a source of heat, a reservoir where water can be stored until the temperature rises to an unstable point, an opening through which the hot water and steam can escape, and underground channels for resupplying water after an eruption.
(10) Favorable conditions for geysers exist in regions of geologically recent volcanic activity, especially in areas of more than average precipitation.

For the most part, geysers are located in three regions of the world: New Zealand, Iceland, and the Yellowstone National Park area of the United States. The most famous geyser in the world is Old Faithful in Yellowstone Park. Old Faithful erupts almost every hour, rising to a
(15) height of 125 to 170 feet and expelling more than ten thousand gallons during each eruption.

1. What does this passage mainly discuss?

   (A) The Old Faithful geyser in Yellowstone National Park
   (B) The nature of geysers
   (C) The ratio of temperature to pressure in underground water
   (D) Regions of geologically recent volcanic activity

2. In order for a geyser to erupt

   (A) hot rocks must rise to the surface of the earth
   (B) water must flow underground
   (C) it must be a warm day
   (D) the earth must not be rugged or broken

3. The word "approximately" in line 3 could best be replaced by

   (A) repeatedly
   (B) correctly
   (C) generally
   (D) certainly

GO ON TO THE NEXT PAGE ➡

4. As depth increases

   (A) pressure increases but temperature does not

   (B) temperature increases but pressure does not

   (C) both pressure and temperature increase

   (D) neither pressure nor temperature increases

5. The word "it" in line 4 refers to

   (A) water

   (B) depth

   (C) pressure

   (D) surface

6. Where in the passage does the author refer to the necessary conditions for geysers to be active?

   (A) Lines 7–9

   (B) Lines 5–6

   (C) Lines 2–5

   (D) Lines 1–2

7. Where is Old Faithful located?

   (A) New Zealand

   (B) Iceland

   (C) The United States

   (D) England

8. How often does Old Faithful erupt?

   (A) Every 10 minutes

   (B) Every 60 minutes

   (C) Every 125 minutes

   (D) Every 170 minutes

9. The word "expelling" in line 15 is closest in meaning to

   (A) heating

   (B) discharging

   (C) supplying

   (D) wasting

10. Which conditions does a geyser require to function?

   (A) A source of heat, a place for water to collect, an opening, and underground channels

   (B) An active volcano nearby and a water reservoir

   (C) Channels in the earth and heavy rainfall

   (D) Volcanic activity, underground channels, and steam

Questions 11–20

     The question has often been asked why the Wright brothers were able to succeed in an effort in which so many others had failed. Many explanations have been offered, but three reasons are most often cited. First, they were a team. Both men worked well together, read the same books, located and shared information, talked incessantly about the possibility of manned flight, and served as a consistent source of inspiration and encouragement to each other. Quite simply, two geniuses are better than one.

     They were also both glider pilots. Unlike some other engineers who experimented with the theories of flight, Orville and Wilbur Wright experienced the practical side of their work by building and flying in kites and gliders. Each craft was slightly better than the last, incorporating in it the knowledge that they had gained from previous failures. They had realized from their experiments that the most serious problem in manned flight would be stabilizing and maneuvering the aircraft once it was airborne. While others concentrated their efforts on the problem of achieving lift for take-off, the Wright brothers focused on developing a three-axis

GO ON TO THE NEXT PAGE

3 3 3 3 3 3 3 3 3 3 3

control for their aircraft. By the time that the brothers started to build an airplane, they were
(15) already among the best glider pilots in the world, and they knew the problems of flying first
hand.

In addition, the Wright brothers had designed more effective wings for the airplane than
had been previously engineered. Using a wind tunnel, they tested more than two hundred different wing designs, recording the effects of slight variations in shape on the pressure of air
(20) on the wings. The data from these experiments allowed the Wright brothers to construct a su-
perior wing for their craft.

In spite of all these advantages, however, the Wright brothers might not have succeeded
had they not been born at precisely the opportune moment in history. Attempts to achieve
manned flight in the early nineteenth century were doomed because the steam engines that
(25) powered the aircrafts were too heavy in proportion to the power that they produced. But by
the end of the nineteenth century, when the brothers were experimenting with engineering options, a relatively light internal combustion engine had already been invented, and they were
able to bring the ratio of weight to power within acceptable limits for flight.

11. What is the author's main point in this passage?

(A) The reasons why the Wright brothers
    succeeded in manned flight
(B) The advantage of the internal combus-
    tion engine in the Wright brothers'
    experiments
(C) The Wright brothers' experience as
    pilots
(D) The importance of gliders to the devel-
    opment of airplanes

12. The word "cited" in line 3 is closest in
    meaning to which of the following?

(A) disregarded
(B) mentioned
(C) considered
(D) proven

13. The word "incessantly" in line 4 could best
    be replaced by which of the following?

(A) confidently
(B) intelligently
(C) constantly
(D) optimistically

14. What kind of experience did the Wright
    brothers have that distinguished them from
    their competitors?

(A) They were geniuses.
(B) They were glider pilots.
(C) They were engineers.
(D) They were inventors.

15. According to the Wright brothers, what was
    the most serious problem in constructing a
    manned aircraft?

(A) Achieving take-off
(B) Stabilizing during take-off
(C) Maneuvering after take-off
(D) Controlling the landing

16. The word "maneuvering" in line 12 could
    best be replaced by

(A) releasing
(B) controlling
(C) understanding
(D) recovering

GO ON TO THE NEXT PAGE

3 3 3 3 3 3 3 3 3 3 | 3

17. How did the Wright brothers build the wings for their airplanes?

   (A) By copying the wings of gliders they had flown
   (B) By experimenting with different wing designs in a wind tunnel
   (C) By using wings that had been developed by other engineers
   (D) By collecting data from scientific literature

18. The word "they" in line 25 refers to

   (A) the Wright brothers
   (B) aircraft
   (C) engines
   (D) attempts

19. The word "doomed" in line 24 is closest in meaning to

   (A) destined to fail
   (B) difficult to achieve
   (C) taking a risk
   (D) not well planned

20. What was the problem with the steam engines used in earlier aircraft?

   (A) They were too small to power a large plane.
   (B) They were too light to generate enough power.
   (C) They did not have internal combustion power.
   (D) They did not have enough power to lift their own weight.

Questions 21–30

    The influenza virus is a single molecule composed of millions of individual atoms. Although bacteria can be considered a type of plant, secreting poisonous substances into the body of the organism they attack, viruses, like the influenza virus, are living organisms
Line themselves. We may consider them regular chemical molecules since they have strictly de-
(5) fined atomic structure; but on the other hand, we must also consider them as being alive since they are able to multiply in unlimited quantities.

    An attack brought on by the presence of the influenza virus in the body produces a temporary immunity, but, unfortunately, the protection is against only the type of virus that caused the influenza. Because the disease can be produced by any one of three types, referred to as A,
(10) B, or C, and many strains within each type, immunity to one virus will not prevent infection by another type or strain.

    Approximately every ten years, worldwide epidemics of influenza called pandemics occur. Thought to be caused by new strains of type-A virus, these pandemic viruses have spread rapidly, infecting millions of people. Epidemics or regional outbreaks have appeared
(15) on the average every two or three years for type-A virus, and every four or five years for type-B virus.

21. With what topic is the passage primarily concerned?

   (A) The influenza virus
   (B) Immunity to disease
   (C) Bacteria
   (D) Chemical molecules

22. According to this passage, bacteria are

   (A) poisons
   (B) very small
   (C) larger than viruses
   (D) plants

GO ON TO THE NEXT PAGE ➤

3   3   3   3   3   3   3   3   3   3   3

23. The word "themselves" in line 4 refers to

   (A) molecules
   (B) bacteria
   (C) substances
   (D) viruses

24. The word "strictly" in line 4 could best be replaced by

   (A) unusually
   (B) completely
   (C) broadly
   (D) exactly

25. Why does the writer say that viruses are alive?

   (A) They have a complex atomic structure.
   (B) They move.
   (C) They multiply.
   (D) They need warmth and light.

26. The atomic structure of viruses

   (A) is variable
   (B) is strictly defined
   (C) cannot be analyzed chemically
   (D) is more complex than that of bacteria

27. The word "unlimited" in line 6 could best be replaced by which of the following?

   (A) very small
   (B) very large
   (C) very similar
   (D) very different

28. How does the body react to the influenza virus?

   (A) It prevents further infection to other types and strains of the virus.
   (B) It produces immunity to the type and strain of virus that invaded it.
   (C) It becomes immune to types A, B, and C viruses, but not to various strains within the types.
   (D) After a temporary immunity, it becomes even more susceptible to the type and strain that caused the influenza.

29. The author names all of the following as characteristics of pandemics EXCEPT

   (A) they spread very quickly
   (B) they are caused by type-A virus
   (C) they are regional outbreaks
   (D) they occur once every ten years

30. The word "strains" in line 13 is closest in meaning to

   (A) theories
   (B) injuries
   (C) varieties
   (D) weaknesses

Questions 31–40

   A green I-538 form is used by international students in order to obtain permission from the Immigration and Naturalization Service (INS) to transfer from one college or university to another college or university in the United States. If you are planning to transfer, remember that
Line you must obtain permission before leaving the university where you are currently studying.
(5)   You must complete the form I-538, have it signed by the foreign student advisor or a designated official of the college, and submit it to the District Office of the Immigration and Naturalization Service together with the form I-20 from your new school and the small, white form I-94 that was affixed to your passport when you entered the country.

GO ON TO THE NEXT PAGE

3 3 3 3 3 3 3 3 3 3 | 3

Submitting the signed I-538 and other documents does not automatically ensure permis-
(10) sion to transfer. Only an official of Immigration can decide, and each request is reviewed on a
case by case basis. Students who have not completed one term of study at the school that issued them their first I-20 are not advised to file for permission to transfer until they have completed one term there since most such requests are denied.

It is generally not necessary to make an appointment since the written documentation usu-
(15) ally provides all the necessary information; however, some cases require a personal interview.
Should you need to see an INS officer, you will be notified.

31. What is this passage mainly about?

(A) The Immigration and Naturalization Ser-
vice
(B) How to get a passport
(C) How to obtain permission to transfer
from one university to another
(D) Studying in the United States

32. What is a transfer form called?

(A) I-20
(B) I-94
(C) I-538
(D) I-520

33. The word "currently" in line 4 is closest in
meaning to

(A) now
(B) later
(C) before
(D) always

34. Who must sign the transfer form?

(A) The foreign student advisor at the new
school
(B) The foreign student advisor at the cur-
rent school
(C) The student
(D) The Immigration officer

35. The phrase "affixed to" in line 8 could best
be replaced by

(A) guaranteed for
(B) fastened on
(C) verified by
(D) misplaced from

36. In order for you to transfer, permission must
be granted by an official at the

(A) foreign student advisor's office
(B) new university
(C) Immigration office
(D) passport office

37. Under which circumstances should students
wait to transfer?

(A) When they are in their first term of study
at a school
(B) When the permission to transfer is not
ensured
(C) When they do not have a valid passport
(D) When they do not have an Immigration
official to decide the case

38. The word "there" in line 13 refers to

(A) the school where the student wants to
transfer
(B) the school that issued the I-20
(C) the local INS office
(D) the immigration office that issued the
original permission

GO ON TO THE NEXT PAGE ▶

39. If you want to transfer, what should you do?

(A) Travel to the new university immediately so that the foreign student advisor can help you.
(B) Study at the university where you have permission until you receive a new permission from Immigration.
(C) Sign an I-538 form and leave it at your current university before traveling to the new university.
(D) Leave the country so that you can enter on another I-20 from the new university.

40. Where in the passage does the author explain the circumstances for a personal interview?

(A) Lines 9–10
(B) Lines 4–8
(C) Lines 14–16
(D) Lines 11–13

Questions 41–50

    Although most universities in the United States are on a semester system, which offers classes in the fall and spring, some schools observe a quarter system comprised of fall, winter, spring, and summer quarters. The academic year, September to June, is divided into three
Line quarters of eleven weeks each beginning in September, January, and March; the summer quar-
(5) ter, June to August, is composed of shorter sessions of varying length.

    There are several advantages and disadvantages to the quarter system. On the plus side, students who wish to complete their degrees in less than the customary four years may take advantage of the opportunity to study year round by enrolling in all four quarters. In addition, although most students begin their programs in the fall quarter, they may enter at the begin-
(10) ning of any of the other quarters. Finally, since the physical facilities are kept in operation year round, the resources are used efficiently to serve the greatest number of students. But there are several disadvantages as well. Many faculty complain that the eleven-week term is simply not long enough for them to cover the material required by most college courses. Students also find it difficult to complete the assignments in such a short period of time.

(15)   In order to combine the advantages of the quarter system with those of the semester system, some colleges and universities have instituted a three-term trimester system. In fourteen weeks, faculty and students have more time to cover material and finish course requirements, but the additional term provides more options for admission during the year and accelerates the degree programs for those students who wish to graduate early.

41. Which of the following would be the best title for this passage?

(A) Universities in the United States
(B) The Academic Year
(C) The Quarter System
(D) The Semester System

42. A semester system

(A) has eleven-week sessions
(B) is not very popular in the United States
(C) gives students the opportunity to study year round
(D) has two major sessions a year

GO ON TO THE NEXT PAGE

3 3 3 3 3 3 3 3 3 3 3

43. How many terms are there in a quarter system?

    (A) Four regular terms and one summer term
    (B) Three regular terms and one summer term
    (C) Two regular terms and two summer terms
    (D) One regular term and four summer terms

44. When is the academic year?

    (A) September to August
    (B) June to August
    (C) August to June
    (D) September to June

45. The word "customary" in line 7 could best be replaced by

    (A) agreeable
    (B) traditional
    (C) lengthy
    (D) limited

46. When may students begin studying in a school that uses a quarter system?

    (A) September
    (B) Summer semester only
    (C) At the beginning of any quarter
    (D) At the beginning of the academic year

47. The word "them" in line 13 refers to

    (A) faculty
    (B) weeks
    (C) courses
    (D) material

48. The word "instituted" in line 16 is closest in meaning to

    (A) established
    (B) considered
    (C) recommended
    (D) attempted

49. Which of the following characteristics does NOT apply to trimesters?

    (A) They allow students to graduate early.
    (B) They provide more options for admission.
    (C) They are long enough to cover the course material.
    (D) They last eleven weeks.

50. Where would this passage most probably be found?

    (A) In a college catalog for a university in the United States
    (B) In a general guide to colleges and universities in the United States
    (C) In an American newspaper
    (D) In a dictionary published in the United States

THIS IS THE END OF THE READING COMPREHENSION SECTION OF TOEFL MODEL TEST 6.

IF YOU FINISH BEFORE 55 MINUTES HAS ENDED, CHECK YOUR WORK ON SECTION 3 ONLY.

DO NOT READ OR WORK ON ANY OTHER SECTION OF THE TEST.

STOP   STOP   STOP   STOP   STOP   STOP   STOP

END OF TOEFL MODEL TEST 6.

To check your answers for Model Test 6, refer to the Answer Key on page 464. For an explanation of the answers, refer to the Explanatory Answers for Model Test 6 on page 513.

MODEL TEST 7—ANSWER SHEET

Section 1 | Section 2 | Section 3

Section 1

1. Ⓐ Ⓑ Ⓒ Ⓓ
2. Ⓐ Ⓑ Ⓒ Ⓓ
3. Ⓐ Ⓑ Ⓒ Ⓓ
4. Ⓐ Ⓑ Ⓒ Ⓓ
5. Ⓐ Ⓑ Ⓒ Ⓓ
6. Ⓐ Ⓑ Ⓒ Ⓓ
7. Ⓐ Ⓑ Ⓒ Ⓓ
8. Ⓐ Ⓑ Ⓒ Ⓓ
9. Ⓐ Ⓑ Ⓒ Ⓓ
10. Ⓐ Ⓑ Ⓒ Ⓓ
11. Ⓐ Ⓑ Ⓒ Ⓓ
12. Ⓐ Ⓑ Ⓒ Ⓓ
13. Ⓐ Ⓑ Ⓒ Ⓓ
14. Ⓐ Ⓑ Ⓒ Ⓓ
15. Ⓐ Ⓑ Ⓒ Ⓓ
16. Ⓐ Ⓑ Ⓒ Ⓓ
17. Ⓐ Ⓑ Ⓒ Ⓓ
18. Ⓐ Ⓑ Ⓒ Ⓓ
19. Ⓐ Ⓑ Ⓒ Ⓓ
20. Ⓐ Ⓑ Ⓒ Ⓓ
21. Ⓐ Ⓑ Ⓒ Ⓓ
22. Ⓐ Ⓑ Ⓒ Ⓓ
23. Ⓐ Ⓑ Ⓒ Ⓓ
24. Ⓐ Ⓑ Ⓒ Ⓓ
25. Ⓐ Ⓑ Ⓒ Ⓓ
26. Ⓐ Ⓑ Ⓒ Ⓓ
27. Ⓐ Ⓑ Ⓒ Ⓓ
28. Ⓐ Ⓑ Ⓒ Ⓓ
29. Ⓐ Ⓑ Ⓒ Ⓓ
30. Ⓐ Ⓑ Ⓒ Ⓓ
31. Ⓐ Ⓑ Ⓒ Ⓓ
32. Ⓐ Ⓑ Ⓒ Ⓓ
33. Ⓐ Ⓑ Ⓒ Ⓓ
34. Ⓐ Ⓑ Ⓒ Ⓓ
35. Ⓐ Ⓑ Ⓒ Ⓓ
36. Ⓐ Ⓑ Ⓒ Ⓓ
37. Ⓐ Ⓑ Ⓒ Ⓓ
38. Ⓐ Ⓑ Ⓒ Ⓓ
39. Ⓐ Ⓑ Ⓒ Ⓓ
40. Ⓐ Ⓑ Ⓒ Ⓓ
41. Ⓐ Ⓑ Ⓒ Ⓓ
42. Ⓐ Ⓑ Ⓒ Ⓓ
43. Ⓐ Ⓑ Ⓒ Ⓓ
44. Ⓐ Ⓑ Ⓒ Ⓓ
45. Ⓐ Ⓑ Ⓒ Ⓓ
46. Ⓐ Ⓑ Ⓒ Ⓓ
47. Ⓐ Ⓑ Ⓒ Ⓓ
48. Ⓐ Ⓑ Ⓒ Ⓓ
49. Ⓐ Ⓑ Ⓒ Ⓓ
50. Ⓐ Ⓑ Ⓒ Ⓓ

Section 2

1. Ⓐ Ⓑ Ⓒ Ⓓ
2. Ⓐ Ⓑ Ⓒ Ⓓ
3. Ⓐ Ⓑ Ⓒ Ⓓ
4. Ⓐ Ⓑ Ⓒ Ⓓ
5. Ⓐ Ⓑ Ⓒ Ⓓ
6. Ⓐ Ⓑ Ⓒ Ⓓ
7. Ⓐ Ⓑ Ⓒ Ⓓ
8. Ⓐ Ⓑ Ⓒ Ⓓ
9. Ⓐ Ⓑ Ⓒ Ⓓ
10. Ⓐ Ⓑ Ⓒ Ⓓ
11. Ⓐ Ⓑ Ⓒ Ⓓ
12. Ⓐ Ⓑ Ⓒ Ⓓ
13. Ⓐ Ⓑ Ⓒ Ⓓ
14. Ⓐ Ⓑ Ⓒ Ⓓ
15. Ⓐ Ⓑ Ⓒ Ⓓ
16. Ⓐ Ⓑ Ⓒ Ⓓ
17. Ⓐ Ⓑ Ⓒ Ⓓ
18. Ⓐ Ⓑ Ⓒ Ⓓ
19. Ⓐ Ⓑ Ⓒ Ⓓ
20. Ⓐ Ⓑ Ⓒ Ⓓ
21. Ⓐ Ⓑ Ⓒ Ⓓ
22. Ⓐ Ⓑ Ⓒ Ⓓ
23. Ⓐ Ⓑ Ⓒ Ⓓ
24. Ⓐ Ⓑ Ⓒ Ⓓ
25. Ⓐ Ⓑ Ⓒ Ⓓ
26. Ⓐ Ⓑ Ⓒ Ⓓ
27. Ⓐ Ⓑ Ⓒ Ⓓ
28. Ⓐ Ⓑ Ⓒ Ⓓ
29. Ⓐ Ⓑ Ⓒ Ⓓ
30. Ⓐ Ⓑ Ⓒ Ⓓ
31. Ⓐ Ⓑ Ⓒ Ⓓ
32. Ⓐ Ⓑ Ⓒ Ⓓ
33. Ⓐ Ⓑ Ⓒ Ⓓ
34. Ⓐ Ⓑ Ⓒ Ⓓ
35. Ⓐ Ⓑ Ⓒ Ⓓ
36. Ⓐ Ⓑ Ⓒ Ⓓ
37. Ⓐ Ⓑ Ⓒ Ⓓ
38. Ⓐ Ⓑ Ⓒ Ⓓ
39. Ⓐ Ⓑ Ⓒ Ⓓ
40. Ⓐ Ⓑ Ⓒ Ⓓ

Section 3

1. Ⓐ Ⓑ Ⓒ Ⓓ
2. Ⓐ Ⓑ Ⓒ Ⓓ
3. Ⓐ Ⓑ Ⓒ Ⓓ
4. Ⓐ Ⓑ Ⓒ Ⓓ
5. Ⓐ Ⓑ Ⓒ Ⓓ
6. Ⓐ Ⓑ Ⓒ Ⓓ
7. Ⓐ Ⓑ Ⓒ Ⓓ
8. Ⓐ Ⓑ Ⓒ Ⓓ
9. Ⓐ Ⓑ Ⓒ Ⓓ
10. Ⓐ Ⓑ Ⓒ Ⓓ
11. Ⓐ Ⓑ Ⓒ Ⓓ
12. Ⓐ Ⓑ Ⓒ Ⓓ
13. Ⓐ Ⓑ Ⓒ Ⓓ
14. Ⓐ Ⓑ Ⓒ Ⓓ
15. Ⓐ Ⓑ Ⓒ Ⓓ
16. Ⓐ Ⓑ Ⓒ Ⓓ
17. Ⓐ Ⓑ Ⓒ Ⓓ
18. Ⓐ Ⓑ Ⓒ Ⓓ
19. Ⓐ Ⓑ Ⓒ Ⓓ
20. Ⓐ Ⓑ Ⓒ Ⓓ
21. Ⓐ Ⓑ Ⓒ Ⓓ
22. Ⓐ Ⓑ Ⓒ Ⓓ
23. Ⓐ Ⓑ Ⓒ Ⓓ
24. Ⓐ Ⓑ Ⓒ Ⓓ
25. Ⓐ Ⓑ Ⓒ Ⓓ
26. Ⓐ Ⓑ Ⓒ Ⓓ
27. Ⓐ Ⓑ Ⓒ Ⓓ
28. Ⓐ Ⓑ Ⓒ Ⓓ
29. Ⓐ Ⓑ Ⓒ Ⓓ
30. Ⓐ Ⓑ Ⓒ Ⓓ
31. Ⓐ Ⓑ Ⓒ Ⓓ
32. Ⓐ Ⓑ Ⓒ Ⓓ
33. Ⓐ Ⓑ Ⓒ Ⓓ
34. Ⓐ Ⓑ Ⓒ Ⓓ
35. Ⓐ Ⓑ Ⓒ Ⓓ
36. Ⓐ Ⓑ Ⓒ Ⓓ
37. Ⓐ Ⓑ Ⓒ Ⓓ
38. Ⓐ Ⓑ Ⓒ Ⓓ
39. Ⓐ Ⓑ Ⓒ Ⓓ
40. Ⓐ Ⓑ Ⓒ Ⓓ
41. Ⓐ Ⓑ Ⓒ Ⓓ
42. Ⓐ Ⓑ Ⓒ Ⓓ
43. Ⓐ Ⓑ Ⓒ Ⓓ
44. Ⓐ Ⓑ Ⓒ Ⓓ
45. Ⓐ Ⓑ Ⓒ Ⓓ
46. Ⓐ Ⓑ Ⓒ Ⓓ
47. Ⓐ Ⓑ Ⓒ Ⓓ
48. Ⓐ Ⓑ Ⓒ Ⓓ
49. Ⓐ Ⓑ Ⓒ Ⓓ
50. Ⓐ Ⓑ Ⓒ Ⓓ

$$1 \quad 1 \quad 1 \quad 1 \quad 1 \quad 1 \quad 1 \quad 1 \quad 1 \quad 1 \quad 1$$

Model Test 7
Short Form

Section 1:
Listening Comprehension

50 QUESTIONS 40 MINUTES

In this section of the test, you will have an opportunity to demonstrate your ability to understand conversations and talks in English. There are three parts to this section with special directions for each part. Answer all the questions on the basis of what is stated or implied by the speakers in this test. When you take the actual TOEFL test, you will not be allowed to take notes or write in your test book. Try to work on this Model Test in the same way.

Part A

Directions: In Part A, you will hear short conversations between two people. After each conversation, you will hear a question about the conversation. The conversations and questions will not be repeated. After you hear a question, read the four possible answers in your book and choose the best answer. Then, on your answer sheet, find the number of the question and fill in the space that corresponds to the letter of the answer you have chosen.

1. (A) The weather.
   (B) A speech.
   (C) Their friend's child.
   (D) A trip.

2. (A) The man should leave the dorm.
   (B) The apartment would be noisy, too.
   (C) The man should not find an apartment.
   (D) The man is working too hard.

3. (A) He is a TV repairman.
   (B) He is a bell boy.
   (C) He is a tailor.
   (D) He is a security guard.

4. (A) He does not have a checking account.
   (B) His wife usually balances the check book.
   (C) He does not like to reconcile his account.
   (D) The secretary is not very helpful.

5. (A) The man and woman are eating lunch now.
   (B) The man will call the woman to arrange for lunch.
   (C) The man and woman have lunch at the same time.
   (D) The woman does not want to have lunch with the man.

6. (A) Send two transcripts to San Diego State.
   (B) Prepare two transcripts.
   (C) Give two transcripts to the woman, and send one to San Diego State.
   (D) Give the woman three transcripts.

7. (A) He wants lettuce, pickles, onions, mustard, mayonnaise, and catsup.
   (B) The sandwich should have only catsup on it.
   (C) Mustard and catsup are enough for him.
   (D) He is ordering french fries and a Coke as well.

GO ON TO THE NEXT PAGE

1 1 1 1 1 1 1 1 1 1 1

8. (A) At a lake.
   (B) At a telephone store.
   (C) At a lawn and garden supply.
   (D) At a garage.

9. (A) Leave a note for the professor.
   (B) Give a note to the professor.
   (C) Wait to speak with the professor.
   (D) Go to the professor's class.

10. (A) She is not ready to go.
    (B) She is cold.
    (C) She is always late.
    (D) She has a new coat.

11. (A) She will have two major fields of study.
    (B) She prefers teaching.
    (C) She does not talk with the woman very often.
    (D) She cannot make up her mind.

12. (A) His guests will enjoy it.
    (B) It is too large.
    (C) He will only eat half of it.
    (D) It weighs eight pounds.

13. (A) Cooking.
    (B) Laundry.
    (C) Shopping.
    (D) The time of day.

14. (A) The graduation list has an error on it.
    (B) The man had already graduated.
    (C) The man's name is the same as that of another student.
    (D) The graduation will not be until next spring.

15. (A) Talk with the woman.
    (B) Use the copy machine.
    (C) Leave.
    (D) Wait in line behind the woman.

16. (A) She did not apply yet.
    (B) She is still not sure.
    (C) She has decided to compete.
    (D) She already has a scholarship.

17. (A) It will be difficult.
    (B) He would rather be alone.
    (C) The woman is welcome.
    (D) There is a large group.

18. (A) He does not like the woman.
    (B) He does not usually study at the library.
    (C) He has received a letter.
    (D) He will not go to the library.

19. (A) Invite the man to lunch.
    (B) Talk with the man for twenty minutes.
    (C) Remind the man that they will have lunch.
    (D) Wait for the man.

20. (A) The office is usually crowded.
    (B) There aren't usually any people in the office.
    (C) Only a few people work in the office.
    (D) The office is closed today.

21. (A) Toronto.
    (B) Plane fares.
    (C) Little towns.
    (D) The woman's vacation.

22. (A) Call the Student Center.
    (B) Try again later.
    (C) Talk to her instead of Mrs. Best.
    (D) Come to her office for help.

23. (A) He wants to go to the grocery store.
    (B) He prefers to go out to eat.
    (C) He does not want very much to eat.
    (D) He is not interested in dinner.

24. (A) Neither the man nor the woman was in class on Friday.
    (B) The woman was at the airport while the man was in class.
    (C) The man was with his mother while the woman was in class.
    (D) The man and the woman were in New York together.

GO ON TO THE NEXT PAGE ➤

1   1   1   1   1   1   1   1   1   1   1

25. (A) Returning home is not very expensive.
    (B) There hasn't been any time to think about the trip.
    (C) The time has passed quickly.
    (D) He expected to be more enthusiastic.

26. (A) The plane did not take off on time.
    (B) The flight was cancelled.
    (C) She almost missed her flight.
    (D) The taxi never arrived.

27. (A) She always eats in the snack bar.
    (B) She used to eat in the snack bar.
    (C) She occasionally eats in the snack bar.
    (D) She has never eaten in the snack bar.

28. (A) The man should rest.
    (B) The man's health has improved.
    (C) The man worries too much.
    (D) The man is very ill.

29. (A) He does not have a television.
    (B) He likes to watch television with the woman.
    (C) He used to watch too much television.
    (D) He does not enjoy watching television.

30. (A) He does not have a topic for his project yet.
    (B) He needs more than thirty-five participants.
    (C) He is discouraged about the research.
    (D) He lost some data for his research project.

Part B

Directions: In this part of the test, you will hear longer conversations. After each conversation, you will hear several questions. The conversations and questions will not be repeated.

After you hear a question, read the four possible answers in your book and choose the best answer. Then, on your answer sheet, find the number of the question and fill in the space that corresponds to the letter of the answer you have chosen.

Remember, you are **not** allowed to take notes or write on your test pages.

31. (A) He was referred by another doctor.
    (B) He needs a routine check up for school.
    (C) He has a medical emergency.
    (D) He must have some tests done.

32. (A) The doctor will not be in the office on that date.
    (B) The man must have his blood tests a week before the appointment.
    (C) The application for the insurance plan is due on the first.
    (D) Mr. Franklin cannot be available on the first.

33. (A) May 29 at two o'clock.
    (B) May 30 at four-thirty.
    (C) June 1 at two o'clock.
    (D) June 3 at four-thirty.

34. (A) Get a physical.
    (B) Submit an application.
    (C) Have blood tests.
    (D) Enroll in an insurance plan.

35. (A) The student's final grade in a course.
    (B) The professor's error.
    (C) The student's midterm exam.
    (D) The professor's book.

GO ON TO THE NEXT PAGE ▶

1 1 1 1 1 1 1 1 1 1 1 **1**

36. (A) In a doctor's office.
    (B) In a college professor's office.
    (C) In Rick's office.
    (D) At a driver's license center.

37. (A) B–
    (B) C +
    (C) D
    (D) F

38. (A) He did not do well on the
        midterm exam.
    (B) He failed the final exam.
    (C) He was often absent.
    (D) The system was not fair.

Part C

Directions: In this part of the test, you will hear several short talks. After each talk, you will hear some questions. The talks and questions will not be repeated.

After you hear a question, read the four possible answers in your book and choose the best answer. Then, on your answer sheet, find the number of the question and fill in the space that corresponds to the letter of the answer you have chosen.

39. (A) The course requirements.
    (B) The syllabus for the course.
    (C) The textbook for the course.
    (D) The attendance policy.

40. (A) Read them before class.
    (B) Read them after the discussion.
    (C) Read them following the lecture.
    (D) Read them before the midterm.

41. (A) A midterm and a final exam.
    (B) A midterm and either a final exam or a
        project.
    (C) A midterm and a paper or a presenta-
        tion.
    (D) A midterm, a project, and a final exam.

42. (A) Call or send an e-mail to the professor.
    (B) Let the secretary know.
    (C) Do extra assignments.
    (D) Come in during office hours to make up
        the class.

43. (A) To compare earth with other planets.
    (B) To explain a theory of the formation of
        diamonds.
    (C) To introduce a group of astronomers
        from the University of Arizona.
    (D) To criticize Marvin Ross.

44. (A) Venus and Saturn.
    (B) Saturn and Uranus.
    (C) Uranus and Neptune.
    (D) Neptune and Venus.

45 (A) Ice clouds are present on both planets.
    (B) Scientists have seen them through tele-
        scopes.
    (C) Conditions are favorable.
    (D) The planets are very large.

46. (A) He is studying it at the University of
        Arizona.
    (B) He agrees with it.
    (C) He is interested in it.
    (D) He thinks it is a joke.

47. (A) The Constitution.
    (B) The electoral college.
    (C) Political parties.
    (D) The election of 1800.

GO ON TO THE NEXT PAGE

1 1 1 1 1 1 1 1 1 1 1

48. (A) To give an example of an election before the electoral college was formed.
    (B) To explain how candidates are nominated.
    (C) To illustrate why there is a separate vote for vice president.
    (D) To demonstrate how well the system works.

49. (A) Each political party nominates electors.
    (B) Congress chooses electors.
    (C) Candidates select their party's electors.
    (D) The people present names to the electoral college.

50. (A) The people vote directly for the candidates.
    (B) The electors vote for their party's candidate.
    (C) The registered voters choose the electors.
    (D) The Congress holds elections.

THIS IS THE END OF THE LISTENING COMPREHENSION SECTION OF TOEFL MODEL TEST 7.

DO NOT READ OR WORK ON ANY OTHER SECTION OF THE TEST.

2 2 2 2 2 2 2 2 2 2 2

Section 2:
Structure and Written Expression

40 QUESTIONS 25 MINUTES

This section is designed to measure your ability to recognize language that is appropriate for standard written English. There are two types of questions in this section, with special directions for each type.

Structure

Directions: Questions 1–15 are incomplete sentences. Beneath each sentence you will see four words or phrases, marked (A), (B), (C), and (D). Choose the **one** word or phrase that best completes the sentence. Then, on your answer sheet, find the number of the question and fill in the space that corresponds to the letter of the answer you have chosen. Fill in the space so that the letter inside the oval cannot be seen.

1. Often a team of engineers is ------ .

   (A) work on one project
   (B) on one project work
   (C) working on one project
   (D) to working on one project

2. ------ in the world export diamonds.

   (A) Only little nations
   (B) Only few nations
   (C) Only a little nations
   (D) Only a few nations

3. A vacuum will neither conduct heat nor ------ .

   (A) transmit sound waves
   (B) transmitting sound waves
   (C) sound waves are transmitted
   (D) the transmission of sound waves

4. To relieve pain caused by severe burns, prevent infection, and treat for shock, ------ .

   (A) taking immediate steps
   (B) to take immediate steps
   (C) taken steps immediately
   (D) take immediate steps

5. All the cereal grains ------ grow on the prairies and plains of the United States.

   (A) but rice
   (B) except the rice
   (C) but for rice
   (D) excepting rice

6. Besides rain, ------ is seldom pure.

   (A) water naturally
   (B) natural water
   (C) water of nature
   (D) the nature's water

7. Burrowing animals provide paths for water in soil, and so do the roots of plants ----- .

   (A) decaying and they dying
   (B) when they die and decay
   (C) they die and decay
   (D) when they will die and decay

8. ------ a busy city, Pompeii was virtually destroyed by the eruption of Mount Vesuvius in 79 A.D.

   (A) Once
   (B) It was once
   (C) Once it was
   (D) That once

GO ON TO THE NEXT PAGE

2 2 2 2 2 2 2 2 2 2

9. In his autobiography, *The Education of Henry Adams,* Adams attempted to show that his generation ------ .

   (A) did not know how to live in a technological society
   (B) did not know living in a technological society
   (C) was not knowing how live in a technological society
   (D) had not known living in a technological society

10. The FDA was set up in 1940 ------ that maintain standards for the sale of food and drugs.

    (A) to enforce the laws
    (B) to enforcing laws
    (C) enforcing laws
    (D) enforced the laws

11. Green and magenta are complementary colors located opposite each other on the color wheel, ------ .

    (A) and blue and yellow so
    (B) and too blue and yellow
    (C) and so blue and yellow do
    (D) and so are blue and yellow

12. Doublestars orbit ------ .

    (A) each to the other
    (B) each other
    (C) each other one
    (D) other each one

13. John F. Kennedy was the youngest president of the United States and ------ to be assassinated.

    (A) the fourth
    (B) fourth
    (C) four
    (D) the four

14. Oscillatona, one of the few plants that can move about, ------ a wavy, gliding motion.

    (A) having
    (B) has
    (C) being
    (D) with

15. ------ a teacher in New England, Webster wrote the *Dictionary of the American Language.*

    (A) It was while
    (B) When
    (C) When was
    (D) While

Written Expression

Directions: In questions 16–40, each sentence has four underlined words or phrases. The four underlined parts of the sentence are marked (A), (B), (C), and (D). Identify the **one** underlined word or phrase that must be changed in order for the sentence to be correct. Then, on your answer sheet, find the number of the question and fill in the space that corresponds to the letter of the answer you have chosen.

16. The bridge at Niagara Falls spans the longer unguarded border in the history of the world,
            (A)   (B)
    symbolizing the peace and goodwill that exist between Canada and the United States.
                                        (C)   (D)

17. Nitrogen must be combine with another element such as hydrogen or oxygen to be useful in
                (A)   (B)   (C)   (D)
    agriculture or industry.

GO ON TO THE NEXT PAGE

2   2   2   2   2   2   2   2   2   2   **2**

18. In ancient times and throughout the Middle Ages, many people believed that the earth is motionless.
                                                                    (A)   (B)   (C) (D)

19. Anyone reproducing copyrighted works without permission of the holders of the copyrights are
              (A)   (B)
    breaking the law.
        (C)   (D)

20. Supersonic transport such the Concorde will probably be widely accepted as soon as problems of
                         (A)   (B)   (C)
    noise and atmospheric pollution are resolved.
                                          (D)

21. It is generally believed that Thomas Jefferson was the one who had researched and wrote the
        (A)   (B)
    Declaration of Independence during the months prior to its signing in July 1776.
                                                                        (C)   (D)

22. Because not food is as nutritious for a baby as its mother's milk, many women are returning to the
                 (A)   (B)   (C)   (D)
    practice of breast feeding.

23. In the sixteenth century, François Vieta, a French mathematician, used the vowels a, e, i, o, u,
                  (A)   (B)
    to represent a unknown number.
        (C)   (D)

24. Increasing involvement in agriculture by large corporations has resulted in what is known as
                                                        (A)   (B)   (C)
    agribusiness—that is, agriculture with business techniques, including heavy capitalization,

    specialization of production, and to control all stages of the operation.
                                              (D)

25. Civil engineers had better planning to use steel supports in concrete structures built on unstable
        (A)   (B)   (C)   (D)
    geophysical sites.

26. Aristotle systematically set out the various forms of the syllogism that has remained an important
                  (A)   (B)   (C)   (D)
    reference for logic.

GO ON TO THE NEXT PAGE

2 2 2 2 2 2 2 2 2 2 **2**

27. If the oxygen supply in the atmosphere was not replenished by plants, it would soon be exhausted.
                        (A)   (B)   (C)   (D)

28. With his father's guidance, Mozart begun playing the clavier at the age of three and composing at
        (A)   (B)   (C)   (D)
    the age of five.

29. The practical and legal implications of euthanasia, the practice of causing the death of a person

    suffering from an incurable disease, are so controversial as it is illegal in most countries.
        (A)   (B) (C)   (D)

30. Programs such as Head Start were developed to prepare children from deprived situations to enter
                    (A)   (B)   (C)
    school without to experience unusual difficulties.
                    (D)

31. Since lightning was probably significant in the formation of life, understanding it might help us
                                                                                    (A)   (B)

    to understanding life itself.
        (C)   (D)

32. Starfishes and sea urchins, members of the echinoderms or spiny skinned animals, are particularly
                                                                                        (A)

    interested because of their unusual structures.
        (B)   (C)   (D)

33. Almost poetry is more enjoyable when it is read aloud.
        (A)   (B)   (C)   (D)

34. It is essential that cancer is diagnosed and treated as early as possible in order to assure a
                                (A)   (B)   (C)   (D)
    successful cure.

35. Vasco da Gama, accompanied by a large crew and a fleet of twenty ships, were trying
                                (A)   (B)
    to establish Portuguese domination in Africa and India during the sixteenth century.
        (C)   (D)

36. Gold, silver, and copper coins are often alloyed with harder metals to make them hard as enough
                                                            (A)   (B)   (C)   (D)
    to withstand wear.

GO ON TO THE NEXT PAGE

2 2 2 2 2 2 2 2 2 2 **2**

37. A vine climbs from one tree to another, continuing to grow and support itself even when the
                                                              (A)   (B)

    original supporting tree is not longer alive.
                 (C)   (D)

38. After Dr. Werner Arber discovered restriction enzymes, Drs. Daniel Nathan, Hamilton Smith, and
                           (A)

    him were awarded the Nobel prize for their research in that field.
    (B)   (C)   (D)

39. Although the Indians and the Eskimo had lived for centuries in Canada and the United States,
                                                                    (A)

    when the European settlers came in the seventeenth century, the newcomers began a systematic
                                      (B)

    effort to push them further into the wilderness and to take the land from their.
           (C)   (D)

40. Sometime ants keep smaller insects that give off honeydew, milking them regularly and even
    (A)   (B)   (C)

    building barns to shelter them.
                    (D)

THIS IS THE END OF THE STRUCTURE AND WRITTEN EXPRESSION
SECTION OF TOEFL MODEL TEST 7.

IF YOU FINISH BEFORE 25 MINUTES HAS ENDED, CHECK YOUR
WORK ON SECTION 2 ONLY.

DO NOT READ OR WORK ON ANY OTHER SECTION OF THE TEST.

STOP   STOP   STOP   STOP   STOP   STOP   STOP

3 3 3 3 3 3 3 3 3 3 3

Section 3:
Reading Comprehension

50 QUESTIONS 55 MINUTES

Directions: In this section you will read several passages. Each one is followed by a number of questions about it. For questions 1–50, you are to choose the **one** best answer, (A), (B), (C), or (D), to each question. Then, on your answer sheet, find the number of the question and fill in the space that corresponds to the letter of the answer you have chosen.

Answer all questions about the information in a passage on the basis of what is **stated** or **implied** in that passage.

Questions 1–10

Throughout history, the search for salt has played an important role in society. Where there was no salt near, it was brought from great distances. Thus, salt became one of the most important articles of early trade. Records show that in areas of scarcity, salt was traded ounce
Line for ounce for gold. Rome's major highway was called the *Via Salaria*, that is, the Salt Road.
(5) Along that road, Roman soldiers transported salt crystals from the salt flats at Ostia up the Tiber River. In return, they received a *salarium* or salary, which was literally money paid to soldiers to buy salt. The old saying "worth their salt," which means to be *valuable*, derives from the custom of payment during the Empire. The caravan trade of the Sahara was also primarily an exchange of goods for salt. Among ancient peoples there, to eat salt with another
(10) person was an act of friendship. Slaves were often purchased with salt. Salt was so important in the Middle Ages that governments retained salt trade as a monopoly, or levied taxes on its purchase. By then, people's social rank was demonstrated by where they sat at the table, above or below the salt.

Even today, in some remote regions of the world, salt is a luxury item. In fact, in a few iso-
(15) lated areas of Southeast Asia and Africa, cakes made of salt are still used for money.

1. What does the passage mainly discuss?

(A) The old saying "worth their salt"
(B) The Roman Empire
(C) Salt
(D) Ancient trade

2. The word "scarcity" in line 3 could best be replaced by

(A) influence
(B) deprivation
(C) demand
(D) progress

3. What was the rate of exchange for salt and gold in areas where salt was a scarce commodity?

(A) One to one
(B) One to two
(C) One to ten
(D) One to sixteen

GO ON TO THE NEXT PAGE

3 3 3 3 3 3 3 3 3 3 3

4. According to the passage, where were salt flats located?

   (A) Rome
   (B) Tiber
   (C) Ostia
   (D) Salaria

5. What does the Latin word *salarium* mean?

   (A) Salt
   (B) Salary
   (C) Soldiers
   (D) The Salt Road

6. If a man is "worth his salt," he is

   (A) a soldier
   (B) a thirsty person
   (C) a valuable employee
   (D) a highly paid worker

7. The word "retained" in line 11 could best be replaced by which of the following?

   (A) reserved
   (B) transferred
   (C) denied
   (D) designated

8. Who enjoyed a monopoly on the sale of salt?

   (A) Soldiers of the Roman Empire
   (B) Traders in the Sahara
   (C) Governments in the Middle Ages
   (D) People of high social rank

9. The word "then" in line 12 refers to

   (A) ancient times
   (B) the Roman Empire
   (C) the Middle Ages
   (D) early modern times

10. The word "remote" in line 14 is closest in meaning to

   (A) distant
   (B) prosperous
   (C) traditional
   (D) irresistible

Questions 11–20

Smallpox was the first widespread disease to be eliminated by human intervention. In May, 1966, the World Health Organization (WHO), an agency of the United Nations, was authorized to initiate a global campaign to eradicate smallpox. The goal was to eliminate the
Line disease in one decade. At the time, the disease posed a serious threat to people in more than
(5) thirty nations. Because similar projects for malaria and yellow fever had failed, few believed that smallpox could actually be eradicated, but eleven years after the initial organization of the campaign, no cases were reported in the field.

The strategy was not only to provide mass vaccinations but also to isolate patients with active smallpox in order to contain the spread of the disease and to break the chain of human
(10) transmission. Rewards for reporting smallpox assisted in motivating the public to aid health workers. One by one, each smallpox victim was sought out, removed from contact with others, and treated. At the same time, the entire village where the victim had lived was vaccinated.

By April of 1978, WHO officials announced that they had isolated the last known case of the disease, but health workers continued to search for new cases for two additional years to
(15) be completely sure. In May, 1980, a formal statement was made to the global community. Today smallpox is no longer a threat to humanity. Routine vaccinations have been stopped worldwide.

GO ON TO THE NEXT PAGE ▶

3 3 3 3 3 3 3 3 3 3 **3**

11. Which of the following is the best title for the passage?

    (A) The World Health Organization
    (B) The Eradication of Smallpox
    (C) Smallpox Vaccinations
    (D) Infectious Diseases .

12. The word "threat" in line 4 could best be replaced by

    (A) debate
    (B) humiliation
    (C) risk
    (D) bother

13. What was the goal of the campaign against smallpox?

    (A) To decrease the spread of smallpox worldwide
    (B) To eliminate smallpox worldwide in ten years
    (C) To provide mass vaccinations against smallpox worldwide
    (D) To initiate worldwide projects for smallpox, malaria, and yellow fever at the same time

14. According to the passage, what was the strategy used to eliminate the spread of smallpox?

    (A) Vaccinations of entire villages
    (B) Treatment of individual victims
    (C) Isolation of victims and mass vaccinations
    (D) Extensive reporting of outbreaks

15. The word "isolated" in line 13 is closest in meaning to

    (A) restored
    (B) separated
    (C) attended
    (D) located

16. How was the public motivated to help the health workers?

    (A) By educating them
    (B) By rewarding them for reporting cases
    (C) By isolating them from others
    (D) By giving them vaccinations

17. The word "they" in line 13 refers to
    (A) health workers
    (B) officials
    (C) victims
    (D) cases

18. Which statement does NOT refer to smallpox?

    (A) Previous projects had failed.
    (B) People are no longer vaccinated for it.
    (C) The World Health Organization mounted a worldwide campaign to eradicate the disease.
    (D) It was a serious threat.

19. It can be inferred that

    (A) no new cases of smallpox have been reported this year
    (B) malaria and yellow fever have been eliminated
    (C) smallpox victims no longer die when they contract the disease
    (D) smallpox is not transmitted from one person to another

20. When was the formal announcement made that smallpox had been eradicated?

    (A) 1966
    (B) 1976
    (C) 1978
    (D) 1980

GO ON TO THE NEXT PAGE

3 3 3 3 3 3 3 3 3 3 | 3

Questions 21–30

The nuclear family, consisting of a mother, father, and their children, may be more an American ideal than an American reality. Of course, the so-called traditional American family was always more varied than we had been led to believe, reflecting the very different *Line* racial, ethnic, class, and religious customs among different American groups, but today diver-
(5) sity is even more obvious.

The most recent government statistics reveal that only about one third of all current American families fit the traditional mold of two parents and their children, and another third consists of married couples who either have no children or have none still living at home. Of the final one third, about 20 percent of the total number of American households are single peo-
(10) ple, usually women over sixty-five years of age. A small percentage, about 3 percent of the total, consists of unmarried people who choose to live together; and the rest, about 7 percent, are single parents, with at least one child.

There are several reasons for the growing number of single-parent households. First, the number of births to unmarried women has increased dramatically. In addition, a substantial
(15) number of adults become single parents as a result of divorce. Finally, a small percentage of deaths result in single-parent families. Today, these varied family types are typical, and there-fore, normal.

In addition, close friends have become a more important part of family life than ever before. The vast majority of Americans claim that they have people in their lives whom they
(20) regard as family although they are not related. A view of family that only accepts the tradi-tional nuclear arrangement not only ignores the reality of modern American family life, but also undervalues the familial bonds created in alternative family arrangements. Apparently, many Americans are achieving supportive relationships in family forms other than the tradi-tional one.

21. With what topic is the passage mainly con-cerned?

(A) The traditional American family
(B) The nuclear family
(C) The current American family
(D) The ideal family

22. The author implies that

(A) there have always been a wide variety of family arrangements in the United States
(B) racial, ethnic, and religious groups have preserved the traditional family struc-ture
(C) the ideal American family is the best structure
(D) fewer married couples are having chil-dren

23. The word "current" in line 6 could best be replaced by which of the following?

(A) typical
(B) present
(C) perfect
(D) traditional

24. According to the passage, married couples whose children have grown or who have no children represent

(A) 33 ⅓ percent of households
(B) 20 percent of households
(C) 7 percent of households
(D) 3 percent of households

GO ON TO THE NEXT PAGE ➡

3 3 3 3 3 3 3 3 3 3 3

25. The word "none" in line 8 refers to

(A) parents
(B) children
(D) couples
(D) families

26. How many single people were identified in the survey?

(A) One third of the total surveyed
(B) One fourth of the total surveyed
(C) One fifth of the total surveyed
(D) Less than one tenth of the total surveyed

27. Who generally constitutes a one-person household?

(A) A single man in his twenties
(B) An elderly man
(C) A single woman in her late sixties
(D) A divorced woman

28. The phrase "the rest" in line 11 could best be replaced by

(A) those easily forgotten
(B) those remaining
(C) a small number
(D) a significant group

29. Where in the passage does the author refer to the value of close friends?

(A) Lines 6–8
(B) Lines 10–12
(C) Lines 15–17
(D) Lines 18–20

30. The word "undervalues" in line 22 is closest in meaning to

(A) does not appreciate
(B) does not know about
(C) does not include
(D) does not understand

Questions 31–40

Noise, commonly defined as unwanted sound, is another environmental pollutant. Particularly in congested urban areas, the noise produced as a byproduct of our advancing technology causes physical and psychological harm, and detracts from the quality of life for those who
Line are exposed to it.
(5)   Unlike the eye, the ear has no lid; therefore noise penetrates without protection. Loud noises instinctively signal danger to any organism with a hearing mechanism, including human beings. In response, heartbeat and respiration accelerate, blood vessels constrict, the skin pales, and muscles tense. In fact, there is a general increase in functioning brought about by the flow of adrenaline released in response to fear, and some of these responses persist even
(10) longer than the noise, occasionally as long as thirty minutes after the sound has ceased.
Because noise is unavoidable in a complex, industrial society, we are constantly responding in the same ways that we would respond to danger. Recently, researchers have concluded that noise and our response may be much more than an annoyance. It may be a serious threat to physical and psychological health and well-being, causing damage not only to the ear and
(15) brain but also to the heart and stomach. We have long known that hearing loss is America's number one nonfatal health problem, but now we are learning that some of us with heart disease and ulcers may be victims of noise as well. In addition, the psychic effect of noise is very important. Nervousness, irritability, tension, and anxiety increase, affecting the quality of rest during sleep, and the efficiency of activities during waking hours.

GO ON TO THE NEXT PAGE ➤

3   3   3   3   3   3   3   3   3   3   3

31. What is the author's main point?

    (A) Noise may pose a serious threat to our physical and psychological health.
    (B) Loud noises signal danger.
    (C) Hearing loss is America's number one nonfatal health problem.
    (D) The ear is not like the eye.

32. What is the author's definition of noise?

    (A) Unwanted sound
    (B) A byproduct of technology
    (C) Physical and psychological harm
    (D) Congestion

33. What was probably the topic of the paragraph that preceded this passage?

    (A) Environmental pollutants
    (B) Urban areas
    (C) Technology
    (D) Disease

34. The word "congested" in line 2 could best be replaced by

    (A) hazardous
    (B) polluted
    (C) crowded
    (D) rushed

35. It can be inferred from this passage that the eye

    (A) responds to fear
    (B) enjoys greater protection than the ear
    (C) increases functions
    (D) is damaged by noise

36. According to the passage, people respond to loud noises in the same way that they respond to

    (A) annoyance
    (B) danger
    (C) damage
    (D) disease

37. The word "accelerate" in line 7 is closest in meaning to

    (A) decline
    (B) interrupt
    (C) increase
    (D) cease

38. The word "it" in line 4 refers to

    (A) noise
    (B) harm
    (C) life
    (D) technology

39. According to the author, which of the following is true?

    (A) Noise is not a serious problem today.
    (B) Noise is America's number-one problem.
    (C) Noise is an unavoidable problem in an industrial society.
    (D) Noise is a complex problem.

40. The phrase "as well" in line 17 is closest in meaning to which of the following?

    (A) after all
    (B) also
    (C) instead
    (D) regardless

GO ON TO THE NEXT PAGE

3 **3** **3** **3** **3** **3** **3** **3** **3** **3**

Questions 41–50

Very few people in the modern world obtain their food supply by hunting and gathering in the natural environment surrounding their homes. This method of harvesting from nature's provision is the oldest known subsistence strategy, and has been practiced for at least the last
Line 2 million years. It was, indeed, the only way to obtain food until rudimentary farming and the
(5) domestication of animals was introduced about 10,000 years ago.

Because hunter-gatherers have fared poorly in comparison with their agricultural cousins, their numbers have dwindled, and they have been forced to live in marginal environments such as deserts, forests, or arctic wastelands. In higher latitudes, the shorter growing season has restricted the availability of plant life. Such conditions have caused a greater dependence
(10) on hunting and, along the coasts and waterways, on fishing. The abundance of vegetation in the lower latitudes of the tropics, on the other hand, has provided a greater opportunity for gathering a variety of plants. In short, the environmental differences have restricted the diet and have limited possibilities for the development of subsistence societies.

Contemporary hunter-gatherers may help us understand our prehistoric ancestors. We
(15) know from observation of modern hunter-gatherers in both Africa and Alaska that a society based on hunting and gathering must be very mobile. While the entire community camps in a central location, a smaller party harvests the food within a reasonable distance from the camp. When the food in the area is exhausted, the community moves on to exploit another site. We also notice a seasonal migration pattern evolving for most hunter-gatherers, along with a strict
(20) division of labor between the sexes. These patterns of behavior may be similar to those practiced by mankind during the Paleolithic Period.

41. With which of the following topics is the passage primarily concerned?

(A) The Paleolithic period
(B) Subsistence farming
(C) Hunter-gatherers
(D) Marginal environments

42. Which is the oldest subsistence strategy?

(A) Migrating
(B) Domesticating animals
(C) Farming
(D) Hunting and gathering

43. The word "rudimentary" in line 4 could best be replaced by

(A) crude
(B) inconsistent
(C) neglectful
(D) careless

44. When was hunting and gathering introduced?

(A) Ten million years ago
(B) Two million years ago
(C) Ten thousand years ago
(D) Two thousand years ago

45. The word "dwindled" in line 7 is closest in meaning to

(A) disagreed
(B) decreased
(C) disappeared
(D) died

46. The phrase "such conditions" in line 9 refers to

(A) greater dependence
(B) higher altitudes
(C) plant life
(D) shorter growing season

GO ON TO THE NEXT PAGE

3   3   3   3   3   3   3   3   3   3   3

47. What conditions exist in lower latitudes?

(A) Greater dependence on hunting
(B) More coasts and waterways for fishing
(C) A shorter growing season
(D) A large variety of plant life

48. How can we learn more about the hunter-gatherers of prehistoric times?

(A) By studying the remains of their camp sites
(B) By studying similar contemporary societies
(C) By studying the prehistoric environment
(D) By practicing hunting and gathering

49. The word "exploit" in line 18 is closest in meaning to

(A) use
(B) find
(C) take
(D) prepare

50. What are some characteristics of hunter-gatherers?

(A) They are mobile, tending to migrate seasonally.
(B) They share the same responsibilities equally between the sexes.
(C) They camp in a central location when they are tired.
(D) They have many social celebrations.

THIS IS THE END OF THE READING COMPREHENSION SECTION OF TOEFL MODEL TEST 7.

IF YOU FINISH BEFORE 55 MINUTES HAS ENDED, CHECK YOUR WORK ON SECTION 3 ONLY.

DO NOT READ OR WORK ON ANY OTHER SECTION OF THE TEST.

END OF TOEFL MODEL TEST 7.

To check your answers for Model Test 7, refer to the Answer Key on page 465. For an explanation of the answers, refer to the Explanatory Answers for Model Test 7 on page 522.

MODEL TEST 8—ANSWER SHEET

———— Section 1 ————

1 2 3 4 5 6 7 8 9 10 11 12 13 14 15 16 17 18 19 20 21 22 23 24 25 26 27 28 29 30
Ⓐ Ⓑ Ⓒ Ⓓ (for each)

31 32 33 34 35 36 37 38 39 40 41 42 43 44 45 46 47 48 49 50 51 52 53 54 55 56 57 58 59 60
Ⓐ Ⓑ Ⓒ Ⓓ (for each)

61 62 63 64 65 66 67 68 69 70 71 72 73 74 75 76 77 78 79 80
Ⓐ Ⓑ Ⓒ Ⓓ (for each)

———— Section 2 ————

1 2 3 4 5 6 7 8 9 10 11 12 13 14 15 16 17 18 19 20 21 22 23 24 25 26 27 28 29 30
Ⓐ Ⓑ Ⓒ Ⓓ (for each)

31 32 33 34 35 36 37 38 39 40 41 42 43 44 45 46 47 48 49 50 51 52 53 54 55 56 57 58 59 60
Ⓐ Ⓑ Ⓒ Ⓓ (for each)

———— Section 3 ————

1 2 3 4 5 6 7 8 9 10 11 12 13 14 15 16 17 18 19 20 21 22 23 24 25 26 27 28 29 30
Ⓐ Ⓑ Ⓒ Ⓓ (for each)

31 32 33 34 35 36 37 38 39 40 41 42 43 44 45 46 47 48 49 50 51 52 53 54 55 56 57 58 59 60
Ⓐ Ⓑ Ⓒ Ⓓ (for each)

61 62 63 64 65 66 67 68 69 70
Ⓐ Ⓑ Ⓒ Ⓓ (for each)

1 1 1 1 1 1 1 1 1 1 1 1

Model Test 8
Long Form

Section 1:
Listening Comprehension

80 QUESTIONS 50 MINUTES

In this section of the test, you will have an opportunity to demonstrate your ability to understand conversations and talks in English. There are three parts to this section with special directions for each part. Answer all the questions on the basis of what is stated or implied by the speakers in this test. When you take the actual TOEFL test, you will not be allowed to take notes or write in your test book. Try to work on this Model Test in the same way.

Part A

Directions: In Part A, you will hear short conversations between two people. After each conversation, you will hear a question about the conversation. The conversations and questions will not be repeated. After you hear a question, read the four possible answers in your book and choose the best answer. Then, on your answer sheet, find the number of the question and fill in the space that corresponds to the letter of the answer you have chosen.

1. (A) She is not his advisor.
   (B) She is not polite.
   (C) She does not have a course request form.
   (D) She will help the man.

2. (A) A TV.
   (B) A computer.
   (C) A room.
   (D) A door.

3. (A) He is lost.
   (B) He needs an apartment.
   (C) He will not move.
   (D) He doesn't know what he will do.

4. (A) It is better to send it.
   (B) The document is too long.
   (C) The fax machine is not working.
   (D) She does not want to do it.

5. (A) He is seven years old.
   (B) He is seventeen years old.
   (C) He is twenty-four years old.
   (D) He is thirty-one years old.

6. (A) 712-98-6504.
   (B) 721-98-6504.
   (C) 712-98-7504.
   (D) 721-98-7504.

7. (A) They are friends and classmates.
   (B) The man is a student in the woman's class.
   (C) They are colleagues at school.
   (D) The man is a teaching assistant for the woman.

8. (A) He should buy comfortable shoes.
   (B) He likes sports.
   (C) He does not get much exercise.
   (D) He is more active now than he used to be.

9. (A) Pay the extra two dollars.
   (B) Mark the suit rush.
   (C) Bring the suit back tomorrow.
   (D) Wait until four o'clock.

GO ON TO THE NEXT PAGE

1 1 1 1 1 1 1 1 1 1 1 1

10. (A) Get the man some glasses.
    (B) Sit together.
    (C) Move to the front of the room.
    (D) Have an argument.

11. (A) Be a teacher.
    (B) Study business.
    (C) Work part time.
    (D) Own a restaurant.

12. (A) She has one child.
    (B) She has three children.
    (C) She has four children.
    (D) She has five children.

13. (A) He liked Montreal in the winter.
    (B) He liked Montreal spring, summer, and
        fall.
    (C) He liked Montreal all year round.
    (D) He did not like Montreal.

14. (A) A concert.
    (B) A park.
    (C) A shopping center.
    (D) A college campus.

15. (A) Today is Saturday.
    (B) The store is closed on weekends.
    (C) Tomorrow is a holiday.
    (D) The store will be closed next Tuesday.

16. (A) He missed a test.
    (B) He lost his syllabus.
    (C) He didn't turn in his composition.
    (D) His teacher won't help him.

17. (A) Get a gift wrapped.
    (B) Pay for a purchase.
    (C) Get a haircut.
    (D) Go to the men's room.

18. (A) He will place a wager.
    (B) He will play.
    (C) He will watch.
    (D) He will go.

19. (A) Use will power.
    (B) Chew gum.
    (C) Wear a nicotine patch.
    (D) Join a support group.

20. (A) He wants the woman to stop criticizing
        him.
    (B) He agrees with the woman.
    (C) He needs the woman's help.
    (D) He is going to give the money back to
        the woman.

21. (A) Driving.
    (B) Taking a test.
    (C) Waiting for the woman.
    (D) Cleaning the room.

22. (A) She likes to watch TV.
    (B) She likes to go to school.
    (C) She likes to work.
    (D) She likes "Star Trek."

23. (A) The chicken is not good.
    (B) She will not prepare a sandwich for
        the man.
    (C) She is not hungry.
    (D) She agrees with the man.

24. (A) A friend's house.
    (B) A coffee shop.
    (C) A hotel.
    (D) A health club.

25. (A) The man is not qualified for the class.
    (B) She doesn't have time to talk to the
        man.
    (C) They can resolve the problem.
    (D) There is a lot to do.

26. (A) The tour is too long.
    (B) The bus is too small.
    (C) He does not like to travel.
    (D) He does not want to say.

GO ON TO THE NEXT PAGE ➤

1 1 1 1 1 1 1 1 1 1 1

27. (A) He is asking where to buy a ticket.
    (B) He is telling the woman to leave.
    (C) He is calling the woman a liar.
    (D) He is congratulating the woman.

28. (A) Check the menu.
    (B) Eat alone.
    (C) Leave the table.
    (D) Pay for his own meal.

29. (A) Her roommate got the assistantship.
    (B) She is not going to take a full load.
    (C) Teaching is more difficult than studying.
    (D) The man is correct.

30. (A) He lives in the dorm.
    (B) He will help the woman.
    (C) He has to work on Saturday.
    (D) He keeps his promises.

31. (A) It is not dark outside yet.
    (B) She is not a very good driver.
    (C) She cannot find her car.
    (D) She needs a ride home from class.

32. (A) She is ill.
    (B) She has not seen a doctor.
    (C) She is a pharmacist.
    (D) She does not know which medicine she needs.

33. (A) Help the man.
    (B) Say goodbye to the man.
    (C) Agree with the man.
    (D) Apologize to the man.

34. (A) She already has an ID card.
    (B) She does not need her picture taken.
    (C) She is ready to leave.
    (D) She does not know where to go.

35. (A) The man should invite his friends to dinner.
    (B) The man's friends should come to his house.
    (C) The man could take a plant to his friends.
    (D) The man likes candy.

36. (A) Go with the man.
    (B) Look on the other side of the hall.
    (C) Get a different room.
    (D) Return to the front desk.

37. (A) She had only a few hours sleep.
    (B) The bed was hard.
    (C) She slept very well.
    (D) Her dreams were good.

38. (A) She was not involved in the accident.
    (B) She was not hurt badly.
    (C) She had her seat belt on.
    (D) She died in a car accident.

39. (A) The basement was the first floor.
    (B) The second floor was the first floor.
    (C) The first floor was downstairs.
    (D) The ground floor was the first floor.

40. (A) He is too busy to answer the phone.
    (B) He will talk on the phone.
    (C) He must buy another phone.
    (D) He wants the phone gift wrapped.

41. (A) She is not going to go to work today.
    (B) She can talk by phone for a short time before work.
    (C) She will visit the man.
    (D) She does not want to see the man.

42. (A) The application was lost.
    (B) The process takes about three weeks.
    (C) The response is probably in the mail.
    (D) The man should be patient.

43. (A) Ask for another card.
    (B) Approve the purchase.
    (C) Put the numbers in the computer again.
    (D) Give the card back to the man.

44. (A) She doesn't know how to use a computer.
    (B) She found the man's books for him.
    (C) She works in a library.
    (D) She is writing a paper for a class.

GO ON TO THE NEXT PAGE

1 1 1 1 1 1 1 1 1 1 1

45. (A) He does not want to go to Georgia State.
    (B) He would have liked going to Georgia State.
    (C) He was frightened about changing schools.
    (D) He will not transfer until next year.

46. (A) She wants to use her passport for ID.
    (B) She does not have a driver's license.
    (C) She prefers to pay with a credit card.
    (D) She does not have any checks.

47. (A) They visit her in Montgomery.
    (B) They moved to Florida.
    (C) They live in the same town as the woman.
    (D) They have their homes in different cities.

48. (A) Many people have asked for a Spanish-English dictionary.
    (B) He does not know where to find the dictionary.
    (C) A Spanish-English dictionary is very expensive.
    (D) Some dictionaries include both Spanish and English entries.

49. (A) Playing tennis.
    (B) Managing stress.
    (C) Getting exercise.
    (D) Losing weight.

50. (A) Long Beach is the woman's destination.
    (B) The man is driving.
    (C) San Diego is less than one hundred miles away.
    (D) She has not arrived at Long Beach yet.

51. (A) The class was not interesting.
    (B) The notes were important.
    (C) The exam was difficult.
    (D) The book was helpful.

52. (A) He was polite to the committee.
    (B) The meeting went very well.
    (C) Additional members are needed for the committee.
    (D) The committee did not meet.

Part B

Directions: In this part of the test, you will hear longer conversations. After each conversation, you will hear several questions. The conversations and questions will not be repeated.

After you hear a question, read the four possible answers in your book and choose the best answer. Then, on your answer sheet, find the number of the question and fill in the space that corresponds to the letter of the answer you have chosen.

Remember, you are **not** allowed to take notes or write on your test pages.

53. (A) Because he failed a class.
    (B) Because he needs some advice.
    (C) Because he was caught plagiarizing.
    (D) Because he stole a book.

54. (A) He says he didn't understand.
    (B) He says someone else did it.
    (C) He says he is sorry.
    (D) He says he needs a tutor.

55. (A) By expelling him.
    (B) By giving him a failing grade in the course.
    (C) By warning him.
    (D) By sending him to the Learning Resources Center.

GO ON TO THE NEXT PAGE

1 1 1 1 1 1 1 1 1 1 1

56. (A) To come back to his office.
    (B) To get a tutor to help him.
    (C) To use his own ideas next time.
    (D) To go to another university.

57. (A) Whether to go to graduate school.
    (B) If she wants to transfer or not.
    (C) Which job to accept.
    (D) What to do about her grades.

58. (A) The prestige of a large school.
    (B) The friends she has made.
    (C) The attitude of the teachers.
    (D) The opportunities for employment.

59. (A) He is not interested.
    (B) He gives her advice.
    (C) He shares his plans.
    (D) He just listens without comment.

60. (A) Go to a large graduate institution.
    (B) Continue his friendship with the
        woman.
    (C) Finish his degree at another school.
    (D) Schedule job interviews.

61. (A) A friend of the man.
    (B) A telephone sales person.
    (C) A shopper.
    (D) A long distance telephone operator.

62. (A) MasterCard.
    (B) Visa.
    (C) American Express.
    (D) Diner's Club.

63. (A) Wilsen.
    (B) Welson.
    (C) Wilson.
    (D) Walsin.

64. (A) One brown and white shirt, size $16\frac{1}{2}$.
    (B) Two brown and white shirts, size 34.
    (C) One brown shirt and one white shirt,
        both size $16\frac{1}{2}$.
    (D) Two brown shirts and one white one, all
        size 34.

Part C

Directions: In this part of the test, you will hear several short talks. After each talk, you will hear some questions. The talks and questions will not be repeated.

After you hear a question, read the four possible answers in your book and choose the best answer. Then, on your answer sheet, find the number of the question and fill in the space that corresponds to the letter of the answer you have chosen.

65. (A) A law.
    (B) A pick-up service.
    (C) A fine.
    (D) A town.

66. (A) Steel and aluminum cans.
    (B) Newspapers and paper bags.
    (C) Plastic bags and magazines.
    (D) Jars and bottles.

67. (A) They should be rinsed and the lids and
        labels should be removed.
    (B) They should be crushed flat.
    (C) They should be wrapped in newspapers.
    (D) They should be put in paper or plastic
        bags.

GO ON TO THE NEXT PAGE

1 1 1 1 1 1 1 1 1 1 1

68. (A) $5.00.
    (B) $15.00.
    (C) $25.00.
    (D) $100.00.

69. (A) Anthropology.
    (B) The definition of culture.
    (C) Subcultures in America.
    (D) Informal conversation.

70. (A) Customs.
    (B) Ethnic groups.
    (C) Values.
    (D) Familiarity with the arts.

71. (A) It must be considered appropriate by
        small groups within society.
    (B) It must be acquired by visiting muse-
        ums, galleries, and theaters.
    (C) It must be commonly shared by a group.
    (D) It must be comprised of many diverse
        ethnic groups.

72. (A) A museum or a gallery.
    (B) An informal culture.
    (C) A smaller group within the entire
        society.
    (D) The behaviors, beliefs, attitudes and val-
        ues of the majority society.

73. (A) Women's health issues.
    (B) The World Health Organization.
    (C) Children with H.I.V.
    (D) AIDS.

74. (A) Homosexual men.
    (B) Heterosexual men.
    (C) Homosexual women.
    (D) Heterosexual women.

75. (A) 19 percent.
    (B) 33 percent.
    (C) 66 percent.
    (D) 90 percent.

76. (A) Children.
    (B) Teens.
    (C) Women and young children.
    (D) Men.

77. (A) Educational programs.
    (B) Summer programs.
    (C) Elderhostel programs.
    (D) College programs.

78. (A) The courses are offered for credit.
    (B) There are final exams.
    (C) Anyone may participate.
    (D) College faculty teach the classes.

79. (A) In dormitories.
    (B) In hotels near campus.
    (C) In homes near campus.
    (D) In tents at campsites.

80. (A) Write the national office.
    (B) Call your local college.
    (C) Listen to the radio station.
    (D) Attend an Elderhostel meeting.

**THIS IS THE END OF THE LISTENING COMPREHENSION SECTION
OF TOEFL MODEL TEST 8.**

DO NOT READ OR WORK ON ANY OTHER SECTION OF THE TEST.

  STOP STOP STOP **STOP** STOP STOP STOP

2 2 2 2 2 2 2 2 2 2 2

Section 2:
Structure and Written Expression

60 QUESTIONS 35 MINUTES

This section is designed to measure your ability to recognize language that is appropriate for standard written English. There are two types of questions in this section, with special directions for each type.

Structure

Directions: Questions 1–30 are incomplete sentences. Beneath each sentence you will see four words or phrases, marked (A), (B), (C), and (D). Choose the **one** word or phrase that best completes the sentence. Then, on your answer sheet, find the number of the question and fill in the space that corresponds to the letter of the answer you have chosen. Fill in the space so that the letter inside the oval cannot be seen.

1. The consistency of protoplasm and that of glue ------- .

   (A) they are alike
   (B) are similar to
   (C) are similar
   (D) the same

2. The lights and appliances in most homes use alternating current ------- .

   (A) instead direct current
   (B) instead of direct current
   (C) that instead direct current
   (D) for direct current instead

3. When Franklin Roosevelt decided to run for a fourth term, the opposition said that he was ------- .

   (A) so old
   (B) too old
   (C) oldest
   (D) very older

4. The decomposition of microscopic animals at the bottom of the sea results in an accumulation of ------- in porous rocks.

   (A) the oil
   (B) oil
   (C) an oil
   (D) oils

5. The U.S. postal service policy for check approval includes a requirement that two pieces of identification ------- .

   (A) must present
   (B) presented
   (C) be presented
   (D) for presentation

6. Nerve impulses ------- to the brain at a speed of about one hundred yards per second.

   (A) sending sensations
   (B) to send sensations
   (C) send sensations
   (D) sensations

7. Although exact statistics vary because of political changes, ------- separate nation states are included in the official lists at any one time.

   (A) more than two hundred
   (B) as much as two hundred
   (C) many as two hundred
   (D) most that two hundred

GO ON TO THE NEXT PAGE

2 **2** **2** **2** **2** **2** **2** **2** **2** **2** **2**

8. ------- owe much of their success as a group to their unusual powers of migration.

(A) That birds
(B) A bird
(C) The bird
(D) Birds

9. Research in the work place reveals that people work for many reasons ------- .

(A) money beside
(B) money besides
(C) beside money
(D) besides money

10. Seals can ------- because they have a thick layer of blubber under their fur.

(A) keep them warm
(B) keep themselves warm
(C) they keep warm
(D) keep their warm

11. Both liquids and gases flow freely from a container because they have ------- .

(A) not definite shape
(B) none definite shape
(C) nothing definite shape
(D) no definite shape

12. One of Shaw's -------, *Pygmalion*, was the story that formed the basis for the musical play *My Fair Lady*.

(A) greatest work
(B) greatest works
(C) the greatest work
(D) the greatest works

13. Although the scientific community had hoped that the field of transplantation -------- , the shortage of organ donors has curtailed research.

(A) progress
(B) had progressed
(C) would progress
(D) progressing

14. The seed heads of teasel plants raise the nap on coarse tweed cloth ------- than do the machine tools invented to replace them.

(A) more efficiently
(B) efficiently
(C) more efficient
(D) most efficient

15. ------- unknown quantities is the task of algebra.

(A) To found
(B) Find
(C) The find
(D) Finding

16. The yearly path of the sun around the heavens ------- .

(A) is known as the ecliptic
(B) known as the ecliptic
(C) it is known to be ecliptic
(D) knowing as the ecliptic

17. A dolphin ------- a porpoise in that it has a longer nose.

(A) different
(B) differs
(C) different than
(D) differs from

18. ------- like MacDonalds and Kentucky Fried Chicken have used franchising to extend their sales internationally.

(A) Chain's restaurants
(B) Chains restaurants
(C) Chain restaurant
(D) Chain restaurants

19. Uranus is just ------- to be seen on a clear night with the naked eye.

(A) bright enough
(B) enough brightly
(C) as enough bright
(D) bright as enough

GO ON TO THE NEXT PAGE ▶

2 2 2 2 2 2 2 2 2 2 2

20. Before Alexander Fleming discovered penicillin, many people died ------- .

(A) infected with simple bacteria
(B) from simple bacterial infections
(C) infections were simple bacteria
(D) infecting of simple bacteria

21. That most natural time units are not simple multiples of each other ------- in constructing a calendar.

(A) it is a primary problem
(B) is a primary problem
(C) a primary problem is
(D) a primary problem

22. An abstract painter and a pioneer of Surrealism, ------- and symbolic images.

(A) Miró's works are characterized by bright colors
(B) the works of Miró are characterized by bright colors
(C) Miró is famous for works characterized by bright colors
(D) bright colors characterize the works of Miró

23. ------- the plow is being displaced by new techniques that protect the land and promise more abundant crops.

(A) As a whole
(B) Wholly
(C) On a whole
(D) The whole

24. In excess of 80 percent of the UN's budget is used ------- the economic development of member nations.

(A) support
(B) supporting
(C) the support
(D) to support

25. The bacteria in milk is destroyed when ------- to at least 62°C.

(A) it be heated
(B) it heated
(C) it is heated
(D) it will be heated

26. In order for people who spoke different languages to engage in trade ------- , they often developed a simplified language called *pidgin*.

(A) with each the other
(B) with each to the other
(C) with each another
(D) with each other

27. The two main ------- are permanent magnets and electromagnets.

(A) kinds of magnets
(B) kind of magnets
(C) kind magnets
(D) kinds magnets

28. The Supreme Court does not hear a case unless ------- , except those involving foreign ambassadors.

(A) a trial
(B) already tried
(C) it already trying
(D) it has already been tried

29. According to a recent survey, ------- doctors do not have a personal physician.

(A) a large amount of
(B) large amount of
(C) a large number of
(D) large number of

30. There are many beautifully preserved historic buildings ------- .

(A) in Beacon Street in Boston
(B) in Beacon Street at Boston
(C) on Beacon Street in Boston
(D) at Beacon Street on Boston

GO ON TO THE NEXT PAGE

2 2 2 2 2 2 2 2 2 2 2

Written Expression

Directions: In questions 31–60, each sentence has four underlined words or phrases. The four underlined parts of the sentence are marked (A), (B), (C), and (D). Identify the **one** underlined word or phrase that must be changed in order for the sentence to be correct. Then, on your answer sheet, find the number of the question and fill in the space that corresponds to the letter of the answer you have chosen.

31. The prime rate is the rate of interest that a bank will <u>charge</u> when <u>it</u> <u>borrows</u> money to <u>its</u> best
                                                              (A)   (B) (C)   (D)
    clients.

32. When a pregnant woman <u>smokes</u>, the <u>blood supply</u> to the uterus is <u>affected</u>, <u>reduction</u> oxygen to
                            (A)   (B)   (C)   (D)
    the fetus.

33. The area <u>where</u> a <u>microchip</u> is manufactured must <u>be</u> the <u>most cleanest</u> environment possible.
              (A)   (B)   (C)   (D)

34. Before his death <u>in 1943</u>, in an effort to encourage <u>less dependence</u> on one crop by the South,
                     (A)   (B)
    George Washington Carver <u>is</u> responsible for developing hundreds of industrial <u>uses</u> for peanuts
                             (C)   (D)
    and sweet potatoes.

35. <u>Sodium</u>, usually a metal, and chlorine, usually a gas, <u>they</u> react <u>to form</u> the solid sodium chloride,
    (A)   (B)   (C)
    or <u>table salt</u>.
       (D)

36. Mathematics <u>is</u> <u>such important</u> field and serves so many of the sciences that <u>it</u> is a prerequisite
                (A)   (B)   (C)
    <u>for studying</u> every scientific discipline.
    (D)

37. Studies of job satisfaction are unreliable because there <u>is</u> so <u>many</u> variables and <u>because</u> the
                                                            (A)   (B)   (C)
    admission of dissatisfaction <u>may be viewed</u> as a personal failure.
                                 (D)

38. Champlain <u>founded</u> a base at Port Royal <u>in 1605</u>, and <u>builds</u> a fort at <u>Quebec</u> three years later.
              (A)   (B)   (C)   (D)

GO ON TO THE NEXT PAGE ▶

39. A calorie is the quantity of heat required to rise one gallon of water one degree centigrade at one
   (A)   (B)   (C)   (D)
   atmospheric pressure.

40. Natural gas often occurs both together with petroleum in the minute pores of rocks such as
                    (A)   (B)   (C)   (D)
   sandstone and limestone.

41. There is no limit to the diversity to be finding in the cultures of people throughout the world.
           (A)   (B)   (C)   (D)

42. Sloths spend most of its time hanging upside down from trees and feeding on leaves and fruit.
               (A)   (B)   (C)   (D)

43. Although blood lets a residue in urine and stool samples, it cannot always be detected without the
               (A) (B)   (C)   (D)
   aid of a microscope.

44. The native people in the Americas were referred to as Indians because, according to the believe at
                                           (A)   (B)   (C)
   the time, Christopher Columbus had reached the East Indies.
                                    (D)

45. A barometer is a device with a sealed metal chamber designed to reading the changes in the
       (A)   (B)   (C)
   pressure of air in the atmosphere.
            (D)

46. Cotton fiber, like other vegetable fibers, are composed mostly of cellulose.
                 (A) (B)   (C)   (D)

47. Almost all life depends to chemical reactions with oxygen to produce energy.
       (A)   (B)   (C)   (D)

48. It may be argued that modern presidents have far great responsibilities than their predecessors did.
              (A)   (B)   (C)   (D)

49. The audible range of frequencies for human beings usually lays between 20 and 20,000 Hz.
                                    (A)   (B)   (C)   (D)

50. Many grasshoppers can produce sounds by rub their hind legs against their wings.
     (A)   (B)   (C)   (D)

GO ON TO THE NEXT PAGE

2   2   2   2   2   2   2   2   2   2   2

51. Henry Wadsworth Longfellow was not only a poet and an author but also presided the modern
                                                                    (A)   (B)
    language department at Harvard University for more than eighteen years.
                                              (C)   (D)

52. Some important characteristics of the Baroque style was a renewed interest in ornamentation and a
                                                        (A)   (B)
    powerful use of both light and shade.
             (C)   (D)

53. The understanding electricity depends on a knowledge of atoms and the subatomic particles of
        (A)   (B)
    which they are composed.
        (C)   (D)

54. If England had not imposed a tax on tea two hundred and twenty years ago, will the United States
    (A)   (B)   (C) (D)
    have remained part of the British Commonwealth?

55. Scientific fish farming, known as aquaculture, has existed for more than 4000 years, but scientists
                            (A)   (B)
    who make research in this field are only recently providing the kind of information that growers
        (C)
    need to increase production.
            (D)

56. The concept of lift in aerodynamics refers to the relationship among the increased speed of air
                                        (A)   (B)   (C)
    over the top of a wing and the higher pressure of the slower air underneath.
                                                        (D)

57. The Greek historian Herodotus reported that one hundred thousand men are employed for twenty
                                                                         (A)   (B)
    years to build the Great Pyramid at Gizeh.
         (C)   (D)

58. New synthetic materials have improved the construction of artificial body parts by provide both
                          (A)   (B)   (C)   (D)
    the power and the range of action for a natural limb.

59. The Cabinet consists of secretaries of departments, who report to the president, give him advice,
               (A)   (B)
    and helping him make decisions.
        (C)   (D)

GO ON TO THE NEXT PAGE

3   3   3   3   3   3   3   3   3   3   3

60. Each of the Intelsat satellites <u>remain</u> in a <u>fixed</u> position from which they relay radio signals to
                                         (A)   (B)

   <u>more than</u> seventy <u>earth stations</u>.
      (C)   (D)

THIS IS THE END OF THE STRUCTURE AND WRITTEN EXPRESSION SECTION OF TOEFL MODEL TEST 8.

IF YOU FINISH BEFORE 35 MINUTES HAS ENDED, CHECK YOUR WORK ON SECTION 2 ONLY.

DO NOT READ OR WORK ON ANY OTHER SECTION OF THE TEST.

Section 3:
Reading Comprehension

70 QUESTIONS 65 MINUTES

Directions: In this section you will read several passages. Each one is followed by a number of questions about it. For questions 1–70, you are to choose the **one** best answer, (A), (B), (C), or (D), to each question. Then, on your answer sheet, find the number of the question and fill in the space that corresponds to the letter of the answer you have chosen.

Answer all questions about the information in a passage on the basis of what is **stated** or **implied** in that passage.

Questions 1–10

     The Richter scale is a numerical logarithmic scale developed and introduced by American seismologist Charles R. Richter in 1935. The purpose of the scale is to measure the amplitude of the largest trace recorded by a standard seismograph one hundred kilometers from the epi-
Line center of an earthquake. Tables have been formulated to demonstrate the magnitude of any
(5) earthquake from any seismograph. For example, for a one-unit increase in magnitude, there is an increase of times thirty in released energy. To put that another way, each number on the Richter scale represents an earthquake ten times as strong as one of the next lower magnitude. Specifically, an earthquake of magnitude 6 is ten times as strong as an earthquake of magnitude 5.
(10)   The Richter scale considers earthquakes of 6.75 as great and 7.0 to 7.75 as major. An earthquake that reads 4 to 5.5 would be expected to cause localized damage, and those of magnitude 2 may be felt. It is estimated that almost one million earthquakes occur each year, but most of them are so minor that they pass undetected. In fact, more than one thousand earthquakes of a magnitude of 2 or less occur every day.

1. What does this passage mainly discuss?

   (A) Earthquakes
   (B) The Richter scale
   (C) Charles F. Richter
   (D) Seismography

2. In what kind of textbook would this passage most likely be found?

   (A) History
   (B) Biography
   (C) Geology
   (D) Mathematics

3. According to information in the passage, what does the Richter scale record?

   (A) The distance from the epicenter
   (B) The amplitude of the largest trace
   (C) The degree of damage
   (D) The location of the epicenter

4. The word "standard" in line 3 could be replaced by

   (A) reliable
   (B) complex
   (C) conventional
   (D) abandoned

GO ON TO THE NEXT PAGE

3   3   3   3   3   3   3   3   3   3   3

5. What is the value of the tables?

(A) They allow us to interpret the magnitude of earthquakes.
(B) They help us to calculate our distance from earthquakes.
(C) They record all earthquakes.
(D) They release the energy of earthquakes.

6. The word "those" in line 11 refers to

(A) magnitudes
(B) damage
(C) earthquakes
(D) energy

7. According to the Richter scale, which of the following numbers would indicate that there had probably been damage to the immediate area only?

(A) 7.0
(B) 6.0
(C) 5.0
(D) 2.0

8. The word "undetected" in line 13 is closest in meaning to

(A) with no damage
(B) with no notice
(C) with no name
(D) with no problem

9. How does each number on the Richter scale compare?

(A) Each number is one hundred times as strong as the previous number.
(B) Each magnitude is ten times stronger than the previous magnitude.
(C) The strength of each magnitude is one less than the previous magnitude.
(D) The scale decreases by five or six for each number.

10. The author mentions all of the following in the explanation of the Richter scale EXCEPT

(A) it was introduced in 1935
(B) it was developed by an American seismologist
(C) it detects all earthquakes
(D) it measures the magnitude of earthquakes

Questions 11–20

Charles Ives, now acclaimed as the first great American composer of the twentieth century, had to wait many years for the recognition he deserved. The son of a bandmaster, Ives entered Yale at twenty to study composition with Horatio Parker, but after graduation, he did not
Line choose to pursue a career in music. He suspected correctly that the public would not accept the
(5)   music he wrote. Even the few conductors and performers he tried to interest in his compositions felt that they were unplayable. Instead, he became a successful insurance executive, building his company into the largest agency in the country in only two decades. Even during that busy time, he still dedicated himself to composing music in the evenings, on weekends, and during vacations. Although he occasionally hired musicians to play one of his works pri-
(10) vately for him, he usually heard his music only in his imagination.

After he recovered from a serious heart attack, he became reconciled to the fact that his ideas, especially the use of dissonance and special effects, were just too different for the

GO ON TO THE NEXT PAGE

3 3 3 3 3 3 3 3 3 3 3

musical mainstream. Determined to share his music with the few people who might appreciate it, he published his work privately and distributed it free.

(15)   In 1939, when Ives was sixty-five, American pianist John Kirkpatrick played *Concord
Sonata* in Town Hall. The reviews were laudatory. One reviewer proclaimed it "the greatest
music composed by an American." By 1947, Ives was famous. His *Second Symphony* was
presented to the public in a performance by the New York Philharmonic, fifty years after it
had been written. The same year, Ives received the Pulitzer prize. He was seventy-three.

11. What does the passage mainly discuss?

(A) Modern musical composition
(B) Charles Ives' life
(C) The Pulitzer prize
(D) Career choices

12. The word "suspected" in line 4 could best be
replaced by

(A) desired
(B) guessed
(C) worried
(D) recalled

13. Why didn't the public appreciate Ives'
music?

(A) It was not performed for a long
time.
(B) It was very different from the
music of the time.
(C) The performers did not play it
well.
(D) He did not write it down.

14. The word "they" in line 6 refers to

(A) conductors
(B) performers
(C) interest
(D) compositions

15. The phrase "became reconciled to" in line 11
is closest in meaning to

(A) accepted
(B) repeated
(C) disputed
(D) neglected

16. How did Ives make a living for most of his life?

(A) He conducted a band.
(B) He taught musical composition.
(C) He owned an insurance company.
(D) He published music.

17. How did Ives first share his music?

(A) By publishing free copies
(B) By playing it himself
(C) By hiring musicians to perform
(D) By teaching at Yale

18. Where was Ives' work first publicly performed?

(A) New York
(B) Europe
(C) Yale University
(D) Town Hall

19. How was the performance of *Concord
Sonata* received?

(A) There were no reviews.
(B) The musicians felt it was unplayable.
(C) The public would not accept it.
(D) It established Ives as an important com-
poser.

20. In what year did Ives receive the Pulitzer
prize?

(A) 1939
(B) 1947
(C) 1965
(D) 1973

GO ON TO THE NEXT PAGE

3   3   3   3   3   3   3   3   3   3   **3**

Questions 21–30

     Bats are not the dirty, bloodthirsty monsters that they are portrayed to be in vampire films. These animals groom themselves carefully like cats and only rarely carry rabies. Of the hundreds of species of bats, only three rely on blood meals. In fact, the majority eat fruit, insects,
Line spiders, or small animals. They consume an enormous number of pests, pollinate many vari-
(5) eties of plant life, and help reforest barren land by excreting millions of undigested seeds.

     Almost all bats use echolocation to navigate, especially at night. As they fly, they emit a series of high-pitched squeaks at the rate of about fifty per minute. As these signals bounce off objects in their path, an echo is detected by the bats' sensitive ears which informs them of the direction and distance of obstacles so that they can undertake corrective or evasive action. But
(10) bats are not blind as widely assumed. In fact, all species of bats can see, probably about as well as human beings.

     It is also a little-known fact that bats are highly social creatures. Thousands or even millions of individual bats may belong to a colony, hanging upside down in caves or in trees. Within their social systems, bats assume specialized roles. Some may guard the entrance to
(15) their caves, others may scout for food, and still others may warn the colony of approaching danger. A nursery colony may be part of a larger colony to provide mother bats with a safe, supportive environment in which to rear their young.

21. What is the author's opinion of bats?

  (A) They are dirty and they carry rabies.
  (B) They are like the monsters in vampire films.
  (C) They are clean, helpful members of the animal world.
  (D) They are not very important in the animal world.

22. According to the passage, how are bats like cats?

  (A) They both carry rabies.
  (B) Cats groom themselves, and so do bats.
  (C) Both cats and bats eat pests.
  (D) Bats use echolocation, and cats do, too.

23. What do most bats eat?

  (A) Blood meals
  (B) Fruit and insects
  (C) Leaves and trees
  (D) Large animals

24. The word "enormous" in line 4 could best be replaced by

  (A) very heavy
  (B) very regular
  (C) very large
  (D) very necessary

25. Which of the following are NOT characteristic of most bats?

  (A) They pollinate plants.
  (B) They have specialized roles in their colony.
  (C) They use echolocation.
  (D) They eat blood.

26. How do bats help reforest the land?

  (A) By eating pests
  (B) By hanging upside down in trees at night
  (C) By excreting seeds
  (D) By taking evasive action

27. The word "emit" in line 6 is closest in meaning to

  (A) send
  (B) continue
  (C) find
  (D) stop

GO ON TO THE NEXT PAGE

28. According to the passage, how do bats navigate?

   (A) By responding to the echoes of their signals bouncing off objects
   (B) By warning the colony of approaching danger with high squeaks
   (C) By beating their wings fifty times per minute
   (D) By using their sensitive ears to hear the noises in their environment

29. Where in the passage does the author refer to the visual range of bats?

   (A) Lines 4–5
   (B) Lines 6–7
   (C) Lines 7–9
   (D) Lines 10–11

30. The word "Some" in line 14 refers to

   (A) social systems
   (B) specialized roles
   (C) bats
   (D) colonies

Questions 31–40

     The fact that most Americans live in urban areas does not mean that they reside in the center of large cities. In fact, more Americans live in the suburbs of large metropolitan areas than in the cities themselves.
Line   The Bureau of Census regards any area with more than 2500 people as an urban area, and
(5) does not consider boundaries of cities and suburbs. According to the Bureau, the political boundaries are less significant than the social and economic relationships and the transportation and communication systems that integrate a locale. The term used by the Bureau for an integrated metropolis is an MSA, which stands for Metropolitan Statistical Area. In general, an MSA is any area that contains a city and its surrounding suburbs and has a total population
(10) of 50,000 or more.
     At the present time, the Bureau reports more than 280 MSAs, which together account for 75 percent of the U.S. population. In addition, the Bureau recognizes eighteen megapolises, that is, continuous adjacent metropolitan areas. One of the most obvious megapolises includes a chain of hundreds of cities and suburbs across ten states on the East Coast from Massachusetts to Vir-
(15) ginia, including Boston, New York, and Washington, D.C. In the Eastern Corridor, as it is called, a population of 45 million inhabitants is concentrated. Another megapolis that is growing rapidly is the California coast from San Francisco through Los Angeles to San Diego.

31. Which of the following would be the best title for the passage?

   (A) Metropolitan Statistical Areas
   (B) Types of Population Centers
   (C) The Bureau of Census
   (D) Megapolises

32. Where do most Americans live?

   (A) In the center of cities
   (B) In the suburbs surrounding large cities
   (C) In rural areas
   (D) In small towns

33. According to the Bureau of Census, what is an urban area?

   (A) An area with 2500 people or more
   (B) An area with at least 50,000 people
   (C) The eighteen largest cities
   (D) A chain of adjacent cities

GO ON TO THE NEXT PAGE ➡

3 3 3 3 3 3 3 3 3 3 3

34. Which of the following are NOT considered important in defining an urban area?

(A) Political boundaries
(B) Transportation networks
(C) Social relationships
(D) Economic systems

35. The word "integrate" in line 7 is closest in meaning to

(A) benefit
(B) define
(C) unite
(D) restrict

36. According to the Bureau of Census, what is an MSA?

(A) The center of a city with a population of 50,000 people to the boundaries of the surrounding suburbs
(B) A city and its suburbs with a total population of at least 50,000 people
(C) The surrounding suburbs of a city with a total population of 50,000 people
(D) Any area with a total population of 50,000 people

37. How many MSAs are there in the United States?

(A) 10
(B) 18
(C) 280
(D) 2500

38. Where in the passage does the author suggest that three-quarters of the U.S. population now resides in MSAs?

(A) Lines 4–5
(B) Lines 8–10
(C) Lines 11–12
(D) Lines 15–16

39. A megapolis is

(A) one of the ten largest cities in the United States
(B) one of the eighteen largest cities in the United States
(C) one of the one hundred cities between Boston and Washington
(D) any number of continuous adjacent cities and suburbs

40. How many people live in the Eastern Corridor?

(A) 4 to 5 million
(B) 10 million
(C) 45 million
(D) 75 million

Questions 41–50

Rainforests circle the globe for twenty degrees of latitude on both sides of the equator. In that relatively narrow band of the planet, more than half of all the species of plants and animals in the world make their home. Several hundred different varieties of trees may grow in a
Line single acre, and just one of those trees may be the habitat for more than ten thousand kinds of
(5) spiders, ants, and other insects. More species of amphibians, birds, insects, mammals, and reptiles live in rainforests than anywhere else on earth.

Unfortunately, half of the world's rainforests have already been destroyed, and at the current rate, another 25 percent will be lost by the year 2000. Scientists estimate that as many as

GO ON TO THE NEXT PAGE

fifty million acres are destroyed annually. In other words, every sixty seconds, one hundred
(10) acres of rainforest is being cleared. By the time you finish reading this passage, two hundred
acres will have been destroyed! When this happens, constant rains erode the former forest
floor, the thin layer of soil no longer supports plant life, and the ecology of the region is
altered forever. Thousands of species of plants and animals are condemned to extinction and,
since we aren't able to predict the ramifications of this loss to a delicate global ecology, we
(15) don't know what we may be doing to the future of the human species as well.

41. What is the point of view that the author expresses in this passage?

(A) The author believes that the rainforest
will survive.
(B) The author believes that preserving the
rainforest is important to the global
ecology.
(C) The author believes that he can predict
the future of global ecology.
(D) The author believes that the extinction of
species is a natural process.

42. The word "relatively" in line 2 could best be
replaced by

(A) temporarily
(B) typically
(C) comparatively
(D) extremely

43. According to the passage, more than half of
all the species of plants and animals

(A) live in twenty rainforests
(B) live in several hundred different varieties
of trees
(C) live in a forty-degree band of latitude
(D) live in areas where the rainforest has
been cleared

44. What is the meaning of the word "just" in
line 4?

(A) fairly
(B) only
(C) correctly
(D) precisely

45. How many of the world's rainforests are
projected to be destroyed by the year 2000
if the current rate continues?

(A) All of them will be gone.
(B) Three-quarters of them will be gone.
(C) Half of them will be gone.
(D) One-quarter of them will be gone.

46. What is the current rate of destruction?

(A) One acre per minute
(B) One acre per second
(C) One hundred acres per minute
(D) Two hundred acres per hour

47. The word "this" in line 11 refers to

(A) the destruction of the acres
(B) the reading of the passage
(C) the erosion of the forest floor
(D) the constant rains

48. The word "constant" in line 11 could best be
replaced by which of the following?

(A) useless
(B) natural
(C) dirty
(D) continual

49. The word "altered" in line 13 is closest in
meaning to

(A) changed
(B) terminated
(C) harmed
(D) invaded

GO ON TO THE NEXT PAGE

50. What will NOT happen if the rainforest continues to be cleared?

(A) The land will be eroded by the rains.
(B) Many species of plants and animals that depend on the rainforest will become extinct.
(C) The future of the human species may be changed.
(D) The rainforest will grow, but at a much slower rate.

Questions 51–60

Human memory, formerly believed to be rather inefficient, is really more sophisticated than that of a computer. Researchers approaching the problem from a variety of points of view have all concluded that there is a great deal more stored in our minds than has been generally sup-
Line posed. Dr. Wilder Penfield, a Canadian neurosurgeon, proved that by stimulating their brains
(5) electrically, he could elicit the total recall of specific events in his subjects' lives. Even dreams and other minor events supposedly forgotten for many years suddenly emerged in detail.

The memory trace is the term for whatever is the internal representation of the specific information about the event stored in the memory. Assumed to have been made by structural changes in the brain, the memory trace is not subject to direct observation but is rather a theo-
(10) retical construct that we use to speculate about how information presented at a particular time can cause performance at a later time. Most theories include the strength of the memory trace as a variable in the degree of learning, retention, and retrieval possible for a memory. One theory is that the fantastic capacity for storage in the brain is the result of an almost unlimited combination of interconnections between brain cells, stimulated by patterns of activity. Re-
(15) peated references to the same information supports recall. Or, to say that another way, improved performance is the result of strengthening the chemical bonds in the memory.

51. With what topic is the passage mainly concerned?

(A) Wilder Penfield
(B) Neurosurgery
(C) Human memory
(D) Chemical reactions

52. The word "formerly" in line 1 could best be replaced by

(A) in the past
(B) from time to time
(C) in general
(D) by chance

53. Compared with a computer, human memory is

(A) more complex
(B) more limited
(C) less dependable
(D) less durable

54. The word "that" in line 2 refers to

(A) the computer
(B) the efficiency
(C) the sophistication
(D) the memory

GO ON TO THE NEXT PAGE

3 3 3 3 3 3 3 3 3 3 3

55. According to the passage, researchers have concluded that

(A) the mind has a much greater capacity for memory than was previously believed
(B) the physical basis for memory is clear
(C) different points of view are valuable
(D) human memory is inefficient

56. How did Penfield stimulate dreams and other minor events from the past?

(A) By surgery
(B) By electric stimulation
(C) By repetition
(D) By chemical stimulation

57. The word "elicit" in line 5 is closest in meaning to

(A) prove
(B) prevent
(C) cause
(D) reject

58. According to the passage, the capacity for storage in the brain

(A) can be understood by examining the physiology
(B) is stimulated by patterns of activity
(C) has a limited combination of relationships
(D) is not influenced by repetition

59. The word "bonds" in line 16 means

(A) promises
(B) agreements
(C) connections
(D) responsibilities

60. All of the following are true of a memory trace EXCEPT that

(A) it is probably made by structural changes in the brain
(B) it is able to be observed
(C) it is a theoretical construct
(D) it is related to the degree of recall

Questions 61–70

   The Federal Reserve System is an independent agency of the United States government that helps oversee the national banking system. Since 1913 the Federal Reserve System, commonly called the Fed, has served as the central bank for the United States. It consists of twelve
Line District Reserve Banks and their branch offices, along with several committees and councils.
 (5) All national commercial banks are required by law to be members of the Fed, and all deposit-taking institutions are subject to regulations by the Fed regarding the amount of deposits that must be held in reserve and, therefore, are not available for loans. The most powerful body is the seven-member Board of Governors in Washington, appointed by the President and confirmed by the Senate.
(10)   The System's primary function is to control monetary policy by influencing the cost and availability of money and credit through the purchase and sale of government securities. If the Federal Reserve provides too little money, interest rates tend to be high, borrowing is expensive, business activity slows down, unemployment goes up, and there is a danger of recession. If there is too much money, interest rates decline, and borrowing can lead to excess demand,
(15) pushing up prices and fueling inflation.
   The Fed has several responsibilities in addition to controlling the money supply. In collaboration with the U.S. Department of the Treasury, the Fed puts new coins and paper currency into circulation by issuing them to banks. It also supervises the activities of member banks abroad, and regulates certain aspects of international finance.

GO ON TO THE NEXT PAGE

3 3 3 3 3 3 3 3 3 3 3

61. Which of the following would be the most appropriate title for this passage?

(A) Banking
(B) The Federal Reserve System
(C) The Board of Governors
(D) Monetary Policies

62. The word "oversee" in line 2 is closest in meaning to

(A) supervise
(B) maintain
(C) finance
(D) stimulate

63. The word "confirmed" in line 9 could best be replaced by

(A) modified
(B) considered
(C) examined
(D) approved

64. The principal responsibility of the Federal Reserve System is

(A) to borrow money
(B) to regulate monetary policies
(C) to print government securities
(D) to appoint the Board of Governors

65. The word "securities" in line 11 is intended to mean

(A) debts
(B) bonds
(C) protection
(D) confidence

66. What happens when the Federal Reserve provides too little money?

(A) Demand for loans increases.
(B) Unemployment slows down.
(C) Interest rates go up.
(D) Businesses expand.

67. According to the information in this passage, what causes inflation?

(A) High unemployment rates
(B) Too much money in the economy
(C) Very high fuel prices
(D) A limited supply of goods

68. The word "them" in line 18 refers to

(A) responsibilities
(B) the money supply
(C) coins and paper currency
(D) circulation

69. Where in the passage does the author mention the responsibilities of the Fed to banks overseas?

(A) Lines 1–3
(B) Lines 5–7
(C) Lines 10–11
(D) Lines 18–19

70. Which professor would probably give this lecture?

(A) Criminal Justice
(B) History
(C) Economics
(D) Political Science

GO ON TO THE NEXT PAGE

THIS IS THE END OF THE READING COMPREHENSION SECTION
OF TOEFL MODEL TEST 8.

IF YOU FINISH BEFORE 65 MINUTES HAS ENDED, CHECK YOUR
WORK ON SECTION 3 ONLY.

DO NOT READ OR WORK ON ANY OTHER SECTION OF THE TEST.

STOP   STOP   STOP   STOP   STOP   STOP   STOP

END OF TOEFL MODEL TEST 8.

To check your answers for Model Test 8, refer to the Answer Key on page 465. For an explanation of the answers, refer to the Explanatory Answers for Model Test 8 on page 530.

6

ANSWER KEYS FOR THE TOEFL REVIEW EXERCISES AND MODEL TESTS

ANSWER KEY—EXERCISES FOR STRUCTURE AND WRITTEN EXPRESSION

Patterns

Problems 1–15

Problem		Part A	Part B
Problem	1	(A)	(A) have
Problem	2	(C)	(A) to evolve
Problem	3	(D)	(B) smoking
Problem	4	(D)	(B) permitting
Problem	5	(C)	(A) saw
Problem	6	(D)	(B) fly
Problem	7	(A)	(C) must have originated
Problem	8	(C)	(A) reproducing
Problem	9	(A)	(B) must mate
Problem	10	(A)	(B) knew how
Problem	11	(B)	(C) used to moving
Problem	12	(A)	(B) advertise
Problem	13	(D)	(A) use
Problem	14	(D)	(D) changed
Problem	15	(B)	(A) don't park

Review Exercise: Problems 1–15

1 (A)
2 (A)
3 (B)
4 (C) to have
5 (C) recover
6 (B) used to roam
7 (B) to resemble
8 (C) have served
9 (D) must be producing
10 (A) ran

Problems 16–26

Problem		Part A	Part B
Problem	16	(A)	(C) turn
Problem	17	(A)	(D) appraised
Problem	18	(A)	(A) printed
Problem	19	(A)	(A) continue
Problem	20	(B)	(D) (to) nourish
Problem	21	(A)	(B) turns *or* will turn
Problem	22	(A)	(C) will have to pay *or* may have to pay
Problem	23	(D)	(D) would occur
Problem	24	(C)	(A) had
Problem	25	(A)	(B) would be
Problem	26	(A)	(C) unless they complete

Review Exercise: Problems 16–26

1 (D)
2 (B)
3 (C)
4 (C) pasteurize
5 (C) found
6 (B) follow
7 (D) delivered
8 (A) drive
9 (A) Unless there are complications
10 (A) were

Problems 27–41

Problem		Part A	Part B
Problem	27	(D)	(B) be used
Problem	28	(D)	(B) appear
Problem	29	(B)	(A) be
Problem	30	(B)	(B) for making *or* to make
Problem	31	(C)	(C) measured
Problem	32	(A)	(C) by high frequency radiation
Problem	33	(C)	(B) to be constructed
Problem	34	(D)	(D) repairing *or* to be repaired
Problem	35	(A)	(A) It is believed
Problem	36	(C)	(D) have buried
Problem	37	(C)	(A) preserved
Problem	38	(D)	(C) will have succeeded
Problem	39	(C)	(A) would be
Problem	40	(B)	(B) is losing
Problem	41	(B)	(D) should be discontinued

Review Exercise: Problems 27–41

1 (C)
2 (C)
3 (D)
4 (B) register
5 (D) is known as
6 (B) to maintain
7 (C) will have been
8 (A) to practice
9 (B) are born
10 (A) he would be able

Problems 42–140

Problem		Part A	Part B
Problem	42	(A)	(B) he
Problem	43	(B)	(A) she
Problem	44	(C)	(C) him
Problem	45	(A)	(D) for them
Problem	46	(D)	(C) his
Problem	47	(D)	(A) his hands and feet
Problem	48	(A)	(A) which
Problem	49	(B)	(A) who
Problem	50	(B)	(D) himself
Problem	51	(D)	(D) each other
Problem	52	(C)	(C) eight or ten computers
Problem	53	(C)	(A) Religion
Problem	54	(B)	(A) Space
Problem	55	(B)	(A) people
Problem	56	(C)	(A) Progress
Problem	57	(B)	(C) pieces of equipment
Problem	58	(B)	(A) kind of tool
Problem	59	(C)	(A) Spelling *or* To spell
Problem	60	(A)	(A) The writing of
Problem	61	(B)	(A) ~~it is~~
Problem	62	(A)	(C) an
Problem	63	(A)	(A) The philosophy
Problem	64	(C)	(A) Soil
Problem	65	(D)	(B) no
Problem	66	(C)	(A) causes
Problem	67	(C)	(D) little news
Problem	68	(A)	(A) Much
Problem	69	(C)	(B) a little
Problem	70	(A)	(A) Only a few early scientists
Problem	71	(C)	(A) The number
Problem	72	(C)	(A) Most of *or* Almost all of
Problem	73	(A)	(B) enough earnings
Problem	74	(C)	(B) secure enough
Problem	75	(D)	(D) another *or* the other
Problem	76	(C)	(B) the rest *or* the rest of them
Problem	77	(A)	(C) the first
Problem	78	(C)	(A) Sex education
Problem	79	(A)	(B) four-stage
Problem	80	(C)	(A) surprising
Problem	81	(A)	(B) so expensive
Problem	82	(A)	(A) such a brilliant scientist *or* so brilliant a scientist

Problem		Part A	Part B
Problem	83	(B)	(C) too
Problem	84	(A)	(D) very long
Problem	85	(B)	(B) good
Problem	86	(B)	(B) the same
Problem	87	(A)	(C) similar
Problem	88	(C)	(D) like
Problem	89	(C)	(C) the same temperature as
Problem	90	(B)	(D) as deep as
Problem	91	(B)	(D) different from
Problem	92	(A)	(B) differ from *or* are different from
Problem	93	(C)	(A) as much as
Problem	94	(A)	(A) more than
Problem	95	(C)	(C) as many as
Problem	96	(B)	(C) more efficient
Problem	97	(C)	(B) most
Problem	98	(C)	(B) worse
Problem	99	(B)	(A) efficiently
Problem	100	(C)	(A) the more intense
Problem	101	(A)	(B) like that of England
Problem	102	(B)	(D) than those of Eastern ladies
Problem	103	(D)	(D) among
Problem	104	(A)	(D) on
Problem	105	(A)	(B) in April
Problem	106	(B)	(B) besides
Problem	107	(A)	(D) but *or* except
Problem	108	(A)	(D) instead of
Problem	109	(B)	(D) such as
Problem	110	(A)	(A) In spite of *or* Despite
Problem	111	(C)	(C) because
Problem	112	(C)	(D) from eating
Problem	113	(C)	(D) for studying *or* to study
Problem	114	(C)	(C) taxing
Problem	115	(A)	(D) to 1852
Problem	116	(A)	(A) and
Problem	117	(A)	(C) as well as
Problem	118	(D)	(D) also easy to install
Problem	119	(B)	(C) but
Problem	120	(C)	(D) too
Problem	121	(B)	(D) should
Problem	122	(B)	(B) so that
Problem	123	(B)	(D) complete
Problem	124	(D)	(C) the plane is
Problem	125	(D)	(A) Whenever
Problem	126	(C)	(B) widely

Problem	Part A	Part B		Problem	Part A	Part B
Problem 127	**(D)**	**(B)** fast		Problem 134	**(D)**	**(A)** the fourth of July *or* July fourth
Problem 128	**(C)**	**(A)** Sometimes				
Problem 129	**(B)**	**(B)** does the same major league baseball team win		Problem 135	**(B)**	**(C)** as high as
				Problem 136	**(C)**	**(B)** as a whole
				Problem 137	**(B)**	**(B)** that
Problem 130	**(D)**	**(A)** Once		Problem 138	**(B)**	**(A)** which
Problem 131	**(A)**	**(A)** While		Problem 139	**(B)**	**(C)** use
Problem 132	**(D)**	**(B)** no longer		Problem 140	**(B)**	**(D)** use
Problem 133	**(C)**	**(A)** since 1930				

Style

Problems 1–30

Problem	Part A	Part B
Problem 1	**(C)**	**(C)** were
Problem 2	**(A)**	**(A)** was
Problem 3	**(C)**	**(B)** gave
Problem 4	**(A)**	**(B)** was
Problem -5	**(B)**	**(B)** enables
Problem 6	**(C)**	**(C)** makes
Problem 7	**(C)**	**(A)** is
Problem 8	**(B)**	**(A)** There are
Problem 9	**(B)**	**(C)** is
Problem 10	**(A)**	**(C)** needs
Problem 11	**(D)**	**(D)** its
Problem 12	**(B)**	**(C)** their
Problem 13	**(D)**	**(C)** one's *or* his
Problem 14	**(C)**	**(B)** its native habitat
Problem 15	**(B)**	**(A)** Having designed

Problem	Part A	Part B
Problem 16	**(D)**	**(C)** find
Problem 17	**(C)**	**(B)** to develop
Problem 18	**(B)**	**(D)** to use as currency
Problem 19	**(B)**	**(B)** rapidly
Problem 20	**(B)**	**(A)** an old one *or* an ancient one
Problem 21	**(C)**	**(A)** ~~its~~
Problem 22	**(B)**	**(A)** raised
Problem 23	**(C)**	**(A)** lies
Problem 24	**(B)**	**(B)** sits
Problem 25	**(A)**	**(D)** telling
Problem 26	**(C)**	**(C)** let
Problem 27	**(A)**	**(B)** lend
Problem 28	**(B)**	**(C)** do
Problem 29	**(A)**	**(B)** depends on
Problem 30	**(B)**	**(B)** differ

Cumulative Review Exercises for Structure and Written Expression

Cumulative Review Exercise for Verbs

1. In the entire history of the solar system, thirty billion planets may ~~has~~ *have* been lost or destroyed.

2. A victim of the influenza virus usually ~~with~~ *has* headache, fever, chills, and body ache.

3. Rubber is a good insulator of electricity, and so ~~does~~ *is* glass.

4. Light rays can make the desert ~~appears~~ *appear* to be a lake.

5. It is essential that nitrogen ~~is~~ *be* present in the soil for plants to grow.

✓ 6. A great many athletes have managed to overcome serious physical handicaps.

7. If the eucalyptus tree ~~was~~ *were* to become extinct, the koala bear would also die.

✓ 8. Various species must begin their development in similar ways, since the embryos of a fish and a cat appear to be very similar during the early stages of life.

9. Some teachers argue that students who *are* used to using a calculator may forget how to do mental calculations.

10. Last year Americans ~~spended~~ *spent* six times as much money for pet food as they did for baby food.

11. Secretaries are usually eligible for higher salaries when they know how *to take OR know* ~~shorthand~~ shorthand.

12. A new automobile needs to *be* tuned up after the first five thousand miles.

✓13. Financial planners usually recommend that an individual save two to six months' income for emergencies.

✓14. If a baby is held up so that the sole of the foot touches a flat surface, well-coordinated walking movements will be triggered.

15. Generally, the use of one building material in preference to another indicates that it *is* found in large quantities in the construction area and does an adequate job of protecting the inhabitants from the weather.

Cumulative Review Exercise for Pronouns

✓ 1. College students like to entertain themselves by playing Frisbee, a game of catch played with a plastic disk instead of a ball.

2. The final member of the Bach family, Dr. Otto Bach, died in 1893, taking with ~~he~~ *him* the musical genius that had entertained Germany for two centuries.

3. When recessive genes combine ~~with each the other one~~ *with each other OR with one another*, a child with blue eyes can be born to parents both of whom have brown eyes.

✓ 4. Almost all of the people who ultimately commit suicide have made a previous unsuccessful attempt to kill themselves or have threatened to do so.

5. Officials at a college or university must see a student's transcripts and financial guarantees prior to ~~them~~ *their* issuing him or her a form I-20.

6. Through elected officials, a representative democracy includes citizens like you and ~~I~~ *me* in the decision-making process.

7. It was ~~her~~ *she*, Anne Sullivan, who stayed with Helen Keller for fifty years, teaching and encouraging her student.

8. To appreciate what the hybrid corn breeder does, it is necessary to understand how corn reproduces ~~its~~. *itself*

9. Most foreign students realize that it is important for ~~they~~ *them* to buy health insurance while they are living in the United States, because hospital costs are very high.

✓10. Top management in a firm is usually interpreted to mean the president and the vice-presidents that report to him or her.

✓11. The barnacle produces glue and attaches itself to ship bottoms and other places.

✓12. Peers are people of the same general age and educational level with whom an individual associates.

13. When an acid and a base neutralize ~~one the other~~ *each other* OR *one another*, the hydrogen from the acid and the oxygen from the base join to form water.

14. About two thirds of the world is inhabited by people ~~which~~ *who* are severely undernourished.

15. In order for a caller to charge a call from another location to his home telephone number, the operator insists on ~~him~~ *his* using a credit card or waiting until someone at the home number can verify that charges will be paid.

Cumulative Review Exercise for Nouns

1. Tuition at state universities has risen by one hundred fifty-~~dollar~~ *dollars*.

2. Although polyester was very popular and is still used in making clothing, ~~cloths~~ *cloth* made of natural fibers is more fashionable today.

3. ~~The~~ peace in the world is the goal of the United Nations.

4. ~~Dam~~ *A dam* is a wall constructed across a valley to enclose an area in which water is stored.

5. ~~The~~ light travels in a straight line.

✓ 6. To hitchhike in the United States is very dangerous.

7. The ptarmigan, like a large number of Arctic ~~animal~~ *animals*, is white in winter and brown in summer.

8. Even children in elementary school are assigned ~~homeworks~~ *homework*.

9. Spirituals were influenced by ~~a~~ music from the African coast.

10. ~~The stare~~ *Staring* OR *To stare* at a computer screen for long periods of time can cause severe eyestrain.

11. There are two ~~kind~~ *kinds* of major joints in the body of a vertebrate, including the hinge joint and the ball and socket joint.

12. ~~That~~ an earthquake of magnitude eight on the Richter Scale occurs once every five or ten years.

13. *The art*
~~Art~~ of colonial America was very functional, consisting mainly of useful objects such as furniture and household utensils.

14. *produce*
To ~~producing~~ one ton of coal it may be necessary to strip as much as thirty tons of rock.

15. *piece of*
A mail that is postmarked on Monday before noon and sent express can be delivered the next day anywhere in the United States.

Cumulative Review Exercise for Adjectives and Adjective-Related Structures

1. Today's modern TV cameras require only a ~~few~~ *little* light as compared with earlier models.

✓ 2. Diamonds that are not good enough to be made into gems are used in industry for cutting and drilling.

3. Cane sugar contains ~~not~~ *no* vitamins.

4. Humorist Will Rogers was brought up on a cattle ranch in the Oklahoma Indian territory, but the life of a cowboy was not ~~excited~~ *exciting* enough for him.

✓ 5. One of the most distinctive features of Islamic architecture is the arch.

6. It is impossible to view Picasso's *Guernica* without feeling ~~badly~~ *bad* about the fate of the people portrayed.

✓ 7. The Erie was so large a canal that more than eighty locks and twenty aqueducts were required.

8. ~~An~~ *A* usual treatment for the flu is to drink plenty of liquids.

9. The United States did not issue any stamps until 1847 when one was printed for use east of the Mississippi and ~~one~~ another for use west of the Mississippi.

10. Red corpuscles are so numerous that a thimbleful of ~~human's~~ *human* blood would contain almost ten thousand million of them.

11. The Malay Archipelago is the world's largest group of islands, forming a ten-thousand-~~islands~~ *island* chain.

12. Some ~~property~~ *properties* of lead are its softness and its resistance.

13. Aristotle is considered the father of ~~the~~ logic.

14. Metals such as iron and magnesium are quite common, but are mostly found in silicates, making them ~~so~~ *too* expensive to extract.

15. *The history*
~~History~~ of the war in Vietnam is just being written.

Cumulative Review Exercise for Comparatives

1. One object will not be the same weight ~~than~~ *as* another object because the gravitational attraction differs from place to place on the earth's surface.

✓ 2. An identical twin is always the same sex as his or her twin because they develop from the same zygote.

3. As many *as* 100 billion stars are in the Milky Way.

4. Compared with numbers fifty years ago, there are twice ~~more~~ *as many* students in college today.

5. The ~~valuablest~~ *most valuable* information we currently have on the ocean floors is that which was obtained by oceanographic satellites such as Seasat.

6. The oxygen concentration in the lungs is higher than *that of* the blood.

7. Since the earth is spherical, the larger the area, the ~~worser~~ *worse* the distortion on a flat map.

✓ 8. The eyes of an octopus are remarkably similar to those of a human being.

9. The terms used in one textbook may be different *from those of* another text.

10. In 1980, residential utility bills were as high *as* sixteen hundred dollars a month in New England.

✓11. When the ratio of gear teeth is five : one, the small gear rotates five times as fast as the large gear.

12. Although lacking in calcium and vitamin A, grains have ~~most~~ *more* carbohydrates than any other food.

13. The more narrow the lens diameter, the ~~more great~~ *greater* the depth of field.

14. No fingerprint is exactly ~~alike~~ *like* another.

15. There is disagreement among industrialists as to whether the products of this decade are inferior to *those of* the past.

Cumulative Review Exercise for Prepositions

1. It is possible to find the weight of anything that floats ~~for~~ *by* weighing the water that it displaces.

2. Metals such *as* copper, silver, iron, and aluminum are good conductors of electricity.

3. The Mother Goose nursery rhymes have been traced back to a collection that appeared in England ~~on~~ *in* 1760.

✓ 4. In making a distinction between butterflies and moths, it is best to examine the antennae.

5. None of the states but ~~for~~ Hawaii is an island.

6. ~~Beside~~ *Besides* copper, which is the principal metal produced, gold, silver, lead, zinc, iron, and uranium are mined in Utah.

7. This year, ~~beside~~ *besides* figuring standard income tax, taxpayers might also have to compute alternative minimum tax.

8. Jet engines are used instead *of* piston engines for almost all but the smallest aircraft.

9. Trained athletes have slower heart rates because ~~of~~ their hearts can pump more blood with every beat.

10. Tools ~~as such~~ *such as* axes, hammerstones, sickles, and awls were made by Paleolithic man using a method called pressure flaking.

11. Despite ~~of~~ *or In spite of* some opposition, many city authorities still fluoridate water to prevent tooth decay.

12. The White House is ~~on~~ *at* 1700 Pennsylvania Avenue.
    The White House is on Pennsylvania Avenue.

✓13. Ice skating surfaces can be made of interlocking plastic squares instead of ice.

14. In supply side economics, a balanced budget results from ~~to reduce~~ *reducing* government spending.

✓15. All of the Native Americans but the Sioux were defeated by the European settlers.

Cumulative Review Exercise for Conjunctions

✓ 1. Foreign students who are making a decision about which school to attend may not know exactly where the choices are located.

2. In the future, classes taught by television will be equipped with boom microphones in the classrooms so *that* students can stop the action, ask their questions, and receive immediate answers.

✓ 3. The Colosseum received its name not for its size but for a colossally large statue of Nero near it.

4. A wind instrument is really just a pipe arranged so *that* air can be blown into it at one end.

5. It is very difficult to compute how much ~~does an item cost~~ *an item costs* in dollars when one is accustomed to calculating in another monetary system.

6. Adolescence, or the transitional period between childhood and adulthood, is not only a biological concept but *also* a social concept.

7. Light is diffused when it ~~will strike~~ *strikes* a rough surface.

✓ 8. The koala bear is not a bear at all, but a marsupial.

✓ 9. Ferns will grow wherever the soil is moist and the air is humid.

10. Although most rocks contain several minerals, limestone contains only one, and marble ~~is~~ *does* too.

11. Learners use both visual and auditory ~~as well that~~ *as well as* analytical means to understand a new language.

12. In a recent study, many high school students did not know where ~~were important geographical entities~~ *important geographical* on the map of the United States. *entities were*

13. It is not only lava but *also* poisonous gases also that cause destruction and death during the eruption of a volcano.

14. Until recently West Point did not admit women and neither *did* Annapolis.

✓15. The Federal Trade Commission may intervene whenever unfair business practices, particularly monopolies, are suspected.

Cumulative Review Exercise for Adverbs and Adverb-Related Structures

1. Not once ~~Lincoln has been~~ *has Lincoln been* painted smiling.

2. The first Skylab crew was launched on ~~twenty-fifth May~~ *may twenty-fifth OR the twenty-fifth of May*, 1973.

3. ~~Wholly~~ *As a whole*, artificial insemination has contributed to the quality of maintaining dairy herds.

4. Thor Heyerdahl worked ~~diligent~~ *diligently* to prove his theory of cultural diffusion.

✓ 5. The Navajos have lived in Arizona for almost one thousand years.

6. ~~That~~ once a serious problem, measles can now be prevented by a vaccine.

7. Because the British fleet arrived ~~lately~~ *late* off the Yorktown Peninsula, the French were able to control the seas, thereby aiding the United States during the Revolution.

8. When the chemicals inside a cell ~~not~~ *no* longer produce ions, the cell stops functioning.

9. The common goldfish may live as long *as* twenty-five years.

10. ~~When~~ *While* a mechanic working at odd jobs, Elisha Otis invented the elevator.

✓11. Sometimes students fail to score well on examinations because they are too nervous to concentrate.

✓12. Alligators are no longer on the endangered species list.

✓13. The standard for atomic weight has been provided by the carbon isotope C12 since 1961.

14. ~~That it was~~ once a busy mining settlement, Virginia City is now a small town with a population of one thousand people.

15. Not until the late Middle Ages ~~glass did become~~ *did glass become* a major construction material.

Cumulative Review Exercise for Sentences and Clauses

1. Since 1927, ~~that~~ the Academy Awards have been given for outstanding contributions to the film industry.

✓ 2. The Guggenheim Museum is cast in concrete with a smooth finish and curving walls that offer a unique backdrop for the art exhibited there.

✓ 3. Solar panels that convert sunlight into electricity are still not being exploited fully.

4. During a total eclipse of the Sun ~~that~~ the Earth *moves* ~~moving~~ into the shadow of the Moon.

5. Founded by John Smith, ~~that~~ Jamestown became the first successful English colony in America.

✓ 6. A chameleon is a tree lizard that can change colors in order to conceal itself in the vegetation.

7. Many of the names of cities in California ~~that~~ are adapted from the Spanish language because of the influence of early missionaries and settlers from Spain.

✓ 8. The oceans, which cover two-thirds of the Earth's surface, are the object of study for oceanographers.

9. Sports heros in the United States earn salaries that ~~they~~ are extraordinarily high in comparison with those of most other occupations.

10. The atoms of elements ~~that joining~~ *join* together to form compounds or molecules.

✓11. Rafts made from the trunks of trees may have been the earliest vehicles.

12. The idea of a set ~~which~~ is the most fundamental concept in mathematics.

✓13. Water that has had the minerals removed is called "soft" water.

14. Feelings of superiority based on pride in cultural achievements and characteristics ~~that calling~~ *is called* ethnocentrism.

✓15. Skeletal muscles are voluntary muscles which are controlled directly by the nervous system.

Cumulative Review Exercise for Point of View

1. Until she died at the age of forty, Marilyn Monroe ~~is~~ *was* the most glamorous star in Hollywood.

2. American colleges ~~do~~ *did* not have very many foreign students learning English full time before 1970.

✓ 3. Ted Kennedy told the American people that he could not run for president for personal reasons.

4. George Washington Carver was one of the first educators who ~~try~~ *tried* to establish schools of higher education for blacks.

5. Before the 1920s, no women ~~will have~~ *had* voted in national elections in the United States.

6. Styles that ~~have been~~ *were* popular in the 1940s have recently reappeared in high-fashion boutiques.

✓ 7. Since his murder, John Lennon has become a legend among those who had been his fans.

✓ 8. When Lyndon Johnson became president in 1963, he had already served in politics for thirty-two years.

9. Early TV programs like the "Arthur Godfrey Show" ~~are beginning~~ *began* as radio programs.

10. Dr. Howard Evans of Colorado State University reported that insects ~~solve~~ *would solve* the food shortage if we could adjust to eating them.

11. The year that James Smithson died, he ~~was leaving~~ *left* a half million dollars to the United States government to found the Smithsonian Institute.

✓12. Mary Decker said that she ran every day to train for the Olympics.

13. A liquid crystal is among the few unstable molecular arrangements that are on the borderline between solids and liquids and whose molecules ~~were~~ *are* easily changed from one to the other.

14. The chestnut tree used to be an important species in the Eastern forests of the United States until a blight ~~kills~~ *killed* a large number of trees.

15. The Cincinnati Reds ~~win~~ *won* the championship several years ago.

Cumulative Review Exercise for Agreement

1. Thirty-five thousand dollars ~~are~~ *is* the average income for a four-person family living in a medium-sized community in the United States.

2. Mary Ovington, along with a number of journalists and social workers, ~~were~~ *was* instrumental in establishing the Negro National Committee, now called the NAACP.

3. Fossils show that early people ~~was~~ *were* only four feet six inches tall on the average.

✓ 4. Each of the Medic Alert bracelets worn by millions of Americans who suffer from diabetes and drug allergic reactions is individually engraved with the wearer's name.

5. The Yon Ho, which is still in use today and is recognized as one of the world's great canals, ~~date~~ *dates* from the sixth century.

✓ 6. Since the Federal Deposit Insurance Corporation started guaranteeing bank accounts of $100,000 or less, there is no reason for small investors to fear losing their savings.

7. One hundred eighty-six thousand miles per second ~~are~~ *is* the speed of light.

8. It is believed that dodo birds forgot how to fly and eventually became extinct because there ~~was~~ *were* no natural enemies on the island of Mauritius, where they lived.

9. Several arid areas in Arizona ~~has~~ *have* been irrigated and reclaimed for cultivation.

10. The nucleus of a human cell except those of eggs and sperm ~~contain~~ *contains* forty-six thread-like structures called chromosomes.

✓11. In spite of its fragile appearance, a newborn infant is extremely sturdy.

protects

12. The ozone layer, eight to thirty miles above the earth, ~~protect~~ us from too many ultraviolet rays.

✓13. Although amendments have been added, not once has the American Constitution been changed.

travels

14. Michael Jackson, with members of his band, ~~travel~~ to key cities to give concerts and make public appearances.

✓15. Over 90 percent of the world's population now uses the metric system.

Cumulative Review Exercise for Introductory Verbal Modifiers

the royal family of Japan

1. Having ruled since the sixth century, ~~the present emperor of Japan~~ has a long and noble tradition.

✓ 2. Built on 230 acres, the palace of Versailles is one of the showplaces of France.

✓ 3. Believing that true emeralds could not be broken, Spanish soldiers in Pizarro's expedition to Peru tested the jewels they found by pounding them with hammers.

4. Adopted as the laws of the former British colonies after the Revolutionary War, Canada was

the Articles of Confederation invited Canada . . .

~~invited to become a member of the Confederation under the Articles of Confederation.~~

✓ 5. After surrendering in 1886 and being imprisoned in Florida and Alabama, the Apache chief Geronimo became a farmer and lived out his life on a military reservation in Oklahoma.

animals decrease their respiration

6. While hibernating, ~~the respiration of animals decreases.~~

Lavoisier introduced

7. To improve the study of chemical reactions, ~~the introduction of~~ effective quantitative methods ~~by Lavoisier.~~

✓ 8. Migrating in a wedge formation, a goose conserves energy by flying in the air currents created by the goose ahead of it.

✓ 9. Invented in China about 105 A.D., paper was manufactured in Baghdad and later in Spain four hundred years before the first English paper mill was founded.

the Mayan culture collapsed

10. After lasting for six centuries, ~~it has never been explained why the Mayan culture collapsed.~~

Lincoln died

11. Wounded by an assassin's bullet while he was watching a play at the Ford Theater, ~~death came to Lincoln~~ a few hours after being shot.

✓12. While viewing objects under a microscope, Robert Hooke discovered that all living things were made up of cells.

Alcatraz . . .

13. Located in San Francisco Bay and nicknamed the "Rock," ~~dangerous criminals were once incarcerated in Alcatraz.~~

✓14. Having calculated the length of time for the first voyages to the moon, Kepler wrote that passengers would have to be drugged.

✓15. To prepare the fields for planting and irrigation, farmers use laser beams.

Cumulative Review Exercise for Parallel Structure

1. We are indebted to the Arabs not only for reviving Greek works but also ~~they introduced~~ *for introducing* useful ideas from India.

2. A century ago in America, all postal rates were determined not by weighing the mail but *by* measuring the distance that the mail had to travel.

3. The four basic elements that make up all but 1 percent of terrestrial matter include carbon, hydrogen, nitrogen, and oxygen ~~is also~~.

4. The three thousand stars visible to the naked eye can be seen because they are either extremely bright or ~~they are~~ relatively close to the earth.

5. George Kaufman distinguished himself as a newspaperman, a dramatic critic, and ~~he was~~ a successful playwright.

6. To apply for a passport, fill out the application form, attach two recent photographs, and ~~taking~~ *take* it to your local post office or passport office.

7. Shakespeare was both a writer and ~~he acted~~ *an actor*.

8. To save on heating and ~~finding~~ *(to) find* cheaper labor are two of the most common reasons that companies give for moving from the Midwest to the South.

9. Both plants and animals have digestive systems, respiratory systems, and ~~reproduce~~ *reproductive systems*.

10. Pollution control involves identifying the sources of contamination, ~~development~~ *developing* improved or alternative technologies and sources of raw material, and persuading industries and citizens to adopt them either voluntarily or legally.

11. Tobacco was considered a sacred plant, and it was used to indicate friendship and ~~concluded~~ *(to) conclude* peace negotiations between Indians and whites.

12. The kidneys ~~both~~ eliminate *both* water and salt.

13. A person who purchases a gun for protection is six times more likely to kill a friend or relative than ~~killing~~ *to kill* an intruder.

✓14. The Brooklyn Bridge was remarkable not only for the early use of the pneumatic caisson but also for the introduction of steel wire.

15. Microwaves are used for cooking, for telecommunications, and ~~also~~ *for* medical diagnosis ~~is made from them~~.

Cumulative Review Exercise for Redundancy

1. Many dentists now say that plaque can cause damage ~~of a more serious nature and degree~~ to teeth than cavities.
   more serious

2. The most common name in the world ~~it~~ is Mohammad.

3. The idea for the Monroe Doctrine was originally ~~first~~ proposed not by Monroe but by the British Secretary for Foreign Affairs, George Canning.
   OR was first proposed

4. That comets' tails are caused by solar wind ~~it~~ is generally accepted.

5. One hundred thousand earthquakes are felt every year, one thousand of which cause severe ~~serious~~ damage.   *OR serious damage*

6. Irving Berlin, America's most prolific songwriter, ~~he~~ never learned to read or write music.

7. The corporation, which is by far the most influential form of business ownership, is a comparatively new ~~innovation~~.
   organization

8. That the earth and the moon formed simultaneously ~~at the same time~~ is a theory that accounts for the heat of the early atmosphere surrounding the earth.
   OR formed at the same time

9. The longest mountain range, the Mid-Atlantic Range, is ~~not~~ hardly visible because most of it lies under the ocean.

10. The Navajo language was used ~~in a successful manner~~ as a code by the United States in World War II.
    successfully

11. One of the magnificent Seven Wonders of the Ancient World was the enormous ~~large~~ statue known as the Colossus of Rhodes.
    OR the large statue

12. ~~It is~~ The first digit that appears on any zip code ~~that it~~ refers to one of ten geographical areas in the United States.

13. Limestone formations growing downward from the roofs of caves ~~that they~~ are stalactites.

14. All matter is composed of molecules or atoms that are in motion ~~in a constant way~~.
    constantly

15. ~~The fact~~ that the earth rotates wasn't known until ~~the years of~~ the 1850s.

Cumulative Review Exercise for Word Choice

1. The ~~manage~~ of a small business requires either education or experience in sales and accounting.
   management

✓ 2. Because of the traffic in ancient Rome, Julius Caesar would not let anyone use a wheeled vehicle on the streets during the day.

3. Occasionally dolphins need to ~~raise~~ to the surface of the water to take in oxygen.
   rise

4. Thomas Jefferson's home, which he designed and built, ~~sets~~ on a hill overlooking the Virginia countryside.
   sits

5. Once, the gold reserve of the United States Treasury was saved when J.P. Morgan, then the richest man in America, ~~borrowed~~ *lent* more than fifty million dollars' worth of gold to the federal government.

✓ 6. Dreams may be the expression of fears and desires that we are not conscious of during our waking hours.

7. Ice has the same ~~hard~~ *hardness* as concrete.

✓ 8. We might never have heard about Daniel Boone had he not told a schoolmaster his stories about the frontier.

9. Terrorists are capable ~~to~~ *of* hijacking planes and taking hostages in spite of security at international airports.

10. It is not the TOEFL but the academic preparation of a student that is the best indicator of his ~~successfully~~ *success*.

11. Some business analysts argue that the U.S. automobile industry is suffering because Congress will not impose heavier import duties, but others say that the cars themselves are inferior ~~with~~ *to* the foreign competition.

12. Lotteries are used to ~~rise~~ *raise* money for the states that sponsor them.

13. When a human being gets hurt, the brain excretes a chemical called enkaphalin to numb the ~~painful~~ *pain*.

14. Benjamin Franklin ~~told~~ *said* that the turkey should be our national bird.

✓15. The prime rate is the rate of interest that a bank will charge when it lends money to its best clients.

ANSWER KEY—EXERCISES FOR READING COMPREHENSION

Problem 1. Previewing

A black hole is a region of space created by the total gravitational collapse of matter. It is so intense that nothing, not even light or radiation, can escape. In other words, it is a one-way surface through which matter can fall inward but cannot emerge.

Some astronomers believe that a black hole may be formed when a large star collapses inward from its own weight. So long as they are emitting heat and light into space, stars support themselves against their own gravitational pull with the outward thermal pressure generated by heat from nuclear reactions deep in their interiors. But if a star eventually exhausts its nuclear fuel, then its unbalanced gravitational attraction could cause it to contract and collapse. Furthermore, it could begin to pull in surrounding matter, including nearby comets and planets, creating a black hole.

The topic is black holes.

Problem 2. Reading for Main Ideas

For more than a century, despite attacks by a few opposing scientists, Charles Darwin's theory of evolution by natural selection has stood firm. Now, however, some respected biologists are beginning to question whether the theory accounts for major developments such as the shift from water to land habitation. Clearly, evolution has not proceeded steadily but has progressed by radical advances. Recent research in molecular biology, particularly in the study of DNA, provides us with a new possibility. Not only environmental changes but also genetic codes in the underlying structure of DNA could govern evolution.

The main idea is that biologists are beginning to question Darwin's theory.
A good title would be "Questions about Darwin's Theory."

Problem 3. Using Contexts for Vocabulary

1. *To auction* means to sell.

2. *Proprietor* means an owner.

3. *Formerly* means in the past.

4. *To sample* means to try or to taste.

5. *Royalty* means payment.

Problem 4. Scanning for Details

To prepare for a career in engineering, a student must begin planning in high school. Mathematics and science should form the core curriculum. For example, in a school where sixteen credit hours are required for high school graduation, four should be in mathematics, one each in chemistry, biology, and physics. The remaining credits should include four in English and at least three in the humanities and social sciences. The average entering freshman in engineering should have achieved at least a 2.5 grade point average on a 4.0 scale in his or her high school. Although deficiencies can be corrected during the first year, the student who needs additional work should expect to spend five instead of four years to complete a degree.

1. What is the average grade point for an entering freshman in engineering?

   2.5

2. When should a student begin planning for a career in engineering?

   in high school

3. How can a student correct deficiencies in preparation?

   by spending five years

4. How many credits should a student have in English?

   four

5. How many credits are required for a high school diploma?

   sixteen

Problem 5. Making Inferences

When an acid is dissolved in water, the acid molecule divides into two parts, a hydrogen ion and another ion. An ion is an atom or a group of atoms which has an electrical charge. The charge can be either positive or negative. If hydrochloric acid is mixed with water, for example, it divides into hydrogen ions and chlorine ions.

A strong acid ionizes to a great extent, but a weak acid does not ionize so much. The strength of an acid, therefore, depends on how much it ionizes, not on how many hydrogen ions are produced. It is interesting that nitric acid and sulfuric acid become greatly ionized whereas boric acid and carbonic acid do not.

1. What kind of acid is sulfuric acid?

   A strong acid ionizes to a great extent, and sulfuric acid becomes greatly ionized.
   Conclusion: Sulfuric acid is a strong acid.

2. What kind of acid is boric acid?

   A weak acid does not ionize so much and boric acid does not ionize greatly.
   Conclusion: Boric acid is a weak acid.

Problem 6. Identifying Exceptions

All music consists of two elements—expression and design. Expression is inexact and subjective, and may be enjoyed in a personal or instinctive way. Design, on the other hand is exact and must be analyzed objectively in order to be understood and appreciated. The folk song, for example, has a definite musical design which relies on simple repetition with a definite beginning and ending. A folk song generally consists of one stanza of music repeated for each stanza of verse.

Because of their communal, and usually uncertain origin, folk songs are often popular verse set to music. They are not always recorded, and tend to be passed on in a kind of musical version of oral history. Each singer revises and perfects the song. In part as a consequence of this continuous revision process, most folk songs are almost perfect in their construction and design. A particular singer's interpretation of the folk song may provide an interesting expression, but the simple design that underlies the song itself is stable and enduring.

1. All of the following is true of a folk song EXCEPT

✓ There is a clear start and finish.
✓ The origin is often not known.
   The design may change in the interpretation.
✓ Simple repetition is characteristic of its design.

Problem 7. Locating References

The National Road, also known as the Cumberland Road, was constructed in the early 1800s to provide transportation between the established commercial areas of the East and Northwest Territory. By 1818, the road had reached Wheeling, West Virginia, 130 miles
Line from its point of origin in Cumberland, Maryland. The cost was a monumental thirteen thou-
(5) sand dollars per mile.

Upon reaching the Ohio River, the National Road became one of the major trade routes to the western states and territories, providing Baltimore with a trade advantage over neighboring cities. In order to compete, New York state authorized the construction of the Erie Canal, and Philadelphia initiated a transportation plan to link it with Pittsburgh. Towns along the
(10) rivers, canals, and the new National Road became important trade centers.

1. The word "its" in line 4 refers to *the road.*

2. The word "it" in line 9 refers to *the canal.*

Problem 8. Referring to the Passage

In September of 1929, traders experienced a lack of confidence in the stock market's ability to continue its phenomenal rise. Prices fell. For many inexperienced investors, the drop produced a panic. They had all their money tied up in the market, and they were pressed to
Line sell before the prices fell even lower. Sell orders were coming in so fast that the ticker tape at
(5) the New York Stock Exchange could not accommodate all the transactions.

To try to reestablish confidence in the market, a powerful group of New York bankers agreed to pool their funds and purchase stock above current market values. Although the buy orders were minimal, they were counting on their reputations to restore confidence on the part of the smaller investors, thereby affecting the number of sell orders. On Thursday, October
(10) 24, Richard Whitney, the Vice President of the New York Stock Exchange and a broker for the J.P. Morgan Company, made the effort on their behalf. Initially, it appeared to have been successful, then, on the following Tuesday, the crash began again and accelerated. By 1932, stocks were worth only twenty percent of their value at the 1929 high. The results of the crash had extended into every aspect of the economy, causing a long and painful depression,
(15) referred to in American history as the Great Depression.

1. Where in the passage does the author refer to the reason for the stock market crash? *Lines 1-3.*

2. Where in the passage does the author suggest that there was a temporary recovery in the stock market? *Lines 11-12.*

Cumulative Review Exercise for Reading Comprehension

1. Ⓐ Ⓑ Ⓒ ●
2. ● Ⓑ Ⓒ Ⓓ
3. Ⓐ Ⓑ ● Ⓓ
4. ● Ⓑ Ⓒ Ⓓ
5. Ⓐ Ⓑ ● Ⓓ
6. ● Ⓑ Ⓒ Ⓓ
7. Ⓐ Ⓑ ● Ⓓ
8. Ⓐ Ⓑ ● Ⓓ
9. Ⓐ ● Ⓒ Ⓓ
10. Ⓐ Ⓑ ● Ⓓ

ANSWER KEY—MODEL TESTS

Model Test 1—Short Form

Section 1: Listening Comprehension

1. (A)	6. (C)	11. (B)	16. (D)	21. (C)	26. (C)	31. (A)	36. (C)	41. (D)	46. (A)
2. (C)	7. (A)	12. (A)	17. (C)	22. (B)	27. (D)	32. (C)	37. (B)	42. (C)	47. (A)
3. (B)	8. (A)	13. (B)	18. (C)	23. (D)	28. (A)	33. (C)	38. (B)	43. (C)	48. (C)
4. (A)	9. (D)	14. (D)	19. (B)	24. (B)	29. (C)	34. (D)	39. (C)	44. (D)	49. (C)
5. (A)	10. (B)	15. (C)	20. (A)	25. (C)	30. (C)	35. (D)	40. (B)	45. (B)	50. (B)

Section 2: Structure and Written Expression

1. (D)	5. (C)	9. (A)	13. (A)	17. (A)	21. (A)	25. (D)	29. (B)	33. (B)	37. (A)
2. (C)	6. (B)	10. (D)	14. (D)	18. (D)	22. (B)	26. (C)	30. (A)	34. (B)	38. (C)
3. (B)	7. (C)	11. (A)	15. (C)	19. (A)	23. (A)	27. (C)	31. (D)	35. (D)	39. (B)
4. (C)	8. (B)	12. (B)	16. (B)	20. (B)	24. (A)	28. (A)	32. (D)	36. (C)	40. (A)

Section 3: Reading Comprehension

1. (B)	6. (A)	11. (B)	16. (C)	21. (C)	26. (B)	31. (B)	36. (C)	41. (A)	46. (A)
2. (A)	7. (B)	12. (A)	17. (C)	22. (D)	27. (B)	32. (B)	37. (B)	42. (C)	47. (D)
3. (D)	8. (B)	13. (B)	18. (B)	23. (A)	28. (C)	33. (B)	38. (A)	43. (A)	48. (C)
4. (B)	9. (C)	14. (D)	19. (C)	24. (B)	29. (C)	34. (D)	39. (B)	44. (A)	49. (B)
5. (A)	10. (A)	15. (B)	20. (B)	25. (D)	30. (A)	35. (A)	40. (B)	45. (D)	50. (B)

Model Test 2—Short Form

Section 1: Listening Comprehension

1. (D)	6. (B)	11. (C)	16. (A)	21. (D)	26. (D)	31. (B)	36. (C)	41. (B)	46. (B)
2. (B)	7. (B)	12. (B)	17. (C)	22. (D)	27. (A)	32. (A)	37. (B)	42. (D)	47. (B)
3. (D)	8. (B)	13. (D)	18. (A)	23. (D)	28. (C)	33. (C)	38. (B)	43. (A)	48. (C)
4. (B)	9. (D)	14. (A)	19. (C)	24. (B)	29. (D)	34. (B)	39. (D)	44. (C)	49. (B)
5. (D)	10. (B)	15. (B)	20. (B)	25. (C)	30. (B)	35. (B)	40. (C)	45. (A)	50. (C)

Section 2: Structure and Written Expression

1. (A)	5. (A)	9. (A)	13. (B)	17. (C)	21. (A)	25. (B)	29. (C)	33. (A)	37. (C)
2. (A)	6. (B)	10. (C)	14. (B)	18. (C)	22. (A)	26. (B)	30. (C)	34. (C)	38. (B)
3. (C)	7. (A)	11. (A)	15. (B)	19. (D)	23. (A)	27. (C)	31. (C)	35. (A)	39. (D)
4. (C)	8. (B)	12. (C)	16. (D)	20. (B)	24. (B)	28. (D)	32. (C)	36. (B)	40. (D)

Section 3: Reading Comprehension

1. (C)	6. (D)	11. (A)	16. (D)	21. (D)	26. (B)	31. (A)	36. (C)	41. (B)	46. (B)
2. (D)	7. (B)	12. (A)	17. (D)	22. (D)	27. (C)	32. (D)	37. (B)	42. (A)	47. (C)
3. (C)	8. (C)	13. (D)	18. (B)	23. (D)	28. (A)	33. (B)	38. (C)	43. (B)	48. (B)
4. (A)	9. (B)	14. (D)	19. (B)	24. (D)	29. (C)	34. (A)	39. (B)	44. (D)	49. (B)
5. (B)	10. (A)	15. (C)	20. (C)	25. (B)	30. (C)	35. (A)	40. (A)	45. (B)	50. (C)

Model Test 3—Short Form

Section 1: Listening Comprehension

1. (A)	6. (C)	11. (A)	16. (A)	21. (A)	26. (B)	31. (C)	36. (B)	41. (C)	46. (B)
2. (B)	7. (D)	12. (D)	17. (D)	22. (B)	27. (A)	32. (C)	37. (B)	42. (A)	47. (D)
3. (C)	8. (D)	13. (A)	18. (B)	23. (A)	28. (C)	33. (A)	38. (C)	43. (A)	48. (C)
4. (B)	9. (A)	14. (C)	19. (B)	24. (C)	29. (A)	34. (C)	39. (B)	44. (C)	49. (B)
5. (C)	10. (D)	15. (C)	20. (A)	25. (D)	30. (B)	35. (D)	40. (C)	45. (B)	50. (A)

Section 2: Structure and Written Expression

1. (C)	5. (C)	9. (A)	13. (C)	17. (B)	21. (B)	25. (A)	29. (B)	33. (A)	37. (C)
2. (B)	6. (B)	10. (C)	14. (A)	18. (C)	22. (D)	26. (B)	30. (B)	34. (A)	38. (A)
3. (A)	7. (D)	11. (C)	15. (B)	19. (B)	23. (D)	27. (B)	31. (B)	35. (A)	39. (D)
4. (C)	8. (C)	12. (A)	16. (A)	20. (A)	24. (C)	28. (B)	32. (D)	36. (D)	40. (D)

Section 3: Reading Comprehension

1. (A)	6. (C)	11. (A)	16. (D)	21. (B)	26. (A)	31. (C)	36. (B)	41. (D)	46. (C)
2. (D)	7. (B)	12. (C)	17. (D)	22. (D)	27. (B)	32. (A)	37. (B)	42. (D)	47. (A)
3. (C)	8. (D)	13. (C)	18. (A)	23. (C)	28. (C)	33. (A)	38. (A)	43. (A)	48. (A)
4. (D)	9. (C)	14. (D)	19. (C)	24. (A)	29. (A)	34. (A)	39. (D)	44. (B)	49. (A)
5. (B)	10. (C)	15. (C)	20. (B)	25. (C)	30. (C)	35. (C)	40. (C)	45. (C)	50. (C)

Model Test 4—Short Form

Section 1: Listening Comprehension

1. (B)	6. (B)	11. (A)	16. (A)	21. (B)	26. (A)	31. (B)	36. (A)	41. (D)	46. (C)
2. (C)	7. (D)	12. (C)	17. (C)	22. (A)	27. (C)	32. (C)	37. (A)	42. (B)	47. (A)
3. (A)	8. (D)	13. (A)	18. (B)	23. (D)	28. (D)	33. (D)	38. (D)	43. (C)	48. (C)
4. (A)	9. (D)	14. (B)	19. (B)	24. (A)	29. (A)	34. (D)	39. (D)	44. (D)	49. (C)
5. (B)	10. (C)	15. (C)	20. (B)	25. (D)	30. (A)	35. (D)	40. (A)	45. (A)	50. (D)

Section 2: Structure and Written Expression

1. (D)	5. (A)	9. (A)	13. (C)	17. (D)	21. (A)	25. (A)	29. (B)	33. (D)	37. (C)
2. (B)	6. (C)	10. (D)	14. (D)	18. (B)	22. (A)	26. (B)	30. (C)	34. (D)	38. (D)
3. (B)	7. (B)	11. (C)	15. (B)	19. (C)	23. (C)	27. (D)	31. (D)	35. (C)	39. (A)
4. (B)	8. (C)	12. (B)	16. (C)	20. (A)	24. (B)	28. (C)	32. (A)	36. (C)	40. (C)

Section 3: Reading Comprehension

1. (A)	6. (C)	11. (B)	16. (C)	21. (D)	26. (D)	31. (B)	36. (B)	41. (A)	46. (A)
2. (C)	7. (D)	12. (A)	17. (C)	22. (C)	27. (D)	32. (C)	37. (D)	42. (C)	47. (B)
3. (B)	8. (B)	13. (A)	18. (A)	23. (D)	28. (C)	33. (B)	38. (B)	43. (B)	48. (B)
4. (A)	9. (A)	14. (B)	19. (B)	24. (A)	29. (A)	34. (C)	39. (A)	44. (C)	49. (B)
5. (B)	10. (B)	15. (A)	20. (C)	25. (A)	30. (D)	35. (A)	40. (C)	45. (C)	50. (D)

Model Test 5—Short Form

Section 1: Listening Comprehension

1. (A)	6. (C)	11. (B)	16. (B)	21. (B)	26. (C)	31. (A)	36. (B)	41. (C)	46. (C)
2. (C)	7. (C)	12. (C)	17. (D)	22. (A)	27. (B)	32. (A)	37. (C)	42. (C)	47. (D)
3. (D)	8. (C)	13. (A)	18. (B)	23. (B)	28. (C)	33. (B)	38. (D)	43. (C)	48. (A)
4. (D)	9. (B)	14. (D)	19. (A)	24. (B)	29. (A)	34. (C)	39. (C)	44. (A)	49. (B)
5. (B)	10. (B)	15. (B)	20. (C)	25. (D)	30. (B)	35. (C)	40. (B)	45. (A)	50. (C)

Section 2: Structure and Written Expression

1. (A)	5. (B)	9. (A)	13. (D)	17. (D)	21. (B)	25. (D)	29. (B)	33. (B)	37. (B)
2. (C)	6. (C)	10. (C)	14. (D)	18. (B)	22. (A)	26. (A)	30. (D)	34. (B)	38. (C)
3. (C)	7. (A)	11. (C)	15. (C)	19. (B)	23. (B)	27. (D)	31. (A)	35. (B)	39. (C)
4. (B)	8. (A)	12. (C)	16. (B)	20. (A)	24. (A)	28. (A)	32. (D)	36. (B)	40. (D)

Section 3: Reading Comprehension

1. (A)	6. (D)	11. (A)	16. (D)	21. (D)	26. (C)	31. (A)	36. (C)	41. (A)	46. (B)
2. (A)	7. (A)	12. (B)	17. (A)	22. (B)	27. (A)	32. (B)	37. (B)	42. (B)	47. (D)
3. (A)	8. (D)	13. (D)	18. (A)	23. (B)	28. (A)	33. (A)	38. (A)	43. (D)	48. (C)
4. (C)	9. (B)	14. (B)	19. (C)	24. (C)	29. (C)	34. (C)	39. (A)	44. (B)	49. (B)
5. (B)	10. (A)	15. (A)	20. (B)	25. (C)	30. (C)	35. (D)	40. (C)	45. (A)	50. (B)

Model Test 6—Short Form

Section 1: Listening Comprehension

1. (C)	6. (C)	11. (A)	16. (A)	21. (A)	26. (D)	31. (D)	36. (A)	41. (A)	46. (B)
2. (D)	7. (C)	12. (C)	17. (B)	22. (D)	27. (A)	32. (B)	37. (B)	42. (C)	47. (A)
3. (B)	8. (C)	13. (C)	18. (B)	23. (A)	28. (A)	33. (A)	38. (C)	43. (A)	48. (B)
4. (B)	9. (B)	14. (B)	19. (C)	24. (C)	29. (B)	34. (A)	39. (B)	44. (C)	49. (D)
5. (B)	10. (C)	15. (C)	20. (C)	25. (A)	30. (B)	35. (C)	40. (B)	45. (B)	50. (B)

Section 2: Structure and Written Expression

1. (B)	5. (B)	9. (C)	13. (C)	17. (C)	21. (D)	25. (B)	29. (B)	33. (C)	37. (A)
2. (A)	6. (D)	10. (D)	14. (A)	18. (C)	22. (D)	26. (C)	30. (D)	34. (C)	38. (C)
3. (D)	7. (C)	11. (D)	15. (C)	19. (B)	23. (B)	27. (D)	31. (B)	35. (B)	39. (D)
4. (B)	8. (C)	12. (D)	16. (C)	20. (A)	24. (A)	28. (A)	32. (D)	36. (C)	40. (A)

Section 3: Reading Comprehension

1. (B)	6. (A)	11. (A)	16. (B)	21. (A)	26. (B)	31. (C)	36. (C)	41. (B)	46. (C)
2. (B)	7. (C)	12. (B)	17. (B)	22. (D)	27. (B)	32. (C)	37. (A)	42. (D)	47. (A)
3. (C)	8. (B)	13. (C)	18. (C)	23. (D)	28. (B)	33. (A)	38. (B)	43. (B)	48. (A)
4. (C)	9. (B)	14. (B)	19. (A)	24. (D)	29. (C)	34. (B)	39. (B)	44. (D)	49. (D)
5. (A)	10. (A)	15. (C)	20. (D)	25. (C)	30. (C)	35. (B)	40. (C)	45. (B)	50. (B)

Model Test 7—Short Form

Section 1: Listening Comprehension

1. (C)	6. (C)	11. (B)	16. (C)	21. (D)	26. (C)	31. (B)	36. (B)	41. (D)	46. (C)
2. (A)	7. (A)	12. (B)	17. (C)	22. (A)	27. (C)	32. (C)	37. (C)	42. (A)	47. (B)
3. (B)	8. (D)	13. (B)	18. (D)	23. (D)	28. (A)	33. (A)	38. (C)	43. (B)	48. (C)
4. (C)	9. (A)	14. (B)	19. (D)	24. (A)	29. (D)	34. (C)	39. (B)	44. (C)	49. (A)
5. (B)	10. (A)	15. (B)	20. (A)	25. (D)	30. (B)	35. (A)	40. (A)	45. (C)	50. (C)

Section 2: Structure and Written Expression

1. (C)	5. (A)	9. (A)	13. (A)	17. (A)	21. (B)	25. (B)	29. (B)	33. (A)	37. (D)
2. (D)	6. (B)	10. (A)	14. (B)	18. (D)	22. (A)	26. (D)	30. (D)	34. (A)	38. (B)
3. (A)	7. (B)	11. (D)	15. (D)	19. (B)	23. (D)	27. (B)	31. (C)	35. (B)	39. (D)
4. (D)	8. (A)	12. (B)	16. (B)	20. (A)	24. (D)	28. (B)	32. (B)	36. (D)	40. (A)

Section 3: Reading Comprehension

1. (C)	6. (C)	11. (B)	16. (B)	21. (C)	26. (C)	31. (A)	36. (B)	41. (C)	46. (D)
2. (B)	7. (A)	12. (C)	17. (B)	22. (A)	27. (C)	32. (A)	37. (C)	42. (D)	47. (D)
3. (A)	8. (C)	13. (B)	18. (A)	23. (B)	28. (B)	33. (A)	38. (A)	43. (A)	48. (B)
4. (C)	9. (C)	14. (C)	19. (A)	24. (A)	29. (D)	34. (C)	39. (C)	44. (B)	49. (A)
5. (B)	10. (A)	15. (B)	20. (D)	25. (B)	30. (A)	35. (B)	40. (B)	45. (B)	50. (B)

Model Test 8—Long Form

Section 1: Listening Comprehension

1. (A)	9. (A)	17. (D)	25. (C)	33. (A)	41. (C)	49. (C)	57. (B)	65. (B)	73. (D)
2. (B)	10. (C)	18. (C)	26. (C)	34. (C)	42. (D)	50. (D)	58. (C)	66. (C)	74. (A)
3. (C)	11. (A)	19. (C)	27. (D)	35. (C)	43. (C)	51. (C)	59. (C)	67. (A)	75. (D)
4. (C)	12. (B)	20. (A)	28. (D)	36. (B)	44. (C)	52. (B)	60. (A)	68. (D)	76. (C)
5. (D)	13. (B)	21. (B)	29. (A)	37. (C)	45. (B)	53. (C)	61. (B)	69. (B)	77. (C)
6. (A)	14. (D)	22. (C)	30. (B)	38. (C)	46. (A)	54. (A)	62. (B)	70. (D)	78. (D)
7. (B)	15. (A)	23. (B)	31. (C)	39. (B)	47. (D)	55. (C)	63. (C)	71. (C)	79. (A)
8. (C)	16. (A)	24. (C)	32. (C)	40. (A)	48. (A)	56. (B)	64. (C)	72. (C)	80. (B)

Section 2: Structure and Written Expression

1. (C)	7. (A)	13. (C)	19. (A)	25. (C)	31. (C)	37. (A)	43. (B)	49. (C)	55. (C)
2. (B)	8. (D)	14. (A)	20. (B)	26. (D)	32. (D)	38. (C)	44. (C)	50. (D)	56. (B)
3. (B)	9. (D)	15. (D)	21. (B)	27. (A)	33. (D)	39. (D)	45. (C)	51. (B)	57. (A)
4. (B)	10. (B)	16. (A)	22. (C)	28. (D)	34. (C)	40. (B)	46. (C)	52. (A)	58. (D)
5. (C)	11. (D)	17. (D)	23. (A)	29. (C)	35. (B)	41. (B)	47. (B)	53. (A)	59. (C)
6. (C)	12. (B)	18. (D)	24. (D)	30. (C)	36. (B)	42. (B)	48. (B)	54. (D)	60. (A)

Section 3: Reading Comprehension

1. (B)	8. (B)	15. (A)	22. (B)	29. (D)	36. (B)	43. (C)	50. (D)	57. (C)	64. (B)
2. (C)	9. (B)	16. (C)	23. (B)	30. (C)	37. (C)	44. (B)	51. (C)	58. (B)	65. (B)
3. (B)	10. (C)	17. (A)	24. (C)	31. (B)	38. (C)	45. (B)	52. (A)	59. (C)	66. (C)
4. (C)	11. (B)	18. (D)	25. (D)	32. (B)	39. (D)	46. (C)	53. (A)	60. (B)	67. (B)
5. (A)	12. (B)	19. (D)	26. (C)	33. (A)	40. (C)	47. (A)	54. (D)	61. (B)	68. (C)
6. (C)	13. (B)	20. (B)	27. (A)	34. (A)	41. (B)	48. (D)	55. (A)	62. (A)	69. (D)
7. (C)	14. (D)	21. (C)	28. (A)	35. (C)	42. (C)	49. (A)	56. (B)	63. (D)	70. (C)

EXPLANATORY ANSWERS FOR THE TOEFL MODEL TESTS

Model Test 1—Short Form

Section 1: Listening Comprehension

1. **(A)** Since the man says that he can have the prescription for the woman in about ten minutes, it must be concluded that she will wait. Prescriptions are filled at drugstores in the United States. Choices (B), (C), and (D) are not mentioned and may not be concluded from information in the conversation.

2. **(C)** Since the man says that there aren't any seats left, it must be concluded that he has to stand when he takes the bus to work. Choice (B) refers to the woman's suggestion, not to the man's response. Choices (A) and (D) are not mentioned and may not be concluded from information in the conversation.

3. **(B)** Since the woman says that she does not have time, it must be concluded that she is not interested in the nomination. Choice (C) contradicts the fact that she does not have time. Choice (D) contradicts the fact that the woman, not the man, was nominated. Choice (A) is not mentioned and may not be concluded from information in the conversation.

4. **(A)** *Who cares* means that it isn't important (that her advisor might be offended). Choices (B), (C), and (D) are not mentioned and may not be concluded from information in the conversation.

5. **(A)** Since the woman says that her new apartment is closer to work, it must be concluded that her old apartment was too far from work. Choice (B) refers to the use of "old" in the conversation to mean "previously used" or "former," not to the condition of the apartment. Choice (C) refers to the name of the street, not to the location of the apartment. Choice (D) is not mentioned and may not be concluded from information in the conversation.

6. **(C)** Because the woman says that the invitation sounds "great," and she thanks the man for asking her, it must be concluded that she would go out with the man on another occasion. Choice (A) contradicts the fact that she responds so positively while refusing the invitation. Choices (B) and (D) contradict the fact that she has plans to attend a lecture.

7. **(A)** *In good shape* is an idiomatic expression that means the item is in good condition. Choice (B) contradicts the fact that the man thinks the bike is new, and that the woman says it is in good shape. Choice (C) contradicts the fact that the speakers are talking about a bike that is able to be seen. Choice (D) contradicts the fact that the woman got the bike almost five years ago.

8. **(A)** *I wish* is an idiomatic expression that means the speaker views the situation as worse than described, and wishes it were only as bad as stated. Choices (B), (C), and (D) are not paraphrases of the expression.

9. **(D)** The woman offers to fix supper and to stay at home in order to please the man, but she says that she would rather go out. Choices (A) and (B) refer to what the woman offers to do, not to what she wants to do. Choice (C) is not mentioned and may not be concluded from information in the conversation.

10. **(B)** According to the woman, Mr. Baker is out to lunch. Choices (A) and (C) refer to where Mr. Williams is, not to where Mr. Baker is. Choice (D) misinterprets Mr. Baker's last name as an occupation.

11. **(B)** Since the woman asks for the man's professional opinion, and he recommends settling out of court, it must be concluded that she will come to an agreement. Choice (A) contradicts the fact that the man is probably a lawyer. Choice (C) refers to the woman's question, not to her conclusion. Choice (D) contradicts the fact that the man thinks the case can be settled out of court.

12. **(A)** The man says that he would rather have something cold. Choices (B), (C), and (D) refer to what the man likes, not to what he wants. (Refer to Patterns, Problem 8 in the Review of Structure and Written Expression.)

13. **(B)** ". . . it isn't too far to walk [to the shopping center]." Choice (A) contradicts the fact that he is already giving the woman information about the shopping center. Choices (C) and (D) are alternative possibilities that the man mentions before making his suggestion.

14. **(D)** Since the man says that he is just checking the schedule now, it must be concluded that he has not registered yet. Choice (A) contradicts the fact that he is checking the schedule for a class. Choices (B) and (C) are not mentioned and may not be concluded from information in the conversation.

15. **(C)** To *not mind* is an idiomatic expression that means the speaker will not be bothered by an activity or situation. Choices (A), (B), and (D) are not paraphrases of the expression.

16. **(D)** "She'd better see someone at the Counseling Center." Choices (A), (B), and (C) are not mentioned and may not be concluded from information in the conversation.

17. **(C)** From the reference to getting the "bill corrected," it must be concluded that the speakers are talking about a mistake on a bill. The word "letter" in Choice (D) refers to a letter that they have received, not to a letter that they have written. Choices (A) and (B) are not mentioned and may not be concluded from information in the conversation.

18. **(C)** *Please go on* is an idiomatic expression that means the speaker wants the other person to continue. Choices (A), (B), and (D) are not paraphrases of the expression.

19. **(B)** Since the man apologizes for going ahead of the woman in line, he will most probably allow her to go ahead of him. Choice (A) contradicts the fact that it is the man, not the woman, who apologizes. Choice (C) contradicts the fact that he has already apologized. Choice (D) is not mentioned and may not be concluded from information in the conversation.

20. **(A)** *Not again* is an idiomatic expression that means the speaker is impatient with some kind of repeated behavior or activity. Choice (C) contradicts the fact that she does not know about the party until the man informs her. Choices (B) and (D) are not mentioned and may not be concluded from information in the conversation.

21. **(C)** *That's too bad* is an idiomatic expression that means the speaker is sorry about the news. Choice (D) contradicts the fact that the woman thought the professor would give the man an extension. Choices (A) and (B) are not mentioned and may not be concluded from information in the conversation.

22. **(B)** Since the woman asks the man whether the computer is plugged in, it must be concluded that she wants him to check the plug. Choices (A), (C), and (D) are not mentioned and may not be concluded from information in the conversation.

23. **(D)** Since the woman did not feel like going to the reception after returning from a long trip, it must be concluded that she was tired. Choice (B) contradicts the fact that she is not surprised about the reception. Choices (A) and (C) are not mentioned and may not be concluded from information in the conversation.

24. **(B)** Since the man says that they should have left already, it must be concluded that they are late. Choice (A) is not likely because of the woman's suggestion that they make a call. Choices (C) and (D) are not mentioned and may not be concluded from information in the conversation.

25. **(C)** Since the woman says that she has her rent paid until the 15th, she will probably stay where she is living until the 15th. The reference to half a month in Choice (A) refers to the fact that the woman already has her rent paid until the 15th, not to what she will do. Choice (B) contradicts the fact that the woman, not the man, is planning to move. Choice (D) contradicts the fact that the woman mentions having her rent paid.

26. **(C)** Since the man expresses surprise, it must be concluded that he thought she had not taken the placement test. Choice (A) contradicts the fact that the man was surprised. Choices (B) and (D) are not mentioned and may not be concluded from information in the conversation.

27. **(D)** *Good deals* is an idiomatic expression that means the prices are competitive. Choices (B) and (C) contradict the fact that the man says "Good for you" which expresses approval. Choice (A) is not mentioned and may not be concluded from information in the conversation.

28. **(A)** Since the man mentions that Gary has to be in Miami, he implies that he may not be able to come. Choice (D) contradicts the fact that he said he would be here for her birthday. Choices (B) and (C) are not mentioned and may not be concluded from information in the conversation.

29. **(C)** To *catch cold* is an idiomatic expression that means to get sick. Choices (A), (B), and (D) are not paraphrases of the expression, and may not be concluded from information in the conversation.

30. **(C)** To be *swamped* is an idiomatic expression that means to be very busy. Choices (A), (B), and (D) are not paraphrases of the expression, and may not be concluded from information in the conversation.

31. **(A)** "Would you like a cup of coffee?" Choices (B), (C), and (D) are mentioned later in the conversation, not at the beginning.

32. **(C)** The speakers keep returning to the coffee as a point of discussion. Choices (A), (B), and (D) are mentioned briefly in the conversation, but not as a main point of discussion.

33. **(C)** "The last time I was there [at the Student Center] it was so crowded that I had to wait in line for almost an hour." "Let's go somewhere else then." Choice (A) contradicts the fact that they still want a cup of coffee. Choice (D) is the reason that the woman suggests their going to the Student Center, not the reason that they decide not to go. Choice (B) is not mentioned and may not be concluded from information in the talk.

34. **(D)** "Let's go to the library. There's another vending machine downstairs by the telephones." The woman says that she has a test at three o'clock, but Choice (A) is not mentioned as a reason to go to the library. The telephones in Choice (B) are near the vending machines, but the speakers do not mention using them. Choice (C) is not mentioned as a reason to go to the library. The woman suggests that the man complain about losing his money, but she does not suggest where he might be able to do so.

35. **(D)** "I need your technical writing class. . . . In that case, I'll sign an override for you." Choice (A) contradicts the fact that he went early to registration. Choice (B) contradicts the fact that his advisor signed his course request. Choice (C) contradicts the fact that the course will not be taught until fall semester.

36. **(C)** ". . . I'll sign an override. . . . Take this form back to the registration area and they'll get you in." Choice (D) refers to something that the professor tells Mike to do, not to something that Mike wants the professor to do. Choices (A) and (B) are not mentioned and may not be concluded from information in the conversation.

37. **(B)** ". . . I can't graduate without your class." Choice (A) contradicts the fact that he plans to graduate in the spring. Choices (C) and (D) are not mentioned and may not be concluded from information in the conversation.

38. **(B)** ". . . I'll sign an override for you." Choice (A) refers to the suggestion that the professor makes at the beginning of the conversation, not to what he actually decides to do. Choices (C) and (D) are not mentioned and may not be concluded from information in the conversation.

39. **(C)** ". . . background music, more commonly known as MUZAK." Choice (A) is one kind of MUZAK, but it contradicts the fact that MUZAK can be upbeat songs, too. Choice (B) is one place where MUZAK is played, but it contradicts the fact that MUZAK can be played in the workplace and the supermarket, too. Choice (D) contradicts the fact that MUZAK is more than a pleasant addition to the environment.

40. **(B)** "In one survey, overall productivity increased by thirty percent, although five to ten percent is the average." Choice (D) refers to one survey, not to the average. Choices (A) and (C) are not mentioned and may not be concluded from information in the talk.

41. **(D)** ". . . stimulus progression . . . starts with a slow, soft song . . . and builds up . . . to an upbeat song . . . programmed . . . when people are generally starting to tire." Choice (A) refers to the first stage of stimulus progression, not to the total progression. Choices (B) and (C) refer to varieties of MUZAK, not to stimulus progression.

42. **(C)** "In supermarkets, slow music can influence shoppers to walk slower and buy more." Choice (D) contradicts the fact that it can influence shoppers to buy more. Choices (A) and (B) are not mentioned and may not be concluded from information in the talk.

43. **(C)** ". . . Community College offers a series of video telecourses to meet the needs of students who prefer to complete coursework in their homes." Choices (A) and (B) are secondary themes used to develop the main theme of the talk. Choice (D) is not men-

tioned and may not be concluded from information in the conversation.

44. **(D)** "Some telecourses will also be broadcast on KCC-TV's 'Sun-Up Semester.'" Choice (A) contradicts the fact that students should call the Community College Distance Learning Program to register. Choice (C) contradicts the fact that a listing of courses is printed in the television guide. Choice (B) is not mentioned and may not be concluded from information in the conversation.

45. **(B)** "To register for a telecourse, phone the Community College. . . " Choice (A) contradicts the fact that the program is designed to meet the needs of students who are not able to come to campus. Choices (C) and (D) are not mentioned and may not be concluded from information in the conversation.

46. **(A)** ". . . you can use either an 800 telephone number or an e-mail address to contact your instructor." Choices (B), (C), and (D) are not mentioned and may not be concluded from information in the conversation.

47. **(A)** "I would like to outline the development of the Sapir-Whorf Hypothesis concerning the relationship between language and culture." Choices (B), (C), and (D) are secondary themes that are used to develop the main theme of the lecture.

48. **(C)** "In 1936, he [Whorf] wrote 'An American Indian Model of the Universe,' which explored the implications of the Hopi verb system . . ." Choice (A) refers to historical linguistics, not to the languages that Whorf used in his research. Choices (B) and (D) are not mentioned and may not be concluded from information in the talk.

49. **(C)** ". . . 'linguistic relativity' which states, at least as a hypothesis, that the grammar of a man's language influences the manner in which he understands reality and behaves with respect to it." Choice (D) contradicts the fact that grammar influences cultural behavior. Choices (A) and (B) are not mentioned and may not be concluded from information in the talk.

50. **(B)** ". . . it [linguistic relativity] came to be called the Sapir-Whorf Hypothesis." Choice (A) is incomplete because it does not include the name of Whorf. Choice (C) includes the name of Boas, who contributed to the hypothesis but was not named in it. Choice (D)

refers to a paper written by Whorf regarding the Hopi verb system, not to linguistic relativity.

Section 2: Structure and Written Expression

1. **(D)** *Since* is used with *have* and a participle before a specific time such as *1970*. Choices (A) and (B) may be used before a specific time, but not with *have* and a participle. Choice (C) may be used with *have* and a participle before a quantity of time, not before a specific time. (Refer to Patterns, Problem 133, page 210.)

2. **(C)** *Used to* requires a verb word. When preceded by a form of *be*, *used to* requires an *-ing* form. In spoken English, Choice (A) may sound correct, but *use to* is not acceptable in written English. In Choices (B) and (D), *used to* preceded by a form of *be* may be used with an *-ing* form, not with a verb word. "He is used to trading," and "he was used to trading," would also be correct. (Refer to Patterns, Problem 11, page 53.)

3. **(B)** A cardinal number is used after a noun. *The* is used with an ordinal number before a noun. Choice (A) is incomplete because there is no verb after *who*. Choices (C) and (D) are redundant. (Refer to Patterns, Problem 77, page 142.)

4. **(C)** *But also* is used in correlation with the inclusive *not only*. Choice (B) would be used in correlation with *both*. Choices (A) and (D) are not used in correlation with another inclusive. (Refer to Patterns, Problem 118, page 192.)

5. **(C)** A form of *have* with someone such as *General Lee* and a verb word expresses a causative. Choice (A) is an infinitive, not a verb word. Choice (B) is a participle. Choice (D) is an *-ing* form. (Refer to Patterns, Problem 18, page 63.)

6. **(B)** In scientific results, a present form in the condition requires a present or future form in the result. Choice (A) is a past, not future form. Choices (C) and (D) are present forms but they are auxiliary verbs. (Refer to Patterns, Problem 21, page 67.)

7. **(C)** For scientific results, a present form in the condition requires a present or future form in the result. Choices (A), (B), and (D)

are not conditional statements. (Refer to Patterns, Problem 21, page 67.)

8. **(B)** When two nouns occur together, the first noun functions as an adjective. In Choice (A), the form *mathematic* does not exist as a singular noun. Choice (C) does not agree with the plural *people* to which it refers. Choice (D) is not logical because it implies ownership of the *teachers* by *mathematics*. (Refer to Patterns, Problem 78, page 144.)

9. **(A)** Ideas in a series should be expressed by parallel structures. Only *to sell* in Choice (A) provides for parallelism with the infinitive *to increase*. Choices (B), (C), and (D) are not parallel. (Refer to Style, Problem 17, page 240.)

10. **(D)** In contrary-to-fact clauses, *were* is the only accepted form of the verb BE Choices (A), (B), and (C) are forms of the verb BE, but they are not accepted in contrary-to-fact clauses. (Refer to Patterns, Problem 25, page 72.)

11. **(A)** The anticipatory clause *it is generally believed that* introduces a subject and verb, *Java Man. . .is.* In Choices (B) and (C) the verb *is* is repeated. Choice (D) may be used as a subject clause preceding a main verb, not preceding a subject and verb. "That it is generally believed that Java Man, who lived before the first Ice Age, is the first manlike animal *is* the result of entries in textbooks" would also be correct. (Refer to Patterns, Problem 35, page 35.)

12. **(B)** Only Choice (B) may be used with a noncount noun such as *money*. Choices (A), (C), and (D) may be used with count nouns. (Refer to Patterns, Problem 67, page 129.)

13. **(A)** *Because* is used before a subject and verb to introduce cause. Choices (B), (C), and (D) are not accepted for statements of cause. (Refer to Patterns, Problem 111, page 183.)

14. **(D)** An adjective clause modifies a noun in the main clause. *That provides food* modifies *the one*. Choice (A) is a subject and verb without the clause marker *that*. Choice (B) is a clause marker *that* with an *-ing* form, not a verb. Choice (C) is a verb without a clause marker. (Refer to Patterns, Problem 140, page 219.)

15. **(C)** *Had better* requires a verb word. Choice (A) is an infinitive, not a verb word. Choice

(B) reverses the order of the phrase to mean to *improve one's health*. Choice (D) is a past form, not a verb word. (Refer to Patterns, Problem 12, page 55.)

16. **(B)** Ideas in a series should be expressed by parallel structures. *To take* should be *taking* to provide for parallelism with the *-ing* forms *mailing* and *calling*. (Refer to Style, Problem 17, page 240.)

17. **(A)** A past form in the condition requires either *would* or *could* and a verb word in the result. Because the past form *planted* is used in the condition, *will* should be *would* in the result. (Refer to Patterns, Problem 23, page 69.)

18. **(D)** In order to refer to an *increase* in the rate of inflation, *rises* should be used. *To raise* means to move to a higher place. *To rise* means to increase. (Refer to Style, Problem 22, page 247.)

19. **(A)** *Drank* should be *drunk* because the auxiliary *has* requires a participle. *Drank* is a past form. *Drunk* is a participle. (Refer to Patterns, Problem 36, page 87.)

20. **(B)** Ideas after exclusives should be expressed by parallel structures. *To hunt* should be *in hunting* to provide for parallelism with the phrase *in planting*. (Refer to Style, Problem 18, page 241.)

21. **(A)** *Capable* should be *capability*. *Capable* is an adjective. *Capability* is a noun. (Refer to Style, Problem 30, page 257.)

22. **(B)** *Effect on* is a prepositional idiom. *In* should be *on*. (Refer to Style, Problem 29, page 255.)

23. **(A)** The word order for a passive sentence is a form of BE followed by a participle. *Call* should be *called*. (Refer to Patterns, Problem 31, page 81.)

24. **(A)** Using words with the same meaning consecutively is repetitive. *Seldom* should be deleted because *seldom* means *almost never*. (Refer to Style, Problem 20, page 244.)

25. **(D)** Because it is a prepositional phrase, *as grass* should be *like grass*. *As* functions as a conjunction. *Like* functions as a preposition. (Refer to Patterns, Problem 88, page 156.)

26. **(C)** Ideas in a series should be expressed by parallel structures. *It is* should be deleted to provide for parallelism with the adjectives *interesting*, *informative*, and *easy*. (Refer to Style, Problem 17, page 240.)

27. **(C)** Activities of the dead logically establish a point of view in the past. *Lives* should be *lived* in order to maintain the point of view. (Refer to Style, Problem 4, page 224.)

28. **(A)** A verb word must be used in a clause after an impersonal expression. *Is not* should be *not be* after the impersonal expression *it is essential*. (Refer to Patterns, Problem 29, page 78.)

29. **(B)** There must be agreement between subject and verb. *Has* should be *have* to agree with the plural subject, *two*. (Refer to Style, Problem 5, page 226.)

30. **(A)** *Who* should be *whom* because it is the complement of the clause *many people consider*. *Who* functions as a subject. *Whom* functions as a complement. (Refer to Patterns, Problem 49, page 103.)

31. **(D)** *By* expresses means before an *-ing* form. *Refine* should be *refining* after the preposition *by*. (Refer to Patterns, Problem 114, page 186.)

32. **(D)** There must be agreement between pronoun and antecedent. *Their* should be *its* to agree with the singular antecedent *atmosphere*. (Refer to Style, Problem 11, page 232.)

33. **(B)** Multiple numbers are usually followed by the phrase *as much as*. *More than* should be *as much as* after the multiple number *twice*. (Refer to Patterns, Problem 93, page 162.)

34. **(B)** Most adverbs of manner are formed by adding *-ly* to adjectives. *Broad* should be *broadly* to qualify the manner in which the speaking was done. (Refer to Patterns, Problem 126, page 202.)

35. **(D)** A present tense verb is used after *when* to express future. *Will limit* should be *limit*. (Refer to Patterns, Problem 123, page 198.)

36. **(C)** *More prettier* should be *prettier*. Because *pretty* is a two-syllable adjective that ends in *y*, the comparative is formed by changing the *y* to *i* and adding *-er*. *More* is used with two-syllable adjectives that do not end in *y*. (Refer to Patterns, Problem 96, page 165.)

37. **(A)** Plural count nouns are used after a number or a reference to a number of items. *Term* should be *terms*. (Refer to Patterns, Problem 52, page 107.)

38. **(C)** Because the verb *to fail* requires an infinitive in the complement, *recognizing* should be *to recognize*. (Refer to Patterns, Problem 2, page 42.)

39. **(B)** *Form* should be *formation*. Although both are nouns derived from verbs, the *-ation* ending is needed here. *Form* means the structure. *Formation* means the process of forming over time. (Refer to Style, Problem 30, page 257.)

40. **(A)** *From* is used with *to* to express a time limit. *In* should be *From*. (Refer to Patterns, Problem 115, page 187.)

Section 3: Reading Comprehension

1. **(B)** "The Process of Photosynthesis" is the best title because it states the main idea of the passage. The other choices are secondary ideas which are used to develop the main idea. Choice (A) describes the process in the form of an equation. In Choice (C), the parts of plants are named because of their roles in the process. Choice (D) is one of the products of the process.

2. **(A)** ". . . under suitable conditions of temperature and moisture, the green parts of plants use carbon dioxide from the atmosphere and release oxygen to it . . . . In photosynthesis, carbohydrates are synthesized from carbon dioxide and water." In Choice (B), the water is a necessary condition for photosynthesis, not a result of it. In Choice (D), water does not interrupt, but rather encourages the process. Choice (C) is not mentioned and may not be concluded from information in the passage.

3. **(D)** "These exchanges are the opposite of those that occur in respiration." Choices (A), (B), and (C) refer to processes which occur in photosynthesis, not to processes which are the opposite.

4. **(B)** ". . . the green parts of plants use carbon dioxide from the atmosphere and release oxygen to it. Oxygen is the product of the reaction." The water referred to in Choice (A) and the carbon referred to in Choice (C) are used in photosynthesis, but neither one is mentioned as occurring in excess as a result of the process. Choice (D) refers to the natural substance in the chloroplasts of plants, not to a chemical combination of carbon dioxide and water.

5. **(A)** In the context of this passage, "stored" is

closest in meaning to "retained." Choices (B), (C), and (D) are not accepted definitions of the word.

6. **(A)** ". . . radiant energy from the sun is stored as chemical energy." In Choice (B), it is water, not energy from the sun, which is conducted from the xylem to the leaves. Choice (C) contradicts the fact that energy from the sun is the source of the chemical energy used in decomposing carbon dioxide and water. Choice (D) is incorrect because it is oxygen, not energy, that is released one to one for each molecule of carbon dioxide used.

7. **(B)** "The products of their decomposition [carbon dioxide and water] are recombined into a new compound, which is successively built up into more and more complex substances." Choices (A), (C), and (D) would change the meaning of the sentence.

8. **(B)** In the context of this passage, "successively" is closest in meaning to "in a sequence." Choices (A), (C), and (D) are not accepted definitions of the word.

9. **(C)** "At the same time, a balance of gases is preserved in the atmosphere." Energy from the sun, referred to in Choice (A), and carbon dioxide, referred to in Choice (B), are used in the process of photosynthesis, not produced as a result of it. Choice (D) is not mentioned and may not be concluded from information in the passage.

10. **(A)** Choice (B) is mentioned in lines 9–10. Choice (C) is mentioned in lines 7–8. Choice (D) is mentioned in lines 8–9. Water, not oxygen, is absorbed by the roots.

11. **(B)** The other choices are secondary ideas that are used to develop the main idea, "the Nobel prizes." Choices (A), (C), and (D) are historically significant to the discussion.

12. **(A)** "The Nobel prizes . . . were made available by a fund bequeathed for that purpose . . . by Alfred Bernhard Nobel." Because of the reference to *bequeath*, it must be concluded that Nobel left money in a will. In Choice (B), Nobel was the founder of the prizes, not a recipient. Choice (C) refers to the place where Nobel was born, not to where he is living now. Since Nobel has bequeathed funds, it must be concluded that he is dead and could not serve as chairman of a committee as in Choice (D).

13. **(B)** "The Nobel prizes, awarded annually . . ."

Because of the reference to *annually*, it must be concluded that the prizes are awarded once a year. Choices (A), (C), and (D) are not mentioned and may not be concluded from information in the passage.

14. **(D)** In the context of this passage, "outstanding" could best be replaced by "exceptional." Choices (A), (B), and (C) are not accepted definitions of the word.

15. **(B)** In the context of this passage, "will" refers to "a legal document." Choices (A), (C), and (D) are not accepted definitions of the word in this context.

16. **(C)** "The Nobel prizes [are] awarded annually for distinguished work in chemistry, physics, physiology or medicine, literature, and international peace." Since there is no prize for music, a composer, in Choice (C) would not be eligible for an award. Choice (A) could be awarded a prize for literature. Choice (B) would be awarded a prize for medicine. Choice (D) could be awarded a prize for peace.

17. **(C)** "Candidates are judged by Swedish and Norwegian academies and institutes on the basis of their [the candidates] contribution to humankind." Choices (A), (B), and (D) would change the meaning of the sentence.

18. **(B)** "The prizes . . . are administered by the Nobel Foundation." Choice (A) refers to the person who presents the awards, not to the administrator of the trust. Choice (C) refers to the organization that endowed a prize for economics. Choice (D) refers to the judges.

19. **(C)** In the context of this passage, "appropriate" is closest in meaning to "suitable." Choices (A), (B), and (D) are not accepted definitions of the word.

20. **(B)** "The awards are . . . presented . . . on December 10 . . . on the anniversary of his [Alfred Nobel's] death." Choice (A) is incorrect because it is a tribute to Nobel, not to the King of Sweden. Choice (D) contradicts the fact that the Nobel Foundation, not the Central Bank of Sweden, administers the trust. Choice (C) is not mentioned and may not be concluded from information in the passage.

21. **(C)** The other choices are secondary ideas that are used to develop the main idea, "the development of opera." Choices (A), (B), and (D) are historically significant to the discussion.

22. **(D)** "The usually accepted date for the beginning of opera as we know it is 1600." Choice (A) refers to Greek tragedy, the inspiration for modern opera. Choices (B) and (C) are not mentioned and may not be concluded from information in the passage.

23. **(A)** "Although stage plays have been set to music since the era of the ancient Greeks, when the dramas of Sophocles and Aeschylus were accompanied by lyres and flutes, the usually accepted date for the beginning of opera as we know it [the opera] is 1600." Choices (B), (C), and (D) would change the meaning of the sentence.

24. **(B)** ". . . composer Jacopo Perí produced his famous *Euridice*, generally considered to be the first opera." Choice (A) refers to the form of musical story that inspired Perí, not to the opera that he wrote. Choice (C) refers to the wife of Henry IV for whose marriage the opera was written, not to the title of the opera. Choice (D) refers to the group of musicians who introduced the opera form, not to the title of an opera written by them.

25. **(D)** "As part of the celebration of the marriage of King Henry IV . . . Jacopo Perí produced his famous *Euridice*." Choice (A) contradicts the fact that *Euridice* was produced in Florence, the native city of King Henry's wife and the place where the wedding was celebrated. Choice (B) refers to Greek tragedy, not to modern opera. Choice (C) is improbable because *Euridice* has become so famous.

26. **(B)** ". . . a group of Italian musicians called the Camerata began to revive the style of musical story that had been used in Greek tragedy." In Choice (A), musicians in the Camerata were Italian, not Greek. Choice (C) contradicts the fact that the center of the Camerata was Florence, Italy. King Henry IV referred to in Choice (D) was a patron of opera, but the name given to his court was not mentioned and may not be concluded from information in the passage.

27. **(B)** In the context of this passage, "revive" could best be replaced by "resume." Choices (A), (C), and (D) are not accepted definitions of the word.

28. **(C)** In the context of this passage, "plots" is closest in meaning to "stories." Choices (A), (B), and (D) are not accepted definitions of the word.

29. **(C)** "They called their compositions *opera in musica* or musical works. It is from this phrase that the word 'opera' is borrowed." Choice (A) refers to the origin of the plots for opera, not to the term. Choice (B) contradicts the fact that the Camerata was a group of Italian musicians. Choice (D) refers to the composer of the first opera.

30. **(A)** "The recitative . . . is also a solo. . . ." Choice (B) is an example of a musical piece written for two voices, not one voice. Choice (C) refers to a musical drama, which may contain duets and choruses as well as several solos. The lyre in Choice (D) refers to a musical instrument that was used to accompany the players in Greek tragedy, not to a solo.

31. **(B)** The author's main purpose is to describe the nature of sunspots. Choice (A) contradicts the fact that there is no theory that completely explains sunspots. Choices (C) and (D) are important to the discussion, and provide details that support the main idea.

32. **(B)** In the context of this passage, "controversial" is closest in meaning to "open to debate." Choices (A), (C), and (D) are not accepted definitions of the word.

33. **(B)** ". . . great storms on the surface of the sun hurl streams of solar particles into the atmosphere." *Storms* refer to disturbances of wind. Choice (A) contradicts the fact that great storms have been identified as the cause of particles being hurled into space. In Choice (C), there are storms, not rivers on the surface of the sun. Choice (D) refers to what happens as a result of the particles being hurled into space.

34. **(D)** In the context of this passage, "articles" refers to "small pieces of matter." Choices (A), (B), and (C) are not accepted definitions of the word.

35. **(A)** ". . . streams of solar particles [are hurled] into the atmosphere." Because of the reference to *particles*, it must be concluded that the matter is very small. Choices (B), (C), and (D) are not mentioned and may not be concluded from information in the passage.

36. **(C)** ". . . the controversial sunspot theory." Because the theory is controversial, it must be concluded that it is subject to disagreement. Choice (B) contradicts the fact that the

theory is controversial. Choices (A) and (D) are not mentioned and may not be concluded from information in the passage.

37. **(B)** "About five percent of the spots are large enough so that they [the spots] can be seen without instruments; consequently, observations of sunspots have been recorded for several thousand years." Choices (A), (C), and (D) would change the meaning of the sentence.

38. **(A)** In the context of this passage, "consequently" could best be replaced by "as a result." Choices (B), (C), and (D) are not accepted definitions of the word.

39. **(B)** "Sunspots . . . tend to occur in pairs." Choices (A) and (C) refer to possibilities for arrangements, but not to the configuration in which sunspots usually occur. Choice (D) is not mentioned in the range of numbers for sunspots, from one to more than one hundred. The number *one thousand* refers to the number of years sunspots have been recorded, not to the number in a configuration.

40. **(B)** ". . . several models attempt to relate the phenomenon [of sunspots] to magnetic fields along the lines of longitude from the north and south poles of the sun." Choice (A) is incorrect because the magnetic fields are on the sun, not the earth. Choice (C) is incorrect because the storms are on the sun, not on the earth. Choice (D) contradicts the fact that several models attempt to relate sunspots to magnetic fields.

41. **(A)** The other choices are secondary ideas that are used to develop the main idea, "Technological Advances in Oceanography." Choices (B), (C), and (D) are important to the discussion, and provide details that support the main idea.

42. **(C)** In the context of this passage, "sluggish" is closest in meaning to "slow moving." Choices (A), (B), and (D) are not accepted definitions of the word.

43. **(A)** "Because of undersea pressure that affected their speech organs, communication among divers was difficult or impossible." Choices (B), (C), and (D) are not mentioned and may not be concluded from information in the passage.

44. **(A)** "Direct observations of the ocean floor are made not only by divers but also by deep-diving submarines." Choices (B), (C), and (D) contradict the fact that observations are made by deep-diving submarines as well as by divers.

45. **(D)** "Direct observations of the ocean floor are made. . .by deep-diving submarines." Choice (A) contradicts the fact that some of the vehicles are manned. Choice (B) refers to the divers, not to the undersea vehicles. Choice (C) contradicts the fact that undersea vehicles have overcome some of the limitations of divers.

46. **(A)** In the context of this passage, "cruise" could best be replaced by "travel at a constant speed." Choices (B), (C), and (D) are not accepted definitions of the word.

47. **(D)** "Radio-equipped buoys can be operated by remote control in order to transmit information back to the land-based laboratories." Choices (A), (B), and (C) are not mentioned and may not be concluded from information in the passage.

48. **(C)** Choice (A) is mentioned in lines 14–15. Choice (B) is mentioned in lines 13–14. Choice (D) is mentioned in line 13. Choice (C) refers to computers, not to satellites.

49. **(B)** "Recently, many oceanographers have been relying more on satellites and computers than on research ships or even submarine vehicles because the satellites and computers can supply a greater range of information more quickly and more efficiently." Choices (A), (C), and (D) would change the meaning of the sentence.

50. **(B)** "Some of mankind's most serious problems, especially in the areas of energy and food, may be solved by the results of these undersea observations." Data about weather are recorded by buoys, but weather control referred to in Choice (A) is not mentioned as a problem to be resolved. Choices (C) and (D) may be true, but they are not mentioned and may not be concluded from information in the passage.

Model Test 2—Short Form

Section 1: Listening Comprehension

1. **(D)** *To flatter* means to look better. Choice (C) refers to what the man, not the woman, thinks of the picture. The opinions in Choices (A) and (B) are not mentioned and may not be concluded from information in the conversation.

2. **(B)** *You don't mean it* is an idiomatic expression that means the speaker is surprised. Choice (C) contradicts the fact that the man is surprised by the large turn out. Choices (A) and (D) are not mentioned and may not be concluded from information in the conversation.

3. **(D)** Since the woman points out the sign on the door, she implies that the man should look at it. Choices (A), (B), and (C) are not mentioned and may not be concluded from information in the conversation.

4. **(B)** From the reference to the *Miami flight*, it must be concluded that they are talking about a flight. The word *minutes* in Choice (A) refers to the schedule of the flight, not to the time. The city in Choice (D) refers to the destination of the flight, not to the topic of conversation. Choice (C) is not mentioned and may not be concluded from information in the conversation.

5. **(D)** Since the woman expressed interest in and enthusiasm for the opportunity to do a project for extra credit, it must be concluded that she intends to do one. Choice (A) contradicts the fact that the woman is already taking a class from Professor Wilson. Choice (C) contradicts the fact that the reference to "extra" is to extra credit, not to an extra class. Choice (B) is not mentioned and may not be concluded from information in the conversation.

6. **(B)** Listen carefully for the distinction between the words *angry* and *hungry*. Because the woman says that Paul would tell them if he were angry, it must be concluded that Paul would tell them if there were a problem. In choices (A) and (C), the word *angry* is confused with the word *hungry*. Choice (B) refers to what the woman, not the man, thinks about Paul.

7. **(B)** Because Miss Brown will use paper, paints, and brushes at the high school, it must be concluded that she will teach art. Choice (A) is improbable because she bought art supplies, including paints and brushes. Choice (D) contradicts the fact that Miss Brown will use her purchases at the high school. Choice (C) is not mentioned and may not be concluded from information in the conversation.

8. **(B)** From the references to *cashing a check* and having an *account*, it must be concluded that the conversation took place at a bank. It is not customary to cash a check at the post office in Choice (A). A check may be cashed for purchases at an airport or a drugstore, but it is not probable that one would have an account at the places referred to in Choices (C) and (D).

9. **(D)** From the references to being *dizzy* and having *chest pain*, it must be concluded that the woman is ill. Choice (A) misinterprets the word *lately* which means *recently*. Choices (B) and (C) are not mentioned and may not be concluded from information in the conversation.

10. **(B)** Since the woman says that her briefcase is smaller and it doesn't have a lock, it must be concluded that the man's briefcase is larger with a lock. Choice (A) contradicts the fact that his briefcase is almost, not exactly, like that of the woman. Choice (C) contradicts the fact that his briefcase is larger. Choice (D) contradicts the fact that the speakers are comparing their briefcases.

11. **(C)** To *drop by* is an idiomatic expression that means to visit. Choices (A) and (D) contradict the fact that Mr. Smith will visit Mr. Jacobs. Choice (B) contradicts the fact that the speakers are confirming the appointment.

12. **(B)** Since the woman gives the man directions, he will probably take them. Choice (A) contradicts the fact that the man is asking for directions from a stranger. Choice (C) contradicts the fact that the woman has given him directions already. Choice (D) contradicts the fact that the woman says the directions are easy.

13. **(D)** Since the woman says that there were a couple of As, it must be concluded that several other students received A grades. Choice (B) contradicts the fact that she refers to other As, implying that she received one. Choices (A) and (C) are not mentioned and may not be concluded from information in the conversation.

14. **(A)** Since the man says that the clock is fast, it must be concluded that the woman still has time to finish. Choice (B) contradicts the fact that there is only a half hour left in the work day. Choice (D) contradicts the fact that the man knows the clock is fast. Choice (C) is not mentioned and may not be concluded from information in the conversation.

15. **(B)** *To not agree more* means to agree very much. Choices (A) and (D) misinterpret the phrase *couldn't agree more* as a negative. Choice (C) is not mentioned and may not be concluded from information in the conversation.

16. **(A)** The man says that he has to go to class. Choice (B) refers to what the woman, not the man, is going to do. Choices (C) and (D) are not mentioned and may not be concluded from information in the conversation.

17. **(C)** *Meaning to* is an idiomatic expression that means intention on the part of the speaker. To "get back with" someone means to return a call or otherwise communicate. Choice (B) contradicts the fact that a message was left on the machine. Choice (D) contradicts the fact that the man acknowledges the message. Choice (A) is not mentioned and may not be concluded from information in the conversation.

18. **(A)** To be *out* is an idiomatic expression that means to be absent. Choices (B), (C), and (D) are not paraphrases of the expression, and may not be concluded from information in the conversation.

19. **(C)** *Could not feel better* is an idiomatic expression that means to feel very good. Choice (D) contradicts the fact that the interview has already taken place. Choices (A) and (B) are not mentioned and may not be concluded from information in the conversation.

20. **(B)** "Check with the secretary before going in. . ." Choice (A) contradicts the fact that the woman has already given him directions to the Math Department. Choice (C) contradicts the fact that the woman tells him to check with the secretary first. Choice (D) is not mentioned and may not be concluded from information in the conversation.

21. **(D)** "Why don't you just get a cake. . ." Choice (A) contradicts the fact that the woman tells him to get a cake at the bakery. Choice (B) refers to the man's idea, not to the woman's suggestion. Choice (C) is not mentioned and may not be concluded from information in the conversation.

22. **(D)** Since Tom is often absent, and there is doubt that he will be present for the final exam, it must be concluded that Tom is not very responsible. Choices (A), (B), and (C) are not mentioned and may not be concluded from information in the conversation.

23. **(D)** *Are we still on* is an idiomatic expression that is used to confirm a date. Choice (C) refers to the woman's feelings, not to the man's feelings. Choices (A) and (B) are not mentioned and may not be concluded from information in the conversation.

24. **(B)** Since the woman mentions the fact that the apartment is expensive, it must be concluded that she is concerned about the rent. Choice (A) contradicts the fact that she thinks the apartment is beautiful. Choices (C) and (D) are not mentioned and may not be concluded from information in the conversation.

25. **(C)** Since the woman must have the course to graduate and Dr. Collin's section is closed, she will probably enroll in the section marked "staff." Choice (A) contradicts the fact that Dr. Collin's section is closed. Choice (B) contradicts the fact that the woman is distressed because she is planning to graduate soon. Choice (D) contradicts the fact that she needs the course to graduate and is more interested in the course than in the instructor.

26. **(D)** "This is just preboarding of children and people who need assistance." Choice (A) contradicts the fact that it is preboarding, not the final call. Choice (B) contradicts the fact that it is preboarding for the San Antonio flight. Choice (C) is not mentioned and may not be concluded from information in the conversation.

27. **(A)** Since the woman says that it takes six

weeks to receive the score, she implies that the man should wait for the results to be mailed. Choice (B) refers to the man's plan, not to the woman's suggestion. Choice (C) contradicts the fact that the man has already taken the test and is waiting for the score. Choice (D) contradicts the fact that the woman tells him not to worry.

28. **(C)** *Hold on* is an idiomatic expression that means the speaker wants the other person to wait. Choice (B) contradicts the fact that he can use the coupon to purchase the other size. Choice (D) contradicts the fact that the purchase is measured in ounces, not in clothing sizes. Choice (A) is not mentioned and may not be concluded from information in the conversation.

29. **(D)** Since the man says that he is ready to go, he will probably leave. Choices (A) and (B) contradict the fact that he has just had his car washed. Choice (C) contradicts the fact that the woman advises him not to tip.

30. **(B)** To *make the most of* something is an idiomatic expression that means to take advantage of an opportunity. Choices (A), (C), and (D) are not paraphrases of the expression, and may not be concluded from information in the conversation.

31. **(B)** ". . . I was wondering whether you could keep an eye on the house?" Choice (C) refers to the fact that the man wants to drop the keys off, not to a date. Choice (D) refers to the reason that the man needs a favor, not to the purpose of his call. Choice (A) is not mentioned and may not be concluded from information in the conversation.

32. **(A)** "I thought that since you are just down the street. . ." Choice (D) contradicts the fact that she gets home from work about six. Choices (B) and (C) are not mentioned and may not be concluded from information in the conversation.

33. **(C)** "Do you want me to water them, [the plants] too?" Choices (A), (B), and (D) refer to chores that the man asked the woman to do, not to the favor that Melissa offers to do.

34 **(B)** "I'll bring the keys over tonight. . ." Choice (A) refers to the woman, not to the man. Choice (C) contradicts the fact that he is leaving the day after tomorrow. Choice (D) is not mentioned and may not be concluded from information in the conversation.

35. **(B)** "It [the video] was about stress." Choices (A), (C), and (D) are secondary themes used to develop the main theme of the video.

36. **(C)** "They said that women usually don't get the same level of care that men do. . ." Choice (D) contradicts the fact that the heart attacks suffered by women are likely to be more serious. Choices (A) and (B) are not mentioned and may not be concluded from information in the conversation.

37. **(B)** "Really it was [good]." Choice (A) contradicts the fact that he explains the video to the woman. Choice (C) contradicts the fact that he encourages the woman to view it. Choice (D) contradicts the fact that he was surprised by the report on the number of women who have heart attacks.

38. **(B)** "It's on reserve in the library. . ." Choice (A) refers to the fact that the man and woman have already discussed the video tape, not to what the woman will do. Choice (C) contradicts the fact that tapes on reserve cannot be checked out. Choice (D) refers to what the woman will do after she sees the video.

39. **(D)** Elizabeth Barrett Browning is the main topic of this lecture. Choices (A), (B), and (C) are secondary topics that are used to develop the main topic of the lecture.

40. **(C)** "In part because the sovereign was a woman, there was great support for a movement to break with the tradition of a male Poet Laureate." Choice (A) contradicts the fact that Elizabeth Barrett was not married at the time that she was considered for the title of Poet Laureate. Choice (B) contradicts the fact that *Sonnets from the Portuguese* was not published at the time that she was considered for the title. Choice (D) is not mentioned and may not be concluded from information in the talk.

41. **(B)** ". . . she married Robert Browning, himself a gifted poet, and they fled to Florence, Italy." The place in Choice (C) refers to the title of one of Elizabeth's most famous works, *Sonnets from the Portuguese*, not to a place where she lived. The place in Choice (D) refers to the country where she lived before, not after her marriage. Choice (A) is not mentioned and may not be concluded from information in the talk.

42. **(D)** "*Aurora Leigh*, her longest work, appeared in 1856, only five years before her

death in 1861." Choice (A) refers to the date when Elizabeth Barrett was suggested to replace the Poet Laureate, not to the date of her death. Choice (B) refers to the date when her son was born, one year before she published her collected works in 1850. Choice (C) refers to the date when *Aurora Leigh* was published, five years before her death.

43. **(A)** The driver's talk includes information about schedules, regulations, and facilities. Choices (B) and (C) are secondary themes used to support the main purpose of the talk. Choice (D) is not mentioned and may not be concluded from information in the talk.

44. **(C)** ". . . with changes in Saint Louis for Kansas City and points west." Choice (A) refers to a rest stop on the way to Saint Louis, not to the place where passengers change buses to go to Kansas City. Choice (B) refers to a dinner stop on the way to Saint Louis. Choice (D) refers to the final destination of the bus, after it has already passed through Saint Louis.

45. **(A)** "That number [of the coach] is 4-1-1-8." Choices (B), (C), and (D) misinterpret and reverse the numbers.

46. **(B)** "Relax and enjoy your trip . . . ." Because the driver has finished his announcements and invited the passengers to relax and enjoy the trip, it must be concluded that he will start the bus and begin the trip. Choices (A), (C), and (D) may occur later during the trip, not right after the announcements.

47. **(B)** The contributions of biology to medicine are the main topic of this lecture. Choices (A), (C), and (D) are secondary topics that are used to develop the main topic of the lecture.

48. **(C)** "Hippocrates . . . began . . . to apply scientific method to the problems of diagnosis and the treatment of diseases. . . . he kept careful records of symptoms and treatments." Choice (A) refers to the work of Aristotle, not Hippocrates. Choice (B) refers to the work of Sir Joseph Lister. Choice (D) refers to a theory that Hippocrates discarded in favor of the scientific method, not to his work.

49. **(B)** "Because of his great contribution to the field, Aristotle has been called the father of biology." Choice (A) refers to the father of modern medicine, not to the father of biol-

ogy. Choice (C) refers to the author of *Materia Medica*. Choice (D) refers to the physician who established the science of immunization.

50. **(C)** ". . . the English physician and anatomist William Harvey discovered a mechanism for the circulation of the blood in the body." Choice (A) refers to a contribution by Louis Pasteur, not by William Harvey. Choice (B) refers to a contribution by Edward Jenner. Choice (D) refers to a reference book that was a contribution by Dioscorides.

Section 2: Structure and Written Expression

1. **(A)** In some dependent clauses, the clause marker is the subject of the dependent clause. *Which* refers to *the soybeans*, and is the subject of the verb *can be used*. Choices (B) and (D) do not have clause markers. Choice (C) is a clause marker that refers to a person, not to *soybeans*. (Refer to Patterns, Problem 138, page 217.)

2. **(A)** Only Choice (A) may be used with a count noun like *species* and a number. Choices (C) and (D) may be used with non-count nouns. Choice (B) may be used with count nouns without a number. "As many species of finch have been identified" would also be correct. (Refer to Patterns, Problem 95, page 164.)

3. **(C)** When the degree of one quality, *the price*, is dependent upon the degree of another quality, *the demand*, two comparatives are required, each of which must be preceded by *the*. Choice (A) is a comparative, but it is not preceded by *the*. Choices (B) and (D) are not accepted comparative forms. (Refer to Patterns, Problem 100, page 169.)

4. **(C)** *So* is used with an adjective to express cause. Choice (A) may be used before a noun, not before an adjective such as *big*. Choices (B) and (D) may not be used to express cause before a clause of result such as *that there are four time zones*. "The United States is very big" would be correct without the clause of result. (Refer to Patterns, Problem 81, page 147.)

5. **(A)** Ideas in a series should be expressed by parallel structures. Only Choice (A) has three parallel *-ing* forms. Choices (B), (C),

and (D) are not parallel. (Refer to Style, Problem 17, page 240.)

6. **(B)** *Would rather* is used with a verb word to express the preference of a subject for himself. *Would rather* is used with a past form to express the preference of a subject for another person. In Choice (A), a past form, not a verb word, should be used to refer to *you*. Choice (C) is a present, not a past form. Choice (D) is incomplete because it does not include a verb word after the past auxiliary. "Most agents would rather you did something about it" would also be correct. (Refer to Patterns, Problem 13, page 56.)

7. **(A)** An introductory verbal phrase should immediately precede the noun that it modifies. Only Choice (A) provides a noun that could be logically modified by the introductory verbal phrase *upon hatching. Swimming, the knowledge,* and *how to swim* could not logically *hatch* as would be implied by Choices (B), (C), and (D). (Refer to Style, Problem 15, page 237.)

8. **(B)** Comparative forms are usually followed by *than. Highest* in Choices (A) and (C) may be used to compare more than two decks. Choice (D) correctly compares *this deck* with *any other one,* but *that,* not *than,* follows the comparative. (Refer to Patterns, Problem 96, page 165.)

9. **(A)** An adjective is used before *enough* to express sufficiency. In Choice (B), *as* is unnecessary and incorrect. In Choice (C), the adjective is used after, not before *enough.* In Choice (D), the adjective is used after, not before *enough,* and the word *as* is unnecessary and incorrect. (Refer to Patterns, Problem 74, page 138.)

10. **(C)** *Calcium* is the subject of the verb *is.* Choice (A) may be used with the word *that.* Choice (B) may be used as a subject clause preceding a main verb. Choice (D) may be used preceding a subject and verb. "It is calcium *that* is necessary for the development of strong bones and teeth." "That calcium is necessary for the development of strong bones and teeth *is* known," and "Although calcium is necessary for strong bones and teeth, *other minerals are* also important" would also be correct. (Refer to Style, Problem 19, page 243.)

11. **(A)** For scientific results, a present form in the condition requires a present or future form in the result. Only Choice (C) introduces a conditional. (Refer to Patterns, Problem 21, page 67.)

12. **(C)** A negative phrase introduces inverted order. *Only after* requires an auxiliary verb, subject, and main verb. In Choices (A) and (D) the subject precedes the auxiliary. In Choice (B) there is no subject. (Refer to Patterns, Problem 129, page 206.)

13. **(B)** A negative phrase introduces inverted order. *Not until* requires an auxiliary verb, subject, and main verb. In Choice (A) there is no auxiliary. In Choices (C) and (D), there is no subject and no auxiliary. (Refer to Patterns, Problem 129, page 206.)

14. **(B)** The verb *to fail* requires an infinitive in the complement. Choice (A) is an *-ing* form, not an infinitive. Choice (C) is a complex infinitive, but it may not be used with the present tense verb *fails.* Choice (D) is a verb word. (Refer to Patterns, Problem 2, page 42.)

15. **(B)** The verb phrase *to approve of* requires an *-ing* form in the complement. *-Ing* forms are modified by possessive pronouns. Choices (A) and (D) are infinitives, not *-ing* forms. Choice (C) is an *-ing* form, but it is modified by a subject, not a possessive pronoun. (Refer to Patterns, Problem 4, page 45.)

16. **(D)** *There* introduces inverted order, but there must still be agreement between subject and verb. *Was* should be *were* to agree with the plural subject *several kinds.* (Refer to Style, Problem 8, page 229.)

17. **(C)** The verb *had* establishes a point of view in the past. *Serves* should be *served* in order to maintain the point of view. (Refer to Style, Problem 1, page 221.)

18. **(C)** Because *required courses* is a plural count noun, *much* should be *many. Much* is used with noncount nouns. *Many* is used with count nouns. (Refer to Patterns, Problem 68, page 130.)

19. **(D)** There must be agreement between subject and verb. *Produce* should be *produces* to agree with the singular subject *a thunderhead.* (Refer to Style, Problem 7, page 228.)

20. **(B)** *The same like* is a combination of *the same as* and *like. Like* should be *as* in the

phrase with *the same*. (Refer to Patterns, Problem 86, page 153.)

21. **(A)** *Despite of* is a combination of *despite* and *in spite of*. Either *despite* or *in spite of* should be used. (Refer to Patterns, Problem 110, page 182.)

22. **(A)** There must be agreement between subject and verb. *Has* should be *have* to agree with the plural subject *so many people*. (Refer to Style, Problem 10, page 231.)

23. **(A)** *Behave* should be *behavior*. *Behave* is a verb. *Behavior* is a noun. (Refer to Style, Problem 30, page 257.)

24. **(B)** There must be agreement between subject and verb. *Are* should be *is* to agree with the singular subject *one*. (Refer to Style, Problem 9, page 230.)

25. **(B)** *Whom* should be *who* because it is the subject of the verb *is*. *Whom* functions as a complement. *Who* functions as a subject. (Refer to Patterns, Problem 49, page 103.)

26. **(B)** *So* is commonly used as a purpose connector in spoken English, but *so that* should be used in written English. (Refer to Patterns, Problem 122, page 197.)

27. **(C)** The two words in an infinitive should not be divided by an adverb of manner. *Clearly* should be placed at the end of the sentence. (Refer to Patterns, Problem 126, page 202.)

28. **(D)** A verb word must be used in a clause after the verb *to insist*. *Will not smoke* should be *not smoke*. (Refer to Patterns, Problem 27, page 76.)

29. **(C)** In order to refer to a city which has been *occupying a place, lying* should be used. *To lay* means to put in a place. *To lie* means to occupy a place. (Refer to Style, Problem 23, page 248.)

30. **(C)** *Invent* should be *invention*. *Invent* is a verb. *Invention* is a noun. (Refer to Style, Problem 30, page 257.)

31. **(C)** *Larger* should be *largest*. Because there are more than two masses of nerve tissue in the human body, a superlative form must be used. (Refer to Patterns, Problem 97, page 166.)

32. **(C)** Ideas in a series should be expressed by parallel structures. *Writing* should be *to write* to provide for parallelism with the infinitives *to understand* and *to read*. (Refer to Style, Problem 17, page 240.)

33. **(A)** *Like* is a preposition. *Alike* should be *like*. (Refer to Patterns, Problem 88, page 156.)

34. **(C)** *Capable of* is a prepositional idiom. *To perform* should be *of performing*. (Refer to Style, Problem 29, page 255.)

35. **(A)** Repetition of the subject by subject pronoun is redundant. *It* should be deleted. (Refer to Style, Problem 21, page 245.)

36. **(B)** A form of BE is used with the participle in passive sentences. *Said* should be *is said*. (Refer to Patterns, Problem 41, page 92.)

37. **(C)** *But* should be *but also*, which is used in correlation with the inclusive *not only*. (Refer to Patterns, Problem 118, page 192.)

38. **(B)** *Commonly* should be *common*. *Commonly* is an adverb. *Common* is an adjective. (Refer to Style, Problem 30, page 257.)

39. **(D)** Ideas in a series should be expressed by parallel structures. *Swimming* should be *swim* to provide for parallelism with the verb words *walk*, *watch*, and *fish*. (Refer to Style, Problem 17, page 240.)

40. **(D)** There must be agreement between pronoun and antecedent. *Its* should be *their* to agree with the plural antecedent *books*. (Refer to Style, Problem 11, page 232.)

Section 3: Reading Comprehension

1. **(C)** "Communication" is the best title because it states the main idea of the passage. The other choices are all examples of communication that provide details in support of the main idea.

2. **(D)** "Whereas speech is the most advanced form of communication. . . ." Choice (A) contradicts the fact that there are many ways to communicate without speech including signals, signs, symbols, and gestures. Choice (B) is incorrect because the advances are dependent upon speech; speech is not dependent upon the advances. Choice (C) is not mentioned and may not be concluded from information in the passage.

3. **(C)** "The basic function of a signal is to impinge upon the environment in such a way that it attracts attention. . . ." Choices (A) and (D) refer to symbols, not signals. Choice (B) refers to communication based on speech.

4. **(A)** In the context of this passage, "impinge

on" is closest in meaning to "intrude." Choices (B), (C), and (D) are not accepted definitions of the word.

5. **(B)** "The basic function of a signal is to impinge upon the environment in such a way that it [the signal] attracts attention, as, for example, the dots and dashes of a telegraph circuit." Choices (A), (C), and (D) would change the meaning of the sentence.

6. **(D)** In the context of this passage, "potential" could best be replaced by "possibility." Choices (A), (B), and (C) are not accepted definitions of the word.

7. **(B)** In the context of this passage, "intricate" could best be replaced by "complicated." Choices (A), (C), and (D) are not accepted definitions of the word.

8. **(C)** ". . . applauding in a theater provides performers with an auditory symbol." A telegraph circuit was cited as an example of Choice (A). A stop sign and a barber pole were cited as examples of Choice (B). Waving and handshaking were cited as examples of Choice (D).

9. **(B)** ". . . means of communication intended to be used for long distances and extended periods are based upon speech. Radio, television, and telephone are only a few." Choices (A), (C), and (D) are not mentioned and may not be concluded from information in the passage.

10. **(A)** "There are many ways of communicating without using speech. Signals, signs, symbols, and gestures may be found in every known culture." Choice (B) contradicts the fact that symbols are more difficult to describe than either signals or signs. Choice (C) contradicts the fact that signals, signs, symbols, and gestures may be found in every known culture. Choice (D) contradicts the fact that gestures such as waving and handshaking also communicate certain cultural messages.

11. **(A)** The passage is a statement of policies for making application to the Graduate School. In Choice (B), there is a policy for students with senior status who wish to take graduate courses, but there is no information how to obtain senior status. Choices (C) and (D) are not mentioned and may not be concluded from information in the passage.

12. **(A)** A university catalog provides information about admissions policies. It is not cus-

tomary to find this kind of information in the places referred to in Choices (B), (C), and (D).

13. **(D)** "Application for admission to the Graduate School at this university must be made on forms provided by the Director of Admissions." Choice (A) refers to the official whose recommendation is necessary for an undergraduate to register for graduate work, not to the official from whom a student must secure application forms for admission. Choice (B) refers to the official to whom transcripts and degrees must be sent and whose approval is necessary for an undergraduate to register for graduate work. Choice (C) refers to the place from which transcripts and degrees, not application forms, should be requested.

14. **(D)** "Both the application and the transcripts must be on file at least one month prior to the registration date." Choices (A), (B), and (C) are not mentioned and may not be concluded from information in the passage.

15. **(C)** "Both the application and the transcripts must be on file at least one month prior to the registration date, and must be accompanied by a nonrefundable ten-dollar check or money order. . ." Choices (A), (B), and (D) cannot be modified by the word "nonrefundable."

16. **(D)** In the context of this passage, "in advance of" is closest in meaning to "prior to." Choices (A), (B), and (C) are not accepted definitions of the phrase.

17. **(D)** Choice (A) is mentioned in lines 12–14. Choice (B) is mentioned in lines 13–14. Choice (C) is mentioned in lines 14–15. Choice (D) is not mentioned and may not be concluded from information in the passage.

18. **(B)** In the context of this passage, "status" could best be replaced by "classification." Choices (A), (C), and (D) are not accepted definitions of the word.

19. **(B)** "Students who have already been admitted to the Graduate School but were not enrolled during the previous semester should reapply for admission . . . ." Choice (A) contradicts the fact that students who were not enrolled during the previous semester must reapply for admission. Choice (C) contradicts the fact that students who were enrolled during the previous semester do not

need to reapply. Choice (D) refers to the procedure for undergraduate admission to graduate work, not to the procedure for students who have already been admitted to the Graduate School.

20. **(C)** "An undergraduate student . . . may register for graduate work with the recommendation of the chairperson of the department and the approval of the Dean of the Graduate School." Choice (A) contradicts the fact that an undergraduate student may register for graduate work with the recommendation of the department chairperson and the approval of the Dean of the Graduate School. Choice (D) contradicts the fact that certain requirements are set for undergraduate students who wish to register for graduate work, including senior status and completion of all but ten hours of course work required for graduation. Choice (B) is not mentioned and may not be concluded from information in the passage.

21. **(D)** Choices (A), (B), and (C) are important to the discussion, and provide details that support the primary topic, "the content, form, and effects of fertilizer."

22. **(D)** In the context of this passage, "essential" could best be replaced by "required." Choices (A), (B), and (C) are not accepted definitions of the word.

23. **(D)** ". . . a formula consisting of three numbers, . . . which designate the percentage content of nitrogen, phosphoric acid, and potash, in the order stated." Choices (A), (B), and (C) may not be concluded from information in the formula 3-6-4 (3 percent nitrogen, 6 percent phosphoric acid, and 4 percent potash).

24. **(D)** Since the last number in the formula represents the percentage content of potash, and since the last number is the smallest, it must be concluded that potash has the smallest percentage content. Choice (A) refers to the number 4 in the formula. Choices (B) and (C) are the substances found in phosphoric acid which refers to the number 8 in the formula.

25. **(B)** Since the content of nitrogen is represented by the first number in the formula, it must be concluded that there is 5 percent nitrogen in the fertilizer. The number in Choice (A) refers to the quantity of numbers in the formula. The percentage in Choice (C) refers to potash. The percentage in Choice (D) refers to phosphoric acid.

26. **(B)** In the context of this passage, "designate" could best be replaced by "specify." Choices (A), (C), and (D) are not accepted definitions of the word.

27. **(C)** "Recently, liquids have shown an increase in popularity . . . ." Choice (A) refers to a form of fertilizers that used to be used, but was found to be less convenient, not to a form that is more popular than ever. Choices (B) and (D) contradict the fact that solids in the shape of chemical granules are easy to store and apply.

28. **(A)** "Formerly, powders were also used, but these [powders] were found to be less convenient than either solids or liquids." Choices (B), (C), and (D) would change the meaning of the sentence.

29. **(C)** In the context of this passage, "convenient" is closest in meaning to "easy to use." Choices (A), (B), and (D) are not accepted definitions of the word.

30. **(C)** "Too much fertilizer on grass can cause digestive disorders in cattle and in infants . . . ." Choice (A) refers to the fact that local research provides recommendations for the safe and appropriate use of fertilizer, not to what happens when too much is used. Choice (B) contradicts the fact that too much fertilizer accelerates the growth of algae. Choice (D) refers to the fact that there are no harmful effects when the fertilizer is used according to recommendations, not to the results when too much is used. It contradicts the fact that more fertilizer than necessary can damage the crop.

31. **(A)** The other choices are secondary ideas that are used to develop the main idea, "the evolution of the horse." Choices (B), (C), and (D) are significant steps in the evolution.

32. **(D)** Choice (A) is mentioned in lines 5–6. Choice (B) is mentioned in lines 4–5. Choice (C) is mentioned in lines 1–3. The Miocene Age is the earliest historical period mentioned in the passage.

33. **(B)** In the context of this passage, "instigated" could best be replaced by "caused." Choices (A), (C), and (D) are not accepted definitions of the word.

34. **(A)** Because of the reference to *climatic*

conditions and *grasslands,* it must be concluded that the hipparions migrated to Europe to feed in developing grasslands. Choice (B) contradicts the fact that information about the evolution of the horse has been documented by fossil finds. Choice (C) contradicts the fact that the European colonists brought horses to North America where the species had become extinct. Choice (D) contradicts the fact that the evolution of the horse has been recorded from its beginnings through all of its evolutionary stages.

35. **(A)** "... a horse crossed ... from Alaska into the grasslands of Europe." Because of the reference to *grasslands,* it must be concluded that the hipparions migrated to Europe to feed in developing grasslands. Choice (B) contradicts the fact that the European colonists brought horses to North America where the species had become extinct. Choice (D) contradicts the fact that the evolution of the horse has been recorded from its beginnings through all of its evolutionary stages.

36. **(C)** "... smaller than the hipparion, the anchitheres was completely replaced by it." Choice (A) refers to the very early form of the horse, not to the hipparion. Choice (B) contradicts the fact that the hipparion was a more highly evolved form than the anchitheres. Choice (D) contradicts the fact that the hipparion was about the size of a small pony.

37. **(B)** "Less developed and smaller than the hipparion, the anchitheres was completely replaced by it [the hipparion."] Choices (A), (C), and (D) would change the meaning of the sentence.

38. **(C)** In the context of this passage, "extinct" is closest in meaning to "nonexistent." Choices (A), (B), and (D) are not accepted definitions of the word.

39. **(B)** "... both the anchitheres and the hipparion had become extinct in North America, where they had originated." Choices (A) and (C) refer to the hipparions, but not to the anchitheres. Choice (D) refers only to the very early evolutionary form of the horse, not to the hipparion and the anchitheres, which were later forms.

40. **(A)** "At the beginning of the Pliocene Age, a horse ... crossed ... into the grasslands of Europe. The horse was the hipparion. ... The hipparion encountered ... the anchitheres, which had previously invaded Europe ... probably during the Miocene Period." Because the anchitheres invaded Europe during the Miocene and was already there when the hipparion arrived in the Pliocene, it must be concluded that the Miocene Period was prior to the Pliocene Period. By the Pleistocene referred to in Choices (B) and (C), the anchitheres and the hipparion had become extinct. Therefore, the Pleistocene Period must have been after both the Miocene and the Pliocene.

41. **(B)** Choice (B) is the author's main purpose because the story refers to the beard throughout. It is not clear whether Grace actually took the photograph as stated in Choice (A). Choices (C) and (D) are not mentioned and may not be concluded from information in the passage.

42. **(A)** In the context of this passage, "fascinated" could best be replaced by "interested." Choices (B), (C), and (D) are not accepted definitions of the word.

43. **(B)** In the context of this passage, "flickering" is closest in meaning to "burning unsteadily." Choices (A), (C), and (D) are not accepted definitions of the word.

44. **(D)** "The man in the photograph was unsmiling, but his eyes were kind." Choice (A) contradicts the fact that the man was unsmiling. Choice (B) contradicts the fact that the little girl suggested his growing a beard after she had seen the photograph. Choice (C) contradicts the fact that the man had hollow cheeks.

45. **(B)** "I was looking at the photograph, as I always did before I went to sleep." Choices (A), (C), and (D) are not mentioned as activities that the little girl did every night. She planned her letter before she went to sleep, but she did not write it at that time.

46. **(B)** "That night I could not sleep, thinking about the letter that I would write." Choices (A), (C), and (D) are not mentioned and may not be concluded from information in the passage.

47. **(C)** "Then I would explain to him the real purpose of my letter. I would ... suggest that he grow whiskers." Choice (B) is incorrect because the little girl suggested that his daughter write to her, but it was not the real purpose of her letter. In Choice (D), the man

did visit the little girl, but she had not asked him to do so in her letter. Choice (A) is not mentioned and may not be concluded from information in the passage.

48. **(B)** "I have no speech to make and no time to make it [a speech] in." Choices (A), (C), and (D) would change the meaning of the sentence.

49. **(B)** " 'Ladies and Gentlemen,' he said, 'I have no speech to make.' " In Choice (A), from the salutation, it must be concluded that there was more than one person at the train station. Choice (C) contradicts the fact that Lincoln did not make a speech. Choice (D) is incorrect because he took the little girl's advice, and it must be concluded that he was not offended by her letter. The president called her his "little friend."

50. **(C)** A surprise ending is a literary device that an author may use to build the interest and curiosity of the reader. Choices (A), (B), and (D) do not refer to literary devices.

Model Test 3—Short Form

Section 1: Listening Comprehension

1. **(A)** Since the woman agrees with the man, it must be concluded that she will not go home for spring vacation. Choice (C) contradicts the fact that she will be graduating in May. Choices (B) and (D) are not mentioned and may not be concluded from information in the conversation.

2. **(B)** From the reference to serving *coffee* with *lunch*, it must be concluded that the conversation took place at a restaurant. Coffee may be bought at a grocery store, but it is not customary to serve lunch at any of the places referred to in Choices (A), (C), and (D).

3. **(C)** From the reference to *the assignment for Monday*, it must be concluded that the speakers are talking about homework. Choices (A), (B), and (D) are all mentioned in the conversation in reference to the assignment.

4. **(B)** Because of the woman's suggestion that the man lock the door at night and because the man assures her that no one will break in, it must be concluded that the woman thinks someone will enter. Choices (A), (C), and (D) are not mentioned and may not be concluded from information in the conversation.

5. **(C)** Since the man asks about her brother's birthday gift, and the woman has not purchased one yet, it must be concluded that she needs a gift for her brother. Choice (A) contradicts the fact that she has been thinking about what to get him for his birthday. Choice (D) contradicts the fact that her brother has not received the gift yet. Choice (B) is not mentioned and may not be concluded from information in the conversation.

6. **(C)** *Cramming* is an idiomatic expression that means studying a lot, especially just before a test. Choices (A), (B), and (D) contradict the fact that the man is confident about being ready for the test.

7. **(D)** Since the woman refers to Mr. Adams as her husband, it must be concluded that she is Mrs. Adams. Choice (A) refers to Mr. Miller, not to the woman. Choice (C) contradicts the fact that her husband is at work. Choice (B) is not mentioned and may not be concluded from information in the conversation.

8. **(D)** Because *don't be too sure* means that the speaker is skeptical, it must be concluded that the man doubts what the woman says. He believes that Jack will quit his job. Choices (B) and (C) refer to what the woman, not the man, believes. Jack is trying to sell his house, but Choice (A) is not mentioned and may not be concluded from information in the conversation.

9. **(A)** Since the man says that he needs a book for an English course, it must be concluded that he will buy the textbook. Choice (C) contradicts the fact that he is already in the bookstore. Choice (D) contradicts the fact that he needs a book for the course. Choice (B) is not mentioned and may not be concluded from information in the conversation.

10. **(D)** Since the woman argues that the other dress is more comfortable, it must be concluded that she will wear the more comfortable one. Choice (B) contradicts the fact that

she has a new dress. Choice (C) contradicts the fact that she prefers a dress that the man did not choose. Choice (A) is not mentioned and may not be concluded from information in the conversation.

11. **(A)** To *turn someone off* is an idiomatic expression that means the speaker does not like something or someone. Choice (D) contradicts the fact that the woman does not like the class. Choice (C) contradicts the fact that the woman thinks Professor Collins is a great person. Choice (B) is not mentioned and may not be concluded from information in the conversation.

12. **(D)** The woman said that she stayed home. Choices (A) and (B) refer to the place where the woman was planning to go, not to the place where she went. She had not been feeling well, but Choice (C) was not mentioned and may not be concluded from information in the conversation.

13. **(A)** To *not put off* is an idiomatic expression that means to stop postponing. Choices (B) and (C) contradict the fact that the woman has not made an appointment yet. Choice (D) is not mentioned and may not be concluded from information in the conversation.

14. **(C)** To be *used to something* is an idiomatic expression that means to be accustomed to something. Choices (A), (B), and (D) are not paraphrases of the expression, and may not be concluded from information in the conversation.

15. **(C)** To *get caught up* is an idiomatic expression that means to bring work or assignments up to date. Choice (B) contradicts the fact that the man says he knows what time it is. Choices (A) and (D) are not mentioned and may not be concluded from information in the conversation.

16. **(A)** *Meaning to* is an idiomatic expression that means to intend. To "have someone over" means to invite them to one's home. Choice (B) contradicts the fact that he wants to invite her to his home. Choices (C) and (D) are not mentioned and may not be concluded from information in the conversation.

17. **(D)** To *pass* is an idiomatic expression that means to lose a turn. Choices (A), (B), and (C) are not paraphrases of the expression, and may not be concluded from information in the conversation.

18. **(B)** To *look into something* is an idiomatic expression that means to investigate. Choice (A) refers to the woman's conclusion, not to the man's intention. Choices (C) and (D) are not mentioned and may not be concluded from information in the conversation.

19. **(B)** To *take care of something* is an idiomatic expression that means to be responsible for it. Choices (A), (C), and (D) are not paraphrases of the expression, and may not be concluded from information in the conversation.

20. **(A)** Since the man says that they should take the opposite direction from the announcer's recommended route, he implies that the announcer is often wrong. Choices (B), (C), and (D) are not mentioned and may not be concluded from information in the conversation.

21. **(A)** To *get mixed up* is an idiomatic expression that means to become confused. Choice (C) contradicts the fact that the man understands the lectures. Choices (B) and (D) are not mentioned and may not be concluded from information in the conversation.

22. **(B)** To *have it made* is an idiomatic expression that means to be very fortunate. Choices (C) and (D) contradict the fact that when asked, the woman responds that she knows Randy. Choice (A) is not mentioned and may not be concluded from information in the conversation.

23. **(A)** To *turn in* is an idiomatic expression that means to submit. "Ahead of time" means early. Choice (C) contradicts the fact that she wants to turn in the paper before it is due. Choice (D) contradicts the fact that she is ready to turn the paper in. Choice (B) is not mentioned and may not be concluded from information in the conversation.

24. **(C)** Since the woman reminds the man that he has never heard her sing, she implies that she is not a good singer. Choice (A) refers to the man's suggestion, not to the woman's preference. Choices (B) and (D) are not mentioned and may not be concluded from information in the conversation.

25. **(D)** "You have to take it [the class] in order to graduate." Choice (A) refers to the man's attitude, not to the woman's opinion. Choice (B) contradicts the fact that the class is required for graduation. Choice (C) is not men-

tioned and may not be concluded from information in the conversation.

26. **(B)** "He'd better trade that car in [for a different car]." Choices (A), (C), and (D) are not mentioned and may not be concluded from information in the conversation.

27. **(A)** ". . . the T.A. said to get into a study group and quiz each other." Choice (B) refers to the type of exam that they will be given, not to the T.A.'s suggestion. Choice (C) refers to quizzes, but the T.A. suggests that they "quiz each other," which means to ask each other questions. Choice (D) contradicts the fact that the professor recommends studying alone, not in a group.

28. **(C)** Since the woman goes to get a pen, it must be concluded that she will sign the form. Choice (A) contradicts the fact that the woman says he doesn't need an appointment. Choice (B) refers to the pen that the woman, not the man, will use. Choice (D) contradicts the fact that the man is asked to wait for the woman.

29. **(A)** "I'd better make one more draft." A "draft" is a revision of written work. Choice (D) refers to the man's suggestion, not to what the woman is going to do. Choices (B) and (C) are not mentioned and may not be concluded from information in the conversation.

30. **(B)** "That's what I thought [that the computer. . . scheduled for the fifth]." Choice (C) refers to the woman's original statement, not to her final conclusion. Choice (D) contradicts the fact that payments are still due. Choice (A) refers to an error made by the woman, not the computer.

31. **(C)** "I'm waiting for the number seven [bus] myself." Choice (A) contradicts the fact that the woman and the man have never met before. Choice (D) contradicts the fact that she wishes it would rain and cool off. The woman moved to Florida with her mother, but Choice (B) is not mentioned and may not be concluded from information in the conversation.

32. **(C)** "I don't remember it ever being so hot and dry in March before." Choice (A) refers to the weather in Indiana, not in Florida. Choice (B) refers to the weather on the day of the conversation, which is noted as not being usual. Choice (D) contradicts the fact

that the man cannot remember it ever being so hot and dry in March.

33. **(A)** "You're from Florida then." "I was born in New York, but I've lived here [in Florida] for ten years now." Choice (B) refers to the place where the man was born, not to where the conversation takes place. Choice (C) refers to the place where the woman would like to be, not to where she is now. Choice (D) refers to the place where the woman lived before she moved to Florida.

34. **(C)** "It never comes exactly on the half-hour as it should." The number in Choice (A) refers to the amount of time that the woman has been waiting, not to when the bus is scheduled to pass. Choice (B) refers to the time of the conversation. Choice (D) is not mentioned and may not be concluded from information in the conversation.

35. **(D)** ". . . I need three letters of recommendation. Would you be willing to write me one?" Choice (A) contradicts the fact that Betty is already in the professor's seminar class. Choice (C) refers to additional information that the professor gives to Betty, not to the purpose of her call. Choice (B) is not mentioned and may not be concluded from information in the conversation.

36. **(B)** "I think you are an excellent candidate for graduate school." Choice (A) contradicts the fact that Betty is already taking the seminar. Choice (D) contradicts the fact that the professor does not recall the deadline for applications. Choice (C) is not mentioned and may not be concluded from information in the conversation.

37. **(B)** "The committee meets on April 30." Choices (A) and (D) refer to the person who will receive the letter, not to who will make the decision. Choice (C) refers to the person who will make a recommendation.

38. **(C)** "The committee meets on April 30, so all the materials must be submitted before then." Choice (A) contradicts the fact that the materials must be submitted before April 30. Choices (B) and (D) are not mentioned and may not be concluded from information in the conversation.

39. **(B)** Because the speaker talks about "trade," "manufacturing," and "competition," it must be concluded that he is a professor of business. It is not as probable that the professors

and lecturers mentioned in Choices (A), (C), and (D) would discuss trade.

40. **(C)** "To maintain this favorable balance of trade, England went to fantastic lengths to keep secret the advanced manufacturing processes . . ." Choice (D) contradicts the fact that it was the colony (America), not England, that stole the plans. Choices (A) and (B) are not mentioned and may not be concluded from information in the talk.

41. **(C)** "Determined to take nothing in writing, Slater memorized the intricate designs for all the machines in an English textile mill. . . ." Choices (A) and (B) contradict the fact that Slater, in partnership with Brown, opened a mill in the United States in the state of Rhode Island. Choice (D) contradicts the fact that he took nothing in writing.

42. **(A)** ". . . in part as a result of Slater and Brown, America had changed from a country of small farmers and craftsmen to an industrial nation . . . ." Choices (B), (C), and (D) are not mentioned and may not be concluded from information in the talk.

43. **(A)** "So many different kinds of writing have been called essays, it is difficult to define exactly what an essay is." Choices (B), (C), and (D) are secondary themes used to develop a definition of the essay.

44. **(C)** ". . . four characteristics that are true of most essays." Choices (A), (B), and (D) are secondary themes used to develop the main theme of the talk.

45. **(B)** ". . . an essay [is] a short, prose composition with a personal viewpoint that discusses one topic." Choice (B) contradicts the fact that an essay is written in prose, not poetry.

46. **(B)** ". . . let's brainstorm some topics for your first essay assignment." Choices (A), (C), and (D) are not mentioned and may not be concluded from information in the conversation.

47. **(D)** The main purpose of this talk is to summarize Jefferson's life. Choices (A), (B), and (C) are secondary themes in the life of Jefferson.

48. **(C)** "Although Jefferson was a Republican, he at first tried to cooperate with Alexander Hamilton, a Federalist. . . ." Choice (A) refers to Jefferson's opinion of Hamilton's political affiliation. Choice (B) refers to Hamilton, not Jefferson. Choice (D) is not

mentioned and may not be concluded from information in the talk.

49. **(B)** "He [Jefferson] and Federalist Aaron Burr received an identical vote, but the Republican Congress elected to approve Jefferson as president." Choice (A) contradicts the fact that Jefferson and Burr received an identical vote. Choices (C) and (D) are not mentioned and may not be concluded from information in the conversation.

50. **(A)** "Thomas Jefferson was a statesman, a diplomat, an author, and an architect. . . . Not a gifted public speaker, he was most talented as a literary draftsman." Choices (B), (C), and (D) are all mentioned as attributes of Jefferson.

Section 2: Structure and Written Expression

1. **(C)** *Most* is used before a noncount noun to express a quantity that is larger than half the amount. A singular verb follows the noncount noun. Choice (A) does not have a verb. In Choice (B), the verb is before, not after the noun. In Choice (D), *the* is used before *most*. (Refer to Patterns, Problem 72, page 135.)

2. **(B)** An adjective is used before *enough* to express sufficiency. In Choice (A), *goodly* is ungrammatical. The adverbial form of the adjective *good* is *well*. In Choice (C), *as* is unnecessary and incorrect. In Choice (D), the adjective is used after, not before *enough*. (Refer to Patterns, Problem 74, page 138.)

3. **(A)** *The* can be used before a noncount noun that is followed by a qualifying phrase. *Population* should be *the population* before the qualifying phrase *of the Americas*. (Refer to Patterns, Problem 63, page 125.)

4. **(C)** An adjective clause modifies a noun in the main clause. *That the earliest cultures evolved* modifies *the way*. Choice (A) is a clause marker *that* and a noun. Choice (B) is a verb and a noun. Choice (D) is a clause marker *which* and a noun. (Refer to Patterns, Problem 140, page 219.)

5. **(C)** A sentence has a subject and a verb. Choice (A) is redundant because the subject pronoun *it* is used consecutively with the subject *calculus*. Choice (B) has the marker *that* to introduce a main clause. Choice (D) is

redundant because it has a verb that replaces the main verb *can reduce*. (Refer to Patterns, Problem 137 and Style, Problem 21, pages 216 and 245.)

6. **(B)** Subject-verb order and a negative verb with *either* expresses negative agreement. Negative agreement with *neither* requires verb-subject order and an affirmative verb. In Choice (A), verb-subject order is reversed. In Choice (C), verb-subject order is reversed, and *neither* is used at the beginning, not at the end of the clause. In Choice (D) *either*, not *neither*, is used with verb-subject order and an affirmative verb. "Neither does Mexico" would also be correct. (Refer to Patterns, Problem 121, page 195.)

7. **(D)** A sentence has a subject and a verb. Choice (A) does not have a verb. Choices (B) and (C) introduce a main clause subject and verb. (Refer to Patterns, Problem 137, page 216.)

8. **(C)** The anticipatory clause *it is accepted that* introduces a subject and verb, *the formation . . . began*. Choices (B), (C), and (D) are incomplete and ungrammatical. (Refer to Patterns, Problem 35, page 35.)

9. **(A)** The word order for a passive sentence is a form of BE followed by a participle. Only Choice (A) has the correct word order. Choice (B) does not have a BE form. Choice (C) has a HAVE, not a BE form. Choice (D) is a present tense verb, not BE followed by a participle. (Refer to Patterns, Problem 31, page 81.)

10. **(C)** Subject-verb order is used in the clause after a question word connector such as *how much*. In Choice (A), subject-verb order is reversed. In Choice (B), the auxiliary *does* is unnecessary and incorrect. In Choice (D), the verb *are* is repetitive. "The Consumer Price Index lists how much every car *is*" would also be correct. (Refer to Patterns, Problem 124, page 199.)

11. **(C)** A logical conclusion about the past is expressed by *must have* and a participle. Choices (A), (B), and (D) are not logical because they imply that the theater will act to restore itself. (Refer to Patterns, Problem 7, page 49.)

12. **(A)** The verb *to want* requires an infinitive complement. Choice (B) is an *-ing* form, not an infinitive. Choice (C) is a verb word.

Choice (D) is ungrammatical. (Refer to Patterns, Problem 2, page 42.)

13. **(C)** An introductory verbal phrase should immediately precede the noun that it modifies. Only Choice (C) provides a noun which could be logically modified by the introductory verbal phrase, *after seeing the movie*. Neither *the book* nor *the reading* could logically *see a movie* as would be implied by Choices (A), (B), and (D). (Refer to Style, Problem 15, page 237.)

14. **(A)** An introductory phrase should immediately precede the subject noun that it modifies. It does not have a main verb. Choices (B) and (C) contain both subjects and verbs. Choice (D) does not modify the subject noun, *Carl Sandburg*. (Refer to Patterns, Problem 131, page 208.)

15. **(B)** A form of *make* with someone such as *us* and a verb word expresses a causative. Choice (A) is an *-ing* form, not a verb word. Choice (C) is a past form. Choice (D) is an infinitive. (Refer to Patterns, Problem 16, page 61.)

16. **(A)** *Responsible for* is a prepositional idiom. *Responsible the* should be *responsible for the*. (Refer to Style, Problem 29, page 78.)

17. **(B)** A form of BE is used with the participle in passive sentences. *Practice* should be *practiced*. (Refer to Patterns, Problem 31, page 81.)

18. **(C)** There must be agreement between pronoun and antecedent. *Their* should be *our* to agree with the second person antecedent *those of us*. (Refer to Style, Problem 11, page 232.)

19. **(B)** *Wrote* should be *written* because the auxiliary *had* requires a participle. *Wrote* is a past form. *Written* is a participle. (Refer to Patterns, Problem 36, page 87.)

20. **(A)** *Would have* and a participle in the result require *had* and a participle in the condition. Because *would have won* is used in the result, *would have* should be *had* in the condition. (Refer to Patterns, Problem 24, page 71.)

21. **(B)** There must be agreement between pronoun and antecedent. *Which* should be *who* to refer to the antecedent *Shirley Temple Black*. *Which* refers to things. *Who* refers to persons. (Refer to Patterns, Problem 48, page 102.)

22. **(D)** Comparative forms are usually followed

by *than.* After the comparative *more reasonable, as* should be *than.* (Refer to Patterns, Problem 96, page 165.)

23. **(D)** *To know* should be *to know how* before the infinitive *to use. To know* is used before nouns and noun clauses. *To know how* is used before infinitives. (Refer to Patterns, Problem 10, page 52.)

24. **(C)** *There* introduces inverted order, but there must still be agreement between subject and verb. *Has been* should be *have been* to agree with the plural subject *two major factions.* (Refer to Style, Problem 8, page 229.)

25. **(A)** In order to refer to occupying a place on the battlefields, *lain* should be used. *To lay* means to put in a place, and the participle is *laid. To lie* means to occupy a place, and the participle is *lain.* (Refer to Style, Problem 23, page 248.)

26. **(B)** *Purposeful* should be *purposes. Purposeful* is an adjective. *Purposes* is a noun. (Refer to Style, Problem 30, page 257.)

27. **(B)** *Large* should be *largest.* Because there were more than two ethnic groups, a superlative form must be used. (Refer to Patterns, Problem 97, page 166.)

28. **(B)** The determiner *a* is used before a singular count noun. *Results* should be *result.* (Refer to Patterns, Problem 62, page 123.)

29. **(B)** Most adverbs of manner are formed by adding *-ly* to adjectives. *Calm* should be *calmly* to qualify the manner in which the talking should be done. (Refer to Patterns, Problem 126, page 202.)

30. **(B)** When the degree of one quality, *the heat,* is dependent upon the degree of another quality, *the humidity,* two comparatives are used, each preceded by *the. The worst* should be *the worse* because it is a comparative. (Refer to Patterns, Problem 100, page 169.)

31. **(B)** A dependent clause modifies an independent clause. *Which are* should be *are* to provide a verb for the subject *statistical data,* of the independent clause. (Refer to Patterns, Problem 138, page 217.)

32. **(D)** Ideas in a series should be expressed by parallel structures. *The Assassinate* should be *The Assassination of* to provide for parallelism with the nouns *Causes, Economy,* and *Strategies.* (Refer to Style, Problem 17, page 240.)

33. **(A)** *Despite of* is a combination of *despite*

and *in spite of.* Either *despite* or *in spite of* should be used. (Refer to Patterns, Problem 110, page 182.)

34. **(A)** Because it is a prepositional phrase, in a comparison *as every nation* should be *like every nation. As* functions as a conjunction. *Like* functions as a preposition. (Refer to Patterns, Problem 88, page 156.)

35. **(A)** A verb word must be used in a clause after the phrase "It is necessary." *Met* should be *meet. Met* is a past form. *Meet* is a verb word. (Refer to Patterns, Problem 29, page 78.)

36. **(D)** The verb *forbid* may be used with either an infinitive or an *-ing* complement. *From owning* should be *to own.* The *-ing* form *owning* would require the possessive pronoun modifier *their.* (Refer to Patterns, Problem 3, page 43 and Patterns, Problem 46, page 100.)

37. **(C)** *More cheaper* should be *cheaper.* Because *cheap* is a one-syllable adjective, the comparative is formed by adding *-er. More* is used with two-syllable adjectives that do not end in *-y.* (Refer to Patterns, Problem 96, page 165.)

38. **(A)** The verb *thought* establishes a point of view in the past. *Will* should be *would* in order to maintain the point of view. (Refer to Style, Problem 2, page 222.)

39. **(D)** Because the verb *enjoy* requires an *-ing* form in the complement, *to play* should be *playing.* (Refer to Patterns, Problem 3, page 43.)

40. **(D)** Ideas in a series should be expressed by parallel structures. *To plant* should be *planting* to provide for parallelism with the *-ing* forms *plowing* and *rotating.* (Refer to Style, Problem 17, page 240.)

Section 3: Reading Comprehension

1. **(A)** "Webster's Work" is the best title because it states the main idea of the passage. Choice (B) is incorrect because Webster's dictionaries represent only part of the work referred to in the passage. Choices (C) and (D) are mentioned briefly in the discussion, but are not the most important topics.

2. **(D)** In the context of this passage, "inadequate" could best be replaced by "unsatisfactory." Choices (A), (B), and (C) are not accepted definitions of the word.

3. **(C)** ". . . he discovered how inadequate the available schoolbooks were for the children of a new and independent nation. . . . In response to the need for truly American textbooks, Webster published *A Grammatical Institute of the English Language*." Choice (A) is a result of having written *A Grammatical Institute*, not a reason for writing it. Choice (B) contradicts the fact that British books were available, but not appropriate. Choice (D) is not mentioned and may not be concluded from information in the passage.

4. **(D)** ". . . *The American Spelling Book* . . . provided him with a considerable income for the rest of his life." Choices (A), (B), and (C) are all publications by Webster, but the income afforded by each is not mentioned and may not be concluded from information in the passage.

5. **(B)** "Published in two volumes in 1828, *An American Dictionary of the English Language* . . . ." The numbers referred to in Choices (A), (C), and (D) are not mentioned and may not be concluded from information in the passage.

6. **(C)** "Published . . . in 1828, *An American Dictionary of the English Language* has become the recognized authority for usage . . . ." Choice (A) refers to the date that Webster finished his study of English and began writing the dictionary. Choice (B) refers to the date that Webster began work on the dictionary. Choice (D) refers to the date that Webster finished writing the dictionary, not to the date that it was published.

7. **(B)** "[His] purpose in writing [*An American Dictionary of the English Language*] was to demonstrate that the American language was developing distinct meanings, pronunciations, and spellings from those of British English." Choice (C) contradicts the fact that Webster promoted new spelling forms instead of the British forms which had been accepted by earlier authorities. Choice (D) occurred as a result of the publication, but it was not Webster's purpose in publishing *An American Dictionary of the English Language*. Choice (A) is not mentioned and may not be concluded from information in the passage.

8. **(D)** "Webster's purpose in writing it [the dictionary] was to demonstrate that the American language was developing distinct meanings, pronunciations, and spellings from those of British English." Choices (A), (B), and (C) would change the meaning of the sentence.

9. **(C)** In the context of this passage, "distinct" is closest in meaning to "different." Choices (A), (B), and (D) are not accepted definitions.

10. **(C)** "He [Webster] is responsible for advancing the form . . . color . . . instead of colour." Choices (A), (B), and (D) are British English spellings.

11. **(A)** Choice (A) is the author's main purpose because the passage refers to the San Andreas Fault specifically. The general information referred to in Choices (B), (C), and (D) is not mentioned and may not be concluded from information in the passage.

12. **(C)** In the context of this passage, "originates" could best be replaced by "begins." Choices (A), (B), and (D) are not accepted definitions of the word.

13. **(C)** ". . . the San Andreas Fault . . . originates . . . six hundred miles from the Gulf of California and runs north. . . ." Choices (A), (B), and (D) contradict the fact that the fault runs north.

14. **(D)** ". . . the San Andreas Fault . . . runs north in an irregular line. . . ." The word *uneven* in Choice (D) means irregular. Choice (A) contradicts the fact that the line is irregular. Choices (B) and (C) are not mentioned and may not be concluded from information in the passage.

15. **(C)** "Its western side always moves north in relation to its eastern side." Choices (A), (B), and (D) contradict the fact that the western side always moves north, not in any other direction.

16. **(D)** "It's western side always moves north in relation to its [the fault's] eastern side." Choices (A), (B), and (C) would change the meaning of the sentence.

17. **(D)** "Intermittent" means "occasional." Choices (A), (B), and (C) are not accepted definitions of the word.

18. **(A)** "Californians have long anticipated the recurrence of what they refer to as the "Big One," a destructive earthquake. . . ." Choices (B), (C), or (D) would change the meaning of the sentence.

19. **(C)** "Tremors are not unusual along the San Andreas Fault. . . ." Choice (B) contradicts the fact that tremors are not unusual. Choices (A) and (D) are not mentioned and may not be concluded from information in the passage.

20. **(B)** "The San Andreas Fault is a fracture at the congruence of two major plates of the earth's crust." Choice (A) refers to the plates, not to the fracture. Choices (C) and (D) refer to the results of the movement along the fracture, not to the fault.

21. **(B)** "The Structure of an Insect" is the best title because it states the main idea of the passage. Choice (C) is a secondary idea that is used to develop the main idea. Choices (A) and (D) are not mentioned and may not be concluded from information in the passage.

22. **(D)** Because the passage is a statement of scientific facts written from an objective point of view, it must be concluded that the purpose is to inform. Choices (A) and (B) are improbable because the passage is not written from a subjective point of view. Choice (C) is improbable because of the scientific content.

23. **(C)** "Features of the mouth parts are very helpful in classifying the many kinds of insects." Choices (A), (B), and (D) are discussed, but not as a basis for classification.

24. **(A)** In the context of this passage, "majority" is closest in meaning to "more than half." Choices (B), (C), and (D) are not accepted definitions of the word.

25. **(C)** ". . . the maxillae which serve to direct food into the mouth between the jaws." Choice (A) refers to mandibles, not to maxillae. Choice (B) refers to sharp stylets. Choice (D) refers to expanding labium.

26. **(A)** "A labrum above and a labium below are similar to an upper and lower lip." Choice (B) is compared to Choice (D). Choice (C) is discussed, but not compared to anything.

27. **(B)** ". . . the coiled drinking tube . . . called the proboscis . . . [is] composed . . . of modified maxillae." Choice (A) refers to food, not to the proboscis that is used in reaching it. Choices (C) and (D) are not mentioned and may not be concluded from information in the passage.

28. **(C)** "In a mosquito or an aphid, mandibles and maxillae are modified to sharp stylets." The insect referred to in choice (A) has mandibles similar to jaws, not sharp stylets. The insect referred to in Choice (B) has a proboscis. The insect referred to in Choice (D) has a sponge-like mouth pad.

29. **(A)** In the context of this passage, "drill through" could best be replaced by "penetrate." Choices (B), (C), and (D) are not accepted definitions of the phrase.

30. **(C)** "In a housefly, the expanding labium forms a spongelike mouth pad that it [the housefly] can use to stamp over the surface of food." Choices (A), (B), and (D) would change the meaning of the sentence.

31. **(C)** The other choices are secondary ideas that are used to develop the primary topic, "interest." Choice (A) refers to the relationship of interest to banks. Choices (B) and (D) figure in the formula for computing interest.

32. **(A)** In the context of this passage, "sum" could best be replaced by "amount." Choices (B), (C), and (D) are not accepted definitions of the word.

33. **(A)** In the context of this passage, "fixed" is closest in meaning to "definite." Choices (B), (C), and (D) are not accepted definitions of the word.

34. **(A)** "Principal is the term used for the money that is borrowed, and the rate of interest is the percent per year of the principal charged for its [the principal's] use." Choices (B), (C), and (D) would change the meaning of the sentence.

35. **(C)** "Interest = Principal × Rate × Time." One dollar at four percent for one year is $1 × .04 × 1, or $.04. Choices (A), (B), and (D) may not be computed on the basis of the formula in the passage.

36. **(B)** "The rate is expressed as a decimal fraction." Choices (A) and (C) are whole numbers, not decimal fractions. Choice (D) is a common, not a decimal fraction.

37. **(B)** "Although the time may be less than, equal to, or greater than one year, most applications for loans are periods of less than one year." Choices (A) and (C) refer to other options, but not to the time for most applications. Choice (D) refers to the commercial year.

38. **(A)** In the context of this passage, "periods" refers to time. Choices (B), (C), and (D) are not accepted definitions of the word.

39. **(D)** "For purposes of computing interest for short periods, the commercial year or 360

days is commonly used. . ." Choices (A), (B), and (C) refer to situations that require the calendar year or 365 days, not the commercial year.

40. **(C)** "Interest is the sum charged for borrowing money." Choice (A) is a definition of principal, not interest. Choice (B) is a definition of the interest rate per time period. Choice (D) is not mentioned and may not be concluded from information in the passage.

41. **(D)** The primary topic is the characteristics of protozoans. Choices (A), (B), and (C) are important to the discussion and provide details that support the primary topic.

42. **(D)** In the context of this passage, "minute" could best be replaced by "very small." Choices (A), (B), and (C) are not accepted definitions of the word.

43. **(A)** "The protozoans, minute, aquatic creatures . . ." Choices (B), (C), and (D) contradict the fact that the protozoans are aquatic.

44. **(B)** "The protozoans . . . [consist] of a single cell of protoplasm. . . ." Choices (A), (C), and (D) contradict the fact that the cell of a protozoan is composed of protoplasm.

45. **(C)** "The Sarcodina, which include amoebae. . . ." Choices (A) and (B) refer to two other groups of protozoans that do not include amoebae. Choice (D) refers to the basis of classification for the three major groups of protozoans.

46. **(C)** ". . . a large nucleus that regulates growth but decomposes during reproduction. . ." Choice (A) refers to the small, not the large nucleus. Choice (B) contradicts the fact that the small nucleus contains the genetic code for the large nucleus. Choice (D) contradicts that fact the large nucleus decomposes during reproduction.

47. **(A)** "Protozoans are considered animals because. . .they do not live on simple organic compounds." Choices (B) and (C) refer to characteristics of some protozoans, not to a reason why they are considered animals. Choice (D) contradicts the fact that they have only one cell, although current research is calling that into question.

48. **(A)** In the context of this passage, "uniformly" is closest in meaning to "in the same way." Choices (B), (C), and (D) are not accepted definitions of the word.

49. **(A)** "Current research into this phenomenon along with investigations carried out with advanced microscopes may necessitate a redefinition of what constitutes a protozoan, even calling into question the basic premise that they [protozoans] have only one cell." Choices (B), (C), and (D) would change the meaning of the sentence.

50. **(C)** Choice (A) is mentioned in lines 18–19. Choice (B) is mentioned in lines 1–2. Choice (D) is mentioned in lines 19–20. Protozoans consist of a single cell, although in the case of Ciliata, the cell may have a larger nucleus and a smaller nucleus.

Model Test 4—Short Form

Section 1: Listening Comprehension

1. **(B)** *That's not too bad* is an idiomatic expression that means it is acceptable. Choice (C) contradicts the fact that the man feels the price was acceptable for the repairs. Choice (D) contradicts the fact that the car needed only a few minor repairs. Choice (A) is not mentioned and may not be concluded from information in the conversation.

2. **(C)** *I wish I could* is an idiomatic expression that means the speaker would like to but is not able to do something. Choice (A) refers to a party that the Association, not the woman, will have. Choice (B) refers to what the woman would like to do, not to what she will probably do. Choice (D) is not mentioned and may not be concluded from information in the conversation.

3. **(A)** Since they have just enough time to get there, it must be concluded that they will leave immediately. Choices (B), (C), and (D) are not mentioned and may not be concluded from information in the conversation.

4. **(A)** The man said that he went to see the foreign student advisor. Choice (D) refers to what the advisor did, not to what the man did himself. The Passport Office is in Washington, D.C., but Choices (B) and (C) are not mentioned and may not be concluded from information in the conversation.

5. **(B)** Since the woman thanks the man sarcastically, it must be concluded that the man was not helpful. Choice (A) refers to the man's comment, not to the woman's response. Choice (C) contradicts the fact that the woman does not have an account at the bank. Choice (D) refers to the woman's request, not to what she means by her response to the man.

6. **(B)** "I'd write a rough draft and ask Dr. Tyler to look at it." A "rough draft" is a preliminary version. Choice (C) contradicts the fact that the woman says to show the draft to Dr. Tyler, not to her. Choices (A) and (D) are not mentioned and may not be concluded from information in the conversation.

7. **(D)** To *put up with* is an idiomatic expression that means to tolerate. It must be concluded that the students do not like Dr. Clark. Choices (A), (B), and (C) are not paraphrases of the expressions, and may not be concluded from information in the conversation.

8. **(D)** "Saturday afternoon would be the earliest that you could have them." Choice (A) contradicts the fact that the shirts will be ready on Saturday afternoon. Choice (B) contradicts the fact that the man cannot have the shirts on Friday morning. Choice (C) is not mentioned and may not be concluded from information in the conversation.

9. **(D)** From the references to *food* as well as to *music* and *flowers*, it must be concluded that the conversation took place at a restaurant. Music would be heard at a concert, and flowers would be found at a flower shop, but it is not customary to serve food at any of the places referred to in Choices (A), (B), and (C).

10. **(C)** According to Anne, Fred is in class. Choice (A) refers to the time when Fred will come home, not to where he is now. Choice (B) refers to where Larry is, not to where Fred is. Choice (D) refers to where Anne is.

11. **(A)** Since the man has asked for the next bus, and it leaves at ten o'clock, it must be concluded that he will take the ten o'clock bus. Choice (B) refers to his missing the first bus by five minutes, not to what he will do now. Choices (C) and (D) contradict the fact that the man asked for the next bus.

12. **(C)** The references to a *textbook* and a *movie* in Choices (B) and (D) relate to the assignment for the class. Choice (A) is not mentioned and may not be concluded from information in the conversation.

13. **(A)** "As soon as I make the final corrections on the original." Choice (B) refers to what the man asked the woman to do, not to what she will do. Choice (D) contradicts the fact that she was ready to make the corrections on the original. Choice (C) is not mentioned and may not be concluded from information in the conversation.

14. **(B)** Since the man asks whether the woman is Sally Harrison's sister, it must be concluded that he assumed the women were sisters.

Choice (A) refers to who the woman is, not to the man's assumption. Choices (C) and (D) contradict the fact that the woman is Sally Harrison's cousin.

15. **(C)** Since the woman says that she can't find her pen, it must be concluded that finding her pen is the problem. Choices (A), (B), and (D) are not mentioned and may not be concluded from information in the conversation.

16. **(A)** Because John agreed to arrive at eight-thirty but the man estimates that he won't arrive until nine o'clock, or one half-hour later, it must be concluded that John is usually late. Choice (B) refers to the time when John agreed to arrive, not to a conclusion that the man wants us to make. Choice (C) contradicts both the fact that John had agreed to come and the fact that the man estimates John's arrival at nine o'clock. Choice (D) contradicts the fact that the man estimates John's arrival one half-hour after he has agreed to arrive.

17. **(C)** "If only we hadn't spent so much money on our vacation [we would have money for the house]." Choice (B) may be true but it is not what the woman means by her comment. Choices (A) and (D) are not mentioned and may not be concluded from information in the conversation.

18. **(B)** To *not know up from down* is an idiomatic expression that means to get confused. Choice (A) contradicts the fact that the man and woman both saw the presentation. Choice (D) contradicts the fact that he was confused. Choice (C) is not mentioned and may not be concluded from information in the conversation.

19. **(B)** Since the man wants to talk to Janet, he implies that he wants to get her opinion. Choices (A), (C), and (D) are not mentioned and may not be concluded from information in the conversation.

20. **(B)** Since the woman can't keep up with the baby, it must be concluded that the baby is very active. Choice (D) contradicts the fact that the woman says the baby is walking. Choices (A) and (C) are not mentioned and may not be concluded from information in the conversation.

21. **(B)** "... it didn't turn out quite like I thought it would." Choice (A) contradicts the fact that the man knows how it turned out. Choice (C)

contradicts the fact that the man says the experiment is finished. Choice (D) is not mentioned and may not be concluded from information in the conversation.

22. **(A)** Since the man expresses exasperation about the woman's attention to her classes, he implies that she does not put much effort in her studies. Choice (D) is true, but it is not what the man implies by his comment. Choices (B) and (C) are not mentioned and may not be concluded from information in the conversation.

23. **(D)** "... I'd try some over-the-counter medication..." Choice (A) refers to the woman's plan, not to the man's suggestion. Choice (B) refers to the idiom "do the job" which means to cure. Choice (C) refers to the place to buy nonprescription medicine [over the counter], not to the man's suggestion.

24. **(A)** To *give it all you've got* is an idiomatic expression that means to try your best. Choices (B), (C), and (D) are not paraphrases of the expression, and may not be concluded from information in the conversation.

25. **(D)** *Just about to* is an idiomatic expression that means the person is ready. Choice (A) contradicts the fact that she greets Robert in a familiar way. Choices (B) and (C) are not mentioned and may not be concluded from information in the conversation.

26. **(A)** Since the woman denies the man's request for a few more minutes, it must be concluded that the man must stop working on the test. Choice (B) contradicts the fact that the man cannot have a few more minutes to finish. Choice (D) contradicts the fact that the test is in progress, not about to start. Choice (C) is not mentioned and may not be concluded from information in the conversation.

27. **(C)** Since the man thinks they are using a different book this semester, he implies that the textbook may have been changed. Choice (D) contradicts the fact that they are discussing plans for this semester. Choices (A) and (B) are not mentioned and may not be concluded from information in the conversation.

28. **(D)** Since the woman questions whether Sally would like a bike, she implies that Sally may prefer a different gift. Choice (A) refers to the man's idea, not to the woman's comment. Choices (B) and (C) are not mentioned

and may not be concluded from information in the conversation.

29. **(A)** Since the man responds in dismay, it must be inferred that he does not want to give Carol a ride. Choice (B) contradicts the fact that the woman offered Carol a ride with the man. Choices (C) and (D) are not mentioned and may not be concluded from information in the conversation.

30. **(A)** ". . . get some rest and try it again later." Choices (B) and (D) contradict the fact that the woman recommends rest. Choice (C) is not mentioned and may not be concluded from information in the conversation.

31. **(B)** ". . .the question is not whether the metric system should be introduced in the United States, but rather, how it should be introduced." Choice (A) contradicts the fact that the question is not whether the metric system should be introduced. Choices (C) and (D) are not mentioned and may not be concluded from information in the discussion.

32. **(C)** "They [cans and packages] are marked in both ounces and grams. . . . And the weather reporters on radio and TV give the temperature readings in both degrees Fahrenheit and degrees Celsius now. . . . Some road signs have the distances marked in both miles and kilometers. . . ." Choice (A) contradicts the fact that the temperature readings are in both degrees Fahrenheit and degrees Celsius. Choice (B) contradicts the fact that the road signs have distances marked in both miles and kilometers. Choice (D) contradicts the fact that cans and packages are marked in both ounces and grams.

33. **(D)** "I [Professor Baker] agree that a gradual adoption is better for those of us who have already been exposed to the English system of measurement. But I would favor teaching only metrics in the elementary schools." Choice (A) refers to the woman's suggestion, not to Professor Baker's opinion. The opinions expressed in Choices (B) and (C) are not mentioned and may not be concluded from information in the discussion.

34. **(D)** Because Professor Baker invites a free exchange of ideas, and does not criticize his students, it must be concluded that he is cooperative. The words in Choices (A), (B), and (C) do not describe Professor Baker's manner in the conversation.

35. **(D)** "I'm calling to make a reservation for a flight from Houston to Atlanta." Choices (A), (B), and (C) are all discussed, but they are not the main purpose of the conversation.

36. **(A)** ". . . if you stay over Saturday night and return on Sunday. . . the ticket will be even cheaper." Choice (B) contradicts the fact that the man is calling one month early. Choice (C) contradicts the fact that she offers to mail the tickets or save them for him in the office. Choice (D) refers to one or two alternatives, not to the woman's suggestion.

37. **(A)** "I'll just keep it [the reservation] for May 19th." Choices (B), (C), and (D) refer to the alternatives, not to the decision that the man made.

38. **(D)** "I'll pick them up. . . . after two o'clock." Choices (A), (B), and (C) are not mentioned and may not be concluded from information in the conversation.

39. **(D)** ". . . an extensive research effort, which, in cooperation with private industry, has transferred technology to the international marketplace." Choices (A), (B), and (C) are secondary themes used to develop the main theme of the talk.

40. **(A)** "Hundreds of everyday products can be traced back to the space mission, including cordless electric tools, airtight food packaging. . . . ultrasound. . ." Choice (A) is not mentioned and may not be concluded from information in the talk.

41. **(D)** "First used to detect flaws in spacecraft, ultrasound is now standard equipment in almost every hospital. . ." Choice (A) refers to implants and pacemakers, not to ultrasound. Choices (B) and (C) are not mentioned and may not be concluded from information in the conversation.

42. **(B)** ". . . archaeologists have been able to explore the earth. . . cities. . . have been located . . . and the sea floor has been mapped using photographs from outer space." Choices (A), (C), and (D) are not mentioned and may not be concluded from information in the conversation.

43. **(C)** The tour guide discusses the history, economy, and landmarks of San Francisco. Choices (A), (B), and (D) are secondary themes used to support the main purpose of the talk, an orientation to the City of San Francisco.

44. **(D)** ". . . the name was changed from Yerba Buena to San Francisco." Choice (A) refers to the name of the bridge, not a settlement. Choice (B) refers to a mission established before Yerba Buena was settled. Choice (C) refers to a military post established before the settlement of Yerba Buena.

45. **(A)** ". . . in 1848, with the discovery of gold, the population grew to ten thousand." Choice (B) refers to what happened in 1869, not 1848. Choice (C) refers to what happened in 1937. Choice (D) refers to what happened in 1862.

46. **(C)** "The bridge, which is more than one mile long, spans the harbor from San Francisco to Marin County. . . ." Choice (A) refers to the length of the Port of San Francisco, not to the length of the Golden Gate Bridge. Choice (B) refers to the altitude of the city. The number in Choice (D) refers to the number of tons of cargo handled at the Port of San Francisco every year.

47. **(A)** "Today we will discuss Transcendentalism. . . ." Choices (B), (C), and (D) are secondary themes that are used to develop the main theme of the lecture.

48. **(C)** "Today we will discuss Transcendentalism, which is a philosophical and literary movement that developed in New England in the early nineteenth century." Choices (A), (B), and (D) are not mentioned and may not be concluded from information in the talk.

49. **(C)** "This group [the Transcendental Club] was the advance guard of a reaction against the rigid Puritanism of the period, especially insofar as it emphasized society at the expense of the individual." Choices (A) and (D) refer to the Transcendental Club, not to the Puritans. Choice (B) contradicts the fact that the Transcendental Club reacted against the Puritans.

50. **(D)** "Thoreau built a small cabin along the shores of Walden Pond . . . he published an account of his experiences in *Walden*. . . ." Choices (A), (B), and (C) are not mentioned and may not be concluded from information in the talk.

Section 2: Structure and Written Expression

1. **(D)** A dependent clause modifies an independent clause. Choice (A) has two clause markers, *which* and *that*. Choice (B) is a verb followed by a noun and a clause marker. Choice (C) does not have a clause marker. (Refer to Patterns, Problem 138, page 217.)

2. **(B)** A passive infinitive is used to express purpose. Choice (A) is a noun. Choice (C) is an -ing form. Choice (D) is a present verb. (Refer to Patterns, Problem 33, page 33.)

3. **(B)** A cardinal number is used after a noun. *The* is used with an ordinal number before a noun. In Choices (A) and (C) an ordinal number is used after, not before a noun. Choice (D) is incomplete because it does not include *the* before the ordinal number. (Refer to Patterns, Problem 77, page 142.)

4. **(B)** *As soon as* is an idiom that introduces a limit of time. The phrase *as soon as* is followed by a noun and a simple present verb. Choice (A) is a modal and a verb word, not a simple present verb. Choice (D) is a noun. Choice (C) uses a present but not a simple present form. (Refer to Patterns, Problem 135, page 213.)

5. **(A)** A form of *make* with someone such as *all Americans* and a verb word expresses a causative. Choice (B) is an infinitive, not a verb word. Choice (D) is an -ing form. Choice (C) does not have a verb form. (Refer to Patterns, Problem 16, page 61.)

6. **(C)** Negative agreement with *neither* requires verb-subject order and an affirmative verb. Affirmative agreement requires subject-verb order, an affirmative verb and *too* or *also*. Choices (A) and (D) have negative, not affirmative, verbs with *too* and *also*. Choice (B) reverses verb-subject order with *neither*. (Refer to Patterns, Problem 121, page 195.)

7. **(B)** Ideas in a series should be expressed by parallel structures. Only *to finish* in Choice (B) provides for parallelism with the infinitive *to answer*. Choices (A), (C), and (D) are not parallel. (Refer to Style, Problem 17, page 240.)

8. **(C)** *Weathering* is the subject of the verb *is*. Choices (A) and (B) are redundant and indirect. Choice (D) is an -ing form, not a verb. (Refer to Style, Problem 19, page 243.)

9. **(A)** Subject-verb order is used in the clause after a question word connector such as *what time*. In Choice (B), subject-verb order is

reversed. In Choice (C), the auxiliary *does* is unnecessary and incorrect. In Choice (D), the connector is after, not before the subject and verb. (Refer to Patterns, Problem 124, page 199.)

10. **(D)** The verb *to consider* requires an *-ing* form in the complement. Choice (A) is an infinitive, not an *-ing* form. Choice (B) is a participle. Choice (C) is a verb word. (Refer to Patterns, Problem 3, page 43.)

11. **(C)** A form of *have* with something such as a *tooth* and a participle expresses a causative. Choice (A) is an *-ing* form, not a participle. Choice (B) is an infinitive. Choice (D) is a verb word. (Refer to Patterns, Problem 18, page 63.)

12. **(B)** A negative phrase introduces inverted order. *Not until* requires an auxiliary verb, subject, and main verb. In Choice (A), the subject precedes the auxiliary. In Choice (C), there is no auxiliary. In Choice (D), there is no auxiliary and no subject. (Refer to Patterns, Problem 129, page 206.)

13. **(C)** Object pronouns are used after prepositions such as *by*. Choice (A) is a reflexive pronoun, not an object pronoun. Choices (B) and (D) are possessive pronouns. "The work was done *by herself*" without the repetitive word *alone* would also be correct. (Refer to Patterns, Problem 45, page 99.)

14. **(D)** An appositive does not require connectors or an additional subject. Choices (A) and (C) include connecting conjunctions. Choice (B) is an anticipatory it clause, not an appositive. (Refer to Style, Problem 7, page 228.)

15. **(B)** Consecutive order must be maintained, along with parallel structure. (Refer to Patterns, Problem 75 and Style, Problem 17, pages 139 and 240.)

16. **(C)** Most adverbs of manner are formed by adding *-ly* to adjectives. *Rapid* should be *rapidly* to qualify the manner in which automatic data processing has grown. (Refer to Patterns, Problem 126, page 202.)

17. **(D)** *As well as* should be *and*, which is used in correlation with *both*. (Refer to Patterns, Problem 116, page 189.)

18. **(B)** *Near* does not require a preposition. *Near to* should be *near*. *Nearby* would also be correct. (Refer to Style, Problem 29, page 255.)

19. **(C)** Because adjectives are used after verbs of the senses, *badly* should be *bad* after the verb *feel*. *Badly* functions as an adverb. *Bad* functions as an adjective. (Refer to Patterns, Problem 85, page 151.)

20. **(A)** Repetition of the subject by a subject pronoun is redundant. *They* should be deleted. (Refer to Style, Problem 21, page 245.)

21. **(A)** *Despite of* is a combination of *despite* and *in spite of*. *Despite of* should be either *despite* or *in spite of*. (Refer to Patterns, Problem 110, page 182.)

22. **(A)** Object pronouns are used after prepositions. *We* should be *us* after the preposition *of*. (Refer to Patterns, Problem 45, page 99.)

23. **(C)** Because dates require ordinal numbers, *twelve* should be *twelfth*. (Refer to Patterns, Problem 134, page 211.)

24. **(B)** *Influence* should be *influential*. *Influence* is a noun. *Influential* is an adjective. (Refer to Style, Problem 30, page 257.)

25. **(A)** In order to refer to an increase in the cost of living, *a rise* not *a raise* should be used. *A raise* is an increase in salary. *A rise* is an increase in price, worth, quantity, or degree. (Refer to Style, Problem 22, page 247.)

26. **(B)** A verb word must be used in a clause after an impersonal expression. *Maintains* should be *maintain* after the impersonal expression *it is imperative*. (Refer to Patterns, Problem 29, page 78.)

27. **(D)** *Such as* introduces the example *shrimps and clams* which must refer to a plural antecedent. *Sea creature* should be *sea creatures*. (Refer to Patterns, Problem 109, page 181.)

28. **(C)** Ideas in a series should be expressed by parallel structures. *Encouraging* should be *to encourage* to provide for parallelism with the infinitive *to discourage*. (Refer to Style, Problem 17, page 240.)

29. **(B)** *Combination* should be *combine*. *Combination* is a noun. *Combine* is a verb. (Refer to Style, Problem 30, page 257.)

30. **(C)** *Presumable* should be *presumably*. *Presumable* is an adjective. *Presumably* is an adverb. (Refer to Style, Problem 30, page 257.)

31. **(D)** Using words with the same meaning consecutively is repetitive. *Words* should be deleted because *speaking* implies the use of *words*. (Refer to Style, Problem 20, page 244.)

32. **(A)** The verb *reported* establishes a point of view in the past. *Discovers* should be *discovered* in order to maintain the point of view. (Refer to Style, Problem 2, page 222.)

33. **(D)** *Either* should be *both* which is used in correlation with the inclusive *and*. (Refer to Patterns, Problem 116, page 189.)

34. **(D)** Because the verb *refuse* requires an infinitive in the complement, *giving* should be *to give*. (Refer to Patterns, Problem 2, page 42.)

35. **(C)** There must be agreement between subject and verb. *Has* should be *have* to agree with the plural subject *the few cities*. (Refer to Style, Problem 9, page 230.)

36. **(C)** Comparative forms are usually followed by *than*. After the comparative *more important*, *as* should be *than*. (Refer to Patterns, Problem 96, page 165.)

37. **(C)** Object pronouns should be used after prepositions. *Who* should be *whom* after the preposition *to*. (Refer to Patterns, Problem 49, page 103.)

38. **(D)** Ideas in a series should be expressed by parallel structures. *Increasing* should be *to increase* to provide for parallelism with the infinitive *to enrich*. (Refer to Style, Problem 17, page 240.)

39. **(A)** *Would have* and a participle in the result requires *had* and a participle in the condition. Because *would not have evolved* is used in the result, *did not filter out* should be *had not filtered out* in the condition. (Refer to Patterns, Problem 24, page 71.)

40. **(C)** A verb word must be used in a clause after the verb *to require*. *Reports* should be *report*. "Everyone who holds a nonimmigrant visa" is the subject of the clause. (Refer to Patterns, Problem 27, page 76.)

Section 3: Reading Comprehension

1. **(A)** The other choices are secondary ideas that are used to develop the main idea, "precipitation." Choices (B), (C), and (D) provide details and examples.

2. **(C)** "Precipitation [is] commonly referred to as rainfall." Choices (A), (B), and (D) are not mentioned and may not be concluded from information in the passage.

3. **(B)** "Precipitation, commonly referred to as rainfall, is a measure of the quantity of water in the form of either rain, hail, or snow." Choice (A) is incomplete because it does not include hail and snow. Humidity referred to in Choices (C) and (D) is not mentioned and may not be concluded from information in the passage.

4. **(A)** "The average annual precipitation over the whole of the United States is thirty-six inches." Choice (B) refers to the formula for computing precipitation, not to the annual rainfall over the United States. Choice (C) refers to the amount of rain recorded in New York State, not in the United States. Choice (D) refers to the total annual precipitation recorded in New York State.

5. **(B)** "A general formula for computing the precipitation of snowfall is that ten inches of snow is equal to one inch of precipitation." Forty inches of snow divided by 10 inches per one inch of precipitation is four inches, or one-third foot. Choices (A), (C), and (D) may not be computed on the basis of the formula in the passage.

6. **(C)** In the context of this passage, "proximity to" is closest in meaning to "nearness to." Choices (A), (B), and (D) are not accepted definitions of the phrase.

7. **(D)** ". . .the Pacific Coast receives more annual precipitation than the Atlantic Coast." Choices (A), (B), and (C) refer to the prevailing winds, not to the highest annual precipitation.

8. **(B)** Choice (A) is mentioned in lines 14–16. Choice (C) is mentioned in lines 9–10. Choice (D) is mentioned in lines 9–10. Choice (B) is not mentioned and may not be concluded from information in the passage.

9. **(A)** In the context of this passage, "substantially" could best be replaced by "fundamentally." Choices (B), (C), and (D) are not accepted definitions of the word.

10. **(B)** "East of the Rocky Mountains, the annual precipitation decreases substantially from that [precipitation] west of the Rocky Mountains." Choices (A), (C), and (D) would change the meaning of the sentence.

11. **(B)** Because the information relates to graduate courses, it is most probable that the passage would be found in a graduate catalog. Choice (A) contradicts the fact that the information is about graduate, not undergraduate, courses. It is less probable that this kind of

information would be distributed in a class as in Choices (C) and (D).

12. **(A)** Because the style of the passage is objective, it must be concluded that the purpose of the passage is to inform. Choices (B), (C), and (D) would require a less objective style, with more subjective commentary.

13. **(A)** In the context of this passage, "prerequisites" is closest in meaning to "courses required before enrolling." Choices (B), (C), and (D) are not accepted definitions of the word.

14. **(B)** "Certain graduate courses, generally those [graduate courses] devoted to introductory material, are numbered 400 for undergraduate students who qualify to take them and 600 for graduate students." Choices (A), (C), and (D) would change the meaning of the sentence.

15. **(A)** "Courses with the numbers 800 or above are open only to graduate students." Choices (B) and (C) may refer to both graduate and undergraduate students. Part-time and full-time students are restricted on the basis of the number of hours that they may take, not on the basis of the courses that they may take. Choice (D) contradicts the fact that courses numbered 800 or above are open to graduate, not undergraduate students.

16. **(C)** "Courses designed for students seeking a professional degree carry a 500 number for undergraduate students and a 700 number for graduate students." The number in Choice (A) refers to an undergraduate, not to a graduate registration. Choice (B) refers to an introductory course with an undergraduate equivalent of 420, not to a professional course with an undergraduate equivalent of 520. Choice (D) refers to a graduate course with no undergraduate equivalent.

17. **(C)** "A full-time graduate student is expected to take courses which total ten to sixteen credit hours. . . . A part-time graduate student must register for a minimum of five credit hours." The student referred to in Choice (A) would be required to register for a minimum of ten, not eight, credit hours. Choice (B) is ambiguous because it may refer to either a part-time or a full-time student. Choice (D) is not mentioned and may not be concluded from information in the passage.

18. **(A)** Choice (B) is mentioned in lines 2–3. Choice (C) is mentioned in lines 3–4. Choice (D) is mentioned in lines 3–4. Courses numbered 99 or below are special interest courses that do not carry academic credit and will not count toward the number of hours needed to complete graduation requirements.

19. **(B)** "A part-time graduate student must register for a minimum of five credit hours." Choices (A) and (D) contradict the fact that introductory courses for graduate students are numbered 600. Choice (C) contradicts the fact that students holding assistantships are expected to enroll for fewer hours.

20. **(C)** In the context of this passage, "under any circumstances" is closest in meaning to "without exception." Choices (A), (B), and (D) are not accepted definitions of the phrase.

21. **(D)** Choices (A), (B), and (C) are important to the discussion, and provide details that support the main topic, "women's suffrage."

22. **(C)** In the context of this passage, "ban" most nearly means to "prohibit." Choices (A), (B), and (D) are not accepted definitions of the word.

23. **(D)** In the context of this passage, "supported" could best be replaced by "promoted." Choices (A), (B), and (C) are not accepted definitions of the word.

24. **(A)** "They [women] became involved primarily in order to better their living conditions and the conditions of others." Choices (B), (C), and (D) are not mentioned and may not be concluded from information in the passage.

25. **(A)** In the context of this passage, "primarily" is closest in meaning to "above all." Choices (B), (C), and (D) are not accepted definitions of the word.

26. **(D)** "When the Civil War ended. . . .the Fifteenth Amendment . . . granted . . . suffrage to blacks. . ." *Suffrage* means the right to vote. Choice (B) contradicts the fact that the bill was presented to Congress in 1878, not immediately after the Civil War. Choice (C) refers to the fact that the eastern states resisted the women's suffrage bill, not the end of the Civil War. Choice (A) is not mentioned and may not be concluded from information in the passage.

27. **(D)** *Suffrage* means the right to vote; the

exercise of such a right. Choice (A) is a definition of the word *suffering*, not *suffrage*. Choices (B) and (C) are related to the word *suffrage*, but they are not accepted definitions of it.

28. **(C)** ". . . the Nineteenth Amendment granted women the right to vote." Choice (A) refers to the Fifteenth not the Nineteenth Amendment. Choice (B) refers to the Fourteenth Amendment. Choice (D) is not mentioned and may not be concluded from information in the passage.

29. **(A)** "A women's suffrage bill had been presented to every Congress since 1878 but it [the bill] continually failed to pass until 1920, when the Nineteenth Amendment granted women the right to vote." Choices (B), (C), and (D) would change the meaning of the sentence.

30. **(D)** ". . . 1920 when the Nineteenth Amendment granted women the right to vote." Choice (A) refers to the date when the Civil War ended. Choice (B) refers to the date when the Fifteenth Amendment was adopted granting blacks, not women, the right to vote. Choice (C) refers to the date when the bill to grant women the right to vote was presented to Congress, not to the date that it was passed and became law.

31. **(B)** The other choices are secondary topics that are used to develop the primary topic, "characteristics and varieties of the *Acacia*." Choices (A), (C), and (D) are important details and examples.

32. **(C)** "Only about a dozen of the three hundred Australian varieties grow well in the southern United States." Choice (A) refers to the number of species identified, not to the number that grow well in the United States. Choice (B) refers to the number of species that grow well in Australia, not in the southern United States. Choice (D) refers to the number of species that have flowers, not to the total number of species that grow well in the southern United States.

33. **(B)** "Although nearly five hundred species of *Acacia* have been identified, only about a dozen of the three hundred Australian varieties grow well in the southern United States, and of these, [varieties] only three are flowering." Choices (A), (C), and (D) would change the meaning of the sentence.

34. **(C)** "The *Silver Wattle*, although very similar to the *Bailey Acacia*, grows twice as high." Choice (A) refers to the *Sydney Golden Wattle*, not to the *Silver Wattle*. Choices (B) and (D) refer to the *Black Acacia*.

35. **(A)** In the context of this passage, "flat" most nearly means "smooth." Choices (B), (C), and (D) are not accepted definitions of the word.

36. **(B)** In the context of this passage, "showy" could best be replaced by "elaborate." Choices (A), (C), and (D) are not accepted definitions of the word.

37. **(D)** ". . . the *Black Acacia* or *Blackwood*, has dark green leaves and unobtrusive blossoms." The species referred to in Choices (A), (B), and (C) have fragrant clusters of yellow flowers.

38. **(B)** ". . .the *Black Acacia* is valuable for its dark wood which is used in making cabinets and furniture." Choices (A), (C), and (D) are not mentioned and may not be concluded from information in the passage.

39. **(A)** In the context of this passage, "highly prized" is closest in meaning to "valuable." Choices (B), (C), and (D) are not accepted definitions of the phrase.

40. **(C)** ". . .the pale yellow blossoms appear in August in Australia." Choice (A) refers to the month that the *Acacia* blooms in the United States, not in Australia. Choices (B) and (D) refer to the reversal of seasons in the northern and southern hemispheres, but not to the blossoming of the *Acacia*.

41. **(A)** "A History of New York City" is the best title because it states the main idea of the passage. Choices (C) and (D) are details used to develop the main idea. Choice (B) is not specific enough.

42. **(C)** "Peter Minuit . . . negotiated with Indian chiefs for the purchase of Manhattan Island for merchandise. . . ." Choices (A) and (B) refer to the value of the merchandise, not to what the Indians received. Choice (D) refers to where the Dutch settlements were located.

43. **(B)** ". . .Dutch settlements in North America known as New Amsterdam. . . ." Choice (C) refers to the location of the land that was purchased from the Indians. Choices (A) and (D) are not mentioned and may not be concluded from information in the passage.

44. **(C)** In the context of this passage, "heterogeneous" could best be replaced by "diverse." Choices (A), (B), and (D) are not accepted definitions of the word.

45. **(C)** ". . .offers, generous by the standards of the era, were extended throughout Europe. Consequently, the settlement became the most heterogeneous of the North American colonies." Choice (A) contradicts the fact that it was New Amsterdam, not the Dutch West India Company, that the English acquired. Choices (C) and (D) are not mentioned and may not be concluded from information in the passage.

46. **(A)** In the context of this passage, "formidable" is closest in meaning to "powerful." Choices (B), (C), and (D) are not accepted definitions of the word.

47. **(B)** ". . . New Amsterdam was renamed New York in honor of the Duke." Choices (A), (C), and (D) are not mentioned and may not be concluded from information in the passage.

48. **(B)** "After the war, it [New York] was selected as the first capital of the United States." Choices (A), (C), and (D) would change the meaning of the sentence.

49. **(B)** "After the war, it [New York] was selected as the first capital of the United States." Choice (A) refers to the former name for New York, which had already been changed when it became the first capital. Choices (C) and (D) refer to cities that became the capital after New York.

50. **(D)** "Three centuries after his initial trade . . . Minuit's tiny investment was worth more than seven billion dollars." Choice (A) refers to the date that the Dutch purchased Manhattan Island from the Indians. Choice (B) refers to the date one century after the purchase. Choice (C) refers to the date three decades after the purchase.

Model Test 5—Short Form

Section 1: Listening Comprehension

1. **(A)** "Maybe its [the problem is] in the cable." Choice (B) contradicts the fact that Channel 17 has a good picture. Choices (C) and (D) are not mentioned and may not be concluded from information in the conversation.

2. **(C)** Since the woman says that Mr. Davis is in conference now, it must be concluded that Mr. Davis cannot talk with Mr. Ward now. Choice (A) contradicts the fact that Mr. Ward, not Mr. Davis, wants to talk. Choice (B) contradicts the fact that Mr. Ward is with the Office of Immigration. Choice (D) is not mentioned and may not be concluded from information in the conversation.

3. **(D)** The woman offers to go to the movie in order to please the man, but she says that she is a little tired, indicating that she does not want to go out. Choice (A) is incorrect because it is the woman, not the man, who is tired. Choice (B) refers to what the man, not the woman, wants to do. Choice (C) is incorrect because the man suggests that they go out after dinner, not for dinner.

4. **(D)** The man offers to get some paper at the bookstore. Choice (A) is incorrect because it is the woman, not the man, who wants to borrow some typing paper. Choice (B) contradicts the fact that the man doesn't have any paper either. Choice (C) is not mentioned and may not be concluded from information in the conversation.

5. **(B)** ". . . walk three more blocks . . ." Since the woman gives directions for walking, it must be concluded that the man is not driving a car. Choice (C) contradicts the fact that the man calls the woman *Miss*. Choices (A) and (D) are not mentioned and may not be concluded from information in the conversation.

6. **(C)** Because the man said that the team played poorly and because both he and his father left the game at half time, it must be concluded that they thought that the game was unsatisfactory. Choice (A) contradicts the fact that the man's father left the game at half time with his son. Choices (B) and (D) contradict the fact that the man said the team played poorly.

7. **(C)** To *fall through* is an idiomatic expression that means not to happen as planned. Choice (D) contradicts the fact that he planned to go to summer school. Choices (A) and (B) are not mentioned and may not be concluded from information in the conversation.

8. **(C)** From the references to a *nurse* and the *emergency room*, it must be concluded that the conversation took place at a hospital. Because the nurse directs the man to an elevator, the conversation must have taken place outside, not inside, an elevator, as in Choice (D). It is not customary to find an emergency room in the places referred to in Choices (A) and (B).

9. **(B)** Choices (A), (C), and (D) are mentioned in reference to the main topic of discussion, the apartment.

10. **(B)** Since the woman mentions that Dr. Taylor does not interact with her in class despite her good grades, she implies that she is not sure how Dr. Taylor feels. Choices (C) and (D) contradict the fact that she was the only one who received an A on her paper. Choice (A) is not mentioned and may not be concluded from information in the conversation.

11. **(B)** Since the man says that he already knows what he wants to order, it must be concluded that he is going to order lunch. Choice (A) contradicts the fact that the man knows what he wants without looking at the menu. Choice (D) contradicts the fact that the man has not seen the list of specials on the menu. Choice (C) is not mentioned and may not be concluded from information in the conversation.

12. **(C)** Since the man inquires whether she has asked Sandy, he implies that she should ask her. Choice (A) refers to the payment for participation, not to the man's suggestion. Choice (B) refers to the woman's request, not to the man's suggestion. Choice (D) refers to the experiment in psychology, not to a person that the woman should see.

13. **(A)** Because *either* means that the speaker is including herself in her statement, it must be concluded that the woman did not go to the meeting. The man said that he did not go because of a headache. Choice (B) contradicts the use of the word *either* in the woman's question. Choice (C) contradicts the man's negative response to the question of whether he went to the meeting. Choice (D) contradicts both the use of the word *either* and the man's negative response.

14. **(D)** Since the man says that he will only need the books for a few days, it must be concluded that he will return the books by the due date. Choice (A) contradicts the fact that he only needs the books for a few days. Choice (B) contradicts the fact that the books have a due date for return. Choice (C) contradicts the fact that the speakers are talking about more than one book.

15. **(B)** A *collect call* means that the money is collected from the person receiving the call. Choice (A) refers to the identity of the woman, not to who will pay for the call. Choice (C) refers to the identity of the man. Choice (D) is not mentioned and may not be concluded from information in the conversation.

16. **(B)** "How about [buying] a nice pen?" Choice (C) refers to the card that the woman has already purchased, not to the man's idea. Choice (D) contradicts the fact that the man offers a suggestion for a gift. Choice (A) is not mentioned and may not be concluded from information in the conversation.

17. **(D)** To *not make up one's mind* is an idiomatic expression that means to be undecided. Choices (A) and (C) contradict the fact that she is still considering both alternatives. Choice (B) contradicts the fact that she has a choice.

18. **(B)** "I've probably had enough exercise for one day." Choice (A) contradicts the fact that they are on the way home. Choices (C) and (D) are not mentioned and may not be concluded from information in the conversation.

19. **(A)** Since the woman asks whether the man can work and go to school, she implies that he may be taking on too much. Choices (B), (C), and (D) are not mentioned and may not be concluded from information in the conversation.

20. **(C)** Since the man suggests that the woman buy postcards, it must be concluded that she should send postcards to her family. Choice (B) contradicts the fact that she does not have time to write a letter. Choice (A) refers to the man's family, not to the woman's family. Choice (D) is not mentioned and may not be concluded from information in the conversation.

21. **(B)** Choices (A), (C), and (D) are all mentioned as they relate to the main topic of the conversation, where the woman will go to school.

22. **(A)** To *cost an arm and a leg* is an idiomatic expression that means to be very expensive. Choices (B), (C), and (D) are not paraphrases of the expression, and may not be concluded from information in the conversation.

23. **(B)** Since the man says that ticket number 32 is in room 27, the woman will probably go to room 27. Choice (A) contradicts the fact that the woman already has a ticket. Choice (C) refers to the number of the ticket, not to the number of the room. Choice (D) contradicts the fact that the man has already seen her ticket.

24. **(B)** Since the teachers gave flowers to all of the honors students, and the woman has a flower, it must be concluded that she is an honors student. Choice (A) contradicts the fact that she has a flower that was presented at the reception. Choice (D) contradicts the fact that she received a flower for students. Choice (C) is not mentioned and may not be concluded from information in the conversation.

25. **(D)** ". . . Take it over next term." Choices (B) and (C) contradict the fact that the woman says to drop the class. Choice (A) is not mentioned and may not be concluded from information in the conversation.

26. **(C)** "To earn enough money for next year's tuition." Choice (A) refers to the place where Margaret works, not to where she stays. Choice (B) contradicts the fact that she is working at the motel. Choice (D) is not mentioned and may not be concluded from information in the conversation.

27. **(B)** "[The seat belt law is]. . . only for the driver and the passengers in the front seat." Choice (A) contradicts the fact that there is a law for the driver and passengers in the front seat. Choice (C) contradicts the fact that the woman says he is okay as he is, implying that he is sitting in the back seat and does not need a seat belt. Choice (D) is not mentioned and may not be concluded from information in the conversation.

28. **(C)** Since the woman used to teach English, the man is not surprised that she likes the course. *No wonder* is an idiomatic expression

that means the information is logical. Choice (D) refers to the woman's interest, not to the course. Choices (A) and (B) are not mentioned and may not be concluded from information in the conversation.

29. **(A)** Since they are discussing potential group members and their value to a presentation, it must be concluded that they are planning to make a presentation. Choice (B) contradicts the fact that the second woman says they should ask Jane. Choices (C) and (D) are not mentioned and may not be concluded from information in the conversation.

30. **(B)** Since the man explains that the procedure requires her to take a number, the woman will probably do it. Choice (A) contradicts the fact that there is no line. Choices (C) and (D) are not mentioned and may not be concluded from information in the conversation.

31. **(A)** ". . . in my experience, a free offer usually starts out free, and ends up costing the usual price or more. . ." Choices (B) and (D) are mentioned by the man during the conversation, but the woman perceives correctly that his purpose is to sell her magazine subscriptions. Choice (C) is not mentioned and may not be concluded from information in the conversation.

32. **(A)** "[I subscribe to] news magazines mostly." Choice (B) contradicts the fact that she subscribes to several magazines. Choice (C) contradicts the fact that she refuses to take solicitations over the phone. Choice (D) contradicts the fact that she repeatedly refers to "we" when she is talking about subscribing to magazines.

33. **(B)** ". . . ends up costing the usual price or more. . ." Choice (A) contradicts the fact that she used to subscribe to the magazines that the man has to offer. Choices (C) and (D) are not mentioned and may not be concluded from information in the conversation.

34. **(C)** "Thank you, anyway." Choice (A) contradicts the fact that the woman refuses to take solicitations over the phone. Choices (B) and (D) are not mentioned and may not be concluded from information in the conversation.

35. **(C)** "We all agree that British English and American English are different. Right? . . . But not so different that it prevents us from

understanding each other." Choices (A), (B), and (D) are secondary points of discussion that are used to develop the main topic of the discussion.

36. **(B)** "Words like *theater* and *center* end in *-re* in England instead of *-er*." Choice (A) is the American, not the British English spelling. Choices (C) and (D) are not mentioned and may not be concluded from information in the discussion.

37. **(C)** "I remember seeing an English movie where the actors kept calling their apartment a *flat*." Choice (A) is the American, not the British meaning of the word. Choices (B) and (D) refer to the context in which the woman heard the British usage.

38. **(D)** "We all agree that British English and American English are different. . . . But not so different that it prevents us from understanding each other." Choice (A) refers to the man's opinion at the beginning of the discussion, not to the opinion of the class at the conclusion of the discussion. The opinions expressed in Choices (B) and (C) are not mentioned and may not be concluded from information in the discussion.

39. **(C)** "On his third exploratory voyage, as captain of two ships. . . Captain James Cook came upon. . . the Hawaiian Islands." Choices (A), (B), and (D) are secondary themes used to develop the main theme of the talk.

40. **(B)** ". . . as captain in charge of two ships, the *Resolution* and the *Discovery*, he came upon a group of uncharted islands. . . ." Choice (A) refers to the fact that this was Cook's third voyage to explore the Pacific Ocean, not to the name of his ship. In Choice (C), the word *resolution* is confused with the word *revolution*. *England* in Choice (D) refers to the country that commissioned Cook, not to the name of his ship.

41. **(C)** "The women cared for the children and made clothing." Choice (A) refers to what the men, not the women, did. Choices (B) and (D) include the duties of both the men and the women.

42. **(C)** ". . . Cook demanded that the king be taken as a hostage until the boat was returned. . . . In the fighting that followed, Cook and four other crewmen were killed." Choice (B) contradicts the fact that the islanders, not the crew, became ill. Choice (D)

contradicts the fact that the islanders, not Cook, stole a boat. Choice (A) is not mentioned and may not be concluded from information in the conversation.

43. **(C)** "Alloys are mixtures that have been deliberately combined in specific proportion for a definite purpose." Choice (A) refers to natural combinations of metals, not to alloys. Choice (B) is true, but incomplete because it does not mention the specific purposes. Choice (D) is not mentioned and may not be concluded from information in the conversation.

44. **(A)** ". . . alloys are mixtures that have been deliberately combined in specific proportion for a definite purpose." Choice (B) refers to properties of some metals, not to what the speaker says in general about the properties of alloys. Choice (D) refers to impure metals, not to alloys. Choice (C) is not mentioned and may not be concluded from information in the conversation.

45. **(A)** "In the aircraft industry, there is a need for metals that are both strong and light." Choice (D) contradicts the fact that the metals referred to are alloys. Choices (B) and (C) are not mentioned and may not be concluded from information in the conversation.

46. **(C)** "Both [alloys and combinations in nature] are mixtures, but alloys are mixtures that have been deliberately combined in specific proportion for a definite purpose." Choice (A) contradicts the fact that metals that occur accidentally in nature are impure. Choice (B) contradicts the fact that combinations of metals occur accidentally in nature. Choice (D) contradicts the fact that both alloys and combinations of metals that occur in nature are mixtures.

47. **(D)** "My report is on local control of schools." Choices (A), (B), and (C) are secondary themes used to develop the main theme of the report.

48. **(A)** ". . .the board. . .must approve the recommendations of the superintendent." Choice (B) contradicts the fact that the board is either elected by the people or appointed by the mayor. Choice (D) contradicts the fact that the superintendent carries out the policies of the board, not the reverse. Choice (C) is not mentioned and may not be concluded from information in the report.

49. **(B)** ". . .the board [is] often made up of community leaders who are not professional educators. . ." Choice (A) contradicts the fact that the board is not made up of professional educators. Choices (C) and (D) are not mentioned and may not be concluded from information in the report.

50. **(C)** "The function of the national department is. . .supervising the compliance of schools with national legislation." Choice (A) contradicts the fact that the school board establishes the policies. Choice (B) contradicts the fact that the school board makes decisions about the curriculum in the local district. Choice (D) contradicts the fact that local school boards are elected by the people or appointed by the mayor.

Section 2: Structure and Written Expression

1. **(A)** Most adverbs of manner are formed by adding -ly to adjectives. Choices (B) and (D) are redundant and indirect. Choice (C) is ungrammatical because the adverb *fast* does not have an -ly ending. (Refer to Patterns, Problem 126, page 202.)

2. **(C)** *Next to* is a prepositional idiom which means *near*. Choices (A), (B), and (D) are not idiomatic. (Refer to Style, Problem 29, page 255.)

3. **(C)** *But also* is used in correlation with the inclusive *not only*. Choice (A) would be used in correlation with *not*, not in correlation with *not only*. Choices (B) and (D) are not used in correlation with another inclusive. (Refer to Patterns, Problem 118, page 192.)

4. **(B)** Ideas in a series should be expressed by parallel structures. Only *an officer in the Navy* in Choice (B) provides for parallelism with the noun *a lawyer*. Choices (A), (C), and (D) are not parallel. (Refer to Style, Problem 17, page 240.)

5. **(B)** Subject-verb order is used in the clause after a question word connector such as *what*. In Choices (A) and (D), subject-verb order is reversed. In Choice (C), the auxiliary *did* is unnecessary and incorrect. (Refer to Patterns, Problem 124, page 199.)

6. **(C)** Comparisons must be made with logically comparable nouns. Choices (A) and (D) are redundant and indirect. Choice (B) makes an illogical comparison of *a salary* with *a teacher*. Only Choice (C) compares two salaries. (Refer to Patterns, Problem 102, page 172.)

7. **(A)** The verb *to expect* requires an infinitive in the complement. Choices (B), (C), and (D) are not infinitives. (Refer to Patterns, Problem 3, page 43.)

8. **(A)** Subject-verb order is used in the clause after a question word connector such as *where*. In Choice (B), there is no question word connector. In Choice (C), the subject-verb order is reversed. In Choice (D), the question word connector is used after, not before the subject and verb. (Refer to Patterns, Problem 124, page 199.)

9. **(A)** The verb phrase *to look forward to* requires an -ing form in the complement. Choices (B) and (D) are not -ing forms. Choice (C) is *be* and an -ing form. (Refer to Patterns, Problem 4, page 45.)

10. **(C)** *As well as* is used in correlation with the inclusive *and*. Choices (A) and (B) would be used in clauses of comparison, not correlation. Choice (D) is incomplete because it does not include the final word *as*. (Refer to Patterns, Problem 117, page 190.)

11. **(C)** *Because of* is used before nouns such as *a misunderstanding* to express cause. Choice (D) is used before a subject and verb, not a noun, to express cause. Choices (A) and (B) are not accepted for statements of cause. (Refer to Patterns, Problem 111, page 183.)

12. **(C)** Affirmative agreement with *so* requires verb-subject order and an affirmative verb which refers to the verb in the main clause. Choices (A) and (B) have verb-subject order, but the verbs DO and HAVE do not refer to the verb BE in the main clause. In Choice (D), *so* is used at the end, not at the beginning, of the clause and there is no verb. (Refer to Patterns, Problem 120, page 194.)

13. **(D)** The anticipatory clause *it was in 1848 that* introduces a subject and verb, *gold was discovered*. Choice (A) may be used preceding a subject and verb without *that*. Choice (B) may be used as a subject clause preceding a main verb. Choice (C) is redundant and indirect. "Because in 1848 gold was discovered at Sutter's Mill, the California Gold Rush began," and "That in 1848 gold was discovered at Sutter's Mill was the

cause of the California Gold Rush" would also be correct. (Refer to Patterns, Problem 35, page 35.)

14. **(D)** There must be agreement between pronoun and antecedent. Choices (A), (B), and (C) do not agree in number, gender, and case with the singular, neuter, objective antecedent *crime rate*. Choice (A) is plural. Choice (B) is masculine. Choice (C) is possessive. (Refer to Style, Problem 11, page 232.)

15. **(C)** Comparative forms for three-syllable adverbs are usually preceded by *more* and followed by *than*. Choice (A) is followed by *as*. Choice (B) is preceded by *as*. Choice (D) is not preceded by *more*. (Refer to Patterns, Problem 96, page 165.)

16. **(B)** Most adverbs of manner are formed by adding *-ly* to adjectives. *Careful* should be *carefully* to qualify the manner in which you must listen. (Refer to Patterns, Problem 126, page 202.)

17. **(D)** There must be agreement between subject and verb, not between the verb and words in the appositive after the subject. *Were* should be *was* to agree with the singular subject *gunpowder*. (Refer to Style, Problem 7, page 228.)

18. **(B)** *Developing* should be *development*. Although both are nouns derived from verbs, the *-ment* ending is preferred. *Developing* means progressing. *Development* means the act of developing or the result of developing. (Refer to Style, Problem 30, page 257.)

19. **(B)** There must be agreement between subject and verb. *Is* should be *are* to agree with the plural subject *manufacturers*. (Refer to Style, Problem 5, page 226.)

20. **(A)** There must be agreement between pronoun and antecedent. *Which* should be *who* to refer to the antecedent *the person*. *Which* refers to things. *Who* refers to persons. (Refer to Patterns, Problem 48, page 102.)

21. **(B)** *So* is commonly used as a purpose connector in spoken English, but *so that* should be used in written English. (Refer to Patterns, Problem 122, page 197.)

22. **(A)** *Despite of* is a combination of *despite* and *in spite of*. *Despite of* should be either *despite* or *in spite of*. (Refer to Patterns, Problem 110, page 182.)

23. **(B)** *So* is used with an adjective to describe a cause. *As* should be *so* with the adjective *high* to describe why most young people cannot afford to buy homes. (Refer to Patterns, Problem 81, page 147.)

24. **(A)** Ideas in a series should be expressed by parallel structures. *Taking* should be *to take* to provide for parallelism with the infinitive *to see*. (Refer to Style, Problem 17, page 240.)

25. **(D)** Because adjectives are used after verbs of the senses, *sweetly* should be *sweet* after the verb *smell*. *Sweetly* is an adverb. *Sweet* is an adjective. (Refer to Patterns, Problem 85, page 151.)

26. **(A)** *Chose* should be *chosen* because the auxiliary *having* requires a participle. *Chose* is a past form. *Chosen* is a participle. (Refer to Patterns, Problem 36, page 87.)

27. **(D)** *Equal to* is a prepositional idiom. *As* should be *to*. (Refer to Style, Problem 29, page 255.)

28. **(A)** *May* and a verb word in the result require a past form in the condition. Because *may have* is used in the result, *having* should be *had* in the condition. (Refer to Patterns, Problem 23, page 69.)

29. **(B)** *As well as* should be *and*, which is used in correlation with the inclusive *both*. (Refer to Patterns, Problem 116, page 189.)

30. **(D)** Ideas in a series should be expressed by parallel structures. *Stressful* should be *stress* to provide for parallelism with the nouns *predisposition*, *drugs*, or *infection*. (Refer to Style, Problem 17, page 240.)

31. **(A)** *I* should be *me* because it is the appositive complement of the clause *they asked*. *I* functions as a subject. *Me* functions as a complement. (Refer to Patterns, Problem 44, page 97.)

32. **(D)** Either an infinitive or a clause with a verb word must be used after an impersonal expression. *For trying* should be either *to try* or *that one try* after the impersonal expression *it is very important*. (Refer to Patterns, Problem 29, page 78.)

33. **(B)** There must be agreement between subject and verb. *Were* should be *was* to agree with the singular subject *what happened*. (Refer to Style, Problem 9, page 230.)

34. **(B)** *Novels* should be *novelists*. Although both are nouns, *novels* refer to books and manuscripts. *Novelists* refer to the writers. (Refer to Style, Problem 30, page 257.)

35. **(B)** A verb word must be used in a clause after the verb *to require*. *Is* should be *be*. (Refer to Patterns, Problem 27, page 76.)

36. **(B)** Most adverbs of manner are formed by adding *-ly* to adjectives. *Perfect* should be *perfectly* to qualify the manner in which the doctor has diagnosed the problem. (Refer to Patterns, Problem 126, page 202.)

37. **(B)** In order to refer to nurses not allowing you to give blood, *let* should be used. *To leave* means to go. *To let* means to allow. (Refer to Style, Problem 26, page 252.)

38. **(C)** There must be agreement between pronoun and antecedent. *Their* should be *its* to agree with the singular antecedent *a turtle*. (Refer to Style, Problem 11, page 232.)

39. **(C)** Ideas in a series should be expressed by parallel structures. *He invented* should be *the inventor of* to provide for parallelism with *the editor* and *a diplomatic representative*. (Refer to Style, Problem 17, page 240.)

40. **(D)** The verb *thought* establishes a point of view in the past. *Has* should be *had* in order to maintain the point of view. (Refer to Style, Problem 2, page 222.)

Section 3: Reading Comprehension

1. **(A)** Choices (B) and (D) are secondary ideas that are used to develop the main idea, "the development of Newton's Laws." Choice (C) is not mentioned and may not be concluded from information in the passage.

2. **(A)** In the context of this passage, "predecessors" refers to "those who came before." Choices (B), (C), and (D) are not accepted definitions of the word.

3. **(A)** *Prior to* means before in time, order, or importance. Choices (B), (C), and (D) are not accepted definitions of the phrase.

4. **(C)** "Prior to Newton, Aristotle had established that the natural state of a body was a state of rest." Choice (A) refers to the scientist who established the behavior of falling objects, not the natural state of a body. Choice (B) refers to the scientist who established the laws of motion of planets around the sun. Choice (D) refers to the scientist who established three laws based in part upon the premise that the natural state of a body is a state of rest, not to the scientist who established the premise originally.

5. **(B)** "Prior to Newton, Aristotle had established that the natural state of a body was a state of rest, and that unless a force acted upon it [the body] to maintain motion, a moving body would come to rest." Choices (A), (C), and (D) would change the meaning of the sentence.

6. **(D)** "Galileo had succeeded in correctly describing the behavior of falling objects." Choice (A) refers to the scientist who described the natural state of a body, not the behavior of falling objects. Choice (B) refers to the scientist who deduced three laws of motion. Choice (C) refers to the scientist who described the motion of planets around the sun.

7. **(A)** "Huygens recognized that a change in the direction of motion involved acceleration, just as did a change in speed." Choice (B) contradicts the fact that acceleration is required for a change in direction. Choice (C) contradicts the fact that acceleration is required for a change in speed. Choice (D) contradicts both the fact that acceleration is required for a change in direction and the fact that it is required for a change in speed.

8. **(D)** "It was primarily from Galileo and Kepler that Newton borrowed." Choices (A), (B), and (C) include less important sources.

9. **(B)** In the context of this passage, "momentum" is closest in meaning to "speed." Choices (A), (C), and (D) are not accepted definitions of the word.

10. **(A)** "(1) a body at rest remains at rest. . ." Choice (B) refers to actions and reactions. Choices (C) and (D) refer to all of Newton's laws, not specifically to the law that describes inertia.

11. **(A)** "The Father of American Public Education" is the best title because it states the main idea of the passage. Choice (C) is a detail used to develop the main idea. Choices (B) and (D) are not specific enough.

12. **(B)** ". . .his father and older brother died, and he [Mann] became responsible for supporting his family." Choice (A) contradicts the fact that he went to school for two or three months, not six months a year. Choice (C) contradicts the fact that he had a brother. Choice (D) contradicts the fact that several teachers helped him study.

13. **(D)** In the context of this passage, "strug-

gles" could best be replaced by "difficult times." Choices (A), (B), and (C) are not accepted definitions of the word.

14. **(B)** In the context of this passage, "regret" could best be replaced by "disappointment." Choices (A), (C), and (D) are not accepted definitions of the word.

15. **(A)** "Mann was recognized as the father of public education." Choice (B) contradicts the fact that Horace Mann exercised an enormous influence. Choices (C) and (D) are unlikely since his influence resulted in a change in the school system.

16. **(D)** "Horace Mann exercised an enormous influence during the critical period. . .that brought into existence the American graded elementary school." Choice (B) refers to the older system that was replaced by the graded elementary school. The state board in Choice (A) refers to the organization for which Horace Mann served as secretary, not to a school system. Choice (C) refers to the fact that the graded elementary school was substituted for the older district system. It was not called a substitute system however.

17. **(A)** In the context of this passage, "mandatory" is closest in meaning to "required." Choices (B), (C), and (D) are not accepted definitions of the word.

18. **(A)** "Mann's ideas were developed and distributed in twelve annual reports to the state of Massachusetts." Choice (B) contradicts the fact that the reports were distributed in the state of Massachusetts. Choice (C) refers to speeches that he made, but the location of them is not mentioned and may not be concluded from information in the passage. Mann established school libraries, referred to in Choice (D), but his books are not mentioned and their presence in the libraries may not be concluded from information in the passage.

19. **(C)** ". . .the Massachusetts reforms later served as a model for the nation." Choice (A) contradicts the fact that the reforms were considered quite radical at the time. Choice (B) contradicts the fact that they served as a model for the nation. Choice (D) is not mentioned and may not be concluded from information in the passage.

20. **(B)** "Be ashamed to die until you have won some victory for humanity." Choices (A),

(C), and (D) are not mentioned specifically as part of Mann's philosophy.

21. **(D)** "A Brief History of Population and Overpopulation" is the best title because it states the main idea of the passage. The other choices are secondary ideas that are used to develop the main idea. They are all significant to the historical discussion.

22. **(B)** "World population totaled about 500 million in 1650. It doubled in the period from 1650 to 1850." Choice (A) refers to the population in 1650. Choice (C) refers to the population today. Choice (D) refers to the population projected for the year 2000.

23. **(B)** "It [population] doubled in the period from 1650 to 1850." In Choice (A), 500 refers to the total population in the year 1650, not to a date. In Choice (C), the population increased ten, not two times. In Choice (D), the population will have increased seven, not two times.

24. **(C)** "Today the population is more than five billion. . .reaching seven billion by the turn of the century." Since world population in the year 2000 will reach seven billion and the population today is five billion, the population in the year 2000 will exceed that of today by seven less five billion, or two billion. Choice (A) refers to the population in the year 1650. Choice (B) refers to the population today. Choice (D) refers to the population in the year 2000.

25. **(C)** "Thomas Malthus, an English economist. . ." Choices (A), (B), and (D) contradict the fact that Malthus was an economist.

26. **(C)** "He suggested that because world population tended to increase more rapidly than the food supply, a continual strain was exerted upon available resources." Choices (A), (B), and (D) are not accepted definitions of the word "resources."

27. **(A)** "With recent advances in science. . . some of the limiting factors in population growth have been lessened. The result is overpopulation." Choice (B) is one of the limiting factors of population growth, not a cause of overpopulation. Choice (C) is a result of overpopulation, not a cause. Choice (D) is one of the recommendations to alleviate overpopulation.

28. **(A)** In the context of this passage, "obvious" could best be replaced by "clear." Choices

(B), (C), and (D) are not accepted definitions of the word.

29. **(C)** In the context of this passage, "lasting" is closest in meaning to "permanent." Choices (A), (B), and (D) are not accepted definitions of the word.

30. **(C)** "International organizations have recommended programs to encourage general economic development in target areas along with a decrease in birth rates to effect a lasting solution." Choice (A) refers to a limiting factor, not to a recommendation to alleviate overpopulation. Choice (B) refers to a cause of overpopulation. Choice (D) may be true, but it is not mentioned and may not be concluded from information in the passage.

31. **(A)** "Organic architecture, that is, natural architecture. . . ." Choice (B) refers to a rule rejected by organic architecture, not to another name for it. Choices (C) and (D) refer to the fact that organic architecture may be varied but always remains true to natural principles. Neither principle architecture nor varied architecture was cited as another name for organic architecture however.

32. **(B)** In the context of this passage, "ultimately" could best be replaced by "eventually." Choices (A), (C), and (D) are not accepted definitions of the word.

33. **(A)** "Organic architecture—that is, natural architecture—may be varied in concept and form, but it [the architecture] is always faithful to natural principles." Choices (B), (C), and (D) would change the meaning of the sentence.

34. **(C)** In the context of this passage, "upheld" is closest in meaning to "promoted." Choices (A), (B), and (D) are not accepted definitions of the word.

35. **(D)** "Form does not follow function; form is inseparable from function." Choice (A) contradicts the fact that form does not follow function. Choices (B) and (C) contradict the fact that form is inseparable from function.

36. **(C)** "Organic architecture rejects. . .mere aesthetics. . .to remain true to the nature of the site. . .If this natural principle is upheld, then a bank cannot be built to look like a Greek temple." Choice (A) contradicts the fact that a bank cannot be built to look like a Greek temple. Choice (B) contradicts the

fact that organic architecture remains true to the nature of the site. Choice (D) contradicts the fact that organic architecture rejects mere aesthetics.

37. **(B)** "Natural principles then, are principles of design, not style. . . . Like a sculptor, the organic architect views the site and materials as an innate form that shapes and develops organically from within. Choice (C) refers to the geometric themes mentioned later in the passage. Choice (D) contradicts the fact that the author emphasizes design, not style. Choice (A) is not mentioned and may not be concluded from information in the passage.

38. **(B)** "For the most part, these structures find their geometric themes in the contours of the land. . ." Choices (A), (C), and (D) refer to other themes in the passage.

39. **(A)** In the context of this passage, "obscured" is closest in meaning to "difficult to see." Choices (B), (C), and (D) are not accepted definitions of the word.

40. **(C)** ". . .a building should. . .respect the natural characteristics of the setting to create harmony with its natural environment." Choices (A), (B), and (D) contradict the fact that nature should be respected.

41. **(A)** Choices (B), (C), and (D) are important to the discussion and provide details that support the main point that there were both laboratory and literary alchemists.

42. **(B)** In the context of the passage, "authentic" could best be replaced by "genuine." Choices (A), (C), and (D) are not accepted definitions of the word.

43. **(D)** "The earliest authentic works on European alchemy are those [works] of the English monk Roger Bacon and the German philosopher St. Albertus Magnus." Choices (A), (B), and (C) would change the meaning of the sentence.

44. **(B)** "The earliest authentic works on European alchemy are those of the English monk Roger Bacon and the German philosopher St. Albertus Magnus." Choice (A) contradicts the fact that Roger Bacon was English and St. Albertus Magnus was German. Choice (C) contradicts the fact that Roger Bacon was a monk and St. Albertus Magnus was a philosopher. Choice (D) is not mentioned and may not be concluded from information in the passage.

45. **(A)** ". . .inferior metals such as lead and mercury were removed by various degrees of imperfection from gold." Choices (B), (C), and (D) are not mentioned and may not be concluded from information in the passage.

46. **(B)** ". . .base metals could be transmuted to gold by blending them with a substance even more perfect than gold. This elusive substance was referred to as the 'philosopher's stone.' " Choices (A) and (D) contradict the fact that the "philosopher's stone" was more perfect than gold. Choice (C) contradicts the fact that the "philosopher's stone" was an element that alchemists were searching for, not another name for their art.

47. **(D)** "In their treatises they [Roger Bacon and St. Albertus Magnus] . . .asserted that. . .base metals could be transmuted to gold. . . ." Choice (A) contradicts the fact that Roger Bacon wrote one of the earliest authentic works on alchemy. Choice (B) contradicts the fact that Roger Bacon and St. Albertus Magnus held the same premise. Choice (C) is not mentioned and may not be concluded from information in the passage.

48. **(C)** "Most of the early alchemists were artisans . . . ." Choice (B) refers to the second group, not the first group of alchemists. Choices (A) and (D) are not mentioned and may not be concluded from information in the passage.

49. **(B)** In the context of this passage, "cryptic" could be replaced by "secret." Choices (A), (C), and (D) are not accepted definitions of the word.

50. **(B)** ". . . it was the literary alchemist who was most likely to produce a written record; therefore, much of what is known about the science of alchemy is derived from philosophers rather than from the alchemists who labored in laboratories." Choice (A) is true, but it is not the reason that we know about the history of alchemy. Choices (C) and (D) are not mentioned and may not be concluded from information in the passage.

Model Test 6—Short Form

Section 1: Listening Comprehension

1. **(C)** Since the man exclaims about the price of gasoline, it must be concluded that he thinks it is very expensive. Choice (A) contradicts the fact that it [the price of gas] will probably be higher next month. Choice (B) refers to the woman's opinion, not to what the man thinks. Choice (D) contradicts the fact that the man could not believe the price.

2. **(D)** Since the woman says that Ellen is interested in African art *too*, it must be concluded that she is also interested. Choice (A) refers to Ellen, not to the woman. Choice (C) contradicts the fact that Ellen is the man's sister, not the woman's sister. Choice (B) is not mentioned and may not be concluded from information in the conversation.

3. **(B)** According to the woman, she has to study for her qualifying examinations. Choices (A) and (C) contradict the fact that the woman says she is tempted to go. Choice (D) is incorrect because the woman is taking a qualifying examination [for a degree]. She is not trying to qualify in order to play tennis.

4. **(B)** "I have an attendance requirement for undergraduates, but not for graduate students." Choice (A) contradicts the fact that she has a policy for undergraduates. Choice (C) contradicts the fact that the woman says "no" when she is asked whether attendance will count toward the grade. Choice (D) contradicts the fact that the woman has an attendance requirement for undergraduates, but not for this class, which implies that it is a graduate course.

5. **(B)** Since the man asks where to buy a cake, and the woman recommends a bakery, it must be concluded that the man will go to a bakery. Choice (A) contradicts the fact that the man wants to buy a cake. Choice (C) refers to the name of a bakery, not to what the man will do. Choice (D) refers to the name of another bakery.

6. **(C)** From the references to *financial reports*, *books*, and *accounts*, it must be concluded

that the man is an accountant. It is not as probable that any of the persons referred to in Choices (A), (B), and (D) would be handling *accounts* and *financial reports*.

7. **(C)** The woman says that Ali is a part-time student this term. Choice (A) is incomplete because Ali is studying at the university and the American Language Institute. The number in Choice (B) refers to the number of classes that Ali is taking at the Institute, not at the university. Choice (D) is incorrect because it is the man in the conversation, not Ali, who is surprised. The woman says that Ali's situation is not surprising.

8. **(C)** To *just miss* someone is an idiomatic expression that means that the person has already left. Choices (A), (B), and (D) are not paraphrases of the expression and may not be concluded from information in the conversation.

9. **(B)** Choices (A), (C), and (D) are all mentioned in reference to the main topic of the conversation, the woman's teeth.

10. **(C)** Because the foreign student advisor is Mrs. Jones, not Miss Jones, we know that she is married. Choice (A) is incorrect because it is Mrs. Jones, not Mr. Adams, who is the new foreign student advisor. Choice (B) contradicts the fact that Mrs., not Mr., Jones, is the foreign student advisor. In Choice (D), it is Mr. Adams, not the foreign student advisor, who is not here.

11. **(A)** *I'm afraid not* is an idiomatic expression that means unfortunately not. Choice (B) contradicts the fact that she did not get a letter. Choice (D) contradicts the fact that she is disappointed. Choice (C) refers to the fact that she received a bill, but it is not mentioned and may not be concluded from information in the conversation.

12. **(C)** Since the woman asks where she can find a telephone, she will probably make a phone call. Choice (D) contradicts the fact that the plane has already departed. Choices (A) and (B) are not mentioned and may not be concluded from information in the conversation.

13. **(C)** *Sold out* is an idiomatic expression that means there are none left. Choice (A) contradicts the fact that she has already tried to buy her books at the bookstore. Choice (D) contradicts the fact that she tried to buy the

books. Choice (B) is not mentioned and may not be concluded from information in the conversation.

14. **(B)** "You'd better leave a few minutes early." Choice (C) refers to the time the man has to be there, not to the time he should leave. Choices (A) and (D) are not mentioned and may not be concluded from information in the conversation.

15. **(C)** To *make fun of* is an idiomatic expression that means to ridicule. Choices (A), (B), and (D) are not paraphrases of the expression, and may not be concluded from information in the conversation.

16. **(A)** A *put down* is an idiomatic expression that means an insult. Choices (B), (C), and (D) are not paraphrases of the expression, and may not be concluded from information in the conversation.

17. **(B)** "Can you watch my book bag?" Choice (D) contradicts the fact that the man wants the woman to stay with his book bag. Choices (A) and (C) are not mentioned and may not be concluded from information in the conversation.

18. **(B)** *I hear you* is an idiomatic expression that means the speaker understands the other person's point of view. Choice (C) refers to the woman's feelings about the apartment, not to the man's feelings about the conversation. Choices (A) and (D) are not paraphrases of the expression, and may not be concluded from information in the conversation.

19. **(C)** Since Mike's brother is using the car while Mike is away, it must be concluded that Mike is in Florida as planned. Choice (A) contradicts the fact that Mike's brother is using his car. Choice (B) refers to Mike, not to his brother. Choice (D) contradicts the fact the Mike's brother is here and Mike is in Florida.

20. **(C)** "You'd better start working on that project." Choice (B) contradicts the fact that the man has not started yet. Choices (A) and (D) are not mentioned and may not be concluded from information in the conversation.

21. **(A)** To *settle something once and for all* is an idiomatic expression that means to arrive at a permanent solution. Choice (B) contradicts the fact that they are going to settle the problem now. Choice (C) contradicts the fact that the woman gives the telephone number to the

man. Choice (D) contradicts the fact that the woman has the telephone number.

22. **(D)** *Why not?* is an idiomatic expression that means the speaker agrees with the other person's plan. Choices (A), (B), and (C) are not paraphrases of the expression, and may not be concluded from information in the conversation.

23. **(A)** Since the woman registers surprise, it must be concluded that she thought the couple would not get married. Choices (B) and (C) contradict the fact that the woman made her comment about the wedding, not the honeymoon. The size of the wedding in Choice (D) is not mentioned and may not be concluded from information in the conversation.

24. **(C)** *What's the point?* is an idiomatic expression that means the speaker does not believe that the suggestion will be helpful. Choices (A), (B), and (D) are not paraphrases of the expression, and may not be concluded from information in the conversation.

25. **(A)** Since the woman says "I suggest that you call your sponsor," the man will probably do it. Choice (B) contradicts the fact that the check isn't here. Choices (C) and (D) are not mentioned and may not be concluded from information in the conversation.

26. **(D)** *Don't give up* is an idiomatic expression that means keep trying. Choices (A), (B), and (C) are not paraphrases of the expression, and may not be concluded from information in the conversation.

27. **(A)** Since the man complains that there wasn't anybody to help him, he implies that he could have used help. Choice (D) contradicts the fact that he made a complaint. Choices (B) and (C) are not mentioned and may not be concluded from information in the conversation.

28. **(A)** ". . . my insurance rates went up. . ." Choice (B) contradicts the fact that he was not cited. Choice (C) contradicts the fact that no one was injured. Choice (D) contradicts the fact that the man knows it was not his fault.

29. **(B)** Since the man expresses surprise that Vanesa was accepted to Yale, and comments about the TOEFL requirement, he must have assumed Vanesa would not make a high enough score. Choice (A) refers to Vanesa's plan, not to the man's assumption. Choice

(C) contradicts the fact that the man was surprised by her acceptance. Choice (D) is not mentioned and may not be concluded from information in the conversation.

30. **(B)** *Is this seat taken?* is an idiomatic expression that means the speaker would like permission to sit down. Choices (A), (C), and (D) are not paraphrases of the expression, and may not be concluded from information in the conversation.

31. **(D)** "I've been sick. . . . Now I'm worried about getting caught up." Choice (A) refers to the fact that the man has been sick, but he is not sick now. Choice (B) contradicts the fact that he stayed out of the hospital. Choice (C) contradicts that fact that he has not missed any quizzes.

32. **(B)** "I was hoping you'd let me make a copy of your notes." Choice (C) refers to the offer that she makes, not to what Gary asks Margaret to do. Choices (A) and (D) are not mentioned and may not be concluded from information in the conversation.

33. **(A)** ". . . why don't we get together. . . so that I can explain [my notes] to you." Choice (B) contradicts the fact that he hasn't missed any quizzes. Choices (C) and (D) are not mentioned and may not be concluded from information in the conversation.

34. **(A)** Since Margaret agrees to let Gary borrow her notes, it must be concluded that she is helpful. Choices (B), (C), and (D) cannot be concluded from information in the conversation.

35. **(C)** ". . .I was wondering whether he has an earlier appointment available on the same day [as my regular appointment]." Choice (A) contradicts the fact that he has an appointment at three o'clock on Wednesday. Choice (B) contradicts the fact that he asked for an early appointment. Choice (D) refers to what the man ultimately decided to do, not to the purpose of his call.

36. **(A)** ". . .Dr. Benjamin is tied up in a meeting until noon, and he has two appointments scheduled before yours. . . ." Choices (B), (C), and (D) contradict the fact that Dr. Benjamin has a meeting and appointments on Wednesday.

37. **(B)** "There is a later appointment time open . . . at four-thirty . . . or . . . Thursday morning at ten." Choice (A) refers to the man's regular

appointment time, not to the new appointment that the secretary offered to make. Choice (D) refers to what the man wanted to do, not to what the secretary offered to do. Choice (C) was not mentioned and may not be concluded from information in the conversation.

38. **(C)** "I think I'll just rearrange my own schedule so I can keep my regular appointment." Choices (A), (B), and (D) are not mentioned and may not be concluded from information in the conversation.

39. **(B)** The main topic of this talk is F. Scott Fitzgerald's work. The other topics are secondary themes used to develop the main topic.

40. **(B)** "Fitzgerald had a great natural talent, but he became a compulsive drinker." Choice (A) contradicts the fact that Fitzgerald had a great natural talent. Choices (C) and (D) contradict the fact that he never made the adjustments necessary to a maturing writer in a changing world.

41. **(A)** "He wrote novels that describe the post-war American society. . .caught up in the rhythms of jazz." Choice (C) contradicts the fact that his novels describe post-war society, not war experiences. Choices (B) and (D) are not mentioned and may not be concluded from information in the talk.

42. **(C)** ". . . I am going to run the video version of *The Great Gatsby*, and then we'll divide up into groups to talk about it." Choices (A), (B), and (D) are not mentioned and may not be concluded from information in the talk.

43. **(A)** ". . .let me tell you a little bit about chamber music." Choice (B) is a detail used to develop the main purpose of the talk. Choices (C) and (D) are not mentioned and may not be concluded from information in the talk.

44. **(C)** ". . . any combination of instruments can be used for chamber music." Choice (B) contradicts the fact that chamber music has been written for the recorder, harpsichord and viola. Choice (D) contradicts the fact that piano, strings, and woodwinds are the most popular. Choice (A) is not mentioned and may not be concluded from information in the talk.

45. **(B)** "This evening the University Quartet will perform two of the later pieces by

Bach." Choices (A) and (D) are true, but they are not the reason that the speaker mentions Bach. Choice (C) contradicts the fact that Bach wrote music after vocal chamber music was popular.

46. **(B)** "Ladies and Gentlemen, the University Quartet." Choices (A), (C), and (D) are mentioned earlier in the talk.

47. **(A)** "Health food is a general term applied to all kinds of foods that are considered more healthful than the types of food widely sold in supermarkets." Although Choices (B), (C), and (D) are all mentioned in the talk, they are secondary ideas used to develop the main idea.

48. **(B)** "A narrower classification of health food is natural food. This term [natural food] is used to distinguish between types of the same food." Choice (A) refers to foods like refined sugar, but is not mentioned as a term to distinguish between types of the same food. Choice (C) refers to food grown on a particular kind of farm. Choice (D) refers to organic foods that are not refined after harvest.

49. **(D)** ". . .the allegations that. . .vitamin content is greatly reduced in processed foods." Choices (A), (B), and (C) contradict the fact that vitamin content is reduced.

50. **(B)** "Eat health foods, preferably the organic variety." Choice (A) contradicts the fact that the speaker has provided detailed information in the talk. Choice (C) contradicts the fact that the speaker recommends eating health foods. Choice (D) may not be concluded from the manner in which the talk was delivered.

Section 2: Structure and Written Expression

1. **(B)** A verb word is used after the subject in impersonal expressions such as *it is important that*. Choices (A) and (D) are modals with a verb word. Choice (C) is a third person present tense verb. (Refer to Patterns, Problem 29, page 78.)

2. **(A)** *Because* is used before a subject and verb to introduce cause. Choices (B) and (C) are not accepted for statements of cause. Choice (D) is used before a noun, not before a subject and verb. (Refer to Patterns, Problem 111, page 183.)

3. **(D)** The anticipatory clause *it was in 1607 that* introduces a subject and verb, *the English settled*. Choice (A) is wordy and indirect. Choice (B) may be used as part of a subject clause preceding a main verb. Choice (C) may be used without *that* preceding a subject and verb. "That in 1607 the English settled in Jamestown *has changed* the history of the Americas," and "Because in 1607 the English settled in Jamestown, *the history* of the Americas *has changed*" would also be correct. (Refer to Patterns, Problem 35, page 35.)

4. **(B)** Multiple comparatives like *twice* are expressed by the multiple followed by the phrase *as much as*. Choice (A) is a multiple number followed by the phrase *more than*. Choices (C) and (D) reverse the order of the multiple number and the phrase. (Refer to Patterns, Problem 93, page 162.)

5. **(B)** The verb phrase *to insist on* requires an *-ing* form in the complement. *-Ing* forms are modified by possessive pronouns. Choice (A) is an infinitive modified by an object pronoun. Choice (C) is an *-ing* form, but it is modified by a subject, not a possessive pronoun. Choice (D) is a verb word. (Refer to Patterns, Problem 3 and Patterns, Problem 46, pages 43 and 100.)

6. **(D)** *The* must be used with a superlative. Choices (A), (B), and (C) are wordy and ungrammatical. (Refer to Patterns, Problem 97, page 166.)

7. **(C)** Singular and plural expressions of noncount nouns such as *equipment* occur in idiomatic phrases, often *piece* or *pieces of*. Choices (A), (B), and (D) are not idiomatic. (Refer to Patterns, Problem 57, page 117.)

8. **(C)** There must be agreement between subject and verb. *Have* should be *has* to agree with the singular subject *triangle*. (Refer to Style, Problem 5, page 226.)

9. **(C)** A sentence has a subject and a verb. Choice (A) is the subject, but there is no main clause verb. Choices (B) and (D) introduce a main clause subject and verb. (Refer to Patterns, Problem 137, page 216.)

10. **(D)** For scientific results, a present form in the condition requires a present or future form in the result. Only Choice (D) introduces a conditional. (Refer to Patterns, Problem 21, page 67.)

11. **(D)** *The same* is used with a quality noun such as *age*, and *as* in comparisons. *As* is used with a quality adjective such as *old*, and *as*. Choice (A) is a quality adjective, not a noun, with *to*. In Choice (B), *the same* is used with *than*, not *as*. In Choice (C), *as old* is used with *like*, not *as*. "As old as" would also be correct. (Refer to Patterns, Problem 89, page 157.)

12. **(D)** *Such* is used with a noun phrase to express cause before *that* and a subject and verb that expresses result. Choice (A) does not have a subject. Choice (B) does not have a subject or verb. Choice (C) is not a *that* clause. (Refer to Patterns, Problem 82, page 148.)

13. **(C)** *Would* and a verb word must be used in the clause that follows *had hoped*. Choices (A) and (D) are phrases, not clauses. Choice (B) is a clause, but it does not include *would*. (Refer to Patterns, Problem 39, page 90.)

14. **(A)** *So* is used with an adjective to express cause before *that* and a subject and verb that expresses result. *Old* should be *so old*. (Refer to Patterns, Problem 81, page 147.)

15. **(C)** *Used to* requires a verb word. When preceded by a form of BE, *used to* requires an *-ing* form. In Choice (A), *used to* requires a verb word, not an *-ing* form. In Choice (B), *used to* preceded by a form of BE may be used with an *-ing* form, not an infinitive. Choice (D) uses the incorrect form, *use to*. (Refer to Patterns, Problem 11, page 53.)

16. **(C)** There must be agreement between pronoun and antecedent. *Their* should be *its* to refer to the singular antecedent *Pickerel Frog*. (Refer to Style, Problem 11, page 232.)

17. **(C)** Repetition of the subject by a subject pronoun is redundant. *It* should be deleted. (Refer to Style, Problem 21, page 245.)

18. **(C)** *Bored with* is a prepositional idiom. *Of* should be *with*. (Refer to Style, Problem 29, page 255.)

19. **(B)** Because a verb word must be used in a clause after the verb *to require*, *must write* should be *write*. (Refer to Patterns, Problem 27, page 76.)

20. **(A)** Using words with the same meaning consecutively is repetitive. *Enough* should be deleted because *sufficient* means *enough*. (Refer to Style, Problem 20, page 244.)

21. **(D)** Ideas in a series should be expressed by

parallel structures. *They drive* should be *driving* to provide for parallelism with the *-ing* forms *babysitting* and *working*. (Refer to Style, Problem 17, page 240.)

22. **(D)** There must be agreement between pronoun and antecedent. *Their* should be *our* to agree with the second person antecedent *those of us*. (Refer to Style, Problem 12, page 233.)

23. **(B)** There must be agreement between subject and verb. *Are* should be *is* to agree with the singular subject *support*. (Refer to Style, Problem 5, page 226.)

24. **(A)** An introductory verbal phrase should immediately precede the noun that it modifies. *Living in New York* is not logical because an *apartment* cannot live. A logical phrase would be *located* in New York. (Refer to Style, Problem 15, page 237.)

25. **(B)** Ideas after inclusives should be expressed by parallel structures. *Energy* should be *saves energy* or *conserves energy* to provide for parallelism with the phrase *saves time*. (Refer to Style, Problem 18, page 241.)

26. **(C)** *So* is commonly used as a purpose connector in spoken English, but *so that* should be used in written English. (Refer to Patterns, Problem 122, page 197.)

27. **(D)** The adverbial phrase *in 1975* establishes a point of view in the past. *Is* should be *was* in order to maintain the point of view. (Refer to Style, Problem 3, page 223.)

28. **(A)** In order to refer to a flag being *moved to a higher place*, *raised* should be used. *To raise* means to move to a higher place. *To rise* means to go up without assistance or to increase. (Refer to Style, Problem 22, page 247.)

29. **(B)** Because the verb phrase *to get through* requires an *-ing* form in the complement, *to lay* should be *laying*. (Refer to Patterns, Problem 4, page 45.)

30. **(D)** Superlatives are used to compare three or more. They are formed by adding *-est* to adjectives. *The greater* should be *the greatest* to compare Wright with all other modern architects. (Refer to Patterns, Problem 97, page 166.)

31. **(B)** The adverb *previously* establishes a point of view in the past. *Is* should be *was* in order to maintain the point of view. (Refer to Style, Problem 3, page 223.)

32. **(D)** There must be agreement between subject and verb. *Is* should be *are* to agree with the plural subject *groups*. (Refer to Style, Problem 5, page 226.)

33. **(C)** *Impossibility* should be *impossible*. *Impossibility* is a noun. *Impossible* is an adjective. (Refer to Style, Problem 30, page 257.)

34. **(C)** *Began* should be *begun* because the auxiliary *had* requires a participle. *Began* is a past form. *Begun* is a participle. (Refer to Patterns, Problem 36, page 87.)

35. **(B)** A form of BE is used with the participle in passive sentences. *Cannot proved* should be *cannot be proved*. (Refer to Patterns, Problem 41, page 92.)

36. **(C)** Redundant, indirect phrases should be avoided. *In a correct manner* is a redundant pattern. The adverb *correctly* is simple and more direct. (Refer to Style, Problem 19, page 243.)

37. **(A)** Using words with the same meaning consecutively is repetitive. *First* should be deleted because *original* means *first*. (Refer to Style, Problem 20, page 244.)

38. **(C)** The noun in the appositive must agree with the antecedent. *Tree* should be *trees* to agree with the antecedent *conifers*. (Refer to Style, Problem 14, page 235.)

39. **(D)** Ideas in a series should be expressed by parallel structures. *Decorations* should be *decorated* to provide for parallelism with *cast* and *carved*. (Refer to Style, Problem 17, page 240.)

40. **(A)** Most adverbs of manner are formed by adding *-ly* to adjectives. *Secure* should be *securely* to qualify the manner in which the tiles were fastened. (Refer to Patterns, Problem 126, page 202.)

Section 3: Reading Comprehension

1. **(B)** The other choices are secondary ideas used to develop the main idea, "the nature of geysers." Choices (A), (C), and (D) are subtopics that provide details and examples.

2. **(B)** "A geyser is the result of underground water under the combined conditions of high temperatures and increased pressure beneath the surface of the earth." Choice (A) contradicts the fact that water, not hot rocks, rises to the surface. Choice (C) contradicts the fact that the hot rocks are in the earth's interior,

not on the surface. Choice (D) contradicts the fact that the water seeps down in cracks and fissures in the earth.

3. **(C)** In the context of this passage, "approximately" could best be replaced by "generally." Choices (A), (B), and (D) are not accepted definitions of the word.

4. **(C)** "Since temperature rises. . .and pressure increases with depth. . ." Choices (A), (B), and (D) contradict the fact that both temperature and pressure increase with depth.

5. **(A)** "Since temperature rises approximately 1°F for every sixty feet under the earth's surface, and pressure increases with depth, water that seeps down in cracks and fissures until it [water] reaches very hot rocks in the earth's interior becomes heated to a temperature in excess of 290°F." Choices (B), (C), and (D) would change the meaning of the sentence.

6. **(A)** "In order to function, then, a geyser must have a source of heat, a reservoir where water can be stored until the temperature rises to an unstable point, an opening through which the hot water and steam can escape, and underground channels for resupplying water after an eruption." Choices (B), (C), and (D) refer to other themes in the passage.

7. **(C)** ". . .geysers are located in. . .the Yellowstone National Park area of the United States. . . . Old Faithful [is] in Yellowstone Park." Choices (A) and (B) refer to locations where geysers occur, but not to the location of Old Faithful. Choice (D) is not mentioned and may not be concluded from information in the passage.

8. **(B)** "Old Faithful erupts almost every hour." The number in Choice (A) refers to the number of thousand gallons of water that is expelled during an eruption, not to the number of minutes between eruptions. The numbers in Choices (C) and (D) refer to the number of feet to which the geyser rises during an eruption.

9. **(B)** In the context of this passage, "expelling" is closest in meaning to "discharging." Choices (A), (C), and (D) are not accepted definitions of the word.

10. **(A)** ". . .a geyser must have a source of heat, a reservoir where water can be stored . . . , an opening through which the hot water and steam can escape, and underground channels

. . . . Favorable conditions for geysers exist in regions of geologically recent volcanic activity. . .in areas of more than average precipitation." Choice (C) includes some of, but not all, the necessary conditions. Choices (B) and (D) contradict the fact that the volcanic activity should be recent, but not active.

11. **(A)** Choice (A) is the author's main point because the reasons for success are referred to throughout the passage. Choices (B), (C), and (D) are each specific reasons for success.

12. **(B)** In the context of this passage, "cited" is closest in meaning to "mentioned." Choices (A), (C), and (D) are not accepted definitions of the word.

13. **(C)** "Incessantly" means "constantly." Choices (A), (B), and (D) are not accepted definitions of the word.

14. **(B)** "They were also both glider pilots. Unlike some other engineers who experimented with the theories of flight, [they] experienced the practical side. . . ." Choices (A), (C), and (D) were all true of the Wright brothers, but these experiences were not different from those of their competitors.

15. **(C)** "They had realized. . .that the most serious problem in manned flight would be stabilizing and maneuvering the aircraft once it was airborne." Choices (A) and (B) refer to the problems that were perceived by other inventors, not by the Wright brothers. Choice (D) is not mentioned and may not be concluded from information in the passage.

16. **(B)** In the context of this passage, "maneuvering" could best be replaced by "controlling." Choices (A), (C), and (D) are not accepted definitions of the word.

17. **(B)** "Using a wind tunnel, they tested more than two hundred different wing designs. . . ." Choice (C) contradicts the fact that the Wright brothers were testing their own designs. Choices (A) and (D) are not mentioned and may not be concluded from information in the passage.

18. **(C)** "Attempts to achieve manned flight in the early nineteenth century were doomed because the steam engines that powered the aircraft were too heavy in proportion to the power that they [the engines] produced." Choices (A), (B), and (D) would change the meaning of the sentence.

19. **(A)** In the context of this passage, "doomed"

is closest in meaning to "destined to fail." Choices (B), (C), and (D) are not accepted definitions of the word.

20. **(D)** ". . .they were able to bring the ratio of weight to power within acceptable limits for flight." From the reference to the ratio of weight to power and *acceptable limits,* it must be concluded that previous engines did not have acceptable limits of weight to power and, thus, did not have enough power to lift their own weight. Choice (B) contradicts the fact that the engines were relatively heavy. Choice (C) contradicts the fact that they were experimenting with internal combustion engines. The size in Choice (A) is not mentioned and may not be concluded from information in the passage.

21. **(A)** The other choices are secondary ideas used to develop the main idea, "the influenza virus." Choices (B), (C), and (D) are subtopics that provide details and examples.

22. **(D)** ". . .bacteria can be considered a type of plant. . ." Choice (A) refers to the secretions of bacteria, not to the bacteria themselves. Although it may be true that bacteria are very small, as in Choice (B), or larger than viruses, as in Choice (C), this information is not mentioned and may not be concluded from reading the passage.

23. **(D)** "Although bacteria can be considered a type of plant, secreting poisonous substances into the body of the organism they attack, viruses, like the influenza virus, are living organisms themselves [the viruses.]" Choices (A), (B), and (C) would change the meaning of the sentence.

24. **(D)** In the context of this passage, "strictly" could best be replaced by "exactly." Choices (A), (B), and (C) are not accepted definitions of the word.

25. **(C)** ". . .we must also consider them [viruses] as being alive since they are able to multiply in unlimited quantities." Choice (A) is the reason that we must consider them as regular chemical molecules, not the reason that we must consider them as being alive. Choices (B) and (D) are not mentioned and may not be concluded from information in the passage.

26. **(B)** ". . .they [viruses] have strictly defined atomic structure. . . ." Choice (A) contradicts the fact that viruses have a strictly defined

atomic structure. Choice (C) contradicts the fact that we may consider them as regular chemical molecules. Although Choice (D) is implied, it may not be concluded from information in the passage.

27. **(B)** "Unlimited" means "without limits;" very large. Choices (A), (C), and (D) are not accepted definitions of the word.

28. **(B)** ". . .the protection is against only the type of virus that caused the influenza." Choices (A) and (C) contradict the fact that the protection is against only the one type of virus. Choice (D) is not mentioned and may not be concluded from information in the passage.

29. **(C)** Choice (A) is mentioned in lines 13–14. Choice (B) is mentioned in lines 13–14. Choice (D) is mentioned in lines 12–13. Epidemics, not pandemics, are regional outbreaks.

30. **(C)** In the context of this passage, "strains" is closest in meaning to "varieties." Choices (A), (B), and (D) are not accepted definitions of the word.

31. **(C)** The other choices are secondary ideas used to develop the main idea, "how to obtain permission to transfer."

32. **(C)** "A green I-538 form is used . . . to transfer from one university to another . . ." Choice (A) refers to the permission form from the new school. Choice (B) refers to the white form affixed upon entry to passports. Choice (D) is not mentioned and may not be concluded from information in the passage.

33. **(A)** In the context of this passage, "currently" is closest in meaning to "now." Choices (B), (C), and (D) are not accepted definitions of the word.

34. **(B)** ". . .you must obtain the permission before leaving the university where you are currently studying. You must complete the form I-538, have it signed by the foreign student advisor. . . ." Choice (A) contradicts the fact that the foreign student advisor at the old, not the new school, must help the student with his or her transfer. Although the student must also sign the transfer form, Choice (C) is not mentioned and may not be concluded from information in the passage. Choice (D) refers to the person who gives the permission, not to the person who signs the transfer form.

35. **(B)** In the context of this passage, "affixed

to" could best be replaced by "fastened on." Choices (A), (C), and (D) are not accepted definitions of the phrase.

36. **(C)** "Only an official of Immigration can decide each [transfer] case." Choice (A) refers to the person who must sign the I-538, not to the person who will give permission to transfer. Choice (B) refers to the person who must issue the I-20 permission to attend the new school, not to the person who will give permission to leave the current school and transfer to the new one. Choice (D) is not mentioned and may not be concluded from information in the passage.

37. **(A)** "Students who have not completed one term of study at the school that issued them their first I-20 are not advised to file for permission to transfer until they have completed one term." Choice (D) refers to the form I-538 and other documents that do not insure permission to transfer. Choices (B) and (C) are not mentioned and may not be concluded from information in the passage.

38. **(B)** "Students who have not completed one term of study at the school that issued them their first I-20 are not advised to file for permission to transfer until they have completed one term there [at the school that issued the I-20]." Choices (A), (C), and (D) would change the meaning of the sentence.

39. **(B)** ". . .remember that you must obtain the permission [from Immigration] before leaving the university where you are currently studying." Choices (A) and (C) contradict the fact that the permission must be obtained before traveling. Signing an I-538 does not guarantee permission. Choice (D) is not mentioned and may not be concluded from information in the passage.

40. **(D)** ". . . however, some cases require a personal interview. Should you need to see an INS officer, you will be notified." Choices (A), (B), and (C) refer to other themes in the passage.

41. **(B)** "The Academic Year" is the best title because it states the main idea of the passage. The other choices are secondary ideas used to develop the main idea.

42. **(D)** ". . .a semester system, which offers classes in the fall and spring. . ." Choices (A) and (C) refer to a quarter system, not to a semester system. Choice (B) contradicts the fact that most universities in the United States are on a semester system.

43. **(B)** "The academic year. . .is divided into three quarters . . .[and] the summer quarter. . . ." Choices (A), (C), and (D) contradict the fact that the academic year has three quarters from September through June when the summer quarter begins.

44. **(D)** "The academic year, [is] September to June. . . ." Choice (A) is the academic year and summer sessions. Choice (B) is summer sessions. Choice (C) is not mentioned as a division in the academic calendar.

45. **(B)** In the context of this passage, "customary" could best be replaced by "traditional." Choices (A), (C), and (D) are not accepted definitions of the word.

46. **(C)** "Most students begin. . .in the fall quarter, but they may enter at the beginning of any of the other quarters." Choices (A) and (D) refer to the time when most students actually do begin, not to the time when they may begin. Choice (B) refers to one quarter when students may begin, but it contradicts the fact that they may begin in any of the other three semesters as well.

47. **(A)** "Many faculty complain that the eleven-week term is simply not long enough for them [the faculty] to cover the material required by most college courses." Choices (B), (C), and (D) would change the meaning of the sentence.

48. **(A)** In the context of this passage, "instituted" is closest in meaning to "established." Choices (B), (C), and (D) are not accepted definitions of the word.

49. **(D)** Choice (A) is mentioned in lines 18–19. Choice (B) is mentioned in line 18. Choice (C) is mentioned in lines 16–17. Quarters, not trimesters, last eleven weeks.

50. **(B)** "Although most universities in the United States are on a semester system. . . , some schools observe a quarter system. . . ." In Choice (A), it is not as probable that a college catalog for a specific school would mention other schools and systems. Choice (C) is possible, but not as probable as Choice (B). A dictionary entry, as in Choice (D), would be much shorter.

Model Test 7—Short Form

Section 1: Listening Comprehension

1. **(C)** From the reference to *he*, it must be concluded that they are talking about a person. Choices (A), (B), and (D) refer to things, not persons.

2. **(A)** *Why not* means you should. Choice (C) contradicts the fact that the woman says to move into an apartment. Choices (B) and (D) are not mentioned and may not be concluded from information in the conversation.

3. **(B)** From the reference to *the TV* and *the heat control* as well as the question *anything else, Ma'am*? it must be concluded that the man is a bell boy. A TV repairman in Choice (A) might show the woman how to turn on the TV, but it is not customary for him to mention the heat control. It is not as probable that the persons mentioned in Choices (C) and (D) would be showing the woman how to turn on the TV and the heat.

4. **(C)** To *put off* is an idiomatic expression that means to procrastinate. Since the man kept putting it off, it must be concluded that he does not like to balance his account. Choice (A) contradicts the fact that he has a checkbook. Choice (B) contradicts that fact that his wife was waiting for him to balance it. Choice (D) contradicts the fact that the secretary helped him by balancing his checkbook.

5. **(B)** Because the man suggests that they have lunch, and the woman responds that the idea sounds good, inviting him to call her, it must be concluded that the man will call the woman to arrange for lunch. Choice (A) contradicts the fact that the invitation is for the future. Choice (D) contradicts the fact that the woman invites the man to give her a call. Choice (C) is not mentioned and may not be concluded from information in the conversation.

6. **(C)** Since the woman needs one transcript for San Diego State and two for herself, the man will probably send one to San Diego State and give two to her. Choice (A) contradicts the fact that she only needs one for San Diego State. Choice (B) contradicts the fact that she needs a total of three transcripts.

Choice (D) refers to the total number of transcripts that the woman requested, not to how many she wants to take herself.

7. **(A)** *Everything* is an idiomatic expression that means all the condiments, usually including lettuce, pickle, onions, mustard, mayonnaise, and catsup. Choices (B), (C), and (D) are not paraphrases of the expression.

8. **(D)** From the reference to the *parts*, the *water hose*, and being able to *drive* it, it must be concluded that the conversation took place at a garage. It is not customary to fix a car at any of the places referred to in Choices (A), (B), and (C).

9. **(A)** "You can just leave a note." Choice (C) refers to the woman's plan, not to the man's suggestion. Choices (B) and (D) are not mentioned and may not be concluded from information in the conversation.

10. **(A)** Because the woman says that it is *only* six o'clock, it must be concluded that she is not ready to go. Choices (B) and (D) are possible reasons for wearing a coat, but they do not refer to the question, *are you ready*? Choice (C) is not mentioned and may not be concluded from information in the conversation.

11. **(B)** Since Susan chose education for her major, it must be concluded that she prefers teaching. Choice (D) contradicts the fact that she declared her major. Choices (A) and (C) are not mentioned and may not be concluded from information in the conversation.

12. **(B)** ". . . that's [the roast is] too big. . ." Choices (A) and (C) contradict the fact that he wants another roast, not the large one. Choice (D) refers to the weight of the roast, not to what the man says about it.

13. **(B)** From the reference to the *clothes* being *dry* it must be concluded that they are talking about laundry. The times in Choice (D) refer to the number of minutes required to dry clothes, not to the time of day. Choices (A) and (C) are not mentioned and may not be concluded from information in the conversation.

14. **(B)** Since the woman saw the man's name on the graduation list, she had assumed that he

had already graduated. Choice (C) refers to the man's explanation, not to the woman's assumption. Choice (D) refers to the man's plan for graduation. Choice (A) is not mentioned and may not be concluded from information in the conversation.

15. **(B)** Because the man wants to know whether the woman is in line, it must be concluded that he wants to move ahead and use the copy machine. Choices (A), (C), and (D) are not mentioned and may not be concluded from information in the conversation.

16. **(C)** To *go for it* is an idiomatic expression that means to compete. Choices (A) and (D) contradict the fact that she is competing now. Choice (B) contradicts the fact that she has decided.

17. **(C)** *By all means* is an idiomatic expression that means certainly in response to a question or in this case, that the woman is welcome to join the man. Choices (A), (B), and (D) are not paraphrases of the expression.

18. **(D)** Since the man says he is waiting for the mail to come, he implies that he will not go to the library with the woman. Choice (C) contradicts the fact that he is waiting for the mail which has not yet arrived. Choices (A) and (B) are not mentioned and may not be concluded from information in the conversation.

19. **(D)** The woman says that she is calling because she can't remember whether the man is supposed to pick her up, or she is supposed to pick him up. Choice (A) contradicts the fact that they already have plans to meet for lunch. Choice (B) refers to how long before the man will pick her up, not how long they will talk on the phone. Choice (C) contradicts the fact that the woman says she is calling because she, not the man, can't remember the plans.

20. **(A)** Because it is strange to see only a few people in the office, it must be concluded that the office is usually crowded. Choice (B) contradicts the fact that it is strange to see only a few people there. Choices (C) and (D) are not mentioned and may not be concluded from information in the conversation.

21. **(D)** "How was your vacation?" Choices (A), (B), and (C) are all mentioned as they relate to the main topic of the conversation, the woman's vacation.

22. **(A)** "Did you try her at the Student Center?"

Choices (B), (C), and (D) are not mentioned and may not be concluded from information in the conversation.

23. **(D)** *I couldn't care less* is an idiomatic expression that means the speaker is not interested. Choices (A), (B), and (C) are not paraphrases of the expression, and may not be concluded from information in the conversation.

24. **(A)** Since the man asks whether or not the woman was in class on Friday and uses the word *either,* it must be concluded that he was not in class on that day. Choice (B) contradicts the fact that the man was not in class. Choice (C) contradicts the fact that the woman was not in class. Choice (D) contradicts the fact that the woman's mother, not the man and the woman, was in New York.

25. **(D)** Since the man says that he is not as excited as he thought he would be, it must be concluded that he expected to be more enthusiastic. Choices (A), (B), and (C) are not mentioned and may not be concluded from information in the conversation.

26. **(C)** *Just barely* is an idiomatic expression that means almost not. Choice (A) refers to the taxi, not the plane, being late. Choice (B) contradicts the fact that the man made the flight. Choice (D) contradicts the fact that the taxi arrived late.

27. **(C)** *Now and then* is an idiomatic expression that means occasionally. Choices (A), (B), and (D) contradict the fact that the woman eats in the snack bar occasionally.

28. **(A)** To *take it easy* is an idiomatic expression that means to rest. Choice (B) refers to the man's comment, not to the woman's observation. Choice (C) contradicts the fact that the man warns the woman not to worry. Choice (D) refers to the fact that the man was sick in the past, not that he is sick now.

29. **(D)** Since the man says "neither do I" when the woman comments about not watching TV, it must be concluded that he does not enjoy watching television either. Choice (B) contradicts the fact that neither the man nor the woman enjoy watching television. Choices (A) and (C) are not mentioned and may not be concluded from information in the conversation.

30. **(B)** Since the man has thirty-five subjects and that is not enough, it must be concluded

that he needs more than thirty-five participants. Choice (A) contradicts the fact that he has started working on the project. Choice (C) contradicts the fact that he feels he has a good start. Choice (D) is not mentioned and may not be concluded from information in the conversation.

31. **(B)** "I just need a recent physical in order to get enrolled in a new insurance plan at school." Choice (A) contradicts the fact that Bob is a patient of Dr. Norman, and does not need a referral. Choice (C) contradicts the fact that it is not a medical emergency. Choice (D) is true, but it is not why the man called for an appointment.

32. **(C)** "I have to turn in the application [for the insurance plan] on the first." Choice (B) is true but it is not a problem as regards the June 1 date. Choices (A) and (D) are not mentioned and may not be concluded from information in the conversation.

33. **(A)** "I'll take the twenty-ninth at two o'clock." Choice (B) is the date that the woman presents as an alternative, not the date the man chooses. The exact times for the dates in Choices (C) and (D) are not mentioned and may not be concluded from information in the conversation.

34. **(C)** ". . . you will need to come in a week before the appointment. . . to get a blood work-up." Choices (A) and (B) refer to the requirements for the insurance plan. Choice (D) refers to the reasons for the physical.

35. **(A)** "I want to talk to you about my final grade." Choice (C) is mentioned as an argument for changing the grade. Choice (D) refers to the professor's grade book, not to what prompted the conversation. Choice (B) is not mentioned and may not be concluded from information in the conversation.

36. **(B)** From the reference to a *grade*, a *grade book*, a *test*, *exams*, a *course*, and *class*, it must be concluded that the conversation is taking place in a college professor's office. Choice (C) contradicts the fact that Rick brought his test with him to the meeting. Choices (A) and (D) are not mentioned and may not be concluded from information in the conversation.

37. **(C)** "Well, I was surprised to get a D. . ." Choice (A) and Choice (B) refer to the grades that Rick claims he should have got,

not to the grade that he received. Choice (D) refers to the grade that Rick received in class participation, not to the grade that he received for the course.

38. **(C)** "You received an F in class participation because you missed too many days, and that brought your grade down." Choice (A) contradicts the fact that Rick got a B on the midterm exam. Choice (B) contradicts the fact that Rick passed the final with a C. Choice (D) contradicts the fact that Dr. Wilson gave Rick a syllabus on the first day of class and the grading system was outlined in it.

39. **(B)** ". . . I'd like to point out a few important features on the syllabus." Choices (A), (C), and (D) are all secondary themes used to develop the main purpose of the talk.

40. **(A)** ". . . it is better to read the assigned pages before you come to class so that you will be prepared to participate in the discussion that follows the lecture." Choices (B) and (C) contradict the fact that the reading should be done before the lecture and discussion. Choice (D) is not mentioned and may not be concluded from information in the talk.

41. **(D)** ". . .you have a midterm. . .and a final. . . . That leaves 25 points for the project. . ." Choice (A) contradicts the fact that there is also a project. Choice (B) contradicts the fact that both the final and the project are required. Choice (C) contradicts the fact that a final exam is required.

42. **(A)** "If you must miss class for whatever reason, please get in touch with me." Choices (B), (C), and (D) are not mentioned and may not be concluded from information in the talk.

43. **(B)** The main purpose of this lecture is to explain a theory of the formation of diamonds on Neptune and Uranus. Choices (A), (C), and (D) are mentioned during the explanation, but are not central to the theory.

44. **(C)** ". . .the seventh and eighth planets from our sun, Uranus and Neptune. . . ." Choice (B) mentions Uranus, but not Neptune. Choice (D) mentions Neptune, but not Uranus. The planets in Choice (A) are not mentioned and may not be concluded from information in the talk.

45. **(C)** ". . .the pressure on these planets. . . could set up conditions whereby diamonds

might form." Choices (A) and (D) are mentioned, but are not the reason that scientists provided for their theory. Choice (B) is not mentioned and may not be concluded from information in the talk.

46. **(C)** "Today I'm going to share a rather interesting theory with you." Choice (D) contradicts the fact that he believes that the theory is interesting. Choices (A) and (B) are not mentioned and may not be concluded from information in the talk.

47. **(B)** ". . .a system whereby a representative group of citizens called the electoral college would be responsible for making the choice." Choices (A), (C), and (D) are secondary themes used to develop the main theme of the talk.

48. **(C)** ". . .when Aaron Burr and Thomas Jefferson received an equal number of votes, the system had to be changed to provide for separate voting for president and vice-president." Choice (A) contradicts the fact that the electoral college voted for Burr and Jefferson. Choice (D) contradicts the fact that the system had to be changed. Choice (B) is not mentioned and may not be concluded from information in the talk.

49. **(A)** ". . .the [political] parties nominated candidates and then chose electors. . ." Choices (B), (C), and (D) contradict the fact that the parties make the nominations.

50. **(C)** ". . .vote by the people for electors is called the popular vote. . ." Choice (A) refers to direct vote, not popular vote. Choice (B) occurs after the popular vote. Choice (D) is not mentioned and may not be concluded from information in the talk.

Section 2: Structure and Written Expression

1. **(C)** An -ing form is used with the auxiliary BE. (Refer to Patterns, Problem 40, page 91.)

2. **(D)** Both a few and a little are used after only, but a few must be used with the count noun nations. (Refer to Patterns, Problem 70, page 132.)

3. **(A)** Ideas after exclusives should be expressed by parallel structures. Only transmit in Choice (A) provides for parallelism with the verb word conduct. Choices (B),

(C), and (D) are not parallel. (Refer to Style, Problem 18, page 241.)

4. **(D)** A verb word is used as an imperative after an introductory verbal modifier that is an infinitive of purpose. (Refer to Style, Problem 16, page 238.)

5. **(A)** But means except. "All of the cereal grains except rice" would also be correct. (Refer to Patterns, Problem 107, page 178.)

6. **(B)** When two nouns are used consecutively, the first often functions as an adjective. Choices (A), (C), and (D) are redundant and unidiomatic. (Refer to Patterns, Problem 78, page 144.)

7. **(B)** A present tense verb is used after when to express future. (Refer to Patterns, Problem 123, page 198.)

8. **(A)** Once means at one time in the past. Once is used in an introductory phrase with a busy city to modify the noun Pompeii. (Refer to Patterns, Problem 130, page 207.)

9. **(A)** To know how is used before infinitives to express ability. Choices (B) and (D) do not include the word how and they are followed by an -ing form, not an infinitive. In Choice (C), there is a verb word, not an infinitive after knowing how. (Refer to Patterns, Problem 10, page 52.)

10. **(A)** An infinitive is used to express purpose. (Refer to Patterns, Problem 30, page 80.)

11. **(D)** Affirmative agreement with so requires verb-subject order and an affirmative verb that refers to the verb in the main clause. Choices (A) and (B) have no verb. In Choice (C), the auxiliary verb do is used after, not before the subject, and does not refer to the verb are in the main clause. (Refer to Patterns, Problem 120, page 194.)

12. **(B)** Each other is used to express mutual acts. Choices (A), (C), and (D) are not idiomatic. "One another" would also be correct. (Refer to Patterns, Problem 51, page 105.)

13. **(A)** A cardinal number is used after a noun. The is used with an ordinal number before a noun. Choice (B) is incomplete because it does not include the before the ordinal number. Choice (C) is not used after a noun. Choice (D) is incomplete because it does not have a -th ending. "President four" would also be correct. (Refer to Patterns, Problem 77, page 142.)

14. **(B)** Every sentence must have a main verb. Choices (A), (C), and (D) are not main verbs. (Refer to Patterns, Problem 1, page 41.)

15. **(D)** *While* means at the same time. *While* is used in an introductory phrase with *a* to modify the noun *Webster*. (Refer to Patterns, Problem 131, page 208.)

16. **(B)** *The longer* should be *the longest*. Because there are more than two unguarded borders in the history of the world, a superlative form must be used. (Refer to Patterns, Problem 97, page 166.)

17. **(A)** A form of BE is used with participle in passive sentences. *Combine* should be *combined*. (Refer to Patterns, Problem 31, page 81.)

18. **(D)** The clause *many people believed* establishes a point of view in the past. *Is* should be *was* to maintain the point of view. (Refer to Style, Problem 1, page 221.)

19. **(B)** There must be agreement between subject and verb. *Are* should be *is* to agree with the singular subject *anyone*. (Refer to Style, Problem 9, page 230.)

20. **(A)** *Such* should be *such as*, which introduces the example *the Concorde*. (Refer to Patterns, Problem 109, page 181.)

21. **(B)** *Wrote* should be *written* because the auxiliary *had* requires a participle. *Wrote* is a past form. *Written* is a participle. (Refer to Patterns, Problem 36, page 87.)

22. **(A)** *Not* should be *no*. *No* before a noun means *not any*. (Refer to Patterns, Problem 65, page 127.)

23. **(D)** *A* should be *an* before the vowel sound *u* in *unknown*. *A* is used before consonant sounds. *An* is used before vowel sounds. (Refer to Patterns. Problem 62, page 123.)

24. **(D)** Ideas in a series should be expressed by parallel structures. *To control* should be *the control of* to provide for parallelism with the nouns *capitalization* and *specialization*. (Refer to Style, Problem 17, page 240.)

25. **(B)** *Had better* requires a verb word. *Planning* should be *plan* after *had better*. (Refer to Patterns, Problem 12, page 55.)

26. **(D)** There must be agreement between subject and verb. *Has* should be *have* to agree with the plural subject *various forms*. (Refer to Style, Problem 5, page 226.)

27. **(B)** In contrary-to-fact clauses, *were* is the only accepted form of the verb BE. *Was*

should be *were*. (Refer to Patterns, Problem 25, page 72.)

28. **(B)** *Begun* should be *began* because a past form is required to refer to Mozart's childhood. *Begun* is a participle. *Began* is a past form. (Refer to Patterns, Problem 5, page 46.)

29. **(B)** *As* should be *that* to introduce a clause of result after *so* and an adjective. (Refer to Patterns, Problem 81, page 147.)

30. **(D)** *To experience* should be *experiencing* after the preposition *without*. *-Ing* nouns and noun forms are used after prepositions. (Refer to Patterns, Problems with Prepositions, pages 174–189.)

31. **(C)** *Understanding* should be *understand* or *to understand* after the causative *help*. (Refer to Patterns, Problem 20, page 65.)

32. **(B)** *Interested* should be *interesting* to modify *animals*. The interesting animals cause us to be interested. (Refer to Patterns, Problem 80, page 146.)

33. **(A)** *Almost* should be *most*. "Almost all of the poetry" would also be correct. (Refer to Patterns, Problem 72, page 135.)

34. **(A)** A verb word must be used in a clause after an impersonal expression. *Is* should be *be* after the impersonal expression *it is essential*. (Refer to Patterns, Problem 29, page 78.)

35. **(B)** There must be agreement between subject and verb. *Were* should be *was* to agree with the singular subject *Vasco da Gama*. The phrase of accompaniment, *accompanied by a large crew and a fleet of twenty ships*, is not the subject. (Refer to Style, Problem 6, page 227.)

36. **(D)** An adjective is used before *enough* to express sufficiency. *As* should be deleted. (Refer to Patterns, Problem 74, page 138.)

37. **(D)** *No longer* is an idiom that means *not any more*. *Not* should be *no* before *longer*. (Refer to Patterns, Problem 132, page 209.)

38. **(B)** *Him* should be *he* because it is part of the subject, with *Drs. Daniel Nathan* and *Hamilton Smith*, of the verb *were awarded*. *He* functions as a subject. *Him* functions as a complement. (Refer to Patterns, Problem 42, page 95.)

39. **(D)** Object pronouns are used after prepositions. *Their* should be *them* after the preposition *from*. (Refer to Patterns, Problem 45, page 99.)

40. **(A)** In order to refer to *occasionally, sometimes* should be used. *Sometimes* means occasionally. *Sometime* means at some time in the future. (Refer to Patterns, Problem 128, page 204.)

Section 3: Reading Comprehension

1. **(C)** The other choices are secondary ideas that are used to develop the main idea, "salt" Choices (A), (B), and (D) are historically significant to the discussion.

2. **(B)** In the context of this passage, "scarcity" could best be replaced by "deprivation." Choices (A), (C), and (D) are not accepted definitions of the word.

3. **(A)** "Records show that in areas of scarcity, salt was traded ounce for ounce for gold." Choices (B), (C), and (D) contradict the fact that salt was traded ounce for ounce, or one to one, for gold.

4. **(C)** ". . .Roman soldiers transported salt crystals from the salt flats at Ostia. . . ." Choice (A) refers to the origin of the soldiers, not the salt. Choice (B) refers to the river that served to unite the salt flats with Rome. Choice (D) refers to the road over which the salt was transported.

5. **(B)** ". . .they [the soldiers] received a *salarium* or salary . . ." Choice (D) contradicts the fact that the Latin word for the Salt Road is *Via Salaria*, not *salarium*. The Latin words for Choices (A) and (C) are not mentioned and may not be concluded from information in the passage.

6. **(C)** "The old saying 'worth their salt'. . . means to be *valuable*. . ." Choices (A), (B), and (D) contradict the fact that "worth his salt" means valuable.

7. **(A)** In the context of this passage, "retained" could best be replaced by "reserved." Choices (B), (C), and (D) are not accepted definitions of the word.

8. **(C)** ". . .in the Middle Ages. . .governments retained salt trade as a monopoly." Choices (A) and (B) refer to people who traded salt, not to those who had a monopoly on the sale. Choice (D) refers to people who sat above the salt at the table, not to those who had a monopoly.

9. **(C)** "By then [the Middle Ages] people's social rank was demonstrated by where they sat at the table, above or below the salt." Choices (A), (B), and (D) would change the meaning of the sentence.

10. **(A)** In the context of this passage, "remote" is closest in meaning to "distant." Choices (B), (C), and (D) are not accepted definitions of the word.

11. **(B)** "The Eradication of Smallpox" is the best title because it states the main idea of the passage. The other choices are secondary ideas that are used to develop the main idea. Choice (A) refers to the organization that initiated the campaign to eradicate smallpox. Choice (C) refers to one of the methods used to contain the spread of the disease. Choice (D) refers to the kind of disease that smallpox is.

12. **(C)** In the context of this passage, "threat" could best be replaced by "risk." Choices (A), (B), and (D) are not accepted definitions of the word.

13. **(B)** "The goal was to eliminate the disease in one decade." Choice (A) contradicts the fact that the goal was to eliminate the disease, not to decrease the spread of it. Choice (C) refers to a procedure for eliminating the disease, not to a goal. Choice (D) refers to projects that had already failed to eliminate malaria and yellow fever.

14. **(C)** "The strategy was not only to provide mass vaccinations but also to isolate patients . . ." Choice (A) refers to only one part of the strategy. It contradicts the fact that individual victims were treated. Choice (B) refers to only one part of the strategy. It contradicts the fact that entire villages were vaccinated. Choice (D) refers to a method to locate both villages and individuals for treatment.

15. **(B)** In the context of this passage, "isolated" is closest in meaning to "separated." Choices (A), (C), and (D) are not accepted definitions of the word.

16. **(B)** "Rewards for reporting smallpox assisted in motivating the public." Choices (A), (C), and (D) refer to procedures for eliminating the spread of the disease, not to ways to motivate the public to help health workers.

17. **(B)** "By April of 1978, WHO officials announced that they [the officials] had isolated the last known case of the disease, but health workers continued to search for new

cases for two additional years to be completely sure." Choices (A), (C), and (D) would change the meaning of the sentence.

18. **(A)** " . . . the World Health Organization was authorized to initiate a global campaign to eradicate smallpox. . . . Today smallpox is no longer a threat [as it was in the past]. . . . Routine vaccinations have been stopped. . ." Choices (B), (C), and (D) refer to smallpox. Choice (A) refers to malaria and yellow fever.

19. **(A)** " . . .eleven years after the initial organization of the campaign, no cases [of smallpox] were reported in the field." Choice (B) contradicts the fact that similar projects for malaria and yellow fever had failed. Choice (C) contradicts the fact that no cases are being reported. Choice (D) contradicts the fact that patients had to be isolated to contain the spread of the disease.

20. **(D)** "In May, 1980, a formal statement was made to the global community." Choice (A) refers to the date that the campaign was authorized. Choice (B) refers to the date that was set as a goal for eradicating the disease. Choice (C) refers to the date that the last known case was isolated.

21. **(C)** The other choices are secondary ideas that are used to develop the main idea, "the current American family." Choices (A), (B), and (D) are classifications of families among those included in the current American family.

22. **(A)** " . . .the so-called traditional American family was always more varied than we had been led to believe, reflecting the very different racial, ethnic, class, and religious customs among different American groups." Choice (B) contradicts the fact that customs are different among these groups. Choices (C) and (D) are not mentioned and may not be concluded from information in the passage.

23. **(B)** "Current" means "present." Choices (A), (C), and (D) are not accepted definitions of the word.

24. **(A)** " . . . another third consists of married couples who either have no children or have none still living at home." Choice (B) refers to the percentage of single people. Choice (C) refers to single, usually divorced parents, with at least one child. Choice (D) refers to

unmarried people who choose to live together.

25. **(B)** "The most recent government statistics reveal that only about one third of all current American families fit the traditional mold of two parents and their children, and another third consists of married couples who either have no children or have none [no children] still living at home." Choices (A), (C), and (D) would change the meaning of the sentence.

26. **(C)** "Of the final one third, about 20 percent of the total number of American households are single people. . ." Choice (A) refers to the final one third, not to the 20 percent who are single. Choices (B) and (D) contradict the fact that 20 percent equals one fifth.

27. **(C)** " . . . about 20 percent . . . are single people, usually women over sixty-five years of age." Choice (C) refers to 7 percent, not to the majority of one-person households. Choices (A) and (B) are not mentioned and may not be concluded from information in the passage.

28. **(B)** In the context of this passage, "the rest" could best be replaced by "those remaining." Choices (A), (C), and (D) are not accepted definitions of the phrase.

29. **(C)** "In addition, close friends have become a more important part of family life than ever before." Choices (A), (B), and (D) refer to other themes in the passage.

30. **(A)** In the context of this passage, "undervalues" is closest in meaning to "does not appreciate." Choices (B), (C), and (D) are not accepted definitions of the word.

31. **(A)** The other choices are secondary ideas that are used to develop the main idea that "noise may pose a serious threat to our physical and psychological health." Choices (B), (C), and (D) are all true, but they are details, not the main idea.

32. **(A)** "Noise, commonly defined as unwanted sound. . ." Choices (B) and (D) refer to the origins of noise, not to definitions of it. Choice (C) refers to the effects of noise.

33. **(A)** "Noise, commonly defined as unwanted sound, is another environmental pollutant." Choices (B), (C), and (D) refer to topics at the end of the paragraph, not at the beginning where a transition from the preceding topic would occur.

34. **(C)** In the context of this passage, "congested" could best be replaced by "crowded." Choices (A), (B), and (D) are not accepted definitions of the word.

35. **(B)** "Unlike the eye [which has a lid], the ear has no lid; therefore noise penetrates without protection." Choices (A), (C), and (D) are not mentioned and may not be concluded from information in the passage.

36. **(B)** "Loud noises instinctively signal danger. . . we are constantly responding [to noise] in the same ways that we would respond to danger." Choice (A) contradicts the fact that noise and our response to it may be more than an annoyance. Choices (C) and (D) refer to the results of our response to noise, not to the source of our response.

37. **(C)** In the context of this passage, "accelerate" is closest in meaning to "increase." Choices (A), (B), and (D) are not accepted definitions of the word.

38. **(A)** "Particularly in congested urban areas, the noise produced as a byproduct of our advancing technology causes physical and psychological harm, and detracts from the quality of life for those who are exposed to it [noise]." Choices (B), (C), and (D) would change the meaning of the sentence.

39. **(C)** ". . .noise is unavoidable in a complex industrial society. . ." Choice (A) contradicts the fact that it [noise] is a serious threat to physical and psychological well-being. Choice (B) refers to hearing loss, which is America's number one nonfatal health problem, not to noise. Choice (D) refers to an industrial society, not to noise.

40. **(B)** In the context of this passage, "as well" is closest in meaning to "also." Choices (A), (C), and (D) are not accepted definitions of the phrase.

41. **(C)** Choices (A), (B), and (D) are important to the discussion and provide details that support the main topic, "hunter-gatherers."

42. **(D)** "This method of harvesting from nature's provision [hunting and gathering] is the oldest known subsistence strategy." Choice (A) refers to a practice engaged in by hunter-gatherers in order to locate new sources of food, not to the subsistence strat-egy. Choices (B) and (C) refer to later strategies for subsistence.

43. **(A)** In the context of this passage, "rudimentary" could best be replaced by "crude." Choices (B), (C), and (D) are not accepted definitions of the word.

44. **(B)** "This method [hunting and gathering] has been practiced for at least the last 2 million years." Choice (C) refers to the date when farming and the domestication of animals, not hunting and gathering, was introduced. Choices (A) and (D) are not mentioned and may not be concluded from information in the passage.

45. **(B)** In the context of this passage, "dwindled" is closest in meaning to "decreased." Choices (A), (C), and (D) are not accepted definitions of the word.

46. **(D)** ". . .the shorter growing season has restricted the availability of plant life. Such conditions [the shorter growing season] have caused a greater dependence on hunting, and, along the coasts and waterways, on fishing." Choices (A), (B), and (D) would change the meaning of the sentence.

47. **(D)** "The abundance of vegetation in the lower latitudes. . . has provided a greater opportunity for gathering a variety of plants." Choices (A), (B), and (C) refer to the higher latitudes, not to the lower latitudes.

48. **(B)** "Contemporary hunter-gatherers may help us understand our prehistoric ancestors." Choices (A), (C), and (D) may be good ways to learn about prehistoric times, but they are not mentioned and may not be concluded from information in the passage.

49. **(A)** In the context of this passage, "exploit" is closest in meaning to "use." Choices (B), (C), and (D) are not accepted definitions of the word.

50. **(A)** ". . .a society based on hunting and gathering must be very mobile. . . .We also notice a seasonal migration pattern." Choice (B) contradicts the fact that there is a strict division of labor between the sexes. In Choice (C), it is the food supply that becomes exhausted, not the hunter-gatherers. Choice (D) is not mentioned and may not be concluded from information in the passage.

Model Test 8—Long Form

Section 1: Listening Comprehension

1. **(A)** Because the woman refuses to sign and tells the man that he has to get his advisor's signature, we must conclude that she is not the man's advisor. In Choice (B), although she says she is sorry, that is not the reason she cannot sign the form. Choice (C) contradicts the fact that the man asks her to sign a course request form. In Choice (D), it is true that he needs his advisor's signature, but that is not the reason the woman cannot sign the form.

2. **(B)** From the references to the *next screen*, *this key*, and *Enter*, it must be concluded that they are working on a computer. Two people may view a TV screen as in Choice (A), or try to find a room as in Choice (C), or open a door as in Choice (D), but it is not customary for a TV or a door to have function keys.

3. **(C)** *No way* is an idiomatic expression that means it is not going to happen. Choice (A) misinterprets the phrase *no way* to mean directions. Choice (B) contradicts the fact that he will not move from the apartment he is in. Choice (D) contradicts the fact that he gives the woman a definitive answer to her question.

4. **(C)** When a *machine* is *down*, the machine is not working. Choice (A) is incorrect because it is the woman, not the man, who wants to use Federal Express. Choice (B) contradicts the fact that the man says the report is only two pages long. Choice (D) contradicts the fact that the woman says she is sorry that she cannot fax the report.

5. **(D)** If Jim is seven years older than the woman, and the woman is twenty-four, then Jim must be twenty-four plus seven, or thirty-one years old. Choice (A) refers to the number of years older than the woman Jim is, not to his age. Choice (B) would make him seven years younger than the woman. Choice (C) refers to the age of the woman.

6. **(A)** Choice (A) is a direct quotation from the conversation. Choice (B) is the number that the man said before he corrected himself. Choices (C) and (D) confuse the number 7 with the number 6.

7. **(B)** Since the woman is grading the man's test, it must be concluded that the man is a student in the woman's class. It is not likely that classmates and colleagues in Choices (A) and (C) would grade each other's tests. Choice (D) is not mentioned and may not be concluded from information in the conversation.

8. **(C)** Since the woman says the man does not jog, play basketball, or walk, she implies that he does not get much exercise. Choice (A) refers to the man's opinion, not to the woman's remark. Choice (D) contradicts the fact that he used to walk with the woman. Choice (B) is not mentioned and may not be concluded from information in the conversation.

9. **(A)** Because the man says he absolutely has to have the suit, and rush service costs two dollars extra, it must be concluded that the man will pay the extra two dollars. Choice (B) refers to what the woman, not the man, will do. Choices (C) and (D) contradict the fact that the man needs the suit by four o'clock tomorrow.

10. **(C)** Since the man suggests that they sit closer to the front and the woman agrees, they will probably move to the front of the room. Choice (B) contradicts the fact that they are already sitting together. Choice (D) contradicts the fact that the woman agrees with the man. Choice (A) is not mentioned and may not be concluded from information in the conversation.

11. **(A)** Because the woman says that she will have her teaching certificate in one more year, it must be concluded that she wants to be a teacher. Choice (B) contradicts the fact that she will have her teaching certificate. In Choice (C), she works part-time, but whether she studies part-time is not mentioned and may not be concluded from information in the conversation. Choice (D) is not mentioned and may not be concluded from information in the conversation.

12. **(B)** Since she has one girl and twin [two] boys, the woman has three children. Choice (A) refers to the number of daughters she has, not to the number of children. The

number in Choice (C) refers to the age of her daughter. The number in Choice (D) refers to the age of her twin sons.

13. **(B)** Because the man objected to the cold winter but said he liked Montreal the rest of the year, it must be concluded that he liked Montreal in the spring, summer, and fall. Choice (A) contradicts the fact that the man objected to the cold winter. Choice (C) contradicts the fact that the man liked Montreal most of the time. Choice (D) contradicts the fact that the man said "yes" when he was asked if he liked living in Montreal.

14. **(D)** From the reference to a *lot reserved for faculty*, it must be concluded that the conversation took place on a college campus. A concert in Choice (A) may take place at an auditorium, but it is not customary to have reserved parking for faculty at a concert. Choice (B) misinterprets the word *park* to mean a public recreation area. A shopping area in Choice (C) may have shops, but it is not customary to have reserved parking for faculty.

15. **(A)** Since it is usually a one-day rental, and the woman expects to return the tape tomorrow [Sunday when the store is closed], it must be Saturday today. Choice (B) contradicts the fact that the store is open on Friday and Saturday. Choice (C) contradicts the fact that Monday, not tomorrow [Sunday], is a holiday. Choice (D) contradicts the fact that the tape is due back on Tuesday.

16. **(A)** Because the teacher is explaining her policy for make-up tests, it must be concluded that the man missed a test. Choice (C) is incorrect because the essay refers to the type of questions on the make-up test, not to a composition. Choice (D) contradicts the fact that the woman is offering to give him a make-up test. Choice (B) is not mentioned and may not be concluded from information in the conversation.

17. **(D)** Since the man asks for a restroom, he will probably go to the men's room. Choices (A) and (C) refer to places near the restroom, not to what the man will do. Choice (B) is not mentioned and may not be concluded from information in the conversation.

18. **(C)** *You bet* means certainly. Choice (A) misinterprets the word *bet* to mean a wager. Choice (B) contradicts the fact that the man will watch. Choice (D) is not mentioned and may not be concluded from information in the conversation.

19. **(C)** The woman says she got a nicotine patch. Choices (A), (B), and (D) refer to the methods that the man has used to quit smoking in the past.

20. **(A)** *Back off* means to stop. Choice (B) misinterprets the word *okay* to indicate agreement. Choices (C) and (D) are not mentioned and may not be concluded from information in the conversation.

21. **(B)** From the reference to *time* and putting a *name* on your *papers*, it must be concluded that the man is taking a test. Choices (A), (C), and (D) are not mentioned and may not be concluded from information in the conversation.

22. **(C)** The woman says that work keeps her busy and she enjoys it. Choice (A) contradicts the fact that she says she doesn't watch much TV. Choice (B) misinterprets the word *learning* to mean school. Choice (D) contradicts the fact the she responds negatively when she is asked whether she likes "Star Trek."

23. **(B)** When someone says *that's tough*, it means they don't care or they aren't going to do anything about it. Choices (A), (C), and (D) misinterpret the meaning of the phrase *that's tough*.

24. **(C)** From the references to a *key*, *complimentary breakfast*, and a *pool*, it must be concluded that this conversation took place in a hotel lobby. A friend may give you a key as in Choice (A), but it is not customary to call breakfast at a friend's house a *complimentary* breakfast. A restaurant may serve breakfast as in Choice (B), but it is not customary to be given a *key* to a restaurant. A health club may give you a *key* and may have a *pool* as in Choice (D), but it is not customary to have a *complimentary breakfast* at a health club.

25. **(C)** To *work it out* is an idiomatic expression that means to resolve a problem. Choice (B) contradicts the fact that she asks the man to sit down. Choices (A) and (D) are not mentioned and may not be concluded from information in the conversation.

26. **(C)** To *not be too big on* something means to not like it very much. Choice (D) contradicts

the fact that he responds to the woman's question. Choices (A) and (B) are not mentioned and may not be concluded from information in the conversation.

27. **(D)** *Way to go* means congratulations. Choices (A), (B), and (C) misinterpret the meaning of the phrase *way to go*.

28. **(D)** *Separate checks* is an idiomatic expression that means each person will pay for his or her own meal. Choices (A), (B), and (C) are not paraphrases of the expression, and may not be concluded from information in the conversation.

29. **(A)** "You must be thinking of my roommate [who got an assistantship]." Choice (B) contradicts the fact that she will be studying full time. Choice (D) contradicts the fact that the man has confused the woman with her roommate. Choice (C) is not mentioned and may not be concluded from information in the conversation.

30. **(B)** Since the man wants to arrange a time, it must be concluded that he will help the woman. Choice (C) contradicts the fact that he will be at the woman's dorm on Saturday. Choices (A) and (D) are not mentioned and may not be concluded from information in the conversation.

31. **(C)** *I wish I knew* is an idiomatic expression that means one does not know. Choices (A), (B), and (D) are not paraphrases of the expression, and may not be concluded from information in the conversation.

32. **(C)** Since the woman is dispensing medication from a doctor's prescription, it must be concluded that she is a pharmacist. Choices (A), (B), and (D) contradict the fact that the man, not the woman, needs medication.

33. **(A)** *Give me a hand* is an idiomatic expression that means to help. Choices (B), (C), and (D) are not paraphrases of the expression, and may not be concluded from information in the conversation.

34. **(C)** To be *on one's way* is an idiomatic expression that means to be ready to leave. Choices (A), (B), and (D) are not paraphrases of the expression, and may not be concluded from information in the conversation.

35. **(C)** ". . . you could get a plant." Choice (D) refers to the fact that the man considered taking candy to his friends, not to the woman's suggestion. Choices (A) and (B) are not mentioned and may not be concluded from information in the conversation.

36. **(B)** Since the woman's room number is 119, and the man points out that the odd numbers are on the other side, the woman will probably look on the other side of the hall. Choices (A), (C), and (D) are not mentioned and may not be concluded from information in the conversation.

37. **(C)** To *sleep like a rock* is an idiomatic expression that means to sleep very well. Choices (A), (B), and (D) are not paraphrases of the expression, and may not be concluded from information in the conversation.

38. **(C)** "If Sue hadn't had her seat belt on [but she did have it on] she would have been killed [but she was not killed]." Choice (A) contradicts the fact that Sue was in the accident. Choice (D) contradicts the fact that she was not killed. Choice (B) is not mentioned and may not be concluded from information in the conversation.

39. **(B)** Since the man needs to go downstairs to get to the first floor, he must have assumed that the second floor was the first floor. Choice (A) contradicts the fact that the man needs to go downstairs, not upstairs, to find the first floor. Choices (C) and (D) refer to the woman's explanation, not to the man's assumption.

40. **(A)** To be *all tied up* is an idiomatic expression that means to be busy. Choices (B), (C), and (D) are not paraphrases of the expression, and may not be concluded from information in the conversation.

41. **(C)** To *drop by* is an idiomatic expression that means to visit. Choice (A) contradicts the fact that she is on her way to work. Choice (B) contradicts the fact that the purpose of the phone call is to set up a visit, not to have a conversation. Choice (D) contradicts the fact that she wants to visit the man.

42. **(D)** Since the woman assures the man that it takes a long time to process the application, she implies that he should be patient. Choice (B) contradicts the fact that it takes six weeks, not three weeks, to process. Choices (A) and (C) are not mentioned and may not be concluded from information in the conversation.

43. **(C)** Since the man asks her to try it again, the woman will probably put the numbers in the computer again. Choices (A), (B), and (D) are not mentioned and may not be concluded from information in the conversation.

44. **(C)** Since the woman is showing the man how to use a computer in order to find books, it must be concluded that she is a librarian. Choice (A) contradicts the fact that she is showing the man how to use a computer. Choice (B) contradicts the fact that the man is going to find the books he needs. Choice (D) contradicts the fact that she is helping the man, not doing her own research.

45. **(B)** *I'm afraid not* is an idiomatic expression that means unfortunately not. Choice (A) contradicts the fact that the man feels it is unfortunate not to go. Choice (D) contradicts the fact that he will not transfer next year. Choice (C) is not a paraphrase of the expression and may not be concluded from information in the conversation.

46. **(A)** Since the woman offers her passport, it must be concluded that she wants to use it for ID. Choice (C) refers to the identification required, not to the method of payment. Choice (D) contradicts the fact that she is paying with a traveler's check. Choice (B) is not mentioned and may not be concluded from information in the conversation.

47. **(D)** Her brother is in Birmingham, her sister is in Mobile, and her parents are in Florida. Choice (B) refers to her parents, not to the rest of the family. Choice (C) contradicts the fact that no family members living in the same town were mentioned. Choice (A) is not mentioned and may not be concluded from information in the conversation.

48. **(A)** *You and everybody else* is an idiomatic expression that means many people. Choices (B), (C), and (D) are not mentioned and may not be concluded from information in the conversation.

49. **(C)** "What happened to your exercise program?" Choice (A) is mentioned as one of several options for exercise. Choice (B) refers to physical stress on the knees, not to stress management. Choice (D) is not mentioned and may not be concluded from information in the conversation.

50. **(D)** Since the man tells the woman how far it is to Long Beach, it must be concluded that she has not arrived there yet. Choice (A) contradicts the fact that the woman wants to know how far it is to San Diego, not to Long Beach. Choice (C) contradicts the fact that it is fifty miles plus ninety miles, or one hundred forty miles to San Diego. Choice (B) is not mentioned and may not be concluded from information in the conversation.

51. **(C)** *A real bear* is an idiomatic expression that means very difficult, especially in reference to a test or examination. Choice (D) refers to the man's statement, not to the woman's comment. Choices (A) and (B) are not mentioned and may not be concluded from information in the conversation.

52. **(B)** *I couldn't have been more pleased* is an idiomatic expression that means the speaker was very pleased. Choice (D) contradicts the fact that the man was pleased with the meeting. Choices (A) and (C) were not mentioned and may not be concluded from information in the conversation.

53. **(C)** "You are here because you are accused of plagiarism." Choice (A) refers to the fact that the professor gave him a failing grade, not to the reason why the student is in the dean's office. The dean gives the student some advice, but Choice (B) is not mentioned as a reason for his being in the dean's office. Choice (D) is incorrect because the dean refers to the fact that plagiarism is intellectual theft, not to the theft of a book.

54. **(A)** "That [using ideas with a citation] is what I don't understand." Choice (D) refers to the dean's suggestion that the student get a tutor, not to the student's excuse. Choices (B) and (C) are not mentioned and may not be concluded from information in the conversation.

55. **(C)** "I'm going to give you a warning this time." Choice (A) refers to the dean's decision to expel the student if he ever sees him in his office for a similar offense. Choice (B) refers to the professor's, not the dean's, punishment of the student. Choice (D) refers to the advice, not the punishment, that the dean gave the student.

56. **(B)** "I suggest that you go over to the Learning Resources Center for some tutoring." Choices (A), (C), and (D) are not mentioned and may not be concluded from information in the conversation.

57. **(B)** "I'm trying to decide whether to stay here or to transfer to a larger school." Choices (A), (C), and (D) are not mentioned and may not be concluded from information in the conversation.

58. **(C)** ". . .your teachers know you, and they really seem to care about you." Choices (A) and (D) refer to the advantages of a larger school, not to what she likes about the college she is attending. Choice (B) is not mentioned and may not be concluded from information in the conversation.

59. **(C)** ". . .I'm planning to go to graduate school, so my plan is to get really good grades here, and try to get into a well-known university for my master's degree." Choice (A) contradicts the fact that he listens to the woman. Choice (D) contradicts the fact that he tries to understand her point of view, and shares his plans. Choice (B) is not mentioned and may not be concluded from information in the conversation.

60. **(A)** ". . . try to get into a well-known university for my master's degree." Choice (C) contradicts the fact that his plan is to get good grades in the undergraduate program at his current school. Choices (B) and (D) are not mentioned and may not be concluded from information in the conversation.

61. **(B)** "And what would you like to order, Mr. Wilson?" In Choice (A), it is not customary for friends to address each other by last names. Choice (C) refers to the man, not to the woman. Choice (D) refers to the fact that the woman and the man are talking by phone, probably long distance, but the woman is not requesting the kind of information that an operator would.

62. **(B)** "Visa, then." Choices (A) and (C) refer to the credit cards that the woman names as possibilities for payment. Choice (D) refers to the card that the man wanted to use, not to the card he actually did use.

63. **(C)** "W-I-L-S-O-N." Choices (A), (B), and (D) confuse the names of the vowel letters in English.

64. **(C)** "Two shirts . . . 16 1/2 . . . a brown one and a white one." Choice (A) is incorrect because the order is for one, not two shirts. The number in Choice (B) refers to the page in the catalog, not to the size. The number in

Choice (D) refers to the page in the catalog, and the order is for three, not two shirts.

65. **(B)** ". . .a home pick-up service for your recyclable items . . . called CURBSIDE. . . ." Choice (A) refers to House Bill 592, not to CURBSIDE. Choice (C) refers to the one-hundred-dollar fine for failure to separate recyclables from trash. Choice (D) is not mentioned and may not be concluded from information in the talk.

66. **(C)** "No magazines or plastic bags will be accepted." Choices (A), (B), and (D) are all mentioned after the question, "What can you recycle?"

67. **(A)** "To prepare the recyclables for pickup, just remove lids and labels from containers and rinse them." Choice (D) is incorrect because paper bags, not plastic bags, must be used to prepare newspapers. Choices (B) and (C) are not mentioned and may not be concluded from information in the talk.

68. **(D)** ". . .a one-hundred-dollar fine for failure to separate recyclables. . . ." Choice (A) refers to the charge for the blue recycling container, not to the fine. Choice (B) refers to the yearly service rate for CURBSIDE. Choice (C) is incorrect because the number refers to the percentage by which communities hope to reduce materials going to landfills, not to a dollar amount for a fine.

69. **(B)** The other choices are secondary ideas that are used to develop the main idea, "the definition of culture." Choices (A), (C), and (D) are mentioned in reference to the definition.

70. **(D)** "In informal conversation, the word *culture* refers to a desirable personal attribute . . . and that's what most people think of when they hear the word culture." Choices (A), (B), and (C) refer to the definition of *culture* in anthropology, not in informal conversation.

71. **(C)** "For a thought or activity to be included as part of a culture, it must be commonly shared by or considered appropriate for the group." Choice (A) refers to a subculture, not a culture. Choice (B) refers to the word *culture* as it is understood in informal conversation. Choice (D) refers to the United States and societies like it.

72. **(C)** ". . .the smaller groups within the larger society have shared customs that are specific

to their group . . . a subculture." Choices (A) and (B) refer to an informal definition of culture, not to subcultures. Choice (D) refers to a definition of culture by an anthropologist, not to a definition of a subculture.

73. **(D)** ". . . ten to twelve million adults and one million children worldwide had contracted H.I.V., the virus that causes AIDS. . . [and] there appears to be a change in the characteristics of AIDS victims." Choice (B) refers to the organization that issued the report. Choices (A) and (C) are secondary themes used to develop the main theme of the talk.

74. **(A)** "In the 1980s, homosexual men in large urban areas accounted for approximately two thirds of all AIDS cases." Choices (B) and (D) refer to the majority of new adult cases today, not in the 1980s. Choice (C) is not mentioned and may not be concluded from information in the talk.

75. **(D)** "Today almost 90 percent of new adult infections result from heterosexual contact." Choice (A) misinterprets the numbers nineteen and ninety. The percentage in Choice (C) refers to the percentage of AIDS cases attributed to male homosexuals in the 1980s. Choice (B) is not mentioned and may not be concluded from information in the talk.

76. **(C)** "By the year 2000, it is now expected that the majority of AIDS victims will be heterosexual women and their young children." Choice (A) refers to only part of the population, and does not include women. Choices (B) and (D) are not mentioned in the estimate and may not be concluded from information in the talk.

77. **(C)** "One of the most successful educational programs for adults is the Elderhostel. . ." Choices (A), (B), and (D) are secondary themes that are used to develop the main theme of the talk.

78. **(D)** "Although courses are not offered for credit, and no exams are required, the classes are taught by highly qualified faculty at the host college." Choice (A) contradicts the fact that the courses are not offered for credit. Choice (B) contradicts the fact that no exams are required. Choice (C) contradicts the fact that Elderhostel is for people over the age of sixty.

79. **(A)** "Students usually live in dormitories. . ." Choices (B), (C), and (D) are not mentioned

and may not be concluded from information in the talk.

80. **(B)** ". . .call your local college." Choice (C) refers to the fact that the talk is an announcement on radio, but no additional announcements are mentioned. Choices (A) and (D) are not mentioned and may not be concluded from information in the talk.

Section 2: Structure and Written Expression

1. **(C)** *Similar* is used after the two nouns *protoplasm* and *glue* to compare them. Choice (A) is redundant because the pronoun *they* is used consecutively after the nouns to which it refers. Choice (B) has the same meaning as the correct answer, but *similar to* is used before, not after, the second noun compared. Choice (D) does not have a verb. (Refer to Patterns, Problem 87, page 154.)

2. **(B)** *Instead of* is used before a noun to indicate replacement. "The lights and appliances in most homes use alternating current instead" would also be correct. (Refer to Patterns, Problem 108, page 179.)

3. **(B)** *Too old* means *excessively old*. Choice (A) may be used to introduce a clause of result, not to conclude a sentence. Choice (C) is ungrammatical because *the* must be used with a superlative. Choice (D) is ungrammatical because *very* is not used with a comparative. (Refer to Patterns, Problem 83, page 149.)

4. **(B)** *Oil* is a noncount noun because it is a liquid that can change shape, depending on the shape of the container. Choices (A) and (C) have articles before a noncount noun. Choice (D) is an adjective, not a noun. (Refer to Patterns, Problem 53, page 109.)

5. **(C)** The verb word *be* must be used in a clause after the noun *requirement*, which is derived from the subjunctive verb *require*. Choice (A) is a modal and a verb word, not a verb word. Choice (B) is a past form of the verb. Choice (D) is a prepositional phrase. (Refer to Patterns, Problem 28, page 77.)

6. **(C)** Every sentence must have a main verb. Choices (A), (B), and (D) are not main verbs. (Refer to Patterns, Problem 1, page 41.)

7. **(A)** *More than* is used before a specific number to express an estimate. "As many as two

hundred" would also be correct. (Refer to Patterns, Problem 94, page 163.)

8. **(D)** No article before a noncount noun or a plural count noun means *all*. Choice (A) would be an incomplete sentence because it is missing a main verb. Choices (B) and (C) contain articles and would change the meaning of the sentence. (Refer to Patterns, Problem 64, page 126.)

9. **(D)** *Besides* is used before a noun or an adjective. It means *in addition to*. Choices (A) and (C) include the word *beside*, which means *near*, not *besides*. In Choice (B), the word *besides* is used after, not before, the noun. (Refer to Patterns, Problem 106, page 177.)

10. **(B)** A reflexive pronoun is used when the subject and complement refer to the same person. Only *themselves* in Choice (B) is a reflexive pronoun. *Them* in Choice (A) is an object pronoun. *They* in Choice (C) is a subject pronoun. *Their* in Choice (D) is a possessive pronoun. (Refer to Patterns, Problem 50, page 104.)

11. **(D)** *No* is used before a noun phrase like *definite shape*. *Not* in Choice A should be used before a verb. *None* in Choice (B) and *nothing* in Choice (C) are pronouns that are used instead of the noun phrase. (Refer to Patterns, Problem 65, page 127.)

12. **(B)** The count noun meaning of *work* is an *artistic creation*. Choices (A) and (C) refer to the noncount meaning, *labor*. Choice (D) is ungrammatical. (Refer to Patterns, Problem 54, page 111.)

13. **(C)** *Would* and a verb word must be used in the clause that follows *had hoped*. Choice (A) is a verb word, but it does not include *would*. Choice (B) completes a clause but it does not include *would*. Choice (D) is an *-ing* form that completes a phrase, not a clause. (Refer to Patterns, Problem 39, page 90.)

14. **(A)** The comparative of a three-syllable adverb is formed by using *more* before the adverb and *than* after the adverb. Choice (B) is an adverb, but it is not a comparative with *more*. Choices (C) and (D) are an adjective comparative and superlative, not adverbs. (Refer to Patterns, Problem 99, page 168.)

15. **(D)** Either an *-ing* form or an infinitive may be used as the subject of a sentence. Choice (A) is an infinitive that means *to establish*, not *to identify*. Choice (B) is a verb word. Choice (C) is a noun. "To find"

would also be correct. (Refer to Patterns, Problem 59, page 119.)

16. **(A)** The word order for a passive sentence is BE followed by a participle. Choice (B) is a participle, but the form of BE is missing. Choice (C) is redundant because the pronoun *it* is used consecutively after the subject *path*. Choice (D) is an *-ing* form, not a passive. (Refer to Patterns, Problem 31, page 81.)

17. **(D)** To *differ from* is a verb that expresses difference. Because Choices (A) and (C) are not verbs, the sentence would not have a main verb in it. Choice (B) is a verb, but the preposition *from* is missing. "A dolphin is different from a porpoise" would also be correct. (Refer to Patterns, Problem 92, page 161.)

18. **(D)** When two nouns occur together, the first noun functions as an adjective. Choice (A) is not logical because it implies ownership of the *restaurants* by a *chain*. In Choice (B), the adjective is plural, but adjectives in English do not change form to agree in number with the nouns they modify. In Choice (C), the singular noun *restaurant* does not agree with the two nouns, *MacDonalds* and *Kentucky Fried Chicken,* to which it refers. (Refer to Patterns, Problem 78, page 144.)

19. **(A)** An adjective is used before *enough* to express sufficiency. In Choice (B), there is an adverb used after *enough*. In Choice (C), the adjective is used after, not before, *enough*, and the word *as* is unnecessary and incorrect. In Choice (D), the word *as* is unnecessary and incorrect. (Refer to Patterns, Problem 74, page 138.)

20. **(B)** *From* introduces cause. Choices (A), (C), and (D) are not idiomatic. (Refer to Patterns, Problem 112, page 184.)

21. **(B)** *That most natural time units are not simple multiples of each other* functions as the noun phrase subject of the main verb *is*. Choice (A) is redundant because the pronoun *it* is used consecutively after the noun phrase subject. In Choice (C), the usual subject-verb-object order of English sentences is reversed. Choice (D) does not include a main verb. (Refer to Patterns, Problem 61, page 121.)

22. **(C)** An introductory verbal phrase should immediately precede the noun that it modifies. Only Choice (C) provides a noun that could be logically modified by the

introductory verbal phrase *an abstract painter and a pioneer of Surrealism*. *Miró's works*, *the works of Miró*, and *bright colors* could not logically be *a painter and a pioneer* as would be implied by Choices (A), (B), and (D). (Refer to Style, Problem 15, page 237.)

23. **(A)** *As a whole* means *generally*. Choice (B) means *completely*. Choice (C) is not idiomatic. Choice (D) is redundant because it is a noun subject used consecutively with the noun subject *the plow*. (Refer to Patterns, Problem 136, page 214.)

24. **(D)** An infinitive is used to express purpose. (Refer to Patterns, Problem 30, page 80.)

25. **(C)** A present tense verb is used after *when* to express future. (Refer to Patterns, Problem 123, page 198.)

26. **(D)** *Each other* is used to express mutual acts. Choices (A), (B), and (C) are not idiomatic. "One another" would also be correct. (Refer to Patterns, Problem 51, page 105.)

27. **(A)** *Kinds of* is used before the plural count noun *magnets* to express classification. *Kind* in Choices (B) and (C) is used before a singular count noun or a noncount noun. In Choice (D), the preposition *of* is missing. (Refer to Patterns, Problem 58, page 118.)

28. **(D)** *Unless* introduces a subject and verb that express a change in conditions. Choices (A), (B), and (C) do not have a subject and verb. (Refer to Patterns, Problem 26, page 74.)

29. **(C)** *A large number of* is used before the plural count noun *doctors*. Choice (A) is used before a noncount noun, not a plural count noun. In Choices (B) and (D), the article *a* is missing. (Refer to Patterns, Problem 71, page 134.)

30. **(C)** *On* is used before the street name *Beacon*. *In* is used before the city *Boston*. Choices (A), (B), and (D) all use inappropriate prepositions before the street name *Beacon*. Choices (B) and (D) use inappropriate prepositions before the city *Boston*. (Refer to Patterns, Problem 104, page 175.)

31. **(C)** In order to refer to giving money to customers, *lend* not *borrow* should be used. To *borrow* means to take and give back. To *lend* means to give and take back. (Refer to Style, Problem 27, page 253.)

32. **(D)** *Reduction* should be *reducing*. Although both are derived from the same verb,

reduction means a decrease; *reducing* means causing a reduction. (Refer to Style, Problem 30, page 257.)

33. **(D)** *Most cleanest* should be *cleanest*. Because *clean* is a one-syllable adjective, the superlative is formed by adding *-est*. *Most* is used with two-syllable adjectives that do not end in *-y*. (Refer to Patterns, Problem 97, page 166.)

34. **(C)** Activities of the dead logically establish a point of view in the past. *Is* should be *was* in order to maintain the point of view. (Refer to Style, Problem 4, page 224.)

35. **(B)** Repetition of the subject by a subject pronoun is redundant. *They* should be deleted. (Refer to Style, Problem 21, page 245.)

36. **(B)** *Such* is used with *a* or *an* before an adjective and a noun to describe a cause. *Such important* should be *such an important* before the noun *field*. (Refer to Patterns, Problem 82, page 148.)

37. **(A)** *There* introduces inverted order, but there must still be agreement between subject and verb. *Is* should be *are* to agree with the plural subject, *so many variables*. (Refer to Style, Problem 8, page 229.)

38. **(C)** The adverbial phrase *in 1605* establishes a point of view in the past. *Builds* should be *built* in order to maintain the point of view. (Refer to Style, Problem 3, page 223.)

39. **(D)** In order to refer to a gallon of water being *moved to a higher place*, *raise* not *rise* should be used. To *raise* means to move to a higher place. To *rise* means to go up without assistance; to increase. (Refer to Style, Problem 22, page 247.)

40. **(B)** Using words with the same meaning consecutively is repetitive. *Both* should be deleted because *together* implies that *both* are included. (Refer to Style, Problem 20, page 244.)

41. **(B)** The participle is used after a form of BE in a passive sentence. *Finding* should be *found* after *to be*. (Refer to Patterns, Problem 31, page 81.)

42. **(B)** There must be agreement between pronoun and antecedent. *Its* should be *their* to agree with the plural antecedent *sloths*. (Refer to Style, Problem 11, page 232.)

43. **(B)** In order to refer to retaining residue, *leave* not *let* should be used. *To let* means to

permit. *To leave* means to let someone or something remain. (Refer to Style, Problem 26, page 252.)

44. **(C)** *Believe* should be *belief*. *Believe* is a verb. *Belief* is a noun. (Refer to Style, Problem 30, page 257.)

45. **(C)** An infinitive is used to express purpose. To *reading* should be to *read*. (Refer to Patterns, Problem 30, page 80.)

46. **(C)** There must be agreement between subject and verb. *Are* should be *is* to agree with the singular subject *cotton fiber*. The phrase of comparison *like other vegetable fiber* modifies the subject. (Refer to Style, Problem 5, page 226.)

47. **(B)** *Depends on* is a prepositional idiom. *To* should be *on*. (Refer to Style, Problem 29, page 255.)

48. **(B)** *Great* should be *greater*. Because *great* is a one-syllable adjective, the comparative is formed by adding *-er*. (Refer to Patterns, Problem 96, page 165.)

49. **(C)** In order to refer to a range of frequencies, *lies* should be used. *To lie* means to occupy a place. *To lay* means to put. (Refer to Style, Problem 23, page 248.)

50. **(D)** *By* expresses means before an *-ing* form. *Rub* should be *rubbing* after the preposition *by*. (Refer to Patterns, Problem 114, page 186.)

51. **(B)** Ideas after inclusives should be expressed by parallel structures. *Presided* should be *the chairman of* to provide for parallelism with the nouns *poet* and *author*. (Refer to Style, Problem 18, page 241.)

52. **(A)** There must be agreement between subject and verb. *Was* should be *were* to agree with the plural subject *some important characteristics*. The phrase of description *of the Baroque style* modifies the subject. (Refer to Style, Problem 5, page 226.)

53. **(A)** An *-ing* form may be used as the subject of a sentence. *The understanding* should be *understanding* or *the understanding of* electricity. (Refer to Patterns, Problem 59 and Problem 60, pages 119–120.)

54. **(D)** *Had* and a participle in the condition requires *would have* and a participle in the result. *Will* should be *would*. (Refer to Patterns, Problem 24, page 71.)

55. **(C)** *Do* is usually used before complements that describe work and chores. *Make* should be *do* before the complement *research*. (Refer to Style, Problem 28, page 254.)

56. **(B)** *Among* refers to three or more nouns. *Between* refers to two nouns. *Among* should be *between* to refer to the two nouns *speed* and *pressure*. (Refer to Patterns, Problem 103, page 174.)

57. **(A)** The construction of the Great Pyramid took place in the past. In addition, the verb *reported* establishes a point of view in the past. *Are* should be *were*, to maintain the point of view. (Refer to Style, Problem 2, page 222.)

58. **(D)** *By* expresses means before an *-ing* form. *Provide* should be *providing*. (Refer to Patterns, Problem 114, page 186.)

59. **(C)** Ideas in a series should be expressed by parallel structures. *Helping* should be *help* to provide for parallelism with the verb words *report* and *give*. (Refer to Style, Problem 17, page 240.)

60. **(A)** There must be agreement between subject and verb. *Remain* should be *remains* to agree with the singular subject *each*. (Refer to Style, Problem 9, page 230.)

Section 3: Reading Comprehension

1. **(B)** The other choices are secondary ideas that are used to develop the main idea, "the Richter scale." Choices (A), (C), and (D) are important to the discussion as they relate to the Richter scale.

2. **(C)** A geology book would have a reference to the Richter scale. It would be unlikely that we would find a passage on the measurement of earthquakes in any of the texts in Choices (A), (B), and (D).

3. **(B)** The Richter scale was developed "to measure the amplitude of the largest trace. . . ." Choices (A) and (D) refer to the placement of the seismograph in order to record the amplitude. Choice (C) refers to the numerical reference that estimates the degree of damage.

4. **(C)** In the context of this passage, "standard" could best be replaced by "conventional." Choices (A), (C), and (D) are not accepted definitions of the word.

5. **(A)** The "tables have been formulated to demonstrate the magnitude of any earthquake. . . ." Choice (D) refers to the release of energy, one of the factors that is

considered in formulating the magnitude. Choices (B) and (C) are not mentioned in reference to the value of the tables.

6. **(C)** "An earthquake that reads 4 to 5.5 would be expected to cause localized damage, and those [earthquakes] of magnitude 2 may be felt." Choices (A), (B), and (D) would change the meaning of the sentence.

7. **(C)** "An earthquake that reads 4 to 5.5 would be expected to cause localized damage. . . ." Choice (A) refers to a major earthquake. Choice (D) refers to an earthquake that could be felt. Choice (B) is not specifically explained on the scale described in the reading passage.

8. **(B)** In the context of this passage, "undetected" is closest in meaning to "with no notice." Choices (A), (C), and (D) are not accepted definitions of the word.

9. **(B)** ". . . each number on the Richter scale represents an earthquake ten times as strong as one of the next lower magnitude." Choices (A), (C), and (D) contradict the fact that each magnitude is ten times stronger than the previous one.

10. **(C)** Choice (A) is mentioned in lines 1–2. Choice (B) is mentioned in lines 1–2. Choice (D) is mentioned in lines 4–5. Choice (C) contradicts the fact that minor earthquakes go undetected.

11. **(B)** The passage mainly discusses Charles Ives' life, including references to the details referred to in Choices (A), (C), and (D).

12. **(B)** In the context of this passage, "suspected" could best be replaced by "guessed." Choices (A), (C), and (D) are not accepted definitions of the word.

13. **(B)** ". . .the use of dissonance and special effects was just too different for the musical mainstream." Choice (A) is true, but is not a reason that the public did not appreciate his music. Choice (D) contradicts the fact the he wrote music. In Choice (C), although the performers felt his music was unplayable, there is no reference to the fact that they did not play it well.

14. **(D)** "Even the few conductors and performers he tried to interest in his compositions felt that they [the compositions] were unplayable." Choices (A), (B), and (C) would change the meaning of the sentence.

15. **(A)** In the context of this passage, "became

reconciled" is closest in meaning to "accepted." Choices (B), (C), and (D) are not accepted definitions of the word.

16. **(C)** ". . .he became a successful insurance executive. . . ." Choice (A) refers to his father's profession. Choice (B) refers to Horatio Parker's profession. Although it is true that Ives published his own music as in Choice (D), he did not make a living from it.

17. **(A)** ". . .he published his work privately and distributed it free." Choice (C) refers to the fact that he occasionally hired musicians to play his works, but they were private, not public performances. Choices (B) and (D) are not mentioned and may not be concluded from information in the passage.

18. **(D)** ". . .John Kirkpatrick played *Concord Sonata* in Town Hall." Choice (A) refers to the place where his *Second Symphony* was performed, eight years later. Choice (C) refers to the place where Ives studied, not to the place where his first work was performed. Choice (B) is not mentioned and may not be concluded from information in the passage.

19. **(D)** ". . .the greatest music composed by an American." Choice (A) contradicts the fact that the reviews were laudatory. Choices (B) and (C) refer to Ives' music prior to the *Concord Sonata* performance.

20. **(B)** "The same year [1947] Ives received the Pulitzer prize." Choice (A) refers to the year that the *Concord Sonata* was performed, not to the year that Ives received the Pulitzer prize. The number 65 in Choice (C) refers to Ives' age when his music was first performed. The number 73 in Choice (D) refers to Ives' age when he received the prize, not to the year he received it.

21. **(C)** Because the author states that bats are "not . . . dirty . . . groom themselves carefully . . . and help reforest barren land," it must be concluded that the author views bats as clean, helpful members of the animal world. Choice (A) contradicts the author's statements that bats are not dirty and only rarely carry rabies. Choice (B) contradicts the author's statement that bats are not the monsters that they are portrayed in vampire films. Choice (D) contradicts the author's statement that bats consume pests, pollinate

plants, and reforest land, all of which are important contributions to the animal world.

22. **(B)** "These animals [bats] groom themselves carefully like cats. . . ." Choices (A), (C), and (D) are mentioned as characteristics of bats, but not in reference to cats.

23. **(B)** ". . .the majority [of bats] eat fruit, insects, spiders or other small animals." Choice (A) contradicts the fact that only three species rely on blood meals. Choice (D) contradicts the fact that bats eat small, not large animals. Choice (C) is not mentioned and may not be concluded from information in the passage.

24. **(C)** In the context of this passage, "enormous" could best be replaced by "very large." Choices (A), (B), and (D) are not accepted definitions of the word.

25. **(D)** "Of the hundreds of species of bats, only three rely on blood meals." Choice (A) contradicts the fact that bats pollinate many varieties of plant life. Choice (B) contradicts the fact that bats assume specialized roles within their social system. Choice (C) contradicts the fact that almost all bats use echolocation.

26. **(C)** "They. . .help reforest barren land by excreting millions of undigested seeds." Choices (A), (B), and (D) all refer to the activities of bats, but not to how they reforest the land.

27. **(A)** In the context of this passage, "emit" is closest in meaning to "send." Choices (B), (C), and (D) are not accepted definitions of the word.

28. **(A)** "As these signals bounce off objects in their path, an echo is detected by the bats' sensitive ears and they undertake corrective or evasive action." Choice (B) refers to one of the roles of bats within their social system, not to their navigational skills. Choice (C) is incorrect because the number fifty refers to the number of high-pitched squeaks per minute, not to the number of times bats beat their wings. Choice (D) is true, but the specific noises they hear are the echoes referred to in Choice (A).

29. **(D)** "But bats are not blind as widely assumed. In fact, all species of bats can see, probably about as well as human beings." Choices (A), (B), and (C) refer to other themes in the passage.

30. **(C)** "Some [bats] may guard the entrance to

their caves, others may scout for food, and still others may warn the colony of approaching danger." Choices (A), (B), and (D) would change the meaning of the sentence.

31. **(B)** The passage includes descriptions of various kinds of population centers. Choices (A) and (D) are two kinds of population centers described in the passage. Choice (C) refers to the source of the information about population centers, not to the topic of the passage.

32. **(B)** ". . .more Americans live in the suburbs of large metropolitan areas than in the cities themselves." Choice (A) contradicts the statement that more Americans live in the suburbs. Choices (C) and (D) are not mentioned and may not be concluded from information in the passage.

33. **(A)** "The Bureau of Census regards any area with more than 2500 people as an urban area. . . ." Choice (B) refers to an MSA, not to an urban area. The number in Choice (C) refers to megapolises, not to urban areas. Choice (D) refers to the definition of a megapolis.

34. **(A)** ". . .the political boundaries are less significant than the social and economic relationships and the transportation and communication systems. . . ." Because the political boundaries are less significant, it must be concluded that the factors in Choices (B), (C), and (D) are more significant.

35. **(C)** In the context of this passage, "integrate" is closest in meaning to "unite." Choices (A), (B), and (D) are not accepted definitions of the word.

36. **(B)** ". . .an MSA is any area that contains a city and its surrounding suburbs, and has a total population of 50,000 or more." Choice (A) contradicts the fact that an MSA includes the surrounding suburbs. Choice (C) contradicts the fact that an MSA includes the city. Choice (D) is too general because it does not specify that a city and its surrounding suburbs must be included.

37. **(C)** ". . .the bureau reports more than 280 MSAs. . . ." The number in Choice (A) refers to the number of states in the Eastern Corridor, not to the number of MSAs. The number in Choice (B) refers to the number of megapolises. The number in Choice (D) refers to the number of people in an urban area.

38. **(C)** Three quarters is 75 percent. There is no

similar reference in the lines referred to in Choices (A), (B), and (D).

39. **(D)** ". . .the bureau recognizes eighteen megapolises, that is, continuous adjacent metropolitan areas." Choices (A), (B), and (C) contradict the fact that a megapolis includes more than one adjacent city.

40. **(C)** "In the Eastern Corridor, as it is called, a population of forty-five million inhabitants is concentrated." In Choice (A), the number *forty-five* is misinterpreted as *four to five*. The number in Choice (B) refers to the number of states included in the Eastern Corridor. The number in Choice (D) refers to the percentage of the population living in 280 MSAs.

41. **(B)** Because the author says "unfortunately" when he refers to the destruction of the rainforests, it must be concluded that he believes preserving the rainforest is important. Choices (A) and (C) contradict the statement that we aren't able to predict the ramifications. Choice (D) contradicts the statement that we don't know what the loss of other species may be doing to the future of the human species.

42. **(C)** In the context of this passage, "relatively" could best be replaced by "comparatively." Choices (A), (B), and (D) are not accepted definitions of the word.

43. **(C)** "Rainforests circle the globe for twenty degrees of latitude on both sides of the equator. . . . In that . . . band . . . more than half of all species . . . make their home." The number in Choice (A) refers to the degrees of latitude, not to the number of rainforests. The number of varieties of trees in Choice (B) refers to the habitat in a single acre of rainforest, not to the habitat for half the species. Choice (D) contradicts the fact that plants and animals cannot survive where the rainforest has been cleared.

44. **(B)** Although Choices (A), (C), and (D) are definitions of the word "just," the meaning in the context of the sentence is "only."

45. **(B)** If half of the rainforests are already destroyed, and 25 percent will be lost by the year 2000, then 50 percent plus 25 percent, or 75 percent, will be destroyed. The percentage in Choice (C) refers to the additional destruction. The percentage in Choice (D) refers to the current destruction. The percentage in Choice (A) is not mentioned and may

not be computed from information in the passage.

46. **(C)** "Every sixty seconds, one hundred acres of rainforest is being cleared." There are sixty seconds in one minute. Choice (A) is a misinterpretation of the word *one* for *one hundred*. Choice (B) would compute to sixty acres per sixty seconds, not one hundred acres. Choice (D) would compute to 3.3 acres per sixty seconds.

47. **(A)** "When this happens [the destruction of the acres], constant rains erode the former forest floor, and the ecology of the region is altered forever." Choices (B), (C), and (D) would change the meaning of the sentence.

48. **(D)** In the context of this passage, "constant" could best be replaced by "continual." Choices (A), (B), and (C) are not accepted definitions of the word.

49. **(A)** In the context of this passage, "altered" is closest in meaning to "changed." Choices (B), (C), and (D) are not accepted definitions of the word.

50. **(D)** ". . .constant rains erode the former forest floor, and the ecology of the region is altered forever." Choices (A), (B), and (C) are all mentioned in the passage as the results of clearing the rainforest.

51. **(C)** The other choices are secondary ideas that are used to develop the main idea, "human memory." Choices (A), (B), and (D) are important to the discussion, but are not the main topic.

52. **(A)** In the context of this passage, "formerly" could best be replaced by "in the past." Choices (B), (C), and (D) are not accepted definitions of the word.

53. **(A)** "Human memory . . . is really more sophisticated than that of a computer." Choice (B) contradicts the statement that human memory is more sophisticated. Choices (C) and (D) are not mentioned and may not be concluded from information in the passage.

54. **(D)** "Human memory, formerly believed to be rather inefficient, is really more sophisticated than that [the memory] of a computer." Choices (A), (B), and (C) would change the meaning of the sentence.

55. **(A)** ". . .there is a great deal more stored in our minds than has been generally supposed." Choice (B) contradicts the statement that the

physical basis for memory is not yet understood. Choice (C) refers to the fact that researchers have approached the problem from a variety of points of view, but it may not be concluded that different points of view are valuable. Choice (D) contradicts the statement that memory was formerly believed to be inefficient, but is really sophisticated.

56. **(B)** ". . .by stimulating their brains electrically, he could elicit the total recall of specific events." Choice (A) refers to the fact that Penfield was a neurosurgeon, but he did not rely on surgery to elicit dreams. Choice (C) refers to the procedure for supporting recall. Choice (D) refers to the way that performance is improved in memory, not to the procedure for eliciting dreams.

57. **(C)** In the context of this passage, "elicit" is closest in meaning to "cause." Choices (A), (B), and (D) are not accepted definitions of the word.

58. **(B)** ". . .the . . . capacity for storage in the brain is the result of an almost unlimited combination of interconnections . . . stimulated by patterns of activity." Choice (A) contradicts the fact that the physical basis for memory is not yet understood. Choice (C) contradicts the statement that storage in the brain is the result of an almost unlimited combination of interconnections. Choice (D) contradicts the fact that repeated references to the same information supports recall.

59. **(C)** Although Choices (A), (B), and (D) are definitions of the word "bonds," the meaning in the context of the sentence is "connections."

60. **(B)** Choice (A) is mentioned in lines 8–9. Choice (C) is mentioned in lines 9–10. Choice (D) is mentioned in lines 14–16. Choice (B) contradicts the fact that the memory trace is not subject to direct observation.

61. **(B)** The other choices are secondary ideas that are used to develop the main idea, "the Federal Reserve System." Choices (A), (C), and (D) are important to the discussion as they relate to the Federal Reserve System.

62. **(A)** In the context of this passage, "oversee" is closest in meaning to "supervise." Choices (B), (C), and (D) are not accepted definitions of the word.

63. **(D)** In the context of this passage, "con-firmed" could best be replaced by "approved." Choices (A), (B), and (C) are not accepted definitions of the word.

64. **(B)** "The System's primary function is to control monetary policy by influencing the cost and availability of money and credit through the purchase and sale of government securities." Choice (A) refers to the effect of regulation on the public, not to the System's responsibility. Choice (D) contradicts the statement that the Board of Governors is appointed by the President. Choice (C) is not mentioned and may not be concluded from information in the passage.

65. **(B)** Although Choices (A), (C), and (D) are definitions of the word "securities," the meaning in the context of the sentence is "bonds."

66. **(C)** "If the Federal Reserve provides too little money, interest rates tend to be high, borrowing is expensive, business activity slows down, unemployment goes up. . . ." Choice (A) contradicts the fact that interest rates are high and borrowing is expensive. Choice (B) contradicts the fact that unemployment goes up. Choice (D) contradicts the fact that business activity slows down.

67. **(B)** "If there is too much money, interest rates decline, and borrowing can lead to excess demand, pushing up prices and fueling inflation." Choice (A) contradicts the statement that during times of too little money, unemployment goes up. Choice (C) misinterprets the word *fuel* to mean *oil*. Choice (D) is not mentioned and may not be concluded from information in the passage.

68. **(C)** "In collaboration with the U.S. Department of the Treasury, the Fed puts new coins and paper currency into circulation by issuing them [coins and paper currency] to banks." Choices (A), (B), and (D) would change the meaning of the sentence.

69. **(D)** "It also supervises the activities of member banks abroad, and regulates certain aspects of international finance." Choices (A), (B), and (C) refer to other themes in the passage.

70. **(C)** Because the lecture is about the Federal Reserve System's effect on the economy, it must be concluded that an economics professor would probably give the lecture. The professors mentioned in Choices (A), (B), and (D) might lecture about related fields of study.

THE TEST
OF WRITTEN
ENGLISH (TWE)

Questions and Answers Concerning the Test of Written English (TWE)

The Test of Written English (TWE) is the essay component of the Test of English as a Foreign Language (TOEFL).

What Is the Purpose of the TWE?

The purpose of the TWE is to provide you with an opportunity to display the kind of writing that you will be required to do in college or university courses.

When Will the TWE Be Given?

The TWE will be given before the international TOEFL examination on five of the test dates every year. It will not be given before institutional TOEFL examinations, but many institutions will require their own writing sample.

How Do I Register for the TWE?

Register for the TOEFL on the dates specified as administrations that will include the TWE. You cannot register to take only the TWE. Both the TWE and the TOEFL must be taken on the same day.

How Much Does the Test Cost?

The TWE is free of charge for those who register to take the TOEFL on the specified administration dates.

How Many Questions Are There on the TWE?

There is only one question on each TWE. To maintain security, no topic will ever be used again, and different questions may be used on the same date for different test centers around the world.

What Types of Topics Are Used?

The TWE includes a number of academic writing tasks that are typical of those required in college and university courses. There are three types of topics commonly used on the TWE:
1. *Argument.* Argue both sides of an issue, and take a position.
2. *Persuasion.* Agree or disagree with a statement, and support your opinion.
3. *Extension.* Based on several examples that support an argument, choose another example and give reasons for the choice.

The topics are very general, and do not require any specialized knowledge of the subject in order to answer them.

How Long Is the Test?

After you have had a few minutes to read the directions, you will be given 30 minutes to plan, write, and revise your essay.

How Should I Begin?

You will find space on your test to make notes and organize your thoughts before you begin writing your final copy. You will not be graded on your organization. A perfect outline will not raise your score.

You should organize in any way that is helpful to you, either by making a list, an outline, notes, or a drawing. You may use English or your first language to organize your essay.

How Much Should I Write?

You should try to write between 200 and 300 words. An essay with three to five short paragraphs should be enough to demonstrate your writing ability. Remember, your essay will be scored on quality, not on quantity.

How Is the TWE Scored?

The test is scored on a scale of 1 to 6. A score between two points on the scale—5.5, 4.5, 3.5, 2.5, 1.5—can also be reported. The following guidelines are used by readers:

6 shows consistent proficiency
- Is well organized
- Addresses the topic
- Includes examples and details
- Has few errors in grammar and vocabulary

5 shows inconsistent proficiency
- Is well organized
- Addresses the topic
- Includes fewer examples and details
- Has more errors in grammar and vocabulary

4 shows minimal proficiency
- Is adequately organized
- Addresses most of the topic
- Includes some examples and details
- Has errors in grammar and vocabulary that occasionally confuse meaning

3 shows developing proficiency
- Is inadequately organized
- Addresses part of the topic
- Includes few examples and details
- Has many errors in grammar and vocabulary that confuse meaning

2 shows little proficiency
- Is disorganized
- Does not address the topic
- Does not include examples and details
- Has many errors in grammar and vocabulary that consistently confuse meaning

1 shows no proficiency
- Is disorganized
- Does not address the topic
- Does not include examples and details
- Has so many errors in grammar and vocabulary that meaning is not communicated

Will My Essay Be Scored For Neatness?

You will not receive a score for neatness; however, the readers must be able to understand what you have written in order to score your essay. Write legibly. Do not write in either very small or very large letters. Do not skip lines or leave large margins.

Who Will Score My Essay?

Your test will be scored by professional teachers of English as a Second Language, rhetoric and composition teachers at secondary schools, colleges, and universities in the United States and Canada. Each essay will be graded by two readers working independently. When the two scores differ by more than one point, a third teacher will read and score your essay. The third teacher is always the chief reader, and will make a final decision.

If you write an essay on a topic other than the one you have been assigned, your test will not be scored.

How Does My Score on the TWE Affect My Score on the Multiple-Choice TOEFL?

At this time, the results of the TWE will not affect the total TOEFL score. The results will appear separately on the score report. It will not be included in the computation of the total TOEFL score, and will not affect your score on the multiple-choice TOEFL.

Review of Written English

There are three steps that most good writers follow in organizing their writing. You should use these steps when you write a short composition like that on the TWE. First, tell your reader what you are going to write. Second, write it. Third, tell your reader what you wrote.

To look at these steps another way, your composition should have three parts:
1. A good beginning
2. Several good comments
3. A good ending

In this review of written English, we will discuss and give examples of the three parts of a short composition, using the types of topics that you will find on the TWE.

A Good Beginning

This is where you tell the reader what you are going to write. A good beginning has certain requirements.

A good beginning is short. Two or three sentences is enough to tell your reader how you plan to approach the topic.

A good beginning is direct. In the case of a chart or graph, state the relationship between the two charts or the parts of the chart in your first sentence. In the case of a comparison, state both sides of the argument in your first sentence. In a short composition, you don't have enough time for indirect approaches.

A good beginning is an outline. The second sentence usually outlines the organization. It gives the reader a general idea of your plan.

Good Comments

This is where you write.

Good comments include several points. A short composition may have between two and five points. Usually, the writer selects three. In the case of a chart or graph, the number may be determined by the number of variables on it. In the case of a comparison, three reasons is a standard argument.

Good comments are all related. All of the comments should relate to the general statement in the first sentence.

Good comments are logical. The points should be based on evidence. In the case of a chart or graph, the evidence should come from information on the chart or graph. In the case of a comparison, the evidence should come from sources that can be cited, such as a television program that you have seen, an article that you have read in a magazine, a book that you have read, or a lecture that you have heard.

Good comments are not judgments. Opinions should be identified by phrases such as, "in my view," "in my opinion," or "it seems to me that." Furthermore, opinions should be based on evidence. Opinions that are not based on evidence are judgments. Judgments usually use words like "good" or "bad," "right" or "wrong." Judgments are not good comments.

A Good Ending

This is where you tell the reader what you wrote.

A good ending is a summary. The last sentence is similar to the first sentence. In a short composition, a good ending does not add new information. It does not introduce a new idea.

A good ending is not an apology. A good ending does not apologize for not having said enough or for not having had enough time.

Example Test

The following example test would receive a score of 6 on the TWE. It is well organized, it addresses the topic, it includes examples and details, and it has some but not many errors in grammar and vocabulary.

Read and study this example test before you complete the eight model tests included here for practice.

Example Test

Some students in the United States work while they are earning their degrees in college; others receive support from their families. How should a student's education be supported? Argue both sides of the issue and defend your position.

Notes

friends praise initiative

(WORK) — future employers be impressed

student satisfaction

friends praise efforts for family

(FAMILY) — future employees not expect

every family member benefit society

Some students in the United States work while they are earning their degrees; others receive support from their families. Both approaches

Line have advantages and disadvantages. In this

(5) essay, I will name some of the advantages of each approach, and I will argue in favor family support.

In a society where independence and individual accomplishment are value, a

(10) student who earned his degree by working would be greatly admired. Friends would praise him for his initiative and perseverence. Future employers might be impressed by his work record. He might derive greater

(15) satisfaction from his personal investment in it.

On the other hand, in a society where cooperation and family dependence are value, a student who received support

(20) would be better understood. Friends would praise him for his efforts on behalf of his family. Future employers would not expect a work record from a student. He might feel greater

(25) responsibility toward others in his family because the accomplishment was shared.

(30)

(35)

Thus, not one but every family member would assured some opportunity or benefit.

For my part, I must argue in favor of family support. While I study at an American University, my older brother will send me money every month. When I finish my degree and find a good job, I will send my younger sister to a school or university. It may not be a better way, but it is the way that my society rewards.

Reader's Comments

This writing sample is well organized with a good topic sentence and good support statements. It addresses the question, and does not digress from the topic. There is a logical progression of ideas. Excellent language proficiency, as evidenced by a variety of grammatical structures and appropriate vocabulary. There are only a few grammatical errors that have been corrected below:

Line 7	in favor of
Line 9	are valued
Lines 18–19	are valued
Line 28	would be assured

SCORE: 6

Test of Written English (TWE) Model Tests

When you take a model examination, you should use one sheet of paper, both sides. Time each model test carefully. After you have read the topic, you should spend 30 minutes writing. For results that would be closest to the actual testing situation, it is recommended that an English teacher score your test, using the guidelines on pages 547–548 of this book.

Model Test 1

Many people enjoy participating in sports for recreation; others enjoy participating in the arts. Give the benefits of each, take a position, and defend it.

Notes

Model Test 2

Read and think about the following statement:
    Pets should be treated like family members.
Do you agree or disagree with the statement? Give reasons to support your opinion.

Notes

Model Test 3

Many people have learned a foreign language in their own country; others have learned a foreign language in the country in which it is spoken. Give the advantages of each and support your viewpoint.

Notes

Model Test 4

In your opinion, what is the best way to choose a marriage partner? Use specific reasons and examples why you think this approach is best.

Notes

Model Test 5

Some people believe that it is very important to make large amounts of money, while others are satisfied to earn a comfortable living. Analyze each viewpoint and take a stand.

Notes

Model Test 6

Advances in transportation and communication like the airplane and the telephone have changed the way that nations interact with each other in a global society. Choose another technological innovation that you think is important. Give specific reasons for your choice.

Notes

Model Test 7

Leaders like John F. Kennedy and Martin Luther King have made important contributions to humanity. Name another world leader you think is important. Give specific reasons for your choice.

Notes

Model Test 8

Read and think about the following statement: The college years are the best time in a person's life. Do you agree or disagree with the statement? Give reasons to support your opinion.

Notes

APPENDIX

TRANSCRIPT FOR THE LISTENING COMPREHENSION SECTIONS OF TOEFL MODEL TESTS 1 – 8

The following is the transcript for the Listening Comprehension sections for each of the eight model TOEFL tests included in this book. Note that the Listening Comprehension sections always appear as Section 1 of the examinations. Each Listening Comprehension section on each examination has three parts and each of these parts has separate instructions.

When you take the model tests in this book as a preliminary step in your preparation for the actual examination, you should use the audiocassettes. These include Listening Comprehension sections for all eight tests.

If you have someone read the TOEFL transcript to you, be sure that he or she understands the timing sequences. The reader should work with a stop watch or with a regular watch with a second hand in order to keep careful track of the timed pauses between questions. The total amount of time for each section is noted both on the transcript and on the model tests. In addition, the time for the pauses between questions is also given on the transcript. Be sure that the reader speaks clearly and at a moderately paced rate. For results that would be closest to the actual testing situation, it is recommended that three persons be asked to read, since some of the Listening Comprehension sections utilize dialogues.

Model Test 1
Short Form

Section 1:
Listening Comprehension

50 QUESTIONS 40 MINUTES

In this section of the test, you will have an opportunity to demonstrate your ability to understand conversations and talks in English. There are three parts to this section, with special directions for each part. Answer all the questions on the basis of what is stated or implied by the speakers in this test. When you take the actual TOEFL test, you will not be allowed to take notes or write in your test book. Try to work on this Model Test in the same way.

Part A

Directions: In Part A, you will hear short conversations between two people. After each conversation, you will hear a question about the conversation. The conversations and questions will not be repeated. After you hear a question, read the four possible answers in your book and choose the best answer. Then, on your answer sheet, find the number of the question and fill in the space that corresponds to the letter of the answer you have chosen.

1. Woman: I need some aspirin, please, and I'd also like to get this prescription filled.
    Man: Fine. Here's your aspirin. I can have the prescription for you in about ten minutes.
    Narrator: What will the man probably do?

(Note: There should be a 12-second pause after each test question in this section.)

2. Woman: If I were you I'd take the bus to work. Driving in that rush-hour traffic is terrible.
    Man: But by the time the bus gets to my stop, there aren't any seats left.
    Narrator: What does the man mean?

3. Man: If I nominate you for president, will you accept the nomination?
    Woman: I really don't have time.
    Narrator: What does the woman mean?

4. Woman: I'd like to take Dr. Sullivan's section of Physics 100, but my advisor is teaching it too, and I don't want her to be offended.
   Man: Who cares?
   Narrator: What does the man mean?

5. Man: Where are you living now? I went to see you at your old apartment on University Avenue and it was empty.
   Woman: I'm living in the city. It's closer to work.
   Narrator: What does the woman imply about her old apartment?

6. Man: Let's go to the dance at the Student Center on Friday.
   Woman: Sounds great, but I'm going to a lecture. Thanks for asking me though.
   Narrator: What does the woman imply?

7. Man: That's a nice bike. Is it new?
   Woman: No. I got it almost five years ago, but it's still in good shape.
   Narrator: What does the woman mean?

8. Man: How much did your books cost? Two hundred dollars?
   Woman: I wish!
   Narrator: What does the woman mean?

9. Man: Would you rather eat at home or go out tonight?
   Woman: I'd rather go out, but I don't mind fixing supper at home if you'd rather not go.
   Narrator: What does the woman want to do?

10. Man: Good afternoon. This is Dick Williams at World Travel Agency. Is Mr. Baker there?
    Woman: He's out to lunch. I'll be glad to take a message.
    Narrator: What does the woman say about Mr. Baker?

11. Woman: I'd appreciate your professional opinion. Do you think that I should sue the company?
    Man: Not really. I think that we can settle this out of court.
    Narrator: What will the woman probably do?

12. Woman: Would you like some hot coffee or tea?
    Man: I do like them both, but I'd rather have something cold.
    Narrator: What does the man want to drink?

13. Woman: How can I get to the shopping center from here?
    Man: You can take a bus or a taxi, but it isn't too far to walk.
    Narrator: What does the man suggest the woman do?

14. Man: Have you found a class yet?
    Woman: I'm just checking the schedule now.
    Narrator: What can be inferred about the man?

15. Woman: Do you mind if I turn on the radio for awhile?
    Man: No, I don't mind.
    Narrator: What does the man mean?

16. Man: I'm worried about Anna. She's really been depressed lately. All she does is stay in
                her room all day.
    Woman: That sounds serious. She'd better see someone at the Counseling Center.
    Narrator: What does the woman suggest Anna do?

17. Man: What's this? Another letter from the phone company?
    Woman: Oh no. I wonder what we have to do to get that bill corrected?
    Narrator: What are the speakers talking about?

18. Woman: If you have a few minutes, I'd like to talk with you about my project.
    Man: Please go on.
    Narrator: What does the man mean?

19. Woman: Excuse me. I was in line here first.
    Man: Oh, I'm sorry. I didn't realize that you were waiting.
    Narrator: What will the man probably do?

20. Man: The neighbors are going to have another party.
    Woman: Not again!
    Narrator: What does the woman imply?

21. Man: Dr. Franklin said I couldn't have an extension.
    Woman: That's too bad. I really thought he would give you one.
    Narrator: What does the woman mean?

22. Man: I can't get my computer printer to work.
    Woman: Is it plugged in?
    Narrator: What does the woman imply?

23. Man: We missed you at the reception on Saturday.
    Woman: Yes. I just didn't feel up to it after such a long trip.
    Narrator: What does the woman mean?

24. Man: We really should have left already.
    Woman: Maybe we ought to call and let them know.
    Narrator: What problem do the man and woman have?

25. Man: Have you moved out of your apartment yet?
    Woman: No. I'm paid up until the 15th.
    Narrator: What is the woman probably going to do?

26. Woman: Mary Anne took the math placement test.
    Man: So, she *finally* did it!
    Narrator: What had the man assumed about Mary Anne?

27. Woman: I got my car at Discount Automotive.
    Man: Good for you. They have some really good deals.
    Narrator: What does the man mean?

28. Woman: Gary said he would be here for my birthday.
    Man: But he has to be in Miami that day, doesn't he?
    Narrator: What does the man imply about Gary?

29. Woman: Where have you been? I haven't seen you in class all week.
    Man: I caught cold, so I stayed in.
    Narrator: What does the man mean?

30. Man: Let's go get a pizza.
    Woman: I'm swamped. Maybe another time.
    Narrator: What does the woman mean?

Part B

Directions: In this part of the test, you will hear longer conversations. After each conversation, you will hear several questions. The conversations and questions will not be repeated.

After you hear a question, read the four possible answers in your book and choose the best answer. Then, on your answer sheet, find the number of the question and fill in the space that corresponds to the letter of the answer you have chosen.

Remember, you are **not** allowed to take notes or write on your test pages.

<u>Questions 31–34.</u> Listen to a conversation between two college students.

    Man: Would you like a cup of coffee?
    Woman: Yes. That would be good.
    Man: Cream and sugar?
    Woman: Please.
    Man: Oh, no.
    Woman: What's the matter?
    Man: This machine is out of order.
    Woman: Did you lose your money?
    Man: I sure did.
    Woman: You ought to complain. These machines are always out of order.
    Man: Well, I still want a cup of coffee, don't you?
    Woman: Let's go to the restaurant at the Student Center.
    Man: I don't know. The last time I was there it was so crowded that I had to wait in line for almost an hour.
    Woman: Really? Let's go somewhere else then. I can't be too long because I have a test at three o'clock.
    Man: Okay. Let's go to the library. There's another vending machine downstairs by the telephone.

    Narrator: 31. What prompted the conversation?

(Note: There should be a 12-second pause after each test question in this section.)

          32. What do the speakers mainly discuss?

          33. Why didn't the couple go to the restaurant at the Student Center?

          34. Why did they decide to go to the library?

Questions 35–38. Listen to a conversation with a professor.

Man:	Professor Day, may I see you for a minute?
Woman:	Sure. Come on in, Mike. What's the matter?
Man:	I've got a problem.
Woman:	Okay.
Man:	I need your technical writing class. And, I knew I had to have it so I went early to registration, but by the time I got to the front of the line, it was closed. See, my advisor signed my course request and everything. I was just too far back in the line.
Woman:	That's a big class already, Mike. If it's closed, that means I have fifty students in it.
Man:	I'm not surprised. It's supposed to be a really good class.
Woman:	Can't you take it next year? We offer it every fall.
Man:	Well, that's the problem. I'm supposed to be graduating this spring. But, of course, I can't graduate without your class.
Woman:	I see. In that case, I'll sign an override for you. It looks like there will be fifty-one. Take this form back to the registration area and they'll get you in.
Man:	Thanks, Professor Day. I really appreciate this!
Narrator:	35. What is Mike's problem?
	36. What does Mike want Professor Day to do?
	37. What does Mike say about graduation?
	38. What does Professor Day decide to do?

Part C

Directions: In this part of the test, you will hear several short talks. After each talk, you will hear some questions. The talks and questions will not be repeated.

After you hear a question, read the four possible answers in your book and choose the best answer. Then, on your answer sheet, find the number of the question and fill in the space that corresponds to the letter of the answer you have chosen.

Questions 39–42. Listen to a talk by a business instructor.

Today's lecture is about the effects of background music on employee performance and retail sales. As you know, every day millions of people in offices and factories around the world do their work to the accompaniment of background music, more commonly known as MUZAK. But did you know that MUZAK is more than a pleasant addition to the environment? Studies show that this seemingly innocent background music can be engineered to control behavior. In fact, MUZAK can improve employee performance by reducing stress, boredom, and fatigue. In one survey, overall productivity increased by thirty percent, although five to ten percent is the average.

The key to MUZAK's success is something called stimulus progression, which means quite simply that the background music starts with a slow, soft song that is low in stimulus value and builds up gradually to an upbeat song that is high in stimulus value. The fastest, loudest sounds are programmed for about ten-thirty in the morning, and two-thirty in the afternoon when people are generally starting to tire.

Besides employee performance, MUZAK can increase sales. In supermarkets, slow music can influence shoppers to walk slower and buy more. In restaurants, fast music can cause customers to eat quickly so that the same number of tables may be used to serve more people during peak times such as the lunch hour.

Narrator: 39. What is MUZAK?

(Note: There should be a 12-second pause after each test question in this section.)

40. What is the average increase in productivity when MUZAK is introduced?

41. What is stimulus progression?

42. How does MUZAK influence sales in supermarkets?

Questions 43–46. Listen to a public service announcement.

Community College understands that everyone who wants to attend college will not be able to come to campus. So, as part of the Distance Learning Program, Community College offers a series of video telecourses to meet the needs of students who prefer to complete coursework in their homes, at their convenience.

These telecourses are regular college credit classes taught on video cassette tapes by a Community College professor. To use the materials for the course, you will need your own VHS type VCR player. Some telecourses will also be broadcast on KCC7-TV's "Sun-Up Semester." This program airs from six o'clock in the morning to seven-thirty, Monday through Friday, and a complete listing of courses is printed in your regular television guide.

To register for a telecourse, phone the Community College Distance Learning Program at 782-6394. The course syllabus, books, and videotapes will be available at the Community College bookstore. During the first week of classes, your instructor will contact you to discuss the course and answer any questions you might have about the course requirements. Then, throughout the rest of the semester, you can use either an 800 telephone number or an e-mail address to contact your instructor.

Narrator: 43. What is this announcement mainly about?

44. Why does the speaker mention the "Sun-Up Semester"?

45. How can students register for a course?

46. How can students contact the instructor?

Questions 47–50. Listen to a talk by a college professor.

When Edward Sapir was teaching at Yale, Benjamin Lee Whorf enrolled in his class. Whorf was recognized for his investigations of the Hopi language, including his authorship of a grammar and a dictionary. Even in his early publications, it is clear that he was developing the theory that the very different grammar of Hopi might indicate a different manner of conceiving and perceiving the world on the part of the native speaker of Hopi.

In 1936, he wrote "An American Indian Model of the Universe," which explored the implications of the Hopi verb system with regard to the Hopi conception of space and time.

Whorf is probably best known for his article, "The Relation of Habitual Thought and Behavior to Language," and for the three articles that appeared in 1941 in the *Technology Review*.

In these articles, he proposed what he called the principle of "linguistic relativity," which states, at least as a hypothesis, that the grammar of a language influences the manner in which the speaker understands reality and behaves with respect to it.

Since the theory did not emerge until after Whorf had begun to study with Sapir, and since Sapir had most certainly shared in the development of the idea, it came to be called the Sapir-Whorf Hypothesis.

Narrator: 47. What central theme does the lecture examine?

48. Which languages did Whorf use in his research?

49. According to the lecturer, what is linguistic relativity?

50. What is another name for linguistic relativity?

Model Test 2
Short Form

Section 1:
Listening Comprehension

50 Questions 40 Minutes

In this section of the test, you will have an opportunity to demonstrate your ability to understand conversations and talks in English. There are three parts to this section with special directions for each part. Answer all the questions on the basis of what is stated or implied by the speakers in this test. When you take the actual TOEFL test, you will not be allowed to take notes or write in your test book. Try to work on this Model Test in the same way.

Part A

Directions: In Part A, you will hear short conversations between two people. After each conversation, you will hear a question about the conversation. The conversations and questions will not be repeated. After you hear a question, read the four possible answers in your book and choose the best answer. Then, on your answer sheet, find the number of the question and fill in the space that corresponds to the letter of the answer you have chosen.

1. Woman: That picture certainly flatters Susan. Don't you think so?
   Man: As a matter of fact, I think it makes her look older than she really is.
   Narrator: What does the woman say about the picture?

(Note: There should be a 12-second pause after each test question in this section.)

2. Woman: Well, let me see. Fifty had registered, but everyone didn't show up. I believe that we had twenty-five from the Middle East and at least fifteen from Latin America.
   Man: You don't mean it!
   Narrator: What had the man assumed?

3. Man: Excuse me. Could you tell me when Dr. Smith has office hours?
   Woman: Not really, but there's a sign on the door I think.
   Narrator: What does the woman imply that the man should do?

4. Man: Could you please tell me if the Miami flight will be arriving on time?
   Woman: Yes, sir. It should be arriving in about ten minutes at Concourse C.
   Narrator: What are the speakers discussing?

5. Man: I heard that Professor Wilson will let you do a project for extra credit.
   Woman: That's great! I could use some.
   Narrator: What is the woman probably going to do?

6. Man: Is Paul angry?
   Woman: If he were, he'd tell us.
   Narrator: What does the woman say about Paul?

7. Man: Miss Brown bought some paper, paints, and brushes.
   Woman: I'll bet she'll use them at the high school.
   Narrator: What will Miss Brown probably do at the high school?

8. Man: I'd like to cash a check, please. I have an account here.
   Woman: Fine. Just make it out to "cash."
   Narrator: Where did this conversation most probably take place?

9. Man: Now, what seems to be the trouble, Mrs. Stephens?
   Woman: I've been very dizzy lately, and last night I had some chest pain.
   Narrator: What is the woman's problem?

10. Man: My briefcase is just like yours, isn't it?
    Woman: Almost. Mine is smaller, but it doesn't have a lock. I think I'd rather have had one
               like yours.
    Narrator: What can be inferred about the man's briefcase.

11. Woman: Hello, Mr. Jacobs. This is Tim Smith's secretary. I'm calling to confirm his appoint-
               ment with you today at two o'clock.
    Man: Thank you for calling. I'll expect Mr. Smith to drop by this afternoon.
    Narrator: What does the man mean?

12. Man: Could you tell me the best way to get to Grove City? I'm not from around here.
    Woman: That's easy. Just take Route Eighteen West all the way there.
    Narrator: What will the man probably do?

13. Man: I heard you got an A on the final exam. I think you're the only one who did!
    Woman: Not really. There were a couple of other As.
    Narrator: What does the woman mean?

14. Woman: Oh, no. It's five o'clock already and I haven't finished typing these letters.
    Man: Don't worry. That clock is half an hour fast.
    Narrator: What does the man mean?

15. Man: It's much better to wait until tomorrow to go. Don't you agree?
    Woman: Yes. I couldn't agree more.
    Narrator: What does the woman mean?

16. Man: I have to go to class because I have a test, but if I could, I'd go with you to the movie.
    Woman: That's too bad. I wish that you could come along.
    Narrator: What is the man going to do?

17. Woman: I left a message on your answering machine a couple of days ago.
    Man: Yes. I've been meaning to get back with you.
    Narrator: What does the man mean?

18. Man: I think it's my turn.
    Woman: Sorry you had to wait so long. One of my cashiers is out today.
    Narrator: What does the woman mean?

19. Woman: How did your interview go?
    Man: I couldn't feel better about it! The questions were very fair, and I seemed to find an answer for all of them.
    Narrator: What does the man say about the interview?

20. Man: Could you please tell me what room Dr. Robert Davis is in?
    Woman: Yes, he's in the Math Department on the fourth floor. Check with the secretary before going in, though.
    Narrator: What does the woman suggest that the man do?

21. Man: I have to take a dish to a potluck, but I'm a terrible cook. Maybe I'll just stay home.
    Woman: Why don't you just get a cake at the bakery?
    Narrator: What does the woman suggest the man do?

22. Man: Tom wasn't in class again today!
    Woman: I know. I wonder whether he'll show up for the final exam.
    Narrator: What can be inferred about Tom?

23. Man: Are we still on for tonight?
    Woman: I'm looking forward to it.
    Narrator: What does the man mean?

24. Man: What do you think of this apartment?
    Woman: It's beautiful, but it's kind of expensive, isn't it?
    Narrator: What does the woman mean?

25. Woman: So the course *is* closed. This is terrible! I have to have it to graduate.
    Man: You're okay. Just Dr. Collin's section is closed. There is another section that's still open, but nobody knows who's teaching it. It's marked "staff."
    Narrator: What will the woman probably do?

26. Woman: Was that the final boarding call for the San Antonio flight?
    Man: No. This is just preboarding for children and people who need assistance.
    Narrator: What does the man say about the boarding call?

27. Man: I still haven't received my score on the GMAT test. Maybe I should call to check on it.
     Woman: Don't worry so much. It takes at least six weeks to receive your score.
     Narrator: What does the woman think that the man should do?

28. Woman: Sorry, sir. The coupon is only valid when you buy the forty-four-ounce size.
     Man: Oops. You're right. Hold on a minute while I get the other size.
     Narrator: What does the man mean?

29. Man: I'm ready to go. Are you supposed to tip the guys at the car wash?
     Woman: Only if they finish your car by hand. Not if it goes through the machine like yours did.
     Narrator: What will the man probably do?

30. Man: You've been doing a lot of traveling, haven't you?
     Woman: Yes. We want to make the most of our time here.
     Narrator: What does the woman mean?

Part B

Directions: In this part of the test, you will hear longer conversations. After each conversation, you will hear several questions. The conversations and questions will not be repeated.

After you hear a question, read the four possible answers in your book and choose the best answer. Then, on your answer sheet, find the number of the question and fill in the space that corresponds to the letter of the answer you have chosen.

Remember, you are **not** allowed to take notes or write on your test pages.

Questions 31–34. Listen to a telephone conversation between friends.

Man: Hi, Melissa. This is Brian.
Woman: Oh, hi, Brian. What's happening?
Man: Actually, I'm calling you for a favor.
Woman: Oh?
Man: Yes. My friends and I are going to go to Florida for spring break, and I was wondering whether you could keep an eye on the house? I thought that since you are just down the street. . .
Woman: When will you be gone?
Man: We're leaving day after tomorrow and we'll be back next Sunday, so that would be about five days.
Woman: Unhuh. That's okay then. I'll be here. What do you want me to do?
Man: Just come over every day and give the cats some food and fresh water. I'll leave the cans of cat food out on the kitchen counter.
Woman: Sure. I can do that. How about all those house plants you've got? Do you want me to water them, too?
Man: That would be great! I'll bring the keys over tonight if that's okay.
Woman: Sure. I get home from work about six, and I'll be here all evening.
Man: Oh, I almost forgot. Would you please get the mail out of the box and put it on the table in the kitchen?
Woman: Sure.
Man: Thanks, Melissa.
Woman: No problem.

Narrator: 31. Why did Brian call Melissa?

(Note: There should be a 12-second pause after each test question in this section.)

        32. What do we learn about Melissa from this conversation?

        33. What does Melissa offer to do?

        34. What will Brian probably do tonight?

Questions 35–38. Listen to a conversation between two college students.

Man:	What did you think about the video we were supposed to watch for Professor Stephen's class?
Woman:	I didn't see it. Was it good?
Man:	Really it was. It was about stress.
Woman:	How to relieve stress?
Man:	Not really. More the effects of stress on the national health.
Woman:	Oh.
Man:	But it was interesting, though.
Woman:	Really?
Man:	Yes. I think they said that one out of nine women age forty-five through sixty-five will have a heart attack.
Woman:	I'm surprised at that.
Man:	I was, too. Oh, another thing. They said that women usually don't get the same level of care that men do, so the heart attack is likely to be more serious.
Woman:	Why is that?
Man:	Because many members of the medical profession still think of a heart attack as a male problem, so they don't recognize the symptoms in their women patients.
Woman:	Well, it does sound like an interesting video. I'm going to try to see it before class next time so I'll be ready for the discussion.
Man:	It's on reserve in the library, so you can't check it out, but you can use one of the viewing rooms. It's only an hour long.

Narrator: 35. What was the video about?

        36. What did the students learn about women?

        37. How did the man feel about the video?

        38. What will the woman probably do?

Part C

Directions: In this part of the test, you will hear several short talks. After each talk, you will hear some questions. The talks and questions will not be repeated.

After you hear a question, read the four possible answers in your book and choose the best answer. Then, on your answer sheet, find the number of the question and fill in the space that corresponds to the letter of the answer you have chosen.

Questions 39–42. Listen to a lecture by an English intructor.

The romance and marriage of Elizabeth Barrett to Robert Browning inspired some of the greatest love poems written in the English language. Elizabeth, without a doubt the greatest woman poet of the Victorian period, was born in Durham County, England, in 1806. Her first important publication was *The Seraphim and Other Poems* which appeared in 1838.

By 1843, she was so widely recognized that her name was suggested to replace the late Poet Laureate as the official national poet of England. In part because the sovereign was a woman, there was great support for a movement to break with the tradition of a male Poet Laureate. Nevertheless, she lost the competition to William Wordsworth.

A short time later, she married Robert Browning, himself a gifted poet, and they fled to Florence, Italy. A play, *The Barretts of Wimpole Street*, recounts their confrontation with Elizabeth's father and their eventual elopement against his wishes.

While living in Florence, their only son was born. A year later, in 1850, Elizabeth published her collected works, along with a volume of new poems entitled *Sonnets from the Portuguese*, so named because her husband often called her his "Portuguese." *Aurora Leigh*, her longest work, appeared in 1856, only five years before her death in Italy in 1861.

Narrator: 39. What is the main topic of this lecture?

(Note: There should be a 12-second pause after each test question in this section.)

40. According to the lecturer, what was one reason that Elizabeth Barrett was considered for the title of Poet Laureate?

41. Where did Elizabeth and Robert Browning live after their elopement?

42. When did Elizabeth Barrett Browning die?

Questions 43–46. Listen to a talk by a tour bus driver.

Good afternoon ladies and gentlemen, and welcome aboard your Scenic Cruiser Bus to Saint Louis, Memphis, and New Orleans with changes in Saint Louis for Kansas City and points west.

This coach is scheduled to arrive in Saint Louis at eight o'clock. You will have a fifteen-minute rest stop at Bloomington at three o'clock and a half-hour dinner stop at Springfield at five-thirty.

Through passengers on this coach are scheduled to arrive in Memphis at seven o'clock tomorrow morning and in New Orleans at five o'clock tomorrow afternoon. Please don't forget the number of your coach when reboarding. That number is four-one-one-eight. Again, that number is four-one-one eight.

Let me remind you that federal regulations prohibit smoking cigarettes, pipes, or cigars inside the coach. If you wish to smoke, kindly wait for a rest stop.

This coach is restroom-equipped for your comfort and convenience. Please watch your step when moving about in the coach. Relax and enjoy your trip, and thank you for traveling Scenic Cruiser Bus Lines.

Narrator: 43. What is the main purpose of the talk?

44. Where will the passengers change buses to go to Kansas City?

45. What is the number of the coach?

46. What will the driver probably do next?

Questions 47–50. Listen to a lecture by a biology instructor.

Today's lecture will include the most outstanding achievements in biology as it relates to the medical sciences.

Early in Greek history, Hippocrates began to study the human body and to apply scientific method to the problems of diagnosis and the treatment of diseases. Unlike other physicians of his time, he discarded the theory that disease was caused by the gods. Instead, he kept careful records of symptoms and treatments, indicating the success or failure of the patient's cure. He has been recognized as the father of modern medicine.

About a century later, Aristotle began a scientific study of plants and animals, classifying more than five hundred types on the basis of body structure. Because of his great contribution to the field, Aristotle has been called the father of biology.

By the first century A.D., Dioscorides had collected a vast amount of information on plants, which he recorded in the now famous *Materia Medica,* a book that remained an authoritative reference among physicians for fifteen hundred years.

During the Middle Ages, scientific method was scorned in favor of alchemy. Thus, medicine and biology had advanced very little from the time of the ancients until the seventeenth century when the English physician and anatomist William Harvey discovered a mechanism for the circulation of the blood in the body.

Narrator: 47. What is the main topic of this lecture?

48. What was Hippocrates' greatest contribution to medicine?

49. Who is known as the father of biology?

50. What was the contribution made to medicine by William Harvey?

Model Test 3
Short Form

Section 1:
Listening Comprehension

50 QUESTIONS 40 MINUTES

In this section of the test, you will have an opportunity to demonstrate your ability to understand conversations and talks in English. There are three parts to this section with special directions for each part. Answer all the questions on the basis of what is stated or implied by the speakers in this test. When you take the actual TOEFL test, you will not be allowed to take notes or write in your test book. Try to work on this Model Test in the same way.

Part A

Directions: In Part A, you will hear short conversations between two people. After each conversation, you will hear a question about the conversation. The conversations and questions will not be repeated. After you hear a question, read the four possible answers in your book and choose the best answer. Then, on your answer sheet, find the number of the question and fill in the space that corresponds to the letter of the answer you have chosen.

1. Man: It doesn't make any sense for us to go home for spring vacation now.
   Woman: Especially since we'll be graduating in May.
   Narrator: What does the woman mean?

(Note: There should be a 12-second pause after each test question in this section.)

2. Woman: Shall I bring you your coffee now or would you rather have it with your lunch?
   Man: I'd like it now, please.
   Narrator: Where did this conversation most probably take place?

3. Man: Could you please explain the assignment for Monday, Miss Smith?
   Woman: Certainly. Read the next chapter in your textbook and come to class prepared to discuss what you've read.
   Narrator: What are the speakers talking about?

4. Woman: If I were you, I'd be more careful about locking the back door at night.
   Man: Don't worry. No one will break in.
   Narrator: What did the woman imply?

5. Man: Did you buy a birthday present for your brother?
   Woman: I've been thinking about getting him a CD. He likes classical music.
   Narrator: What is the woman's problem?

6. Woman: Are you ready for this?
   Man: I should be. I've been cramming for the past three days.
   Narrator: What does the man mean?

7. Man: Good morning. I'd like to speak to Mr. Adams, please. This is Edward Miller at the Sun Valley Health Center.
   Woman: Mr. Miller, my husband isn't at home. I can give you his business phone if you'd like to call him at work, though.
   Narrator: What can be inferred about the woman?

8. Woman: Jack must have been joking when he said that he was going to quit his job.
   Man: Don't be too sure. He told me that he was trying to sell his house.
   Narrator: What does the man mean?

9. Man: I need a book for English two-twenty-one.
   Woman: All of the textbooks are on the shelves in the back of the store.
   Narrator: What will the man probably do?

10. Man: I was hoping that you'd wear your new dress. It's much prettier.
    Woman: But this one is more comfortable for hot weather.
    Narrator: What can be inferred about the woman?

11. Man: What do you think of Professor Collins?
    Woman: I think he's a great person, but the class just turns me off.
    Narrator: What does the woman mean?

12. Man: I thought that you were going to the convention in Atlanta last Saturday.
    Woman: I was planning to, but I haven't been feeling well.
    Narrator: What can be inferred about the woman?

13. Man: Have you made an appointment with the dentist yet?
    Woman: No. And I really can't put it off anymore.
    Narrator: What will the woman probably do?

14. Woman: How do you like American food?
    Man: I'm used to it now.
    Narrator: What does the man mean?

15. Woman: Are you still studying? It's two o'clock in the morning.
    Man: I know. I just can't seem to get caught up.
    Narrator: What does the man mean?

16. Woman: Let's get together sometime soon.
    Man: Yes. Connie and I have been meaning to have you over.
    Narrator: What does the man mean?

17. Man: It's your turn to call the names on the list if you want to.
    Woman: I think I'll pass this time.
    Narrator: What is the woman going to do?

18. Woman: I'm pretty sure that the deadline for applications has passed.
    Man: Why don't you let me look into it for you?
    Narrator: What does the man mean?

19. Woman: Did you get your tickets?
    Man: I talked to Judy about it, and she took care of it for me.
    Narrator: What does the man mean?

20. Woman: Maybe we should take Front Street this morning. The radio announcer said that traffic was very heavy on the freeway.
    Man: Well, if he says to take Front Street, we should go the other way.
    Narrator: What does the man imply about the radio announcer?

21. Woman: What seems to be the problem?
    Man: Well I understand the lectures but I get mixed up when I try to read the book.
    Narrator: What does the man mean?

22. Man: Do you know Randy Johnson?
    Woman: Yes. He sure has it made, doesn't he?
    Narrator: What does the woman mean?

23. Man: This paper isn't due until next week.
    Woman: Yes, I know. But I wanted to turn it in ahead of time if that's all right.
    Narrator: What does the woman mean?

24. Man: Why don't you do the solo?
    Woman: You've never heard me sing, have you?
    Narrator: What does the woman imply?

25. Man: I can't stand this class!
    Woman: Well, you might as well get used to it. You have to take it in order to graduate.
    Narrator: What does the woman say about the class?

26. Man: That was Dale on the phone. His car broke down on the way here, so he won't be able to make it.
    Woman: He'd better trade that car in.
    Narrator: What does the woman suggest that Dale do?

27. Woman: How are you going to get ready for an oral final?
    Man: The professor said we should study alone, but the T.A. said to get into a study group and quiz each other.
    Narrator: What did the T.A. suggest the students do?

28. Man: I need an advisor's signature on my course request form. Could I make an appointment, please?
    Woman: Oh, well, you don't need to make an appointment. Just wait here. I'll get a pen.
    Narrator: What is the woman going to do?

29. Man: This copy looks good. Why don't you just hand it in?
    Woman: I'd better make one more draft.
    Narrator: What is the woman going to do?

30. Woman: Your loan payment is due on the first. Oh, sorry, the computer has you scheduled for the fifth.
    Man: That's good. That's what I thought.
    Narrator: What had the man assumed about the loan payment?

Part B

Directions: In this part of the test, you will hear longer conversations. After each conversation, you will hear several questions. The conversations and questions will not be repeated.

After you hear a question, read the four possible answers in your book and choose the best answer. Then, on your answer sheet, find the number of the question and fill in the space that corresponds to the letter of the answer you have chosen.

Remember, you are **not** allowed to take notes or write on your test pages.

Questions 31–34. Listen to a conversation between two strangers.

    Man: Excuse me. Have you been waiting long?
    Woman: About ten minutes.
    Man: Did you notice whether the number seven bus has gone by?
    Woman: Not while I've been standing here. I'm waiting for the number seven myself.
    Man: Good. Hot today, isn't it?
    Woman: Yes, it is. I wish that it would rain and cool off.
    Man: Me too. This is unusual for March. I don't remember it ever being so hot and dry in March before.

Woman:	You're from Florida then.
Man:	Not really. I was born in New York, but I've lived here for ten years now.
Woman:	My mother and I have just moved here from Indiana.
Man:	Pretty cold in Indiana, isn't it?
Woman:	Yes. That's why we moved. But we didn't know that it would be so hot here. We should have gone to California. Do you think that we've missed the bus?
Man:	No. It's always a little late.
Woman:	I have twenty to one, but my watch is a little fast.
Man:	Don't worry. It never comes exactly on the half-hour like it should.

Narrator:	31. Why is the woman waiting?

(Note: There should be a 12-second pause after each test question in this section.)

32. According to the conversation, what kind of weather is usual for March?

33. Where does this conversation take place?

34. How often is the bus scheduled to pass their stop?

Questions 35–38. Listen to a telephone call to a professor.

Woman:	Hello, Professor Hayes. This is Betty Peterson. I'm in your senior seminar this semester.
Man:	Oh, yes, Betty. How are you?
Woman:	Just fine, thanks. I'm calling because I'm applying for graduate school, and I need three letters of recommendation. Would you be willing to write me one?
Man:	Why yes, Betty. I'd be happy to. I think you are an excellent candidate for graduate school. Are you applying here or to another university?
Woman:	Here. That's why I think your letter is so important. Everyone on the selection committee knows and respects you.
Man:	Let's see, Dr. Warren is the chair of that committee, isn't she?
Woman:	Yes. So, if you would just write the letter to her, that would be great.
Man:	Okay. And when do you need this? I don't recall the deadline for applications.
Woman:	The committee meets on April 30, so all the materials must be submitted before then.
Man:	All right. I'll send it directly to her office.
Woman:	Thank you. I really appreciate it.
Man:	You're welcome. Glad to do it.

Narrator:	35. Why did Betty call Professor Hayes?

36. What does Professor Hayes think about Betty?

37. Who will decide whether Betty is accepted to the program?

38. When does Betty need to submit all her materials?

Part C

Directions: In this part of the test, you will hear several short talks. After each talk, you will hear some questions. The talks and questions will not be repeated.

After you hear a question, read the four possible answers in your book and choose the best answer. Then, on your answer sheet, find the number of the question and fill in the space that corresponds to the letter of the answer you have chosen.

Questions 39–42. Listen to a lecture by a history professor.

I know that this is probably a digression from the topic of today's lecture, but it is worth noting that although England no longer ruled her former colonies after the eighteenth century, she controlled trade with them by selling products so cheaply that it was not possible for the new countries to manufacture and compete with English prices. To maintain this favorable balance of trade, England went to fantastic lengths to keep secret the advanced manufacturing processes upon which such a monopoly depended.

Enterprising Americans made all kinds of ingenious attempts to smuggle drawings for the most modern machines out of England, but it was an Englishman, Samuel Slater, who finally succeeded.

Although textile workers were forbidden to emigrate, Slater traveled to the United States in secret. Determined to take nothing in writing, he memorized the intricate designs for all the machines in an English textile mill, and in partnership with Moses Brown, a Quaker merchant, recreated the mill in Rhode Island.

Forty-five years later, in part as a result of the initial model by Slater and Brown, America had changed from a country of small farmers and craftsmen to an industrial nation in competition with England.

Narrator: 39. Who is the speaker?

(Note: There should be a 12-second pause after each test question in this section.)

40. According to the speaker, how did England control trade in the eighteenth century?

41. What did Samuel Slater do?

42. What happened as a result of the Slater-Brown partnership?

Questions 43–46. Listen to a talk by a college instructor in an English class.

So many different kinds of writing have been called essays, it is difficult to define exactly what an essay is. Perhaps the best way is to point out four characteristics that are true of most essays. First, an essay is about one topic. It does not start with one subject and digress to another and another. Second, although a few essays are long enough to be considered a small book, most essays are short. Five hundred words is the most common length for an essay. Third, an essay is written in prose, not poetry. True, Alexander Pope did call two of his poems essays, but that word is part of a title, and after all, the "Essay on Man" and the "Essay on Criticism" really are not essays at all. They are long poems. Fourth, and probably most important, an essay is personal. It is the work of one person whose purpose is to share a thought, idea, or point of view. Let me also state here that since an essay is always personal, the term "personal essay" is redundant. Now, taking into consideration all of these characteristics, perhaps we can now define an essay as a short, prose composition with a personal viewpoint that discusses one topic. With that in mind, let's brainstorm some topics for your first essay assignment.

Narrator: 43. What is the instructor defining?

44. What is the main point of the talk?

45. According to the talk, which of the characteristics are NOT true of an essay?

46. What will the students probably do as an assignment?

Questions 47–50. Listen to a talk by a tour guide for Jefferson's home.

Not a gifted public speaker, Thomas Jefferson was most talented as a literary draftsman. Sent to Congress by the Virginia Convention in 1775, he was elected to the committee to draft a declaration of independence from England. Although John Adams and Benjamin Franklin also served on the committee, the composition of the Declaration of Independence belongs indisputably to Jefferson. In 1779, Jefferson was elected governor of the state of Virginia, an office he held until Congress appointed him to succeed Franklin as U.S. minister to France. Upon returning to Washington, he accepted the position of secretary of state.

Although Jefferson was a Republican, he at first tried to cooperate with Alexander Hamilton, a Federalist who was first among President Washington's advisors. When he concluded that Hamilton was really in favor of a monarchy, hostility between the two men sharpened.

Having served as vice-president in John Adams' administration, Jefferson ran for president in the election of 1800. He and Federalist Aaron Burr received an identical vote, but the Republican Congress elected to approve Jefferson as president. The most outstanding accomplishment of his administration was the purchase of the Louisiana Territory from France in 1803. He was easily re-elected in 1804. When he left office four years later, he returned here to Monticello, where he promoted the formation of a liberal university for Virginia.

Narrator: 47. What is the main purpose of this talk?

48. Jefferson was a member of which political group?

49. How did Jefferson become president?

50. According to the lecturer, what was it that Jefferson was NOT?

Model Test 4
Short Form

Section 1:
Listening Comprehension

50 QUESTIONS 40 MINUTES

In this section of the test, you will have an opportunity to demonstrate your ability to understand conversations and talks in English. There are three parts to this section with special directions for each part. Answer all the questions on the basis of what is stated or implied by the speakers in this test. When you take the actual TOEFL test, you will not be allowed to take notes or write in your test book. Try to work on this Model Test in the same way.

Part A

Directions: In Part A, you will hear short conversations between two people. After each conversation, you will hear a question about the conversation. The conversations and questions will not be repeated. After you hear a question, read the four possible answers in your book and choose the best answer. Then, on your answer sheet, find the number of the question and fill in the space that corresponds to the letter of the answer you have chosen.

1. Woman: You'd better take the car to the garage from now on. They charged me seventy-five dollars for a few minor repairs.
   Man: That's not too bad.
   Narrator: What does the man mean?

(Note: There should be a 12-second pause after each test question in this section.)

2. Man: The International Students' Association is having a party Saturday night. Can you come or do you have to work at the hospital?
   Woman: I wish I could.
   Narrator: What will the woman probably do?

3. Woman: I think that the game starts at eight.
   Man: Good. We have just enough time to get there.
   Narrator: What will the speakers probably do?

4. Woman: What did you do after you lost your passport?
   Man: I went to see the foreign student advisor, and he reported it to the Passport Office in Washington.
   Narrator: What did the man do after he lost his passport?

5. Man: If you don't have an account here, I can't cash your check. I'm sorry, but that's the way it is.
   Woman: Well, thanks a lot! You're a big help!
   Narrator: What does the woman mean?

6. Man: I'm not sure what Dr. Tyler wants us to do.
   Woman: If I were you, I'd write a rough draft and ask Dr. Tyler to look at it.
   Narrator: What does the woman suggest the man do?

7. Man: Dr. Clark is the only one teaching statistics this term.
   Woman: You mean we have to put up with her for another semester?
   Narrator: What does the woman mean?

8. Man: Do you think that you can have these shirts finished by Friday morning?
   Woman: I'm sorry. I couldn't possibly get them done by then. Saturday afternoon would be the earliest that you could have them.
   Narrator: What does the woman say about the shirts?

9. Woman: The music and the flowers are lovely.
   Man: Yes. I hope that the food is good.
   Narrator: What kind of place are the speakers probably talking about?

10. Man: Hello, Anne. This is Larry at the office. Is Fred at home?
    Woman: No, Larry. He's in class now. He'll be home for lunch though.
    Narrator: What do we know about Fred?

11. Man: When does the next bus leave for New York?
    Woman: Buses leave for New York every half-hour. You just missed the nine-thirty bus by five minutes.
    Narrator: What will the man probably do?

12. Woman: Did we have an assignment for Monday? I don't have anything written down.
    Man: Nothing to read in the textbook, but we have to see a movie and write a paragraph about it.
    Narrator: What are the speakers discussing?

13. Man: Make thirty copies for me and twenty copies for Mr. Brown.
    Woman: As soon as I make the final corrections on the original.
    Narrator: What is the woman probably going to do?

14. Man: Excuse me. Are you Sally Harrison's sister?
    Woman: No, I'm not. I'm her cousin.
    Narrator: What had the man assumed about the woman?

15. Woman: I can't find my pen. It was right here on the desk yesterday and now it's gone. Have you seen it?
    Man: Yes. I put it in the desk drawer.
    Narrator: What is the woman's problem?

16. Woman: When is John coming?
    Man: Well, he said he'd be here at eight-thirty, but if I know him, it will be at least nine o'clock.
    Narrator: What does the man imply about John?

17. Man: I suppose we should look for a bigger house, but I don't see how we can afford one right now.
    Woman: If only we hadn't spent so much money on our vacation this year.
    Narrator: What does the woman mean?

18. Man: Did you see Jack's presentation?
    Woman: Yes. What happened? He didn't seem to know up from down.
    Narrator: What does the woman imply about Jack?

19. Woman: Shall I send out the invitations?
    Man: Let's hold off on that until I can talk to Janet.
    Narrator: What does the man mean?

20. Man: How's the baby? Is she walking yet?
    Woman: Oh, yes. I can't keep up with her!
    Narrator: What does the woman mean?

21. Woman: How is your experiment coming along?
    Man: It's finished, but it didn't turn out quite like I thought it would.
    Narrator: What does the man mean?

22. Woman: Barbara sure likes to talk on the phone.
    Man: If only she liked her classes as well!
    Narrator: What does the man imply about Barbara?

23. Woman: My allergies are really bothering me. I guess I'll have to go to the doctor.
    Man: If I were you, I'd try some over-the-counter medications first. They usually do the
                job.
    Narrator: What does the man suggest the woman do?

24. Man: What did you decide about the scholarship? Did you fill out the application?
    Woman: I'm going to give it all I've got.
    Narrator: What does the woman mean?

25. Man: Hello, Anne. This is Robert.
    Woman: Oh, hi, Robert. I was just about to call you.
    Narrator: What does the woman mean?

26. Man: Could I have a few more minutes to finish?
    Woman: I'm afraid not. It's a timed test.
    Narrator: What does the woman mean?

27. Woman: The best part is I can use my roommate's book.
    Man: I'm not so sure about that. I think they're using a different book this semester.
    Narrator: What does the man imply?

28. Man: I'm going to get Sally a bike for Christmas.
    Woman: Are you sure she'd like one?
    Narrator: What does the woman imply?

29. Woman: Carol needs a ride downtown, and I said you'd take her.
    Man: Oh no. Please say you didn't!
    Narrator: What can be inferred about the man?

30. Man: I just can't get the answer to this problem! I've been working on it for three hours.
    Woman: Maybe you should get some rest and try it again later.
    Narrator: What does the woman suggest that the man do?

Part B

Directions: In this part of the test, you will hear longer conversations. After each conversation, you will hear several questions. The conversations and questions will not be repeated.

After you hear a question, read the four possible answers in your book and choose the best answer. Then, on your answer sheet, find the number of the question and fill in the space that corresponds to the letter of the answer you have chosen.

Remember, you are **not** allowed to take notes or write on your test pages.

Questions 31–34. Listen to a class discussion.

Baker: It seems to me that the question is not whether the metric system should be intro-
         duced in the United States, but rather, how it should be introduced.
Woman: I think that it should be done gradually to give everyone enough time to adjust.

Man: Yes. Perhaps we could even have two systems for a while. I mean, we could keep the English system and use metrics as an optional system.

Woman: That's what they seem to be doing. When you go to the grocery store, look at the labels on the cans and packages. They are marked in both ounces and grams.

Man: Right. I've noticed that too. And the weather reporters on radio and TV give the temperature readings in both degrees Fahrenheit and degrees Celsius now.

Woman: Some road signs have the distances marked in both miles and kilometers, especially on the interstate highways. What do you think, Professor Baker?

Baker: Well, I agree that a gradual adoption is better for those of us who have already been exposed to the English system of measurement. But I would favor teaching only metrics in the elementary schools.

Man: I see your point. It might be confusing to introduce two systems at the same time.

Narrator: 31. What is the topic under discussion?

(Note: There should be a 12-second pause after each test question in this section.)

32. What changes in measurement in the United States have the students observed?

33. What was Professor Baker's opinion?

34. Which word best describes Professor Baker's attitude toward his students?

Questions 35–38. Listen to a telephone call to a travel agent.

Man: Hi. This is Roger Jackson. I'm calling to make a reservation for a flight from Houston to Atlanta.

Woman: Yes, Mr. Jackson. And what day would you like to travel?

Man: Oh, not until next month. I want to leave on May 15th and return on May 19th. I thought maybe if I called in advance I could get a better fare.

Woman: Yes, you can. But if you stay over Saturday night and return on Sunday, May 20th, the ticket will be even cheaper.

Man: Really? How much cheaper?

Woman: Almost fifty dollars.

Man: Hmnn. But I would have an extra night in a hotel. No. That's okay. I'll just keep it for May 19th.

Woman: All right. Do you have a seating preference?

Man: I'd rather have a window seat.

Woman: Good. There is one available. And do you want me to mail these tickets or will you pick them up?

Man: I'll pick them up. When can I have them?

Woman: Any time after two o'clock.

Man: Great!

Narrator: 35. What is the main purpose of the telephone call?

36. What does the woman suggest?

37. What does the man decide to do?

38. What will the man probably do?

Part C

Directions: In this part of the test, you will hear several short talks. After each talk, you will hear some questions. The talks and questions will not be repeated.

After you hear a question, read the four possible answers in your book and choose the best answer. Then, on your answer sheet, find the number of the question and fill in the space that corresponds to the letter of the answer you have chosen.

<u>Questions 39–42.</u> Listen to "Breakthroughs in Science," a weekly radio program.

Since the National Aeronautical and Space Administration was established in 1961, NASA has been engaged in an extensive research effort, which, in cooperation with private industry, has transferred technology to the international marketplace. Hundreds of everyday products can be traced back to the space mission, including cordless electrical tools, airtight food packaging, water purification systems, and even scratch coating for eye glasses.

In addition, many advances in medical technology can be traced back to NASA laboratories. First used to detect flaws in spacecraft, ultrasound is now standard equipment in almost every hospital for diagnosis and assessment of injuries and disease; equipment first used by NASA to transmit images from space to earth is used to assist in cardiac imaging, and lasers first used to test satellites are now used in surgical procedures. Under-the-skin implants for the continuous infusion of drugs, and small pacemakers to regulate the heart were originally designed to monitor the physical condition of astronauts in space.

Finally, with the help of images that were obtained during space missions, and NASA technology, archaeologists have been able to explore the earth. Cities lost under desert sands have been located and rediscovered, and the sea floor has been mapped using photographs from outer space.

Narrator: 39. What is the talk mainly about?

(Note: There should be a 12-second pause after each test question in this section.)

>   40. Which of the products listed are NOT mentioned as part of the technology developed for space missions?

>   41. According to the speaker, why did NASA develop medical equipment?

>   42. Why does the speaker mention archaeology?

<u>Questions 43–46.</u> Listen to a talk by a tour guide on a bus.

The first permanent settlement was made at this site in 1776, when a Spanish military post was established on the end of that peninsula. During the same year, some Franciscan Fathers founded the Mission San Francisco de Asis on a hill above the post. A trail was cleared from the military post to the mission, and about halfway between the two, a station was established for travelers called *Yerba Buena*, which means "good herbs."

For thirteen years the village had fewer than one hundred inhabitants. But in 1848, with the discovery of gold, the population grew to ten thousand. That same year, the name was changed from Yerba Buena to San Francisco.

By 1862 telegraph communications linked San Francisco with eastern cities, and by 1869, the first transcontinental railroad connected the Pacific coast with the Atlantic seaboard. Today San

Francisco has a population of almost three million. It is the financial center of the West, and serves as the terminus for trans-Pacific steamship lines and air traffic. The port of San Francisco, which is almost eighteen miles long, handles between five and six million tons of cargo annually.

And now, if you will look to your right, you should just be able to see the Golden Gate Bridge. The bridge, which is more than one mile long, spans the harbor from San Francisco to Marin County and the Redwood Highway. It was completed in 1937 at a cost of thirty-two million dollars and is still one of the largest suspension bridges in the world.

Narrator: 43. What is the main purpose of this talk?

44. According to the tour guide, what was the settlement called before it was re-named San Francisco?

45. According to the tour guide, what happened in 1848?

46. How long is the Golden Gate Bridge?

Questions 47–50. Listen to a talk by an English professor.

Transcendentalism began with the formation in 1836 of the Transcendental Club in Boston, Massachusetts, by a group of artists and writers. This group advanced a reaction against the rigid Puritanism of the period, especially insofar as it emphasized society at the expense of the individual.

One of the most distinguished members of the club was Ralph Waldo Emerson, who served as editor of the literary magazine *Dial.* His writing stressed the importance of the individual. In one of his best-known essays, "Self-Reliance," he appealed to intuition as a source of ethics, asserting that people should be the judge of their own actions, without the rigid restrictions of society.

From 1841 to 1843, Emerson entertained in his home the naturalist and author Henry David Thoreau who also became a member of the Transcendental Club. Probably more than any other member, he demonstrated by his life-style the ideas that the group advanced. He preferred to go to jail rather than to pay taxes to the federal government for a war of which he did not approve.

Upon leaving Emerson's home, Thoreau built a small cabin along the shores of Walden Pond near Concord, Massachusetts, where he lived alone for two years. Devoting himself to the study of nature and to writing, he published an account of his experiences in *Walden,* a book which is generally acknowledged as the most original and sincere contribution to literature by the Transcendentalists.

Narrator: 47. What does the lecturer mainly discuss?

48. During which century did the literary movement develop?

49. According to the lecturer, what did the Puritans do?

50. What is *Walden?*

Model Test 5
Short Form

Section 1:
Listening Comprehension

50 Questions 40 Minutes

In this section of the test, you will have an opportunity to demonstrate your ability to understand conversations and talks in English. There are three parts to this section with special directions for each part. Answer all the questions on the basis of what is stated or implied by the speakers in this test. When you take the actual TOEFL test, you will not be allowed to take notes or write in your test book. Try to work on this Model Test in the same way.

Part A

Directions: In Part A, you will hear short conversations between two people. After each conversation, you will hear a question about the conversation. The conversations and questions will not be repeated. After you hear a question, read the four possible answers in your book and choose the best answer. Then, on your answer sheet, find the number of the question and fill in the space that corresponds to the letter of the answer you have chosen.

1. Woman: There's something wrong with the TV. Only Channel Seventeen has a good picture.
   Man: Maybe it's in the cable.
   Narrator: What does the man mean?

(Note: There should be a 12-second pause after each test question in this section.)

2. Man: Hello. I'd like to speak with Mr. Davis, please. This is Thomas Ward with the Office of Immigration.
   Woman: I'm sorry, Mr. Ward. Mr. Davis is in conference now.
   Narrator: What does the woman mean?

3. Man: Let's go to the movies after dinner.
   Woman: Well, I'll go if you really want to, but I'm a little bit tired.
   Narrator: What does the woman mean?

4. Woman: I'm out of typing paper. Will you lend me some?
   Man: I don't have any either, but I'll be glad to get you some when I go to the bookstore.
   Narrator: What is the man going to do?

5. Man: Excuse me, Miss. Could you please tell me how to get to the University City Bank?
   Woman: Sure. Go straight for two blocks, then turn left and walk three more blocks until you get to the drugstore. It's right across the street.
   Narrator: What can be inferred about the man?

6. Woman: How did you and your dad like the football game yesterday?
   Man: Oh, we left at the half-time.
   Narrator: What does the man imply about the game?

7. Woman: Are you still going to summer school at the university near your parent's house?
   Man: That plan kind of fell through because there weren't enough courses.
   Narrator: What does the man mean?

8. Man: Excuse me, nurse. I'm looking for the emergency room. I thought that it was on the first floor.
   Woman: It is. This is the basement. Take the elevator one flight up and turn left.
   Narrator: What kind of place are the speakers probably talking about?

9. Man: How much is the rent for the apartmant?
   Woman: It's three hundred and fifty dollars a month unfurnished or four hundred dollars a month furnished. Utilities are seventy-five dollars extra, not including the telephone.
   Narrator: What are the speakers discussing?

10. Man: Dr. Taylor must have really liked your paper. You were about the only one who got an A.
    Woman: But he never seems to call on me in class.
    Narrator: What does the woman imply?

11. Woman: Would you like to see a lunch menu? The specials are on the back.
    Man: I already know what I want to order.
    Narrator: What is the man going to do?

12. Woman: Do you know anyone who would like to participate in a psychology experiment? It pays ten dollars an hour.
    Man: Have you asked Sandy?
    Narrator: What does the man suggest that the woman do?

13. Woman: Didn't you go to the meeting last night either?
    Man: No. I had a slight headache.
    Narrator: What can be inferred about the meeting?

14. Woman: Your library books are due on December thirteenth. If you haven't finished using them by then, you may renew them once.
    Man: Thank you very much. I only need them for a few days.
    Narrator: What does the man mean?

15. Man: Operator, I want to place a long-distance call collect to Columbus, Ohio. The area code is six-one-four and the number is four-two-nine, seven-five-eight-three.
    Woman: Thank you. I'll ring it for you.
    Narrator: Who will pay for the call?

16. Woman: I have a card, but now I need a farewell gift for my advisor.
    Man: How about a nice pen?
    Narrator: What does the man mean?

17. Man: Are you going to move out of the dorm next semester?
    Woman: I just can't seem to make up my mind.
    Narrator: What does the woman mean?

18. Man: You and I should stop by the gym on the way home.
    Woman: I don't think so. I've probably had enough exercise for one day.
    Narrator: What does the woman imply?

19. Man: I signed the contract.
    Woman: Do you really think you can work and go to school full time?
    Narrator: What does the woman imply?

20. Woman: I owe everyone in my family a letter, but I really don't have time to sit down and write them and it's too expensive to call.
    Man: Why don't you just buy some postcards?
    Narrator: What does the man suggest the woman do?

21. Man: Have you heard from any schools yet?
    Woman: Yes, I was accepted at Kansas State, the University of Oklahoma, and the University of Nebraska, but I'm going to wait until I hear one way or another from the University of Minnesota.
    Narrator: What are the speakers discussing?

22. Woman: Did you see the stereo CD system that Steve just bought?
    Man: I sure did. It must have cost an arm and a leg.
    Narrator: What does the man mean?

23. Woman: I thought I was supposed to take the test in Room 32.
    Man: No. Ticket number 32 is in Room 27.
    Narrator: What will the woman probably do?

24. Man: Where did you get the flower?
    Woman: At the Honor's Reception. The teachers gave them to all of the honors students.
    Narrator: What can be inferred about the woman?

25. Man: Terry is really having trouble in Dr. Wise's class. She's missed too much to catch up.
    Woman: If I were Terry, I'd drop the course, and take it over next semester.
    Narrator: What does the woman suggest that Terry do?

26. Man: Why does Margaret have to work so many hours at the motel?
    Woman: To earn enough money for next semester's tuition.
    Narrator: What does the woman say about Margaret?

27. Man: Do you have a seat-belt law? In my state you can be charged fifty dollars if you get stopped.
    Woman: Yes, we do, too. But only for the driver and the passengers in the front seat. You're okay.
    Narrator: What does the woman say about the seat-belt law?

28. Woman: I used to teach English before I came back to graduate school.
    Man: No wonder you like this course!
    Narrator: What does the man mean?

29. Woman 1:   We should ask Carl to be in our group.
    Woman 2:   We probably ought to ask Jane, too. She's really good at making presentations.
    Narrator: What problem do the women have?

30. Woman: Where is the line?
    Man: No line. You're supposed to take a number.
    Narrator: What will the woman probably do?

Part B

Directions: In this part of the test, you will hear longer conversations. After each conversation, you will hear several questions. The conversations and questions will not be repeated.

After you hear a question, read the four possible answers in your book and choose the best answer. Then, on your answer sheet, find the number of the question and fill in the space that corresponds to the letter of the answer you have chosen.

Remember, you are **not** allowed to take notes or write on your test pages.

Questions 31–34. Listen to a telephone solicitation.

    Man: Is this Mrs. Todd?
    Woman: Yes.
    Man: Mrs. Todd, you have been selected to receive three magazines of your choice absolutely free.
    Woman: Oh, well, thank you very much, but we subscribe to quite a few magazines already.
    Man: Mrs. Todd, this is a free offer. You will receive these magazines at no charge.
    Woman: No, I don't think so.
    Man: What kind of magazines do you subscribe to now?
    Woman: News magazines mostly. We get *Newsday* and *This Week.*
    Man: Well then, you would probably enjoy the *Reporter* and the *Weekly News.*
    Woman: Actually, we used to get both of those magazines.
    Man: Well, then. Why shouldn't you take advantage of this free offer?
    Woman: I'm sorry, but in my experience, a free offer usually starts out free, and ends up costing the usual price or more for the item.
    Man: But. . .
    Woman: Besides, I don't take solicitations over the phone. Thank you, anyway.

    Narrator: 31. What is the main purpose of the call?

(Note: There should be a 12-second pause after each test question in this section.)

    32. What do we know about the woman?

    33. Why wasn't the woman interested in the offer?

    34. How does the woman close the conversation?

Questions 35–38. Listen to a class discussion.

    John: British English and American English are really about the same, aren't they?
    Mary: I don't think so. It seems to me that some of the spellings are different.
    Baker: You're right, Mary. Words like *theater* and *center* end in *re* in England instead of in *er,* the way that we spell them. Let me write that on the board. Can you think of any more examples?
    Mary: The word *color?*

Baker:	Good. In fact, many words that end in *or* in American English are spelled *our* in British English.
John:	I'm still not convinced. I mean, if someone comes here from England, we can all understand what he's saying. The spelling doesn't really matter that much.
Baker:	Okay. Are we just talking about spelling? Or are there some differences in pronunciation and meaning too?
Mary:	Professor Baker?
Baker:	Yes.
Mary:	I remember seeing an English movie where the actors kept calling their apartment a *flat*. Half of the movie was over before I realized what they were talking about.
John:	So there are slight differences in spelling and some vocabulary.
Mary:	And pronunciation, too. You aren't going to tell me that you sound like Richard Burton.
John:	Richard Burton wasn't English. He was Welsh.
Mary:	Okay. Anyway, the pronunciation is different.
Baker:	I think that what we are really disagreeing about is the extent of the difference. We all agree that British English and American English are different. Right?
Mary:	Yes.
John:	Sure.
Baker:	But not so different that it prevents us from understanding each other.
John:	That's what I mean.
Mary:	That's what I mean, too.
Narrator:	35. What do the speakers mainly discuss?
	36. According to this discussion, how is the word *center* spelled in British English?
	37. What does the word *flat* mean in British English?
	38. On what did the class agree?

Part C

Directions: In this part of the test, you will hear several short talks. After each talk, you will hear some questions. The talks and questions will not be repeated.

After you hear a question, read the four possible answers in your book and choose the best answer. Then, on your answer sheet, find the number of the question and fill in the space that corresponds to the letter of the answer you have chosen.

Questions 39–42. Listen to a talk by a history instructor.

On his third exploratory voyage, as captain of two ships, the *Resolution* and the *Discovery,* Captain James Cook came upon a group of uncharted islands that he named the Sandwich Islands as a tribute to his friend, the Earl of Sandwich. Today the islands are known as the Hawaiian Islands. Some historians contend that the islanders welcomed Cook, believing that he was the god Launo, protector of peace and agriculture.

These islanders were short, strong people, with a well-organized social system. The men fished and raised crops, including taro, coconuts, sweet potatoes, and sugar cane. The women cared for the children and made clothing—loin cloths for the men and short skirts for the women. The natives were eager to exchange food and supplies for iron nails and tools, and Cook was easily able to restock his ship.

Because of a severe storm in which the *Resolution* was damaged, it was necessary to return to Hawaii. Now sure that Cook and his crew were men and not gods, the natives welcomed them less hospitably. Besides, diseases brought by the English had reached epidemic proportions. When a small boat was stolen from the *Discovery*, Cook demanded that the king be taken as a hostage until the boat was returned. In the fighting that followed, Cook and four other crewmen were killed.

Narrator: 39. What is the main purpose of this talk?

(Note: There should be a 12-second pause after each test question in this section.)

40. According to the lecturer, what were the two ships commanded by Captain Cook?

41. What did the native women do?

42. What caused the fighting that resulted in Cook's death?

Questions 43–46. Listen to an engineer talk about metals.

An alloy is a substance that is formed by combining a metal with other metals, or nonmetals. For example, brass is an alloy of the metals copper and zinc, and steel is an alloy of the metal iron with the nonmetal carbon.

The special characteristics of metals, such as hardness, strength, flexibility, and weight are called its properties. By the process of alloying, it is possible to create materials with the exact combination of properties for a particular use. In the aircraft industry, there is a need for metals that are both strong and light. Steel is strong but too heavy, whereas aluminum is light but not strong. By alloying aluminum with copper and other metals, a material that is strong enough to withstand the stresses of flight, but light enough to reduce the cost of fuel to lift the craft is created. By alloying steel with nickel and chromium, the steel alloy that results is not only lighter but also stronger than solid steel.

Of course, there is an important difference between the alloys we have used in our examples and the combination of metals that occur accidentally as impure metals. Both are mixtures, but alloys are mixtures that have been deliberately combined in specific proportion for a definite purpose.

Narrator: 43. What is an alloy?

44. What does the speaker say about the properties of alloys?

45. Why does the speaker use the example of the aircraft industry?

46. What is the difference between combinations of metals in nature and alloys?

Questions 47–50. Listen to a student make a presentation to the class.

My report is on local control of schools. First, I was surprised to learn that public schools in the United States are not the same in every state or even from community to community within the state. The reason for differences in organization, curriculum, and school policies is because each school district has a governing board, called the school board, that makes the decisions about the way the schools in their district will be run. Of course, a superintendent is selected by the board to carry out policies and the superintendent is usually a professional educator, but the board, often made up of community leaders who are not professional educators, must approve the recommendations of the superintendent.

There are two ways to organize a school board. In most communities, the board is elected by the people in their local school district. And the members usually serve without pay for three to five years. But in some districts, the school board is appointed by the mayor.

Of course, the federal government has an interest in improving education on a national level, even though schools are controlled locally. But the function of the national department is very different from a department of education in many parts of the world. This national agency is primarily involved in collecting demographics, supporting research and projects, and supervising the compliance of schools with national legislation.

Narrator: 47. What is the presentation mainly about?

48. What is the relationship of the superintendent and the school board?

49. Who serves on the school board?

50. According to the speaker, what is the function of the department of education in the United States?

Model Test 6
Short Form

Section 1:
Listening Comprehension

50 QUESTIONS 40 MINUTES

In this section of the test, you will have an opportunity to demonstrate your ability to understand conversations and talks in English. There are three parts to this section with special directions for each part. Answer all the questions on the basis of what is stated or implied by the speakers in this test. When you take the actual TOEFL test, you will not be allowed to take notes or write in your test book. Try to work on this Model Test in the same way.

Part A

Directions: In Part A, you will hear short conversations between two people. After each conversation, you will hear a question about the conversation. The conversations and questions will not be repeated. After you hear a question, read the four possible answers in your book and choose the best answer. Then, on your answer sheet, find the number of the question and fill in the space that corresponds to the letter of the answer you have chosen.

1. Man: Have you seen the price of gas? I couldn't believe it when I drove into the service station.
   Woman: I know. It has gone up a lot this month and it will probably be even higher next month.
   Narrator: What does the man think about the price of gasoline?

(Note: There should be a 12-second pause after each test question in this section.)

2. Man: Jane, I would like to introduce you to my sister, Ellen.
   Woman: Glad to meet you, Ellen. Bob tells me that you are interested in African art too. In fact, he says that you plan to spend the summer in Zimbabwe.
   Narrator: What does the woman mean?

3. Man: What are you going to do this weekend? Maybe we can play some tennis.
   Woman: Don't tempt me. I have to study for my qualifying examinations. I take them on Monday.
   Narrator: What does the woman mean?

4. Man: Does attendance count toward the grade in this class?
   Woman: No. I have an attendance requirement for undergraduates, but not for graduate students.
   Narrator: What does the woman mean?

5. Women: Where is the best place to buy cakes?
   Man: Well, the Dutch Oven is the best place, but it is closed right now. Why don't you try Mama's Bake Shop on Wells Street?
   Narrator: What will the woman probably do?

6. Woman: How do you like your new job, Bill?
   Man: Fine. This week I have been reading the financial reports and studying the books. Next week I will probably start to handle some of the accounts.
   Narrator: What can be inferred about Bill?

7. Man: Have you talked to Ali lately? I thought that he was studying at the American Language Institute, but yesterday I saw him going into the chemistry lab in the engineering building.
   Woman: That is not surprising. Ali is a part-time student this term. He is taking three classes at the Institute and one class at the university.
   Narrator: What does the woman say about Ali?

8. Man: Hello, Miss Evans? This is Paul Thompson. I would like to talk with my wife, please.
   Woman: Oh, Paul. You just missed her.
   Narrator: What does the woman mean?

9. Man: I would like to take an X-ray, Mrs. Johnson. I can't be sure, but I think you have a small cavity starting in one of your back molars, and if so, I want you to make an appointment before it begins to give you problems.
   Woman: I have been so careful about eating too many sweets, too. I don't know why my teeth get so many cavities.
   Narrator: What are the speakers discussing?

10. Man: I would like to see Mr. Adams, please.
    Woman: Mr. Adams is not here anymore. Mrs. Jones is the foreign student advisor now.
    Narrator: What do we know from this conversation?

11. Man: Hi, Mary. Did you get a letter from your family?
    Woman: I'm afraid not. This is a telephone bill.
    Narrator: What does the woman mean?

12. Man: I am sorry, Miss. Flight six twenty-two has already departed.
    Woman: Oh. All right. Can you please tell me where I can find a telephone?
    Narrator: What will the woman probably do?

13. Man: Have you bought your books yet?
    Woman: I tried to, but the math and English books were sold out.
    Narrator: What does the woman mean?

14. Man: I don't have to be there until seven.
    Woman: The traffic is really bad though. You'd better leave a few minutes early.
    Narrator: What does the woman suggest the man do?

15. Man: You don't like the new graduate assistant, do you?
    Woman: No. He makes fun of his student's mistakes.
    Narrator: What does the woman mean?

16. Woman: Susan told me what you said about my accent.
    Man: I don't know what she told you, but I really didn't mean it as a put down.
    Narrator: What does the man mean?

17. Man: I'll be right back. Can you watch my book bag for a minute?
    Woman: Sure. I'll be glad to.
    Narrator: What does the woman agree to do for the man?

18. Woman: I'm really tired of living in this tiny apartment.
    Man: I hear you.
    Narrator: What does the man mean?

19. Man: Is that Mike's car? I thought you said that Mike was spending spring break in
                Florida.
    Woman: That's Mike's brother. He's using the car while Mike's away.
    Narrator: What does the woman imply?

20. Woman: You'd better start working on that project. It's due in a week.
    Man: I will. I'll get it done.
    Narrator: What does the woman advise the man to do?

21. Woman: Here is the telephone number for customer service.
    Man: Good. Let's settle this once and for all.
    Narrator: What does the man mean?

22. Man: Do you want to go to the International Talent Show?
    Woman: Sure. Why not?
    Narrator: What does the woman mean?

23. Man: Did you know that Bill and Carol are back from their honeymoon?
    Woman: So they *did* get married after all.
    Narrator: What had the woman assumed about Bill and Carol?

24. Man: Are you going to the review session for the test?
    Woman: What's the point?
    Narrator: What does the woman mean?

25. Woman: Your check isn't here. I suggest that you call your sponsor.
    Man: Okay. I'll be back.
    Narrator: What will the man probably do?

26. Woman: I still haven't heard from Columbia University yet.
    Man: I know it looks grim right now, but don't give up!
    Narrator: What does the man mean?

27. Woman: Were you able to find everything you needed?
    Man: There wasn't anybody around in the stacks to help!
    Narrator: What does the man imply?

28. Woman: Were you cited for the accident?
    Man: No. It wasn't my fault and no one was hurt. But my insurance rates went up anyway.
    Narrator: What problem does the man have?

29. Woman: Vanesa got accepted to Yale.
    Man: Really? I thought they required a 600 or 650 on the TOEFL.
    Narrator: What had the man assumed about Vanesa?

30. Man: Is this seat taken?
    Woman: No, it isn't.
    Narrator: What will the man probably do?

Part B

Directions: In this part of the test, you will hear longer conversations. After each conversation, you will hear several questions. The conversations and questions will not be repeated.

After you hear a question, read the four possible answers in your book and choose the best answer. Then, on your answer sheet, find the number of the question and fill in the space that corresponds to the letter of the answer you have chosen.

Remember, you are **not** allowed to take notes or write on your test pages.

Questions 31–34. Listen to a telephone conversation between two college students.

    Man: Hi, Margaret. This is Gary.
    Woman: Oh, hi, Gary. Where have you been? I've missed you in lab.
    Man: I've been sick.
    Woman: Nothing serious, I hope.
    Man: Well, I stayed out of the hospital, but to tell the truth, I was in pretty bad shape. Some kind of flu.
    Woman: That's too bad. Are you better now?
    Man: Well enough to start thinking about school again. Now I'm worried about getting caught up.
    Woman: Let's see, how many labs have you missed?
    Man: Margaret, I got sick three weeks ago, so I am really behind.
    Woman: Let me look at my notebook. I've got it right here.
    Man: Oh, great. I was hoping you'd let me make a copy of your notes.

Woman:	Sure. You can do that, Gary. And I have some good news for you. You haven't missed any quizzes. We haven't had any since you've been gone. Listen, after you have a chance to look at my notes, why don't we get together? If there's anything you don't understand, maybe I can explain it to you. It's hard trying to read someone else's notes.
Man:	That would be perfect. I hate to bother you though.
Woman:	No bother. I'm sure you'd do it for me.

| Narrator: | 31. What is Gary's problem? |

(Note: There should be a 12-second pause after each test question in this section.)

32. What does Gary want Margaret to do?

33. What does Margaret offer to do?

34. What is Margaret's attitude in this conversation?

Questions 35–38. Listen to a telephone call to a university department.

Woman:	Chemical Engineering Department. May I help you?
Man:	Yes. My name is Bob Stephens and I have an appointment with Dr. Benjamin at three o'clock on Wednesday.
Woman:	Three o'clock on Wednesday? Yes. I see it here on his calendar.
Man:	Well, I was wondering whether he has an earlier appointment available on the same day.
Woman:	I'm sorry, Mr. Stephens, but Dr. Benjamin is tied up in a meeting until noon, and he has two appointments scheduled before yours when he gets back from lunch.
Man:	Oh.
Woman:	There is a later appointment time open though, at four-thirty, if that would help you. Or you could see him Thursday morning at ten.
Man:	Hmmm. No thank you. I think I'll just rearrange my own schedule so I can keep my regular appointment.

| Narrator: | 35. Why did the man call the Chemical Engineering Department? |

36. What does the woman say about Dr. Benjamin?

37. What did the secretary offer to do?

38. What did the man decide to do?

Part C

Directions: In this part of the test, you will hear several short talks. After each talk, you will hear some questions. The talks and questions will not be repeated.

After you hear a question, read the four possible answers in your book and choose the best answer. Then, on your answer sheet, find the number of the question and fill in the space that corresponds to the letter of the answer you have chosen.

Questions 39–42. Listen to a lecture by a college English teacher.

There have been a number of important American novelists in this century, but I have chosen F. Scott Fitzgerald for our class because he is one of the more interesting ones. Born in 1896 and educated at Princeton, he wrote novels that describe the post-war American society, very much caught up in the rhythms of jazz.

In 1920, the same year that he published his first book, *This Side of Paradise*, he married Zelda Sayre, also a writer. His most famous book, *The Great Gatsby*, appeared in 1925.

Fitzgerald had a great natural talent, but unfortunately he became a compulsive drinker. A brilliant success in his youth, he never made the adjustments necessary to a maturing writer in a changing world. His later novels, *All the Sad Young Men*, *Tender is the Night*, and *The Last Tycoon*, were less successful, so that when he died in 1940 his books were out of print and he had been almost forgotten.

His reputation now is far greater than it was in his lifetime, especially since the film version of his novel *The Great Gatsby* was released. Now, with that introduction, I am going to run the video version of *The Great Gatsby,* and then we'll divide up into groups to talk about it.

Narrator: 39. What is the main topic of this talk?

(Note: There should be a 12-second pause after each test question in this section.)

40. What does the lecturer tell us about Fitzgerald's later life?

41. According to the lecturer, what do we know about the novels written by F. Scott Fitzgerald?

42. What is the assignment for the class?

Questions 43–46. Listen to a radio announcer.

Before the concert begins, let me tell you a little bit about chamber music. From medieval times through the eighteenth century, musicians in Europe had two options for employment—the church or the nobility. So when they were not performing at religious functions, they were playing in the chambers of stately homes. And they came to be known as chamber players.

Chamber music is written to be performed by a small group, more than one, but fewer than a dozen musicians. Pieces for more than eight players are unusual though, and it is rare to see a conductor. It may surprise you to know that any combination of instruments can be used for chamber music. The most popular are the piano, strings, and woodwinds, but chamber music has been written for other instruments as well.

Early chamber music, let's say the sixteenth and seventeenth centuries, was often written for the recorder, harpsichord, and viola. During the Elizabethan Period, there were many talented composers of chamber music, including William Byrd and Orlando Gibbons. And at that time, vocal chamber music, called madrigal singing, was very popular. Later, both Johann Sebastian Bach and George Frederick Handel wrote trio sonatas for chamber groups. This evening the University Quartet will perform two of the later pieces by Bach. Ladies and gentlemen, the University Quartet.

Narrator: 43. What is the main purpose of the talk?

44. According to the speaker, which instruments are used for chamber music?

45. Why does the speaker mention Johann Sebastian Bach?

46. What will the listeners hear next?

Questions 47–50. Listen to a talk by a radio host.

Health food is a general term applied to all kinds of foods that are considered more healthful than the types of foods widely sold in supermarkets. For example, whole grains, dried beans, and corn oil are health foods. A narrower classification of health foods is natural food. This term is used to distinguish between types of the same food. Fresh fruit is a natural food, but canned fruit, with sugars and other additives, is not. The most precise term of all and the narrowest classification within health foods is organic food, used to describe food that has been grown on a particular kind of farm. Fruits and vegetables that are grown in gardens treated only with organic fertilizers, that are not sprayed with poisonous insecticides, and that are not refined after harvest, are organic foods.

In choosing the type of food you eat, then, you have basically two choices: inorganic, processed foods, or organic, unprocessed foods. A wise decision should include investigation of the allegations that processed foods contain chemicals, some of which are proven to be toxic, and that vitamin content is greatly reduced in processed foods.

Narrator: 47. What is the main idea of this talk?

48. Which term is used to distinguish between types of the same food?

49. What happens to food when it is processed?

50. Which word best describes the speaker's attitude toward health foods?

Model Test 7
Short Form

Section 1:
Listening Comprehension

50 QUESTIONS 40 MINUTES

In this section of the test, you will have an opportunity to demonstrate your ability to understand conversations and talks in English. There are three parts to this section with special directions for each part. Answer all the questions on the basis of what is stated or implied by the speakers in this test. When you take the actual TOEFL test, you will not be allowed to take notes or write in your test book. Try to work on this Model Test in the same way.

Part A

Directions: In Part A, you will hear short conversations between two people. After each conversation, you will hear a question about the conversation. The conversations and questions will not be repeated. After you hear a question, read the four possible answers in your book and choose the best answer. Then, on your answer sheet, find the number of the question and fill in the space that corresponds to the letter of the answer you have chosen.

1. Woman: Their son is very bright.
   Man: Yes, he is. When we saw them in Houston at the convention, I was surprised how clearly he could talk.
   Narrator: What are the speakers discussing?

(Note: There should be a 12-second pause after each test question in this section.)

2. Man: It's so noisy in the dorm I can't get anything done.
   Woman: Why not move into an apartment?
   Narrator: What does the woman mean?

3. Man: You turn on the TV by pulling out this button. The heat control is on the wall. Will there be anything else, Ma'am?
   Woman: No, thank you.
   Narrator: What can be inferred about the man?

4. Woman: Did you balance your checkbook?
   Man: I had my secretary do it because I kept putting it off and my wife was starting to lose patience with me.
   Narrator: What can be inferred about the man?

5. Man: Let's have lunch sometime.
   Woman: Sounds good. Give me a call.
   Narrator: What can we assume from this conversation?

6. Man: How many transcripts do you want me to send to San Diego State?
   Woman: Just one, but I want two for myself.
   Narrator: What will the man probably do?

7. Woman: And what do you want on that?
   Man: Everything, and extra catsup, too, please.
   Narrator: What does the man mean?

8. Man: The problem is I don't have the parts I need to fix the water hose. You can drive it as it is, but you'll have to get it replaced pretty soon.
   Woman: Okay. When the parts come in, give me a call and I'll bring it back.
   Narrator: Where does this conversation probably take place?

9. Woman: I ought to wait until Professor Bloom gets back from class.
   Man: Not really. You can just leave a note. I'll give it to her.
   Narrator: What does the man suggest the woman do?

10. Man: Are you ready? You don't even have your coat on.
    Woman: You've got to be kidding! It's only six o'clock.
    Narrator: What does the woman mean?

11. Woman: Susan told me she was really interested in social work.
    Man: Yes, but when she declared her major she chose education.
    Narrator: What can be inferred about Susan?

12. Woman: That roast weighs about eight pounds.
    Man: Oh, that's too big then. I only want to serve five people. Why don't you give me one about half that size?
    Narrator: What does the man say about the roast?

13. Woman: I wonder whether the clothes are dry yet?
    Man: I don't think so. It usually takes about forty-five minutes, and you just put them in fifteen minutes ago.
    Narrator: What are the speakers talking about?

14. Woman: Congratulations! I saw your name on the graduation list.
    Man: Someone else must have the same name then. I'm not graduating until next spring.
    Narrator: What had the woman assumed?

15. Man: Excuse me. Are you in line for the copy machine?
    Woman: No. We're just talking.
    Narrator: What will the man probably do?

16. Man: Did you ever apply for that scholarship? You weren't sure whether you wanted to compete with all those applicants.
    Woman: I decided to go for it!
    Narrator: What does the woman mean?

17. Woman: May I join you?
    Man: By all means.
    Narrator: What does the man mean?

18. Woman: We're going to the library. Want to come along?
    Man: I'm waiting for the mail to come.
    Narrator: What does the man imply?

19. Woman: I'm calling because I can't remember whether you are supposed to pick me up or I'm supposed to pick you up for lunch.
    Man: I'm supposed to pick you up, in about twenty minutes, okay?
    Narrator: What will the woman probably do?

20. Man: Strange to see only a few people in the office, isn't it?
    Woman: It sure is. I wonder why.
    Narrator: What can be inferred about the office?

21. Man: How was your vacation? You went to Toronto, didn't you?
    Woman: I was going there, but I got a really great fare to Montreal, then I drove to Quebec and some of the little towns in the province.
    Narrator: What are the speakers talking about?

22. Man: Hello. Mrs. Best?
    Woman: She's not here. Did you try her at the Student Center?
    Narrator: What does the woman suggest the man do?

23. Man: Do you want me to get anything special at the grocery store for dinner?
    Woman: I couldn't care less.
    Narrator: How does the woman feel about dinner?

24. Man: Weren't you in class Friday either?
    Woman: No. I had to take my mother to the airport. She went back to New York.
    Narrator: What do we learn about the two students in this conversation?

25. Woman: You must be so excited about going home after four years.
    Man: Not as much as I thought I would be.
    Narrator: What does the man mean?

26. Man: Did you make your flight okay?
    Woman: Just barely. The taxi was late.
    Narrator: What does the woman mean?

27. Man: Do you usually bring your lunch?
    Woman: I eat in the snack bar now and then.
    Narrator: What does the woman mean?

28. Man: I'm much better now. No need to worry.
    Woman: You'd better take it easy though, or you'll get sick again.
    Narrator: What does the woman mean?

29. Woman: I don't like to watch TV that much.
    Man: Neither do I.
    Narrator: What does the man mean?

30. Woman: Did you find enough subjects for your research project?
    Man: Not yet. I have thirty-five though, so that's a good start.
    Narrator: What does the man imply?

Part B

Directions: In this part of the test, you will hear longer conversations. After each conversation, you will hear several questions. The conversations and questions will not be repeated.

After you hear a question, read the four possible answers in your book and choose the best answer. Then, on your answer sheet, find the number of the question and fill in the space that corresponds to the letter of the answer you have chosen.

Remember, you are **not** allowed to take notes or write on your test pages.

Questions 31–34. Listen to a telephone conversation with a receptionist.

    Woman: Dr. Norman's office.
    Man: Hi, this is Bob Franklin. I'm a patient of Dr. Norman.
    Woman: Oh, yes, Mr. Franklin.
    Man: I'm calling to make an appointment with the doctor. It's not an emergency. I just
              need a recent physical in order to get enrolled in a new insurance plan at school.
    Woman: I see. Well, the doctor has several openings on June third.
    Man: Hmnn. Anything sooner than that? I have to turn in the application on the first.
    Woman: Yes. He has May twenty-ninth at two o'clock or May thirtieth at four-thirty.

Man: Oh, good. I'll take the twenty-ninth at two o'clock.
Woman: All right. I have you down. Since it's for a physical, you will need to come in a week
              before the appointment to get a blood work-up.
Man: Oh.
Woman: You can do that without an appointment. Just come into the office before May
              twenty-second, and the nurse will take care of you. That way, the doctor will have
              the results of the tests when he sees you.
Man: Okay.

Narrator: 31. Why does the man need an appointment?

(Note: There should be a 12-second pause after each test question in this section.)

              32. Why is the June first date a problem?

              33. When is the man's appointment?

              34. What must the man do before his appointment?

Questions 35–38. Listen to a conversation with a professor.

Rick: Thank you for seeing me today, Dr. Wilson. I want to talk with you about my final
              grade.
Dr. Wilson: Yes?
Rick: Well, I was surprised to get a D after doing so well on the midterm.
Dr. Wilson: Let's see. I'll just check my grade book here.
Rick: I got a B, Dr. Wilson. I brought my test with me.
Dr. Wilson: Yes, you did. I have it recorded here. And you passed the final with a C.
Rick: Then I should have got a C + or a B–.
Dr. Wilson: Yes, you should have, but the problem was your attendance. Twenty-five percent of
              your grade was calculated on the basis of class participation, and Rick, you just
              didn't participate.
Rick: But I passed the exams.
Dr. Wilson: Yes, I know you did. And you passed the course. D is a passing grade.
Rick: But. . .
Dr. Wilson: I'm sorry, Rick. I gave you a syllabus on the first day of class and the grading sys-
              tem was outlined in it. You received an F in class participation because you missed
              too many days, and that brought your grade down.

Narrator: 35. What prompted this conversation?

              36. Where is this conversation taking place?

              37. What is the grade that Rick received for the course?

              38. Why did Rick receive a lower grade?

Part C

Directions: In this part of the test, you will hear several short talks. After each talk, you will hear some questions. The talks and questions will not be repeated.

After you hear a question, read the four possible answers in your book and choose the best answer. Then, on your answer sheet, find the number of the question and fill in the space that corresponds to the letter of the answer you have chosen.

Questions 39–42. Listen to a professor talk with her students in a college class.

Before we begin our discussion of today's topic, I'd like to point out a few important features on the syllabus. First, please look at the calendar. As you see, we will be meeting for fifteen weeks. The last week of November we will not meet because of the Thanksgiving holiday. But, all of the other dates are listed, along with the reading assignments in your textbook. In general, it is better to read the assigned pages before you come to class so that you will be prepared to participate in the discussion that follows the lecture.

Now, let's look at the course requirements. As you see, you have a midterm examination the last week of October, and a final examination the second week of December. The midterm is worth 25 points and the final is worth 50 points. That leaves 25 points for the project that you will be working on, and you have several choices to fulfill that requirement. You can either write a paper or make a half-hour presentation on a topic of your choice. We'll be talking a bit more about the projects in the next several weeks. Oh, yes, you will notice that I don't factor attendance into the grade, but I do expect you to be here. If you must miss class for whatever reason, please get in touch with me. My office hours are listed on the syllabus, along with my voice mail number and my e-mail address.

Narrator: 39. What does the speaker mainly discuss?

(Note: There should be a 12-second pause after each test question in this section.)

40. What suggestion does the professor make about the reading assignments?

41. What are the course requirements?

42. According to the professor, what should students do if they must be absent?

Questions 43–46. Listen to a talk given on a radio program called "Science News."

Today I'm going to share a rather interesting theory with you. As you already know from your reading material, many scientists believe that the atmosphere of the seventh and eighth planets from our sun, Uranus and Neptune, have an outer film of hydrogen and helium. The atmosphere of Neptune above its methane ice clouds is about 85 percent hydrogen and 15 percent helium, and beneath the clouds, methane concentrations increase to more than 1 percent. The atmosphere of Uranus consists mostly of hydrogen with 2 percent methane and 10 to 20 percent helium, with lesser amounts of ammonia. Because of this, the surfaces of these planets are probably covered with frozen ammonia and methane.

Now Marvin Ross of the Lawrence Livermore National Laboratory in California has postulated that the methane could have separated into the carbon and hydrogen atoms that form it, and furthermore, that at the high pressures common to those planets, the carbon atoms could have been squeezed into a layer of diamonds.

Astronomers at the University of Arizona in Tucson agree that the pressures on these planets, some 200,000 to 6 million times that of Earth's atmosphere, could set up conditions whereby diamonds might form. Moreover, since the two giant planets are each nearly four times the size of the Earth, and each is nearly one-fifth carbon, the quantities of diamonds could be huge.

Narrator: 43. What is the main purpose of this lecture?

44. Which planets are being discussed?

45. Why do the scientists believe that diamonds may have formed?

46. How does the speaker feel about the theory?

Questions 47–50. Listen to a teacher talk to her freshman history class.

In the United States, the people do not elect the president by direct vote. This is so because the men who wrote the Constitution in 1787 believed that ordinary citizens would not be informed enough to make such an important decision, and they created a system whereby a representative group of citizens called the electoral college would be responsible for making the choice. The candidate with the most votes became president, and the candidate receiving the next highest number of votes became vice-president. But in 1800, when Aaron Burr and Thomas Jefferson received an equal number of votes, the system had to be changed to provide for separate voting for president and vice-president.

Later, when political parties had become more influential, the parties nominated candidates and then chose electors to vote for them.

Today, each political party in the state nominates a slate of electors pledged to support the party's nominees for president and vice-president. Each state has the same number of electors in the college as it has members of Congress. On election day, registered voters go to the polls to choose the electors. In most states, the ballots list only the names of the candidates for president and vice-president that the electors have pledged to support. This vote by the people for electors is called the popular vote, and the candidates who receive the most popular votes win all the electoral votes in a state.

Narrator: 47. What is the talk mainly about?

48. Why does the speaker mention Aaron Burr and Thomas Jefferson?

49. How are the people nominated for the electoral college?

50. What is the popular vote?

Model Test 8
Long Form

Section 1:
Listening Comprehension

80 QUESTIONS 50 MINUTES

In this section of the test, you will have an opportunity to demonstrate your ability to understand conversations and talks in English. There are three parts to this section with special directions for each part. Answer all the questions on the basis of what is stated or implied by the speakers in this test. When you take the actual TOEFL test, you will not be allowed to take notes or write in your test book. Try to work on this Model Test in the same way.

Part A

Directions: In Part A, you will hear short conversations between two people. After each conversation, you will hear a question about the conversation. The conversations and questions will not be repeated. After you hear a question, read the four possible answers in your book and choose the best answer. Then, on your answer sheet, find the number of the question and fill in the space that corresponds to the letter of the answer you have chosen.

1. Man: Could you please sign my course request form?
   Woman: I'm sorry. You have to get your advisor's signature on that.
   Narrator: What can be inferred about the woman?

(Note: There should be a 12-second pause after each test question in this section.)

2. Man: Go to the next screen.
   Woman: Okay. Oh, I see! You hit this key and Enter.
   Narrator: What are the speakers discussing?

3. Woman: So what are you going to do? Move out of the apartment?
   Man: No way!
   Narrator: What does the man mean?

4. Man: Can't you just fax the report to me? It can't be more than two pages long.
   Woman: I'm sorry. Our fax machine is down. But I could send it Federal Express if you want.
   Narrator: What does the woman mean?

5. Man: How old is Jim?
   Woman: Well, let's see. I'm twenty-four, and he is seven years older than I am.
   Narrator: What can be inferred about Jim?

6. Woman: What is your social security number?
   Man: Seven-two-one—Wait! That's not right! Seven-one-two. Nine-eight. Six-five-zero-four.
   Narrator: What is the man's social security number?

7. Man: Are you going to pass back our tests today?

   Woman: No. I don't have them all graded yet. But you can pick them up after Wednesday in my office if you don't want to wait until class next Monday.

   Narrator: What is the relationship between the two speakers?

8. Woman: Why do you need running shoes? You never go jogging. You don't play basketball anymore. You don't even walk with me in the mornings.

   Man: I know. I just like to wear them because they're comfortable.

   Narrator: What does the woman imply about the man?

9. Man: I absolutely have to have this suit back by tomorrow at four o'clock.

   Woman: Well, I can mark it rush, but it will cost you two dollars extra.

   Narrator: What will the man probably do?

10. Man: Let's sit closer to the front. I can't see very well.

   Woman: That's a good idea.

   Narrator: What will the man and woman probably do?

11. Man: What do you do?

   Woman: I'm a student right now, so I'm working part time at Pizza Hut. One more year and I'll have my teaching certificate though.

   Narrator: What does the woman want to do?

12. Man: Do you have children?

   Woman: Yes. I have one daughter four years old, and twin boys, five.

   Narrator: What can be inferred about the woman?

13. Woman: Did you like living in Montreal?

   Man: Yes. Most of the time. The weather was really cold in the winter, but the rest of the year was beautiful.

   Narrator: How did the man feel about Montreal?

14. Man: Don't park there. That lot is reserved for faculty. Go up another block past those shops and you'll see a visitor's lot. There! Across the street from the auditorium.

   Woman: Thanks. I don't want to get a ticket.

   Narrator: What kind of place are the speakers probably talking about?

15. Woman: See you tomorrow.

   Man: I don't think so! That video tape isn't due back until Tuesday. We're closed on Sunday and Monday is a holiday. It's usually a one-day rental though.

   Narrator: What can be inferred from this conversation?

16. Man: What can I do?

   Woman: Well, my policy for make-up tests is on the syllabus. You'll have to take an essay test instead of the multiple choice test I gave last Thursday.

   Narrator: What is the man's problem?

17. Man: Excuse me. Is there a restroom out here?

   Woman: No. It's the other way. Past customer service and gift wrap by the beauty salon.

   Narrator: What will the man probably do?

18. Woman: Are you going to watch the play-offs?
    Man: You bet!
    Narrator: What does the man mean?

19. Man: I've got to quit smoking. But how? I've tried chewing gum. I've joined a support group. My will power only lasts about two weeks.
    Woman: It's hard. I smoked for almost ten years. Then I got one of those nicotine patches. Why don't you try it?
    Narrator: What did the woman suggest?

20. Woman: You wouldn't be in this mess if you hadn't charged so much on your credit cards!
    Man: Okay, Linda. Back off!
    Narrator: What does the man mean?

21. Man: How much time do we have left?
    Woman: About ten minutes. Please put your name on your papers before you turn them in.
    Narrator: What is the man most probably doing?

22. Man: Do you like "Star Trek?"
    Woman: Not really. I don't watch much TV, and when I do, I usually turn on the Learning Channel. Mostly I'm not home though. Work keeps me pretty busy, so it's a good thing I enjoy it.
    Narrator: What does the woman imply?

23. Man: I wish I had a chicken sandwich, or maybe grilled cheese.
    Woman: That's tough!
    Narrator: What does the woman mean?

24. Woman: Here's your key. Do you know about the complimentary breakfast? We serve it tomorrow from seven to nine, right behind the pool.
    Man: Yes, thanks. I've stayed here before.
    Narrator: What kind of place are the speakers probably talking about?

25. Man: My research class was cancelled, so now I don't have a full load.
    Woman: Sit down for a minute. I'm sure we can work it out.
    Narrator: What does the woman mean?

26. Woman: How do you like the bus trip so far?
    Man: Well, to tell the truth, I'm not too big on tours.
    Narrator: What does the man mean?

27. Woman: Can you believe it? I won twenty dollars on the lottery last night!
    Man: Way to go!
    Narrator: What does the man mean?

28. Woman: Will that be together, or do you want separate checks?
    Man: Separate, please.
    Narrator: What is the man going to do?

29. Man: Hey, I heard that you got an assistantship.
    Woman: You must be thinking of my roommate. I'm not going to try to teach next year while I'm studying full time.
    Narrator: What does the woman mean?

30. Woman: Would you help me on Saturday when I move out of the dorm?
    Man: When would you like me to be there?
    Narrator: What can be inferred about the man?

31. Man: Where is your car?
    Woman: I wish I knew. I thought I parked it under a light so I could find it when we came out of class.
    Narrator: What is the woman's problem?

32. Woman: I can't give you the medication until your doctor phones in the prescription.
    Man: It should be here. I talked with his office this morning.
    Narrator: What do we know about the woman?

33. Man: Give me a hand, will you?
    Woman: Sure thing.
    Narrator: What did the woman agree to do?

34. Man: You'd better hurry. They're only taking pictures for ID cards until five o'clock.
    Woman: I'm on my way.
    Narrator: What does the woman mean?

35. Man: What is an appropriate gift to take to some friends who have invited you to their house for dinner? I was thinking maybe some candy.
    Woman: That sounds good. Or you could get a plant.
    Narrator: What does the woman suggest?

36. Woman: I can't find my room. It's number 119.
    Man: Oh! The even numbers are on this side, so your room must be on the other side.
    Narrator: What will the woman probably do?

37. Man: How did you sleep last night?
    Woman: Like a rock.
    Narrator: What does the woman mean?

38. Woman: Did you hear about the accident?
    Man: Yes. If Sue hadn't had her seat belt on she would have been killed.
    Narrator: What do we know about Sue?

39. Woman: The ground floor *is* the first floor in the United States. You need to go downstairs.
    Man: No wonder I've been confused.
    Narrator: What had the man assumed?

40. Man: Would you please get the phone, Jan? I'm all tied up right now.
    Woman: Certainly.
    Narrator: What does the man mean?

41. Man: Good morning, Mary. How are you?
    Woman: Oh, fine. I'm just on my way to work, but I thought that I would drop by for a minute.
    Narrator: What does the woman mean?

42. Man: But I sent my application three weeks ago.
    Woman: Well that's why you haven't heard, then. It takes six weeks to process it.
    Narrator: What does the woman imply?

43. Woman: I'm sorry. Your credit card number was not approved. The computer didn't accept it.
    Man: Try it again. There must be some mistake.
    Narrator: What will the woman probably do?

44. Woman: You just select the number one for a title, two for an author, three for a subject, and then you type in the information.
    Man: Thanks for showing me. I'm sure that I can find the books I need now.
    Narrator: What can be inferred about the woman?

45. Woman: Will you be transferring to Georgia State next year?
    Man: I'm afraid not.
    Narrator: What does the man mean?

46. Man: I need to see your driver's license and a major credit card.
    Woman: Even for a traveler's check? I have my passport.
    Narrator: What does the woman mean?

47. Man: Does your family live here in Montgomery?
    Woman: No, I have a brother in Birmingham, and a sister in Mobile, but my parents live in Florida.
    Narrator: What did the woman say about her family?

48. Woman: Excuse me, I'm looking for a good Spanish-English dictionary.
    Man: You and everybody else.
    Narrator: What does the man mean?

49. Man: I never see you out jogging any more. What happened to your exercise program?
    Woman: I walk now. It's less stress on the feet and knees. I've been playing some tennis, too, though.
    Narrator: What are the speakers talking about?

50. Woman: How many miles is it to San Diego?
    Man: Well, it's fifty miles to Long Beach, and Long Beach is about ninety miles from San Diego.
    Narrator: What can be inferred from the conversation?

51. Man: Good thing we studied the book as well as the notes.
    Woman: Even so, that test was a real bear!
    Narrator: What does the woman mean?

52. Woman: How did the meeting go with your doctoral committee?
    Man: I couldn't have been more pleased.
    Narrator: What does the man mean?

Part B

Directions: In this part of the test, you will hear longer conversations. After each conversation, you will hear several questions. The conversations and questions will not be repeated.

After you hear a question, read the four possible answers in your book and choose the best answer. Then, on your answer sheet, find the number of the question and fill in the space that corresponds to the letter of the answer you have chosen.

Remember, you are **not** allowed to take notes or write on your test pages.

Questions 53–56. Listen to a conversation in the dean's office.

Dean:	You are here because you are accused of plagiarism. That is one of the most serious kinds of misconduct at the University. It is intellectual theft.
Student:	But I didn't mean to steal.
Dean:	Maybe not, but copying is stealing.
Student:	I didn't copy.
Dean:	Yes, you did. In this case, you copied from a book instead of from a friend. It's still copying. Look, if you want to use someone else's words, you must put them in quotation marks, and you must cite the source. You know that, don't you?
Student:	Yes, but…
Dean:	Even if you don't copy word for word, but you use someone else's ideas, if those ideas are not widely published, it can still be plagiarism to use them without a citation.
Student:	That is what I don't understand, Dean Conners.
Dean:	Mr. Farr, your professor already gave you a failing grade for the course, and in this case I feel that is punishment enough. I'm going to give you a warning this time. But if you ever come back to my office for a similar offense, I'll have you expelled. In the meantime, if you really don't know how to write a research paper, I suggest that you go over to the Learning Resources Center for some tutoring.

Narrator:	53.	Why is the student in the dean's office?

(Note: There should be a 12-second pause after each test question in this section.)

54. What is the student's excuse?

55. How does the dean punish the student?

56. What advice does the dean give the student?

Questions 57–60. Listen to a conversation between two college students.

Man:	What's bothering you? You've been really quiet tonight.
Woman:	I'm sorry. I'm trying to decide whether to stay here or to transfer to a larger school.
Man:	Well, there are advantages to both, I suppose.
Woman:	That's the problem. I keep thinking that eventually it will be better to have the degree from a larger, more prestigious college, but I really like it here.
Man:	I know what you mean. At a small place like this, we have professors teaching our classes, not graduate students.
Woman:	Exactly. And, besides that, your teachers know you, and they seem to really care about you. I'm not sure it would be like that in a huge university.

Man:	True. So, you are basically happy here, but you are worried about the impression that you will make with a degree from such a small college.
Woman:	Yes. I'm afraid I'll be in a job interview sometime, and the interviewer will say, "And just where *is* your alma mater?"
Man:	I've thought about that myself.
Woman:	And?
Man:	Well, as you know, I'm planning to go to graduate school, so my plan is to get really good grades here, and try to get into a well-known university for my master's degree. I think that will give me the best of both worlds.
Narrator:	57. What is the woman trying to decide?
	58. What does she like about the college she is attending?
	59. How does the man respond to her problem?
	60. What does the man plan to do?

Questions 61–64. Listen to a conversation by telephone.

Woman:	How may I help you?
Man:	I'd like to place an order, please.
Woman:	And will you be paying by credit card?
Man:	Yes.
Woman:	Mastercard, Visa, or American Express?
Man:	Do you take Diner's Club?
Woman:	No.
Man:	Visa, then.
Woman:	The number, please.
Man:	Five-two-seven-seven. Three-four-zero-four. Five-nine-two-one. Six-eight-nine-nine.
Woman:	Expiration date?
Man:	Eight-ninety-six.
Woman:	And the name as it appears on the card.
Man:	Larry E. Wilson. W-I-L-S-O-N.
Woman:	And what would you like to order, Mr. Wilson?
Man:	Two shirts. Like the ones on page thirty-four in the catalog.
Woman:	Yes. I have it. What size do you need?
Man:	Sixteen and a half.
Woman:	Color?
Man:	A brown one and a white one.
Woman:	And your next item?
Man:	That's all.
Narrator:	61. Who is the woman?
	62. How will the man pay for his purchase?
	63. What is the man's name?
	64. What is the man ordering?

Part C

Directions: In this part of the test, you will hear several short talks. After each talk, you will hear some questions. The talks and questions will not be repeated.

After you hear a question, read the four possible answers in your book and choose the best answer. Then, on your answer sheet, find the number of the question and fill in the space that corresponds to the letter of the answer you have chosen.

<u>Questions 65–68.</u> Listen to a public service announcement on radio.

Starting next month you can subscribe to a home pick-up service for your recyclable items. The service, called CURBSIDE, is available for a yearly rate of fifteen dollars plus a one-time charge of five dollars for a blue recycling container. Pick-up will be scheduled for the first and third Wednesday of the month.

What can you recycle? All steel and aluminum cans, glass jars and bottles, newspapers, paper bags, and those plastic containers stamped with a number one or a number two inside a triangle.

To prepare the recyclables for pick-up, just remove lids and labels from containers and rinse them. Bundle newspapers or put them in paper bags. No magazines or plastic bags will be accepted.

Remember, House Bill Five-nine-two requires that every community in the state develop a plan for recycling. Our goal is to reduce the material going to landfills by twenty-five percent. In addition, our community's mandatory recycling law includes a one-hundred-dollar fine for failure to separate recyclables from trash.

You don't have to sign up for CURBSIDE in order to comply with the law. You can bring your recyclables to the Recycling Center on Adams Street if you prefer. CURBSIDE just makes it a little more convenient.

Recycle! It's the law. And it's also the right thing to do.

Narrator: 65. What is CURBSIDE?

(Note: There should be a 12-second pause after each test question in this section.)

66. What materials cannot be recycled?

67. How should recyclables be prepared for recycling?

68. What is the fine for failure to recycle?

<u>Questions 69–72.</u> Listen to a talk by an anthropologist.

In informal conversation, the word *culture* refers to a desirable personal attribute that can be acquired by visiting museums and galleries and by attending concerts and theatrical performances. An educated person who has *culture* is familiar with the finer things produced in civilized society. And that's what most people think of when they hear the word *culture*. In anthropology, however, *culture* is defined in a very different way. To an anthropologist, culture refers to the complex whole of ideas and material objects produced by groups in their historical experience; that is, the learned behaviors, beliefs, attitudes, and values that are characteristic of a particular society. For a thought or activity to be included as part of a culture, it must be commonly shared by or considered appropriate for the group.

Even in a complex society like that of the United States, which comprises many diverse ethnic groups, there are practices common to all Americans, and these practices constitute American culture. In addition, the smaller groups within the larger society have shared customs that are specific to their group. These shared customs represent a subculture within the larger culture. Now, can anyone think of an example of a subculture in the United States?

Narrator: 69. What is the main topic of the talk?

70. According to the speaker, what do most people mean when they use the word *culture* in ordinary conversation?

71. According to the speaker, what do anthropologists mean when they say a thought or activity is to be included as part of culture?

72. According to the speaker, what is a subculture?

Questions 73–76. Listen to a radio program called "To Your Health."

In 1992, the World Health Organization (WHO) reported that ten to twelve million adults and one million children worldwide had contracted H.I.V., the virus that causes AIDS, and they estimated that by the year two thousand, forty million people would be infected. If the current trends continue, however, that estimate will fall far short of actual numbers, which may reach one hundred ten million.

In addition, there appears to be a change in the characteristics of AIDS victims. In the 1980s, homosexual men in large urban areas accounted for approximately two thirds of all AIDS cases. Women and children seemed to be on the periphery of the AIDS epidemic. But today almost ninety percent of new adult infections result from heterosexual contact. Consequently, the rates of exposure and infection are rising for women, with an accompanying rise in the number of children born to them with H.I.V. By the year 2000, it is now expected that the majority of AIDS victims will be heterosexual women and their young children.

Furthermore, research by WHO reveals that women around the world are more susceptible to the AIDS virus for a number of reasons. First, women are biologically more susceptible to all sexually transmitted diseases; second, women tend to have sexual relationships with older men who are more likely to have had multiple partners; and last, the traditional role of the man as the partner in control of the sexual activity inhibits women in many cultures from using protection.

Narrator: 73. What is this talk mainly about?

74. Which segment of the population constituted the majority of AIDS cases in the 1980s?

75. What percentage of new adult infections are resulting from heterosexual contact?

76. Which segment of the population will probably constitute the majority of AIDS cases in the year 2000?

Questions 77–80. Listen to a public service announcement on the radio.

One of the most successful educational programs for adults is the Elderhostel designed for students over the age of sixty. Initiated in 1975 by five colleges in New Hampshire, Elderhostel was originally a one-week summer program for senior citizens combining travel and college residence with enrichment courses. The concept has been so popular that it has grown rapidly to include a network of more than three hundred colleges and universities in all fifty states. Host institutions have expanded to include museums, parks, and other outdoor centers as well as traditional college campuses, and one, two, or three-week programs are now available year round. Although courses are not offered for credit, and no exams are required, the classes are taught by highly qualified faculty at the host college.

To date, hundreds of thousands of students from sixty to one hundred years old have participated in Elderhostel. Students usually live in dormitories, eat in cafeterias, and attend social, recreational, and cultural functions. All services available to students during the academic year are offered to Elderhostel students. Registration fees vary from as little as twenty dollars to as much as three hundred dollars, excluding books and transportation to the campus or community site. For many senior citizens, Elderhostel offers the opportunity for lifelong learning, companionship, and fun.

If you are sixty years old or older and you enjoy learning, call your local college. There is probably an Elderhostel program right in your community.

Narrator: 77. What is this announcement mainly about?

78. Which of the statements is true of Elderhostel?

79. Where do the participants live?

80. What should you do if you are interested in finding out more about the programs?